RESEARCH METHODS FOR LEISURE AND TOURISM

Pearson

At Pearson, we have a simple mission: to help people make more of their lives through learning.

We combine innovative learning technology with trusted content and educational expertise to provide engaging and effective learning experiences that serve people wherever and whenever they are learning.

From classroom to boardroom, our curriculum materials, digital learning tools and testing programmes help to educate millions of people worldwide – more than any other private enterprise.

Every day our work helps learning flourish, and wherever learning flourishes, so do people.

To learn more, please visit us at **www.pearson.com/uk**

Research Methods for Leisure and Tourism

Fifth edition

A. J. VEAL
University of Technology Sydney

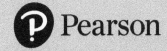 Pearson

Harlow, England • London • New York • Boston • San Francisco • Toronto • Sydney • Dubai • Singapore • Hong Kong
Tokyo • Seoul • Taipei • New Delhi • Cape Town • São Paulo • Mexico City • Madrid • Amsterdam • Munich • Paris • Milan

Pearson Education Limited
KAO Two
KAO Park
Harlow CM17 9NA
United Kingdom
Tel: +44 (0)1279 623623
Web: www.pearson.com/uk

First published 1992 (print)
Second edition published 1997 (print)
Third edition published 2006 (print)
Fourth edition published 2011 (print)
Fifth edition published 2018 (print and electronic)

ISBN: 978-1-292-11529-0 (print)
         978-1-292-11531-3 (PDF)
         978-1-292-21786-4 (ePub)

British Library Cataloguing-in-Publication Data
A catalogue record for the print edition is available from the British Library

Library of Congress Cataloging-in-Publication Data

Names: Veal, Anthony James, author.
Title: Research methods for leisure and tourism / A. J. Veal.
Description: Fifth edition. | Harlow, United Kingdom : Pearson, 2018. |
    Includes bibliographical references and index.
Identifiers: LCCN 2017038217 | ISBN 9781292115290 (print) | ISBN 9781292115313 (pdf) |
    ISBN 9781292217864 (epub)
Subjects: LCSH: Leisure—Research—Methodology. |
    Tourism—Research—Methodology.
Classification: LCC GV14.5 .V43 2018 | DDC 790.1/8072—dc23
LC record available at https://lccn.loc.gov/2017038217

10 9 8 7 6 5 4
22 21 20 19 18

Front cover image © Robert Cadloff/Getty Images
Print edition typeset in 10/12.5 Palatino LT Pro by iEnergizer, Aptara®, Ltd.
Printed and bound in Great Britain by Ashford Colour Press Ltd

NOTE THAT ANY PAGE CROSS REFERENCES REFER TO THE PRINT EDITION

Summary contents

Detailed chapter contents

Supporting resources

Visit **www.pearsoned.co.uk/veal** to find valuable online resources

Companion Website for students
- Annotated links to relevant sites on the web
- Interactive media resources, including video cases, flash animations and extra cases
- A full compendium of part bibliographies for you to print out and take with you to the library
- Online tutorials for SPSS, Excel and Nvivo
- Additional practice data sets

For instructors
- Customisable PowerPoint slides, including key figures and tables from the main text
- A fully updated Instructor's Manual, including sample answers for all question material in the book
- Testbank of question material

Also: The Companion Website provides the following features:
- Search tool to help locate specific items of content
- E-mail results and profile tools to send results of quizzes to instructors
- Online help and support to assist with website usage and troubleshooting

For more information please contact your local Pearson Education sales representative or visit **www.pearsoned.co.uk/veal**

List of figures

List of tables

List of case studies

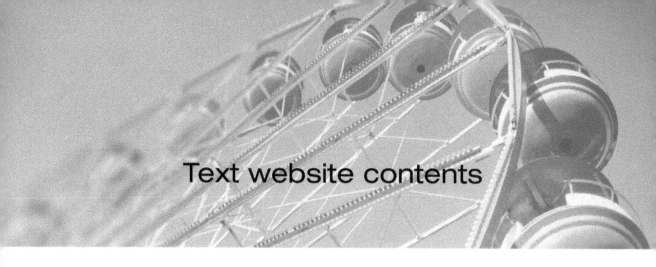

Text website contents

Available at: www.pearsoned.co.uk/veal

Contents at the time of publication; additions/changes may be made over time.

- *PowerPoint* files for each chapter: containing copies of graphics, tables and some dot-point lists.

- Consolidated list of references.

- Chapter 15: copy of NVivo files used.

- Chapter 16 and 17: copies of SPSS files used.

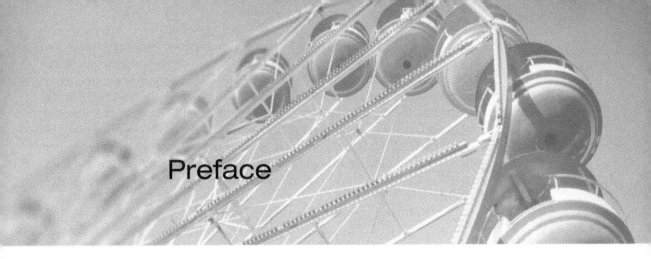

Preface

The first edition of *Research Methods for Leisure and Tourism* was published in 1992, with subsequent editions in 1997, 2006 and 2011. In this fifth edition, in addition to a general updating of sources and versions of software packages, a number of changes have been made, including:

- A substantial expansion of the number of 'subsidiary and cross-cutting methods' in Chapter 5, from 24 in the previous edition to 34, and the addition of a number of policy/management-related research techniques. This reflects the continuing process of innovation apparent in leisure and tourism research.

- A step-by-step introductory guide to the *Endnote* bibliographic/referencing computer package.

- Further discussion of the question of measurement (Chapter 7) – although this remains 'unfinished business'.

- Arrangement of references by chapter rather than in one listing at the end of this text; this makes individual chapters more self-contained. A consolidated listing is provided on the text website.

As in the previous edition, I stress that the software packages used in the text were selected neither as a result of some exclusive arrangement with software publishers nor as a result of an evaluative 'consumer test' of available packages. They are simply the packages with which I am familiar and which have been available to the students in the universities where I have taught. I can vouch for the usefulness of the packages used but am not in a position to compare the packages used with others available.

Efforts have been made to provide additional study materials online at the text website: www.pearsoned.co.uk/veal (see the list of contents).

The aims of the book remain unchanged: to provide a 'how to do it' text and also to offer an understanding of how research findings are generated in order to assist students and practising managers to become knowledgeable consumers of the research of others.

Two companion texts have recently been published: *Research Methods for Arts and Event Management* (A.J. Veal and Christine Burton, Pearson, 2014, ISBN 9780 27372 0829) and *Research Methods in Sport Studies and Sport Management* (A.J. Veal and Simon Darcy, 2014, Routledge, ISBN 9780 27373 6691). The three texts follow the same chapter structure, with much generic material in common, but with sector-specific references, case studies and exercises. In institutions where arts/events and sport studies students are taught together with leisure and tourism studies students, each group of students can use their own subject-specific version of the text with relevant examples and source material.

I am grateful to Professor Simon Darcy, UTS, for on-going support and to Barbara Almond, UTS, for assistance in updating the NVivo section of Chapter 15.

A. J. Veal
University of Technology Sydney
September 2017

Acknowledgements

Figures

Figure 10.11 from Port Hacking Visitor Use Study, Centre for Leisure and Tourism Studies, University of Technology, Sydney (Robertson, R. W., and Veal, A. J. 1987); Figure 15.7 from Screenshot of NVivo_CAQDAS package, Courtesy of QSR International Pty Ltd.; Figure 15.9 from NVivo Software of QSR International, Courtesy of QSR International Pty Ltd.; Figures 15.12, 15.13, 15.14, 15.16 from NVivo Software - QSR International, Courtesy of QSR International Pty Ltd.; Figures 16.7, 16.9 from SPSS Data Editor, Reprint Courtesy of International Business Machines Corporation, © International Business Machines Corporation.; Figure 16.8 from IBM SPSS Statistics Data Editor, Reprint Courtesy of International Business Machines Corporation, © International Business Machines Corporation.

Text

Case Study 11.1 from Managing the "commons" on Cadillac Mountain: a stated choice analysis of Acadia National Park visitors' preferences, *Leisure Science*, 30, 71–86 (Bullock, S.D., & Lawson, S.R 2008); Case Study 14.1 from Leisure, income inequality and the Veblen effect: cross-national analysis of leisure time and sport and cultural activity, *Leisure Studies*, 35(2), 215–240 (Veal, A.J. 2016); Case Study 14.1 from Volunteering and income inequality: cross-national relationships, *Voluntas*, 28(1), 379–399 (Veal, A.J., & Nichols, G 2017), With permission of Springer.

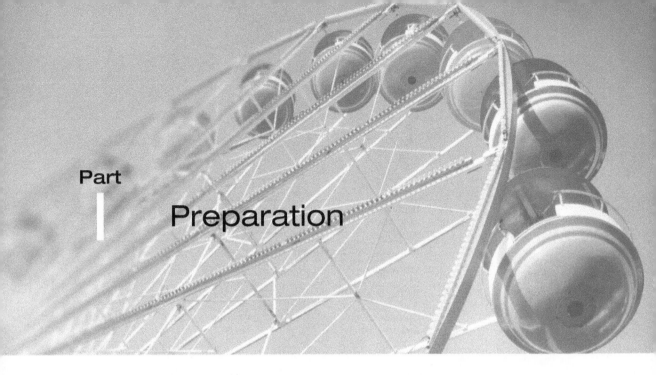

Part

I

Preparation

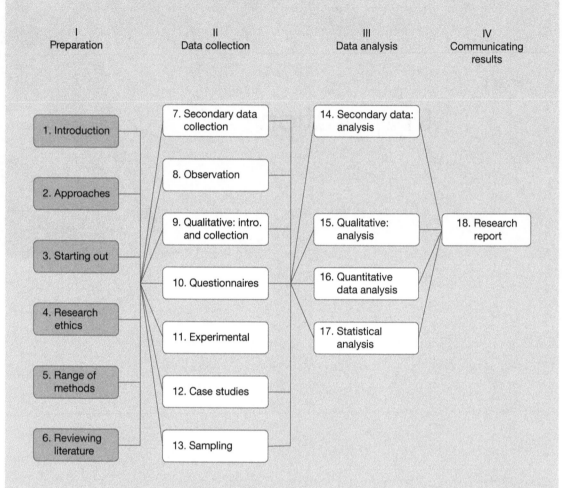

I Preparation	II Data collection	III Data analysis	IV Communicating results

1. Introduction

2. Approaches

3. Starting out

4. Research ethics

5. Range of methods

6. Reviewing literature

7. Secondary data collection

8. Observation

9. Qualitative: intro. and collection

10. Questionnaires

11. Experimental

12. Case studies

13. Sampling

14. Secondary data: analysis

15. Qualitative: analysis

16. Quantitative data analysis

17. Statistical analysis

18. Research report

1

Introduction to research: what, why and who?

1. Introduction

2. What is research?

2.1 Research defined
2.2 Scientific research
2.3 Social science research
2.4 Descriptive, explanatory and evaluative research

3. Why study research?

3.1 In general
3.2 Research in policy-making, planning and management processes

4. Who does research?

4.1 Academics
4.2 Students
4.3 Government, commercial and non-profit organisations
4.4 Managers
4.5 Consultants

5. Who pays?

6. Research outputs

6.1 Academic journal articles
6.2 Professional journal articles
6.3 Conference papers/ presentations
6.4 Books
6.5 Policy/planning/ management reports

7. Terminology

8. Using this text

1. Introduction

Data, information, knowledge and understanding concerning the natural, social and economic environment have become the very basis of cultural and material development in contemporary societies and economies. Controversies over the research basis of global climate change predictions offer a dramatic demonstration of this, as do discussions on crime, education, health and the economy. An understanding of how information and knowledge are generated and utilised and an ability to conduct or commission research relevant to the requirements of an organisation can therefore be seen as key skills for, and as significant components of the education of, managers and policy-makers in any domain. It goes without saying that they are also fundamental to those embarking on a research/academic career.

Research is, however, not just a set of disembodied skills; it exists and is practised in a variety of social, political and economic contexts. The purpose of this text is to provide an introduction to the world of social research in the context of leisure and tourism, as industries and public policy concerns and as fields of academic inquiry and reflection. The aim is to provide a practical guide to the conduct of research, an appreciation of the role of research in the policy-making, planning and management processes of the leisure and tourism sector and a basis for a critical understanding of existing theoretical and applied research.

Research methodology can be seen as universal, but various fields of research – including leisure and tourism studies – have developed their own methodological emphases and bodies of experience. For example, in some fields of enquiry, scientific laboratory experiments are the norm, while in others social surveys are more common. While most of the principles of research are universal, a specialised text such as this reflects the traditions and practices in its fields of focus and draws attention to examples of relevant applications of methods and the particular problems and issues which arise in such applications.

The field of leisure and tourism is a large one, encompassing a wide range of individual and collective human activity. It is an area fraught with problems of definition – for example, in some contexts the word *recreation* is used synonymously with *leisure*, while in others recreation is seen as a distinct and limited part of leisure or even separate from leisure. In some cultures, the term *free time* is used in preference to the word leisure. In some definitions, *tourism* includes *business travel* and *day-trips*, while in others they are excluded. The aim in this study is to be *inclusive* rather than *exclusive*. Leisure refers to both a type of time and groups of activities. It is time relatively free of obligation, such as paid or unpaid work or personal maintenance activity, and activities which typically take place during such time, as indicated in Figure 1.1. There is sufficient overlap between leisure and tourism for them to be covered by a single research methods text like the current one; but in practice, two distinct fields of study exist with their own journals, conferences, institutions and academic courses. Tourism is seen primarily as a leisure activity involving travel away from a person's normal place of residence. Leisure and tourism overlap in activities such as attending cultural or sporting events and in visiting natural and cultural heritage sites. Tourism as an industry

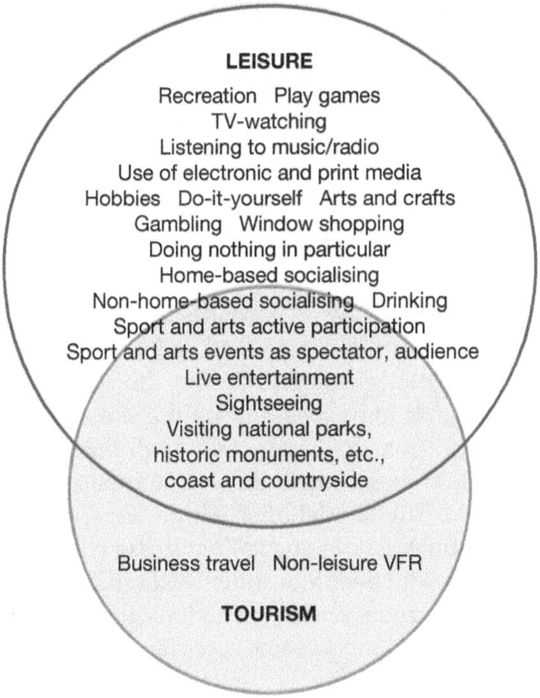

Figure 1.1 Leisure and tourism

also encompasses non-leisure activities, such as business travel or attending conventions, as shown in Figure 1.1, but such travellers invariably engage in leisure activities in addition to the business activity which is the prime motivator for travel. Travelling to visit relatives may also be partly leisure and partly family business. Since the text covers leisure *and* tourism, day-tripping is included, whether it is viewed as part of recreation or tourism. Leisure and tourism are seen as activities engaged in by individuals and groups, but also as service industries which involve public sector, non-profit and commercial organisations.

Most of the text is concerned with *how* to do research; the aim of this opening chapter is to introduce the 'what, why and who' of research. What is it? Why study it? Who does it?

2. What is research?

2.1 Research defined

What is research? The sociologist Norbert Elias defined **research** in terms of its aims, as follows:

> The aim, as far as I can see, is the same in all sciences. Put simply and cursorily, the aim is to make known something previously unknown to human beings. It is to advance human knowledge, to make it more certain or better fitting . . . The aim is . . . discovery. (Elias, 1986: 20)

Discovery – making known something previously unknown – could cover a number of activities, for instance, the work of journalists or detectives. Elias, however, also indicates that research is a tool of 'science' and that its purpose is to 'advance human knowledge' – features which distinguish research from other investigatory activities.

2.2 Scientific research

Scientific research is conducted within the rules and conventions of science. This means that it is based on logic and reason and the systematic examination of evidence. Ideally, within the scientific model, it should be possible for research to be *replicated* by the same or different researchers and for similar conclusions to emerge (although this is not always possible or practicable). It should also contribute to a cumulative body of knowledge about a field or topic. This model of scientific research applies most aptly in the physical or natural sciences, such as physics or chemistry. In the area of *social science*, which deals with people as individuals and social beings with relationships to groups, communities and organisations, the pure scientific model must be adapted and modified, and in some cases largely abandoned.

2.3 Social science research

Social science research is carried out using the methods and traditions of social science. Social science differs from the physical or natural sciences in that it deals with the behaviour of *people* as social beings, and people are less predictable than non-human phenomena. People can be aware of the research being conducted about them and are not therefore purely passive subjects; they can react to the results of research and change their behaviour accordingly. While the fundamental behaviour patterns of non-human phenomena are constant and universal, people in different parts of the world and at different times behave differently. The social world is constantly changing, so it is rarely possible to produce exact replications of research findings at different times or in different places.

2.4 Descriptive, explanatory and evaluative research

Elias's term *discovery* can be seen as, first, the process of finding out – at its simplest, therefore, research might just *describe* what exists. But to 'advance human knowledge, to make it more certain or better fitting' requires more than just the accumulation of information, or facts. The aim is also to provide *explanation* – to explain why things are as they are, and how they might be. In this study, we are also concerned with a third function of research, namely *evaluating* – that is, judging the degree of success or value of policies or programmes. Three types

Table 1.1 Types of research

Descriptive research	Finding out, describing what is.
Explanatory research	Explaining *how* or *why* things are as they are (and using this to predict).
Evaluative research	Evaluation of policies and programmes.

of research can be identified corresponding to these three functions, as shown in Table 1.1. In some cases, particular research projects concentrate on only one of these, but often two or more of the approaches are included in the same research project.

Descriptive research

Descriptive research is very common in the leisure and tourism area, for three reasons: the relative newness of the field, the changing nature of the phenomena being studied and the frequent separation between research and action.

Newness of the field: Since leisure and tourism are relatively new fields of study, there is a need to map the territory. Much of the research, therefore, seeks to discover, describe or map patterns of behaviour in areas or activities which have not previously been studied. In some texts this form of research is termed *exploratory*, which is also appropriate; but the other categories of research, explanatory and evaluative, can also at times be exploratory, so the term *descriptive* is used here. Explanation of what is discovered, described or mapped is often left until later or to other researchers.

Change: Leisure and tourism phenomena are subject to constant change over time, including change in:

● the popularity of different leisure activities or travel destinations;

● the leisure preferences of different social groups (for example, young people or women);

● social and economic conditions in a community;

● available technologies, such as faster transport systems and digital devices;

● availability of built facilities/attractions; and

● policy/management practices, for example, loyalty or membership schemes or online access.

A great deal of research effort in the field is therefore devoted to tracking – or monitoring – changing patterns of behaviour. Hence the importance in leisure and tourism of secondary data sources – that is, data collected by other organisations, such as government statistical agencies – as discussed in Chapter 7.

A complete understanding and explanation of these changing patterns would be ideal, so that the future could be predicted, but this is only partially possible. So providers of leisure and tourism services must be aware of changing social and market conditions whether or not they can be fully explained or understood; they therefore rely on a flow of descriptive research to provide up-to-date information.

Separation: Research of a descriptive nature is often undertaken because that is what is commissioned. For example, a company may commission a *market profile* study or a local council may commission a *cultural needs* study from a research team. However, the actual use of the results of the research, in marketing or planning, is a separate exercise with which the research team is not involved: the research team may simply be required to produce a descriptive study.

One role of descriptive research is in *classification* of phenomena in the field of study. This is discussed in Chapter 2.

Explanatory research

Explanatory research moves beyond description to seek to *explain* the patterns and trends observed. For example:

● A particular type of leisure activity or tourism destination experiences a decline in popularity: an explanation is called for.

● The hosting of an international sporting event gains approval from the government against the wishes of members of the local community: why or how does this happen?

● The arts are patronised by some social groups but not others: what is the explanation for this?

Such questions raise the thorny issue of *causality*: the aim is to be able to say, for example, that there has been an increase in A *because of* a corresponding fall in B. However, while it is one thing to discover that A has increased at the same time as, or just after, B has decreased, it is often a much more demanding task to establish that the rise in A has been *caused* by the fall in B. To establish causality, or the likelihood of causality, requires some sort of theoretical framework to relate the phenomenon under study to specific social, economic and/or political processes, as discussed in Chapter 2.

Once causes are understood, at least partially, the knowledge can be used to *predict*. This is clear enough in the physical sciences: we know that heat causes metal to expand (explanation) – therefore, we know that if we apply a certain amount of heat to a bar of metal, it will expand by a certain amount (prediction). In the biological and medical sciences, this process is also followed, but with less precision: it can be predicted that if a certain treatment is given to patients with a certain disease, then it is *likely* that a certain proportion will be cured. In the social sciences, this approach is also used, but with even less precision. For example, economists have found that demand for goods and services, including leisure and tourism goods and services, responds to price levels. But this does not always happen because so many other factors are involved – such as variation in quality of the goods or services and the activities of competitors. Human beings make their own decisions and are far less predictable than non-human phenomena. Nevertheless, prediction is a key aim of much of the research that takes place in the area of leisure and tourism.

Evaluative research

Evaluative research arises from the need to make judgements on the success or effectiveness of policies, programmes or practices – for example, whether a particular leisure facility or programme is meeting required performance standards or whether a particular tourism promotion campaign has been cost-effective. In the private sector, the level of profit is the main criterion used for such evaluations. In the public sector, where facilities or services are not usually intended to make a cash profit, research effort is required to assess community benefits and even, in some cases such as parks, to assemble data as elementary as levels of use. Evaluative research is highly developed in some areas of public policy, for example education, but is less well developed in the public-sector part of leisure and tourism.

Evaluation is based on the concept of *valuation* and implies a technical or *value-free* process. However, as we shall see, values are never absent from human affairs. When the process is more explicit with respect to values, particularly when research is involved with a process of seeking to change the status quo, it may be referred to as *transformative* (Stewart, 2014).

3. Why study research?

3.1 In general

Why study research? Research or research methods might be studied for a variety of reasons, as listed in Table 1.2.

● First, it is useful to be able to *understand* and *evaluate* research reports and articles encountered in an academic, professional or managerial context. It is advantageous to understand the basis and limitations of such documents.

Table 1.2 Why study research?

1. Understanding research reports, etc.
2. Conducting academic research projects
3. Management tool in:
    – policy-making
    – planning
    – managing
    – evaluating

- Second, many readers of this text may engage in research in an academic environment, where research is conducted for its own sake, in the interests of the pursuit of knowledge – for example for an honours, master's or doctoral thesis.

- Third, most readers will find themselves conducting or commissioning research for professional reasons, as managers or consultants. It is therefore particularly appropriate to consider the role of research in the policy-making, planning and management process.

Of course, for many readers of this text, the immediate challenge is to complete a research-related project as part of an undergraduate or postgraduate programme of study. This text should assist in this task, but it is a means to an end, not an end in itself. Research projects conducted as part of a curriculum are seen as a learning process to equip the student as a consumer, practitioner and/or commissioner of research in professional life.

3.2 Research in policy-making, planning and management processes

All organisations, including those in the leisure and tourism industries, engage in policy-making, planning and managing processes to achieve their goals. A variety of terms is used in this area and the meanings of terms vary according to the context and user. In this text:

- *policies* are considered to be the statements of principles, intentions and commitments of an organisation;

- *plans* are detailed strategies, typically set out in a document, designed to implement policies in particular ways over a specified period of time; and

- *management* is seen as the process of implementing policies and plans.

Although planning is usually associated in the public mind with national, regional and local government bodies, it is also an activity undertaken by the private and non-profit sectors. Organisations such as cinema chains, holiday resort developers and sport promoters are all involved in planning, but their planning activities are less open to public scrutiny than those of government bodies. Private organisations are usually only concerned with their own activities, but government bodies often have a wider responsibility to provide a planning framework for the activities of many public- and private-sector organisations, in the public interest. Examples of policies, plans and management activity in leisure and tourism contexts are given in Table 1.3.

Policies and plans can vary enormously in detail, complexity and formality. Here the process is considered only briefly in order to examine the part played by research. Of the many models of policy-making, planning and management processes that exist, the *rational-comprehensive* model, a version of which is depicted in Figure 1.2, is the most traditional, somewhat idealised, model. It is beyond the scope of this text to discuss the many alternative models which

Table 1.3 Examples of policies, plans and management

	Leisure Centre	Tourism Commission	Arts Centre	National Park
Policy	Maximise use by all age-groups	Extend peak season	Encourage contemporary composers	Increase non-government revenue
Plan	Two-year plan to increase visits by older people by 50%	Three-year plan to increase shoulder season visits by promoting new festivals	Three-year plan to commission new work by contemporary composers	Three-year plan to implement user-pays programme
Management	Implement daily morning keep-fit sessions for older people	Choose marketing themes	Select composers and commission and produce works	Implement user-pays programme

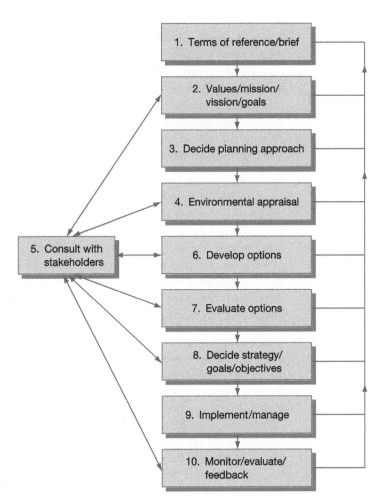

Figure 1.2 The rational/comprehensive planning/management process

seek to more accurately reflect real-world decision-making, but guidance to further reading on this issue is given at the end of the chapter. These alternatives are often 'cut-down' versions of the rational-comprehensive model, emphasising some aspects of this model and de-emphasising, or omitting, others. Thus some reflect the view that it is virtually impossible to be completely *comprehensive* in assessing alternative policies; some reflect the fact that political interests often intervene before 'rational' or 'objective' decisions can be made; while others elevate community/stakeholder consultation to a central rather than supportive role. In nearly all cases the models are put forward as an *alternative* to the rational-comprehensive model, so the latter, even if rejected, remains a universal reference point.

Research plays a part in most models – sometimes curtailed and sometimes enhanced. It is rare that all of the steps shown in Figure 1.2 are followed through in the real world. And it is also rare for research to inform the process in all the ways discussed below. The steps depicted provide an agenda for discussing the many roles of research in policy-making, planning and management processes. Two examples of how the process might unfold in leisure and tourism contexts are given in Table 1.4.

1. *Terms of reference/brief:* The 'terms of reference' or 'brief' for a particular planning or management task sets out the scope and purpose of the exercise. Research can be involved at the beginning of this process, assisting in establishing the terms of reference. For example, existing research showing low levels of sports participation in a community may result in a government policy initiative to increase participation; or research on the effects of climate change on tourism could prompt a government to develop a sustainable tourism plan.

2. *State values/mission/goals:* Statements of the overall mission or goals of the organisation may already be in place if the task in hand is a relatively minor one, but if it is a major undertaking, such as the development of a strategic plan for the whole organisation, then the development of a statement of mission and goals may be part of the exercise. It is very much a task for the decision-making body of an organisation (such as the board or the council) to determine its mission and/or goals, but research may be directly involved when consultation with a large number of stakeholders is involved, as discussed under step 5.

3. *Decide planning approach:* Like research, a range of different methodologies and approaches is available for policy-making and planning. These include: adopting fixed standards of provision; providing opportunity; resource-based planning; meeting demand; meeting the requirements/requests of stakeholders; meeting unmet needs; providing benefits; and increasing participation (Veal, 2016, 2017: Ch. 8). The method/approach selected will determine the type of research to be carried out during the policy-making/planning process: for example, a needs-based approach will require a definition of need and a method for collecting information on needs, while resource-based planning will require identification of the range of heritage,

Table 1.4   Examples of planning/management tasks and associated research

Planning/ Management Process Steps (See Table 1.3)	Young people and sport in a local community		Sustainable tourism in a tourism destination	
	Policy/ Planning/ Management	Associated Research	Policy/ Planning/ Management	Associated Research
1. Terms of reference	Increase young people's participation in sport.	Existing research indicates 40% participation rate.	Develop local sustainable tourism strategy.	Physical survey indicates road capacity reached.
2. Set values/ mission/vision/ goals	Increase participation level to 60% over 5 years.		Develop policy to Increase tourism volume by 50% over 10 years within acceptable environmental impact parameters.	Study of likely increases in tourism demand over 10 years.
3. Decide planning approach	Needs-based, demand-based, etc.: for discussion, see Veal (2016, 2017: Ch. 7).	As below.	Demand-based, stakeholder-based, etc.: for discussion, see Veal (2017: Ch. 10).	As below.
4. Environmental appraisal	Consider existing supply – demand.	Existing programs and infrastructure fully used.	Examine current environmental impacts of tourism and future scenarios.	Extensive physical surveys (traffic + other environ-mental issues) + development of future tourism demand scenarios.
5. Consult stakeholders	Consult sporting clubs, schools, young people.	Survey indicates support among all groups and confirms feasibility.	Consult community and tourism industry provider groups.	Survey + meetings with community and tourism industry provider groups.
6. Develop options	1. Publicity campaign 2. Free vouchers 3. Build more community facilities 4. Provide support to clubs/schools 5. Train leaders/ coaches/teachers	Review of experience of each option in other regions, based on published accounts and a survey.	1. Road-building/ traffic management program 2. Local public transport solution 3. Alternative accommodation development strategies	Survey of experience of similar destinations in similar stages of the tourism life cycle.
7. Evaluate options	Evaluate options 1–5.	Each option costed; on basis of survey evidence, estimate made of cost-effectiveness of each option.	Evaluate options 1 and 2 against range of options in 3.	Options 1 and 2 costed and evaluated against a range of accommodation development strategies (3).

(continued)

Table 1.4 *(continued)*

Planning/ Management Process Steps (See Table 1.3)	Young people and sport in a local community		Sustainable tourism in a tourism destination	
	Policy/ Planning/ Management	**Associated Research**	**Policy/ Planning/ Management**	**Associated Research**
8. *Decide strategy/ objectives*	Options 3 and 4 adopted.	Options 3 and 4 recommended.	Options selected in light of evaluative research.	Options ranked in order of effectiveness and net environmental impact.
9. *Implement – manage*	Implement options 3 and 4.	–	Implement public transport and 3-star accommodation option.	–
10. *Monitor/ evaluate/ feedback*	Assess success in terms of increased participation. Continue program: increase resources for training coaches/ leaders.	Survey indicates participation increase to 45% after 1 year, but shortage of coaches/leaders.	Assess success in terms of tourism numbers and traffic congestion. Develop peak public holiday traffic management plan.	Annual surveys of traffic conditions and tourism numbers undertaken. Persistent peak public holiday congestion problems noted.

cultural and/or environmental resources to be included and processes for data gathering and evaluation.

4. *Environmental appraisal:* An environmental appraisal involves the gathering of relevant information on the broad context of the task at hand. Information may relate to the organisation's internal workings or to the outside world, including actual and potential clients, and the activities of governments and competitors and physical resources. Such information may be readily at hand and may just need collation, or it may require extensive original research.

5. *Consult with stakeholders:* Consultation with *stakeholders* is considered vital by most organisations and, indeed, is a statutory requirement in many forms of public-sector planning. Stakeholders can include employees, clients, visitors, members of the general public, members of boards and councils and neighbouring or complementary organisations. Research can be a significant feature of such consultation, especially when surveys are required to contact large numbers of individuals or organisations.

6. *Develop options:* In order to develop a plan or strategy, it is necessary to consider what policy options are available to pursue the goals of the organisation,

their feasibility, their likely contribution to the achievement of the goals and the best way to implement them. Research can be involved in the process of *identifying* alternative policy or planning options, for example, by providing data on the extent of unmet needs or on stakeholder preferences.

7. *Evaluate options:* Deciding on a strategy involves selecting a course or courses of action from among all the options identified. This choice process may involve a complex procedure requiring research to *evaluate* the alternatives. Typical formal evaluation techniques include *cost–benefit analysis, economic impact analysis* and *environmental and social impact analysis,* and the use of the *importance-performance* technique or *conjoint analysis* (Veal, 2017: ch. 15, 16).

8. *Decide strategy/goals/objectives:* Evaluation processes rarely produce a single best solution or course of action. Thus, for example, option A may be cheaper than option B, but option B produces better outcomes. Final decisions on which strategy to pursue must be taken by the governing body of the organisation – the board or council – based on political and/or personal values. A strategy should involve clear statements of what it is intended to achieve (goals), with measurable outcomes and time-lines (objectives).

9. *Implement – manage:* Implementing a plan or strategy is the field of management. Research can be involved in day-to-day management in investigating improved ways of deploying resources and in providing continuous feedback on the management process – for example, in the form of customer surveys. However, the line between such research and the monitoring and evaluation process is difficult to draw.

10. *Monitor/evaluate:* Monitoring progress and evaluating the implementation of strategies is clearly a process with which research is likely to be involved. The process comes full circle with the feedback step. The data from the monitoring and evaluation step can be fed back into the planning or management cycle and can lead to a revision of any or all of the decisions previously made. The monitoring and evaluation process may report complete success, it may suggest minor changes to some of the details of the policies and plans adopted or it could result in a fundamental re-think, going 'back to the drawing board'.

Of course, not all research is policy/planning/management driven. Research conducted in academic contexts is shaped by the ideas of the researcher in relation to the existing body of knowledge. This is explored in Chapter 3.

4. Who does research?

This book is mainly concerned with how to conduct research, but it also aims to provide an understanding of the research process which will help the reader to become a knowledgeable, critical consumer of the research carried out by

Table 1.5 Who does research?

Group	Motivation/purpose
1. Academics	Part of the job description. Knowledge for its own sake and/or to engage with industry/profession and/or to benefit society.
2. Students	Coursework students: projects as learning medium and/or part of professional training. Research students: adding to knowledge and training/ qualification for a research/academic career.
3. Government, commercial and non-profit organisations	Research to inform policy, monitor performance and aid in decision-making. Relevant to the idea of 'evidence-based policy'.
4. Managers	Research to inform practice, monitor performance and aid in decision-making.
5. Consultants	Research under contract to government, commercial and non-profit organisations.

others. In reading reports of research, it is useful to bear in mind *why* the research has been done, and to a large extent, this is influenced by *who* did the research and *who paid* for it to be done. Who does research is important because it affects the nature of the research conducted and hence shapes the *body of knowledge* which students of leisure and tourism must absorb and which leisure and tourism managers rely on. Leisure and tourism research is undertaken by a wide variety of individuals and institutions, as listed in Table 1.5. The respective roles of these research actors are discussed in turn below.

4.1 Academics

Academics are members of the paid academic staff of academic institutions, including professors, lecturers, tutors and research staff – in North American parlance, the *faculty*. In most academic institutions, professors and lecturers are expected, as part of their contract of employment, to engage in both research and teaching. Typically, a quarter to a third of an academic's time might be devoted to research and writing. Promotion and job security depend partly (some would say mainly) on the achievement of a satisfactory track record in published research. Publication can be in various forms and can be assessed quantitatively and qualitatively as discussed under 'outputs' later in this chapter.

Some research arises from academic interest and some from immediate problems being faced by the providers of leisure or tourism services. Much published academic research tends to be governed by the concerns of the various theoretical disciplines, such as sociology, economics or psychology, which may or may not coincide with the day-to-day concerns of the leisure or tourism industries. In fact, part of the role of the academic researcher is to 'stand apart' from the rest of the world and provide disinterested analysis, which may be critical and may not be seen as particularly supportive by those working in the industry. However, what some see as overly critical and unhelpful, or just plain irrelevant, others may see as insightful and constructive.

A number of applied disciplines focus specifically on aspects of the policy, planning and management process, such as planning, management, marketing or financial management. While academic research in these areas can also be critical rather than immediately instrumental, it is more likely to be driven by the sorts of issues which concern the industry. Generally, academics become involved in funded research of a practically orientated nature when their own interests coincide with those of the agency concerned. For instance, an academic may be interested in ways of measuring what motivates people to attend certain types of event, and this could coincide with an event-organising agency's need for research to assist in developing a marketing strategy. Some academics specialise in such applied areas, so they are very often in a better position to attract funding from industry sources.

4.2 Students

PhD, master's and honours degree students are major contributors to research. In the past, theses (or dissertations, to use the term more common in North America) were available only in hard copy at the library of the university which produced them. Increasingly in recent years, they have become available in digital form and university libraries generally subscribe to various thesis databases (see Chapter 6).

In the science area, research students often work as part of a team, under the direction of a supervisor who may determine what topics will be researched by individual students within a particular funded research programme. In the social sciences, this approach is less common, with students having a wider scope in their selection of research topic.

PhD dissertations are the most significant form of student research, but research done by master's degree and graduate diploma students, and even undergraduates in the form of projects and honours theses, can be a useful contribution to knowledge. Leisure and tourism are not generally well endowed with research funds, so even, for example, a small survey conducted by a group of undergraduates on a particular leisure activity or in a particular locality, or a thorough review of an area of literature, may be of considerable use or interest to others.

4.3 Government, commercial and non-profit organisations

Government, commercial and non-profit organisations conduct or commission research to inform policy, monitor performance or aid in decision-making. A term coined to describe this relationship between policy and research is *evidence-based policy* (Pawson, 2006). Some large organisations have their own in-house research organisations – for example, the Office of National Statistics in the United Kingdom, the Australian Bureau of Statistics in Australia and the

US Forest Service Experiment Stations in the United States. Commercial organisations in leisure and tourism tend to rely on consultants for their social, economic and market research, although equipment manufacturers, for instance in sport, may conduct their own scientific research for product development.

Research reports from these organisations can be important sources of knowledge, especially of a more practically oriented nature. For example, in nearly every developed country, some government agency takes responsibility for conducting nationwide surveys of tourism patterns, and for participation rates in leisure (Cushman et al., 2005), sport (Nicholson et al., 2011) and the arts (Schuster, 2007). This is descriptive research which few other organisations would have the resources or incentive to undertake.

4.4 Managers

Professionals in leisure and tourism who recognise the full extent of the management, policy-making and planning process see research as very much part of their responsibilities. Managers may find themselves carrying out research on a range of types of topic, as indicated in Table 1.6. Since most of the readers of this text will be actual or trainee managers, this is an important point to recognise.

Successful management depends on good information. Much information – for example, sales figures – is available to the manager as a matter of routine and does not require *research*. However, the creative utilisation of such data – for example, to establish market trends – may amount to research. Other types of information can be obtained only by means of specific research projects. In some areas of leisure and tourism management, even the most basic information must be obtained by research. For example, unlike managers of formal ticketed facilities like theatres or stadia, managers of informal and free facilities, such as urban parks or beaches, do not routinely receive information on the level of use of their facilities from sales figures or bookings. To gain such information, it is necessary

Table 1.6 Managers and research

Current customers
Market research: potential customers/community
Environmental appraisal
Organisational performance
• Sales
• Efficiency
• Staff performance/motivation
Competitors
Products
• Existing
• New

to conduct a specific data-gathering exercise, which may not be very sophisticated and therefore might not be viewed as *research* by some. However, being part of the management information system, involving *finding out* and sometimes *explaining* and often requiring the deployment of specific techniques and skills, it qualifies as research for the purposes of this book.

Most managers need to carry out – or commission – research if they want information on their users or customers: for example, where they live (the 'catchment area' of the facility) or their socio-economic characteristics. Research is also a way of finding out about customers' evaluations of the facility or service. It might be argued that managers do not themselves need research skills since they can always commission consultants to carry out research for them. However, managers will be better able to commission good research and evaluate the results if they are familiar with the research process themselves. It is also the case that few managers in leisure and tourism work in an ideal world where funds exist to commission all the research they would like; often the only way they can get research done is to do it using their own 'in-house' skills and time.

4.5 Consultants

Consultants offer their research and advisory services to government and commercial and non-profit organisations. Some consultancy organisations are large, multi-national companies involved in accountancy, management and project development consultancy generally, and who often establish specialised units covering the leisure and/or tourism field. Examples are PricewaterhouseCoopers and Ernst and Young. But there are also many smaller, specialised organisations in the consultancy field. Some academics operate consultancy companies as a 'side-line', either because of academic interest in a particular area or to supplement incomes, or both. Self-employed consultancy activity is common among practitioners who have taken early retirement from leisure or tourism industry employment.

5. Who pays?

Most research requires financial support to cover the costs of paying full-time or part-time research assistants, to pay for research student scholarships, to pay interviewers or a market research firm to conduct interviews or to cover travel costs or the costs of equipment. Research is funded from a variety of sources, as indicated in Table 1.7.

- *Unfunded*: Some research conducted by academics requires little or no specific financial resources over and above the academic's basic salary – for example, theoretical work and the many studies using students as subjects.

Table 1.7 Who pays?

- Unfunded
- University internal funds
- Government-funded research councils
- Private trusts
- Industry – public, commercial or non-profit

- *University internal funds:* Universities tend to use their own funds to support research which is initiated by academic staff and where the main motive is the 'advancement of knowledge'. Most universities and colleges have research funds for which members of their staff can apply.

- *Government-funded research councils:* Governments usually establish organisations to fund scientific research – for example, the UK Economic and Social Research Council and the Australian Research Council. These or similar bodies often also provide scholarships for research students.

- *Private trusts:* Many private trusts or foundations also fund research – for example, the Ford Foundation and the Leverhulme Trust. Trusts have generally been endowed with investment funds by a wealthy individual or from a public appeal.

- *Industry:* Funds may come from the world of practice – for example, from a government department or agency, from a commercial company or from a non-profit organisation such as the governing body of a sport. In this case, the research will tend to be more practically oriented. Government agencies and commercial and non-profit organisations fund research to solve particular problems or to inform them about particular issues relevant to their interests.

6. Research outputs

Research for leisure and tourism planning/management is presented in many forms and contexts. Some of these are listed in Table 1.8 and discussed briefly below. The formats are not all mutually exclusive: a number of them may arise in various aspects in a single research project.

6.1 Academic journal articles

Publication of research in academic journals is considered to be the most prestigious form in academic terms because of the element of *refereeing* or *peer review*. Articles submitted to such journals are assessed (refereed) on an anonymous

Table 1.8 Research report formats

1. Academic journal articles
2. Professional journal articles
3. Conference presentations/papers
4. Books
5. Policy/planning/management reports:
   - Position statements
   - Market profiles
   - Market research
   - Market segmentation/lifestyle/psychographic studies
   - Feasibility studies
   - Leisure/recreation needs studies
   - Tourism strategies/marketing plans
   - Forecasting studies
   - Impact studies
   - Industry/sector studies

basis by two or three experts in the field, as well as by the editors. Editorial activity is overseen by a board of experts in the field, whose names are listed in the journal. Some of the main refereed journals in the leisure and tourism area are listed in Table 1.9.

Academic research and publication is, to a large extent, a 'closed system'. Academics are the editors of the refereed journals and serve on their editorial advisory boards and referee panels. They therefore determine what research is acceptable for publication. Practitioners thus very often find published academic research irrelevant to their needs – this is hardly surprising, since much of it is designed not for the practitioner but for the academic world. This issue is a matter for some debate in the literature (e.g. Dredge, 2015a, 2015b). The student training to become a professional practitioner in the leisure or tourism field should not therefore be surprised to come across scholarly writing on leisure

Table 1.9 Refereed journals in leisure and tourism

- Journal of Leisure Research (USA)
- Leisure Studies (UK)
- Leisure Sciences (USA)
- Society and Leisure (Canada)
- Journal of Policy Research in Tourism, Leisure & Events (UK)
- Annals of Leisure Research (Australia)
- Annals of Tourism Research (USA)
- Tourism Management (UK)
- Journal of Travel Research (USA)
- Event Management (USA)
- International Journal of Event Management Research (Australia/UK)

Table 1.10   Examples of article impact (as at July 2017)

Indicator	Source	Veal et al. (2012) Olympic Games sport legacy	Veal (2012) The leisure society
Views/downloads	Publisher's website	6448	311
Citations in journals	Crossref database	45	8
Citations in journals	Scopus database	56	0
Citations in journals/books etc.	Google Scholar	86	16
Other online mentions	Altmetrics Attention Score	24	2

and tourism which is not suitable for direct practical application to policy, planning and management. This does not mean that it is irrelevant, but simply that it does not necessarily focus explicitly on immediate practical problems.

A key feature of academic journals and the articles they contain is their *impact*; that is, the extent to which the articles are cited in other publications. Databases permit statistics to be automatically collated at the journal, article and author levels. The *impact factor* for a journal for a given year refers to the last two complete calendar years and is the number of citations in the period divided by the number of articles published in the period. Thus, for example, the impact factor for 2016 (referring to years 2014 and 2015) was 1.05 for *Leisure Studies* and 2.27 for *Annals of Tourism Research*. For individual articles, the *impact metrics* can vary enormously, depending not only on the quality of the article but also on the database used and the popularity of the topic. This point is illustrated in Table 1.10, which shows data for two contrasting articles published at about the same time. Such metrics are becoming increasingly significant in assessing the performance of individual academics and research centres/departments.

6.2 Professional journal articles

Journals published by professional bodies for their members rarely include original research, but may publish summaries of research of immediate relevance to practitioners.

6.3 Conference papers/presentations

Some academic conferences publish the papers presented in a hard-copy or online set of *proceedings*. In some cases, such papers have been peer-reviewed and have a status similar to academic journals, but this is rare in leisure and tourism. Typically, research presented at a conference will also be published in journal or book form.

6.4 Books

Academic books can be divided into *textbooks*, like this text, and *monographs*, which may present the results of a single empirical research project or research programme, may be largely theoretical or may be a mixture of the two. Textbooks are not expected to present original research but may provide summaries and guides to research. Edited books with chapters contributed by a number of authors may be closer to the textbook model or, if they contain original research, to the monograph model.

6.5 Policy/planning/management reports

Research conducted by commercial bodies is usually confidential, but that conducted by government agencies is generally available to the public, typically online. Such reports can invariably be found on the websites of national agencies, such as sports councils or tourism commissions and government departments, and local councils. They can take a variety of forms:

- *Position statements:* are similar to the environmental appraisals discussed above in relation to the rational-comprehensive planning model. They are compilations of factual information on the current situation with regard to a topic or issue of concern, and are designed to assist decision-makers to become knowledgeable about the topic or issue and to take stock of such matters as current policies, provision levels and demand. For example, if a local council wishes to develop new policies for heritage conservation in its area, a position statement might be prepared listing what actual and potential heritage properties and attractions currently exist, their ownership, quality, nature and state of preservation, existing policies, rules and regulations and types and level of use.

- *Market profiles:* are similar to position statements, but relate specifically to current and potential consumers and suppliers of a product or service. If an organisation wishes to start a project in a particular tourism or leisure market it will usually require a profile of that market sector. How big is the market? What are its growth prospects? Who are the customers? What sub-sectors does it have? How profitable is it? Who are the current suppliers? Such a profile will usually require considerable research and can be seen as one element in the broader activity of market research.

- *Market research:* is a more encompassing activity. Research on the actual or potential market for a product or service can take place in advance of a service being established but also as part of the ongoing monitoring of the performance of an operation. Market research seeks to establish the scale and nature of the current market – the number of people who use or are likely to use the product or service and their socio-demographic characteristics and expenditure patterns – and actual and potential customer requirements and attitudes.

- *Market segmentation/lifestyle/psychographic studies:* traditionally, market researchers attempted to classify consumers into sub-markets or segments on the basis of their product preferences, including leisure activities and holiday behaviour, and their socio-demographic characteristics such as age, gender, occupation and income. Later they used not only these variables but also information on attitudes, values and behaviour. Such lifestyle *segments* may be developed as part of any survey-based research project, but there are also commercially developed systems which survey companies may apply to a range of market research projects. Examples are discussed in Chapter 5.

- *Feasibility studies:* investigate not only current consumer characteristics and demands, as in a market profile, but also future demand and such aspects as the financial viability and environmental impact of proposed development or investment projects. The decision whether or not to build a new leisure facility or launch a new tourism product is usually based on a feasibility study.

- *Leisure/recreation needs studies:* are a common type of research in leisure planning. These are comprehensive studies, usually carried out for local councils, examining levels of provision and use of leisure facilities and services, levels of participation in leisure activities, and views and aspirations of the population concerning their own leisure preferences and desired provision. In some cases, a needs study also includes a leisure or recreation 'plan', which makes recommendations on future provision; in other cases, the plan is a separate document. It has been argued that so-called leisure needs studies are not needs studies at all, since they do not investigate what people need, but what they want, would like to do or might do in the future.

- *Tourism strategies/tourism marketing plans:* are the tourism equivalent of the leisure/recreation needs study, but rather than referring to the needs of the local population, tourism strategies or marketing plans refer to the tourism demands of non-local populations to be accommodated in a destination area. Such tourism studies usually consider the capacity of the host area to meet the demands of a projected volume of tourism, in terms of accommodation, transport, existing and potential attractions and acceptable levels of environmental impacts.

- *Forecasting studies:* form a key input to many plans. They might provide, for example, projections of demand for a particular leisure activity or for a particular type of tourist accommodation over a 10-year period. Forecasting is intrinsically research-based and can involve predicting the likely effects of future population growth and change, the effects of changing tastes, changing levels of income or developments in technology. Leisure and tourism forecasting have become substantial fields of study in their own right.

- *Impact studies:* large built developments typically require an environmental impact study to be undertaken as part of the process of gaining approval from planning agencies, covering matters such as noise and traffic generation and impacts on natural and cultural heritage. This can also apply to proposed major events, particularly sporting events, which typically require the conduct of an economic impact study to demonstrate that the costs incurred by the hosting of an event will be more than offset by benefits, such as the generation of income, jobs and other types of legacy.

● *Performance appraisals:* organisations, facilities, teams and individuals are often expected to work to achieve a performance target set out in some plan or contract. Regular *performance appraisals* may therefore be undertaken to check progress. For individuals, this may be a comparatively simple process, and the result may be set out in a few pages and, following discussion with a supervisor, lodged on the individual's file. For facilities and organisations, the process will inevitably be more complex and may involve research activity and lengthy reports. A simple example would be measures of customer satisfaction, or public perceptions which typically involve customer and community surveys.

● *Industry/sector studies:* in common with other sectors, organisational stakeholders in leisure and tourism, from time to time, see the need to set out the scale, (economic) significance and impacts of the sector, in an effort to raise the awareness of the sector among governments, other industry sectors, media and the general public.

7. Terminology

Like any field of study and practice, research methods has its own distinct terminology, some of which is familiar to the wider community and some of which is not. Most terms and expressions will be introduced and defined in the appropriate chapters which follow; but some are common to the whole research process, and some key ones are described here.

Subject is used to refer to people providing information or being studied in a research project. For example, if a social survey involves interviews with a sample of 200 people, it involves 200 *subjects*. Some researchers prefer to use the term *participant*, believing that subject implies subjective, suggesting a hierarchical relationship between the researcher and the researched. The term *case* is sometimes used, particularly when the phenomenon being researched is not individual people – for example, organisations, countries, destinations or sports.

Variable refers to a characteristic, behaviour pattern or opinion which varies from subject to subject. Thus, for example, age, income, level of holiday-taking and music preferences are all variables. An *independent* variable is one which is controlled by forces outside the context of the study and which influences *dependent* variables within the scope of the study. Thus, for example, in a study of outdoor recreation, the weather would be an independent variable while the number of people who visit a park would be a dependent variable. In another context, such as the study of climate, the weather could be a dependent variable influenced by such independent variables as the behaviour of the sun and the temperature of the oceans.

8. Using this text

The aim in compiling this text has been to be as comprehensive as possible, to cater for a wide range of potential users and to provide guidance in relation to the diversity of material and issues which readers are likely to encounter in their own reading and research practice. Most users will therefore be selective in their use of the various parts of the text, depending on their interests, needs and time available. Often this process of selection will be guided by a teacher or supervisor. The summaries and diagrammatic outlines of chapter contents, various summary tables and detailed table of contents and index are designed to aid the process of selection and the use of the text as a reference work. It should be emphasised that substantial sections of the text are designed as a working manual to be used alongside actual research activity: this applies particularly to the detailed outline of the research process (Chapter 3) and to the analysis chapters involving computer software (Chapters 15–17).

In Part I, a great deal of material of a general nature is covered. Just a limited number of leisure and tourism examples or illustrations is given, but further references are provided in the Resources sections, and users of the text are encouraged to explore their own examples and applications in the questions and exercises. The application of specific methods is referred to in illustrative leisure and tourism examples in Case Studies in Parts II and III. Readers who have worked in the leisure and tourism industry will be able to relate the theoretical or generic discussions to their own experience and knowledge of the industry and its participants. Those who do not have such work experience nevertheless have experience of leisure facilities, such as local or national parks, cinemas or museums. It is also possible to familiarise oneself, to some extent, with relevant organisations responsible for such facilities via their websites. It should be possible, therefore, to relate the discussion to real-world examples. In some cases, the reader is encouraged to do this in questions and exercises at the end of each chapter. Research is a means to an end. A textbook on research methods is a means to the means. While few people enjoy reading cookbooks for their own sake, some enjoy actually cooking, with or without the aid of a recipe, but everyone enjoys eating good food.

Summary

This chapter addresses the 'What?' of research in defining and introducing the concept of research and describes three types of research with which this text is concerned: descriptive, explanatory and evaluative. The 'Why?' of research is discussed primarily in the context of policy-making, planning and management, since the majority of the users of the text will be studying for a vocational qualification. The links between research and the various stages of policy-making, planning and management are discussed using the rational-comprehensive model as a framework, and attention is drawn to the variety of forms that research reports can take in the management environment. 'Who?' conducts research is an important and often neglected aspect of research: in this chapter, the respective research roles of academics, students, governmental and commercial organisations, consultants and managers are discussed. Finally, there is an introduction to the various formats in which research results may be published, from academic journal articles to a variety of management-related reports.

Test questions

1. What is the difference between research and investigative journalism?

2. Outline the differences between *descriptive*, *explanatory* and *evaluative* research.

3. What are the broad differences between policy-making, planning and management, as presented in this chapter?

4. Summarise the potential role of research in three of the ten steps in the 'rational-comprehensive' model of the policy-making/planning/management process presented in this chapter.

5. Name three of the 12 formats which research reports might take, as put forward in this chapter and outline their basic features.

6. Outline three of the six topics, as put forward in this chapter, on which managers might conduct or commission research.

7. Why does academic research often appear to be irrelevant to the immediate needs of practitioners?

Exercises

1. Choose a leisure or tourism organisation with which you are familiar, or which can be identified online, and outline ways in which it might use research to pursue its objectives.

2. Choose a large leisure or tourism organisation and investigate its research activities from its website. What proportion of its budget does it devote to research? What research has it carried out? How are the results of the research used, by the organisation or others?

3. Select a recent edition of a leisure or tourism journal, such as *Leisure Studies* or *Annals of Tourism Research*, and ascertain for each article why the research was conducted, how it was funded and who or what organisations are likely to benefit from the research and how.

4. Using the same journal edition as in Exercise 3, examine each article and determine whether the research is descriptive, explanatory or evaluative.

Resources

Websites

Harzing's Publish or Perish program: www.harzing.com/resources/publish-or-perish

Publications

- Conjoint analysis: see Chapter 5.

- Descriptive research:
    - leisure: Cushman et al. (2005); Veal (2003);
    - sport: Nicholson et al. (2011); and
    - the arts: Schuster (2007).

- Evaluative research: Blankenship (2010), Henderson and Bialeschki (2010), Jennings (2011), Pollard (1987), Shadish et al. (1991), Veal (2017: Ch. 14, 15), Xiao and Smith (2006).

- Evidence-based policy: Pawson (2006), Ruiz (2004), Solesbury (2002).

- Exploratory research: Stebbins (1997).

- Importance-performance analysis:
    - general: Martilla and James (1977);
    - recreation and parks: Hunt et al. (2003); and
    - tourism: Azzopardi and Nash (2013), Oh (2001).

- Industry sector studies:
    - arts: CEBR (2013), DCMS (2016); and
    - outdoor recreation: Sport and Recreation Alliance (2015).

- Leisure/recreation needs studies: Veal (2009).

- Leisure and tourism forecasting: Archer (1994), Veal (1999, 2017: Ch. 13).

- Models of planning and policy-making:
  - introductory discussions: Parsons (1995: 248ff), Veal (2016, 2017: Ch. 8); and
  - more advanced discussion: Treuren and Lane (2003).

- Relevance of academic research:
  - sport/tourism: Downward (2005); and
  - tourism: Dredge (2015a); comments on Dredge from Minnaert (2015), Mosedale (2015), Scott (2015) and Thomas (2015); and a reply by Dredge (2015b).

- Research in the planning process: Veal (2017).

- Segmentation/psychographics/lifestyle: Chisnall (1991), Veal (1993, 2013), Wells (1974).

- Terminology: Atkinson (2012), Blackshaw and Crawford (2006).

- Tourism research methods: Ritchie and Goeldner (1994), Ryan (1995), Sirakaya-Turk et al. (2011), Smith (2010).

- Tourism strategies/marketing plans: Middleton et al. (2009: Ch. 10).

- Transformative research: Mertens (2009), Stewart (2014).

References

Atkinson, M. (2012). *Key concepts in sport and exercise research methods*. London: Sage.

Azzopardi, E., and Nash, R. (2013). A critical evaluation of importance-performance analysis. *Tourism Management*, 35, 222–33.

Blackshaw, T., and Crawford, G. (2006). *The Sage dictionary of leisure studies*. London: Sage.

Blankenship, D. C. (2010). *Applied research and evaluation methods in recreation*. Champaign, IL: Human Kinetics.

Centre for Economics & Business Research (CEBR) (2013). *The contribution of the arts and culture to the national economy: report for Arts Council England and the National Museums Directors' Council*. London: CEBR.

Chisnall, P. M. (1991). Market segmentation analysis. Chapter 6 of *The essence of marketing research* (pp. 76–91). New York: Prentice-Hall.

Cushman, G., Veal, A. J., and Zuzanek, J. (Eds) (2005). *Free time and leisure participation: international perspectives*. Wallingford, UK: CABI Publishing.

Department for Culture, Media and Sport (DCMS) (2016). *Creative industries economic estimates January 2016*. London: DCMS.

Downward, P. (2005). Critical (realist) reflection on policy and management research in sport, tourism and sports tourism. *European Sport Management Quarterly*, 5(3), 303–20.

Dredge (2015a). Does relevance matter in academic policy research? *Journal of Policy Research in Tourism, Leisure and Events*, 7(2), 173–7.

Dredge, D. (2015b). Does relevance matter in academic research? Further reflections. *Journal of Policy Research in Tourism, Leisure and Events*, 7(2), 195–99.

Elias, N. (1986). Introduction. In N. Elias and E. Dunning (Eds), *Quest for excitement: sport and leisure in the civilizing* process (pp. 19–62). Oxford: Basil Blackwell.

Henderson, K. A., and Bialeschki, D. (2010). *Evaluating leisure services: making enlightened decisions*, 3rd edn. State College, PA: Venture.

Hunt, K. S., Scott, D., and Richardson, S. (2003). Positioning public recreation and park offerings using importance-performance analysis. *Journal of Park and Recreation Administration*, 21(3), 1–21.

Jennings, G. (2011). Evaluation research methods in leisure, recreation and tourism research. In E. Sirakaya-Turk, M. Uysal, W. E. Hammitt and J. J. Vaske (Eds), *Research methods for leisure, recreation and tourism* (pp. 140–61). Wallingford, UK: CABI.

Martilla, J. A., and James, J. C. (1977). Importance-performance analysis. *Journal of Marketing*, 41(1), 77–9.

Mertens, D. M. (2009). *Transformative research and evaluation*. New York: Guilford Press.

Middleton, V. T. C., Fyall, A., and Morgan, M. (2009). *Marketing in travel and tourism*, 4th edn. Oxford: Butterworth-Heinemann.

Minnaert, L. (2015). Does relevance matter in academic policy research? A comment on Dredge. *Journal of Policy Research in Tourism, Leisure and Events*, 7(2), 190–4.

Mosedale, J. (2015). Does relevance matter in academic policy research? A comment on Dredge. *Journal of Policy Research in Tourism, Leisure and Events*, 7(2), 183–6.

Nicholson, M., Hoye, R., and Houlihan, B. (Eds) (2011). *Participation in sport: international policy perspectives*. London: Routledge.

Oh, H. (2001). Revisiting important-performance analysis. *Tourism Management*, 22, 617–27.

Parsons, W. (1995). *Public Policy*. Cheltenham, UK: Edward Elgar.

Pawson, R. (2006). *Evidence-based policy: a realist perspective*. London: Sage.

Pollard, W. E. (1987). Decision making and the use of evaluation research. *American Behavioral Scientist*, 30(6), 661–76.

Ritchie, J. R. B., and Goeldner, C. R. (Eds) (1994). *Travel, tourism and hospitality research*, 2nd edn. New York: John Wiley.

Ruiz, J. (2004). *A Literature review of the evidence base for culture, the arts and sport policy*. Edinburgh: Social Research, Scottish Executive. Available at: www.scotland.gov.uk/Publications/2004/08/19784/41507.

Ryan, C. (1995). *Researching tourist satisfaction: issues, concepts, problems*. London: Routledge.

Schuster, J. M. (2007). Participation studies and cross-national comparison: proliferation, prudence, and possibility. *Cultural Trends*, 16(2), 99–196.

Scott, N. (2015). Does relevance matter in academic policy research? A comment on Dredge. *Journal of Policy Research in Tourism, Leisure and Events*, 7(2), 187–9.

Shadish, W. R., Jr., Cook, T. D., and Leviton, L. C. (1991). *Foundations of program evaluation: theories of practice*. Newbury Park, CA: Sage.

Sirakaya-Turk, E., Uysal, M., Hammitt, W. E., and Vaske, J. J. (Eds) (2011). *Research methods for leisure, recreation and tourism*. Wallingford, UK: CABI.

Smith, S. L. J. (2010). *Practical tourism research*. Wallingford, UK: CABI.

Solesbury, W. (2002). The ascendancy of evidence. *Planning Theory and Practice*, 3(1), 90–6.

Sport and Recreation Alliance (2015). Reconomics: the economic impact of outdoor recreation in the UK: the evidence. London: Sport and Recreation Alliance.

Stebbins, R. A. (1997). Exploratory research as an antidote to theoretical stagnation in leisure studies. *Society & Leisure*, 20(2), 421–34.

Stewart, W. (2014). Leisure research to enhance social justice. *Leisure Sciences*, 36(4), 325–39.

Thomas, H. (2015). Does relevance matter in academic policy research? A comment on Dredge. *Journal of Policy Research in Tourism, Leisure and Events*, 7(2), 178–82.

Treuren, G., and Lane, D. (2003). The tourism planning process in the context of organised interests, industry structure, state capacity, accumulation and sustainability. *Current Issues in Tourism*, 6(1), 1–22.

Veal, A. J. (1993). The concept of lifestyle: a review. *Leisure Studies*, 12(4), 233–52.

Veal, A. J. (1999). Forecasting leisure and recreation. In E. L. Jackson and T. L. Burton (Eds), *Leisure Studies: Prospects for the Twenty-First Century* (pp. 385–98). State College, PA: Venture.

Veal, A. J. (2003). Tracking change: leisure participation and policy in Australia, 1985–2002. *Annals of Leisure Research*, 6(3), 246–78.

Veal, A. J. (2009). *Leisure and the concept of need: U-Plan Project Paper 4*. Available at: www.leisuresource.net, under 'U-Plan'.

Veal, A. J. (2012). The leisure society II: the era of critique, 1980–2011. *World Leisure Journal*, 54(2), 99–140.

Veal, A. J. (2013). Lifestyle and leisure theory. In T. Blackshaw (Ed), *Routledge handbook of leisure studies* (pp. 266–79). London: Routledge.

Veal, A. J. (2016). Policy and planning frameworks. In G. Walker, D. Scott and M. Stodolska (Eds), *Leisure matters* (pp. 287–94). State College, PA: Venture.

Veal, A. J. (2017). *Leisure, sport and tourism: politics, policy and planning*, 4th edn. Wallingford, UK: CABI Publishing.

Veal, A. J., Frawley, S., and Toohey, K. (2012). The sport participation legacy of the Sydney 2000 Olympic Games and other international sporting events hosted in Australia. *Journal of Policy Research in Tourism, Leisure and Events*, 4(2), 155–84.

Wells, W. D. (Ed) (1974). *Life style and psychographics*. Chicago: American Marketing Association.

Xiao, H., and Smith, S. L. J. (2006). The making of tourism research: insights from a social sciences journal. *Annals of Tourism Research*, 33(2), 490–507.

2 Approaches to leisure and tourism research

1. Introduction

The aim of the chapter is to introduce a range of disciplines and paradigms within which leisure and tourism research is conducted.

2. Disciplinary traditions

The bulk of published leisure and tourism research has arisen not from the demands of the leisure and tourism industries, but from the interests of academics who owe allegiance to a particular discipline. Here we examine, very briefly, the contributions from academic disciplines that have been particularly significant in the field, namely:

● sociology and cultural studies,

● economics,

● geography/environmental studies,

● psychology/social psychology,

● history and anthropology,

● political science.

Disciplines are characterised by the particular aspect or dimension of the universe with which they are concerned, the theories which they develop for explanation and the distinctive techniques they use for conducting research. Some commentators refer to leisure studies and tourism studies as disciplines, but since, arguably, they do not meet the criteria for a free-standing discipline, in this text they are seen as multi-disciplinary, cross-disciplinary or inter-disciplinary *fields of study*:

● Multi-disciplinary means that research from a number of disciplines is used – for example, the economics and the sociology of leisure/tourism.

● Cross-disciplinary means that issues, theories, concepts and methods which are common to more than one discipline are involved.

● Inter-disciplinary refers to sub-fields of research which do not fit neatly into any particular discipline – for example, time-budget research.

When reading in the area of leisure and tourism studies, it should be noted that not all commentators keep the wide mix of disciplines consistently in mind. For example, when making comments on 'leisure studies', they may in fact be discussing only 'the sociology of leisure'.

We should also note that there are other fields of study which are generally longer-established than leisure and tourism studies and are variously referred to as disciplines, *applied disciplines* or *fields of study*. The first of these is *cultural studies*, which sits somewhere between sociology and the humanities but, because of its particular history in relation to leisure studies, is best treated together with sociology. Other fields are *management*, *marketing*, *planning* and *education.* However, despite the importance of these fields of study for professional practitioners in the leisure and tourism sectors, they are not examined separately in this chapter because, for research purposes, they generally draw, to varying degrees, on the methods associated with the six disciplines listed earlier.

The relationships between leisure and tourism research and the six disciplines are summarised in Table 2.1, which presents examples of descriptive, explanatory and evaluative research topics/questions addressed by each discipline. Further relevant reading is in the Resources section.

Table 2.1 Disciplines and examples of research questions

Descriptive	Explanatory	Evaluative
Sociology		
• What proportions of the population and of various age, gender, ethnic and socio-economic groups participate in specified leisure activities? • What are the trends in numbers of tourists visiting a particular destination over the last 10 years?	• Why do members of middle-class, highly educated groups make greater use of cultural facilities than members of other groups? • What factors influence rises and falls in tourist visits to a particular tourist destination?	• To what extent have policies designed to boost women's participation in sport been successful? • How successful has a training programme been in increasing locals' employment in the tourism industry?
Geography/environment		
• What is the spatial area from which most users of a particular leisure facility travel? • What impacts does a particular island tourist resort have on the environment?	• What is the relative importance of distance and travel time in affecting use of a particular leisure facility? • How do the different styles of tourism (back-packer, package tour, touring) impact on the environment?	• How effective is the local council in meeting the leisure demands of all neighbourhoods in its area? • How effective is the tourism strategy in protecting the environment from the impacts of tourism?
Economics		
• What proportion of household expenditure is devoted to leisure/tourism goods and services? • What proportion of the labour force works in the leisure and tourism industries?	• What is the relationship between level of income and expenditure on leisure and tourism? • What is the relationship between travel cost and level of visits to a leisure/tourism facility?	• What are the costs and benefits of hosting the Olympic Games? • What has been the economic impact of developing tourism at destination X?

(continued)

Table 2.1 *(continued)*

Descriptive	Explanatory	Evaluative
Psychology/social psychology • What satisfactions do people obtain from engaging in a leisure activity or going on holiday? • What is the level of stress among teenagers?	• To what extent is Maslow's hierarchy of needs relevant to leisure/tourism? • Does leisure activity/going on holiday relieve stress? If so, how lasting is this?	• How effective has a youth sports programme been in enhancing participants' self-esteem? • How effective has a marketing policy been in enhancing visitor satisfaction?
History/anthropology • How has the balance between work and leisure time changed since 1900? • What is the history of the 'Grand Tour'?	• What has been the influence of marketing and materialism on changes in the work/life balance since 1950? • What has caused the growth in gambling over the past 20 years?	• How successful have public policies to increase physical activity been over the past 30 years? • Over the past 30 years, have governments helped or hindered the development of tourism?
Political/policy science • What are the leisure/tourism policies of the major political parties? • What proportion of publicly owned leisure facilities are managed by commercial contract?	• How has changing political philosophy affected leisure and tourism policies in the last two changes of government? • How is power exercised in leisure/tourism contexts?	• How effective are policies directed at 'inclusion' in increasing leisure participation? • How effective have joint public–private partnerships been in leisure/tourism development?

3. Approaches, dimensions, issues, terminology

Here we discuss a number of approaches, dimensions, issues and associated terminology which recur in the research literature and discourses on research, and of which at least a basic understanding is necessary if the literature and the discourses are to be understood. They are listed in Table 2.2. Those terms which arise in pairs, X and Y, are often presented in the literature as X *versus* Y. But X and Y are not always opposed to one another; they are often complementary, so here the form X *and* Y is used. In this text, rather than 'either/or' thinking, the idea of 'both/and' thinking is embraced (Ateljevic, Morgan and Pritchard, 2007: 3). Since it is impossible to analyse all the terms and concepts in detail in this introductory chapter, especially

Table 2.2 Terminology, approaches, dimensions and issues

Terms/concepts	Brief definition	Associated terms
Ontology	Way of looking at the world.	Paradigm, philosophy
Epistemology	Relationship between researcher and the subject of research.	–
Methodology	Ways of gathering and analysing data.	Technique
Positivist	Hypotheses are tested using objectively collected factual data which, if successful, produces scientific laws.	Scientific method, logical empiricist, functionalist, objectivist
Post-positivist	Hypotheses found to be consistent (or not) with the data deemed to be 'not falsified', establishing *probable* facts or laws.	Realist
Interpretive	People provide their own accounts or explanation of situation/behaviour.	Symbolic interaction, phenomenology, phenomenography, grounded theory, subjectivist, intersubjectivity, ethnography.
Critical	Research influenced by beliefs/values critical of the status quo in society.	Standpoint, transformative, emancipatory
Constructivist	People construct their own views of reality and the researcher seeks to discover this.	Social constructivism
Descriptive	Seeks to describe what is.	Exploratory
Explanatory	Seeks to explain relationships between phenomena.	Predictive
Evaluative	Seeks to test policy/management outcomes against benchmarks.	
Qualitative	Research in which words (and possibly images, sounds) are the medium.	
Quantitative	Research in which numbers are the main medium.	
Pragmatism	Located between positivist and interpretive/relativist position; often policy/management-focused	Mixed methods, *bricolage*, eclecticism
Participatory	Researcher and subjects jointly influence the pattern of research.	Action research (see Chapter 5)
Theoretical	Research which results in general propositions about how things/people behave.	Pure
Applied	Use of research to address particular policy/management issues.	Evidence-based

(continued)

Table 2.2   (*continued*)

Terms/concepts	Brief definition	Associated terms
Experimental	Research where the researcher seeks to control all variables.	Controlled experiment
Naturalistic	Research where subjects are researched in their 'natural' environment where the researcher's control is minimal.	Real-life context
Reflexive	The process of examining the relationship between the researcher and the subject of the research.	Intersubjective
Empirical	Research involving data – quantitative or qualitative, or both.	
Non-empirical	Research involving only theory and the literature.	Theoretical
Inductive	Hypotheses/explanations/theory are generated from examination of the data.	Exploratory
Deductive	Data collected to test a priori hypotheses.	Hypothetical-deductive, confirmatory
Primary data	Data gathered by the researcher for the current project.	
Secondary data	Use of existing data gathered by other people/organisations for other purposes.	
Self-reported	Subjects' own accounts of activity/behaviour.	
Observed	Researcher's observation of subjects' activity/behaviour.	Unobtrusive
Validity	The research accurately identifies/measures what is intended.	
Reliability	Repetition of the research would produce similar findings.	
Trustworthiness	Trust which can be placed in qualitative research.	

given that definitions vary in the literature, additional sources are provided in the Resources section of the chapter.

3.1 Ontology, epistemology, methodology

Ontology, epistemology and methodology are frequently encountered in discussions of research approaches, particularly in sociology:

● Ontology refers to the nature of reality assumed – in the positivist paradigm (see the next section), it is assumed that the 'real world' is as seen by the observer, while in interpretive and similar approaches, the observer's perspective is not privileged: it is accepted that 'reality' may be perceived differently by different people/groups.

- Epistemology refers to the relationship between the researcher and the phenomenon being studied. Again, the distinction is most sharply drawn between the positivist and interpretive stance; the positivist researcher seeks to adopt an objective, distanced stance, while the interpretive researcher is more subjective and engaged with the subjects of the study.

- Methodology refers to the ways by which knowledge and understanding are established through research. For example, the method used in the classic positivist approach is the controlled experiment (as discussed in section 3.9), which is only possible in a limited number of leisure and tourism research contexts. The quantitative and qualitative divide, as discussed in section 3.4 of this chapter, also highlights distinctive methodologies. Ideally the choice of method in a study should be closely influenced by the ontological and epistemological perspectives used.

3.2 Positivist, post-positivist, interpretive and critical approaches/paradigms

The positivist, post-positivist and interpretive and critical approaches refer to *paradigms* in the social sciences which are ways of looking at the theoretical/ research world:

- Positivism is a framework of research, similar to that adopted by the natural scientist, in which the researcher sees the phenomena to be studied from the outside, with behaviour to be explained on the basis of data and observations objectively gathered by the researcher, using theories and models developed by the researcher. The classic positivist approach involves the hypothetical-deductive model, which uses a deductive process (as discussed in section 3.4 of this chapter) to test a pre-established hypothesis. If successful, this results in the establishment of 'laws' – for example, Newton's laws of motion. Many commentators are highly suspicious of such attempts to translate natural science approaches into the social sciences, arguing that it is inappropriate to draw conclusions about the causes and motivations of human behaviour on the basis of the type of evidence used in the natural sciences. Botterill and Platenkamp (2012: 147) observe that, despite its significance in the development of tourism research, positivism has 'almost become a term of derision in some circles'.

- Post-positivism is distinguished from the classic positivist approach by some writers (for example Guba and Lincoln, 2006) as an approach in which hypotheses found to be consistent with the data are deemed to be 'not falsified'; researchers do not claim to have discovered the 'truth' but to have established probable facts or laws which are useful until such time as they are supplanted by new theories/laws which provide a fuller or more comprehensive explanation of the available data.

- Interpretive approaches to research place reliance on people providing their own explanations of their situation or behaviour. The interpretive researcher tries to 'get inside' the minds of subjects and see the world from their varied points of view. This of course suggests a more flexible approach to data collection, usually involving qualitative methods and generally an inductive approach. A number of variations exist within this category, as indicated in the 'associated terms' column in Table 2.2, and these are discussed in Chapter 9.

- Critical approaches to research are influenced by particular sets of beliefs or values which are critical of the status quo in society: the most common in leisure and tourism are related to neo-Marxist perspectives, which are critical of the capitalist system, and various feminist perspectives, which are critical of the economic, social and political inequality between men and women. There are numerous other perspectives which researchers may adopt or causes with which they may be associated. One term used for research shaped by such commitments is standpoint research (Humberstone, 2004), while Karla Henderson (2009) has used the term *just research* to refer to research which not only is about diversity and inclusiveness but is committed to its achievement. Ateljevic et al. (2007: 3) see critical tourism scholarship as 'a way of being, a commitment to tourism enquiry which is pro-social justice and equality and anti-oppression: it is an academy of hope'. Other terms used in this context are transformative and emancipatory research. Compared with the 'relativist' position of the interpretive approach, critical theorists/researchers are committed to social change (Chambers, 2007), although how far they wish to go in achieving this is not always clear. Typically, it is declared that positivists are not concerned with social justice or social change, although this is clearly not universally true, as recent empirical work on inequality in Western society demonstrates (e.g. Piketty, 2014; Veal, 2016a; Wilkinson and Pickett, 2009).

Along with parallel debates on quantitative and qualitative research, there is much debate in the leisure and tourism studies literature on the relative merits, suitability and appropriateness of the above alternative approaches to research. However, since leisure and tourism researchers are generally all using a combination of theory and empirical evidence to draw conclusions, the question arises as to how great the underlying, as opposed to surface, differences are between these approaches. Allen Lee (1989), using the terms 'subjectivist' and 'objectivist', argues that a subjectivist case study in organisation studies has similarities to the classic scientific experiment.

In the 1990s, numerous commentators, in calling for more interpretive and qualitative research, referred to positivist, and quantitative, approaches as dominant in leisure and tourism studies. Since the 1990s, with the wide range of research approaches evident in published research, particularly outside North America, this is hard to substantiate. While positivism can be said to be still dominant in tourism, interpretive research is becoming increasingly common there also, although commentary on this is difficult to disentangle from discussions of qualitative versus quantitative research methods (e.g. see Phillimore and Goodson, 2004).

3.3 Descriptive, explanatory, evaluative

In Chapter 1 the differences between descriptive, explanatory and evaluative research were discussed. Two additional points are added here, in regard to the first two categories.

Descriptive research and classification

In addition to the gathering of descriptive data, as discussed in Chapter 1, descriptive research can involve the task of *classification*, which is essential for all fields of research. Thus, for example, physical sciences involve the classification of *elements* and biological science the classification of *species*. In the social sciences, we see the classification of social classes, occupations, age-groups/generations, genders, ethnic groups and household types. Sometimes classificatory systems are functional in nature and are used for convenience; in other cases, they have theoretical significance. For example, as discussed in Chapter 10, people can be classified in occupational groups (manual, professional, managerial, etc.), sometimes referred to as socio-economic status, as a descriptive variable for use in censuses and surveys; or they may be grouped into classes (working, middle, upper-middle), which has much more theoretical significance (Chan and Goldthorpe, 2007). There are numerous examples of classificatory systems in leisure and tourism. Beyond the most common classification of leisure into such groupings as active and passive or sport, social activity, cultural activity and tourism, one of the most well-known systems is Stebbins' Serious Leisure Perspective (Elkington and Stebbins, 2014), which groups leisure activities into serious, casual and project-based forms. In tourism, beyond conventional classifications into domestic/international and leisure/business/visiting friends and relatives, the most well-known classification is Cohen's (1972): organised mass tourist, individual mass tourist, explorer and drifter.

Explanatory research and causality

Explanatory research in particular raises the issue of causality: whether or not A is the cause of B. Labovitz and Hagendorn (1971: 4) state that there are 'at least four widely accepted scientific criteria for establishing causality. These criteria are association, time priority, non-spurious relation and rationale':

- Association is a 'necessary condition for a causal relation' – that is, A and B must be associated in some way. For example, A increases when B decreases.

  There are two characteristics of an association that generally strengthen the conclusion that one variable is at least a partial cause of another. The first is magnitude, which refers to the size or strength of the association . . . The second . . . is consistency. If the relation persists from one study to the next under a variety of conditions, confidence in the causal nature of the relation is increased. (Labovitz and Hagendorn, 1971: 5)

- Time priority means that for A to be the cause of B, A must take place before B.

- Non-spurious relationships are defined as associations between two variables that 'cannot be explained by a third variable' (Labovitz and Hagendorn, 1971: 9). This means that it must be established that there is no third factor, C, which is affecting both A and B.

- Rationale means that statistical or other evidence is not enough; the conclusion that A causes B is not justified simply on the basis of an observed relationship; it should be supported by some plausible, theoretical or logical explanation to suggest how it happens.

These matters are taken up again in Chapter 3 and the chapters in Part III.

3.4 Quantitative and qualitative research

Much leisure and tourism research involves the collection, analysis and presentation of statistical information. Sometimes the information is innately quantitative – for instance, the numbers of people engaging in a list of leisure activities in a year, the number of tourists visiting a particular holiday area or the average income of a group of people. Sometimes the information is qualitative in nature but is presented in quantitative form – for instance, numerical scores obtained by asking people to indicate levels of satisfaction with different services, where the scores range from 1, 'very satisfied', to 5, 'very dissatisfied'.

The *quantitative* approach to research involves numerical data. It relies on numerical evidence to draw conclusions or to test hypotheses. To be sure of the reliability of the results, it is often necessary to study relatively large numbers of people and to use computers to analyse the data. The data can be derived from questionnaire surveys, from observation involving counts, or from administrative sources, such as ticket sales data from a leisure facility or data collected by immigration authorities at airports on the number of tourist arrivals from different origins.

There are three approaches to quantitative research:

- Type A: hypothetical-deductive quantitative research conforms to the hypothetical-deductive model discussed under positivism earlier. Invariably statistical methods and tests, such as the chi-square tests, t-tests, analysis of variance, correlation or regression outlined in Chapter 17, are used. This model is implicit in many discussions of quantitative methods.

- Type B: statistical quantitative research makes use of statistical methods and tests but is not necessarily hypothetical-deductive. It can be descriptive, exploratory and/or deductive.

- Type C: inductive quantitative research is based on numerical data but makes little or no use of statistical tests; its most sophisticated statistical measure is usually the percentage and sometimes means/averages. This type of quantitative research is very common in the British tradition of leisure and tourism research. For example, in reading the British journal *Leisure Studies*, it is notable that, whereas many articles present numerical information, very few utilise the types of statistical tests and techniques discussed in Chapter 17. This is in marked contrast to the leading American *Journal of Leisure Research*, where a substantial proportion of the articles that include numerical data make use of such tests, so are of type A or B. Type C quantitative research is more informal than type B or type A and is closer in approach to qualitative methods.

The *qualitative* approach to research is generally not concerned with numbers but typically with information in the form of words, conveyed orally or in writing. In addition to words, images and sounds *may* also be involved. Definitions offered in the literature often go beyond this minimalist definition to include types of methods which are often associated with qualitative research but, arguably, are not exclusive to the approach. Thus, for example, Denzin and Lincoln (2006: 3) include in their definition the proposition that qualitative research practices 'transform the world', when clearly any type of research may achieve this. Similarly, they state that qualitative research involves a *'naturalistic'* (see section 3.9 in this chapter) approach, when clearly qualitative methods may be deployed in non-naturalistic settings (for example, a laboratory) and quantitative research may take place in 'naturalistic' settings (for example, quantitative observation at a leisure/tourism site).

Qualitative research methods generally make it possible to gather a relatively large amount of information about the research subjects, which may be individuals, places or organisations. But the collection and analysis processes typically place a practical limit on the number of subjects which can be included. The approach involves obtaining a full and rounded account and understanding of the leisure or tourist behaviour, attitudes and/or situation of a few individuals, as opposed to the more limited amount of information which might be obtained in a quantitative study of a large sample of individuals. No claim is therefore made that the sample studied in a qualitative study is representative of a larger population, so that the findings cannot be generalised statistically to the wider population; although, as Szarycz (2009) observes, this principle is often breached in the reporting; Dupuis (1999: 54) makes the same observation.

The methods used to gather qualitative information include observation, informal and in-depth interviewing, participant observation and analysis of texts. Research studying groups of people using non-quantitative, anthropological approaches is referred to as *ethnographic* research or *ethnographic fieldwork*. Such methods were initially developed by anthropologists but have been adapted by sociologists for use in their work.

The question of the differences between, and respective merits of, quantitative and qualitative methods is arguably the most discussed methodological issue in the social sciences and in leisure and tourism research. The discussion is led by proponents of qualitative methods who generally portray themselves as pioneering a novel approach in the face of opposition from proponents of 'traditional' quantitative methods. While the debate can become somewhat partisan, it is now widely accepted that the two approaches complement one another. Leading proponents of qualitative methods Guba and Lincoln (1998: 195) have stated: 'From our perspective, both qualitative and quantitative methods may be appropriate with any research paradigm'. Furthermore, there has been strong support in recent years for *mixed methods* and *pragmatism* discussed in Chapter 5. Other signs of a drawing together of the two approaches are that quantitative research is often based on initial qualitative work, and computers are now being used to analyse qualitative as well as quantitative data.

3.5 Pragmatism

This principle is reflected in the idea of *pragmatism*. As an approach to research, pragmatism emerged in philosophy at the beginning of the twentieth century and involved the proposition that the criterion for valid knowledge should be based not on theoretical or logical rigour alone but also on experience in the real world and practical usefulness in addressing real-world problems. In the social sciences, it has come to refer to an approach to research which is not committed, a priori, to either the post-positivist or interpretive paradigm but may combine them in different parts of the same research exercise. For example, a project might involve a survey of sport participation with quantified results but also some in-depth interviews with participants and non-participants which adds complexity to the notion of 'participation', even challenging the definition used in the survey. That the approach may involve the use of quantitative and/or qualitative methods has also led to the use of the term 'mixed methods' to describe it. Another related term is *bricolage*, a French word referring to the work of a handyman/woman, who is multi-skilled and assembles a miscellany of tools and materials ('bits and pieces') to do the job in hand.

3.6 Participatory research

Typically, the researcher takes total responsibility for the design, conduct and reporting of the research. Some researchers, however, work in fields where the subjects of the research may be involved with the research, in directing the research in a cooperative manner. This can happen in exploratory research in relatively informal environments, such as community groups, but also in open-ended, diagnostic research involving organisations. The approach overlaps with the concept of action research, in which the research is part of a process for bringing about change, with which the researcher is actively involved. Action research is discussed further in Chapter 5.

3.7 Theoretical and applied research

Theoretical research seeks to draw conclusions about the class of phenomena being studied which can be applied to that class of phenomena as a whole, not just the cases or subjects included in the study. Indeed, some theoretical research is non-empirical (see section 3.10 in this chapter), so it does not involve the direct study of cases or subjects, but relies on the existing research literature. Xin, Tribe and Chambers (2013) use the term *conceptual research* to refer to theoretical research which focuses on a particular concept.

Applied research, however, is less universal in its scope: it does not necessarily seek to create wholly *new* knowledge about the world but to apply existing theoretical knowledge to particular problems or issues. Such problems or issues may arise in specific policy, planning or management situations. Policy studies, planning and management are themselves fields of study which have developed a body of theory. Because they are related to areas of practice, they can be seen as *applied disciplines*. In these fields, therefore, there can be such a thing as *applied theory*. The rational-comprehensive model of management portrayed in Table 1.3 is an example of a context for considering the difference between theoretical and applied research: research which might seek to develop or elaborate the model in general would be theoretical; whereas research which simply used the model as a framework for examining a problem in a particular organisation would be called applied. In some discussions of this dimension, the term 'pure' is used rather than 'theoretical'.

3.8 Reflexivity

A reflexive approach to research involves explicit consideration of the relationship between the researcher and the researched. As Davies (1997: 3) points out, all research involves a degree of reflexivity. Thus, for example, in small particle physics the very act of measurement can only be achieved by the researcher causing physical interference with the particle being measured, and this becomes the focus of the research methodology. In questionnaire-based research, interaction between the researcher and the respondent is in the form of the asking of questions: different wording of the questions and the manner in which they are posed affect the answers given. Reflexivity is most often considered in the context of qualitative research, and the deeper the involvement of the researcher with the research subjects, the more relevant it becomes, the most extreme being participant observation. Thus, reflexivity may be related to physical relationships, to culture or power or to a variety of forms of social interaction. In social research, reflexivity is sometimes referred to as intersubjectivity (Glancy, 1993).

In methodologies closer to the classic scientific model, the aim is generally to minimise the impact of the researcher on the research subjects. Description of measures taken to achieve this are confined to the 'methods' section of the research report, although it may be revisited in the conclusions, particularly if the results are less than clear-cut and might be improved in future by changes in the research design. But in interpretive studies involving methods such as participant observation, discussion of the relationship between the researcher and the researched can be a major part of the analysis and reporting process.

3.9 Experimental and naturalistic methods

The experiment is the classic scientific research method: the popular image of the scientist is someone in a white coat in a laboratory, conducting experiments. In the experimental method of research, the scientist aims to control the environment of the subject of the research and measure the effects of controlled change. Knowledge based on the experimental method progresses on the basis that, in a controlled experimental situation, any change in A must have been brought about by a change in B because everything except A and B have been held constant. The experimental researcher therefore aims to produce conditions such that the research will fulfil the requirements for causality discussed earlier in this chapter.

In the world of human beings, with which the social scientist deals, there is much less scope for experiment than in the world of inanimate objects or animals with which natural scientists deal. Some situations do exist where experimentation with human beings in the field of leisure or tourism can take place. For example, it is possible to experiment with:

● variations in design or location of children's play equipment;

● willing subjects in game-playing or decision-making tasks under different conditions or responding to 'stimuli', such as photographs or videos;

● sporting/human movement activity where subjects can be asked to engage in particular forms of physical exercise and their physical and psychological reactions can be measured; and

● management situations, for instance varying prices or advertising strategies in relation to leisure or tourism services.

But many areas of interest to the leisure or tourism researcher are not susceptible to controlled experiment. For instance, the researcher interested in the effect of people's level of income on their behaviour cannot take a group of people and vary their incomes in order to study the effects of income on leisure participation or tourism behaviour – it would be difficult to find people on executive salaries willing voluntarily to spend a year living on a student grant in the interests of research! Furthermore, unlike the natural scientist experimenting with rats, it is not possible to find two groups of humans identical in every respect except for their level of income. Even more fundamentally, it is of course not possible to vary people's social class or race. In order to study these phenomena, it is necessary to use *non-experimental* methods: that is, it is necessary to study differences between people as they exist.

So, for example, in order to study the effects of income on leisure participation patterns or touristic behaviour, it is necessary to gather information on the leisure and travel behaviour patterns of a range of people with different levels of income. But people differ in all sorts of ways, some of which may be related to their level of income and some not. For example, two people with identical income levels can differ markedly in terms of their personalities, their family situation, their physical health and so on. So, in comparing the behaviour of two groups of people, it is difficult to be sure which differences arise as a result of income differences and which as a result of other differences. The results of the research are therefore likely to be less clear-cut than in the case of the controlled experiment.

One term used for studying people in their normal environment – that is, not in a laboratory – is *naturalistic*. In a fully naturalistic study, the researcher would be as unobtrusive as possible so as not to interfere in any way with the normal behaviour of the research subjects. Unlike the laboratory experiment, where as many variables as possible are controlled, the naturalistic researcher would be taking a *holistic* or *systematic* view, in which all relevant known and unknown variables are in operation simultaneously. As Guba and Lincoln (1998: 8) put it, in naturalistic research: 'first, no manipulation on the part of the inquirer is implied and, second, the inquirer imposes no a priori units on the outcome'.

Some observational methods seek to achieve this. Interviews of various types may begin to interfere with the normal or 'natural' behaviour of the subject: the asking of a question can be seen as a sort of loosely controlled experiment. But interviews which take place in a subject's home or at a leisure site or holiday destination are more naturalistic than a focus group session in the office of a market research company which is closer to the experiment end of the experimental–naturalistic continuum. For some types of naturalistic research project, quite extensive interaction may be required between the researcher and the subjects being researched in order to gain an understanding of behaviour in the subject's normal/natural environment.

The experimental method is dealt with in Chapter 11. The survey and qualitative methods discussed in Chapters 7–10 can all be seen as naturalistic but varying in their degrees of naturalism.

3.10 Empirical and non-empirical research

The dichotomy here should probably be between *purely* empirical research, if such a thing exists, and *purely* theoretical research. Empirical research involves the collection and/or analysis of data, which may be quantitative or qualitative, primary or secondary. The research is informed by observations or information from the 'real world'. It is, however, rare for any research project to be exclusively empirical – it is usually informed by some sort of theory or conceptual framework (see Chapter 3), however implicit.

It is possible for the researcher to become carried away with data and their analysis and to forget the theory which should make them *meaningful*. In such cases the disparaging term 'mindless empiricism' is sometimes used to describe this situation. Similarly, theoretical research with no reference to information about the 'real world', however contested the description of that might be, is likely to be of limited value. Typically – and ideally – theoretical and empirical research coexist and enhance each other; indeed, most research projects have complementary theoretical and empirical components.

While empirical studies provide some of the building blocks of a great deal of research and knowledge, non-empirical contributions are needed to review and refine ideas and to place the empirical work in context. A text like this inevitably devotes more space to empirical methods, because they involve more explicit, technical processes which can be described and taught. It cannot, however, be too strongly stressed that a good review of the literature or a thoughtful piece of writing arising from deep, insightful, inspirational thinking about a subject can be worth a hundred, unthinking, surveys!

3.11 Induction and deduction

Induction and deduction refer to alternative approaches to explanation in research. It has been noted that research involves *finding out* and *explaining*. Finding out might be called the 'what?' of research. Explaining might be called the 'how?' and the 'why?' of research.

Finding out involves description and gathering of information. Explaining involves attempting to understand that information: it goes beyond the descriptive. Appropriate research methods can facilitate both these processes. Description and explanation can be seen as part of a circular model of research as illustrated in Figure 2.1.

The research process can work in two ways:

● Deductive: The process starts at point A1 and moves via observation/ description (B) to analysis/testing (C) which confirms or disproves the hypothesis (D1). The process is deductive: it involves deduction, where

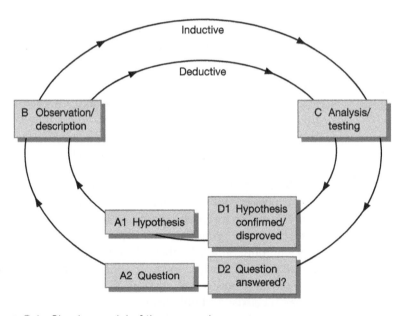

Figure 2.1 Circular model of the research process

the process is based on prior logical reasoning and available evidence from observation or the research literature resulting in a hypothesis to be tested.

- Inductive: The process may begin with a question, at point A2, or it may begin with observation/description, at point B in the diagram; it then moves from analysis (C) to answering, or failing to answer, the question. The process is inductive: the explanation is induced from the data; the data come first and the explanation later.

The concept of a *hypothesis* arises in the deductive process. A hypothesis is a proposition about how something might work or behave – an explanation which may or may not be supported by data, or possibly by more detailed or rigorous argument. A hypothesis may be suggested from informal observation and experience of the researcher or from examination of the existing research literature. As we shall see in Chapter 3, not all research projects involve the use of hypotheses which are associated with the classic positivistic or *hypothetical-deductive* model as discussed earlier in this chapter.

The terms *theory* or *model* could also be included at point D1. When more elaborate hypotheses or a number of inter-related hypotheses are involved, the term theory or model may be used. A theory or model can be similar to a hypothesis, in being propositional, or it may have been subjected to empirical validation – that is, testing against data. A research project may involve a single circuit or a number of circuits of the process, possibly in both directions. Theory and models can also arise out of the inductive process if, for example, the question was a 'why?' question.

Case study 2.1 illustrates the concepts of induction and deduction using an example of the relative popularity of two leisure activities.

In practice, data are rarely collected without at least an informal explanatory model in mind – otherwise, how would the researcher know what data to collect? So there is always an element of deduction in any research. And it is not possible to develop hypotheses and theories without at least some initial information on the topic in hand, however informally obtained; so there is always an element of induction. Thus most research is partly inductive and partly deductive.

There is a tendency, particularly among writers on qualitative methods, to associate quantitative methods with a deductive approach and qualitative methods with inductive approaches. But quantitative research can be, and often is, inductive. For example:

- Factor analysis, as discussed in Chapter 17, is a highly quantitative data manipulation technique which seeks to identify a manageable number of meaningful 'factors' from a large number of variables, such as might be generated from a questionnaire. The technique can be used as an exploratory (i.e. inductive) tool, to discover what, if any, factors might exist in the data, and as a confirmatory (i.e. deductive) tool, to confirm the existence of hypothesised factors.

Case study 2.1   Tennis vs golf – inductive and deductive approaches

The relative popularity of tennis and golf could be studied using an inductive or deductive approach to research and explanation.

A. Inductive

A descriptive survey shows that more people play tennis than play golf. This is just a piece of information; we cannot explain why this is so without additional information and analysis. If the research also reveals that it costs more to play golf than to play tennis, then we could offer the explanation that relative popularity is related to price.

However, qualitative information from the survey might also indicate that more people consider tennis as being fun to play than consider golf to be fun. This suggests that tennis is intrinsically more attractive than golf for many people and its popularity is not related to price but to intrinsic enjoyment.

On the other hand, the research might indicate that there are more tennis courts available than golf courses in the particular community being studied, suggesting that, if there were more golf courses available, then golf would be more popular – implying that popularity is related to availability of facilities.

In this example, a series of possible explanations is being *induced* from the data. In its most fully developed form, the explanation amounts to a theory. In this case, a theory of sports participation might be developed relating levels of participation to costs of participation, intrinsic satisfactions and supply of facilities, perceived attractiveness of the activity and facilities and so on.

B. Deductive

On the basis of reading and existing theory on leisure activities generally, the following two hypotheses are put forward.

> *Hypothesis 1:* if sport A is more expensive to play than sport B, then sport B will be more popular than sport A.

> *Hypothesis 2:* if more facilities are available for sport B than for sport A then sport B will be more than sport A.

To test these hypotheses, a research project is designed to collect information on:

- *the levels of participation in the two sports – tennis and golf;*
- *the costs of participating in the two sports; and*
- *the availability of facilities for the two sports in the study area.*

The two hypotheses would then be tested using the data collected. The data collection and outcomes are limited by the hypotheses put forward. In this example, the idea of 'intrinsic motivation', which featured in the inductive approach, was not identified. In this case, the research is guided from the beginning by the initial hypotheses. The process is deductive.

- Structural equation modelling (SEM), as discussed in Chapter 17, is also a highly quantitative technique; in his book on the technique, Rex Kline notes that computer programs used to analyse data for SEM require the researcher to provide in advance specifications of the model to be tested and observes:

> These *a priori* specifications reflect the researcher's hypotheses, and in total they make up the model to be evaluated in the analysis. In this sense SEM could be viewed as confirmatory [i.e. deductive]. That is, the model is given at the beginning of the analysis, and one of the main questions to be answered is whether it is supported by the data. But, as often happens in SEM, the data may be inconsistent with the model, which means that the researcher must either abandon the model or modify the hypotheses on which it is based. The former option is rather drastic. In practice, researchers more often opt for the second choice, which means the analysis now has a more exploratory [i.e. inductive] nature as revised models are tested with the same data. (Kline, 2005: 10)

Whether hypotheses or theories containing the explanation are put forward at the start of a research project or arise as a result of exploratory data analysis, they represent the key creative part of the research process. Data collection and analysis can be fairly mechanical, but interpretation of data and the development of explanations require at least creativity and, at best, inspiration!

3.12 Objectivity and subjectivity

As indicated in Chapter 1 and in the discussion of the experimental method earlier, the classic stance of the researcher in the natural science research model is as an objective observer. Experiments are set up to prove or disprove a hypothesis. If the data from the experiment are consistent with the hypothesis, the latter is accepted as reflecting the real world until such time as new evidence emerges which is inconsistent with the hypothesis, which is then rejected or modified. In practice, absolute objectivity is impossible since the researcher's selection of one research topic rather than any one of a thousand others suggests a value position: the researcher's choice implies that the selected topic is, in some way, more important than the others. If the research has been funded from a trust or government grant-giving body, the application will invariably have been required to demonstrate the 'social benefits' of the research. When moving into the social science area, it becomes even more difficult to maintain the classic objective stance: thus much research on leisure is conducted because the researcher is convinced of the value of leisure activity to society as a whole or to particular groups within society. In the case of tourism, there may be a belief in the economic benefits it can bring to host communities or, in some cases, concern about its negative consequences or unequal sharing of costs and benefits. Nevertheless, researchers typically seek to be as objective as possible and to report honestly on the results of empirical enquiry, as discussed in Chapter 4.

3.13 Primary and secondary data

In planning a research project, it is advisable to consider whether it is necessary to go to the expense of collecting new information (*primary* data, where the researcher is the first user), or whether existing data (*secondary* data, where the researcher is the secondary user) will do the job. Sometimes existing information is in the form of research already completed on the topic or a related topic; sometimes it arises from non-research sources, such as administration. A fundamental part of any research project is therefore to scour the existing published – and unpublished – sources of information for related research. Existing research might not obviate the need for the originally proposed research, but it may provide interesting ideas and points of comparison with the proposed research.

Even if the research project is to be based mainly on new information, it will usually be necessary also to make use of other, existing, information – such as official government statistics or financial records from a leisure or tourism facility or service. Such information is generally referred to as *secondary data*, as opposed to the *primary data*, which are the new data to be collected in the proposed research. The topic of secondary data is dealt with in Chapters 7 and 14.

3.14 Self-reported and observed data

The best, and often the only, sources of information about people's leisure or tourism behaviour or attitudes are individuals' own reports about themselves. Much leisure and tourism research therefore involves asking people about their past behaviour, attitudes and aspirations, by means of an interviewer-administered or respondent-completed questionnaire (Chapter 10) or by means of an informal, in-depth, semi-structured or unstructured interview (Chapter 9). In some cases, information can be gathered from written sources such as diaries, letters or biographies.

There are some disadvantages to this approach, mainly that the researcher is never sure just how honest or accurate people are in responding to questions. In some instances, people may deliberately or unwittingly distort or 'bend' the truth – for instance, in understating the amount of alcohol they drink or overstating the amount of exercise they take. In other instances, they may have problems of recall, for instance, in remembering just how much money they spent on a recreational or holiday trip some months ago – or even yesterday! In biomedical research, which relies a great deal on subjects/patients accurately reporting such things as symptoms and behaviour, study of the design and practice of such data collection has come to be referred as the 'science of self-report' (Stone et al., 2000).

For some types of information, an alternative to relying on self-report is for the researcher to observe behaviour. For instance, to find out how children use a playground or how adults make use of a resort area or a park, it would probably be better to watch them than to try to ask them about it. Patterns of movement and crowding can be *observed*. Sometimes people leave behind evidence of their behaviour – for instance, the most popular exhibits at a museum will be the ones where the carpet is most worn, and the most used beaches are likely to be those where the most litter is dumped. Generally, these techniques are referred to as *observational* or *unobtrusive* techniques and are dealt with in Chapter 8. Clearly observation does not provide direct information on motives, attitudes and aspirations or past behaviour.

4. Validity, reliability and trustworthiness

The quality of research and the trust which can be placed in it depends on the methods used and the care with which they have been deployed. Two dimensions are generally considered in this context: validity and reliability.

Validity is the extent to which the information presented in the research truly reflects the phenomena which the researcher claims it reflects. *External validity* refers to generalisability or representativeness: to what extent can the results be generalised to a population wider than the particular sample used in the study? This will depend on how the members of the sample are selected, as discussed in Chapter 13. *Internal validity* refers to how accurately the characteristics of the phenomena being studied are represented by the variables used and the data collected – sometimes referred to as *measurement* or *instrument* (for example, questionnaire) *validity* – and the extent to which the study identifies and measures all the relevant variables.

Leisure and tourism research is fraught with difficulties in this area, mainly because empirical research is largely concerned with people's behaviour and with their attitudes, and for information on these the researcher is, in the main, reliant on people's own reports in the form of responses to questionnaire-based and other forms of interview. These instruments are subject to a number of imperfections, which means that the validity of leisure and tourism data can rarely be as certain as in the natural sciences. For example, data on the number of people who have participated in an activity at least once over the last month (a common type of measure used in leisure research) covers a wide range of different types of involvement, from the person who participates for two hours every day to the person who accidentally engaged in the activity just once for a few minutes. So the question of what is a *participant* can be complex. More detailed questioning to capture such complexity can be costly to undertake on a large scale and can try the patience of interviewees, thus increasing the risk that responses will be inaccurate or incomplete.

Reliability is the extent to which research findings would be the same if the research were to be repeated at a later date or with a different sample of subjects. Again, it can be seen that the model is taken from the natural sciences where, if experimental conditions are appropriately controlled, a replication of an experiment should produce identical results wherever and whenever it is conducted. This is rarely the case in the social sciences, because they deal with human beings in differing and ever-changing social situations. While a single person's report of his or her behaviour may be accurate, when it is aggregated with information from other people, it presents a snapshot picture of a group of people, which is subject to change over time, as the composition of the group changes, or as *some* members of the group change their patterns of behaviour. Further, identical questions asked of people in different locations, even within the same country or region, are likely to produce different results because of the varying social and physical environment. This means that the social scientist, including the leisure and tourism researcher, must be very cautious when making general, theoretical, statements on the basis of empirical research. While measures can be taken to ensure a degree of generalisability, strictly speaking, any research findings relate only to the subjects involved, at the time and place the research was carried out.

There is a considerable literature on validity and reliability, particularly related to experimental research and the use of scales (see Chapter 5); sources are indicated in the Resources section at the end of the chapter.

It has been noted that the use of validity and reliability as criteria for assessing the quality of research arose from the positivist tradition and that they are therefore not always fully appropriate for non-positivist research approaches. In qualitative research in particular, the concepts of *trustworthiness* and *authenticity* have been introduced by Guba and Lincoln (1998) to replace validity and reliability. Trustworthiness has four components: credibility (paralleling internal validity), transferability (external validity), dependability (reliability) and confirmability (objectivity). Authenticity includes: fairness and ontological, educative, analytic and tactical authenticity. Because qualitative studies do not follow a regimented process, a detailed explanation of the research process is advisable, as Henderson (2006: 231) has put it: 'A thorough reporting of the process and the results of qualitative data collection and analysis is the key to justifying and assuring that trustworthiness exists in the study.'

Summary

The aim of this chapter is to introduce the disciplinary context and traditions of leisure and tourism research as well as some of the general dimensions and concepts associated with social science research. It begins with a brief overview of the contributions of individual disciplines to leisure and tourism research, covering sociology, geography, economics, psychology/social psychology, history and anthropology and political science. The review indicates that most of the disciplines contributing to leisure and tourism research now use a wide variety of research methods. The second half of the chapter covers a range of generic social science concepts and issues which arise in the literature and with which the leisure and tourism researcher should be familiar. They are: ontology, epistemology and methodology; positivist, post-positivist, interpretive and critical approaches; descriptive, explanatory and evaluative research (as discussed in Chapter 1); qualitative and quantitative research; theoretical and applied research; empirical and non-empirical research; induction and deduction; experimental and non-experimental research; primary and secondary data; self-reported and observed data; and validity and reliability.

Test questions

1. What are the basic differences between theoretical and applied research?

2. What are the basic differences between empirical and non-empirical research?

3. What are the basic differences between the inductive and deductive approaches to research?

4. What are the basic differences between descriptive and explanatory research?

5. What are the basic differences between the positivist and interpretive approaches to research?

6. What are the basic differences between experimental and non-experimental research?

7. What is the basic difference between primary and secondary data?

8. What is the basic difference between self-reported and observed data?

9. What are the basic differences between qualitative and quantitative research?

10. What are validity and reliability?

Exercises

1. Examine any issue of either *Leisure Studies* or *Annals of Tourism Research* and classify the articles into disciplinary areas. Contrast the key questions which each article is addressing.

2. Using the same journal issue as in exercise 1, determine whether the articles are: (a) empirical or non-empirical; (b) deductive or inductive; (c) positivist or interpretive.

3. Using a leisure or tourism journal such as *Leisure Studies* or *Annals of Tourism Research*, select an issue of the journal at two-yearly intervals over 10 years and summarise the apparent change over time in the topics addressed and methods used in the articles.

Resources

- Action research: Greenwood and Levin (2007).
- Approaches to research: Tourism: Smith (2010: Ch. 1).
- *Bricolage*: see Pragmatism/mixed methods.
- Classification:
  - events: Getz (2008);
  - leisure: Tinsley and Eldredge (1995);
  - Serious Leisure Perspective: Elkington and Stebbins (2014), Veal (2016b);
  - sport: Stewart et al. (2003); and
  - tourism: Cohen (1972), McKerchner (2016).
- Conceptual research: Tourism: Xin et al. (2013).
- Critical approach:
  - emancipatory research: Antonio (1989);
  - tourism: Ateljevic et al. (2007), Chambers (2007); and
  - transformative research: Mertens (2009).
- Disciplines:
  - interdisciplinarity: Moran (2010);
  - tourism: Leiper (2000), Tribe (1997); and
  - volunteering: Lockstone-Binney et al. (2010).
- Ethnography:
  - auto-ethnography, leisure: Anderson and Austin (2011);
  - general: Davies (1997);
  - leisure: Chick (2009);
  - sport: Spracklen et al. (2011);
  - sport fandom: Knijnik (2015); and
  - tourism: Cole (2005), Pereiro (2010).
- Experimental methods:
  - leisure: Havitz and Sell (1991).
  - tourism: Oppewal (2011).
- Grounded theory:
  - sport management: Edwards and Skinner (2009: Ch. 17); and
  - tourism: Jennings and Junek (2007).
- Mixed methods: see Pragmatism/mixed methods.
- Participatory research: Heron and Reason (1997).
- Positivism: Botterill and Platenkamp (2012).
- Post-positivism: Henderson (2011), Parry et al. (2013); Tourism: Ryan (2000).

- Pragmatism/mixed methods:
  - *bricolage*: Kincheloe (2001);
  - general: Johnson and Onwuegbuzie (2004), Patton (1988), Tashakkori and Creswell (2007), Tashakkori and Teddlie (2003), Teddlie and Tashakkori (2009);
  - leisure: Henderson (2011);
  - sport: Giacobbi et al. (2005), Rudd and Johnson (2010); and
  - tourism: Molina-Azorín and Font (2016).

- Qualitative methods:
  - leisure: Henderson (2011);
  - sport: Andrews et al. (2005);
  - sport management: Edwards and Skinner (2009); and
  - tourism: Phillimore and Goodson (2004).

- Qualitative versus quantitative research: Allwood (2012), Borman et al. (1986), Bryman (2006), Bryman and Bell (2003: Ch. 21, 22), Godbey and Scott (1990), Henderson (2006), Veal (1994).

- Realism: Pawson (2006).

- Reflexivity: Davies (1997), Donne (2006), Dupuis (1999), Howe (2009); inter-subjectivity: Glancy (1993).

- Self-report: Stone et al. (2000).

- Trustworthiness: Guba and Lincoln (1998), Lincoln and Guba (1985); in tourism: DeCrop (2004), Henderson (2006: 225–36).

- Validity/reliability: Riddick and Russell (2008: 149–53, 179–81), Vaske (2008: 66–75).

References

Allwood, C. M. (2012). The distinction between qualitative and quantitative research methods is problematic. *Quality and Quantity*, 46(5), 1417–29.

Andrews, D. L., Mason, D. S., and Silk, M. L. (Eds) (2005). *Qualitative methods in sports studies*. Oxford: Berg.

Antonio, R. J. (1989). The normative foundations of emancipatory theory: evolutionary versus pragmatic perspectives. *American Journal of Sociology*, 94(4), 721–48.

Ateljevic, I., Morgan, N., and Pritchard, A. (2007). Editors' introduction: promoting an academy of hope in tourism enquiry. In I. Ateljevic, A. Pritchard and N. Morgan (Eds), *The critical turn in tourism studies: innovative research methodologies* (pp. 1–10). Oxford: Elsevier.

Ateljevic, I., Pritchard, A., and Morgan, N. (Eds) (2007). *The critical turn in tourism studies: innovative research methodologies.* Oxford: Elsevier.

Borman, K. M., LeCompte, M. D., and Goetz, J. P. (1986). Ethnographic and qualitative research design and why it doesn't work. *American Behavioral Scientist,* 30(1), 42–57.

Botterill, D., and Platenkamp, V. (2012). *Key concepts in tourism research.* London: Sage.

Bryman, A. (2006). Paradigm peace and the implications for quality. *International Journal of Social Research Methodology,* 9(2), 111–26.

Bryman, A., and Bell, E. (2015). Breaking down the quantitative/qualitative divide, and Mixed methods research. Chapters 26–27 of: *Business research methods,* 4th edn (pp. 625–60). Oxford: Oxford University Press.

Chambers, D. (2007). Interrogating the 'critical' in critical approaches to tourism research. In I. Ateljevic, A. Pritchard and N. Morgan (Eds), *The critical turn in tourism studies: innovative research methodologies* (pp. 105–19). Oxford: Elsevier.

Chan, T. W., and Goldthorpe, J. H. (2007). Class and status: the conceptual distinction and its empirical relevance. *American Sociological Review,* 72, 512–32.

Chick, G. (2009). Leisure and culture: Issues for an anthropology of leisure. *Leisure Sciences,* 20(2), 111–33.

Cohen, E. (1972). Towards a sociology of international tourism. *Social Research,* 39(1), 164–82.

Cole, S. (2005). Action ethnography: using participant observation. In B. W. Ritchie, P. Burns and C. Palmer (Eds), *Tourism Research methods: integrating theory with practice* (pp. 63–72). Wallingford, UK: CABI Publishing.

Davies, C. (1997). *Reflexive ethnography: a guide to researching selves and others.* London: Routledge.

DeCrop, A. (2004). Trustworthiness in qualitative tourism research. In J. Phillimore and L. Goodson (Eds), *Qualitative research in tourism: ontologies, epistemologies and methodologies.* London: Routledge, 156–169.

Denzin, N. K., and Lincoln, Y. S. (Eds) (2006). *Handbook of qualitative research,* 3rd edn. Thousand Oaks, CA: Sage.

Donne, K. (2006). From outsider to quasi-insider at Wodin Watersports: a reflexive account of participant observation in a leisure context. In S. Fleming and F. Jordan (Eds), *Ethical issues in leisure research.* LSA Publication 90, Eastbourne, UK: Leisure Studies Association, 63–82.

Dupuis, S. (1999). Naked truths: towards a reflexive methodology in leisure research. *Leisure Sciences,* 21(1), 43–64.

Edwards, A., and Skinner, J. (2009). *Qualitative research in sport management.* Oxford: Butterworth-Heinemann.

Elkington, S., and Stebbins, R. A. (2014). *The serious leisure perspective*. London: Routledge.

Getz, D. (2008). Event tourism: definition, evolution, and research. *Tourism Management*, 29(3), 403–28.

Giacobbi, P. R., Poczwardowski, A., and Hager, P. (2005). A pragmatic research philosophy for applied sport psychology. *Sport Psychologist*, 19(1), 18–31.

Glancy, M. (1993). Achieving intersubjectivity: the process of becoming the subject in leisure research. *Leisure Studies*, 12(1), 45–60.

Godbey, G., and Scott, D. (1990). Reorienting leisure research – the case for qualitative methods. *Society and Leisure*, 13(1), 189–206.

Greenwood, D. J., and Levin, M. (2007). *Introduction to action research: social research for social change*, 2nd edn. Thousand Oaks, CA: Sage.

Guba, E. G., and Lincoln, Y. S. (1998). Competing paradigms in qualitative research. In N. K. Denzin and Y. S. Lincoln (Eds) *The landscape of qualitative research: theories and* issues (pp. 195–220). Thousand Oaks, CA: Sage,

Guba, E. G., and Lincoln, Y. S. (2006). Paradigmatic controversies, contradictions and emerging confluences. In N. K. Denzin and Y. S. Lincoln (Eds), *Handbook of qualitative research*, 3rd edn. (pp. 191–216). Thousand Oaks, CA: Sage.

Havitz, M. E., and Sell, J. A. (1991). The experimental method and leisure/recreation research: promoting a more active role. *Society and Leisure*, 14(1), 47–68.

Henderson, K. A. (2006). *Dimensions of choice: a qualitative approach to recreation, parks and leisure research*, 2nd edn. State College, PA: Venture.

Henderson, K. A. (2009). *Just* research and physical activity: diversity is more than an independent variable. *Leisure Sciences*, 31(2), 100–5.

Henderson, K. A. (2011). Post-positivism and the pragmatics of leisure research. *Leisure Sciences*, 33(4), 341–6.

Heron, J., and Reason, P. (1997). A participatory inquiry paradigm. *Qualitative Inquiry*, 3(3), 274–94.

Howe, D. (2009). Reflexive ethnography, impairment and the pub. *Leisure Studies*, 28(4), 489–96.

Humberstone, B. (2004). Standpoint research: multiple versions of reality in tourism theorising and research. In J. Phillimore and L. Goodson (Eds), *Qualitative research in tourism: ontologies, epistemologies and methodologies* (pp. 119–36). London: Routledge.

Jennings, G., and Junek, O. (2007). Grounded theory: innovative methodology or a critical turning from hegemonic methodological praxis in tourism studies. In I. Ateljevic, A. Pritchard and N. Morgan (Eds), *The critical turn in tourism studies: innovative research methodologies* (pp. 197–210). Oxford: Elsevier.

Johnson, R. B., and Onwuegbuzie, A. J. (2004). Mixed methods research: a research paradigm whose time has come. *Educational Researcher*, 33(1), 14–26.

Kincheloe, J. L. (2001). Describing the bricolage: conceptualizing a new rigor in qualitative research. *Qualitative Inquiry*, 7(6), 679–92.

Kline, R. B. (2005). *Principles and practice of structural equation modelling*, 2nd edn. New York: Guilford Press.

Labovitz, S., and Hagedorn, R. (1971). *Introduction to social research*. New York: McGraw-Hill.

Lee, A. S. (1989). Case studies as natural experiments. *Human Relations*, 42(2), 117–37.

Leiper, N. (2000). An emerging discipline. *Annals of Tourism Research*, 27(3), 805–9.

Lincoln, Y. S., and Guba, E. G. (1985). *Naturalistic inquiry*. Beverly Hills, CA: Sage.

Lockstone-Binney, L., Holmes, K., Smith, K., and Baum, T. (2010). Volunteers and volunteering in leisure: social science perspectives. *Leisure Studies*, 29(4), 435–55.

McKerchner, B. (2016). Towards a taxonomy of tourism products. *Tourism Management*, 54, 196–208.

Mertens, D. M. (2009). *Transformative research and evaluation*. New York: Guilford Press.

Molina-Azorín, J. F., and Font, X. (2016). Mixed methods in sustainable tourism research: an analysis of prevalence, designs and application in JOST (2005–2014). *Journal of Sustainable Tourism*, 24(4), 549–73.

Moran, J. (2010). *Interdisciplinarity*, 2nd edn. London: Routledge.

Oppewal, H. (2011). Experimental research. In E. Sirakaya-Turk, M. Uysal, W. Hammitt and J. J. Vasle (Eds), *Research methods for leisure, recreation and tourism* (pp. 162–81). Wallingford, UK: CABI.

Patton, M. (1988). Paradigms and pragmatism. In D. Fetterman (Ed.), *Qualitative approaches to evaluation in educational research* (pp. 116-37). Newbury Park, CA: Sage.

Parry, D. C., Johnson, C. W., and Stewart, W. (2013). Leisure research for social justice: a response to Henderson. *Leisure Sciences*, 35(1), 81–7.

Pawson, R. (2006). *Evidence-based policy: a realist perspective*. London: Sage.

Pereiro, X. (2010). Ethnographic research on cultural tourism: an anthropological view. In G. Richards and W. Munsters (Eds), *Cultural tourism research methods* (pp. 173–87). Wallingford, UK: CABI.

Phillimore, J., and Goodson, L. (2004). Progress in qualitative research in tourism. In J. Phillimore and L. Goodson (Eds), *Qualitative research in tourism: ontologies, epistemologies and* methodologies (pp. 3–29). London: Routledge.

Piketty, T. (2014). *Capital in the twenty-first century*. Cambridge, MA: Harvard University Press.

Riddick, C. C., and Russell, R. V. (2008). *Research in recreation, parks, sport, and tourism*, 2nd edn. Champaign, IL: Sagamore.

Rudd, A., and Johnson, R. B. (2010). A call for more mixed methods in sport management research. *Sport Management Review*, 13(1), 14–24.

Ryan, C. (2000). Tourist experiences, phenomenographic analysis, post-postivism and neural network software. *International Journal of Tourism Research*, 2(2), 119–131.

Smith, S. L. J. (2010). *Practical tourism research*. Wallingford, UK: CABI.

Spracklen, K., Timmins, S., and Long, J. (2011). Ethnographies of the imagined, the imaginary and the critically real: blackness, whiteness, the north of England and rugby league. *Leisure Studies*, 29(4), 397–414.

Stewart, B., Smith, A. C. T., and Nicholson, M. (2003). Sport consumer typologies: a critical review. *Sport Marketing Quarterly*, 12(4), 206–16.

Stone, A.A., Turkkan, J. S., et al. (2000). *The science of self-report: implications for research and practice*. Mahwah, NJ: Lawrence Erlbaum.

Szarycz, G. S. (2009). Some issues in tourism research phenomenology: a commentary. *Current Issues in Tourism*, 12(1), 47–58.

Tashakkori, A., and Creswell, J. W. (2007). Exploring the nature of research questions in mixed methods research. *Journal of Mixed Methods Research*, 1(3), 207–11.

Tashakkori, A., and Teddlie, C. (Eds) (2003). *Handbook of mixed methods in social and behavioral research*. Thousand Oaks, CA: Sage.

Teddlie, C., and Tashakkori, A. (Eds) (2009). *Foundations of mixed methods research: integrating quantitative and qualitative approaches in the social and behavioral Sciences*. Thousand Oaks, CA: Sage.

Tinsley, E. A., and Eldredge, B. D. (1995) Psychological benefits of leisure participation: a taxonomy of leisure activities based on their need-gratifying properties. *Journal of Counseling Psychology*, 42(2), 123–32.

Tribe, J. (1997). The indiscipline of tourism. *Annals of Tourism Research*, 24(3), 638–57.

Vaske, J. J. (2008). *Survey research and analysis: applications in parks, recreation and human dimensions*. State College, PA: Venture.

Veal, A. J. (1994). Intersubjectivity and the transatlantic divide: a comment on Glancy (and Ragheb and Tate). *Leisure Studies*, 13(3), 211–16.

Veal, A. J. (2016a). Leisure, income inequality and the Veblen effect: cross-national analysis of leisure time and sport and cultural activity. *Leisure Studies*, 35(2), 215–40.

Veal, A. J. (2016b). The Serious Leisure Perspective and the experience of leisure. *Leisure Sciences*, online at: http://dx.doi.org/10.1080/01490400.2016.1189367.

Wilkinson, R., and Pickett, K. (2009). *The spirit level: why more equal societies almost always do better*. London: Allen Lane.

Xin, S., Tribe, J., and Chambers, D. (2013). Conceptual research in tourism. *Annals of Tourism Research*, 41(1), 66–88.

3 Starting out – research plans and proposals

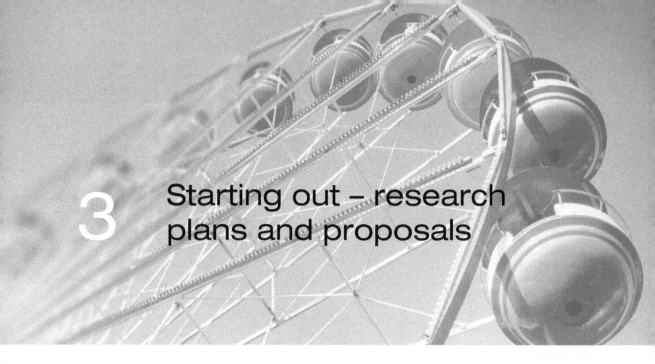

Introduction: elements of the research process

| 1. Select a topic | 1.1 Sources of topics | 1.2 Processes for topic selection | 1.3 Purpose of research |

| 2. Review the literature | 2.1 Introduction: purposes | 2.2 Conducting the review | 2.3 What discipline? |

| 3. Devise conceptual framework | 3.1 The idea | 3.2 Explore/explain relationships | 3.3 Identify/list concepts |
| | 3.4 Define concepts | 3.5 Operationalise concepts | 3.6 Modelling |

| 4. Decide research question(s) | 4.1 Research question, problem or hypothesis? | 4.2 Specific starting point | 4.3 Decision-making models |
| | 4.4 Area of interest | 4.5 Research questions or objectives? | 4.6 Primary and secondary questions |

| 5. List information requirements |

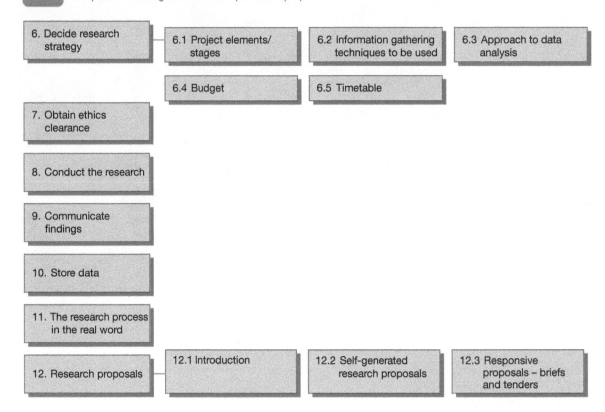

Introduction: elements of the research process

A research plan or proposal must summarise how a research project is to be conducted in its entirety; consequently, preparation of a plan or proposal involves examination of the whole research process from beginning to end. In this chapter, therefore, a certain amount of cross-referencing is required to later chapters, where elements of the process are dealt with in detail.

The research process can be envisaged in a number of ways, but for the purposes of discussion in this chapter, it is divided into 10 main elements, as shown in Figure 3.1. The enormous variety of approaches to research means that all research projects do not follow precisely the sequence or include all the elements set out in the diagram. In particular, the first four elements depicted – selecting the topic, reviewing the literature, devising a conceptual framework and deciding the key research questions – rarely happen in the direct, linear way that the numbered sequence implies: there is generally a great deal of 'to-ing and fro-ing' between the elements. Hence, in Figure 3.1, these elements are depicted on a circle, implying that a number of circuits may be necessary before proceeding to element 5. The bulk of the chapter is structured around the 10 elements in Figure 3.1. This is followed by discussion of research proposals.

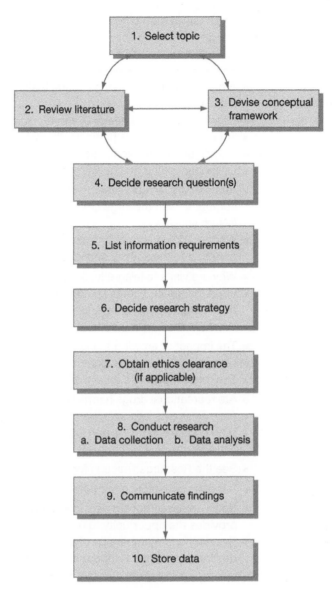

Figure 3.1   Elements in the research process

1. Select a topic

1.1 Sources of topics

How do research topics arise? They may arise from a range of sources, including: the researcher's personal interests; reading research literature; a policy or management problem; an issue of social concern; a popular or media issue;

Table 3.1 Examples of research topics from different sources

Source of topic	Examples of topics
Personal interest (usually combined with one or more of the next five sources)	• A particular sport – trends in participation, participants' motivations/ satisfactions. • Leisure access and needs of a particular ethnic or age group. • Tourism conflicts in a particular (home) locality. • A particular professional group – its ethos, history and future. • Online marketing of a new fitness facility.
The literature	• Remedy the lack of research on *casual leisure*, noted in Veal (2016a), compared with the large amount of research conducted on *serious leisure* activities. • What is known about the leisure activity of 'taking a holiday', as opposed to the activity of choosing a tourism destination?
Policy/management	• Why are visits to leisure facility X declining? • What market segments should be used to develop a strategy for promoting sport X, arts venue Y or tourism destination Z? • What are the leisure needs of community X?
Social	• The impact of growing tourism traffic on a local environment. • Leisure needs of single parents. • The role of sport in a third-world community.
Popular/media	• Are recreational drugs harmful? • Are city streets less safe than they used to be? • Who engages in online gaming and what do they get out of the activity?
Research agendas	• See the Resources section for a listing.
Brainstorming	• A means of exploring the potential of all of the above.
Opportunism	• Newly released government-collected leisure participation/tourism data provides the opportunity to undertake some demand forecasting. • Researcher's membership of a sporting club or a visit to a tourist destination offers an opportunity to conduct a participant survey.

published research agendas; and/or brainstorming, which may draw on a number of the above sources. Examples of topics arising from these sources are shown in Table 3.1.

Personal interest

Personal interest can give rise to a research project in a number of ways. For example, the researcher may be personally involved in a sport or other leisure activity, may be a member of a particular social group, based on gender, ethnicity or occupation, or may live in or have visited a particular tourism location and so be personally aware of certain local issues or problems. Using personal interest as a focus for research has advantages and disadvantages. The advantage lies in the knowledge of the phenomenon which researchers already have, the possibility of access to key individuals and information sources, and the high level of motivation which is likely to be brought to the research. Markula and Denison (2005) suggest that personal experience is a way into the process of exploring potential topics for research in sport, but clearly it can also apply in other forms of leisure and tourism. The disadvantage is that the researcher may be unduly biased and may not be able to view the situation 'objectively'; familiarity with the subject of the research may result in too much being taken for granted so that the researcher cannot 'see the wood for the trees'.

While a particular personal interest in the research topic may be referred to in writing up a research project – generally in a foreword or preface rather than in the main body of the report – it is often not mentioned in formal reports of research, such as journal articles. On the other hand, for some types of qualitative or 'standpoint' research (as discussed in Chapter 2), the researcher's personal relationship with the subjects of the research may be an important aspect of the methodology.

Personal interest may be a component in the process of selecting a research topic, but it does not alone generally provide a sufficient rationale or focus for a research project. It is necessary to develop additional criteria for selection of a specific topic from among the other sources discussed in this section.

The research literature

The research literature is the most common source of topics for academic research. A researchable topic derived from a reading of the literature can take a variety of forms. It may arise from an informal scanning of the literature which stimulates a spark of interest in a topic, or it may arise from a more critical and focused reading. Much reported research is very specific to time and place, so that even a widely accepted theory might be subject to further testing and exploration. Thus it may be that a certain theory or theoretical proposition has never been tested empirically, or it merits further empirical testing for a variety of reasons, as set out in Table 3.2.

A topic may, however, be inspired not by theory but by other material from the literature. For example, a particular research technique might be of interest, and the aim is then to find a suitable setting to explore the use of the technique. An historical account could inspire a researcher to explore the history of an area or an activity or a group of people.

Clearly, therefore, identifying a topic from the literature requires a special, *questioning, exploratory* approach to reading research literature: the aim is to identify not just what the literature *says*, but also what it does *not* say or the *basis* for assertions made. The process of critically reviewing the literature is discussed further below under element 2 of the research process, and in Chapter 6. If the research literature is to be the main source of ideas for a research topic, then the first two elements of the research process – (1) selecting a topic and (2) reviewing the literature – are effectively combined.

Table 3.2   Reasons for re-visiting theories/propositions/observations from the literature

Type of reason	The theory/proposition/ observation history	Example
Geographical	May have been tested only in one country/region	Theory established using US data could be tested in another country. Behaviour patterns of urban residents – are they replicated in rural areas?
Social	May have been established on the basis of the experience of one social group only	Theory based on men's experience – does it apply to women? Theory tested on middle-class subjects – does it apply to working-class people?
Temporal	May be out of date	Theory on youth culture established in the 1980s – is it still valid?
Contextual	May have been established in fields other than leisure/tourism	Wilkinson and Pickett's (2009) study of income inequality and human well-being did not include consideration of leisure. This was remedied in Veal (2016b).
Methodological	May have been tested using only one methodology	Conclusions from a qualitative study could be tested quantitatively.

A policy or management issue/problem

Policy or management topics are often specified by a leisure or tourism organisation, but students or academics interested in policy or management issues can also identify such topics. For example: tourism forecasting is conducted not only by, and at the behest of, government and commercial tourism bodies but also by academics; and surveys of users of leisure or tourist facilities or cost–benefit analyses of programmes and projects can be conducted by interested academics as well as by leisure or tourism service organisations. The difference between industry-sponsored and academically initiated research is that:

- academically initiated research results will often be made public, will generally be presented so as to highlight their more general implications rather than the particular application to the facility or programme being studied, and will be concerned as much with the *methodology* of the study as with its substantive findings; however

- industry-sponsored research results may often not be made public, the wider implications of the research might not be examined and the methodology, while it must be sound, will often not be of particular interest to the sponsoring organisation.

In some cases, academics involved with one or more industry-sponsored projects, the results of which have been reported to the sponsoring organisation, may publish academic articles highlighting particular features for a wider readership.

Research sponsored by government bodies lies somewhere in between these two situations. The results of the research may be very specific but will often not be confidential.

It is common for policy or management topics to be outlined by an organisation in a *brief* or set of *terms of reference* for a funded research or consultancy project. Research organisations – usually consultants – are invited to respond in the form of a competitive *tender* to conduct the project. This type of procedure has its own set of practices and conventions, as discussed later in the chapter in section 12.3.

Social concern

Social concern – of the researcher and/or sections of society at large – can give rise to a wide range of research topics. For example, concern for certain deprived or neglected groups in society can lead to research on the leisure needs or behaviour of members of such groups. Concern for the environment can lead to research on the environmental impact of tourism in sensitive areas. Often such research is closely related to policy or management issues, but the research may have a more limited role, seeking to highlight problems rather than necessarily seeking to devise solutions.

Popular/media

A popular issue can inspire research that seeks to explore popular beliefs or perceptions, especially where it is suspected that these may be inaccurate or contestable. 'Popular' usually means 'as portrayed in the media'. For example, this might be seen as the motivation for much research on media portrayals of such phenomena as sporting crowd violence and 'alienated youth' (Rowe, 1995: 4) or a major controversial leisure or tourism development.

Published research agendas

From time to time public agencies, professional bodies or individual academics publish 'research agendas', based on an assessment, often made by a committee, of the research needs of a field of study. Examples are listed in the Resources section. Often the aim of the body initiating the agenda is to implement the published research agenda itself, but in other cases the idea is for researchers in the field generally – including students – to respond by adopting topics in the agenda for their own research. Students looking for research topics know that if their topic is selected from such a published list, then there will be at least a few people 'out there' who will be interested in the results!

1.2 Processes for topic selection

What makes a viable research topic? There is no single, or simple, answer to this question. In general, it is not the topic itself which is good or bad but the way the research is conceptualised (see element 3 of the research process) and how the research question or questions are framed (element 4). A key question is whether the topic has already been researched by someone else – hence the need for a review of the literature, as discussed in element 2. But even when a topic has already been researched, there is invariably scope for further research – sometimes this is pointed out by the original researcher in concluding comments.

Thus the first four elements of the research process – select topic, review literature, conceptualise, define research questions – form an iterative, often untidy, process, which is invariably difficult, challenging and sometimes frustrating. But it is essential to get this stage right, or the rest of the research effort may be wasted.

Brainstorming

Brainstorming involves a group of two or more people bouncing ideas off one another in discussion to find inspiration or solutions to a problem. Typically, this might be done with the aid of a whiteboard or flip chart to write down ideas as they emerge. It can be seen as a separate source of ideas for a research topic or a way of refining ideas from any or all of the sources discussed earlier.

Opportunism

Sometimes an idea for research is prompted for opportunistic reasons: a data source becomes available. The various government surveys and other data collected for policy and administrative purposes and used for limited and internal policy-related or administrative purposes present constant opportunities for secondary analysis, and this is discussed further in Chapter 7. Membership of an organisation or a visit to a tourist destination or an event may provide the opportunity for participant observation, and the availability of organisational or personal archives may provide an opportunity for historical research. In all these cases, as well as considering the nature and quality of the available data, one or more of the above rationales have to be brought into play to see if conducting a project using the data can be justified. A related phenomenon is *serendipity*, which is the chance discovery of something positive or useful. As Smith and Waddington (2014: 2–3) point out, this is quite common in research generally. It may apply within a research project, with unexpected discoveries from the data, or it may apply to the discovery of a researchable topic. A chance observation of human behaviour, or a chance remark by an acquaintance or in the media, can spark a chain of thought which leads to the development of a research project.

1.3 Purpose of research

The *purposes* of a research project can shape the choice of topic and the subsequent research design. Three types of purpose are discussed here: knowledge

Table 3.3 Purposes of research

Type of purpose/motivation	Features
Knowledge for its own sake	Academic/scientific criteria – but may combine with others below
Ideologically driven:	
• Conservative	• defence/acceptance of the status quo
• Reformist, e.g. social-democratic, environmental	• a more egalitarian society • sustainability
• Radical/critical, e.g. neo-liberal neo-Marxist radical-feminist anti-globalist	• defence/extension of the market • demonstration of class conflict/exploitation • demonstration of patriarchy/women's oppression • demonstrate undesirable features of global market trends
Policy/management:	
• Critical	• Critiques current policy/management – may reflect one or more radical/critical stances above
• Instrumental	• Accepts broad philosophy of organisational milieu being studied

for its own sake, ideological/political purposes and policy/management purposes; and their key features are summarised in Table 3.3. These purposes or motivations for research are often not explicitly stated in research reports, but they are generally implicit. They affect the choice of topic and the overall shaping of the research process.

Knowledge for its own sake

The classic purpose of research is to 'add to knowledge' for its own sake, or for the general good as judged by the researcher. Some researchers continue to be driven by this goal in all or some of their research, and work in an institutional environment, typically a university, where it can be pursued. Much unfunded research undertaken by academics in their own time is of this nature. But even in such a 'pure' situation, other, less noble, although not necessarily illegitimate, purposes may be involved – for example, personal career advancement.

Ideological/political

Many academic researchers are motivated in whole or in part by an ideological or political agenda. It could be said that *all* are so motivated, and in certain areas of the social sciences this is a valid point. Many social scientists might be described as *reformist*, in that they are motivated by a general desire for a more equitable or just society, and their research will tend to be at least consistent with such a goal if not centrally concerned with it. Thus, for example, much leisure research is concerned with equality and inequality of access to leisure opportunities, and much tourism research is concerned with unjust exploitation of host communities. Similarly, in both fields, environmental protection and sustainability is often an implicit or explicit concern.

If none of these concerns is apparent but the research is dealing with social issues, the implicit stance may be taken as *conservative* – implying contentment with the political, social and/or economic *status quo*. In contrast, some researchers are guided by one or more of a number of ideological positions which seek fundamental change in society and might be described as *radical* or *critical*. In Chapter 2, the concept of *standpoint research* was noted. On the right of the political spectrum is radical 'New Right' thinking which endorses market processes, seeks their extension and might be termed *neo-liberal*. Relatively little research in leisure studies adopts this outlook, although it is implicit in some tourism research which is concerned with the economic development of tourism.

By contrast, there are researchers who, as Lincoln (2005: 165) puts it, are 'committed to seeing social science used for democratic and liberalizing social purposes'. Researchers on the left with, for example, neo-Marxist beliefs are often explicit about the political purpose of research. Thus, in the heyday of the neo-Marxist influence on leisure research, Clarke and Critcher (1985: xiii) stated: 'the study of leisure for its own sake . . . is an irrelevancy. The purpose of studying any particular element of the social order is to . . . understand the ways in which one particular element is shaped by other structures . . .'; while, in the epilogue to their book, they discussed how 'socialism as a movement might benefit from an active appreciation of leisure' (p. 232). Researchers with radical feminist beliefs seek to combat patriarchal power: for example, Betsy Wearing (1998: xvi) seeks to develop the concept of leisure as 'a potential site for resistance to and subversion of hegemonic masculinity'. In tourism, Philip Pearce (2005: 15) notes that 'some scholars want to see researchers generate more powerful emancipatory perspectives on social life'.

Policy/management

The purpose of policy or management-related research seems obvious enough: to address policy or management problems. But the stance adopted can vary and can be affected by the ideological positions outlined above. Some research might be seen as *critical*, in that it steps outside the policy or management milieu of the public- or private-sector organisations being studied and adopts a reformist or leftist stance, critiquing processes such as privatisation or managerialism, or seeking to demonstrate the inequitable outcomes of policies or management practices. Research which seeks to make private-sector operations more efficient or profitable and generally accepts the broad philosophical stance of the field being studied can be seen as *instrumental*.

2. Review the literature

2.1 Introduction: purposes

The process of reviewing the existing research literature is sufficiently important for a complete chapter to be devoted to it in this text (Chapter 6). 'Reviewing the literature' is a somewhat academic term referring to the process of identifying and engaging with previously published research relevant to the topic of interest. The process can play a number of roles, as listed in Table 3.4 and discussed further in Chapter 6.

In many cases the review undertaken in the early stages of the research has to be seen as a preliminary or interim literature review only, since time does not always permit a thorough literature review to be completed at the start of a project. Part of the research programme itself may be to explore the literature further. Having investigated the literature as thoroughly as possible, it is usually necessary to proceed with the research project in the hope that all relevant material has been identified. Exploration of the literature will generally continue for the duration of the project. Researchers always run the risk of coming across some previous – or contemporaneous – publication which will completely negate or upstage their work just as they are about to complete it. But that is part of the excitement of research! In fact, unlike the situation in the natural sciences, the risk of this happening in the leisure and tourism field is minimal, since research in this area can rarely be replicated exactly. In the natural sciences, research carried out in, say, California can reproduce exactly the findings of research carried out in, say, London. In leisure and tourism research, however, this is not the case – a set of research procedures carried out in relation to residents of California could be expected to produce very different results from identical procedures carried out in London – or even New York – simply because leisure and tourism research is involved with unique people in varying social settings.

Table 3.4   Roles of the literature in research

- Entire basis of the research
- Source of ideas on topics for research
- Source of information on research already done by others
- Source of methodological or theoretical ideas
- Basis of comparison
- Source of information that is an integral/supportive part of the research
- Definition or refinement of policy intervention (meta-analysis) (see Ch. 6)

2.2 Conducting the review

Where possible, attempts should be made to explore not just published research – the *literature* – but also unpublished and ongoing research. This process is very much hit and miss. Knowing what research is ongoing, or knowing of completed but unpublished research, usually depends on having access to informal networks, although some organisations produce registers of ongoing research projects. Once a topic of interest has been identified, it is often clear, from the literature, where the major centres for such research are located and to discover, from direct approaches or from websites, annual reports or newsletters, what research is currently being conducted at those centres. This process can be particularly important if the topic is a 'fashionable' one. However, in such cases the communication networks are usually very active, which eases the process. In this respect, papers from conferences and seminars are usually better sources of information on current research than books and journals, since the latter have long gestation periods, so that the research reported in them is generally based on work carried out two or more years prior to publication.

As discussed in Chapter 6, a review of the literature should be concluded with a *summary* which provides an overview of the field, its substantive and methodological merits and deficiencies or gaps, and an indication of how such conclusions are related to the research task in hand.

2.3 What discipline?

In an academic context, especially for undergraduate or graduate projects, it is helpful to consider what *discipline(s)* the project relates to. In some cases, this is obvious because the project is linked to a particular disciplinary unit – for example, marketing. In other cases, the project is a capstone exercise in a degree course which may draw on one or more of any of the subjects studied. If a topic does not have an obvious disciplinary label, efforts should be made to identify links with available disciplinary theories and frameworks to demonstrate the knowledge gained during a course of study. For example, if the research topic is to do with the subject of *golf*, searching library catalogues and databases using the keyword 'golf' will undoubtedly produce a certain amount of useful material. But consideration of whether the focus of the study is to be on golf *management*, golf *marketing*, the *social* context of golf or the *motivations* of golf players opens up the possibility of applying relevant theories and relating the research to comparable studies on other phenomena in the area of management, marketing, sociology and psychology, respectively. An important question to ask, therefore, is: what disciplinary field(s) is this research related to? What theories and ideas can be drawn from the literature in this discipline or these disciplines?

3. Devise conceptual framework

3.1 The idea

The development of a conceptual framework is arguably the most important part of any research project and also the most difficult. It is the weakest element in many research projects. A *conceptual framework* involves *concepts* involved in a study and the *hypothesised relationships between them*. Concepts are the building blocks of research – indeed, of knowledge. They are terms which refer to a type or class of object; thus leisure, tourism and sport are concepts, as are power, wealth, love, competition, occupation and gender.

In this discussion, the term conceptual framework has been used to cover a wide range of research situations. Thus such a term can be used in applied research when the framework adopted might relate to such activities as planning or marketing. In such cases, ideas for conceptual frameworks may readily be found in the planning or marketing literature. When the research is more academically/theoretically oriented, the term *theoretical framework* might equally well be used. Miles and Huberman, in their book on *Qualitative Data Analysis*, describe conceptual frameworks as follows:

> A conceptual framework explains, either graphically or in narrative form, the main things to be studied – the key factors, variables or constructs – and the presumed relationships among them. Frameworks can be simple or elaborate, commonsensical or theory-driven, descriptive or causal. (Miles and Huberman, 2013: Ch. 2, e-book)

Different types of research – descriptive, explanatory or evaluative – tend to call for different styles of conceptual framework. *Descriptive research* rarely requires an elaborate conceptual framework, but clear definitions of the concepts involved are required. In some cases, this can nevertheless be a considerable undertaking. For example, considerable thought is required when the descriptive task is to discover people's time use and a taxonomy and associated coding system must be devised for every conceivable form of leisure and non-leisure activity, or when the task is to gather data on the many types of tourist expenditure and activity. Both *explanatory* and *evaluative* research call for well-developed conceptual frameworks which form the basis for the explanatory or evaluative work at the heart of the research.

One reaction to this discussion of conceptual frameworks is to observe that the approach seems inconsistent with the apparently more inductive approach (as discussed in Chapter 2), in which theory is derived from the data rather than data being used to test pre-existing theory. In particular, it seems inconsistent with more open-ended approaches, such as grounded theory, and informal and flexible approaches used in qualitative research. However, as Miles and Huberman indicate, conceptual frameworks are just as vital for qualitative research as for quantitative – arguably more so. In the context of qualitative research, Karla Henderson states:

> A researcher conducting an inductive qualitative study should have a broad research question, conceptual framework, or working hypothesis in mind when beginning a project and, subsequently, as data collection begins. . . . however, a researcher must be willing to let the working hypothesis metamorphose as the study progresses. (Henderson, 2006: 79)

In fact, a conceptual framework need not be a straitjacket: it can be a flexible, evolving device. As discussed in Chapter 9, theory development and data collection and analysis are often intertwined in qualitative research, rather than being sequential. But the researcher rarely starts with an absolutely blank conceptual framework – there is usually some sort of rudimentary framework drawn from the literature or other sources. At the minimum there will be an initial list of relevant concepts with which the researcher is concerned and without which it is difficult to know what questions to ask or what issues to explore. In some cases, the researcher may start with a framework from the literature which is seen as unsatisfactory in some way: the aim of the research, then, is not to validate the framework but to do the opposite and replace it with an improved – and possibly very different – model. The conceptual framework drawn up at the beginning of the research project can be seen as the 'first draft'; as data gathering and analysis proceeds, further drafts will emerge, incorporating new insights arising from the research. The developing conceptual framework becomes the focus of the research process.

The concepts identified and the framework within which they are set determine the whole course of the study. In exploring the conceptual framework for the study, the researcher is asking: what's going on here? What processes are at work or likely to be at work? Sometimes the framework is developed from individual reflection or 'brainstorming', and sometimes it arises from the literature; indeed, an existing framework from the literature might well be used and merely adapted for application in a new situation. Where a number of areas of literature has been reviewed to provide the basis for the research, the skill is to draw the theoretical ideas together into a common framework – even if the aim is to show the incompatibility between two or more perspectives. Such links of course should be clearly and fully explained in the exposition of the framework.

While the devising of a conceptual framework is presented here as a *stage* in a research project, together with 'just thinking' and the review of the literature, it can also be seen as comprising the whole of a theoretical study. Theoretical research typically involves identifying concepts and considering the relationships between them. As noted in Chapter 2, Xin, Tribe and Chambers (2013) refer to this type of research as *conceptual research*, particularly when a theoretical research exercise is focused on a single concept.

The development of a conceptual framework can be thought of as involving four elements, as depicted in Figure 3.2. The element 'Identification of concepts' should, perhaps, be the starting point, but the tendency is to think about

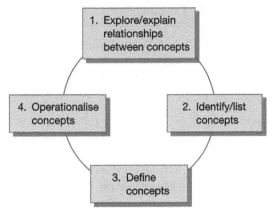

Figure 3.2 Development of a conceptual framework

possible relationships first and then identify and define the concepts involved, as this becomes necessary. In fact the exercise is generally *iterative* – that is, it involves going backwards and forwards, or round and round, between the various elements until a satisfactory solution is reached. The four elements are discussed in turn.

3.2 Explore/explain relationships

Relationships may represent power relationships, influencing factors, money or information flows or simply a sequence of elements in a process. The postulated relationships correspond to the theory – however tentative – which underpins the conceptual framework. Explaining a conceptual framework may be a lengthy and complex process, especially when links with the literature are involved. The example in Table 3.5 is very simple. It shows how the ideas develop from a simple statement (Stage A) to a more complex statement or series of statements (Stage C). In the example, the statements are expressed in the form of hypotheses; they could alternatively be expressed as questions, for example: 'To what extent is the decision influenced by income?'

One aid to the development of a conceptual framework is to use the device of a *concept map*, sometimes referred to as a *mental map* or *relevance tree*. While some concept maps are more self-evident than others, a concept map *is* only an optional aid – a full narrative discussion and explanation always forms the core of the conceptual framework. A concept map merely illustrates or summarises the discussion.

Concept mapping can be seen as a form of visual 'brainstorming' and can be undertaken alone or as part of a group exercise. The idea is to write down, on a piece of paper, board, flip chart or screen, all the concepts which appear to be relevant to a topic, in any order in which they come to mind. Then begin to group the concepts and indicate linkages between them. This is likely to involve

Table 3.5   Exploration of relationships between concepts – example

Stage	Statements/hypotheses (*concepts are in italics*)
A	*Participation* in a leisure or tourism *activity* arises as a result of an individual (or household/family) decision-making process.
B	Whether or not a person participates could depend on a variety of *events and circumstances*, for example: • the *availability of and access to facilities* may be good or bad; • *advertising and promotion* may vary in quantity and influence; • the *cost* of participation may be high or low; and • a *chance event*, such as meeting up with a group of friends, may trigger *participation*.
C	Whether or not individuals participate will also depend on their *characteristics*, such as: • *age*; • *income*; • *personality*; and • *past experience* in participating in that or similar experiences.

a process of trial and error. Figure 3.3 illustrates diagrammatically the framework described in words in Table 3.5. Three versions of the concept map correspond to the three stages, A, B and C, in Table 3.5. The concept map depicts *concepts* – usually in boxes or circles – and the *relationships* between concepts, which are usually represented by lines between the concepts, with or without directional arrows. Different types of concept might be represented by different-shaped boxes and different relationships by different types of line. The process of concept mapping may be conducted using: paper and pencil; 'butcher's paper' or flip charts; a whiteboard, with or without a printing facility; software with graphics capabilities, for example, Microsoft PowerPoint; or specialist software, such as NVivo, as discussed in Chapter 15.

3.3 Identify/list concepts

Concepts are general representations of the phenomena to be studied. Concepts emerge in the discussion of relationships and the concept-mapping process: here we formally identify, recognise and list them. They might involve types of individuals (e.g. manager, customer), groups of individuals (e.g. gang, community) or organisations (e.g. firm, government) or their characteristics or actions. The first column of Table 3.6 lists the concepts encountered in Table 3.5 and Figure 3.3.

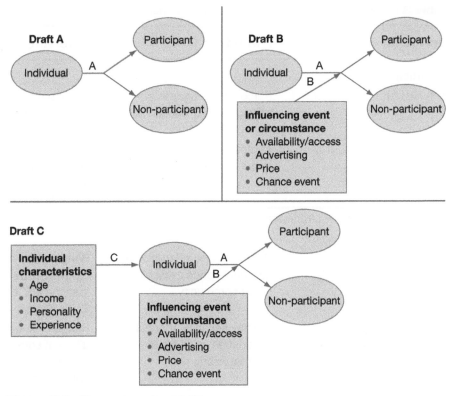

Figure 3.3 Concept map example

3.4 Define concepts

Concepts must be clearly defined for research purposes. Dictionary definitions or definitions from the research literature may be used, but it is often necessary to be selective or adaptive. Table 3.6, column 2, includes suggested definitions for the concepts listed. Definitions might be very rudimentary in the early stages of the exercise and become more detailed and complex with time: as we talk about 'X', we have to clarify 'exactly what we mean' by 'X'.

3.5 Operationalise concepts

The terminology used to describe the process of *operationalisation* depends on whether a concept is quantitative or qualitative in nature or in its treatment:

● Quantitative: operationalisation involves deciding *how the concept might be measured*.

● Qualitative: operationalisation involves deciding how the concept might be *identified, described* or *assessed* when conducting qualitative research, such as in-depth interviews.

Table 3.6   Examples of concepts – definition and operationalisation

Concept*	Definition	Operationalisation
1. Participant		
a. In leisure	Person who engages in relatively freely chosen activity during leisure time.	Participation in activity identified as 'leisure' at least once in preceding year.
b. In tourism	Person who travels away from home for leisure purposes.**	Travel for leisure purposes at least 40 km from home with at least one overnight stay in preceding three months.
2. Influencing event or circumstance		
a. Availability of/access to:		
● Leisure facilities	Preferred leisure facilities at affordable price available in home community.	Range of facilities within day-trip range at or below a various 'benchmark' costs, e.g. £10, £20, £30 a head.
● Tourism opportunities	Holiday services at preferred destination available at affordable price.	Range of two-week holidays of different sorts available at a range of 'benchmark' costs, related to household income.
b. Advertising/promotion	Leisure/tourism advertising/promotion to which individual is exposed.	Individual's recall of a specified list of advertisements/promotions in past three months.
c. Cost (of participation)	Total cost of leisure/tourism experience.	Costs of ranges of activities as indicated in 2a and 2b above.
d. Chance event	Unplanned occurrence which affects decision to participate.	Events which individual claims affected recent decisions to participate: experience, advice from friend/relative, item read or seen in the media.
3. Individual characteristics	Individual attributes (which influence leisure/tourism decisions), e.g.:	
	a. Age	a. Age last birthday
	b. Income	b. Annual household income before tax
	c. Personality	c. Results of Myers–Briggs test
	d. Past leisure/tourism experience	d. Leisure: activities undertaken in past six months; Tourism: trips taken in past five years

* Concepts appearing in Figure 3.3, Draft C.
** NB some definitions of tourism include other purposes, such as business.

Examples of operationalisation of concepts are shown in Table 3.6, column 3. Most of the concepts listed lend themselves to quantification and measurement, at least in part, but concepts 2a, 2b and 2d have qualitative characteristics and could be treated either way. The question of measurement is discussed more fully in Part II of the text, particularly in Chapter 7.

To some extent operationalisation involves thinking ahead as to how information might, in practice, be gathered about a concept: it is an indication of the practical implications of the definition. Often arbitrary or pragmatic choices have to be made in order to 'operationalise' the project. For example, should 'leisure participation' involve 'regular participation' to be of interest in the study, or is 'once a year' adequate? Or, what distance should someone have to be travelling away from home to be classified as a 'tourist' – 40 km or 50 km, or 25 km? These may be arbitrary decisions, or decisions based on the need to gather data which is comparable to other, existing, data. Case study 3.1 presents an example of a discussion of the operationalisation of concepts from the literature.

Case study 3.1   Operationalisation of concepts

Table 3.7 summarises the operationalisation of concepts/variables used in a quantitative/modelling study of visitor user patterns in a theme park in China. The study sought to test a number of propositions concerning how the pattern of use of attractions/rides within a park was affected by the attributes of the attractions/rides and their spatial layout. Some data items were collected by a questionnaire survey of visitors and some from management records and satellite (GIS/Google Earth).

Table 3.7 Examples of operationalisation of concepts

Concept/variable	Operationalisation
Visitor flow	Number of visitors/respondents moving from one park attraction/ride to another in study period.
Distance between attractions/rides	Distance in metres calculated via GIS
Attendance	Total number of respondents who visited an attraction/ride.
Experience value	Respondents' average score of an attraction on a 5-point scale from 1: very low experience value to 5: very high experience value
Attraction/ride capacity	Number of seats
Floor area	Area in sq. m. estimated from Google Earth
Indoor/outdoor attraction/ride	Dummy variable: 1 = indoor 2 = outdoor

Source: Extracted/summarised from Zhang et al. (2017: Table 1)

Table 3.8   Conceptual framework as quantifiable model

Conceptual framework/theory	The frequency of holiday-taking of a particular group is positively related to the group's average level of income
Concepts/variables	H = average number of holiday trips per year
	N = annual income in £000s
Relationship/equation	H = a + bN
Example of calibrated equation (value of a and b found from survey-based research)	H = 0.1 + 0.05N
Use of the equation for prediction of trips when N = £30k.	H = 0.1 + 0.05 × 30 = 0.1 + 1.5 = 1.6 trips a year

3.6 Modelling

A theoretical framework might also be called a *model*, particularly when the research is quantitative in nature. For example, the relationship between holiday-taking and a person's social and economic circumstances could be expressed in quantitative modelling terms as shown in Table 3.8. A survey of holiday-taking would identify various groups with different levels of income and holiday frequency, and statistical analysis could be used to 'calibrate' the equation – that is, find values for the 'parameters' a and b – so that the level of holiday-taking of a particular group could be predicted once the average income of that group was known. In Table 3.8, hypothetical parameter values of 0.1 and 0.05 are presented to illustrate the approach, and an example is given of how such an equation might be used to estimate or predict holiday expenditure of groups with given income levels, now or in the future. The technicalities of the statistical process are not pursued further here, but are touched on again in Chapter 17, when the technique of regression is discussed. More complex models could be developed, including additional variables such as age, occupation, the price of travel, exchange rates and so on. Such models are used to predict future tourism demand to and from different countries and regions.

4. Decide research question(s)

4.1 Research question, problem or hypothesis?

The focus of a research project might be expressed as a *question*, a *problem* or a *hypothesis*.

- A question requires an answer.

- A problem requires a solution.

- A hypothesis is expressed as a statement, which must be proved 'true' (consistent with the evidence), or 'false' (not consistent with the evidence).

The differences and relationships between the question-based approach and the hypothesis-based approach are illustrated in Table 3.9, which uses the *problem* of declining visitor numbers at a leisure/tourism site as an illustrative example to explore a range of possible *answers* in the question form and *testing* in the hypothesis form. Two versions are offered: A, a simple

Table 3.9   The research question vs the hypothesis

Research question	Hypothesis
A. Simple version	
1. *Pose research question:* Why have visitor levels declined in the last two years at site X?	1. *State hypothesis*: Visitor levels declined in the last two years at site X because of the attraction of newer, better-value sites.
2. *Conduct research*	2. *Conduct research*
3. *Answer:* Because of the attraction of newer, better value sites.	3. *Result:* Consistent with the evidence.
B. More detailed version	
1. *Pose research question:* Why have visitor levels declined in the past two years at site X?	1. *Develop hypotheses* Brainstorm/review literature/make enquiries as to range of possible reasons for decline in attendances.
2. *Develop research strategy* Brainstorm/review literature/make enquiries as to range of possible reasons for decline in visits. Compile list of possible reasons: a. attraction of newer, better-value facilities b. declining income in local catchment c. downturn in tourist numbers d. decline in quality of the facility e. increase in prices.	2. *Formulate/state hypotheses:* Visit levels have declined because of: a. attraction of newer, better-value facilities b. declining disposable income in local catchment c. downturn in tourist numbers d. decline in quality of the facility e. increase in prices, or f. a combination of the above.
3. *Conduct research:* Collect evidence/data to discover which reasons are plausible.	3. *Conduct research* Collect evidence/data and test all five hypotheses.
4. *Answer:* Because of the attraction of newer, better-value sites.	4. *Results:* a. Consistent with evidence; b. Not consistent; c. Not consistent; d. Not consistent; e. Not consistent.

version; and B, a more complex version. In each case, the left-hand column uses the question form and the right-hand column uses the hypothesis form. The hypothesis format is more common in the natural sciences, while the research question format is more common in the social sciences. The latter lends itself to descriptive and inductive research, while the former is more appropriate for explanatory and deductive research, as discussed in Chapter 2. For most of the text, the research question format is assumed; but the hypothesis format is integral to certain forms of statistical analysis and so is used in Chapter 17.

4.2 Specific starting point

In some cases, the research *topic* selected by the researcher is quite specific from the beginning and is initially expressed in the form of a question: the subsequent literature review and the conceptual framework are then the process by which this specific issue is analysed and placed in the context of existing knowledge.

4.3 Decision-making models

The conceptual framework can involve a *decision-making model*. That is, the research is designed to explore the causal factors and processes involved in people's decisions to visit a site or destination in order to discover how others might be persuaded to visit, or how existing visitors might be persuaded to visit again. The literature review would involve a review of similar existing models and a review of existing research on the various factors which influence people to choose a destination or visit a leisure site.

4.4 Area of interest

In other cases, the topic is initially quite vague: it is an area of interest without a very specific focus. In such cases, the literature review and the process of developing a conceptual framework help to focus the topic and to determine what exactly should be researched. The aim is to focus the research on one or more very specific questions which can be answered by the research. This is inevitably an iterative process; a question that looks simple and answerable, once subject to thought, reading and analysis, often develops into many questions which become conceptually too demanding to deal with in one project or which cannot be managed in the time and with the resources available. In such a situation, a smaller part of the problem must be isolated for research. This does not mean that the complex, 'big picture' must always be ignored – there is always a case, when writing up a research project, for setting it in its wider context and explaining how and why the particular focus was adopted.

4.5 Research questions or objectives?

Often research projects have a set of practical *objectives*, but these should not be confused with research *questions*. Nor should objectives be confused with the list of *tasks* necessary to conduct the research – as discussed under *research strategy* in section 6 of this chapter. Thus, for example, to say: 'The purpose of this research is to conduct a survey of a group of clients . . .' is to confuse ends with means. The survey, in this case, is being conducted for a purpose, to answer the research question(s), not as an end in itself. Of course, a research question can be embedded in an objective; thus it is possible to say:

> The objective of this research is to answer the following question: Why are attendances falling?

The one possible exception to this rule is the sort of descriptive research project which is aimed at establishing a database for a range of possible future uses. For example, the national statistics offices of most countries conduct the population census every 5 or 10 years as a service to a multitude of users who use the data for a wide range of purposes – so 'conducting a census of the population' could be said to be the objective of the research project. But even in this case, most of the possible future uses are known: the project assumes at least a prior range of policy-oriented research questions related to trends in ageing, educational needs, health matters and so on. Few leisure or tourism researchers find themselves in this sort of 'open-ended' data-collection situation: data should generally not be collected for their own sake or in the hope that they 'might come in useful'; there is invariably an instrumental purpose.

4.6 Primary and secondary questions

In most situations, the idea of *primary* and *subsidiary* questions is helpful. The subsidiary questions are necessary steps towards answering the primary question. For example, in Figure 3.3, while the main research question is to determine what influences leisure participation, one subsidiary question would be to determine the socio-economic characteristics and experience of the people involved in the study, and another would be to determine available facilities and their accessibility, marketing and prices.

5. List information requirements

The research question(s) and the conceptual framework should give rise to a list of *information requirements*. In some cases the information requirements are quite clear and the likely sources of information are straightforward. For example, in Table 3.6 the operationalisation column is, basically, a list of information requirements. Some more complex examples are shown in Appendix 3.1.

6. Decide research strategy

Development of a *research strategy* involves making decisions on a number of aspects of the research process, as listed in Table 3.10.

6.1 Project elements/stages

Often a research project will involve a number of different elements, or 'sub-projects' – for example, gathering of primary and secondary data, or gathering data in different locations or in different time-periods. A project may be devised in stages, particularly when one part is dependent on the findings from another. For example, stage 1 might involve some fieldwork in a particular location and, depending on the outcomes, stage 2 might involve more in-depth work in the same location or conducting work in a second location.

6.2 Information gathering techniques to be used

It is at this stage that alternative information gathering techniques are considered. While the *operationalisation of concepts* and the identification of *information needs* processes may already have indicated certain types of information source, it is here that the detail is determined. For each item in the list of information needs, a range of sources may be possible. Judgement is required to determine just what techniques to use, particularly in the light of time and resources available.

A further review of the literature can be valuable at this stage, concentrating particularly on techniques used by previous researchers, and asking such questions as whether their chosen methods were shown to be limiting or even misguided and whether lessons can be learned from past errors.

Table 3.10   Research strategy components

Identify project elements/stages

Decide information gathering techniques to be used

Decide data analysis techniques to be used

Decide budget

Draw up timetable

The range of information-gathering methods which are most likely to be considered at this stage are those covered in the following chapters of this text:

- utilisation of existing information, including published and unpublished research and secondary data (Chapters 6 and 7);

- observation (Chapter 8);

- qualitative methods, including ethnographic methods, participant observation, informal and in-depth interviews, group interviews or focus groups (Chapter 9);

- questionnaire-based surveys, including household face-to-face surveys, street surveys, telephone surveys, user/site surveys, postal surveys (Chapter 10);

- experimental methods (Chapter 11); and

- the case study approach (Chapter 12).

These individual techniques are not discussed further here since they are covered in general terms in Chapter 5 and in detail in subsequent chapters, as indicated.

Where the process of information gathering involves going out into the field – for instance, to conduct interviews or to undertake observation – the planning of *fieldwork* needs to be considered. In the case of experimental research, the programme of experiments would be considered here. If the proposed research does not involve primary data collection, then this will not be a consideration. Where extensive data collection is involved, then the organisation of fieldwork may be complex, involving recruitment and training of field staff (e.g. interviewers or observers), obtaining of permissions including ethics committee clearance in universities (as discussed in section 7) and organisation of data processing and analysis.

6.3 Approach to data analysis

Data analysis may be simple and straightforward and may follow fairly logically from the type of information collection technique to be used. This is particularly the case when the research is descriptive in nature. In some cases, however, the analysis of data may be complex, and particular thought needs to be given to the time and the skills which will be required to undertake the analysis. Consideration must be given to the format of the data which will be collected and just how its analysis will answer the research questions posed. The planned analysis procedures have implications for data collection. Where qualitative data are to be collected, for example using in-depth interviews, thought must be given as to how the results of the interviews will be analysed. Details of analysis methods which are appropriate and possible for different data-collection techniques are discussed in subsequent chapters, but it must be borne in mind that when planning a project, full consideration should be given to the time and resources required not only to the *collection* of data but also to its *analysis*.

6.4 Budget

In some situations, key aspects of the budget are fixed. For example, students generally have only their own labour available. Research consultants usually have an imposed upper budgetary limit. In other situations, for example when seeking a grant for research from a grant-giving body, or when seeking permission to conduct an 'in-house' project, the proposer of the research is called upon to recommend a budget. Whatever the situation, the task is never easy, since there is rarely enough money available to conduct the ideal research project, so compromises invariably have to be made.

6.5 Timetable

Timetabling is subject to similar overall constraints to budgeting. For example, students are typically required to submit a report by a specified date, and consultants are subject to a fixed externally required completion date. In other situations the researcher can specify the length of time for the project. The research strategy and timetable can be represented in various graphical formats; examples are shown in Figures 3.4 and 3.5.

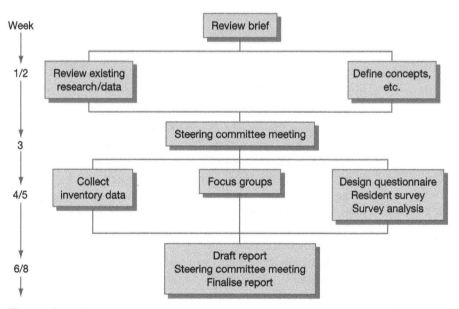

Figure 3.4 Example of research programme diagrammatic representation

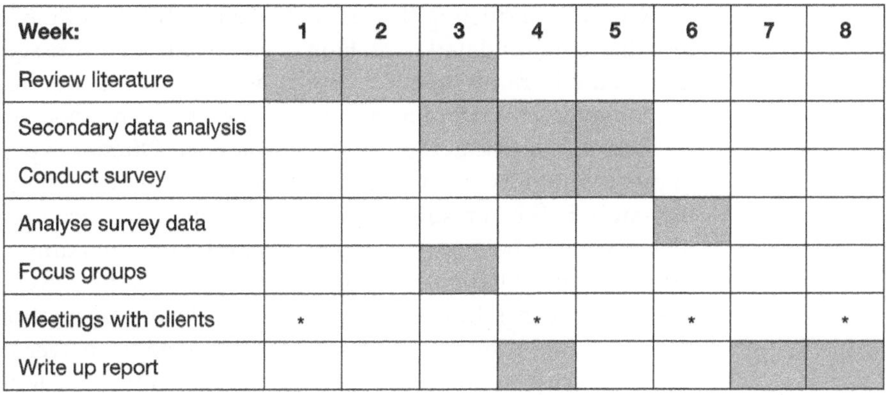

Week:	1	2	3	4	5	6	7	8
Review literature	▓	▓	▓					
Secondary data analysis			▓	▓	▓			
Conduct survey				▓	▓			
Analyse survey data						▓		
Focus groups			▓					
Meetings with clients	*			*		*		*
Write up report				▓			▓	▓

Figure 3.5   Example of research project timetable

7. Obtain ethics clearance

Ethical behaviour is important in research, as in any other field of human activity. Certain ethical considerations, concerned with such matters as plagiarism and honesty in reporting of results, arise in all research; but additional issues arise when the research involves human subjects, in both the biological and social sciences. The principles underlying 'research ethics' are universal – they concern things like honesty and respect for the rights of individuals.

Professional groups, such as market researchers, have established explicit 'codes of ethics' to which members are obliged to adhere. Most universities now have codes of ethics enforced by ethics committees. Typically, undergraduate and graduate projects are covered by a generic code of behaviour, but research proposals for theses and funded research by academics which involve humans or animals must be individually submitted for approval by the University Ethics Committee before the research can proceed. The ethical conduct of research is considered in more detail in Chapter 4.

8. Conduct the research

Element 8 of the research process is divided into two components: (a) data collection and (b) data analysis. These two components have not been presented as two sequential elements because in some research approaches, particularly qualitative methods, they are often intertwined; in other cases there are multiple data collection/analysis tasks in a single research project, with some being contingent on the analytical outcomes of others.

Actually conducting the research is what the rest of the text is about, so it is not discussed in detail here. However, it cannot be stressed enough that good research will rarely result if care is not taken over the preparatory processes discussed in this chapter. In a more positive vein, good preparation can ease the rest of the research process considerably. Often inexperienced researchers move too rapidly from stage 1, selecting the topic, to stage 8, conducting the research. This can result in the collection of data which is of doubtful use, and the researcher being presented with a problem of making sense of information which has been laboriously collected but does not fit into any framework. If the above process is followed, then every item of information collected should have a purpose, since it will have been collected to answer specific questions or to test specific hypotheses. This does not, of course, mean that the unexpected will not happen and 'serendipitous' findings may not arise, nor is it intended to ignore methodologies in which the framework – strategy – data collection/ analysis relationships are iterative in nature. It is intended to ensure that the core intellectual structure of the research is 'front of mind'.

It might be thought that inductive research, grounded theory and various forms of qualitative research require less preparation, but in practice this is rarely the case. As discussed in Chapter 9, in qualitative research it is certainly true that there is often a more fluid, evolutionary structure to the research design, but a sound preparatory base is still vital.

9. Communicate findings

The question of writing up research results is not discussed in detail here because the whole of Chapter 18 is devoted to this topic. Unlike the conduct of the empirical components of research, which inexperienced researchers invariably rush into too quickly, beginning the writing up of results is often delayed too long, so that insufficient time is left to complete it satisfactorily. An outline of the research process, as presented here, can itself be part of the problem, in that it implies that the writing-up process comes right at the end. In fact, the writing of a research report can begin almost as soon as the project begins, since all the early stages, such as the review of the literature and the development of the conceptual framework, can be written up as the project progresses.

10. Store data

Data, in the form of questionnaires, images and audio and video files, in various hard-copy and electronic formats, must be securely stored during the conduct of a project and for a period of time after its conclusion. Particular ethical and legal issues arise in the case of personally identifiable data (these are discussed in Chapter 4). These matters are generally affected by legislation relating to privacy and rights of access to personal records. Some data may also be subject to freedom of information legislation.

Research organisations, such as universities, generally have policies on the minimum length of time for which hard-copy materials, such as questionnaires, and electronic data must be stored after completion of research projects, typically five years. Given the length of time sometimes taken for results to be published, this is seen as a necessary precaution in case errors are detected in published results which may need to be checked back to original data sources – for example, the errors can arise from miscoding of questionnaires or in transferring of data from questionnaires or other sources into electronic form. Given that researchers may move on from institutions before the minimum storage time-period elapses, it is clearly necessary for institutions to have organised archiving and disposal systems. Of course, the ease of electronic storage means that this form of the data will generally be stored indefinitely. Re-analysis of data at a later stage and replication of research for comparative purposes often arises. In the case of longitudinal research, as discussed in Chapter 5, this is intrinsic to the method. This means that the data as stored should be easily accessible and readable by the original researcher and possibly others.

11. The research process in the real world

As noted in the introduction, and as discussed by Smith and Waddington (2014), the research process rarely proceeds in the ordered way depicted in Figure 3.1 and in the above discussion. The 10-element process is an idealised framework which underpins the actual process. It is also the sort of process which has to be outlined when planning the allocation of time in a project and when seeking funding. The idea that the process might not be entirely unidirectional is indicated by the fact that the first four elements are shown as connected in a circular process. Figure 3.6 shows some additional examples of iterative components of the process, and additional events which might occur during the course of research and cause revisions of any element. In some, more inductive research processes, iteration between the data and the research questions and conceptual framework is intrinsic to the approach and this can be conveyed verbally and diagrammatically in research proposals. This is particularly the case with qualitative methods, as discussed in Chapter 9.

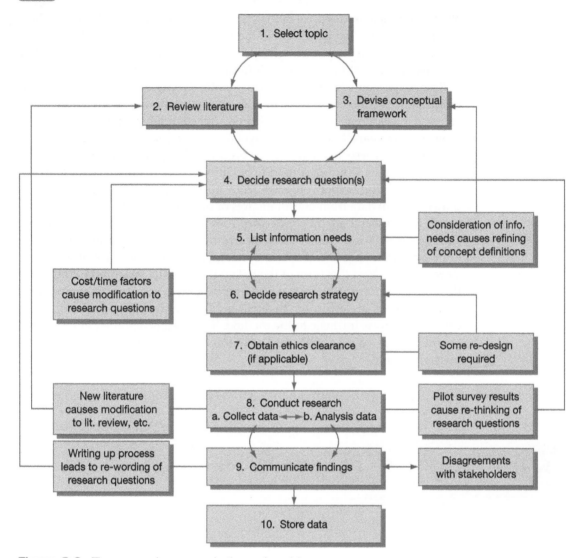

Figure 3.6   The research process in the real world

12. Research proposals

12.1 Introduction

Research proposals of two broad kinds are discussed here.

- *Self-generated* – proposals of the sort prepared by students seeking approval for research for a project or thesis on a topic of their own choosing or by academics seeking funds for a research project of their own devising.

- *Responsive* – proposals prepared by consultants responding to research briefs prepared by potential clients, sometimes simulated in the teaching environment with student projects for real or hypothetical client organisations.

Planners and managers seeking 'in-house' resources to conduct research fall somewhere between the two situations described.

In each case the proposal is a written document, which may or may not be supported by an oral presentation, and which must be convincing to the person or persons who will decide whether the research should go ahead. The writers of a research proposal are faced with the difficult task of convincing the decision-makers of:

- the value of the research;

- the soundness of the proposed approach;

- the valuable and original insights which the proposers will bring to the project; and

- the proposers' personal capabilities to conduct the research.

In some cases the decision-makers will be experts in the field, while in other cases they may be non-experts, so care must be taken to ensure that the proposal is understandable to all concerned. Clarity of expression and succinctness are often the key qualities looked for in these situations.

12.2 Self-generated research proposals

Academic research proposals, for student theses/projects or for academics seeking funding, must provide a rationale for the choice of topic as well as outlining what research is to be done and how. The topic and its treatment must be seen to be appropriate, in terms of scale and complexity, to the particular level of project involved, be it an undergraduate project, a PhD thesis or a funded project involving a team of researchers over a number of years.

In general, the academic research proposal must cover the material dealt with in this chapter. In some cases considerable work will already have been completed before the proposal is submitted. This could apply in the case of a PhD proposal, which might be based on as much as a year of preparatory work, or a proposal from an experienced academic who has been working in a particular field for a number of years. In such cases, the proposal may present considerable completed work on elements 1 to 6 of the research process as discussed earlier. The funding being sought may be required only to conduct the fieldwork part of the research and write up the results – elements 7 to 9 of the process. In other cases little more than the selection of the topic may have been completed, and the proposal outlines a programme of funding to undertake elements 2 to 9 of the process. Some proposals contain a preliminary review of the literature with a proposal to undertake more as part of the project. Some

Table 3.11 Research proposal checklist – self-generated research

Item	Element of Figure 3.1	Chapter
1. Background and justification for selection of topic	1	3
2. (Preliminary) review of the literature	2	3
3. Conceptual/theoretical framework/theoretical discussion	3	3
4. Statement of research questions or hypotheses	4	3
5. Outline of data/information requirements and research strategy	5, 6	3
6. Details of information collection methods: structured by the research strategy, but including:	6	
• outline of any additional literature to be reviewed		6
• summary of any secondary data sources to be used		7
• outline of empirical tasks to be conducted – qualitative and/or quantitative, including, as appropriate:		7–12
• sample/subject selection methods		13
• justification of sample sizes		13
• measures to ensure quality		7-12
7. Consideration of ethical implications	7	4
8. Details of data analysis methods	6	9, 11, 12, 14–17
9. Timetable or work/tasks	6a	3
10. Budget, where applicable, including costing of each element/stage/task	6	3
11. Report/thesis chapter outline or indication of number/type of publications	9	18
12. Other resources, researcher skills/experience/'track record' (necessary when seeking funds)	6d	3

proposals are very clear about the conceptual framework to be used, while in other cases only speculative ideas are presented. While bearing in mind, therefore, that there can be substantial differences between proposals of various types, the checklist in Table 3.11 is offered as a guide to the contents of a proposal. An example of a proposal is provided on the book website.

12.3 Responsive proposals – briefs and tenders

A *brief* is an outline of the research which an organisation wishes to have undertaken. Consultants wishing to be considered to undertake the project must submit a written, costed proposal or *tender*. Usually briefs are prepared by an organisation with a view to a number of consultants competing to obtain the contract to do the research. In some cases potential consultants are first asked, possibly through an advertisement, to indicate their *expression of interest* in the project. This will involve a short statement of the consultants' capabilities, their track record of previous consultancies and the qualifications and experience of staff available. In some cases public bodies maintain a register of accredited consultants with particular interests and capabilities, who may be invited to tender for particular projects. In the light of such statements of interest or information in the register, a *shortlist* of consultants is sent the full brief and invited to submit a detailed proposal. In very large projects some financial compensation may be provided to shortlisted candidates to cover the costs of the work undertaken to prepare a more detailed tender. The successful tender is usually selected not on the basis of price alone (the budget is in any case often a fixed sum indicated in the brief) but also on the quality of the submitted proposal and the track record of the consultants.

Briefs vary in the amount of detail they provide. Sometimes they are very detailed, leaving little scope for consultants to express any individuality in their proposals. In other cases they are very limited and leave a great deal of scope to consultants to indicate proposed methods and approaches. Client organisations experienced in commissioning research can produce briefs which are clear and 'ready to roll'. In other situations it is necessary to clarify the client's meanings and intentions. For example, a client might ask for a study of the 'leisure needs' of a community – in which case it would be necessary to clarify what the client means by 'leisure' – for example, whether home-based leisure, holidays, entertainment, restaurants or nightclubs are to be included. If a client asks for the 'effectiveness' of a programme to be assessed, it may be necessary to clarify whether a statement of objectives or a list of performance criteria for the programme already exists, or whether that must be developed as part of the research.

Paradoxically, problems can arise when client organisations are over-specific about their requirements. For example an organisation may ask for a 'user survey' or 'visitor survey' to be conducted. It is not easy to decide what should be included in such a survey without information on the management or policy issues which the resultant data are intended to address. Is the organisation concerned about declining attendances? Is it wanting to change its 'marketing mix'? Is it concerned about the particular mix of clientele being attracted? Is it concerned about future trends in demand? It would be preferable in such a situation for the client to indicate the nature of the management issue and leave the tenderer to suggest the most suitable research approach to take, which might or might not include a survey.

Sometimes there is a hidden agenda which the potential researcher would do well to become familiar with before embarking on the research. For example, research can sometimes be used as a means to defuse or delay difficult management decisions in an organisation – in the same way that governments often commission 'an inquiry' to delay having to make a decision. An example would be where a leisure or tourism service is suffering declining attendances because of poor maintenance of facilities and poor staff attitudes towards cus-tomers. This is very clear to anyone who walks through the door, but the man-agement decides to commission a 'market study' in the hope that the answer to their problem can be found 'out there' in the market – when in fact, the problem is very much 'in here', and their money might be better spent on improving maintenance and staff training than on research!

A situation where the client's requirements may seem vague is when the research is related not to immediate policy needs but to possible future needs or simply to satisfy curiosity. For example, a manager of a leisure or tourism facility might commission a visitor survey (perhaps because there is spare money in the current year's budget) without having any specific policy or man-agement problems in mind. In that case the research will need to specify hypo-thetical or potential policy or management issues and match the data specifications to them.

What should a proposal contain? The first and golden principle is that it should *address the brief*. It is likely that the brief will have been discussed at great length in the commissioning organisation; every aspect of the brief is likely to be of importance to some individual or section in the organisation, so *all* aspects of the brief should be considered and addressed in the proposal. So, for example, if the brief lists four objectives, it would be advisable for the pro-posal to indicate very clearly how each of the four objectives will be met. A proposal must therefore indicate the following:

● What is to be done?

● How is it to be done?

● When will it be done?

● What will it cost?

● Who will do it?

A typical responsive proposal might include elements as shown in Table 3.12. An example of a brief and successful responsive proposal is provided online.

Table 3.12   Research proposal checklist – responsive research

	Element	Chapter
1. Brief summary of key aspects of the proposal, including any unique approach and particular skills/experience of the consultants		
2. Re-statement of the key aspects of the brief and interpretation/ definition of key concepts		
3. Conceptual framework/theoretical discussion	3	3
4. Research strategy – methods/tasks	6	3
5. Details of information collection methods – structured by the research strategy, but including:	5, 6	

	Element	Chapter
• outline of any additional literature to be reviewed	2	6
• summary of any secondary data sources to be used		7
• outline of fieldwork to be conducted – qualitative and/or quantitative		7–12
• sample/subject selection methods		13
• sample sizes and their justification		13
• measures to ensure quality		
6. Timetable of tasks, including interim reporting/meetings with clients/ draft and final report submission	6	3
7. Budget: costing of each element/stage/task	6	3
8. Chapter outline of report and, if appropriate, details of other proposed reporting formats – e.g. interim reports, working papers, articles	9	18
9. Resources available, staff, track record		3

Summary

This chapter covers the process of planning a research project and preparing a research proposal. It is structured around 10 'elements':

1. selecting the topic;

2. reviewing the literature;

3. devising a conceptual framework;

4. deciding the research questions;

5. listing information needs;

6. deciding a research strategy;

7. obtaining ethics clearance (where relevant);

8. conducting the research;

9. reporting the findings; and

10. storing the data.

The term 'elements' is used rather than 'stages' or 'steps', since the 10 elements do not always occur sequentially in the precise order indicated. In particular, the first elements listed take place in a variety of orders, often in an iterative process.

The overview of the research process is followed by a discussion of research proposals – self-generated proposals, where the researcher initiates the research, and responsive proposals, which are prepared in response to a research brief from a commissioning organisation.

Test questions

1. In this chapter, it is suggested that a research topic might arise from eight different sources – name four of the sources.

2. What is a concept?

3. What is meant by 'operationalisation' of a concept?

4. What is a conceptual framework?

5. What is the difference between a research question and a hypothesis?

6. What are the differences between a self-generated research proposal and a responsive research proposal, and what implications do they have for the content of the two types of proposal?

Exercises

1. The ideal way of learning to do research is to conduct a live research project. Many readers of this text will have already embarked on such a project or will be required to do so as part of their assessment. In this case, the 'exercises' being undertaken will involve progressing through the various tasks discussed in this chapter. The first of these relates to the initial task discussed: selecting a topic. However, the following exercises may also be drawn on.

2. Select three articles from an issue of a leisure or tourism journal and identify the basis of their choice of research topic.

3. Select any article from a copy of a leisure or tourism journal and: (a) identify the key concepts used in the article; and (b) draw a simple concept map to show how the concepts are related.

4. Draw a concept map for a possible research project on either: (a) the effects of American culture on British leisure; (b) the effects of the ageing of the population on trends in tourism in Western countries; or (c) the effects of social media on leisure activity patterns.

5. Choose two of the research agendas listed in the Resources section and, through online exploration, assess the extent to which their suggestions have been followed up.

Resources

The best reading material for this chapter would be examples of successful research grant applications and proposals written in response to tenders. Completed research reports, whether academic or non-academic, vary in the amount of detail they provide about the development of the research process.

• Approaches to research: Hammitt et al. (2011); tourism: Pizam (1994), Ryan (1995).

• Concepts:
  • events: Getz and Andersson (2016: Fig. 2), Quinn (2013);
  • leisure studies: Chick (2009), Harris (2005);
  • sport and exercise research: Atkinson (2012); and
  • tourism: Botterill and Platenkaamp (2013), Chadwick (1994).

• Concept mapping: Brownson et al. (2008), Crowe and Sheppard (2012), Dillard and Bates (2011), Taylor et al. (2012).

• Conceptual frameworks: general: Miles and Huberman (1994: 18–22), D. G. Pearce (2012), P. L. Pearce (2005: 12–17). Examples:
  • adolescent girls and sport/recreational choice: James and Embrey (2005);
  • constraints negotiation and serious leisure: Lyu and Oh (2015);
  • environmental influences on walking and cycling: Pikora et al. (2003);
  • events: community education: Harris (2014);
  • generated from qualitative research (sport): Johnston et al. (1999: 263–74);
  • leisure: Veal et al. (2013: 104–6); Serious Leisure Perspective: Elkington and Stebbins (2014), but see critique: Veal (2016a);
  • mega-events: Kassens-Noor et al. (2015);
  • physical activity in parks: Bedimo-Rung et al. (2005);
  • sport: consumers and organizations: Kim and Traill (2011); elite success: De Bosscher et al. (2006); events: Mazodier et al. (2012); sport-for-development: Schulenkorf (2012); sport tourism: Wäsche and Woll (2010); and
  • tourism: experience: Cutler and Carmichael (2010: Fig. 1.1); general: Pearce (2012); poverty: Zhao and Ritchie (2007).

• Conceptual research: Xin et al. (2013). Examples:
  • authenticity: Heitmann (2011), Wang (1999);
  • lifestyle: Veal (1993: see Box 6.1); and
  • sport event legacy: Thompson et al. (2013).

• Importance-performance analysis: Veal (2017: Ch. 15).

• Proposal writing: Kline (2011); responsive proposals: Smith (2010: 35–9).

- Research agendas:
  - arts/culture: Scullion and Garcia (2005); USA: National Endowment for the Arts (2012);
  - arts and outdoor recreation: Cushman et al. (2010);
  - event tourism: Getz (2008: 413–21);
  - events: Carlsen et al. (2007), Harris et al. (2000), Lai and Li (2014), Mair and Whitford (2013), Weed (2012);
  - human rights and leisure: Veal (2015);
  - leisure: Lynch and Brown (1999);
  - lifestyle sports: Tomlinson et al. (2005);
  - sport: Australian Sports Commission (2004), Brownson et al. (2008), European Platform for Sport Innovation (EPSI) (2008), Owen et al. (2004); and
  - tourism: Ritchie (1994); backpacker tourism: Ateljevic and Hannam (2008); cultural tourism: Lehman, Wickham and Fillis (2014); social impacts: Deery et al. (2012).

- Research process in the real world: Smith and Waddington (2014).

- Selection of a research topic: Howard and Sharp (1983: Ch. 2), Punch (1994); serendipity: Smith and Waddington (2014).

- Stages in the research process: most general and specific research methods texts offer versions, for example: Gratton and Jones (2010: 16), Jennings (2010: 23–4), Long (2007: 17), Mitra and Lankford (1999: 19), Riddick and Russell (2008: 14), Saunders et al. (2009: 11), Vaske (2008: 5).

References

Ateljevic, I., and Hannam, K. (2008). Conclusion: towards a critical agenda for backpacker tourism. In K. Hannam and I. Ateljevic (Eds), *Backpacker tourism: concepts and profiles* (pp. 247–56). Clevedon, UK: Channel View.

Atkinson, M. (2012). *Key concepts in sport and exercise research methods*. London: Sage.

Australian Sports Commission (2004). *Statement of intent: social research agenda, 2004–2008*. Canberra: ASC.

Bedimo-Rung, A. L., Mowen, A. J., and Cohen, D. A. (2005). The significance of parks to physical activity and public health: a conceptual model. *American Journal of Preventive Medicine*, 28(2S2), 159–68.

Botterill, D., and Platenkaamp, V. (2013). *Key concepts in tourism research*. London: Sage.

Brownson, R. C., Kelly, C. M., et al. (2008). Environmental and policy approaches for promoting physical activity in the United States: a research agenda. *Journal of Physical Activity and Health*, 5(4), 488–503.

Carlsen, J., Ali-Knight, J., and Robertson, M. (2007). Access – a research agenda for Edinburgh festivals. *Event Management*, 11(1–2), 3–11.

Chadwick, R. A. (1994). Concepts, definitions, and measures used in travel and tourism research. In J. R. B. Ritchie and C. R. Goeldner (Eds), *Travel, tourism and hospitality research*, 2nd edn (pp. 65–80). New York: John Wiley.

Chick, G. (2009). Culture as a variable in the study of leisure. *Leisure Sciences*, 31(3), 305–10.

Clarke, J., and Critcher, C. (1985). *The Devil makes work: leisure in capitalist Britain.* London: Macmillan.

Crowe, M., and Sheppard, L. (2012). Mind mapping research methods. *Quality and Quantity*, 46(5): 1493–1504.

Cushman, G., Gidlow, B., and Espiner, S. (2010). Developing a national leisure research strategy for New Zealand: arts, outdoor recreation, sport and community recreation. *Annals of Leisure Research*, 13(3), 352–75.

Cutler, S. Q., and Carmichael, B. A. (2010). The dimensions of the tourist experience. In M. Morgan, P. Lugosi and J. R. B. Ritchie (Eds), *The tourism and leisure experience* (pp. 3–26). Bristol: Channel View.

De Bosscher, V., De Knop, P., Van Bottenburg, M., and Shibli, S. (2006). A conceptual framework for analysing sports policy factors leading to international sporting success. *European Sport Management Quarterly*, 6(2), 185–215.

Deery, M., Jago, L., and Fredline, L. (2012). Rethinking social impact of tourism research: a new research agenda. *Tourism Management*, 33, 64–73.

Dillard, J. E., and Bates, D. L. (2011) Leisure motivation revisited: why people recreate. *Managing Leisure*, 16(4), 253–68.

Elkington, S., and Stebbins, R. A. (2014). *The serious leisure perspective: an introduction*. London: Routledge.

European Platform for Sport Innovation (EPSI) (2008). *Building a future of European sports innovation*. Brussels: EPSI.

Getz, D. (2008). Event tourism: definition, evolution and research. *Tourism Management*, 29(3), 403–28.

Getz, D., and Andersson, T. (2016). Analysing whole populations of festivals and events: an application of organizational ecology. *Journal of Policy Research in Tourism, Leisure and Events*, 8(3), 249–73.

Gratton, C., and Jones, I. (2010). *Research methods for sport studies*, 2nd edn. London: Routledge.

Hammitt, W., Aybar-Damali, B., and McGuire, F. A. (2011). Leisure, recreation and tourism research design. In E. Sirakaya-Turk, M. Uysal, W. E. Hammitt and J. J. Vaske (Eds.), *Research methods for leisure, recreation and tourism* (pp. 20–35). Wallingford, UK: CABI.

Harris, D. (2005). *Key concepts in leisure studies*. London: Sage.

Harris, R. (2014). The role of large-scale sporting events in host community education for sustainable development: an exploratory case study of the Sydney 2000 Olympic Games. *Event Management*, 18(2), 207–30.

Harris, R., Jago, L., Allen, J., and Huskens, M. (2000). Towards an Australian event research agenda: first steps. *Event Management*, 6(4), 213–21.

Heitmann, S. (2011). Authenticity in tourism. In P. Robinson, S. Heitmann and P. U. C. Dieke (Eds), *Research themes for tourism* (pp. 45–58). Wallingford, UK: CABI.

Henderson, K. A. (2006). *Dimensions of choice: a qualitative approach to recreation, parks and leisure research, second edition*. State College, PA: Venture.

Howard, K., and Sharp, J.A. (1983). *The management of a student research project*. Aldershot, UK: Gower.

James, K., and Embrey, L. (2005). Adolescent girls' leisure: a conceptual framework highlighting factors that can affect girls' recreational choices. *Annals of Leisure Research*, 5(1), 14–26.

Jennings, G. (2010). *Tourism research, 2nd edn*. Milton, Qld, Australia: John Wiley.

Johnston, L. H., Corban, R. M., and Clarke, P. (1999). Multi-method approaches to the investigation of adherence issues within sport and exercise: qualitative and quantitative techniques. In S. J. Bull (Ed.), *Adherence issues in sport and exercise* (pp. 263–88). Chichester, UK; John Wiley.

Kassens-Noor, E., Wilson, M., Muller, S., Maharaj, B., and Huntoon, L. (2015). Towards a mega-event legacy framework. *Leisure Studies*, 34(6), 665–671.

Kim, Y. K., and Traill, G. (2011). Conceptual framework for understanding relationships between sport consumers and sport organizations: a relationship quality approach. *Journal of Sports Management*, 25(1), 57–69.

Kline, S. F. (2011). Proposal writing. In E. Sirakaya-Turk, M. Uysal, W. E. Hammitt and J. J. Vaske (Eds), *Research methods for leisure, recreation and tourism* (pp. 72–93). Wallingford, UK: CABI.

Lai, K., and Li, Y. (2014). Image impacts of planned special events: literature review and research agenda. *Event Management*, 18(2), 111–26.

Lehman, K., Wickham, M., and Fillis, I. (2014). A cultural tourism research agenda. *Annals of Tourism Research*, 49(2), 156–8.

Lincoln, Y. (2005). Institutional review boards and methodological conservatism: the challenge to and from phenomenological paradigms. In N. K. Denzin and Y. S. Lincoln (Eds), *Handbook of qualitative research, third edition* (pp. 165–90). Thousand Oaks, CA: Sage.

Long, J. (2007). *Researching leisure, sport and tourism: the essential guide*. London: Sage.

Lynch, R., and Brown, P. (1999). Utility of large-scale leisure research agendas. *Managing Leisure*, 4(2), 63–77.

Lyu, S., and Oh, C-O. (2015). Bridging the conceptual frameworks of constraints negotiation and serious leisure to understand benefit realization. *Leisure Sciences*, 37(2), 176–93.

Mair, J., and Whitford, M. (2013). An exploration of events research: event topics, themes and emerging trends. *International Journal of Event and Festival Management*, 4(1), 6–30.

Markula, P., and Denison, J. (2005). Sport and personal narrative. In D. L. Andrews, D. S. Mason and M. L. Silk (Eds), *Qualitative methods in sports studies* (pp.165–84). Oxford: Berg.

Mazodier, M., Quester, P., and Chandon, J. L. (2012). Unmasking the ambushers: conceptual framework and empirical evidence. *European Journal of Marketing*, 46(1/2), 192–214.

Miles, M. B., and Huberman, A. M. (1994). *Qualitative data analysis*, 2nd edn. Thousand Oaks, CA: Sage.

Miles, M. B., and Huberman, A. M. (2013). *Qualitative data analysis*, 3rd edn. Thousand Oaks, CA: Sage, e-book/Kindle version.

Mitra, A., and Lankford, S. (1999). *Research methods in park, recreation, and leisure services*. Champaign, IL: Sagamore.

National Endowment for the Arts (2012). *How art works: the National Endowment for the Arts' Five-year research agenda*. Washington, DC: NEA.

Owen, N., Humpel, N., Leslie, E., Bauman, A., and Sallis, J. F. (2004). Understanding environmental influences on walking: review and research agenda. *American Journal of Preventive Medicine*, 27(1), 67–76.

Pearce, D. G. (2012). *Frameworks for tourism research*. Wallingford, UK: CABI.

Pearce, P. L. (2005). *Tourist behaviour: themes and conceptual schemes*. Clevedon, UK: Channel View.

Pikora, T., Giles-Corti, B., Bull, F., Jamrozic, K., and Donovan, R. (2003). Developing a framework for assessment of the environmental determinants of walking and cycling. *Social Science and Medicine*, 56(6), 1693–1703.

Pizam, A. (1994). Planning a tourism research investigation. In J. R. B. Ritchie and C. R. Goeldner (Eds), *Travel, tourism and hospitality research*, 2nd edn (pp. 91–104). New York: John Wiley.

Punch, M. (1994). Politics and ethics in qualitative research. In N. K. Denzin and Y. S. Lincoln (Eds), *Handbook of qualitative research* (pp. 83–98). Thousand Oaks. CA: Sage.

Quinn, B. (2013). *Key concepts in event management*. London: Sage.

Riddick, C. C., and Russell, R. V. (2008). *Research in recreation, parks, sport, and tourism*, 2nd edn. Champaign, IL: Sagamore.

Ritchie, J. R. B. (1994). Tourism research: policy and managerial priorities for the 1990s and beyond. In D. G. Pearce and R. W. Butler (Eds), *Tourism research: critiques and challenges* (pp. 201–16). London: Routledge.

Rowe, D. (1995). *Popular cultures: rock music, sport and the politics of pleasure*. London: Sage.

Ryan, C. (1995). *Researching tourist satisfaction: issues, concepts, problems*. London: Routledge.

Saunders, M., Lewis, P., and Thornhill, A. (2009). *Research methods for business students*. Harlow, UK: Financial Times-Prentice Hall.

Schulenkorf, N. (2012). Sustainable community development through sport and events: A conceptual framework for sport-for-development projects. *Sport Management Review*, 15(1), 1–12.

Scullion, A., and Garcia, B. (2005). What is cultural policy research? *International Journal of Cultural Policy*, 11(2), 113–26.

Smith, A., and Waddington, I. (Eds) (2014). *Doing real world research in sports studies*. London: Routledge.

Smith, S. L. J. (2010). *Practical tourism research*. Wallingford, UK: CABI.

Taylor, M. J., Higgins, E., Francis, M., and Hulya, F. (2012). A multi-paradigm approach to developing policy for the location of recreational facilities. *Systems Research and Behavioural Science*, 29(3), 240–52.

Thompson, A., Schlenker, K., and Schulenkorf, N. (2013). Conceptualizing sport event legacy. *Event Management*, 17(2), 111–12.

Tomlinson, A., Ravenscroft, N., Wheaton, B., and Gilchrist, P. (2005). *Lifestyle sports and national sport policy: an agenda for research: Report to Sport England*. London: Sport England.

Vaske, J. J. (2008). *Survey research and analysis: applications in parks, recreation and human dimensions*. State College, PA: Venture.

Veal, A. J. (1993). The concept of lifestyle: a review. *Leisure Studies*, 12(4), 233–52.

Veal, A. J. (2015). Human rights, leisure and leisure studies, *World Leisure Journal*, 57(4), 249–72.

Veal, A. J. (2016a). The Serious Leisure Perspective and the experience of leisure. *Leisure Sciences*, 39(3), 205–23.

Veal, A. J. (2016b). Leisure, income inequality and the Veblen effect: cross-national analysis of leisure time and sport and cultural activity. *Leisure Studies*, 35(2), 215–40.

Veal, A. J. (2017). *Leisure, sport and tourism: politics, policy and planning*, 4th edn. Wallingford, UK: CABI Publishing.

Veal, A. J., Darcy, S., and Lynch, R. (2013). *Australian leisure*, 4th edn. Sydney: Pearson Australia.

Wang, N. (1999). Rethinking authenticity in tourist experience. *Annals of Tourism Research*, 26(2), 349–70.

Wäsche, H., and Woll, A. (2010). Regional sports tourism networks: a conceptual framework. *Journal of Sport and Tourism*, 15(3), 191–214.

Wearing, B. (1998). *Leisure and feminist theory*. London: Sage.

Weed, M. (2012). Towards an interdisciplinary events research agenda across sport, tourism, leisure and health. In S. J. Page and J. Connell (Eds), *The Routledge handbook of events* (pp. 57–71). London: Routledge.

Wilkinson, R., and Pickett, K. (2009). *The spirit level: why more equal societies almost always do better*. London: Allen Lane.

Witt, C. A., and Wright, P. L. (1992) Tourist motivation: life after Maslow. In P. Johnston and B. Thomas (Eds), *Choice and demand in tourism* (pp. 33–55). London: Mansell.

Xin, S., Tribe, J., and Chambers, D. (2013). Conceptual research in tourism. *Annals of Tourism Research*, 41(1), 66–88.

Zhang, Y., Li, X., and Su, Q. (2017). Does spatial layout matter to theme park tourist carrying capacity? *Tourism Management*, 61, 82–95.

Zhao, W., and Ritchie, J. R. B. (2007). Tourism and poverty alleviation: an integrative research framework. In C. M. Hall (Ed.), *Pro-poor tourism: who benefits?* (pp. 9–33). Clevedon, UK: Channel View publications.

Appendix 3.1: Examples of conceptual frameworks

1. Market research study

The *aim* of the study is to assess the size and nature of the market for a potential new tourist/leisure attraction.

The *research strategy* (concepts are indicated in italic) is: (1) to obtain information on the general level of *demand* for *this type of attraction* in the community at large, and the *market profile* of visitors to existing similar attractions, using national or regional data; (2) to estimate the *current level of demand* and *future level of demand* for this type of attraction in the specified *market area*, based on *local demand, day-trip demand* and *tourist demand*; (3) to assess *existing provision* of this type of attraction in the locality and the likely *market share* which the new attraction might attract; (4) to conduct a consumer study of *quality* of existing provision to guide developers on the design of the proposed new attraction. Suggested relationships between the concepts are shown in the shaded part of Figure 3.7.

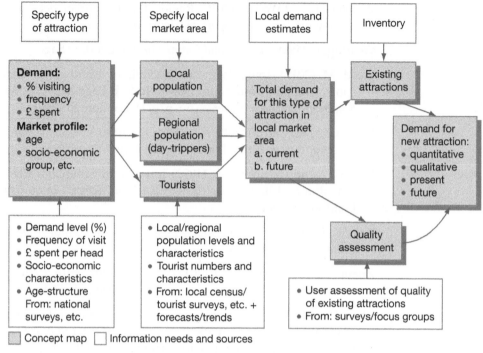

Figure 3.7 Concept map and Information needs for a market research study

The unshaded parts of Figure 3.7 indicate the information needs for the market research study and also suggest some likely sources for this information. The information needs are only indicated in abbreviated form in Figure 3.7: for example, a 'market profile' for a particular type of attraction could involve more than just age and socio-economic group. This is linked to the idea of 'operationalising' concepts.

2. Holiday/leisure facility choice

The example conceptual framework presented in Figure 3.3 relates to leisure participation decision-making, including the decision to take a holiday. A more elaborate version of a framework related to this topic is presented here.

In a paper entitled 'Tourist motivation: life after Maslow', Witt and Wright (1992) seek to move tourist motivation theory beyond reliance on Maslow's famous 'hierarchy of needs'. They review a range of other motivation theories and note that most deal with what people need but do not involve consideration of how such needs will be met and therefore have limited usefulness in the context of tourism studies. They suggest the use of *expectancy theory*, developed largely in the context of work motivation. Expectancy theory models the individual's *expectations* regarding the likelihood of a course of action satisfying his or her needs and the extent to which the need will be satisfied. When applied to holiday destination choice, the model involves consideration of the importance of certain holiday attributes (such as warm climate, interesting

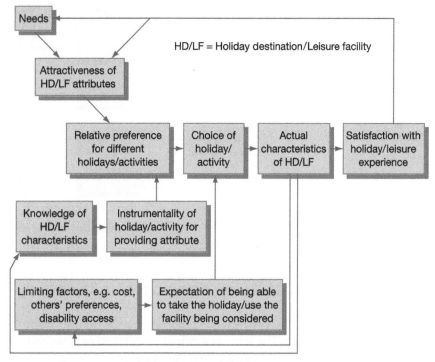

Figure 3.8   Concept map holiday/leisure facility choice
Source: Based on Witt and Wright (1992: 50).

surroundings) in satisfying an individual's needs and the individual's assessment of the extent to which a certain destination has these attributes and is therefore likely to satisfy the individual's needs. Feedback processes suggest that each holiday experienced will contribute to the development of the individual's understanding and knowledge of destination attributes and their relationships with his or her needs. Witt and Wright develop a diagrammatic representation of the model, which serves as a conceptual framework not for a single research project but for research projects on destination choice in general.

The model developed could also apply to non-holiday leisure experiences, so the version presented in Figure 3.8 relates not just to holiday destinations but to holiday destinations and leisure facilities.

3. Performance monitoring

Figure 3.9 presents a generic concept map of research which might be conducted for *performance evaluation*, as indicated in step 8 of the rational-comprehensive model of the management process shown in Figure 1.2. Typically, the progress towards achievement of objectives in a corporate plan or strategy is measured by *key performance indicators* (KPIs), which must often be obtained by some sort of research. Thus, for example, an objective to increase event visitor numbers would have associated with it a KPI which would call for periodic measurement of the number of event visitors.

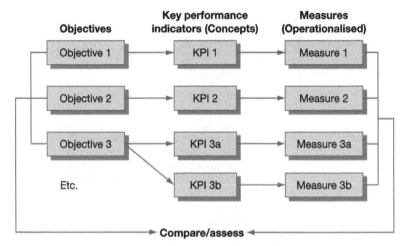

Figure 3.9   Concept map: performance monitoring

4. Customer service quality study

Figure 3.10 concerns a customer service quality study using the SERVQUAL approach. The latter is similar to what is sometimes referred to as the *importance-performance* approach (see the Resources section).

The *aim* of the study is to assess customers' satisfaction with a leisure/tourism facility/service

The *research strategy* (concepts in italic) uses the SERVQUAL approach to customer service quality measurement (see Parasuraman et al., 1985; Howat et al., 2003), which compares customers' *expectations* concerning various *attributes of service quality* with customers' assessment of actual *performance* of the service in regard to those attributes. The *difference* or *disconfirmation* between the two assessments provides information for managers on areas of service quality which require *management action*.

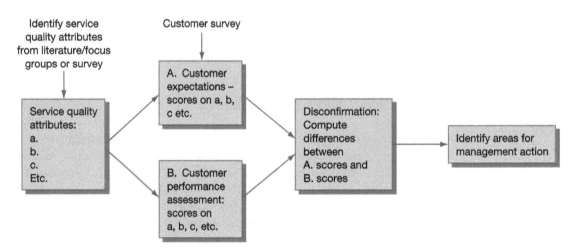

Figure 3.10   Conceptual framework: customer service quality study

4 Research ethics

1. Introduction

2. Institutional oversight of research ethics

3. Ethics in the research process

4. Ethical issues in research

    4.1 Social benefit
    4.2 Researcher competence
    4.3 Subjects' freedom of choice
    4.4 Subjects' informed consent
    4.5 Risk of harm to subjects
    4.6 Honesty/rigour in analysis, interpretation
        and reporting
    4.7 Conflict of interest

5. Access to research information

1. Introduction

Ethical behaviour is important in research, as in any other field of human activity. Ethical considerations, concerned with such matters as plagiarism and honesty in reporting of results, arise in all research, but additional issues arise when the research involves human and animal subjects, in both the biological and social sciences. Increasingly, ethical issues also arise in relation to research which may have an impact on the physical environment. The underlying principles of research ethics are universal: they concern things like honesty and respect for the rights of individuals and animals and the integrity of eco-systems. The issue came to the fore at the end of World War II, when details were revealed of horrific experiments which had been conducted on prisoners in the Nazi concentration camps and certain medical experiments conducted in the United States in the 1960s and 1970s without the consent of the subjects (Loue, 2002). These events raised questions about not only the ethical conduct of research but also the subsequent use of findings from research conducted unethically. The result has been the establishment of international, national, professional and institutional codes of research ethics and their oversight by regulatory organisations.

An example of a code of research ethics is the document on the responsible conduct of research published in 2007 by a consortium of Australian organisations, which covered:

- honesty and integrity;

- respect for human research participants, animals and the environment;

- good stewardship of public resources used to conduct research;

- appropriate acknowledgement of the role of others in research; and

- responsible communication of research results. (NHMRC et al., 2007: 13).

2. Institutional oversight of research ethics

Most universities now have their own codes of research ethics enforced by ethics committees. Typically, undergraduate and graduate projects are covered by a generic code of behaviour, but research proposals for student theses and funded and unfunded research by academics which involve human or animal subjects must be individually submitted for approval by the University Ethics Committee.

Codes of research ethics have intrinsic value in protecting the rights of humans and animals involved in research, but they also serve a professional and organisational function. Researchers may be subject to litigation and risk losing professional indemnity if they are not seen to have adhered to the appropriate code of ethics. A related consideration is the question of public relations and the standing of organisations responsible for the research within the community. Some practices may be ethical, but still give offence, so the value of the data collected using such practices must be weighed against the ill-will which may be generated.

In universities and other research institutions, research projects involving human or animal subjects are subject to approval by an ethics committee. Some universities have established a committee to cover the whole of the university, although usually there are at least two committees, covering human and animal-related research, respectively. In some cases committees cover a single faculty or division. Typically, the approval process involves the completion of an 'Application for Ethics Approval Form' which must provide full details of the rationale for the research, the methods to be used and qualifications of the researchers involved. The *National Ethics Application Form* of the Australian National Health and Medical Research Council (NHMRC, nd), which is a model for the use of Australian research institutions, runs to over 450 items of information.

When ethics committees are faculty/division-specific, a researcher would expect committee members to be familiar with the research methods being used. With university-wide committees, however, committee members possibly might not be familiar with research methods being used by colleagues from very different disciplines, especially those using novel methods. This is believed by some to be the case with some qualitative methods which reflect a very different epistemology from the positivist approach of the natural sciences. This issue is argued by Lincoln (2005), who notes 'increased scrutiny' from research committees in the United States 'largely in response to failures in biomedical research' but spilling over into the social sciences and resulting in 'multiple rereviews of faculty proposals for qualitative research projects and … rereviews and denials of proposed student research (particularly dissertation research) that utilise action research … methods, research in the subjects' own settings (e.g. high schools), and/or research which is predominantly qualitative in nature' (Lincoln, 2005: 167). As processes have become more formalised in areas outside the physical sciences, concerns have been expressed about 'ethics creep' (Haggerty, 2004).

3. Ethics in the research process

Research ethics can be examined in regard to three dimensions: the nature of the ethical issues, the stage or component of the research process where the issues arise and whether the research subject is anonymous or identified.

Regarding the nature of the ethical issues, most codes of ethics and ethical practice are based on the 'golden rule' which relates to all human conduct and is endorsed by most religions, that is, that you should treat others as you yourself would wish to be treated. More specifically, the general principles usually invoked in codes of research ethics are that:

● the research should be *beneficial to society*;

● researchers should be suitably *qualified* and/or appropriately *supervised* to conduct the research;

● subjects should take part *freely*;

- subjects should take part only on the basis of *informed consent;*
- no *harm* should befall the research subjects; and
- data should be honestly and rigorously analysed, *interpreted* and *reported.*

These issues arise in different stages/components of the research process, as summarised in Table 4.1.

Regarding anonymous versus personally identifiable data, in much primary empirical leisure and tourism research, for example on-site questionnaire-based surveys and much observational research, data are collected and stored anonymously: the researcher never knows the names of the subjects, so names are not recorded in any form. However, in some cases the names and contact details of individual subjects are known to the researcher and may be recorded in hard-copy or electronically as part of the data from the research.

The way these three dimensions relate to one another is shown in the examples in Case study 4.1. It can be seen that the question of identifiable subjects relates only to the storage and reporting of results components of the research. The ethical issues are discussed in turn below.

With regard to the design and conduct of research, many codes of ethics deal with practices in laboratories, but this discussion is largely concerned with ethical conduct in the field – that is, with people in their own living environment, including leisure and tourism locations. As far as the reporting of results and storage of data are concerned, the same ethical principles apply, regardless of the methods involved.

Table 4.1 Ethics in the research process

Ethical issue	Design/ organisation	Collection	Analysis/ interpretation	Storing data during project	Reporting	Storing data after project
Social benefit	●					
Researcher competence	●					
Subjects' freedom of choice		●				
Subjects' informed consent		●				
Risk of harm to subjects – anonymous		●				
Risk of harm to subjects – identifiable		●	●	●	●	●
Honesty/rigour in analysis/interpretation			●			
Honesty/rigour in reporting					●	

Case study 4.1	Examples of ethical issues in leisure and tourism research

A. Status of the participant observer in an outdoor adventure setting

Donne (2006) conducted research for a PhD thesis as a participant observer at a watersports outdoor adventure centre involving a study of young people aged 14–16 years who used the centre, and the professional instructors who worked at the centre. Among ethical issues he identifies during the experience were the following:

- In order to gain access to facilities involving contact with children, it was necessary for the researcher to undergo an official police check to ensure that he had no prior criminal record.

- Donne describes the role he chose to play at the centre. Centre staff – mainly instructors – knew he was conducting research, but it was necessary for him to indicate an appropriate level of expertise in watersports since he knew that 'appearing too knowledgeable could have resulted in confrontational situations' with the staff, while 'any pretence of incompetence' could have identified him as a liability. He had personal skills in sailing and windsurfing, was a qualified kayak and canoe instructor and had competed at high level in canoe slalom. He decided to pose as 'an enthusiastic learner with a basic understanding and competence'. This mild level of deception was considered justified in the interests of successfully conducting the research.

- Early on Donne recognised two instructors at the centre whom he had taught in the past and who would be aware of his skill level, and he had to take them into his confidence regarding his 'enthusiastic learner' role.

- When one of the centre instructors, who had been reluctant to be interviewed for the research, challenged Donne to a canoe race, he accepted but then regretted having done so because it placed him in a dilemma as to whether he should deliberately lose the race to secure the instructor's cooperation with the research.

B. Exposure by association in autobiographical research on elite sport coaching

Jones et al. (2006) discuss the example of a doctoral thesis on the relationship between an elite athlete (the researcher) and his coach, using the autobiographical method. The relationship between the two had deteriorated over time, with negative views expressed about the coach in the thesis. While a pseudonym was used for the coach, the author of the thesis was clearly identified and so, for people familiar with the athletics scene, the coach could be identified 'by association'. This was pointed out by one of the thesis examiners.

The paper, involving the student and thesis supervisors, describes how the problem was dealt with in the final, approved, version of the thesis.

C. Deception in recreation/tourism survey research

In a celebrated case in outdoor recreation/tourism research, Moeller et al. (1980a) used incognito interviewers, posing as campers, to investigate campers' attitudes towards pricing using informal interviewing techniques. They discovered different results from those collected by formal interviews conducted by identified interviewers. It was believed that the views expressed to the incognito interviewers, which were more relaxed about possible price increases, were more truthful than views expressed to 'official' interviewers. However, the ethics of this practice raised considerable controversy in the *Journal of Leisure Research* (see Christensen, 1980, Moeller et al., 1980b, LaPage, 1981).

4. Ethical issues in research

4.1 Social benefit

Research on nuclear and chemical weaponry has given rise to the proposition that research should be supported only if its social benefits can be demonstrated. Such an assessment is, of course, subjective. Thus, during the Cold War, it was argued that research on nuclear weapons could be defended on the grounds that peace was maintained as long as each side – the West and the communist bloc – matched each other's weapons, in terms of technological sophistication and quantity, so that neither side would risk attacking the other: the principle of mutually assured destruction (MAD). In contemporary leisure and tourism research, the issues are not as dramatic but can arise in relation to funding sources: for example, should research funding be accepted from tobacco companies or from companies with questionable environmental practices?

Push polls

In 1995, the US National Council on Public Polls issued the following media release about:

> a growing and thoroughly unethical political campaign technique, commonly called 'push polls', masquerading as legitimate political polling. . . . A 'push poll' is a telemarketing technique in which telephone calls are used to canvass vast numbers of potential voters, feeding them false and damaging 'information' about a candidate under the guise of taking a poll to see how this 'information' affects voter preferences. In fact, the intent is to 'push' the voters away from one candidate and toward

the opposing candidate. This is clearly political telemarketing, using innuendo and, in many cases, clearly false information to influence voters; there is no intent to conduct research.

These telemarketing techniques damage the electoral process in two ways. They injure candidates, often without revealing the source of the information. Also, the results of a 'push poll', if released, give a seriously flawed and biased picture of the political situation. (National Council on Public Polls, 1995)

Push polling typically takes place in marginal electorates where a successful telephone campaign can have a significant impact on the election outcome. A typical push poll question would be of the following format: 'Given that candidate X could increase income tax by 50%, whereas candidate Y is committed to no increases in income tax, how does this affect your voting intentions?' The results of the poll are of less interest than the planting of the false or misleading information about candidate X in the listener's mind.

Push polling occurs in the political realm and would rarely be relevant to leisure and tourism, but it highlights the ethical dimension of the use of the 'leading question', which is discussed further in Chapter 10.

4.2 Researcher competence

Research ethics guidelines require that those undertaking research have appropriate levels of training, qualifications and experience, including familiarisation with ethical issues. Occasionally cases in which unqualified individuals are found to have been practising as doctors and even surgeons attract media publicity. The community is shocked that unqualified people should be undertaking such important work and the individuals are duly prosecuted. Such cases represent the extreme of public ethical concern because of the level of risk of harm involved. But the issue of professional competence, while less clear-cut in other areas, is nevertheless applicable. In leisure and tourism research, a researcher who is not competent, through training and/or experience, to conduct research runs the risk of:

- wasting the resources of the funding organisation;
- wasting the time of subjects;
- abusing the goodwill of subjects;
- misleading the users of the research results; and/or
- damaging the reputation of the research organisation.

4.3 Subjects' freedom of choice

It seems obvious that subjects should not be coerced to become involved in research projects, but there are some grey areas. Some of these are institutional and some are intrinsic to the design and nature of the research.

Captive groups

In universities, students are often used as subjects in research. In some places students are *required* to be available for a certain amount of experimental or survey work conducted by academic staff, and in some cases they receive study credit for this involvement. Although, no doubt, students can opt out of such activities, there is moral pressure on them to conform and possibly fear of sanctions if they do not. Clearly it is unethical for the university to allow such undue moral pressure to be brought to bear.

Other captive group cases involve classes of schoolchildren or members of organisations, whose participation is agreed to by the person in charge. Again, while opting out may be possible, in practice it may be difficult, and the subject may be, in effect, coerced. As a consequence, education authorities generally place strict controls on the amount and type of research which may be carried using schoolchildren as subjects. Research in prisons and mental and other hospitals raises similar questions about genuine freedom of choice on the part of the subject.

Children

Research involving children, inside or outside the school setting, raises particular ethical issues. At what age are children able to give informed consent to being involved in research? How does this relate to parents' and carers' rights and obligations? If children below a certain age are not deemed to be able to give consent on their own behalf, in what circumstances, if any, is it appropriate for carers to give consent on the child's behalf? Are there situations where the risk of physical or emotional harm is greater for children than for adults involved with similar research processes?

In general it is believed that particular care should be taken in conducting research involving children because they typically see adults – including researchers – as figures of authority. Thus they may be less likely than adults to exercise their right to non-cooperation. This is not only a human rights issue but can also raise validity issues if children see questions as some sort of performance test and/or feel a need to please the questioner by answering or behaving in certain ways.

Where institutions are involved, such as play centres or schools, those organisations will have their own guidelines, particularly in regard to the requirements for parental permission.

Official surveys

The principle of freedom of choice is constantly infringed by governments: it is an offence, for example, not to complete the official population census forms or to refuse cooperation with a number of other official surveys. In these cases, the 'social benefit' argument relating to the need for accurate and complete data is considered to outweigh the citizen's right to refuse to give information.

Observation

In the case of some types of research where large numbers of subjects are involved – for example, studies of traffic flows, pedestrian movements or crowd behaviour – choice on the part of the subject is impossible. In many observational research situations, if the subjects knew that they were being observed, they might well modify their behaviour and so invalidate the research. This would apply particularly in situations where antisocial, and even illegal, behaviour may be involved. These considerations might apply in research ranging from people's interpersonal behaviour in a gym through to research on the milieu of prostitution, gambling or drinking.

Participant observation

The problem of freedom to participate arises particularly in research using participant observation where, as discussed in Chapter 9, the researcher is a participant in the phenomenon being studied. Examples are presented in Case study 4.1. The whole basis of such research may rely on the researcher being accepted and trusted by the group being investigated: this may not be forthcoming if it is known that the participant is a researcher. If the researcher does 'come clean', there is the risk – even the likelihood – of the subjects modifying their behaviour, thus invalidating the research. To what extent is it ethical for researchers to disguise their identity to the people they are interacting with and studying – in effect, to lie about their identity? When researchers are involved with groups engaging in illegal and/or antisocial activities, for example drug-taking or some youth gangs, where do their loyalties lie? In some research methodologies, a different approach is adopted and fully informed interaction between researcher and subjects is embraced and becomes part of the analysed and reported research.

If it is accepted that the research of this type is permissible, despite the lack of freedom of consent, then the issue of confidentiality in reporting, as discussed later in this chapter, becomes even more critical.

4.4 Subjects' informed consent

In experimental research, where there is a risk, however remote, of physical harm to the subject (for example, where allergies might be involved, or a risk of muscle strains, or even of heart attack), it is clearly necessary for subjects to be fully aware of the risks involved in order to be able to give their 'informed consent' to participate. The level of risk of harm is a matter of judgement, and often only the researcher is fully aware of the extent of risk involved in any given research procedure. This raises the question of the extent to which the subject can ever be 'fully informed'. Subjects can never be as fully informed as the researcher. A judgement has to be made about what is reasonable. In the traditional science laboratory setting, verbal and written explanations of the nature of the research are given to the potential subjects, and they are asked to sign a document indicating their agreement to be involved in the research. A checklist

Table 4.2   Information for research participants: checklist

1. Name of organisation conducting the research
2. Purpose of the research
3. Sponsoring/funding organisation, if applicable
4. Participants and how they are being selected
5. What is required from participants:
   - nature of involvement (interviews, focus groups, etc.)
   - time required for each session
   - number of sessions
   - time-period over which sessions will take place
6. Any risks to the participant
7. Voluntary nature of participation
8. Right of participant to refuse to answer any questions or withdraw at any stage without giving reasons
9. Privacy and security of data
10. Ways in which data will be used
11. Contact details for research project supervisor

regarding the sort of information which should be provided to potential participants is provided in Table 4.2, and an example of a consent form is provided in Figure 4.1. In the case of a single, anonymous questionnaire-based survey, verbal consent is generally considered adequate; but if names are recorded, and lengthy and/or repeated interviews or other types of activity are involved, then written consent is advisable.

A researcher could of course 'go through the motions' of following this procedure but abuse it by providing misleading information about the level of risk – itself an unethical practice. Hence the need for clear institutional guidelines and monitoring of these matters.

Physical or mental risks of harm do not generally arise in leisure and tourism research, but they are only one aspect of being informed. There may be a moral dimension also. For example, some people may object to being involved in research which is being conducted for certain public, political or commercial organisations. So being informed also involves being informed about the purpose of the research and the nature of the sponsor or beneficiary.

In some cases the status of the researcher is ambivalent: for example, when students engaged in a project as part of their learning process in a university course conduct the project on behalf of a real client organisation, or when part-time students conduct research for a university assignment using their fellow employees as subjects or conduct research on competitors. It is clearly unethical for students to identify themselves only as students and not to identify to their informants the organisation which will be the beneficiary of the research.

University of xxxxxxx: School of Leisure and Tourism
Holiday history research project

CONSENT FORM

I confirm that I have read and understood the research project
information sheet for the 'Holiday history research project' and have
had any questions answered to my satisfaction.   _____

I understand that my participation in the study is entirely voluntary
and I may cease to take part at any time without giving reasons.   _____

I agree to take part in the study as described in the information sheet. _____

I agree to interviews/discussion sessions being recorded.   _____

I agree that anonymous quotations from interviews/discussions may
be used in publications.   _____

Name: _____   Date: _____

Signature: _____

Researcher: _____   Date: _____

Signature: _____

Figure 4.1 Example of a consent form

But again, there are some grey areas. In some cases the research would be
invalidated if subjects knew its purpose in detail. For example, responses could
be affected if the subjects knew that a survey was being carried out to see how
respondents reacted to interviewers of differing race or gender. In some attitu-
dinal research, for example on potentially sensitive topics such as race or sex, it
may be thought that responses would be affected if respondents were told too
much about the research and therefore placed 'on their guard'. Clearly such
deception raises ethical issues, and judgements have to be made about whether
the value of the research justifies the use of mild deception.

In some cases the provision of detailed information to informants and obtaining their written consent is neither practicable nor necessary. Thus the typical
leisure or tourism survey:

- is anonymous;

- involves only a short interview (e.g. three or four minutes);

- involves fairly innocuous, mostly non-personal questions; and

- takes place at a facility/site with the agreement of the management or
authorities.

In this type of situation most respondents are not interested in detailed explanations of the research. Most adults are familiar with the typical survey process, and their main concern is that if they are to take part, the interview should
not take up too much of their time! Potential respondents can become impatient

Table 4.3   Ethics guidelines for anonymous questionnaire-based surveys

1. Interviewers should be identified with a badge including their given name and the name of the organisation involved (the host/client organisation or university).

2. Interviewers should be fully briefed about the project so that they can answer questions if asked.

3. If a respondent-completion ('handout') questionnaire is used, a brief description of the purpose of the project should be provided on the questionnaire (typically two or three lines so that it takes just a few seconds to read), with contact telephone numbers of supervisors for those requiring more information.

4. Interviewers approaching potential respondents should introduce themselves and seek cooperation using wording such as the following: 'We are conducting a survey of users of _____, would you mind answering a few questions?'

5. Telephone numbers of supervisors should be available and can be given to respondents if required.

6. A short printed handout may be available with more information for those respondents who are interested.

7. Respondents should not be pressured if they refuse to answer a question or wish to terminate the interview at any time.

with attempts to provide detailed explanations of the research and would prefer to 'get on with it'. Often questions about the purpose of the survey, if they arise at all, do so later during the interview process, when the respondent's interest has been stimulated. A suggested set of guidelines for such survey situations is provided in Table 4.3.

4.5 Risk of harm to subjects

There may be a risk of harm to the subject in the collection of data, in its storage and handling and in publication. Such risks obviously need to be eliminated or minimised, for the sake of the subjects, the researcher and sponsoring organisations and, indeed, the whole research process.

Data-collection process

The risk of harm in data collection arises particularly in medical/biological research, where a subject's physical health may be put at risk by an experimental procedure. The risk of injury may arise in sport-related experimenting and testing: for example, in cases of excessive exertion. Assuming there is appropriate screening and selection of subjects, for example checking on health status, this risk should be minimised by appropriate briefing of subjects and clear explanation and implementation of informed consent procedures discussed earlier.

Risks of harm can also arise in psychological research, where stress and distress can be caused, and in socio-psychological research, where interpersonal relationships could be damaged, although this is very rare in leisure/tourism research. In social research, where most leisure and tourism research falls, the risk of harm in the data-collection process is almost non-existent.

Anxiety during the data-collection process may arise if the subject has concerns about how the data are to be used. This may relate to themselves and their own privacy, which relates to data storage, handling and publication, as discussed in the next sub-section. The harm which may potentially arise if privacy is breached could vary from mild embarrassment to disruption of relationships with friends, colleagues or employers, to loss of reputation and/or position. Concerns may also relate to moral principles, for example the use of data by certain types of corporation or governments, which relates to the 'informed consent' issue discussed earlier. In this case the potential harm is the affront to the subject's moral principles. Both concerns relate to the right of the subject to refuse to answer questions and/or withdraw from the process at any stage.

Data storage and handling

Data storage and handling involve not only hard-copy materials, such as questionnaires, but also digital material, such as audio and video recordings, transcripts and coded data files. Typically, hard-copy data may be kept for several years as the project progresses and the publication process unfolds, and for a minimum period of time after the completion of the project specified by research organisations, typically about five years. Digital data today are likely to be stored indefinitely. The term 'handling' is used as well as storage because, while data may be stored securely in a formal sense, there are issues about who has access to it at the various stages (e.g. coding, data computer entry, transmission) and whether they are aware of and adhere to confidentiality commitments.

Hard-copy data should be protected by an appropriately secure form of storage and digital data by password-protected access.

The risk of harm to the subject due to the way data are stored and handled is affected by whether the information is provided entirely anonymously or the subject's name and/or contact details are known to the researcher and/or recorded. There is an in-between situation which can be termed *partial anonymity*. These three situations are discussed in turn.

1. *Anonymous subjects:* Even in an anonymous situation, informants may be reluctant to give certain types of information to 'a complete stranger'. Where such sensitivity is encountered, the usual approach is to stress the voluntary and anonymous nature of the information-giving process, while respecting the respondent's right to refuse to provide certain types of information.

2. *Partial anonymity:* Often research participants are not randomly drawn from the population but are members of a community or organisation. While the community or organisation may not be named in the publication, as discussed later, it may be in the stored data, and it is possible that individuals or groups could be identified by their position – e.g. the president, secretary, coach, head teacher, team captain. Participants may

therefore have concerns about the security of the data, particularly if they have revealed information about themselves or expressed views about others which they would like to be kept confidential. Much digital information is anonymous because of the use of identification numbers rather than names; but somewhere there will be a list linking names and identification numbers, so the security and confidentially of that list becomes important. In addition to written information, observational research may involve photography and video material which may involve invasion of people's privacy if they are recognisable, even in the most innocent-seeming activities.

3. *Identified subjects:* Privacy is a valued right in Western society and such rights are generally enshrined in laws, which vary in detail between jurisdictions. People can be offended and suffer stress if their affairs are made public or divulged to certain third parties. There is therefore an obligation on the part of the researcher to ensure confidentiality of any personally identifiable data which have been collected.

Situations where personally identifiable data inevitably arise and the nature of the resultant confidentiality issues are summarised in Table 4.4, together with suggested means to reduce risk.

Some routine methods for maintaining individuals' privacy, such as keeping lists of names separate from actual data and use of pseudonyms are indicated, but these measures may not always prevent research subjects from being offended. An important principle, but one that is difficult to prescribe in detail, is that the researcher should be aware of research subjects' sensitivities, whether they be personal, professional, cultural or organisational.

In some research projects, the naming of individuals is inevitably involved – for example, where the number of subjects is small and they are key figures associated with particular high-profile organisations or communities. Where interviews are conducted with such individuals, care must be taken to adopt the journalist's practice of checking whether information is being given 'on the record' or 'off the record'. Thus, in interviews, particularly where sensitive matters arise, it is wise to ask named informants whether they are prepared to be quoted.

In reporting results, the use of false names or numbers to identify individuals, organisations, events, places and communities is the obvious solution. However, this is not always sufficient. The use of false names may protect identities from the world at large, but for those 'in the know', the places and the people involved in the research project may be all too easily identifiable – the partial anonymity situation discussed earlier. Particular care should be taken when dealing with members of close-knit communities: the researcher should be aware of cultural and interpersonal sensitivities within such communities. Such issues are further highlighted in certain types of qualitative research where the research methodology involves gaining the trust and confidence of research subjects. It would be unethical to betray such trust and confidence.

Occasionally this issue can be carelessly exacerbated by the author's own list of 'acknowledgements' if it clearly identifies people, organisations and places!

Table 4.4 Personally identifiable data

Research method	Who is identified?	Identifying information	Why identify?	Issues re storage or publication?	Methods to reduce risk
Postal surveys – quantitative	Sampled members of general public or of organisations	Names + addresses*	Intrinsic to method	Storage	List of names and addresses kept separate from questionnaires and destroyed at end of data collection.
Telephone surveys – quantitative	Sampled members of general public or of organisations	Telephone numbers	Intrinsic to method + quality control	Storage	List of names and addresses kept separate from questionnaires and destroyed at end of data collection.
Interviews – qualitative – individuals	Private individuals	Name + possibly telephone number/ address*	Intrinsic to method	Both	Use of pseudonyms; be aware of sensitivities.
Interviews – qualitative – individuals in organisational roles	Individuals in identifiable public offices (e.g. mayor) or corporate roles (e.g. managing director)	Names, positions, organisation/place/ contact details	Intrinsic to method	Both	Use pseudonyms for individuals, place or organisation, but not always possible. Clarify 'on record'/'off record'; be aware of sensitivities.
Interviews – qualitative – small groups	Members of small groups (e.g. a village, a club or a small business)	Names (possibly addresses*, telephone numbers, surnames may not be involved)	Intrinsic to method	Both, but mainly publication	Use of pseudonyms for individuals, group and place, but not always possible. Clarify 'on record'/'off record'; be aware of sensitivities.
Ethnographic – variety of subjects and qualitative methods	Individuals, separately or as members of a group	Names (possibly addresses*, telephone numbers, surnames may not be involved)	Intrinsic to method	Mainly publication	Use of pseudonyms, but issue may lie in betraying confidence/trust. Be aware of sensitivities.
Longitudinal research: a. Quantitative b. Qualitative	Same subjects are contacted to be studied at intervals over a number of weeks, months, years	Names, addresses*, telephone numbers	Intrinsic to method	a. Storage b. Both	a. Keep names, etc. separate from data. b. Storage: as for a. Publication: use pseudonyms.

*addresses includes email addresses

When data are confidential, measures must be taken to protect that confidentiality through ensuring the security of the raw data, such as interview tapes/transcripts/questionnaires. Specific freedom of information and privacy laws invariably cover the storage of and access to personally identifiable data, including allowing individuals access to their own records and the right to have inaccuracies corrected.

Data can be stored with code-numbers or false names, with a key to the code-numbers or names being kept securely in a place apart from the data.

Mail surveys are an in-between case. If returned questionnaires do not have any identification, then there is no way of identifying non-respondents in order to send reminders. Sending reminders to *everyone* is costly and an irritation to those who have already responded. One solution is to place an identifying number on the provided return *envelope* rather than on the questionnaire, with an assurance that the number will not be transferred to the questionnaire. In some situations a third party, such as a legal firm, is used to receive the questionnaires and pass them on to the researcher in anonymous form.

Confidentiality issues often arise with regard to the relationship between the researcher and the organisation funding the research. In particular, if the funding organisation 'owns' the data, the researcher may wish to protect the confidentiality of informants by *not* passing on to the sponsoring organisation any information which could identify informants by name.

Publication

Many of the considerations discussed in relation to data storage and handling also apply to the publication of results. Any undertaking given to individuals or organisations in regard to anonymity should be respected, and steps should be taken to avoid inadvertent breaches of confidentiality. Typically, issues do not arise at the publication stage with individuals in quantitative research, particularly if they were anonymous from the start. But if the subjects were drawn from a particular geographical community or an organisation, unintended embarrassment could arise. General readers would usually not be able to make the identification, or would not be concerned if they could. But people in the academic or policy community familiar with the research may be able to make the identification, as might interested residents or members of the organisation. So the researcher must be prepared, in ethical terms, for the possibility of such identification and take this into account when writing the research report.

4.6 Honesty/rigour in analysis, interpretation and reporting

The falsification of research results is clearly unethical. There have been some notorious cases in the natural sciences where experimental results have been falsified.

A common practice in quantitative research is to exclude 'outliers' from the analysis. Thus, for example, if a survey of physical recreation found that all respondents participated three times a week or less except for two who participated ten times a week, these two might be termed 'outliers' and excluded from the analysis because they would distort averages. This is generally seen as ethical as long as it is stated in the research report that it has taken place. The same principle could of course apply in qualitative research, although identifying an 'outlier' would be a more complex task.

Researchers are concerned about reporting 'negative findings' or non-findings. This typically does not arise with descriptive research – what is, is – or in evaluative research – the performance of the programme/organisation is as found. The difficulty arises with explanatory research when no apparent 'explanation' is found. But negative findings are of interest and use if the research has been carefully designed. Thus, if the interest is in the effect on variable X of 15 different independent variables and none of them is found to have a significant influence, then this would generally be of interest, in that it suggests that other variables must be at work. In the case of qualitative research, of course, the fact that the 15 variables are not influential in one study does not preclude them from being influential in another study, since the findings would not be generalisable in the same way.

In some cases, negative findings are the result of a limited sample size: there may be an effect, but the small sample size makes it impossible to be confident about it – it is statistically insignificant. With a larger sample it may have been found to be a small, but still significant, relationship. But such findings may be relevant for later studies when considering required sample sizes and may be taken into account in meta-analysis (see Chapter 6), which aggregates the findings of many similar studies. This may seem like purely practical rather than ethical matters but, arguably, there is an ethical obligation to report all the findings of research which might contribute to the development of knowledge.

Authorship and acknowledgements

A clear ethical principle is that all those involved with a research project should receive appropriate acknowledgement of their contribution in any publication. Acknowledgement of funding sources, named informants or collaborators and anonymous research subjects may be made in a footnote or in a preface or acknowledgements section. Difficulties can arise in the case of claims for joint authorship, especially in academic research where careers are dependent on such matters. Judgements have to be made as to whether a research assistant, who may be a research student, has simply undertaken routine work for payment or whether he or she has contributed intellectually to the research.

Typically in team research situations, the name of the team leader, or 'principal investigator', is placed first in the list of authors. However, where the leadership is shared, names may appear in alphabetical order or may be rotated in different publications from a research programme.

Plagiarism

Plagiarism – the use of others' data or ideas without due acknowledgement and, where appropriate, permission – is clearly unethical and is also covered by copyright and intellectual property laws.

4.7 Conflict of interest

The honesty and rigour in designing and conducting research projects and reporting their results may be called into question if researchers and/or the institution they work in are in a position to be unduly influenced by individuals or organisations which may benefit, financially or otherwise, from the research results. This can arise particularly when the beneficiary organisations are funding the research. High-profile examples are pharmacy corporations funding research on the efficacy of medical treatments when they are the manufacturers of the drugs involved, or fossil fuel companies funding research which challenges the legitimacy of climate change research. Most academic journals now require authors to provide statements of any potential conflict of interest, notably the source of any research funds they are in receipt of.

5. Access to research information

Some of the controversies surrounding climate research in recent years have highlighted the issue of rights of access to research information. We have already referred to individuals' rights of access to personal information about them held by public and other corporate bodies, as covered by freedom of information and privacy legislation. But such legislation also covers the public rights of access to information held by public bodies, for example on decision-making processes, a right which is regularly pursued by journalists. While the provisions of legislation vary between jurisdictions, the common principle is that information held by public bodies is *not secret* unless publication would threaten individual privacy, commercial property rights or national security, or unless the costs of compiling information and making it publicly available would be prohibitive. In theory, such provisions apply to research data gathered with the support of public funds and/or held by public research institutions and have implications for the way data sets are stored and the length of time for which they are kept. As noted previously, since most research data in the social sciences are held in digital form, they are, for the most part, potentially storable indefinitely.

It might be thought that if the results of research have been published, there should be no further interest in the raw data. However, as Montford (2010: 134, 379–83) discusses, in the natural sciences *replication* is a key criterion in assessing validity but, as data sets become increasingly complex and expensive to compile, the only way of checking and replicating some types of published research is through access to the authors' original data. Some scientific journals are therefore requiring public (website) archiving of data sets and of the computer code used to analyse them as a condition of publication.

Summary

This chapter considers the ethical, and legal, dimensions of conducting research. It is noted that in universities and other research organisations, the responsible and ethical conduct of research is regulated by codes of conduct and ethics committees. In this chapter we consider mainly issues arising in research involving human subjects. In the biological and physical sciences, consideration is also given to the involvement with animals, and increasingly environmental dimensions are considered. Ethical considerations arise in all components of the research process, including design, data collection, data storage and handling, analysis and interpretation and publication. A number of questions must be answered satisfactorily for a research project to be judged to be ethical. Is the research likely to be of social benefit? Are the researchers involved competent to conduct the research? Are the individuals involved participating voluntarily, without compulsion? Are the individuals taking part fully informed about the purposes and nature of the research – have they given 'informed consent'? Is the risk of harm to subjects at an acceptably low level? Has the analysis and interpretation of data and reporting of the results been undertaken honestly and rigorously? Have all those involved been suitably acknowledged or, where appropriate, included among the authors?

Test questions

1. What are the main ethical issues which arise in research?
2. What is 'informed consent' and what measures should be taken to ensure it?
3. What are the 'grey areas' where participation in research may not be voluntary?
4. What are the main possible sources of harm to participants in social science research?
5. What is plagiarism?

Exercises

1. In conducting interviews with 15-year-olds on leisure activities, a few of the respondents let you know that they take illegal drugs and indicate indirectly who supplies them. Do you tell anyone or maintain confidentiality? Do you include the finding, anonymously, in your research report?
2. Read Christensen's (1980) critique of Moeller et al. (1980a) and the response of Moeller et al. (1980b) and discuss.
3. Establish the extent to which ethical issues are discussed in a volume of a recent leisure or tourism journal.

Resources

Research ethics guidelines

- Market Research Society (UK): www.mrs.org.uk/standards/codeconduct.htm

- NHMRC/ARC/Universities Australia guidelines: www.nhmrc.gov.au/_files_nhmrc/file/publications/synopses/r39.pdf

- Social Research Association (UK): http://the-sra.org.uk/research-ethics/ethics-guidelines/

- University of Technology, Sydney: for undergraduate and postgraduate students: www.gsu.uts.edu.au/policies/hrecguide.html.

Other publications

- Climate change controversies:
  - attacking the science: Montford (2010); and
  - defence: Mann (2012).

- Ethics committees and qualitative research: Atkinson (2014), Haggerty (2004), Lincoln (2005).

- Informed consent: Olivier and Olivier (2001).

- Research ethics:
  - guidelines: Saunders et al. (2009: 183–200);
  - leisure/tourism: Fleming and Jordan (2006);
  - qualitative research: Miles and Huberman (2012: Ch. 3);
  - social sciences: Israel and Hay (2006);
  - sport: Edwards and Skinner (2009), Smith and Waddington (2014); and
  - tourism: Ryan (2005).

- A unique case in leisure research: Christensen (1980), LaPage (1981), Moeller et al. (1980a, 1980b).

References

Atkinson, M. (2014). Mischief managed: ticket scalping, research ethics and involved detachment. In A. Smith and I. Waddington (Eds), *Doing real world research in sports studies* (pp. 74–87). London: Routledge.

Christensen, J. E. (1980). A second look at the informal interview. *Journal of Leisure Research*, 12(2), 183–86.

Donne, K. (2006). From outsider to quasi-insider at Wodin Watersports: a reflexive account of participant observation in a leisure context. In S. Fleming and F. Jordan (Eds), *Ethical issues in leisure research* (pp. 63–82). LSA Publication 90, Eastbourne, UK: Leisure Studies Association.

Edwards, A., and Skinner, J. (2009). *Qualitative research in sport management*. Oxford: Butterworth-Heinemann.

Fleming, S., and Jordan, F. (Eds) (2006). *Ethical issues in leisure research*. LSA Publication 90, Eastbourne, UK: Leisure Studies Association.

Haggerty, K. D. (2004). Ethics creep: governing social science research in the name of ethics. *Qualitative Sociology*, 27(4), 391–414.

Israel, M., and Hay, I. (2006) *Research ethics for social scientists*. Los Angeles, CA: Sage.

Jones, R.L., Potrac, P., Haleem, H., and Cushion, C. (2006). Exposure by association: anonymity and integrity in autobiographical research. In S. Fleming and F. Jordan (Eds) *Ethical issues in leisure research* (pp.45–62). LSA Publication 90, Eastbourne, UK: Leisure Studies Association.

LaPage, W. F. (1981). A further look at the informal interview. *Journal of Leisure Research*, 13(2), 174–76.

Lincoln, Y. (2005). Institutional review boards and methodological conservatism: the challenge to and from phenomenological paradigms. In N. K. Denzin and Y. S. Lincoln (Eds), *Handbook of qualitative research, third edition* (pp. 165–90). Thousand Oaks, CA: Sage.

Loue, S. (2002). *Textbook of research ethics: theory and practice*. New York: Kluwer.

Mann, M. E. (2012). *The hockey stick and the climate wars: dispatches from the front lines*. New York: Columbia University Press.

Miles, M. B., and Huberman, A. M. (2013). *Qualitative data analysis*, 3rd edn. Thousand Oaks, CA: Sage, e-book/Kindle version.

Moeller, G. H., Mescher, M. A. et al. (1980a). The informal interview as a technique for recreation research. *Journal of Leisure Research*, 12(2), 174–82.

Moeller, G. H., Mescher, M. A., et al. (1980b). A response to 'A second look at the informal interview'. *Journal of Leisure Research*, 12(2), 187–88.

Montford, A. W. (2010). *The hockey stick illusion: climategate and the corruption of science*. London: Stacey International.

National Health and Medical Research Council (NHMRC) (nd). *National ethics application form*. Canberra: NHMRC, available at: www.neaf.gov.au/default. aspx (accessed March 2010).

National Health and Medical Research Council (NHMRC)/Australian Research Council (ARC) and Universities Australia (2007). *Australian code for the responsible conduct of research*. Canberra: Australian Government, available at: www.nhmrc.gov.au/filesnhmrc/file/publications/synopses/r39.pdf

National Council on Public Polls (1995). *Push polls*. Press release, 25 May, Clifton, NJ: NCPP, available at: www.ncpp.org/?q=node/41 (accessed March 2010).

Olivier, S., and Olivier, A. (2001). Informed consent in sport science. *Sportscience*, 5(1), online at: http://sportsci.org/jour/0101/so.htm.

Ryan, C. (2005). Ethics in tourism research: objectives and personal perspectives. In B. W. Ritchie, P. Burns and C. Palmer (Eds), *Tourism research methods: integrating theory with practice* (pp. 9–19). Wallingford, UK: CABI Publishing.

Saunders, M., Lewis, P., and Thornhill, A. (2009). *Research methods for business students*. Harlow, UK: Financial Times-Prentice Hall.

Smith, A., and Waddington, I. (Eds) (2014). *Doing real world research in sports studies*. London: Routledge.

5 The range of research methods

1. Introduction – horses for courses

In this chapter the range of alternative research methods and criteria for their use are examined in broad terms, as an introduction to the methods and techniques to be covered in more detail in subsequent chapters.

Choosing appropriate research methods is clearly vital. In this text we espouse the principle that every technique has its place; the important thing is for researchers to be aware of the limitations of any particular method and to take these into account when reporting research results. A *horses for courses* approach is adopted; techniques are not intrinsically *good* or *bad* but are considered to be *appropriate* or *inappropriate* or *feasible* or *not feasible* for the task in hand. Further, it is maintained that it is not a question of good or bad techniques which should be considered, but good or bad *use* of techniques.

2. Major research methods

The range of major methods to be examined is listed in Table 5.1 and are discussed in turn below.

Table 5.1 The range of major methods

Method	Brief description
1. Scholarship	Being well-read about a topic and thinking deeply and creatively about it.
2. Just thinking	The thinking part of scholarship.
3. Existing sources – the literature	Identifying, summarising and evaluating the research literature – part of all research but can be the sole method used in a project.
4. Existing sources – secondary data	Re-use of data originally collected by another organisation for other purposes.
5. Observation	Direct looking at behaviour, or use of still or video cameras.
6. Qualitative methods	Range of methods where the data gathered is in the form of words (or images/sounds), as opposed to quantitative methods, where data are in the form of numbers.
7. Questionnaire-based surveys	Methods using a formal, printed schedule of questions to gather data – the main quantitative method in leisure/tourism research.
8. Experimental method	The researcher controls the environment of the phenomenon being studied, holding all variables constant except those which are the focus of the research.
9. Case study method	The focus of the research is on one or a small number of cases, and typically a number of data-gathering and analysis methods is used.

2.1 Scholarship

Although the dividing line between *scholarship* and *research* can often be diffi-cult to draw, it is useful to consider the differences between the two. Scholarship involves being well-informed about a subject and also thinking critically and creatively about a topic or concept and the accumulated knowledge on it. Scholarship therefore involves *knowing the literature*, but also being able to syn-thesise it, analyse it and critically appraise it. Scholarship is traditionally prac-tised in the role of teacher, but when the results of scholarship are published, they effectively become a contribution to research.

Research involves the generation of new knowledge. Traditionally, this has been thought of as involving the gathering and presentation of new data – empirical research – but clearly this is not a necessary condition for a contribu-tion to be considered research. New insights, critical or innovative ways of looking at old issues, or the identification of new issues or questions – the fruits of scholarship – also contribute to knowledge. Indeed, the development of a new framework or *paradigm* for looking at a field can be far more significant than a minor piece of empirical work using an outmoded paradigm.

2.2 Just thinking

There is no substitute for thinking! Creative, informed thinking about a topic, referred to by Edwards and Skinner (2009) as 'reflection', can be the only process involved in the development and presentation of a piece of research, although it will usually also involve consideration of the literature, as discussed below.

Even when data collection is involved, the difference between an *acceptable* piece of research and an *exceptional* or *significant* piece of research is usually the quality of the creative thought that has gone into it. The researcher needs to be creative in:

- identifying and posing the initial questions or issues for investigation;
- conceptualising the research and developing a research strategy;
- analysing data; and
- interpreting and presenting findings.

Texts on research methods, such as this one, can provide a guide to mechanical processes, but creative thought must come from within the individual researcher – in the same way that the basics of drawing can be taught, but *art* comes from within the individual artist.

2.3 Existing sources – the literature

Virtually no research can be done which would not benefit from some reference to the existing literature, and for most research such reference is essential. It is possible for a research project to consist only of a review of the literature: in comparatively new and multidisciplinary areas of study, such as leisure and tourism, there is a great need for the consolidation of existing knowledge which can come from good literature reviews.

The review of the literature often plays a key role in the formulation of research projects; it indicates the state of knowledge on a topic and is a source of, or stimulant for, ideas, both substantive and methodological.

A review of the literature can be important even when it uncovers no literature on the topic of interest. To establish that *no* research has been conducted on a particular topic, especially when the topic is considered to be of some importance to the field, can be a research finding of some significance in its own right. The literature review process is discussed in detail in Chapter 6.

2.4 Existing sources – secondary data

Clearly, if information is already available which will answer the research questions posed, then it would be wasteful of resources to collect new information for the purpose. As discussed in Chapter 7, large quantities of information are collected and stored by government and other organisations as routine functions of policy-making, management and evaluation, including sales figures and visitor numbers, income and expenditure, staffing, accident reports, crime reports and travel, leisure participation and health data. Such data are referred to as *secondary* data, because their primary use is administrative and research is only a secondary use. Even when such data are not ideal for the research at hand, they can often provide answers to some questions more quickly and at less cost than the collection of new data.

Secondary data need not be quantitative. Historians, for example, use diaries, official documents or newspaper reports as sources. Such sources may be seen as secondary, since they were not initially produced for research purposes; but for historians themselves, some of them are described as primary sources. In policy research, documents such as the annual reports or minutes of meetings of organisations might be utilised.

In some cases data have been collected for research as opposed to administrative purposes but may not have been fully analysed, or they may have been analysed only in one particular way for a particular purpose, or even not analysed at all. Secondary analysis, or re-analysis, of research data is a potentially fruitful, but widely neglected, activity.

2.5 Observation

The technique of observation is discussed in Chapter 8. Observation has the advantage of being unobtrusive – indeed, the techniques involved are sometimes referred to as *unobtrusive* techniques (Kellehear, 1993). Unobtrusive techniques involve gathering information about people's behaviour without their knowledge. While in some instances this may raise ethical questions (see Chapter 4), it clearly has certain advantages over techniques where subjects are aware of the researcher's presence and may therefore modify their behaviour, or where reliance must be placed on subjects' own recall and description of their behaviour, which can be inaccurate or distorted.

Observation may be the only possible technique to use in certain situations: for example, when researching an illicit activity, which people may be reluctant to talk about, or when researching the behaviour of young children (for example, their play patterns) who may be too young to interview.

Observation is capable of presenting a perspective on a situation which is not apparent to the individuals involved. For example, the users of a crowded part of a recreation or tourist area may not be aware of the uncrowded areas available to them – the uneven pattern of use of the site can be assessed only by observation.

Observation is therefore an appropriate technique to use when knowledge of the presence of the researcher is likely to lead to unacceptable modification of subjects' behaviour, and when mass patterns of behaviour not apparent to individual subjects are of interest.

2.6 Qualitative methods

As discussed in Chapter 2, qualitative methods stand in contrast to *quantitative* methods. The main difference between the two groups of techniques is that quantitative methods involve numbers – quantities – whereas qualitative methods rely on words, and sometimes images, as the unit of analysis. In the case of qualitative techniques, the information collected does not generally lend itself to statistical analysis, and conclusions are not based on such analysis.

In consequence there is a tendency for qualitative techniques to involve the gathering of large amounts of relatively detailed information about relatively few cases (people, organisations, facilities, programmes, locations) and for quantitative techniques to involve the gathering of relatively small amounts of data on relatively large numbers of cases. It should be emphasised, however, that this is just a *tendency*. It is not always the case. For example, it is possible for a quantitative research project to involve the collection of, say, 500 items of data on only 20 people and for a qualitative research project to involve the collection of relatively little information on, say, 200 people. Conversely, some questionnaire-based surveys designed to collect quantitative data can involve questionnaires many pages long, which take an hour or more to administer and can collect hundreds of items of data from each respondent. The difference in the two approaches lies in the nature of information collected and the way it is analysed.

In what situations are qualitative techniques used? They tend to be used when one or more of the following situations apply:

- when the focus of the research is on meanings and attitudes (although these can also be studied quantitatively);

- when the situation calls for exploratory theory building rather than theory testing;

Table 5.2 Qualitative data-collection methods

Data collection	Alternative methods names/variations	Description
In-depth interviews	Informal, semi-structured or unstructured interviews	One-on-one interviews with small numbers of individuals, interviewed at length, possibly on more than one occasion, typically using a checklist of topics rather than a formal questionnaire.
Focus groups	Group interviews	Discussions with groups of people (typically 6–12) led by a facilitator.
Observation*	Unobtrusive techniques	The phenomenon of interest is examined by the naked eye or by use of still or video camera.
Participant observation		The researcher becomes a participant in the phenomenon being studied.
Biographical methods	Auto-ethnography	Research subjects are invited to provide their own accounts of events, etc., in written or recorded oral form.
Analysis of texts	Content analysis,* hermeneutics	Analysis and interpretation of the content of published or unpublished texts. May also involve audio-visual materials (images, TV, film, music, radio).
Ethnography	Field research (in anthropology)	Studying groups of people using a mixture of the above methods.

* Can also be quantitative.

- when the researcher accepts that the concepts, terms and issues must be defined by the subjects themselves and not by the researcher in advance; and

- when interaction between members of a group is of interest.

Qualitative techniques are not appropriate when the aim of the research is to make general statements about large populations, especially if such statements call for quantification. Table 5.2 summarises a range of types of qualitative data-collection method, and these are discussed in more detail in Chapter 9.

2.7 Questionnaire-based surveys

A questionnaire is a printed or electronic/web-based list of questions. In a questionnaire-based survey, the same questionnaire is used to interview a sample of respondents. The term questionnaire-*based* survey is used because such surveys can take two formats:

- *interview format*, in which an interviewer, in a face-to-face situation or via telephone, reads out the questions from the questionnaire and records the answers; and

● *respondent-completion format*, in which the respondent reads the questions and writes answers on the questionnaire or on-screen, and no interviewer is involved.

In many discussions of research methods in the literature, 'questionnaires' and 'interviews' are presented as alternatives; this is clearly misleading, since interviews may be conducted using a questionnaire. A more accurate distinction would be made between 'questionnaire-based interviews' and 'informal, in-depth or unstructured interviews', as discussed in relation to qualitative methods earlier in this chapter.

Questionnaire-based surveys are probably the most commonly used method in leisure and tourism research. This is partly because the basic mechanics are relatively easily understood and mastered, but also because so much leisure and tourism research calls for general, quantified statements. Thus, for example, governments want to know how many people engage in sport, managers want to know what proportion of customers are dissatisfied with a service and marketers want to know how many people are in a particular market segment. These examples come from practical policy/management situations, which emphasises that most of the resources for survey research come from the public or private sector of the leisure/tourism industries. Academic papers are very often a secondary spin-off from research which has been sponsored for such purposes.

Unlike qualitative techniques, where the researcher can begin data collection in a tentative way, return to the subjects for additional information and gradually build the data, concepts and explanation, questionnaire-based surveys require researchers to be very specific about their data requirements from the beginning, since they are committed irrevocably to a questionnaire.

A further key feature of questionnaire-based surveys is that they depend on respondents' own accounts of their behaviour, attitudes or intentions. In some situations – for example in the study of 'deviant' behaviour or in the study of activities which are socially approved of (e.g. playing sport) or disapproved of (e.g. smoking or drinking) – this can raise some questions about the validity of the approach, since accuracy and honesty of responses may be called into question.

Questionnaire-based surveys are used when quantified information is required concerning a specific population and when individuals' own accounts of their behaviour and/or attitudes are acceptable as a source of information. They may nevertheless be used to gather qualitative as well as quantitative data by the inclusion of open-ended questions (as discussed in Chapter 10) – although this is not a view shared by all researchers (see, for example, Dupuis, 1999: 45). In one of the earliest questionnaire-based studies of leisure in Australia, in describing their methodology, Scott and U'Ren (1962: xiii) indicated that the questionnaire-based interviews lasted up to three hours, with most taking between one and one and a half hours and, in interviewing, 'verbatim replies were recorded'.

Questionnaire surveys in the leisure and tourism field can be divided into six types, as shown in Table 5.3 and considered in more detail in Chapters 10 and 16.

Table 5.3 Types of questionnaire-based survey

Type	Alternative name	Description
Household survey	Community survey or social survey	People are selected on the basis of where they live and are interviewed in their home.
Street survey	Quota survey or intercept survey	People are selected by stopping them in the street, in shopping malls, etc.
Telephone survey		Interviews are conducted by telephone.
Online survey	Web-based survey	Respondents complete screen-based questionnaire online.
Mail survey	Postal survey	Questionnaires are sent and returned by mail.
Site or user survey	Visitor survey, customer survey, intercept survey	Users of a leisure or tourism facility or site are surveyed on-site.
Captive group survey		Members of groups such as classes of schoolchildren, members of a club or employees of an organisation are surveyed.

2.8 Experimental method

The experimental method is the traditional approach of the natural sciences and involves the researcher controlling the environment in order to study the effects of specified variables, typically in a laboratory setting. The principles of the method were discussed in Chapter 2 and are addressed in more detail in Chapter 11.

2.9 Case study method

A case study involves the study of an example – a case – of the phenomenon being researched. The aim is to seek to understand the phenomenon by studying single examples. Cases can consist of individuals, communities (the community study method as discussed in section 4.3), organisations and whole countries. Invariably, multiple methods are used within the case study, including historical/documentary research, the use of secondary data, interviews and, in the case of communities, questionnaire-based or qualitative surveys. The case study method and its use in leisure and tourism studies is discussed further in Chapter 12.

3. Subsidiary/cross-cutting techniques

The somewhat inelegant term 'subsidiary and cross-cutting' is used to describe a number of techniques which are subsidiary to one or more of the major methods discussed earlier, in that they are a variation on or an application of the major method (e.g. Delphi technique, which uses questionnaires) or cut across a number of major methods (e.g. action research, which can use any or all of the major methods). The techniques discussed here are listed in Table 5.4 and discussed in turn in this chapter. The brief descriptions presented here do not provide a basis for implementing the various techniques, but they summarise their general nature and possibilities. The list indicates the extraordinary diversity of techniques and approaches which exist in social research. Guides to further information and applications are provided in the Resources section.

Table 5.4 Subsidiary, cross-cutting techniques/methods

Technique	Brief description
1. Action research	Research committed to social outcomes, typically involving collaboration with a client organisation.
2. Big data	Analysis of very large electronic/digital data sets: for example, organisations with a large customer base can analyse data from electronic records of customer activity to reveal patterns of behaviour of use in marketing.
3. Conjoint analysis/ Discrete choice experiments	A process for studying people's choice processes by asking people to express preferences for hypothetical products with different combinations of attributes.
4. Content analysis	Quantitative study of printed/written documents or static/moving images (see also qualitative methods).
5. Coupon surveys/ conversion studies	Analysis of returns from 'special offer', 'two for the price of one', etc. vouchers/advertisements.
6. Cross-cultural research	Research involving subjects from two or more cultural backgrounds
7. Delphi technique	Process in which a sample of experts responds to questions about future events in repeated rounds ideally to achieve consensus.
Diary methods	See 'Time-use surveys' (section 3.29).
8. Discourse analysis	Examination of the ways in which language is used in the treatment of a topic, typically in social/political contexts and/or in the popular and/or academic print and other communications media.
9. *En route*/intercept/ cordon surveys	Survey conducted with visitors entering, leaving or travelling to or from a site/destination.
10. Experience sampling method (ESM)	Subjects are 'beeped' or contacted electronically several times a day to record activities/feelings, etc. as they go about day-to-day activities.
11. Historical research	Research on past events.
Latent class analysis	See: 'Multiple correspondence analysis'.
12. Longitudinal studies	Same sample repeatedly surveyed, typically over a number of years.
13. Mapping techniques	Subjects provide graphic representation of components of a problem/ issue/experience, sometimes collaborative.

(continued)

Table 5.4   *(continued)*

Technique	Brief description
14. Media reader/viewer/ listener surveys	Media report on surveys which readers/listeners have been invited to take part in, typically online or via automated phone-in.
15. Meta-analysis	Examination and summary of a number of studies on the same topic, typically with a key outcome measure such as a correlation coefficient.
16. Multiple correspondence/Latent class analysis	Analytical techniques used to group subjects on the basis of comparable behaviour patterns, tastes and socio-demographic and lifestyle characteristics.
17. Netnography	Research using the internet as data source and/or subject.
18. Network analysis	Study of links between individuals and/or organisations involved in an activity.
19. Panel studies	A sample of individuals recruited to a 'panel' who may take part in several surveys over a period of time.
20. People meters	Devices to monitor television viewing patterns.
21. Perceptual mapping	Subjects provide graphic representation of components of a problem/ issue, typically collaborative.
22. Projective techniques	Subjects are asked to respond to hypothetical scenarios.
23. Psychographic/lifestyle studies	Research which gathers data on a wide range of attitudes, values and socio-demographic characteristics and analyses them to determine distinctive psychographic/lifestyle groups or market segments.
24. Q methodology	Process in which subjects rank scale items (see below, item 27) depicted on cards.
25. Quantitative modelling	Quantitative method in which relationships between two or more variables are assessed statistically.
26. Repertory grid/laddering	Pairs of contrasting descriptors for the phenomenon being studied are elicited from respondents to form constructs, and scores on the constructs are analysed to form a perceptual picture.
27. Scales	Development and use of batteries of 'stimulus items' (statements/ questions, features, etc.) to be responded to via Likert-type scales.
28. Scenarios	Subjects asked to judge contrasting (future) scenarios regarding the topic – see projective techniques.
29. Time-use surveys	Survey in which respondents complete a detailed one- to two-day diary of activities.
30. Visitor conversation research	In informal spaces (e.g. museums), selected visitors wear microphones so that their discussion of exhibits can be recorded and analysed.
31. Visual methods	Use of graphical prompts to evoke attitudes etc.
32. Web-based research	Research on, or using, the internet – see also 'netnography'.

3.1 Action research

The common image of research is as a detached process reporting objectively on what is discovered. When a researcher is personally committed to the topic under investigation, whether that be self-interest-related, such as the fortunes of a company, or a social cause, like saving the environment, efforts are still generally made to abide by the rules of science, for ethical reasons or because of the general belief that sound research is more likely to be effective in supporting a cause. Some types of research can, nevertheless, be deliberately designed to involve the researcher in the topic and are intended to be overtly part of the process of bringing about change – such research is termed 'action research'. Typically, action research is also distinguished by being conducted on behalf of, and in association with, one or more organisations, or stakeholders. Indeed, some definitions envisage the action research process as happening within a corporate organisation, with the researcher 'embedded' in the organisation for the duration of the project.

The action research process shown in Figure 5.1 indicates that researchers are involved in the 'action' stages of the process as well as the research stage. There may be various feedback loops in the process as research is conducted to assist the campaign for change and to evaluate outcomes.

There are similarities with the normal research process within an organisation, where step 3 is an internal resource allocation and implementation process. It can also be seen as a quasi-experimental process. Action research is not constrained as to methods or techniques. There is a tendency to see it as a form of qualitative research but, in their introductory text on the subject, Greenwood and Levin state:

> it is wrong to think of action research as 'qualitative' research, yet a great many conventional researchers and far too many action researchers make this error. . . . An action research process must use qualitative, quantitative and/or mixed-method techniques wherever and whenever the conditions and subject an action research team deals with require. (Greenwood and Levin, 2007: 98)

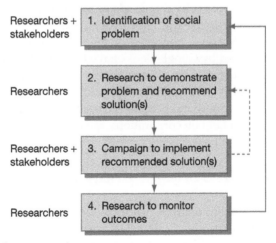

Figure 5.1 Action research process

Action research is less usual in the leisure and tourism context than in some areas of social policy, such as housing or ethnic affairs. One of the earliest studies in the leisure domain was the *Leisure and the Quality of Life* study which was conducted in Britain the 1970s and involved a wide range of leisure-provision projects in four locations (Department of the Environment, 1977). While the study was government-funded, the projects were initiated and overseen by locally established community groups, supported by research teams. The similarity between action research and the experimental method was demonstrated by the fact that the four local projects were referred to as 'experiments', while one of the research papers published as part of the project report was entitled: 'The action research background to the leisure experiments' (Batty, 1977).

3.2 Big data

Big data is a form of secondary data consisting of very large electronic/digital data sets arising from corporate or government activity. Thus, for example, commercial or public organisations with a large client base, often running into the millions, can make use of the data which has accumulated from online and other electronic purchasing records to discover patterns of behaviour and socio-demographic, geographic and temporal relationships which may be of use in marketing (see Case study 14.5).

One of the market phenomena identified by this research activity is the 'long tail', which applies particularly to cultural products like books and recorded music. It is found that, while best-sellers and blockbusters attract most of the publicity, the bulk of the market is accounted for by hundreds or thousands of titles which sell very few copies and may even be only marginally economic. Thus, for example, Anderson (2011: 121) notes that in 2004, the 420 books which sold over 100,000 copies each in the United States accounted for 100 million copies in total, but the 1.1 million titles selling 1000 copies or less each accounted for 230 million copies in total. Centralised online sales through organisations such as Amazon can compile and exploit data patterns of book purchases. Without knowing why thousands of purchasers of book A often also purchase book B, they can use this information to recommend book B to new purchasers of book A (Mayer-Schönberger and Cukier, 2013: 56). The 15 million books scanned and stored by Google Books have been used to examine cultural trends as revealed by the changing content of books published over a period of time. Michel et al. (2011) refer to this sort of analysis as 'culturomics'. Big data practices are relatively new and heighten concerns about the privacy implications of the personal data held by corporations, raising ethics issues when used for research.

3.3 Conjoint analysis

Conjoint analysis is a methodology used to explore people's decision-making processes, including choices of products, such as holiday types, holiday destinations, leisure activities or particular leisure facilities or items of equipment.

In particular, it seeks to discover how various features of products are evaluated by the consumer and how this evaluation influences choices. One way of doing this would be to examine people's actual selections against the attributes of a range of existing products, and there is research which adopts this approach; but it is a complex, 'messy' and possibly expensive process. Furthermore, such research will be constrained by the available products and their features and will not include people for whom existing choices are not attractive and have therefore been rejected altogether. In conjoint analysis, subjects are asked to express their preferences among a range of *hypothetical* products with varying combinations of features. The more features that are considered and the more levels or categories that exist for each feature, the more combinations there will be for consideration. For example, four features, each with four levels/categories, produces 256 different combinations. Selecting combinations for inclusion in a study and analysing the results is the complex mathematical task undertaken by conjoint analysis. The detail is beyond the scope of this text, but further reading is indicated in the Resources section, and the approach is discussed again in Chapter 11 under 'Discrete choice experiments (DCE)'.

3.4 Content analysis

In some fields of inquiry, the focus of research is textual – for example, the content of organisations' annual reports or of politicians' speeches, or the coverage of sport or a major event in the media. The analysis and interpretation of the content of published or unpublished texts is referred to as *content analysis*, often when the analysis is quantitative, or *hermeneutics*, when the analysis is of a more qualitative nature. The technique has not traditionally been widely used in leisure and tourism studies, but with the development of postmodernism and the widening of the scope of *text* to include a wide variety of cultural products such as company documents, advertising material, websites and letters, the approach is attracting increasing attention. Some examples of quantitative studies are listed in the Resources section, and qualitative approaches are discussed in Chapter 9.

3.5 Coupon surveys/conversion studies

In marketing research, use can be made of information from the responses of the public to advertising coupons – that is, where the public is invited in an advertisement to write or telephone for information on a product. The data can be used to indicate the level of interest in the product on offer (compared with other products or with the same product in previous periods) and also to indicate the geographical spread of the interested public. The question then arises as to the extent to which people who respond to such advertising actually become customers. Thus conversion studies are designed to examine the extent to which enquirers *convert* to become customers (Woodside and Ronkainen, 1994).

3.6 Cross-cultural research

In increasingly multi-cultural and globalised societies, researchers are faced with research subjects from different cultural backgrounds. Cultural background or identity may be just one of a number of variables in a study or may be a substantial focus of the research. This calls for appropriate skills and resources in relation to such matters as language and cross-cultural sensitivities. Sources of guidance are indicated in the Resources section.

3.7 Delphi technique

The Delphi technique (named after the classical Greek 'Delphic oracle') is a procedure involving the gathering and analysing of information from a panel of experts on future trends in a particular field of interest. The experts in the field (e.g. leisure or tourism) complete a questionnaire indicating their views on the likelihood of certain developments taking place in future; these views are then collated and circulated to panel members for further comment, a process which might be repeated a number of times before the final results are collated. The technique is used in some areas of business and technological forecasting, and it has been used to a limited extent in leisure and tourism. In this text the technique is not examined explicitly, but to some extent it involves questionnaire design and analysis, as covered in Chapters 10 and 16. A thorough state-of-the-art review has been provided by Donohue and Needham (2009).

3.8 Discourse analysis

Discourse analysis is research on the use of language in relation to a topic/issue in popular and/or academic texts and other communications media. The way language is used, consciously or unconsciously, in relation to a phenomenon, shapes popular and official conceptualisations of that phenomenon. For example, the public view of tourism is likely to be affected if the term is invariably accompanied by the descriptor 'mass' or 'sustainable'. The conscious adoption of one term rather the another – for example, 'rave' rather than 'dance' – signals an intent on the part of the users. In the organisational context, the process is the stock-in-trade of public relations practitioners or 'spin merchants'. Research on this dimension of human interaction typically involves analysis of media and official broadcast and print material on a topic over a period of time – for example Jaimangal-Jones's (2012) examination of the media coverage of dance music events.

3.9 *En route*/intercept/cordon surveys

In tourism research, surveys of tourists while travelling are sometimes referred to as *en route* surveys (Hurst, 1994). Such surveys may be conducted in aeroplanes, at airports or while travelling by car (when travellers are waved into lay-bys for survey purposes with the assistance of police). In this text, this type of survey, which invariably involves a questionnaire, is considered to be a special case of site or user surveys, as discussed in Chapter 10. Since respondents are 'intercepted' at or near a destination, site or attraction, the term *intercept survey* is sometimes used, and if all approaches to the destination, site or attraction are covered, the term *cordon survey* may be used.

3.10 Experience sampling method (ESM)

The experience sampling method (ESM) was pioneered by Mihaly Csikszentmihalyi and his colleagues at the University of Chicago in 1977 (Csikszentmihalyi and Larson, 1977) and can be seen as a development of the time-budget survey/diary method. Alternative names for the technique are *ecological momentary assessment* (EMA) (Smyth and Stone, 2003) and *ambulatory assessment*.

An ESM study typically takes place over a few days, during which, on about eight occasions each day, study participants are alerted by some electronic device – a pager in the early examples, later by watches programmed to 'beep' at certain times and most recently by mobile telephone. When alerted, or as soon as practically possible thereafter, the study participant completes a short questionnaire in a booklet carried with the participant at all times or, in recent versions, responds to questions via text message. Information is gathered on activities being undertaken, where and with whom, and attitudes and feelings. The method has the advantage of recording activities and feelings in real time and in the 'natural' environment of the subject, rather than relying on recall at a later date in a different environment. While the amount of information which can be elicited in any one episode is limited, the cumulative amount of information gathered, together with any information included in a preliminary conventional questionnaire, can be substantial.

The early study by Csikszentmihalyi and Larson (1977) was of adolescents' daily behaviour patterns, while a later study using the method explored adult stress levels related to work and leisure patterns and family interactions (Schneider et al., 2004).

The research approach made possible by ESM has been characterised as *idiographic*, based on the Greek word *idios*, meaning specific to an individual (Conner et al., 2009). This is in contrast to *nomothetic* research, based on the Greek word *nomos*, meaning law, which seeks to establish general scientific laws of behaviour based on studies of a number of individuals. However, unlike qualitative research, which is often idiographic, ESM is generally quantitative in nature since it gathers data from individuals on repeated occasions.

Further developments in this type of electronically aided research include digital tracking using global positioning systems and the electronically activated recorder (EAR). For the EAR, the subject wears a small microphone and recording device which is automatically activated for short periods (for example for 30 seconds, 12 times per hour), thus providing a record of the environments the subject experiences and conversational interaction with people. This has been used in psychological research to track social interaction (Mehl et al., 2001), but there are no known examples in leisure or tourism.

The details of the method are not pursued further in this text, but references to examples of its use are provided in the Resources section.

3.11 Historical research

History is of course a major discipline with its own approaches to research. Historical research arises in the leisure/tourism environment in at least two contexts; biographical research (discussed as a qualitative approach in Chapter 8) and case-study research (discussed in Chapter 11). It can also be seen as a form of secondary data analysis, since historians are invariably dependent on documents contemporary to a period, which were originally compiled for other purposes. As a discipline, history is part of the humanities, although in the context of leisure/tourism research, it clearly extends into the social sciences when history is presented as a partial explanation for contemporary phenomena; for example in research on significant events, such as the Olympic Games, or significant institutions, such as tourism commissions. A major preoccupation of scholars in leisure/tourism is the topic of public policy, notably state subsidies and promotion of sport or the arts, and the history of this phenomenon in various countries is often the focus of research, as indicated in the Resources section. Compared with the social science literature, in historical literature the question of method tends to be down-played or taken for granted. While historical accounts are generally conducted in a scholarly manner, with detailed reference to sources, just how the source material has been used and analysed is not always clear: thus there is rarely a 'methods' section in historically based articles. Historical methods are not pursued in this text, but some sources/examples are indicated in the Resources section.

3.12 Longitudinal studies

Longitudinal studies involve surveying the same sample of individuals periodically over a number of years (Young et al., 1991). Such studies are of course expensive because of the need to keep track of the sample members over the years, and the need to have a large enough sample at the beginning to allow for the inevitable attrition to the sample over time. They are, however, ideal for studying social change and the combined effects of social change and ageing. While longitudinal studies are a recognised technique in the social sciences, and leisure and tourism activity may feature in some studies, there are no known examples specifically focused on leisure or tourism.

Studies of communities can be seen as longitudinal if comparable data are collected at intervals over an extended period of time, even if the same individuals are not interviewed each time; in this case the constant is the community – physical, social and economic – rather than individuals. Such a study was conducted by Donald Getz (1993) in relation to the changing impact of tourism in Spey Valley, Scotland, between 1978 and 1992. He undertook surveys of adults and schoolchildren. While tracking down the children for repeat interviewing in 1992 would have been of interest, it also made sense for Getz to conduct a new survey of schoolchildren with the same age-range as those interviewed in 1978. Chang Huh and Christine Vogt (2008) adopted a similar approach in relation to the impact of tourism on coastal residents over time.

3.13 Mapping techniques

Asking research subjects to draw maps is a method of eliciting spatially-related information. When this refers to people's knowledge and perceptions of their neighbourhood or city, it is referred to as *perceptual mapping* and this is discussed in section 3.21 later in the chapter.

In some cases the idea of mapping is used as an analogue. For example, 'personal meaning mapping' has been used in events research to elicit visitors' conceptual map of meanings of the experience (van Winkle and Falk, 2015). This approach is sometimes referred to as *mind-mapping* (Buzan, 1994; Crowe and Sheppard, 2012). In the cultural sector, compiling a position statement on the cultural resources of a community can be referred to as a *cultural mapping* (see Evans and Foord, 2008: 78–90; British Council, 2010).

3.14 Media reader/viewer/listener surveys

Newspapers, magazines and radio and television stations often run opinion poll-type surveys among their readers, viewers or listeners, often web-based. At the local level, the public's views on an issue may be canvassed by the inclusion of some sort of form in a newspaper, which readers may fill in and return, and radio and television stations often run 'phone in' polls on topical issues. The results of these exercises have entertainment value but should not generally be taken seriously. This is mainly because there is no way of knowing whether either the original population (the readers/listeners/viewers who happen to read, hear or view the item) or the sample of respondents are representative of the population as a whole. In most cases they are decidedly unrepresentative, in that the audiences and readership of particular media outlets tend to have particular socio-economic characteristics, and only those with pronounced views, one way or the other, are likely to become involved in the process. In a recent example, a reader panel survey indicated that 86% of respondents had visited the cinema at least once in the previous year, but national survey data indicates that only 66% do so (*Sydney Morning Herald*, 2016). These exercises should not, of course be confused with surveys sponsored by the media but conducted by reputable survey companies, such as Newspoll or Ipsos.

3.15 Meta-analysis

One approach to research combines features of a literature review and second-ary data analysis and involves a quantitative appraisal of the findings of a number of research projects on the same topic. The technique, known as *meta-analysis* (Glass et al., 1981), is suitable for the sort of research where findings are directly comparable from one study to another – for example, when the key findings are expressed in terms of correlation and regression coefficients between particular variables (see Chapter 17). In a meta-analysis, the reported findings of a large number of individual research projects in the same area pro-vide the basis for further exploration and analysis of the area. Typically, because many studies are involved and must be compared on a common basis, only relatively simple relationships can be examined.

A less formal approach to cross-project appraisal is the *consensus study* in which a group of researchers reviews the accumulated research on a topic and seeks to reach a consensus on the state of knowledge. This is discussed further in Chapter 6.

Examples of meta-analysis in the leisure and tourism area are given in the Resources section.

3.16 Multiple correspondence/latent class analysis

Multiple correspondence analysis (MCA) and latent class analysis are analyti-cal techniques used to group subjects on the basis of comparable behaviour patterns, tastes and socio-demographic (lifestyle) characteristics. They are sim-ilar to cluster and factor analysis (see Chapter 17) but do not require quantita-tive variables. They have been used extensively in analysis of cultural participation patterns and their relationship to class and lifestyle, most notable in the work of Bourdieu (1984). Examples are listed in the Resources section, and they are further discussed in Chapter 17.

3.17 Netnography

The internet and social media in particular are increasingly significant as means of communication. They are therefore key potential sources of information about people's attitudes, values, tastes and behaviour which interest marketers and social and cultural researchers. A set of practices and associated literature have grown up in this area, referred to as *netnography* or *virtual research*. Sources are indicated in the Resources section.

3.18 Network analysis

Many human activities operate through networks involving nodes and links between them, including transport systems, electricity supply systems and telecommunications. A science has developed around this idea and has been

Analogue depiction

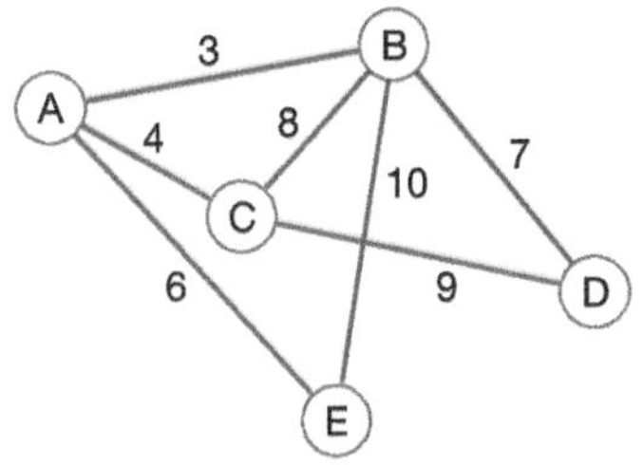

Digital depiction

	A	B	C	D	E
A	0	3	4	0	6
B	3	0	8	7	10
C	4	8	0	9	0
D	0	7	9	0	0
E	6	10	0	0	0

Figure 5.2 A simple network

used to optimise the design of networks. Figure 5.2 shows a simple network represented in analogue and digital format, with the numbers indicating the size of the flows between the nodes (e.g. traffic flows, financial flows, communication). Although it is not possible to pursue this here, this situation clearly lends itself to mathematical analysis, although analysis can be confined to graphical format and can involve qualitative approaches. In terms of data collection, the method involves the identification of the relevant nodes (organisations, destinations) in the system and measuring the extent of links between them. The approach has similarities to the notion of *sociometry* as used in psychotherapy and education research (see Dayton, 2005; Oppenheim, 2000: 254–59).

Tourism clearly involves networks, in terms of traffic flows and the structure of the industry and its interdependencies, and a research literature is developing in the field (Scott et al. 2008). Everyday leisure activity also involves networks, among individuals and groups. The phenomenon of the social networking website is the latest manifestation of this and, indeed, when network analysis is applied at the individual and small group level, it is referred to as *social network analysis*. Numerous surveys of leisure facility and service users over many years have illustrated the importance of friendship networks when they have discovered that 'word of mouth' is a far more significant source of information for most people than any form of advertising. Social network analysis is not common in leisure studies, but has been explored by Patricia Stokowski (1994; Stokowski and Lee, 1991).

3.19 Panel studies

Market research companies often maintain *panels* of individuals for some of their surveys. Panels are made up of a representative cross-section of the public who agree to be on call for a series of surveys over a period of time. Often some financial reward is paid to panel members, but this cost is offset by the savings in not having to continually select and contact new samples of respondents. While managing such panels presents particular problems, the range of survey methods which can be used with panels – by telephone, by mail or by face-to-face interview – is the same as for normal one-off samples (LaPage,

1994). Panel studies can therefore be seen as a particular form of household questionnaire survey.

3.20 People meters

In the early days of radio, and later television, broadcasting, and until the 1990s, the patterns of use of radio and television and relative popularity of programmes were monitored by the use of diaries kept by a sample or panel of listeners/viewers (see section 3.29 on time-use surveys). This process has been conducted by survey companies typically commissioned by a joint broadcasting industry consortium. More recently, for television, devices are installed into the homes of a sample or panel of viewers which record the channel being viewed and even the members of the household viewing at any one time. This information is, of course, vital for commercial channels, since advertisers must be informed as to the size and socio-demographic profile of the audiences for the shows and time slots in which they advertise.

3.21 Perceptual mapping

One of the issues in leisure/tourism planning and marketing is the extent to which the public are well-informed about available facilities and services. This is partly related to information coming through the media, formal marketing activities and personal networks, but can also relate to people's spatial perception of the neighbourhood, city or region in which they live. For example, people are likely to be familiar with their immediate neighbourhood and the route to their place of work or education, but are likely to be less familiar with areas on the other side of town. This can apply particularly to people without cars, notably young people and the elderly. Information on people's *perceptual space* can be elicited by inviting them to draw *perceptual maps* of their environment.

The idea of spatial perception and mapping can be extended to mental processes, so that the process becomes similar to the development of conceptual frameworks, *concept maps*, as discussed in Chapters 3 and 14.

3.22 Projective techniques

Projective techniques might be termed 'what if?' techniques in that they involve subjects responding to hypothetical – projected – situations. For example, subjects might be asked to indicate how they might spend a particular sum of money if given a free choice, or how they might spend additional leisure time if it were made available, or they might be invited to respond to photographs of possible holiday destinations (Ryan, 1995: 124). While the technique can become elaborate and specialised, in this text it is considered to be an extension of questionnaire-based surveys and possibly of focus-group interviews.

3.23 Psychographic/lifestyle research

Psychographic research, as discussed in Chapter 2, gathers data on a wide range of attitudes and socio-demographic characteristics of people and analyses the data to establish groupings or market segments with common characteristics, typically using statistical techniques such as factor and cluster analysis, as discussed in Chapter 17. A number of commercial survey/consultant organisations offer their own psychographic/lifestyle systems to clients to classify survey respondents into segments seen as more meaningful than those based on the usual age, gender and social class.

● The VALS typology (Values, Attitudes and Life Styles), developed in the United States, classifies people into nine segments, as shown in Table 5.5. This system has been widely used in market research, including tourism research (e.g. Shih, 1986). The ACORN (A Classification of Residential Neighbourhoods) was developed in Britain by the commercial survey company CACI and is based on socio-demographic data from census collection areas (see Chapter 7). So, since it does not contain attitude data, it must be classified as a lifestyle rather than a psychographic system. It has five segments divided into 17 sub-segments as shown in Table 5.5 and has been used in leisure research, notably in the annual Sport England Active People Survey (as discussed in Chapter 7).

Table 5.5 Examples of psychographic/lifestyle categories

VALS*	ACORN†	
1. Survivor	1. Wealth achievers	A. Wealthy executives
2. Sustainer		B. Affluent greys (older people)
3. Belonger		C. Flourishing (well-off) families
4. Emulator	2. Urban prosperity	D. Prosperous professionals
5. Achiever		E. Educated urbanites (young urban professionals)
6. I-Am-Me		F. Aspiring singles (mainly urban area students)
7. Experiential	3. Comfortably off	G. Starting out (young couples)
8. Socially conscious		H. Secure families
9. Integrated		I. Settled suburbia (older couples in suburbs)
		J. Prudent pensioners
	4. Moderate means	K. Asian communities
		L. Post-industrial families (older skilled)
		M. Blue-collar roots (manual workers)
	5. Hard-pressed	N. Struggling (low-income) families
		O. Burdened singles (elderly and single parents)
		P. High-rise hardship
		Q. Inner-city adversity

* Values, Attitudes and Lifestyles: Strategic Business Insights (2009).

† A Classification of Residential Neighbourhoods: CACI Ltd (2006).

3.24 Q methodology

Q methodology was developed in the 1930s by physicist/psychologist William Stephenson to examine people's subjective opinions of phenomena. It involves five steps:

1. Definition of the 'concourse', the scope of the phenomenon to be studied – typically in the form of a set of attitude statements (see Chapter 10), but sometimes photographs.

2. Development of the 'Q-sample' or 'Q-set' of stimulus items – typically a set of cards, each containing one of the statements/photographs.

3. Selection of the 'person-sample', 'P-sample' or 'P-set' – the sample of individuals to be involved in the study.

4. Q-sorting – individuals sort the cards into piles arranged along a spectrum – for example, from strongly agree to strongly disagree, scored as in a Likert scale (see Chapter 10). Subjects are required to arrange cards on a provided template in the shape of a bell-shaped 'normal curve' (as shown in Figure 17.1a).

5. Analysis and interpretation – this involves factor analysis of the data (see Chapter 17) to discover themes.

Computer software packages, such a 'PQ Method' are available to analyse the data. Examples of applications in leisure and tourism studies are indicated in the Resources section, and some further technical detail of the method is discussed in Chapter 17.

3.25 Quantitative modelling

The techniques discussed so far are distinguished primarily by their data-collection procedures and in some cases by both their data-collection and analysis procedures. Quantitative modelling is distinguished by an approach to theory and data analysis: the data used are quantitative, but may have been collected by one or more of a variety of methods (e.g. observation, questionnaires, documentary records, experiment). The idea of quantitative modelling was discussed briefly in Chapter 3, where it is noted that hypotheses concerning the relationships between variables may be expressed and tested in the form of models/equations (see Figure 3.11). This approach to research is considered further in Chapter 17, particularly in connection with linear and multiple regression.

3.26 Repertory grid/laddering

Developed by psychologist George Kelly in the 1950s, the repertory grid technique is used from time to time in leisure and tourism research. It can be seen as a formalisation and quantification of perceptual mapping. Research subjects are asked to indicate a range of qualities of the phenomenon being studied and

Friendly						Threatening
Cool						Uncool
Expensive						Cheap
Etc.						

Figure 5.3 Repertory grid example

then the opposite of that quality – for example, friendly – threatening; cool – uncool; expensive – cheap. A number of these *constructs* are elicited – typically up to about 20 – and entered into a grid, as shown in Figure 5.3. Subjects then indicate on the grid where the study object fits on each construct: for example, for the first construct, whether it is closer to the friendly end or the threatening end. This information can be scored and analysed using graphic and/or statistical analyses such as factor analysis (see Chapter 17) at the individual level and/or collectively.

Laddering is a less formal technique which explores a person's underlying feelings and values concerning a product or service through focused questioning. Sources are provided in the Resources section.

3.27 Scales

A scale is a numerical index used to measure constructs or variables which are generally not intrinsically quantitative. Typically, subjects are asked to respond to questions using rating scales, and the scores are combined to produce a scale or index of the phenomenon of interest. In Chapter 10 the development and use of customised scales in questionnaires is discussed, but it is quite common for researchers to make use of standardised scales which have been developed by others. The advantage of the use of existing scales is that researchers are not continually 'reinventing the wheel' by devising their own measure of a particular phenomenon. Widely used scales have generally been subject to considerable testing to ensure validity – that is, that they measure what they are intended to measure. Further, the use of common measures facilitates comparability between studies. The disadvantage is, of course, that any fault in the scale validity may be replicated across many studies, and a fixed scale may not fully reflect different socio-economic environments or change over time.

The use of such scales is widespread, particularly in psychology and related disciplines, but they have not been widely utilised in the mainstream of leisure and tourism research. Some examples are as follows:

● McGuiggan (2000) makes use of the Myers–Briggs Type Indicator, one of the most well-known scales used to assess personality, in a study of the relationship between personality and leisure activity preferences.

● The Leisure Satisfaction Scale (LSS) was developed by Beard and Ragheb (1980) and applied in a tourism context by Ryan and Glendon (1998).

- The Paragraphs About Leisure (PAL) scale, developed by Howard Tinsley and his associates (see Driver et al., 1991), is concerned with a range of psychological benefits derived from participation in leisure activities.

- The Recreation Experience Preference (REP) scale, developed by Bev Driver and associates (Driver et al., 1991), is similar to the PAL but focused particularly on outdoor natural area facilities.

- Researchers in the area of sport and exercise often make use of scales related to physical and mental health, such as that developed by Ware et al. (1994).

Despite the considerable amount of psychologically influenced research using scales in such areas as destination choice and tourist satisfaction (see Woodside et al., 2000 and Mazanec et al., 2001), the use of specialised standardised scales has not emerged prominently in tourism research.

The *Marketing Scales Handbook*, published in a number of volumes by the American Marketing Association (Bruner and Hensel, 1992), lists hundreds of scales used in marketing research, most relating to generic topics such as consumer motivation and attitudes, but others relating to specific settings. A selection of relevance to leisure and tourism is listed in Table 5.6.

Further examples of the use of scales in leisure and tourism research are listed in the Resources section.

Table 5.6 Scales for leisure/tourism-related topics

Listed in Bruner and Hensel (1992)

72	Cooking enjoyment	261	Sports activeness
74	Co-viewing TV (parent/child)	262	Sports enthusiasm
147	Involvement (television)	268	Time management
186	Pleasure	269–70	Time pressure
193	Pricing issues (air travel)	274	Venturesomeness
219	Restriction of TV viewing	277	Volunteerism (benefits)
226	Safety (air travel)	278	Volunteerism (family/job constraints)
227	Satisfaction (air travel)	279	Volunteerism (willingness)

Listed in Bruner et al. (2001)

2	Affect (music)	323	Sensation seeking
48	Attitude toward conservation activity	330–33	Services evaluation (airline features)
154	Experiential response to music	345	Service quality (health club)
180	Imaginal response to music	368	Shopping orientation (recreation)
186	Impulse buying (music)	403–6	Ad. avoidance in various media
217	Involvement (televised soccer match)	436	Attitude toward sex in advertising
239	Need to reexperience music	443	Attitude toward the ad. (humour)
259	Pressure to be thin	938	Work involvement
285	Quality of service (stadium)	939	Work/family conflict
307	Satisfaction (with health club)		

3.28 Scenarios

Scenario writing is a technique developed particularly in the area of forecasting. It involves the devising of alternative pictures of the future as characterised by alternative values of *key variables* and the relationships between them. For example, a simple approach for an exercise at the national level might select the politics of the government in power and the level of unemployment as two key variables. Alternative political scenarios for a country for the year 2025 might envisage either a right-wing conservative government or a left/centrist social democratic government, and high or low economic growth. These two dimensions offer four alternative scenarios, as indicated in Figure 5.4.

3.29 Time-use surveys

There is a long tradition in leisure studies of investigating people's allocation of time between such categories as paid work, domestic work, sleep and leisure (Szalai, 1972; Pentland et al. 1999). The approach has not been widely used in tourism research, when people are away from home, although Douglas Pearce (1988) has suggested its use and noted a few examples. Time-use – or time-budget – research is basically a special case of the household survey, and some reference is made to it in that context in Chapter 10.

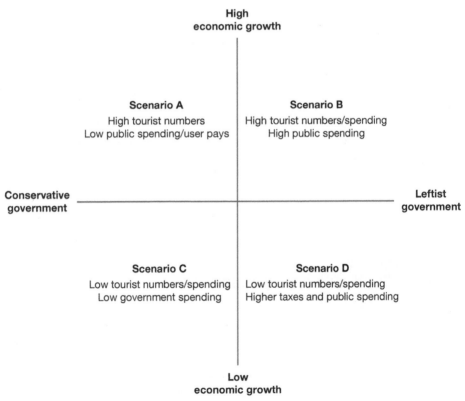

Figure 5.4 Scenarios for the year 2025: two dimensional

3.30 Visitor conversation research

Rather than conduct research with questionnaires or even semi-structured interviews, some researchers have explored the content of facility/service users' own conversations. In the context of the museum as a learning institution, for example, researchers have sought to explore the extent to which visitors are engaging and absorbing the educational message by inviting selected visitors to wear microphones so that their within-group discussions can be recorded and analysed. The technique typically also involves interviews before and/or following the visit, and researchers track the subjects' route and stopping points so that the audio-recording can be linked with appropriate exhibits.

3.31 Visual methods

Visual methods use such visual props as photographs, video, drawings, post-cards, advertising material and internet-based images to explore leisure and tourism phenomena. Rakic and Chambers (2012: 5) note that the visual material can be of three types: secondary sources, such as brochures, collected and subsequently analysed; material, such as a set of photographs, purposely created or selected by the researcher to stimulated responses from individuals; or materials, such as drawings, generated by research subjects.

3.32 Web-based research

Research based entirely on the internet is referred to as netnography and is discussed in section 3.17 of this chapter. More informal use of the World Wide Web is, however, now an integral part of most social research. Up-to-date data and policy documents are much more readily available, and often in more detail, than when researchers were entirely dependent on access to hard-copy materials. The relative ease of access does not, however, absolve researchers from the need to check the validity of the resources being used. Access to online research literature is discussed in Chapter 6.

4. Multiple methods

Many research methods involve the use of more than one method or technique. Three multi-method situations are discussed here, as shown in Table 5.7. The case study method is also a multi-method approach, but this is considered a primary method in this text and so is discussed separately above and in Chapter 12.

Table 5.7 Multiple methods

Technique	Brief description
1. Triangulation	Two or more methods used to focus on the same phenomenon, providing confirmation or differing insights.
2. Community studies	Comprehensive study of a geographical or other community using a variety of data sources.
3. Counting heads	A management task involving various research approaches, needed in situations where usage/visitor numbers are not available from ticket sales.

4.1 Triangulation/mixed methods

Triangulation gets its name from the land surveying method of fixing the position of an object by measuring it from two different positions, with the object being the third point of the triangle. In research, the triangulation method involves the use of more than one research approach in a single study to gain a broader or more complete understanding of the issues being investigated. The methods used are often complementary in that the weaknesses of one approach are complemented by the strengths of another. Triangulation often utilises both qualitative and quantitative approaches in the same study. Duffy (1987: 131) identified four different ways that triangulation can be used in research:

- analysing data in more than one way;
- using more than one sampling strategy;
- using different interviewers, observers and analysts in the one study; and
- using more than one methodology to gather data.

If triangulation methods are to be used in a study, the approaches taken will depend on the imagination and the experience of the researcher. However, it is important that the research question is clearly focused and not confused by the methodology adopted, and that the methods are chosen in accordance with their relevance to the topic. In particular, the *rationale* for using triangulation should be outlined in reporting the research, and the possible weaknesses of one method and the ways in which the additional method has been used to overcome such a weakness should be explained. This is clearly relevant to the issue of validity and reliability discussed in Chapter 2.

Often triangulation is claimed in a study because more than one data source and/or analytical method has been used to address different aspects of the research question, or even different research questions. However, it is when the different data/methods address the *same* question that true triangulation can be said to have occurred. Figure 5.5 presents an example where four data

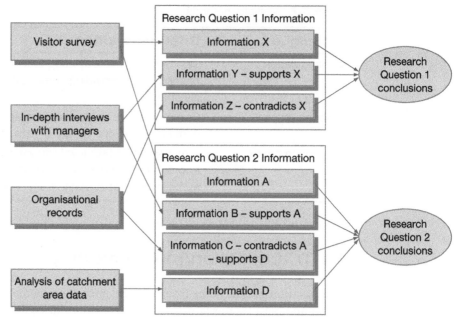

Figure 5.5   Triangulation

collection methods are used to address two research questions. A research report on a project where triangulation is claimed should therefore compare and contrast the findings from the multiple methods. Whether the multiple methods produce similar or different findings should then be an issue for discussion.

Triangulation, as metaphor and method, has, however, been subject to criticism, notably by Blaikie (1991), who argued that, in the original surveying use of triangulation, the two measurements from two different locations are made in the context of the same ontology. In social science terms, this was quantitatively based positivism. The second measurement is not made to overcome the limitations of the first as is often claimed in social research: the two measurements are part of the same process. In the social science situation, two contrasting methodologies may be addressing different questions altogether. To overcome this dilemma in the deployment of multiple methods, Richardson (2005) has used the metaphor of the multi-faceted *crystal* in place of the simple triangle.

Another term used to refer to the utilisation of multiple methods is *mixed methods*, which in turn is sometimes referred to as *pragmatism*. The above comments on triangulation generally apply to mixed methods/pragmatism.

4.2 Counting heads

In virtually all leisure and tourism contexts there is a requirement for information on visitor numbers for planning and management purposes. This calls for what is colloquially referred to as 'counting heads' or, in seated venues, counting 'bums on seats'. In many cases the required information is generated automatically by the ticket sales process. But there are situations where ticket numbers are not available; for example, urban parks, beaches, some museums and galleries and public events and tourist destinations with informal access (e.g. by private vehicle). In other cases, data are available from multiple sources – for example, a tourist destination with a variety of modes of access, or a festival with a combination of free and ticketed events. In these situations, a variety of data-collection methods may be available from which one or more methods may be selected. The methods/sources can be divided into administrative, survey-based and direct counts. Thus, assembling data concerning one site or destination involves consideration of methods addressed in a number of the chapters in Part II, particularly Chapters 7, 8 and 10. This issue is addressed initially in Chapter 7 and information provided in Tables 7.2 and 7.3 and cross-referenced in Chapters 8 and 10.

4.3 Community study as method

As long ago as 1954, Conrad Arensberg presented a case for viewing the community study as a distinct research method, describing it as a naturalistic, comparative method in which

> a problem (or problems) in the nature, interconnections, or dynamics of behavior and attitudes is explored against or within the surround of other behavior and attitudes of the individuals making up the life of a particular community. (Arensberg, 1954: 110)

The key requirement of a community study is, of course, the existence of an identifiable community, and this is generally geographical. Community studies have been a feature of leisure studies from the beginning:

- In the United States, one of the most famous community studies, of 'Middletown', was conducted by Robert and Helen Lynd in 1929 and included three chapters on the use of leisure; while the first major study of leisure, entitled *Leisure: A Suburban Study*, by George Lundberg and his associates (Lundberg, Komorosky and McInerny, 1934), was a study of Westchester County in suburban New York.

- In the United Kingdom, a study of High Wycombe formed part of the earliest major study of leisure conducted in the late 1940s by Rowntree and Lavers (1951) (see Case studies 9.1 and 12.1).

- More recently, there is Derek Wynne's study of the leisure behaviours and lifestyles of residents of a new housing estate near London (Wynne, 1998 – see Case study 12.4).

- In Australia, one of the earliest examples of leisure research, *Leisure: A Social Enquiry* by Scott and U'Ren (1962), was of the leisure participation of residents of a Melbourne suburban housing estate.

- In tourism, studies have been conducted of relatively small host communities: for example, Waldren's (1996, 1997) study of the Mediterranean island of Mallorca.

In effect, community studies are case studies, so the methodological considerations relevant to case studies as discussed in Chapter 12 are also applicable to community studies.

5. Policy/management-related methods

All of the aforementioned approaches and concepts are academically based. While all of these also apply in various ways to research conducted in policy or management contexts, the latter have also given rise to a range of research approaches, which are listed in Table 5.8 with brief descriptions and an indication of the main data-collection methods used in their conduct. They are not discussed in detail, but examples arise from time to time in the Resources sections of later chapters.

Table 5.8 Policy/management-related research approaches/techniques

Approach/ technique	Description	Main data collection and/or analysis methods
Balanced scorecard analysis	A structured system of performance measures applied across the whole of an organisation, beginning with mission/vision, then specifying 'critical success factors' (CSFs), then metrics for four *facets* for each CSF: financial performance, customer perspective, internal processes and innovation and learning.	Mainly management-generated data from the organisation, but could also involve survey results.
Cost-benefit analysis	Evaluation of a project (building, programme, organisation, service) by comparison of the total costs and total benefits using, where possible, monetary measures.	Secondary economic data and surveys of customers.
Demand forecasting	Estimating future participation levels, based on a variety of assumptions and using a variety of techniques.	Secondary and survey-based participation, demographic and economic data
Discrete choice analysis	Research subjects are offered choices of hypothetical products with varying characteristics.	Laboratory-type conditions. (see Chapter 12).

Approach/ technique	Description	Main data collection and/or analysis methods
Evidence-based policy	The idea that public/government policies should be based on, and evaluated on the basis of, empirical evidence.	All, but often mainly quantitative
Importance-performance analysis	Service/product users/visitors are asked to scale the importance of aspects of a service/product and then to scale the actual performance experienced.	Customer surveys
Key performance indicators (KPIs)	The success/failure of policies is assessed on the basis of a number of measurable indicators of performance.	Secondary data (e.g. sales, attendances, profit) or survey-based (e.g. customer satisfaction)
Logic model	Rational management model based on the sequence: initial conditions, needs, problems, resources; action; outcomes; impacts.	Secondary/management-generated data, possibly surveys
Market segmentation	Actual and potential customers for a product or service are grouped into 'segments' on the basis of product preferences and socio-demographic characteristics.	Mostly customer surveys, also use of customer purchasing patterns.
Mystery shopping	Incognito researcher tests product/service and reports back.	Observation (see Chapter 8)
Performance evaluation	Assessment of the success or failure of an organisation, unit or programme based on outcomes compared with stated objectives, often using KPIs	As for KPIs
Resource auditing/ mapping	Compiling a register/inventory of existing or potential resources (e.g. cultural or heritage resources) of an area, for public information or as input to a policy process. See 'mapping' above.	Use of secondary sources, documents, internet, observation, organisational survey
SERVQUAL	Short for 'service quality': similar to importance-performance analysis, but users compare service quality *expectations* with actual quality experienced.	Customer surveys.

6. Choosing methods

The process of choosing appropriate research methods for a research task is part of the whole process of planning and designing a research project, as discussed in Chapter 3. Here, a number of considerations which should be borne in mind are discussed, as listed in Table 5.9.

Table 5.9 Considerations in selecting a research method

---

1. The research question or hypothesis
2. Previous research
3. Data availability/access
4. Resources
5. Time and timing
6. Validity, reliability, generalisability
7. Ethics
8. Uses/users of the findings

6.1 The research question or hypothesis

Much of the decision on how to research a topic is bound up in the basic research question or hypothesis. As discussed in Chapter 3, the 'research question' can take a variety of forms, but generally it will point the researcher in the direction of certain data sources – for example, in relation to employees, customers or organisations. Certain types of data also suggest certain types of analysis.

6.2 Previous research

If the proposed research is closely keyed into the literature and previous research, then the methods used in that research are likely to influence the choice of methods. The aim may be to replicate the methodology used in previous studies to achieve comparability, to improve on the methods used, or to deliberately adopt a contrasting methodology.

6.3 Data availability/access

In some cases an obvious existing data source presents itself and may even have prompted the research in the first place – termed *opportunistic* research in Chapter 2. For example:

- a set of archives of an organisation can provide the basis for historical research;
- official data which have been published but only superficially analysed could be analysed in more depth; and
- access to a sample of people, such as the workforce or customer-base of a company, members of a club or members of an informal interest group can be seen as an opportunity too good to miss.

In other cases *lack* of access shapes the research – for example, ethical or practical issues may preclude some research on children, so data may have to be gathered from parents.

6.4 Resources

Clearly the resources of staff and money will have a major effect on the type and scale of the research to be conducted.

6.5 Time and timing

Time and timing is always a limitation. Most research projects have a time limit. Timing in relation to external events or routines is also often a factor. For example, research using the current year's attendance data must be completed quickly if it is to be used to influence next year's strategic planning; and empirical research on events, such as sporting events or arts festivals, is constrained by their timing.

6.6 Validity, reliability and generalisability

As discussed in Chapter 2:

- *validity* is the extent to which the data collected truly reflect the phenomenon being studied; and

- *reliability* is the extent to which research findings would be the same if the research were to be repeated at a later date, or with a different sample of subjects.

It is also noted in Chapter 2 that these concepts are sometimes replaced in qualitative research by the concept of *trustworthiness*.

As discussed in Chapter 2, generalisability refers to the extent to which the results of the research findings apply to other subjects, other groups and other conditions. The extent to which this is required as an outcome of the research will influence the choice of method.

6.7 Ethics

Ethical issues also limit choices of research method. Reference has already been made to ethical issues surrounding research on children: further examples of ethical issues are discussed in Chapter 4.

6.8 Uses/users of the findings

The uses and users of the research are often taken for granted, but they are an important factor in shaping research. If substantial investment will depend on the results of the research, then a more extensive and thorough-going project will be required than if the research is to used only to generate ideas. When life-and-death issues are at stake – for example, in medical research on the effects of a treatment for a disease – much greater precision is needed in the results than if, for example, a company merely wishes to know the socio-economic characteristics of its customers.

Summary

This chapter complements Chapter 3 in setting out in brief the range of research methods available to the leisure and tourism researcher. It reinforces the message of Chapter 3, that research methods should ideally be selected on the basis of their suitability to answer the research questions posed, not on the basis of some prior preference for a particular method. Initially the 'major' research methods are reviewed, namely: scholarship; 'just thinking'; the use of existing information – the literature and secondary data; observation; qualitative methods; questionnaire-based surveys; case study method; and experimental method.

The first two are included to emphasise that research is not just about deploying techniques but also involves being well-informed about the field and *thinking* about the problems and issues being researched in theoretical and practical terms. The other major methods foreshadow subsequent chapters which deal with them in detail.

The middle section of the chapter briefly introduces a number of approaches and techniques which are subsidiary to one or more of the major methods, in that they are a variation on or an application of the major method, or cut across a number of the major methods. The approaches and techniques covered are listed in Table 5.4.

A section on 'multiple methods' discusses the concept of *triangulation/mixed methods, counting heads* and the *community study* as method.

A brief examination is offered of a range of research/data analysis techniques used in policymaking and management, namely: balanced scorecard analysis; cost-benefit analysis; demand forecasting; discrete choice analysis; evidence-based policy; importance-performance analysis; key performance indicators (KPIs); the logic model; market segmentation; mystery shopping; performance evaluation; resource auditing/mapping; and SERVQUAL.

Finally, factors to be considered in selecting research methods are examined.

Test questions

1. What is 'scholarship'?

2. Table 5.4 lists 32 research methods/techniques. Cover the 'brief description' column and test your own ability to describe each of the items.

3. What is triangulation and why is it used in research?

4. Repeat question 2 using Table 5.8 on policy/management-related techniques.

5. What does counting heads involve?

Exercises

Exercises involving the major methods and subsidiary and cross-cutting methods arise in the subsequent chapters.

Resources

Websites

- Time use: Centre for Time Use Research, USA: www.timeuse.org, International Association for Time Use Research: www.iatur.org.

- Experience sampling method:
  - Society for Ambulatory Assessment: www.ambulatory-assessment.org.
  - Software sites: www.experience-sampling.org, www.cfs.purdue.edu/mfri/pages/PMAT/.

- Q methodology: www.qmethod.org/about.php.

- Longitudinal: UK Longitudinal Studies Centre: www.esrc.ac.uk/research/our-research/centre-for-longitudinal-studies/, Australian Longitudinal Study of Women's Health: www.alswh.org.au.

Publications

Major methods

- See the Resources sections of Chapters 6–12.

- Methodological debate: Borman et al. (1986), Bryman and Bell (2003: 465–478), Dupuis (1999), Henderson (2006), Krenz and Sax (1986), Rojek (1989).

Subsidiary/cross-cutting techniques

- Action research:
  - feminist leisure research: White (2004);

- general: Cole (2005), Greenwood and Levin (2007), McNiff and Whitehead (2002), Reason and Bradbury (2001); and
- sport/community study: Partington and Totten (2012).

- Big data: Anderson (2011), Boyd and Crawford (2012), Hjorth-Andersen (2007), Mayer-Schönberger and Cukier (2013).

- Conjoint analysis: Claxton (1994), Cosper and Kinsley (1984), Jones (1991).

- Content analysis: Scott and Smith (2005), Scott et al. (2012).

- Coupon surveys/conversion studies: Perdue and Botkin (1988), Woodside and Ronkanen (1994).

- Cross-cultural research: Ember and Ember (2009).

- Delphi technique:
  - general: Donohue and Needham (2009), Rowe and Wright (1999);
  - leisure: Moeller and Shafer (1994); and
  - tourism: Garrod and Fyall (2005), Green et al. (1990), Von Bergner and Lohman (2013).

- Diary methods: Bolger et al. (2003), Heimtun (2007). See also time-use methods.

- Discourse analysis: Gee (2010); dance events: Jaimangal-Jones (2012); critical discourse analysis: Locke (2004); tourism company: Palmer and Dunford (2002).

- En route/intercept surveys: Denstadli (2000), Gartner and Hunt (1988), Huang and Confer (2009), Hurst (1994).

- Experience sampling method (ESM): Christensen et al. (2003), Conner et al. (2009), Csikszentmihayli and Larson (1977), Hektner et al. (2006), Mannell and Kleiber (1997: 100–5), Schimmack and Diener (2003), Schneider et al. (2004), Smyth and Stone (2003).

- Historical research: Storey (2004), Williams (2003).

- Laddering:
  - arts/cultural: Guintcheva and Passebois (2009).
  - general: Reynolds and Gutman (1988), Saaka et al. (2004).

- Longitudinal studies:
  - leisure: Scott and Willits (1989, 1998), Warde and Tampubolon (2002);
  - social sciences: Getz (1993), Young et al. (1991);
  - tourism: Huh and Vogt (2008), Ritchie (2005); and
  - the Australian Longitudinal Study on Women's Health includes questions on leisure: see Brown et al. (2009) and project website in the Websites sub-section.

- Mapping techniques/mental maps – mind mapping: Buzan (1994), Crowe & Sheppard (2012); cultural mapping: British Council (2010), Evans and Foord (2008) - see also perceptual mapping.

- Media reader/viewer/listener surveys: Example: *Sydney Morning Herald* (2016).

- Meta-analysis: See Chapter 6.

- Multiple correspondence/latent class analysis: Le Roux and Rouanet (2010), McCutcheon (1987); Philllips and Phillips (2013); examples: Bennett et al. (2009), Bourdieu (1984: 126–31).

- Netnography: Kozinets (1997, 2009); digital leisure: Lupton (2016), Spracklen (2015).

- Network analysis:
  - leisure: Scott et al. (2008), Stokowski (1994);
  - sport tourism: Wasche (2015); and
  - tourism: Casanueva et al. (2016).

- Panel surveys: Kasprzyk et al. (1989), LaPage (1994), Rose (2000).

- People meters: Barnes and Thomson (1994); other modes of media audience research: Patriarche et al. (2014).

- Perceptual mapping: Guy et al. (1990), Pearce (2005: 99–104), Van Winkle and Falk (2015), Walmsley and Jenkins (1991), Young (1999).

- Projective techniques: Oppenheim (2000: Ch. 12), Semeonoff (1976).

- Psychographic/lifestyle research: CACI Ltd (2006), O'Brien and Ford (1988), Strategic Business Insights (2009).

- Q methodology:
  - motivation to visit zoos: Sickler and Fraser (2009);
  - neighbourhood leisure and the elderly: Annear et al. (2009, 2014);
  - principles: McKeown and Thomas (1988); and
  - sport: Annear et al. (2009), Farquhar and Meeds (2007), Grix (2010).

- Quantitative modelling: Crouch and Louviere (2001), Frechtling (1996: 172–9), Hanley et al. (2003), Smith (1995: 140–3).

- Repertory grid:
  - arts: Canning and Holmes (2006);
  - general: Kelly (1955);
  - laddering: Willson and McIntosh (2010);
  - leisure: Stockdale (1984);
  - sport: Feixas et al. (1989); and
  - tourism: Botterill (1989), Coshall (2000), Potter and Coshall (1988).

- Scales:
  - events: Fredline et al. (2002);
  - impact: Ap and Crompton (1998);
  - involvement in leisure: Kyle et al. (2007);
  - Leisure Boredom Scale: Iso-Ahola and Weissinger (1990);
  - leisure/tourism and the Myers–Briggs personality indicator: Allen (1982), McGuiggan (2000, 2001);
  - Life Satisfaction Index: Neugarten et al. (1961);
  - Locus of Control Scale: Levenson (1974);

- marketing: Bruner and Hensel (1992);
- outdoor recreation: Beard and Ragheb (1980), Driver et al. (1991);
- Perceived Leisure Control Scale and Perceived Leisure Competence Scale: Witt and Ellis (1987);
- physical and mental health: Brown et al. (2001), Ware et al. (1994);
- resident surveys: Delamere, (1997, 2001), Delamare et al. (2001); and
- tourism: Hung and Petrick (2010), Ryan and Glendon (1998), Tasci and Ko (2015).

- Scenarios: Bekkers (2010), Page et al. (2010).

- Sociometry: Oppenheim (2000: 254–5).

- Thinking: Edwards and Skinner (2009).

- Time use/budget surveys:
  - children – physical activity: Ridley et al. (2006);
  - leisure: Pentland et al. (1999), Szalai (1972), Zuzanek and Veal (1998);
  - tourism: Pearce (1988).

- Visual methods: Annear et al. (2009, 2014), Burns and Lester (2005), Garrod (2008), Rakic and Chambers (2012).

Multiple methods

- Community studies:
  - leisure-related: Wynne (1986, 1990, 1998);
  - sport-related: Partington and Totten (2012); and
  - tourism-related: Waldren (1996, 1997).

- Counting heads: Gartner and Hunt (1988); see Chapter 8.

- Mixed methods: see Chapter 2, Resources section.

- Triangulation: Blaikie (1991), Bryman and Bell (2003: 482–4); tourism: Hartmann (1988), Northcote and Macbeth (2005), Oppermann (2000).

Policy/management techniques

- Balanced scorecard: Weinstein and Bukovinsky (2009).

- Cost-benefit analysis: Veal (2017: Ch. 14).

- Demand forecasting: Veal (2017: Ch. 13).

- Discrete choice analysis/models: see Chapter 11.

- Evidence-based policy: Pawson (2006), Piggin et al. (2009), Silk et al. (2010).

- Head Counting: Watson and Yip (2011).

- Importance-performance analysis /SERVQUAL:
  - arts venues: Lin (2009), Williams (1998);
  - festivals: Baker and Draper (2013), Tkaczynski and Stokes (2010);
  - general: Martilla and James (1977), Parasuraman et al. (1988), Veal (2017: Ch. 15); and
  - tourism: critical review: Azzopardi and Nash (2013), Oh (2001).

- Key performance indicators: Veal (2017: Ch. 15); arts policy: Evans (2000).

- Logic Model: McLaughlin and Jordan (1999).

- Market segmentation: Funk (2002), Pitts et al. (1994), Salome and Van Bottenburg (2012).

References

Allen, L. R. (1982). The relationship between Murray's personality needs and leisure interests. *Journal of Leisure Research*, 14(1), 63–76.

Anderson, C. (2011). *The long tail: how endless choice is creating unlimited demand.* New York: Random House.

Annear, M. J., Gidlow, B., and Cushman, G. (2009). Neighbourhood deprivation and older adults' preferences for and perceptions of active leisure participation. *Annals of Leisure Research*, 12(2), 96–128.

Annear, M. J., Cushman, G., Gidlow, B., and Keeling, S. (2014). A place for visual research methods in the field of leisure studies? Evidence from two studies of older adults' active leisure. *Leisure Studies*, 33(5), 618–43.

Ap, J. and Crompton, J. L. (1998). Developing and testing a tourism impact scale. *Journal of Travel Research*, 37(2), 120–30.

Arensberg, C. M. (1954). The community-study method. *American Journal of Sociology*, 60(2), 109–24.

Azzopardi, E., and Nash, R. (2013). A critical evaluation of importance-performance analysis. *Tourism Management*, 35, 222–33.

Baker, K. L., and Draper, J. (2013) Importance–Performance analysis of the attributes of a cultural festival. *Journal of Convention and Event Tourism*, 14(2), 104–23.

Barnes, B. E., and Thomson, L. M. (1994). Power to the people (meter): audience measurement technology and media specialization. In J. S. Ettema and D. C. Whitney (Eds), *Audiencemaking: how the media create the audience* (pp. 75–94). Thousand Oaks, CA: Sage.

Batty, A. (1977). The action research background to the leisure experiments. In Department of the Environment, *Leisure and the quality of life: a report on four local experiments* (pp. 3–16). London: HMSO.

Beard, J. G., and Ragheb, M. (1980). Measuring leisure satisfaction. *Journal of Leisure Research*, 12(1), 20–33.

Bekkers, R. (2010). Who gives what when? A scenario study of intentions to give time and money. *Social Science Research*, 39(4), 369–81.

Bennett, T., Savage, M., Silva, E., Warde, A., Gayo-Cal, M., and Wright, D. (2009). *Culture, class, distinction*. London: Routledge.

Blaikie, N. (1991). A critique of the use of triangulation in social research. *Quality and Quantity*, 25(2), 115–36.

Bolger, N., Davis, A., and Rafael, E. (2003). Diary methods: capturing life as it is lived. *Annual Review of Psychology*, 54(4), 579–616.

Borman, K. M., LeCompte, M. D., and Goetz, J. P. (1986). Ethnographic and qualitative research design and why it doesn't work. *American Behavioral Scientist*, 30(1), 42–57.

Botterill, T. D. (1989). Humanistic tourism? Personal constructions of a tourist: Sam visits Japan. *Leisure Studies*, 8(3), 281–94.

Bourdieu, P. (1984). *Distinction: a social critique of the judgement of taste*. London: Routledge.

Boyd, D., and Crawford, K. (2012). Critical questions for big data: provocations for a cultural, technological, and scholarly phenomenon. *Information, Communication and Society*, 15(5), 662–79.

British Council (2010). *Mapping the Creative Industries: a Toolkit*. London: British Council.

Brown, P. R., Brown, W. J., and Powers, J. R. (2001). Time pressure, satisfaction with leisure and health among Australian women. *Annals of Leisure Research*, 4, 1–16.

Brown, W. J., Heesch, K., and Miller, Y. (2009). Life events and changing physical activity patterns in women at different life stages. *Annals of Behavioral Medicine*, 37(3), 294–305.

Bruner, G. C., and Hensel, P. J. (1992). *Marketing scales handbook: a compilation of multi-item measures*. Chicago, IL: American Marketing Association.

Bruner, G. C., James, K. E., and Hensel, P. J. (2001). *Marketing scales handbook: a compilation of multi-item measures*, Vol. 3. Chicago, IL: American Marketing Association.

Bryman, A., and Bell, E. (2003). Breaking down the quantitative/qualitative divide, and Combining quantitative and qualitative research. Chapters 21–2 of *Business research methods* (pp. 465–94). Oxford: Oxford University Press.

Burns, P., and Lester, J. (2005). Using visual evidence: the case of *Cannibal Tours*. In B. W. Ritchie, P. Burns and C. Palmer (Eds), *Tourism research methods: integrating theory with practice* (pp. 49–62). Wallingford, UK: CABI Publishing.

Buzan, T. (1994). *The Mind Map Book: How to Use Radiant Thinking to Maximise your Brain's Untapped Potential*. New York: Dutton.

CACI Ltd (2006). *ACORN user guide*. London: CACI Ltd., available at: www. caci.co.uk/products/product/acornfamily.

Canning, C., and Holmes, K. (2006). Community consultation in developing museum projects: a case study using the repertory grid technique. *Cultural Trends*, 15(4), 275–97.

Casanueva, C., Gallego, A., and Garcia-Sancez, M-R. (2016). Social network analysis in tourism. *Current Issues in Tourism*, 19(12), 1190–1209.

Claxton, J. D. (1994) Conjoint analysis in travel research: a manager's guide. In J. R. B. Ritchie and C. R. Goeldner (Eds), *Travel, tourism and hospitality research*, 2nd edn (pp. 513–52). New York: John Wiley.

Christensen, T. C., Barrett, L. F., Bliss-Moreau, E., Lebo, K., and Kaschub, C. (2003). A practical guide to experience-sampling procedures. *Journal of Happiness*, 4(1), 53–78.

Cole, S. (2005). Action ethnography: using participant observation. In B. W. Ritchie, P. Burns and C. Palmer (Eds), *Tourism research methods: integrating theory with practice* (pp. 63–72). Wallingford, UK: CABI Publishing.

Conner, T. S., Tennen, H., Fleeson, W., and Barrett, L.F. (2009). Experience sampling methods: a modern idiographic approach to personality research. *Social and Personality Psychology*, 3(3), 292–313.

Coshall, J. T. (2000). Measurement of tourists' images: the repertory grid approach. *Journal of Travel Research*, 39, 85–9.

Cosper, R., and Kinsley, B.L. (1984) An application of conjoint analysis to leisure research: cultural preferences in Canada. *Journal of Leisure Research*, 16(3), 224–33.

Crouch, G. I., and Louviere, J. J. (2001) A review of choice modelling research in tourism, hospitality and leisure. In J. A. Mazanec, G. I. Crouch, J. R. B. Ritchie and A. G. Woodside (Eds), *Consumer psychology of tourism, hospitality and leisure*, Vol. 2 (pp. 67–86). Wallingford, UK: CABI Publishing.

Crowe, M., & Sheppard, L. (2012). Mind mapping research methods. *Quality and Quantity*, 46(6), 1493–1504.

Csikszentmihalyi, M., and Larson, R. (1977). The ecology of adolescent activity and experience. *Journal of Youth and Adolescence*, 6(3), 281–94.

Dayton, T. (2005). *The living stage: a step-by-step guide to psychodrama, sociometry and experiential group therapy*. Deerfield Beach, FL: Health Communication Books.

Delamere, T. A. (1997). Development of scale items to measure the social impact of community festivals. *Journal of Applied Recreation Research*, 22(4), 293–315.

Delamere, T. A. (2001). Development of a scale to measure resident attitudes toward the social impacts of community festivals, Part 2: Verification of the scale. *Event Management*, 7(1), 25–38.

Delamere, T. A., Wankel, L. M., and Hinch, T. D. (2001). Development of scale to measure resident attitudes toward the social impacts of community festivals, Part 1: Item generation and purification of the measure. *Event Management*, 7(1), 11–24.

Denstadli, J. M. (2000). Analyzing air travel: a comparison of different survey methods and data collection procedures. *Journal of Travel Research*, 39(4), 4–10.

Department of the Environment (1977). *Leisure and the quality of life: a report on four local experiments*. London: HMSO.

Donohue, H. M., and Needham, R. D. (2009). Moving best practice forward: Delphi characteristics, advantages, potential problems, and solutions. *International Journal of Tourism Research*, 11(3), 415–37.

Driver, B. L., Tinsley, H. E. A., and Manfredo, M. J. (1991) The 'Paragraphs about Leisure' and 'Recreation Experience Preference' scales: results from two inventories designed to assess the breadth of perceived psychological benefits of leisure. In B. L. Driver, P. J. Brown and G. L. Peterson (Eds), *Benefits of leisure* (pp. 263–301). State College, PA: Venture.

Duffy, M. E. (1987). Methodological triangulation: a vehicle for merging qualitative and quantitative research methods. *IMAGE: Journal of Nursing Scholarship*, 19(1), 130–3.

Dupuis, S. (1999). Naked truths: towards a reflexive methodology in leisure research. *Leisure Sciences*, 21(1), 43–64.

Edwards, A., and Skinner, J. (2009). Reflection in sport management research. Chapter 7 of *Qualitative research in sport management* (pp. 151–65). Oxford, UK: Butterworth-Heinemann.

Ember, C. R., and Ember, M. (2009) *Cross-cultural research methods*. Lanham, MD: Altamira Press.

Evans, G. (2000). Measure for measure: evaluating performance and the arts organisation. *Studies in Cultures, Organisations and Societies*, 6(3), 243–66.

Evans, G., & Foord, J. (2008). Cultural mapping and sustainable communities: planning for the arts revisited. *Cultural Trends*, 17(2), 65–96.

Feixas, G., Marti, J., and Villegas, M. (1989): Personal construct assessment of sport teams. *International Journal of Personal Construct Psychology*, 2(1), 49–54.

Frechtling, D. C. (1996). *Practical tourism forecasting*. Oxford: Butterworth-Heinemann.

Fredline, L., Jago, L., and Deery, M. (2003). The development of a generic scale to measure the social impacts of events. *Event Management*, 8(1), 23–37.

Funk, D. (2002). Consumer-based marketing: the use of micro-segmentation strategies for understanding sport consumption. *International Journal of Sports Marketing and Sponsorship*, 4(3), 231–56.

Garrod, B. (2008). Exploring place perception: a photo-based analysis. *Annals of Tourism Research*, 35(2), 381–401.

Garrod, B., and Fyall, A. (2005). Revisiting Delphi: the Delphi technique in tourism research. In B. W. Ritchie, P. Burns and C. Palmer (Eds), *Tourism research methods: integrating theory with* practice (pp. 85–98). Wallingford, UK: CABI Publishing.

Gartner, W., and Hunt, J. D. (1988). A method to collect detailed tourist flow information. *Annals of Tourism Research*, 15(1), 159–72.

Gee, J. P. (2010). *An introduction to discourse analysis*. London: Routledge.

Getz, D. (1993). Impacts of tourism on residents' leisure: concepts and a longitudinal case study of Spey Valley, Scotland. *Journal of Tourism Studies*, 4(2), 33–44.

Glass, G. V., McGaw, B., and Smith, M. L. (1981). *Meta-analysis in social research*. Beverly Hills, CA: Sage.

Green, H., Hunter, C., and Moore, B. (1990). Application of the Delphi technique in tourism. *Annals of Tourism Research*, 17(2), 270–79.

Greenwood, D. J., and Levin, M. (2007). *Introduction to action research*. Thousand Oaks, CA: Sage.

Grix, J. (2010). Introducing 'hard' interpretivism and 'Q' methodology: notes from a project on 'county sport partnerships and governance', *Leisure Studies*, 29(4), 457–67.

Guintcheva, G., and Passebois, J. (2009). Exploring the place of museums in European leisure markets: an approach based on consumer values. *International Journal of Arts Management*, 11(2), 4–16.

Guy, B. S., Curtis, W. W., and Crotts, J.C. (1990). Environmental learning of first-time travelers. *Annals of Leisure Research*, 17(2), 419–31.

Hanley, N., Shaw, W. D., and Wright, R. E. (Eds) (2003). *The new economics of outdoor recreation*. Cheltenham, UK: Edward Elgar.

Hartmann, R. (1988). Combining field methods in tourism research. *Annals of Tourism Research*, 15(1), 88–105.

Heimtun, B. (2007). From principles to practices in feminist tourism research: a call for greater use if the survey method and the solicited diary. In I. Ateljevic, A. Pritchard and N. Morgan (Eds), *The critical turn in tourism studies: innovative research methodologies* (pp. 245–59). Oxford: Elsevier.

Hektner, J. M., Schmidt, J. A., and Csikszentmihayli, M. (Eds) (2006). *Experience sampling method: measuring the quality of everyday life*. Thousand Oaks, CA: Sage.

Henderson, K. A. (2006). *Dimensions of choice: a qualitative approach to recreation, parks and leisure research*, 2nd edn. State College, PA: Venture.

Hjorth-Andersen, C. (2007). Chris Anderson, 'The Long Tail: How Endless Choice is Creating Unlimited Demand': the new economics of culture and commerce. *Journal of Cultural Economics*, 31(3), 235–37.

Huang, C., and Confer, J. (2009) Applying the Tourism Opportunity Spectrum model in nature-based tourism management. *Leisure Management*, 14(4), 247–57.

Huh, C., and Vogt, C. A. (2008). Change in residents' attitudes toward tourism over time: a cohort analytical approach. *Journal of Travel Research*, 46(3), 446–55.

Hung, P., and Petrick, J. F. (2010). Developing a measurement scale for constraints to cruising. *Annals of Tourism Research*, 37(1), 206–28.

Hurst, F. (1994). En route surveys. In J. R. B. Ritchie and C. R. Goeldner (Eds), *Travel, tourism and hospitality research*, 2nd edn (pp. 453–72). New York: John Wiley.

Iso-Ahola, S. E., and Weissinger, E. (1990). Perception of boredom in leisure: conceptualisation, reliability and validity of the leisure boredom scale. *Journal of Leisure Research*, 22(1), 1–17.

Jaimangal-Jones, D. (2012). More than worlds: analyzing the media discourses surrounding dance music events. *Event Management*, 16(3), 305–18.

Jones, R. A. (1991). Enhancing marketing decisions using conjoint analysis: an application in public leisure services. *Society and Leisure*, 14(1), 69–84.

Kaplan, R. S., and Norton, D. P. (2007). Using the balanced scorecard as a strategic management system. *Harvard Business Review*, 84(7), 150–61.

Kasprzyk, D., Duncan, G., Kalton, G., and Singh, M. P. (1989). *Panel surveys*. New York: John Wiley & Sons.

Kellehear, A. (1993). *The unobtrusive researcher: a guide to methods*. Sydney: Allen and Unwin.

Kelly, G. A. (1955). *The psychology of personal constructs*. New York: Norton.

Kozinets, R. V. (1997). 'I want to believe'. A netnography of 'The X-Philes' subculture of consumption. *Advances in Consumer Research*, 24(1), 470–5.

Kozinets, R. V. (2009). *Netnography: doing ethnographic research Online*. London: Sage

Krenz, C., and Sax, G. (1986). What quantitative research is and why it doesn't work. *American Behavioral Scientist*, 30(1), 58–69.

Kyle, G., Absher, J., Norman, W., and Jodice, L. (2007). A modified involvement scale. *Leisure Studies*, 20(4), 399–427.

LaPage, W. F. (1994). Using panels for tourism and travel research. In J. R. B. Ritchie and C. R. Goeldner (Eds), *Travel, tourism and hospitality research*, 2nd edn (pp. 481–6). New York: John Wiley.

Le Roux, B., and Rouanet, H. (2010). *Multiple correspondence analysis*. Thousand Oaks, CA: Sage.

Levenson, H. (1974). Activism and powerful others: distinction within the concept of internal–external control. *Journal of Psychology and Aging*, 1(1), 117–26.

Lin, Y-N. (2009). Importance-performance analysis of the Taipei Fine Arts Museum's services. *Museum Management and Curatorship*, 24(2), 105–21.

Locke, T. (2004). *Critical discourse analysis*. London: Continuum.

Lundberg, G. A., Komarovsky, M., and McInerny, M. A. (1934). *Leisure: a suburban study*. New York: Columbia University Press.

Lupton, D. (2016). Foreword to special issue on digital leisure cultures: lively devices, lively data and lively leisure studies. *Leisure Studies*, 35(6), 709–11.

Mannell, R. C., and Kleiber, D. A. (1997). *A social psychology of leisure*. State College, PA: Venture.

Martilla, J. A., and James, J. C. (1977). Importance-performance analysis. *Journal of Marketing*, 41(1), 77–9.

Mayer-Schönberger, V., and Cukier, K. (2013). *Big data: a revolution that will transform how we live, work and think*. London: John Murray.

Mazanec, J. A., Crouch, G. I., Brent Ritchie, J. R., and Woodside, A. G. (Eds) (2001). *Consumer psychology of tourism, hospitality and leisure*, Vol. 2. Wallingford, UK: CABI Publishing.

McCutcheon, A. L. (1987). *Latent class analysis*. Newbury Park, CA: Sage.

McGuiggan, R. L. (2000). The Myers–Briggs Type Indicator and leisure attribute preference. In A. G. Woodside, G. I. Crouch, J. A. Mazanec, M. Oppermann and M. Y. Sakai (Eds), *Consumer psychology of tourism, hospitality and leisure* (pp. 245–67). Wallingford, UK: CABI Publishing.

McGuiggan, R. L. (2001). What determines our leisure preferences: demographics or personality? In J. A. Mazanec, G. I. Crouch, J. R. B. Ritchie and A. G. Woodside (Eds), *Consumer psychology of tourism, hospitality and leisure*, Vol. 2 (pp. 195–214). Wallingford, UK: CABI Publishing.

McKeown, B., and Thomas, D. (1988). *Q methodology*. Newbury Park, CA: Sage.

McLaughlin, J. A., and Jordan, G. B. (1999). Logic models: a tool for telling your program's performance story. *Evaluation and Program Planning*, 22(1), 65–72.

McNiff, J., and Whitehead, J. (2002). *Action research: principles and practice*. London: Routledge/Falmer.

Mehl, M. R., Pennebaker, J. W., Crow, D. M., Dabbs, J., and Price, J. H. (2001). The Electronically Activated Recorder (EAR): a device for sampling naturalistic daily activities and conversations. *Behavior Research Methods, Instruments, and Computers*, 33(4), 517–23.

Moeller, G. H., and Shafer, E. L. (1994). The Delphi technique: a tool for long-range tourism and travel planning. In J. R. B. Ritchie and C. R. Goeldner (Eds), *Travel, tourism and hospitality research*, 2nd edn (pp. 473–80). New York: John Wiley.

Neugarten, P. L., Havighurst, R. J., and Tobin, S. S. (1961). The measurement of life satisfaction. *Journal of Gerontology*, 16(1), 134–43.

Northcote, J., and Macbeth, J. (2005). Limitations of resident perception surveys for understanding tourism social impacts the need for triangulation. *Tourism Recreation Research*, 30(2), 43–54.

O'Brien, S., and Ford, R. (1988). Can we at last say goodbye to social class? An examination of the usefulness and stability of some alternative methods of measurement. *Journal of the Market Research Society*, 30(3), 289–332.

Oh, H. (2001). Revisiting importance–performance analysis. *Tourism Management*, 22(6), 617–27.

Oppenheim, A. N. (2000). *Questionnaire design, interviewing and attitude measurement: new edition*. London: Pinter.

Oppermann, M. (2000). Triangulation: a methodological discussion. *International Journal of Tourism Research*, 2(2), 141–46.

Page, S. J., Yeoman, I., Connell, J., and Greenwood, C. (2010). Scenario planning as a tool to understand uncertainty in tourism: the example of transport and tourism in Scotland in 2025. *Current Issues in Tourism*, 13(2), 99–137.

Palmer, I., and Dunford, R. (2002). Managing discursive tension: the co-existence of individualist and collaborative discourses in Flight Centre. *Journal of Management Studies*, 39(8), 1045–70.

Parasuraman, A., Zeithaml, V. A., and Berry, L. L. (1988). SERVQUAL: a multiple-item scale for measuring consumer perceptions of service quality. *Journal of Retailing*, 64(1), 12–37.

Partington, J., and Totten, M. (2012). Community sports projects and effective community empowerment: a case study in Rochdale. *Managing Leisure*, 17(1), 29–46.

Patriarche, G., Bilandzic, H., Jenson, J. L., and Jurisic, J. (Eds) (2014). *Audience research methodologies: between innovation and consolidation*. London: Routledge.

Pawson, R. (2006). *Evidence-based policy: a realist perspective*. London: Sage.

Pearce, D. (1988). Tourist time budgets. *Annals of Tourism Research*, 15(1), 106–21.

Pearce, P. L. (2005). *Tourist behaviour: themes and conceptual schemes*. Clevedon, UK: Channel View.

Pentland, W. E., Harvey, A. S., Powell Lawton, M., and McColl, M. A. (Eds) (1999). *Time use research in the social sciences*. New York: Kluwer/Plenum.

Perdue, R. R., and Botkin, M. R. (1988). Visitor survey versus conversion study. *Annals of Tourism Research*, 15(1), 76–87.

Phillips, D., and Phillips, J. (2013) Visualising types: the potential of correspondence analysis. In D. Byrne and C. G. Ragin (Eds), *The Sage handbook of case-based methods* (pp. 148–68). London: Sage.

Piggin, J., Jackson, S. J., and Lewis, M. (2009). Knowledge, power and politics: contesting 'evidence-based' national sport policy. *International Review for the Sociology of Sport*, 44, 87–101.

Pitts, B. G., Fielding, L., and Miller, L. (1994). Industry segmentation theory and the sport industry: Developing a sport industry segment model. *Sport Marketing Quarterly*, 3(1), 15–24.

Potter, R.B., and Coshall, J. (1988). Socio-psychological methods for tourism research. *Annals of Tourism Research*, 15(1), 63–75.

Rakic, T., and Chambers, D. (Eds) (2012). *An introduction to visual research methods in tourism*. London: Routledge.

Reason, P., and Bradbury, H. (Eds) (2001). *Handbook of action research: participative inquiry and practice*. London: Sage.

Reynolds, T. J., and Gutman, J. (1988). Laddering theory, method, analysis and interpretation. *Journal of Advertising Research*, 70(1), 11–15.

Richardson, L. (2005). Writing: a method of inquiry Part I; Qualitative writing. In N. K. Denzin and Y. S. Lincoln (Eds), *Handbook of qualitative research*, 2nd edn (pp. 959–67). Thousand Oaks, CA: Sage.

Ridley, K., Olds, T. S., and Hill, A. (2006). The multimedia activity recall for children and adolescents (MARCA): development and evaluation. *International Journal of Behavioral Nutrition and Physical Activity*, 3(10), 1–11.

Ritchie, B. W. (2005). Longitudinal research methods. In B. W. Ritchie, P. Burns and C. Palmer (Eds), *Tourism research methods: integrating theory with* practice (pp. 131–48). Wallingford, UK: CABI Publishing.

Rojek, C. (1989). Leisure and recreation theory. In E. L. Jackson and T. L. Burton (Eds), *Understanding leisure and recreation: mapping the past and charting the future* (pp. 69–88). State College, PA: Venture.

Rose, D. (Ed.) (2000). *Researching social and economic change: the uses of household panel studies*. London: Routledge.

Rowe, G., and Wright, G. (1999). The Delphi technique as a forecasting tool: issues and analysis. *International Journal of Forecasting*, 15, 353–75.

Rowntree, B. S., and Lavers, G. R. (1951). *English life and leisure: a social study*. London: Longman, Green & Co.

Ryan, C. (1995). *Researching tourist satisfaction: issues, concepts, problems*. London: Routledge.

Ryan, C., and Glendon, I. (1998). Application of leisure motivation scale to tourism. *Annals of Tourism Research*, 25(1), 169–84.

Saaka, A., Sidon, C., and Blake, B. F. (2004) *Laddering: a 'How to do it' Manual – with a Note of Caution*. Research Reports in Consumer Behavior: Methodology Series. Cleveland, OH: Cleveland State University. Available at: http://academic.csuohio.edu/cbresearch/papers/Good%20PDFs/Laddering_A%20How%20to%20do%20it%20manual.pdf.

Salome, L., and Van Bottenburg, M. (2012). Are they all daredevils? Introducing a participation typology for the consumption of lifestyle sports in different settings. *European Sport Management Quarterly*, 12(1), 19–42.

Schimmack, U., and Diener, E. (Eds) (2003). Experience sampling method in happiness research: special issue. *Journal of Happiness Studies*, 3(1).

Schneider, B., Ainbinder, A. M., and Csikszentmihalyi, M. (2004). Stress and working parents. In J. T. Haworth and A. J. Veal (Eds), *Work and leisure* (pp. 145–67). London: Routledge.

Scott, D., and U'Ren, R. (1962). *Leisure: a social enquiry into leisure activities and needs in an Australian housing estate*. Melbourne: F. W. Cheshire.

Scott, D., and Willits, F. K. (1989). Adolescent and adult leisure patterns: a 37-year follow-up study. *Leisure Sciences*, 11(4), 323–35.

Scott, D., and Willits, F. K. (1998). Adolescent and adult leisure patterns: a reassessment. *Journal of Leisure Research*, 30(3), 319–30.

Scott, N., Baggio, R., and Cooper, C. (2008) *Network analysis and tourism*. Clevedon, UK: Channel View.

Scott, N., and Smith, A. E. (2005). Use of automated content analysis techniques for event image assessment. *Tourism Recreation Research*, 30(2), 87–91.

Scott, O. K. M., Hill, B., and Zakus, D. H. (2012). When the home team is not featured: Comparison of two television network commentaries during broadcasts of the 2006 FIFA World Football Cup. *Sport Management Review*, 15, 21–32.

Semeonoff, B. (1976). *Projective techniques*. London: John Wiley & Sons.

Shih, D. (1986). VALS as a tool of tourism marketing research. *Journal of Travel Research*, 25(1), 2–11.

Shrestha, R. K., and Loomis, J. B. (2003). Meta-analytic benefit transfer of outdoor recreation economic values: testing out-of-sample convergent validity. *Environmental and Resource Economics*, 25(1), 79–100.

Sickler, J., and Fraser, J. (2009). Enjoyment in zoos. *Leisure Studies*, 28(3), 313–32.

Silk, M. L., Bush, A., and Andrews, D. L. (2010). Contingent intellectual amateurism, or, the problem with evidence-based research. *Journal of Sport and Social Issues*, 34, 105–28.

Smith, S. L. J. (1995). *Tourism analysis: a handbook*, 2nd edn. Harlow, UK: Longman.

Smyth, J. M., and Stone, A. A. (2003). Ecological momentary assessment research in behavioral medicine. *Journal of Happiness Studies*, 4(1), 35–52.

Snape, R. (2004). The Co-operative Holidays Association and the cultural formation of countryside leisure practice. *Leisure Studies*, 23(2), 143–58.

Spracklen, K. (2015). *Digital leisure, the internet and popular culture*. Basingstoke, UK: Palgrave Macmillan.

Stockdale, J. (1984). People's conceptions of leisure. In A. Tomlinson (Ed.), *Leisure: politics, planning and people* (pp. 86–115). Eastbourne, UK: Leisure Studies Association.

Stokowski, P. A. (1994). *Leisure in society: a network structural perspective*. London: Mansell.

Stokowski, P. A., and Lee, R. G. (1991). The influence of social network ties on recreation and leisure: an exploratory study. *Journal of Leisure Research*, 23(1), 95–113.

Storey, W. K. (2004). *Writing history: a guide for students*. New York: Oxford University Press.

Strategic Business Insights (2009). *The VALS survey*. Menlo Park, CA: Strategic Business Insights.

Sydney Morning Herald (2016). Readers panel, 28 February, p. 36.

Szalai, A. (Ed.) (1972). *The use of time: daily activities of urban and suburban populations in twelve countries*. The Hague: Mouton.

Tasci, A. D. A., and Ko, Y. J. (2015). Travel needs revisited. *Journal of Vacation Marketing*, doi: 10.1177/1356766715617499.

Tkaczynski, A., and Stokes, R. (2010) FESTPERF: a service quality measurement scale for festivals. *Event Management*, 14(1), 69–82.

Van Winkle, C. M., and Falk, J. H. (2015). Personal meaning mapping at festivals: a useful tool for a challenging context. *Event Management*, 19(2), 143–50.

Veal, A. J. (2017). *Leisure, sport and tourism: politics, policy and planning*, 4th edn. Wallingford, UK: CABI Publishing.

Von Bergner, N.M., and Lohman, M. (2013). Future challenges for global tourism: a Delphi survey. *Journal of Travel Research*, 53(4), 420–32.

Waldren, J. (1996). *Insiders and outsiders: paradise and reality in Mallorca*. Providence, RI: Berghahn.

Waldren, J. (1997). We are not tourists – we live here. In S. Abram, J. Waldren and D. V. L. Macleod (Eds), *Tourists and tourism: identifying with people and places* (pp. 51–70). Oxford: Berg.

Walmsley, D. J., and Jenkins, J. M. (1991). Mental maps, locus of control, and activity: a study of business tourists in Coffs Harbour. *Journal of Tourism Studies*, 2(2), 36–42.

Warde, A. and Tampubolon, G. (2002). Social capital, networks and leisure consumption. *Sociological Review*, 50(2), 155–80.

Ware, J. E., Kosinski, M., and Keller, S. D. (1994). *SF 36 physical and mental health summary scales: a user's manual*. Boston, MA: The Health Institute, New England Medical Centre.

Wasche, H. (2015). Interorganizational cooperation in sport tourism: a social network analysis. *Sport Management Review*, 18(4), 542–54.

Watson, R., and Yip, P. (2011). How many were there when it mattered? Estimating the sizes of crowds. *Significance*, 8(5), 104–7.

Weinstein, L., and Bukovinsky, D. (2009). Use of the Balanced Scorecard and performance metrics to achieve operational and strategic alignment in arts and culture not-for-profits. *International Journal of Arts Management*, 11(2), 42–55.

White, J. (2004). Gender, work and leisure. In J. T. Haworth and A. J. Veal (Eds), *Work and leisure* (pp. 67–84). London: Routledge.

Williams, C. (1998). Is the SERVQUAL model an appropriate management tool for measuring service delivery quality in the UK leisure industry? *Managing Leisure*, 3(2), 98–110.

Williams, R. C. (2003). *The historian's toolbox: a student's guide to the theory and craft of history*. Armonk, NY: M. E. Sharpe.

Willson, G., and McIntosh, A. (2010). Using photo-based interviews to reveal the significance of heritage buildings to cultural tourism experiences. In G. Richards and W. Munsters (Eds), *Cultural tourism research methods* (pp. 141–55). Wallingford, UK: CABI.

Witt, P., and Ellis, G. (1987). *The Leisure Diagnostic Battery: user's manual*. State College, PA: Venture.

Woodside, A. G., and Ronkainen, I. A. (1994). Improving advertising conversion studies. In J. R. B. Ritchie and C. R. Goeldner (Eds), *Travel, tourism and hospitality research*, 2nd edn (pp. 481–7). New York: John Wiley.

Woodside, A. G., Crouch, G. I., Mazanec, J. A., Oppermann, M., and Sakai, M. (Eds) (2000). *Consumer psychology of tourism, hospitality and leisure*. Wallingford, UK: CAB International.

Wynne, D. (1986). Living on 'The Heath'. *Leisure Studies*, 5(1), 109–16.

Wynne, D. (1990). Leisure, lifestyle and the construction of social position. *Leisure Studies*, 9(1), 21–34.

Wynne, D. (1998). *Leisure, lifestyle and the new middle class: a case study*. London: Routledge.

Young, C. H., Savola, K. L., and Phelps, E. (1991). *Inventory of longitudinal studies in the social sciences*. Newbury Park, CA: Sage.

Young, M. (1999). Cognitive maps of nature-based tourists. *Annals of Tourism Research*, 26(4), 817–39.

Zuzanek, J., and Veal, A. J. (Eds) (1998). Time pressure, stress, leisure participation and well-being. Special issue of *Loisir et Société/Society and Leisure*, 21(2).

6 Reviewing the literature

1. Introduction – an essential task

The aim of this chapter is to explain the importance, for any research project, of reviewing previous research and being aware of existing writing – the literature – on a topic. In addition, the chapter indicates general sources of information on leisure and tourism studies literature, sets out the mechanics of compiling bibliographies and recording bibliographical references and considers the *process* of reviewing the literature for research purposes.

Reviewing existing research or writing on a topic is a vital step in the research process. The field of leisure and tourism studies comprises relatively new areas of academic enquiry which are wide-ranging and multidisciplinary in nature. Research is not so plentiful in the field that we can afford to ignore research which has already been completed by others. As discussed briefly in Chapters 3 and 5, the literature can serve a number of functions, as indicated in Table 6.1.

The aim of academic research is to add to the body of human knowledge. In most societies, that body of knowledge is generally in written form – the literature. To presume to add to the body of knowledge, it is necessary to be familiar with what knowledge exists and to indicate precisely how the proposed or completed research relates to it. In research which is of a consultancy or policy nature, where the *primary* aim is not to add to knowledge but to use research to assist directly in the solution of policy, planning or management problems, a familiarity with existing knowledge in the area is still vital. Much time and valuable resources can be wasted in 're-inventing the wheel' to devise suitable methodologies to conduct a project, or in conducting projects with inadequate methodologies, when reference to existing work could provide information on tried-and-tested, and failed, approaches.

Identifying relevant literature is often a demanding task. It involves a careful search for information on relevant published and, if necessary, unpublished work; accessing copies of relevant items and reading them;

Table 6.1   The roles of the literature in research

- The entire basis of the research
- Source of ideas on topics for research
- Source of information on research already done by others
- Source of methodological or theoretical ideas
- Source of comparison between your research and that of others
- Source of information that is an integral or supportive part of the research – for example, statistical data on the study area population

making a list of useful items to form a *bibliography*; and assessing and summarising aspects which are salient for the research proposal or the research report in hand.

2. The value of bibliographies

This chapter focuses on reviewing the literature in relation to planned research projects, but the development of a bibliography can be a useful end in itself. It might be thought that modern electronic search methods have made the compilation and publication of bibliographies on specific topics obsolete, but this is not the case. While electronic databases are continually developing, they are still incomplete, especially with regard to:

● older published material;

● 'ephemeral' material, such as conference papers and reports and working papers not produced by mainstream publishers;

● chapters from edited collections of papers; and

● relevant content which is not mentioned in abstracts or keywords.

More importantly, electronic databases do not provide an *evaluation* of material: they rarely distinguish between a substantial research paper and a lightweight commentary with no original content. Furthermore, not all databases are full-text, so electronic systems will be able to identify items only on the basis of their titles or, in some cases, key words and abstracts. A database may not indicate, for example, whether a report on 'recreation activities' includes data on a specific activity, such as golf, or whether a report on 'holiday patterns' mentions a specific form of holiday, such as backpacking. A great deal of useful work can therefore still be done in compiling bibliographies on specific topics, thus helping to consolidate the 'state of the art' and saving other researchers a great deal of time and trouble in searching for material.

Examples of published bibliographies in the leisure and tourism area are listed in the Resources section at the end of the chapter, and considerable scope exists for the development of similar bibliographies on other topics.

3. Searching: sources of information

Where can the researcher look for information on existing published research on a topic? In this section a number of sources is examined, as listed in Table 6.2.

Table 6.2 Sources of information

---

1. Library catalogues
2. Specialist indexes and databases
3. The internet
4. Google Scholar
5. Published bibliographies
6. General leisure/tourism books
7. Reference lists
8. Beyond leisure and tourism

3.1 Library catalogues

Modern libraries have computerised catalogues which are accessible via terminals within the library and also from remote locations via the internet. These online catalogues include information on:

- the library's own physical holdings;

- online materials, including e-books, online versions of journals and database sites such as national governmental statistical offices; and

- in some cases, access to other university and public library catalogues.

The full-text versions of many of the online materials are, like lending rights, available only to registered library members, such as students or academic staff.

Searches can be made on the basis of the titles of publications or using key words assigned to them by the library. This can be very helpful as a starting point in establishing a bibliography. But it is *only* a starting point, particularly for the researcher with a specialist interest.

If search words such as *leisure, tourism, sport* or *the arts* are used, the typical computerised catalogue will produce an enormous number of references, running to the thousands, and far too many to be manageable. But if more specialised terms, such as *female golfers* or *Asian backpackers* are entered, the catalogue will produce few references, sometimes none at all. Whether a large or small number of references is produced, a proportion will be of a 'popular' nature, concerned with, for example, how to play golf, biographies of golfers or backpacker guides to budget accommodation in Europe. Such material may be of interest to some researchers but will be of little use if the researcher is interested in such aspects as levels of participation in golf, the socio-economic characteristics of golfers or trends in the numbers of backpackers.

Neither can a library catalogue indicate, for instance, whether a general report on *sport* or *recreation* or *tourism* includes any reference to a specific leisure activity or a particular type of tourism. Of course, the catalogue will not identify publications which, while they deal with one topic, provide a suitable methodology for studying other topics. Such material can only be identified by actually reading – or at least perusing – original texts.

Catalogues of a library's physical holdings do not contain references of individual chapters in books which are collections of readings, or individual papers in collections of conference papers.

Integrated within library online catalogues is access to on-line versions of journals provided by specialist organisations, such as *EBSCO, Informaworld* and *Ingenta*, and journal publishers, such as *Taylor & Francis* or *Sage*.

3.2 Indexes and databases

Specialist indexes and databases are online resources generally accessed via subscribing libraries. Examples in the leisure and tourism area are as follows:

- The most extensive and well-established index and electronic database of leisure and tourism publications is *Leisure Tourism Database*, published by the UK organisation CABI, available online to subscribing libraries. It contains over 100,000 abstracts sourced from over 6000 periodicals and other publications, including details of books and book chapters. The basic format is publication details and abstracts, but some items are available in full text.

- *SPORTDiscus* is the most comprehensive reference and full-text source for some 500 sport and sports medicine journals, dating back to 1985.

- General online journal databases include *ISI Web of Knowledge* (formerly Social Sciences Citation Index), *CrossRef* and *Scopus*. These cover thousands of social science journals, cross-referenced by author and subject. In addition, items of literature referred to by authors in papers are themselves listed and cross-referenced, so that further writings of any cited author can be followed up. Not all leisure and tourism journals are included in all these databases, but coverage is slowly increasing, year by year.

The advantage of using this type of database is that they ensure a level of reliability by dealing mainly with peer-reviewed material as discussed later in this chapter.

3.3 Searching the internet

Direct searching on the internet using a search engine such as Google has rapidly become second nature to computer users. Such searches are clearly effective when searching for organisational websites but are a rather blunt tool for searching for published material compared with the specialist sources discussed earlier. Extreme caution should be exercised in using internet sources. Some key specialist websites are listed in the Resources section.

3.4 Google Scholar

The Google Scholar website stores bibliographical information related to authors. It does not contain a complete bibliography for the individuals listed, but just those items which have been referenced – or 'cited' – by other authors. It therefore has a similar structure to the above-mentioned online databases, but is not restricted to journal articles.

An example of the information included is that for well-known leisure and tourism author John L. Crompton. A long list of Crompton's publications is presented, arranged in order of number of citations. The first is his article in *Annals of Tourism Research* on 'Motivations for pleasure vacations' which had, in July 2017, 3233 citations. Clicking on the article title provides publication details of the article, and clicking on the citation number brings up a listing of the 3233 publications in which the article has been cited. This is an effective way of identifying other papers on a topic – in this case, vacation motivation. The database can also be searched using key words or individual publication titles.

3.5 Published bibliographies

Reference has already been made to the value of bibliographies on particular topics. Libraries usually have a separate section for bibliographies, and it may be worth browsing in that section, especially when the topic of interest is inter-disciplinary. While many bibliographies have been published in hard-copy form over the years (see the Resources section for examples), the trend recently has been to publish these resources online, typically on university/research centre websites.

3.6 General leisure and tourism publications

The researcher should be aware of publications which contain information on specific activities or aspects of leisure or tourism. For example, Chapter 7 discusses national leisure participation and tourism surveys which contain information on as many as a hundred leisure activities, on tourism flows of different types and on such socio-economic characteristics of participants such as age and income. They are therefore a source of basic statistical information on many topics of interest.

General introductory books on leisure or tourism may have something to say on the topic of interest or may provide leads to other sources of information via the index and bibliography. In addition, in specialist reference books, such as encyclopaedias and handbooks typically include bibliographic references. Examples are listed in Table 6.3.

Searching through such texts, using the contents pages or the index, can be a somewhat 'hit and miss' process but can often be rewarded with leads which could not be gained in any other way. Similarly, scanning through the contents

Table 6.3 Specialist reference books

Encylopaedias

Encyclopedia of Leisure and Outdoor Recreation	Jenkins and Pigram (2003)
Encyclopedia of Tourism	Weaver (2000)
Encyclopedia of Tourism	Jafari (2000)
Encyclopedia of Exercise, Sport and Health	Brukner et al. (2003)
Encyclopedia of Women and Sports	Sherrow (1996)
Encyclopedia of World Sport: from Ancient Times to the Present	Levinson and Christensen (1996)
St. James Encyclopedia of Popular Culture	Pendergast and Pendergast (1999)

Handbooks

A Handbook of Leisure Studies	Rojek, Shaw and Veal (2006)
Routledge Handbook of Leisure Studies	Blackshaw (2013)
Routledge Handbook of Events	Page and Connell (2012)
Sage Handbook of Qualitative Research	Denzin and Lincoln (2005)

pages of key journals, such as *Leisure Studies* or *Annals of Tourism Research*, may produce relevant material which would not be identified by conventional searches.

3.7 Reference lists

Most importantly, the lists of references in the books and articles identified in initial searches will often lead to useful material. Researchers interested in a particular topic should be constantly on the alert for sources of material on that topic in anything they are reading. Sometimes key items are encountered when they are least expected. The researcher should become a 'sniffer dog' obsessed with 'sniffing out' anything of relevance to the topic of interest. In a real-world research situation, this process of identifying as much literature as possible can take months or even years. While a major effort should be made to identify material at the beginning of any research project, it will also be an ongoing exercise, throughout the course of the project.

3.8 Beyond leisure and tourism

Lateral thinking is also an aid to the literature search task. The most useful information is not always found in the most obvious places. Some commentators have remarked on how many researchers fail to look beyond immediate *leisure* or *tourism* material. Leisure and tourism are interdisciplinary areas of study, not disciplines in their own right – they do not have a set of research methods and theories uniquely their own. Much is to be gained from looking outside the immediate area of leisure or tourism studies. For example, if the research involves measurement of *attitudes*, then certain *psychological* literature will be of interest. If the research involves the study of leisure or tourism *markets*, then general *marketing* journals may be useful sources. And, if the research involves the leisure activities of the *elderly*, then *gerontology* journals should be consulted.

3.9 Unpublished research

Where possible, attempts should be made to explore not just published research – the *literature* – but also unpublished and ongoing research. This process is very much hit and miss. Knowing what research is ongoing or knowing of completed but unpublished research usually depends on having access to informal networks, although some organisations produce registers of ongoing research projects. Once a topic of interest has been identified, it is often clear, from the literature, where the major centres for such research are located and to discover, from direct approaches or from websites, annual reports or newsletters, what research is currently being conducted at those centres. This process can be particularly important if the topic is a 'fashionable' one, with a lot of research/writing taking place. However, in such cases the communication networks are usually very active, which eases the process. In this respect papers from conferences and seminars are usually better sources of information on current research than books and journals, since the latter have long gestation periods, so that the research reported in them is generally based on work carried out two or more years prior to publication.

4. Obtaining access to material

If material is not available in a particular library, it can often be obtained through the *inter-library loan* service. This is a system through which loans of books and reports can be made between one library and another. In the case of journal articles, the service usually involves the provision of a digital copy. In theory, any item published in a particular country should be available through this system since it is connected with national copyright libraries – such as the British Lending Library in Boston Spa or the National Library of Australia – where copies of all published items must be lodged by law. Practices vary from library to library, but in academic libraries the service is often available to postgraduate students and to undergraduate students through a member of academic staff.

For researchers working in metropolitan areas, the other obvious source of material is specialist libraries, particularly of government agencies. For example, in London, Sport England and the English Tourist Board libraries are major resources for leisure and tourism researchers. In metropolitan areas and some other regions, there is also often a cooperative arrangement between municipal reference libraries such that particular libraries adopt particular specialist areas – so it can be useful to discover which municipal library service specialises in leisure and/or tourism.

5. Compiling and maintaining a bibliography

What should be done with the material once it has been identified? First, a record should be made of everything which appears to be of relevance. The researcher is strongly advised to start a file listing every item of literature used. This can be of use not only for the current research project but also for future reference – a personal bibliography can be built up over the years. Such record-keeping can be done using cards but is best done on a computer, using a word-processor or a database program, which can also store keywords. This has the attraction that when there is a need to compile a bibliography on another topic in future, a start can be made from your personal bibliography by getting the computer to copy designated items into a new file. In this way, the researcher only ever needs to type out a reference once! Specialist packages, such as *EndNote* and *Pro-Cite*, store reference material in a standard format, but will automatically compile bibliographies in appropriate formats to meet the requirements of different report styles and the specifications of different academic journals.

Case study 6.1 provides a brief guide to the use of EndNote.

Case study 6.1   Using EndNote

The EndNote reference manager software package organises the referencing process for writers of documents and also facilitates online searches for reference material. Documents might include articles, essays, theses or books/book chapters. At the heart of the system is the *Library* created by the writer. This is a list of references contained in a computer file within EndNote. A writer may create a number of Libraries for various purposes, but in this short presentation a single Library is assumed. Once a Library is established, the writer can draw on it for any number of documents with which he or she may be involved, as indicated in Figure 6.1

▶

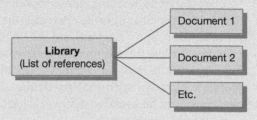

Figure 6.1   EndNote system

Note: in what follows, the Windows operating system and the Microsoft Office Word word-processor is assumed. When EndNote Version 7 is installed on your computer, a tab 'EndNote X7' appears in the top ribbon/toolbar.

To start an EndNote session, click on the *EndNote X7* tab, then on the *Go to EndNote* tab to bring up the EndNote screen.

To create a library:

- On the top ribbon, click on *File* and then *New*.
- Decide where the Library file is to be located – e.g. in one of the 'Libraries' locations indicated, or your own selection on the C: drive or the cloud, etc.
- Give the Library a name – e.g. 'Library_01' – it is automatically given the suffix '.enl'.
- Click on *Save*: the empty Library file will be saved in the specified location and a panel appears with 'Library_01.enl' in the top left hand corner.
- In future sessions, to bring up the Library_01 panel: click on *File*, then *Open Library*.
- The panel has a toolbar with two drop-down menus and 17 icons, the names of which appear if the cursor is moved across them.
- In the first drop-down menu, select your preferred *Output Style* – this is the format in which references are presented in in bibliographies. For example, the American Psychological Association (APA) style is used in a number of leisure studies journals (this is further discussed later in the chapter, under referencing).
- Each library also has an accompanying folder by the same name located in the same location that stores all associated documents and attachments to the individual references within the library. If you wish to send the library file to another person, then the accompanying folder must also be sent as part of the package; otherwise, the Library file will not work.

To add references to the Library:

This can be done in four ways, as outlined below. Each reference added will be given a unique reference number by the software.

1. **Existing reference list**

   There is no straightforward procedure for automatically loading an existing reference list or bibliography into the EndNote system, for example from a Word file. This is because each component of a reference (author, date, title, etc.) needs to be 'tagged' in a way that the EndNote package will recognise. The only solution is to copy and paste, or retype, each component into the Endnote system separately, using process 2 below. (Some suggestions for overcoming this problem can be found on the internet.)

2. **An independent exercise**
   This could apply when the researcher comes across a reference of interest which might be useful for a current or possible project, or is copying from an existing reference list, as discussed above. With the Library_01 panel open:
   - Click on the fifth, *New Reference* icon. The *New Reference* panel appears with a list of reference items (author, title, etc.) appears
   - In the drop-down menu, select the *Reference Type*: e.g., *Journal Article* or *Book*, etc.
   - Type in the reference information in the spaces indicated.
   - Close the *New Reference* panel and the reference appears in the Library_01 panel.
   - A reference record now appears in the Library.

3. **Journal website**
   With Endnote and a Library open on your computer, use your web browser to locate an article on a journal website (obviously, this option is not possible for books, reports, etc.). Click on 'download citation' and select the RIS format option (which is EndNote compatible): the reference details will be added to your Library and will appear in the Library_01 panel. If you are searching in a multiple journal database (e.g. Scopus), multiple articles can be downloaded after eliminating non-relevant items. Within certain journal databases, the PDF file can also be downloaded and automatically attached to each record.

4. **From an online search process.**
   - With Library_01 open,: click on the second icon, *Online Search Mode*.
   - Under *Online Search*, select, for example, *Library of Congress*, and conduct your search: the results are displayed in the panel.
   - Highlight one or more references which you wish to add to your Library, right-click, select *Copy References To* and select a Library.
   - Other databases can be added, in addition to those already provided: notes on this are provided on the book's website.

5. **Google Scholar**
   For users of Google Scholar, under *Settings* there is an option to specify a *Bibliography Manager* with Endnote as one of the options. Once activated, an extra menu item appears under each searched reference, *Import into Endnote*. As with all reference records, double-check that the information imported is accurate

▶

To cite a reference in the text of a paper.

- Place the cursor at the point in your Word document where a reference is required. Click the *EndNote X7* tab.

- Click on the *Insert Citation* icon. The *'EndNote X7 Find and Insert My References'* box appears. In the *Find* box, enter an author name – e.g. Smith. All 'Smith' references in the Library are then listed. Click on the one required. Then click on the insert button. This returns you to your Word document.

- The highlighted reference appears in the text – e.g., (Smith, 2010) – and a copy of the full reference is inserted at the end of the document.

EndNote output styles: EndNote users have access to literally thousands of different types of reference styles that journals and books may require. Many university libraries also contain custom reference output styles for individual universities. EndNote users may also create their own output styles if they cannot find one to suit the requirements of particular journals. These features will save much document preparation time. For further information, see http://endnote.com/downloads/styles.

It takes only seconds to copy out the *full details* of a reference when it is first identified. It is advisable to have a notebook/computer always at hand for such purposes. If this practice is adopted, hours of time and effort can be saved in not having to chase up details of references at a later date. Not only should the details be recorded accurately, as set out below, but also a note should be made about the availability of the material – for example, the library catalogue reference, or the fact that the item is *not* in the library, or that a photocopy or digital copy has been taken.

6. Reviewing the literature

Reviewing the literature on a topic can be one of the most rewarding – and one of the most frustrating – of research tasks. It is a task where a range of skills and qualities needs to be employed – including patience, persistence, insight and lateral thinking.

6.1 Types of literature review

The review of the literature can play a number of roles in a research project, as outlined earlier, and this leads to a number of approaches to conducting a review, as listed in Table 6.4.

Table 6.4 Types of literature review

- Inclusive bibliography
- Systematic review/meta-analysis
- Exploratory
- Instrumental
- Content analysis/hermeneutics

Inclusive bibliography

The *inclusive* approach to reviewing the literature seeks to identify everything that has been written on a particular topic. The compilation of such a bibliography may be a significant achievement in itself, independent of any research project with which it may be connected. It becomes a resource to be drawn on in the future by others. Such a bibliography does not amount to a 'review' of the literature if there is no accompanying commentary, although classification of entries into categories (e.g. books, articles, government reports) or time-periods can be seen as the beginning of such a process. In some cases bibliographies merely list the reference details; in other cases they include abstracts of the contents – in which case they are referred to as *annotated* bibliographies. Examples of inclusive bibliographies are listed in the Resources section.

Systematic reviews/meta-analysis

In previous editions of this text, this type of literature review was referred to as *inclusive/evaluative*, but a term from the health/medical sector, the *systematic review*, has increasingly been adopted in the social sciences, so is now used here. The most well-known study of this type in recent years has been the series of reports by the United Nations Intergovernmental Panel on Climate Change, which evaluated the findings of thousands of scientific publications to draw conclusion regarding climate change and its causes (UNIPCC, 2014). An example of an open-ended, academically motivated review related to the field of leisure is shown in Case study 6.2. It seeks to 'make sense' of the concept of lifestyle, drawing from a wide range of literature. Other examples are listed in the Resources section.

The systematic review is related particularly to the public policy idea of 'evidence-based policy' (Pawson, 2006a). This is based on the idea that any policy designed to deal with a particular problem should be firmly based on all the available research-based evidence on the nature of the problem and/or on effective solutions – 'what works'.

The methodology for systematic reviews, draws on practice in the medical/health policy sector, which is typically concerned with reviewing evidence on the effect of treatments and only with research which conforms to the

Case study 6.2   **The lifestyle and leisure project: systematic review**

This case study is an example of how a project can be built around the activity of reviewing the literature. The project arose from a course I taught to students of the Polytechnic of North London in the 1980s. In searching for relevant material on lifestyle in the literature, I was struck by the fact that, even though it had a serious sociological pedigree, there was a tendency for writers to use the term without defining it and often without discussing it in any detail at all. It was often used as sort of advertising 'buzzword'. Having completed the course, I drew attention to this state of affairs in a conference presentation entitled: 'Lifestyle: concept or buzzword?' (Veal, 1986). Later, I published an article which included a partial review of the substantive literature on lifestyle but also developed the proposition that it could play a role in leisure theory, in place of the then-emerging emphasis on a Marxist view of class (Veal, 1989a). This attracted strident critiques from neo-Marxist/cultural studies (Critcher, 1989) and feminist (Scraton and Talbot, 1989) standpoints, from which I attempted to defend myself (Veal, 1989b).

Despite this negative response, I continued to accumulate reference material on lifestyle. Systematic reviews today typically rely on formal scans of databases to identify publications, but in this case the process was less formal and relied on a 'snowball' process, with one source leading to another. Having identified some 400 references which made substantial use of the term, it seemed appropriate to compile a systematic review for submission to a journal (Veal, 1993). The challenge was to provide some framework for grouping and discussing the diverse range of material. The first task was to identify the histories and associated meanings of lifestyle as used in different disciplines and study areas. These included:

- *Weberian* – early sociological formulation by Max Weber, related to status groups.
- *Sub-cultural* – ways of life associated with different sub-cultural groups (e.g. youth sub-cultures).
- *Psychological* – outlook on life established in the first few years of life.
- *Market research/psychographics* – quantitative analysis of values, attitudes and socio-economic characteristics.
- *Spatial research* – ways of life associated with a type of residential location (e.g. suburban, rural).
- *Leisure styles* – statistical groupings of types of leisure.
- *Socialist lifestyles* – ways of life approved of and planned for by East European communist regimes of the 1960s and 1970s.

A second exercise was to identify a range of dimensions which might be involved in seeking a generic definition for the concept of lifestyle. These were:

- *Activities/behaviour* – e.g. leisure, tourism, consumption, work and home activity patterns.

- *Values and attitudes* – political, moral, aesthetic.
- *Individuals versus groups* – whether a 'lifestyle' is only a group phenomenon.
- *Group interaction* – whether group interaction among individuals adopting particular lifestyles is required to develop and reinforce a lifestyle.
- *Coherence* – whether a lifestyle requires some sort of internal aesthetic or moral coherence.
- *Recognisability* – whether a lifestyle must be recognised by others to exist.
- *Choice* – whether adoption of a *lifestyle* involves choice on the part of an individual, compared with a 'way of life' which might be imposed by circumstances.

Twenty years later, an opportunity arose to update the work in a book chapter (Veal, 2013). The amount of published material available had increased enormously, so that a systematic review would have required more time and resources than were available. An essay format was therefore adopted. It was gratifying to note that, while the concept of lifestyle had not become a strong presence in the field of leisure studies, it had received considerable recognition in the field of sociology, through the work of such figures as Pierre Bourdieu, Anthony Giddens and Ulrick Beck, and that cultural studies concerned with youth sub-cultures, which had a considerable influence on leisure studies in its early days, was abandoning the use of class in favour of the concept of lifestyle.

requirements of the scientific, experimental research model. As discussed in Chapter 11, although much research in the leisure/tourism sector can be seen as experimental in nature, it rarely fully meets all the requirements of this model. Application of the systematic review in sectors such as sport and the arts has therefore become controversial. For example, when Priest et al. (2008) reviewed the literature on policy interventions to boost physical activity in the community, despite locating some 1500 studies on the topic, they found *none* which conformed fully to strict scientific experimental principles. The area of sport has been exposed to this sort of investigation because of the link between sport programmes and the health sciences. However, Long and Hylton (2014) have argued, on the basis of their experience with a review of the literature on sport participation and race (Long et al., 2009), that the approach is not appropriate in the sport sector because of the narrow view of what constitutes 'evidence', in particular its exclusion of qualitative research. Even the leading advocate of evidence-based policy, Ray Pawson (2006b), has argued that research which may be imperfect in the strict scientific sense may, if critically evaluated, provide useful insights.

An even more formalised quantitative approach to analysing the literature is known as *meta-analysis* and involves a systematic, typically quantitative, appraisal of the findings of a number of projects focused on the same topic. The technique is particularly suitable for the sort of research where findings are directly comparable from one study to another – for example, when the key research findings are expressed in terms of correlation or regression coefficients (see Chapter 17). In this approach, the reported findings of the research themselves become the subject of analysis and the number of reported projects can become so large that it is necessary to *sample* from them in the same way that individuals are sampled for empirical research. Examples are listed in the Resources section and, since this can be seen as a form of secondary data analysis, an example is summarised in Case study 14.6 in Chapter 14. While meta-analysis is typically a quantitative methodology, it can also be adapted for qualitative research (Weed, 2005).

Another term used in this general area of systematic reviews of the literature/evidence is 'consensus study', which is typically undertaken by a panel of researchers appointed by a governmental or other organisation. The IPCC exercise referred to earlier is an example. Examples in the leisure sector include the World Leisure Organisation study on leisure and the quality of life (Jackson, 2006) and the International Olympic Committee's review of young people's health and fitness and sport (Mountjoy et al., 2011).

A common variation on the inclusive/evaluative type of review involves a quantitative analysis of temporal trends in the content and/or authorship of the literature in a particular field or in a particular journal. For example, Riley and Love (2000) present an analysis of the contents of four tourism journals since their inception to show the changing proportion of articles using qualitative methodology through the 1970s and 1990s. Henderson (2006: 5) analysed the methodological emphasis in articles in four leisure studies journals over the period 1982–2006.

Exploratory review

The *exploratory* approach is more focused and seeks to discover existing research which might throw light on a specific research question or issue. This is very much the classic literature review which is the norm for academic research and best fits the model of the research process outlined in Chapter 3. Comprehensiveness is not as important as the focus on the particular question or issue. The skill in conducting such a review lies in keeping the question or issue in sight, while 'interrogating' the literature for ideas and insights which may help shape the research. The reviewer needs to be open to useful new ideas but must not be side-tracked into areas which stray too far from the question or issue of interest.

Instrumental review

In the *instrumental* approach the literature is used as a source of suitable ideas on how a particular research project might be tackled. The criterion for selection of literature is not necessarily to present a picture of the state of knowledge on the topic, but merely to identify a useful methodology for the project in hand. A common version of this is the use of pre-existing scales, as discussed in Chapter 5. Numerous researchers investigating leisure experiences have identified the Serious Leisure Perspective (Elkington and Stebbins, 2014) as a framework to be adopted because it provides a helpful list of 'distinguishing qualities' to guide empirical work. Where research is more management orientated, a model such as SERVQUAL, which examines service users' expectations of service quality with their views on the quality of service received (see Appendix 3.1, section 4).

Content analysis and hermeneutics

Content analysis and *hermeneutics* are techniques which involve detailed textual analysis of the contents of a certain body of literature or other documentary source as *texts*. The text becomes a focus of research in its own right rather than merely a report of research. The texts might be, for example, novels, politicians' speeches or the contents of advertising. Content analysis tends to be quantitative, involving, for example, counting the number of occurrences of certain phrases. Hermeneutics tends to be qualitative in nature, the term being borrowed from the traditional approach to analysis and interpretation of religious texts. The essence of this approach is discussed in Chapter 9 in relation to the analysis of in-depth interview transcripts.

6.2 Reading critically and creatively

Reviewing the literature for *research* purposes involves reading the literature in a certain way. It involves being concerned as much with the methodological aspects of the research (which are not always well reported) as the substantive content. That is, it involves being concerned with *how* the conclusions are arrived at as well as with the conclusions themselves. It involves being critical – questioning rather than accepting what is being read. The task is as much to ascertain what is *not* known as it is to determine what *is* known. This is different from reading for other purposes, such as some essay-writing. In the latter instance, a particular substantive critical issue may be explored, but the research basis or overall scope of the literature being discussed may not be an issue.

As material is being read, a number of questions might be asked, as set out in Table 6.5. Some questions relate to individual research items and some to the body of literature as a whole.

It can be helpful to be conscious of the appropriate way in which the contents of an item of literature should be reported when reference is made to the author. A number of styles of reporting are used, including:

- Smith believes . . . thinks . . . is of the opinion that . . .
- Smith argues . . .
- Smith establishes . . .

Table 6.5   Questions to ask when reviewing the literature

---

a. Individual items
- What is the (empirical) basis of this research?
- How does the research relate to other research writings on the topic?
- What theoretical framework is being used?
- What geographical area does the research refer to?
- What social group(s) does the research refer to?
- When was the research carried out, and is it likely still to be empirically valid?

b. In relation to the literature as a whole
- What is the *range* of research that has been conducted?
- What *methods* have generally been used and what methods have been neglected?
- What, in summary, does the existing research tell us?
- What, in summary, does the existing research *not* tell us?
- What contradictions are there in the literature – either recognised or unrecognised by the authors concerned?
- What are the *deficiencies* in the existing research, in substantive or methodological terms?

- Smith observes . . .
- Smith speculates . . .
- Smith puts forward the possibility that . . .
- Smith concludes . . .

An author's opinion or beliefs may be important if the author is someone who deals professionally in opinions and beliefs, such as a politician or cleric, but we generally expect more than just statements of belief from academic literature. An academic may be influenced by particular ideological or religious beliefs. For example, a well-known theorist in the field of leisure, Josef Pieper, author of *Leisure, the Basis of Culture*, was a Catholic priest, and this is not irrelevant to his work. However, if his work had been merely a statement of faith, it would not have been as influential as it has been in the development of leisure theory.

A review of the literature should convey accurately the basis of the material presented, whether it be opinion, the result of argument or presentation of empirical evidence, informal observation or speculation. The type of literature being summarised is therefore important: newspaper and popular and professional magazine articles are not subject to the same checks and balances as academic journal articles; and reports emanating from leisure or tourism organisations or from politically motivated organisations cannot always be relied on to tell 'the truth, the whole truth and nothing but the truth'. Of course, such material may appear in a literature review, but its status and the way it is reported and interpreted should be treated with caution and subtlety.

Care should be taken when referring to textbooks. Textbooks, such as this text, may contain some original contributions from the author but will mostly contain summaries of the state of knowledge in a field, with some material attributed to specific sources and some not. Generally, in a research report, particularly a thesis, original scholarly sources rather than textbooks should be referred to where possible (see also 'Second-hand references' later in this chapter).

As regards the substantive content of the literature, a major challenge for a reviewer is to find some framework to classify and analyse it. In the case of an inclusive literature review, literature might be classified chronologically, by geographical origin or by discipline. For other types of review, themes or issues are likely to be more important. Reviewing the literature in this way can be similar to the development of a conceptual framework for a research project, as discussed in Chapter 3. Some sort of diagrammatic, concept map, approach, as indicated in Figure 6.2, may be helpful. Such a diagram might be devised before starting a review or may be developed, inductively, as the review progresses.

6.3 Summarising

A review of the literature should draw *conclusions* and *implications for the proposed research programme*. It is advisable to complete a review by presenting a *summary* which addresses the second set of questions in Figure 6.1. This summary should lead logically to the research project in hand. It should make clear to the reader just how the proposed research relates to the existing body of literature – whether it is seeking to:

● add to the body of knowledge in a unique way;

● fill a gap in knowledge;

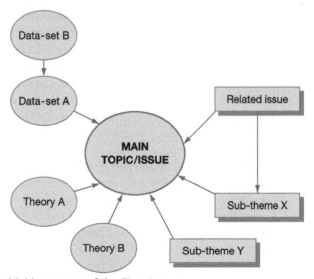

Figure 6.2 Making sense of the literature

- update existing knowledge;

- correct or contradict some aspect of existing knowledge; or

- simply use the literature as a source of ideas or comparison.

When a large amount of literature with similar format is being reviewed, it may be helpful to summarise it in a tabular quasi-meta-analytical form, using headings such as: geographical area covered, sample size, independent variables used, year of survey.

7. Referencing the literature

7.1 The purpose of referencing

What is the purpose of referencing? First, referencing is evidence of the writer's scholarship: it indicates that the particular research report is related to the existing body of knowledge. This is not only of importance to teachers marking student assignments or theses; it is part and parcel of the development of knowledge. Second, references enable the reader of the research report to check sources – either to verify the writer's interpretation of previous research or to follow up areas of interest.

7.2 Recording references

A number of standard or conventional formats, or styles, exist for recording references to the literature. The conventions have been established by leading academic organisations and publishers. Guides are produced by organisations such as the American Psychological Association (2010) and the Australian Government Publishing Service (see DCITA, 2002), to which the reader is referred for more detail. Individual journals publish their required reference format on their websites. The formats presented here follow the APA system quite closely. The important point in a publication is to use a consistent format throughout. If using a system such as EndNote, as discussed earlier, the software offers a range of formats and can convert a set of references to a different format as required.

In what follows, the word *text* refers to the main body of the research report or article. The general format recommended for recording references is as shown in Table 6.6.

In some systems the date is put at the end, but when using the *author/date* or *Harvard* system, as discussed later in this chapter, the date should follow the author name as indicated.

Note that the part of the reference which is in *italic* is the title which would be found in a library catalogue. Thus, what is found in the catalogue is the

Table 6.6 Standard/generic reference formats

- A book or report:

  Author(s), Initials (Year) *Title of book or report in Italic*. Place of publication: Publisher.

- An article from a periodical (journal/magazine/newspaper):

  Author(s), Initials (Year) Title of article. *Title of Periodical in Italic*, Vol. number (Issue number), Page numbers.

name of the periodical, not the title of the article, so the *title of the periodical* is in italic. In the case of a chapter from a book, the title of the book is found in the catalogue, not the title of the chapter, so the *title of the book* is in italic.

Note that the *publisher* of a book is not the same as the *printer* of the book. For example, for this book the *publisher* is Pearson Education, but the *printer* is Jiwabaru (see page iv). References do not need to refer to the printer. Note that it is *not* necessary to refer to the publisher in the case of periodicals.

Some examples of reference formats are set out in Table 6.7 to illustrate the principles.

Table 6.7 Examples of references

1. A book	Veal, A. J. (1987). *Leisure and the future*. London: Allen & Unwin.
2. An edited book	Rojek, C., Shaw, S., and Veal, A. J. (Eds) (2006). *Handbook of leisure studies*. London: Palgrave.
3. A chapter from an edited book	Veal, A. J. (2016). Policy and planning frameworks. In G. Walker, D. Scott and M. Stodolska (Eds), *Leisure matters* (pp. 287–94). State College, PA: Venture
4. A published conference report	Allen, J., Harris, R, Jago, L. K., and Veal, A. J. (Eds) (2000). *Events beyond 2000: conference proceedings Sydney, July 2000*. Sydney: Australian Centre for Event Management, University of Technology Sydney.
5. A published conference paper	Getz, D. (2000). Developing a research agenda for the event management field. In J. Allen et al.* (Eds), *Events beyond 2000: conference proceedings Sydney, July 2000* (pp. 9–20). Sydney: Australian Centre for Event Management, University of Technology Sydney.
6. A government agency authored and published document	Sport England (2012). *Sport England strategy, 2012–17*. London: Sport England.
7. A journal article	Ravenscroft, N. (1993). Public leisure provision and the good citizen. *Leisure Studies*, 12(1), 33–44.

(continued)

Table 6.7 *(continued)*

8. A newspaper article with named author	Hornery, A. (1996). Market researchers facing major hurdles. *Sydney Morning Herald*, 11 April, p. 26.
9. A newspaper item without a named author	*Sydney Morning Herald* (1996). Our green future, 7 June, p. 12.
10. An internet source	Priest, N., Armstrong, R., Doyle, J., and Waters, E. (2008). Interventions implemented through sporting organisations for increasing participation in sport. *Cochrane Database of Systematic Reviews*, 3, no pagination. Available at: www.cochrane.org (accessed 10 October 2016).

(* et al. means 'and others' and can be used in second and subsequent references to a publication, but the first time, all authors/editors should be listed)

Internet references are becoming increasingly common. One of the problems with this medium is that some sources disappear or their website address (URL) changes over time, so that it is difficult for the reader to follow them up. For individual publications, it is often advisable to give the index or 'list of publications' address rather than the often long and complex address of the individual publication. The general principle to be followed is that an internet reference should include all the details which would normally apply to hard-copy items, *plus* the website URL *and* the date accessed. The place of publication is not always clear from the website but can generally be found with a little effort. If accessing a journal article via the internet, it is not necessary to give the website address unless the journal is *only* published electronically. Published style guides are now available for referencing in relation to this evolving medium, for example, *The Columbia Guide to Online Style* (Walker and Taylor, 2006).

Some guidelines suggest that newspaper articles should be referenced with the title of the article rather than, as here, with the author or the name of the newspaper. The important point to note is that, once a style is adopted, it should be consistent throughout the report.

8. Referencing and referencing systems

There are two commonly used referencing systems: the 'author/date' system, sometimes referred to as the 'Harvard' system, and the 'footnote' or 'endnote' system. These two systems are discussed in turn here.

8.1 The author/date or Harvard system

Basic features

In the author/date, or Harvard, system, references to an item of literature are made in the text by using the author's name and the year of the publication; at the end of the paper, report or chapter, references are listed in alphabetical order. Thus, a sentence in a report might be:

> Research on women and leisure in the 1970s and 1980s included work in Britain by Deem (1986), in Canada by Bella (1989), in the United States by Bialeschki and Henderson (1986), and in Australia by Anderson (1975).

Note that authors' initials are not used in these references (unless there are two authors with the same surname). At the end of the report a list of references is provided, arranged in alphabetical order, as follows.

References

Anderson, R. (1975). *Leisure: an inappropriate concept for women*? Canberra: AGPS.

Bella, L. (1989) Women and leisure: beyond androcentrism. In E. L. Jackson and T. L. Burton (Eds). *Understanding leisure and* recreation (pp. 151–80), State College, PA: Venture.

Bialeschki, M. D., and Henderson, K. (1986). Leisure in the common world of women. *Leisure Studies*, 5(3), 299–308.

Deem, R. (1986). *All work and no play? The sociology of women's leisure*. Milton Keynes: Open University Press.

Text style variation

The style of presentation can be varied; for instance, the above statement could be made drawing less explicit attention to specific authors:

> Interest in research on women and leisure was widespread in the 1970s and 1980s in the English speaking world, as work from authors in Britain, Canada, the United States and Australia indicates (Bella, 1989; Bialeschki and Henderson, 1986; Deem, 1986; Anderson, 1975).

Specifics and quotations

When referring to *specific points* from an item of literature, rather than making a general reference to the whole item as above, page references should be given to the specific point of interest. This is particularly important when referring to a specific point from a substantial publication, like a book, for example:

> Aitchison (2003: 135–58) makes the link between gender issues and leisure management practices.

When *quoting* directly from a source, page references should always be given:

> Iso-Ahola makes the point that: 'To survive as an academic field, scholars must supply evidence that their methods of investigation are valid and reliable rather than "soft"' (1980: 49).

A longer quotation would be indented in the page and handled like this:

> Iso-Ahola argues the case for scientific research in the leisure area and states:
>> To survive as an academic field, scholars must supply evidence to the effect that their methods of investigation are valid and reliable rather than 'soft'. This becomes increasingly important in obtaining grants from sources inside and outside academic institutions (Iso-Ahola, 1980: 49).

Advantages and disadvantages

The author/date system is an 'academic' style. Its disadvantage is therefore that referencing is very 'up-front', even obtrusive, in the text. It is not an appropriate style for some practically orientated reports, particularly where the readership is not academic. Large numbers of references using this style tend to 'clutter up' the text and make it difficult to read. The system also has the disadvantage that it does not incorporate footnotes (at the foot of the page) or endnotes (at the end of the chapter). However, one view is that footnotes and endnotes are undesirable anyway – that if something is worth saying, it is worth saying in the text. If notes and asides are nevertheless considered necessary, it is possible to establish a footnote system for this purpose in addition to using the author/date system for references to the literature only. This of course becomes somewhat complex. If footnotes or endnotes are considered necessary, then it is probably best to use the footnote style for everything, as discussed in the next sub-section.

The advantages of the author/date system are that it saves the effort of keeping track of footnote or endnote numbers; it indicates the date of publication to the reader; the details of any one item of literature have to be written out only once; and it results in a tidy, alphabetical list of references at the end of the document.

8.2 Footnote or endnote system

Basic features

The *footnote* style involves the use of numbered references in the text and a list of corresponding numbered references at the foot of the page, at the end of each chapter or at the end of the report or book. The term footnote originates from the time when the notes were invariably printed at the foot of each page – and this can be seen in older books. However, printing footnotes at the bottom of the page came to be viewed as too complex to organise and too expensive to set up for printing, so it was generally abandoned in favour of providing a list of notes at the end of each chapter or at the end of the book. Consequently, *endnotes* are now more common. Ironically, the advent of word-processing has meant that the placing of footnotes at the bottom of the page can now be done automatically by computer. Most word-processing packages offer this feature, automatically making space for the appropriate number of footnotes on each page and keeping track of their numbering and so on.

Publishers have, however, generally adhered to the practice of placing the notes all together at the end of the chapter or book.

The actual number reference in the text can be given in brackets (1) or as a superscript: [1]. Using the footnote system, the paragraph given earlier appears as follows:

> Research on women and leisure in the 1970s and 1980s included Deem's[1] work in Britain, Bella's[2] work in Canada, Bialeschki and Henderson's[3] work in the United States and Anderson's[4] work in Australia.

The list of notes at the end of the report appear in the numerical order in which they appear in the text:

> *Notes*
> 1 Deem, R. (1986). *All work and no play? The sociology of women's leisure.* Milton Keynes: Open University Press.
> 2 Bella, L. (1989). Women and leisure: beyond androcentrism. In E. L. Jackson and T. L. Burton (Eds) *Understanding leisure and recreation.* State College, PA.: Venture, 151–80.
> 3 Bialeschki, M. D., and Henderson, K. (1986). Leisure in the common world of women. *Leisure Studies*, 5(3), 299–308.
> 4 Anderson, R. (1975) *Leisure: an inappropriate concept for women?* Canberra: AGPS.

This format is less obtrusive in the text than the author/date system. In fact, it can be made even less obtrusive by using only one footnote, as follows:

> Research on women and leisure in the 1970s and 1980s included work by research-ers in Britain, Canada, the United States and Australia.[1]

At the end of the report the reference list then appears as follows:

> *Notes*
> 1 In Britain: Deem, R. (1986). All *work and no play? The sociology of women's leisure.* Milton Keynes: Open University Press.
>   In Canada: Bella, L. (1989). Women and leisure: beyond androcentrism. In E. L. Jackson and T. L. Burton (Eds) *Understanding leisure and recreation.* State College, PA.: Venture, 151–80.
>   In the USA: Bialeschki, M. D., and Henderson, K. (1986). Leisure in the common world of women. *Leisure Studies*, 5(3), 299–308.
>   In Australia: Anderson, R. (1975). *Leisure: an inappropriate concept for women?* Canberra: AGPS.

Multiple references

It should never be necessary to write a reference out in full more than once in a document. Additional references to a work already cited can be made using *op. cit.* or references back to previous footnotes. For example, the above paragraph of text might be followed by:

Deem pioneered the study of women and leisure in Britain.[2]

The footnote would then say:

2 Deem, *op. cit.*   *or*   2 See footnote 1.

Specifics, quotations

Page references for specific references or quotations are given in the footnote rather than the text. So the Iso-Ahola quotation given earlier would look like this:

Iso-Ahola makes the point that: 'To survive as an academic field, scholars must supply evidence to the effect that their methods of investigation are valid and reliable rather than "soft"'.[4]

The footnote would then say:

4 Iso-Ahola, S. E. (1980). Tools of social psychological inquiry. Chapter 3 of *The social psychology of leisure and recreation*. Dubuque: Wm. C. Brown, p. 49.

Further quotations from the same work might have footnotes as follows:

5 Iso-Ahola, *op. cit.*, p. 167.

Advantages and disadvantages of the footnote/endnote system

One of the advantages of the footnote system is that it is less obtrusive than the author/date system and it can accommodate authors' notes in addition to references to the literature. A disadvantage of the system is that it does not result in a tidy, alphabetical list of references. This diminishes the convenience of the report as a source of literature references for the reader. Some writers therefore resort to producing a bibliography in addition to the list of references. This results in extra work, since it means that references have to be included a second time (but see the 'Comparing two systems' sub-section). Keeping track of footnotes or endnotes and their numbering is much less of a disadvantage than it used to be, since the word-processing program now takes care of it.

8.3 Comparing two systems

The features, advantages and disadvantages of the two systems, author/date and footnote/endnote, are summarised in Table 6.8.

Table 6.8   Reference systems: features, advantages, disadvantages

Feature	Harvard/author-date	Footnore/endnote
Reference in text	Author (date)	Number, e.g.:[1]
Reference format	Author (date) *Title*. Publishing details.	1. Author *Title*. Publishing details, date.
Reference list format	Alphabetical list at end of report	Numbered list at: • foot of pages, or • end of chapters, or • end of report
Advantages	• alphabetical bibliography • easy to use • date of publication conveyed in text	• unobtrusive in text • can add other notes/comments
Disadvantages	• obtrusive in text • can't add notes	• no alphabetical bibliography

One way of combining the advantages of both systems is for the list of notes in a footnote/endnote system to consist of author/date references and then to provide an alphabetical list of references at the end of the report. So the list of footnotes for the above paragraph would then appear as follows:

Notes
1 Deem (1986).
2 Bella (1989).
3 Bialeschki and Henderson (1986).
4 Anderson (1975).

An alphabetical bibliography would then follow which would be the same as for the author/date system. This approach is particularly useful when making several references to the same document.

9. Referencing issues

9.1 Second-hand references

Occasionally you make a reference to an item which you yourself have not read directly, but which is referred to in another document which you have read. This can be called a *second-hand* reference. It is misleading, somewhat unethical and risky to give a full reference to the original if you have not read it directly yourself. The reference should be given to the second-hand source, *not* to the original. For example:

> Kerlinger characterises research as 'systematic, controlled, empirical, and critical investigation of hypothetical propositions about the presumed relations among natural phenomena' (quoted in Iso-Ahola, 1980: 48).

In this instance, the writer has not read Kerlinger in the original but is relying on Iso-Ahola's quotation from Kerlinger. The Kerlinger item is not listed in the references; only the Iso-Ahola reference is listed. It is ethical to treat the second-hand reference this way, and it is also safe, since any inaccuracy in the quotation then rests with the second-hand source.

In academic research reports – journal articles and theses – second-hand references should be avoided and every effort made to access and refer to the original source.

9.2 Excessive/ambivalent referencing

A certain amount of judgement must be used when a large number of references is being made to a single source. It becomes very tiresome when repeated reference is made to the same source on every other line of a report! One way to avoid this is to be very 'up-front' about the fact that a large section of your literature review is based on a single source. For example, if you are summarising MacCannell's work on tourism, rather than have large numbers of formal references to MacCannell cluttering up the text, it may be preferable to have a separate section of the report and announce it as follows:

> *The work of MacCannell*
> This section of the review summarises MacCannell's (1976) seminal work, *The Tourist: A New Theory of the Leisure Class.* . . .

Subsequently, formal references need only be given when using specific quotations.

Some forms of referencing can be misleading, or at least ambivalent, about who is saying what. An example is the following statement by Bloyce and Smith (2010: 165): 'the Sydney Olympic Park has been described by some as a 'white elephant' (Cashman, 2006: 153)'. This gives the impression that it is Cashman's view that is being reported, whereas he is referring to views expressed in the local media.

9.3 Latin abbreviations

A number of Latin abbreviations is used in referencing and are generally presented in italic, but some publishers have dropped this practice.

et al.   If there are more than two authors of a work, the first author's name and 'et al.' may be used in text references, but all authors should be listed in the bibliography: 'et al.' stands for the Latin *et alia*, meaning 'and the others'.

op. cit.   stands for the Latin *opere citato*, meaning 'in the work cited'.

ibid.   In the footnote system, if reference is made to the same work in consecutive footnotes, the abbreviation ibid. is sometimes used, short for *ibidem*, meaning 'the same'.

Summary

This chapter provides an overview of the process of reviewing the literature, as a research tool in its own right and as an essential element of any research project. It is noted that a literature review can have a number of purposes and can take a number of forms, ranging from being the entire basis of a research project to being the source of ideas and methods for conducting a research project. The mechanics of searching for relevant literature is examined, including library catalogues, published bibliographies and indexes and electronic sources. The process of reviewing the literature is examined, addressing the sorts of questions which should be asked when conducting such a review for research purposes. Finally, the chapter reviews the process of referencing the literature, examining the characteristics and advantages and disadvantages of the author/date or Harvard system and the footnote or endnote system.

Test questions

1. What are the potential uses of the literature review in research?

2. Name three different sources of bibliographical information and their advantages and limitations.

3. What is the difference between conducting a literature review for the purpose of writing an essay compared with providing the context for a research project?

4. What are the advantages and disadvantages of the author/date referencing system compared with the footnote/endnote system?

5. What is a 'second-hand' reference?

Exercises

1. Compile an inclusive bibliography on a topic of your choice, using the sources outlined in this chapter.

2. Choose a research topic and, within a specified time-period:
   a. investigate the literature using a library computerised catalogue and any other electronic database available to you;
   b. explore the literature via literary sources, such as reference lists and indexes in general textbooks, journal contents and lists of references in articles; and
   c. compare the nature and extent of the bibliography arising from the two sources.

Resources

Websites

- CABI Leisure Tourism site: www.cabi.org/leisuretourism/.
- Campbell Collaboration (systematic reviews in the social policy area): www.campbellcollaboration.org.
- Cochrane network (systematic reviews in the health/medical area): www.cochrane.org.
- SPORTDiscus: www.ebscohost.com/academic/sportdiscus-with-full-text.
- World Tourism Organisation: http://publications.unwto.org/.
- YouTube video on conducting a literature review: see Jameson (2013).

Examples of bibliographies

- Disability and tourism: Darcy (1998).
- Olympic Games: Veal (2012).
- Sociology of leisure, early example: Meyersohn (1958).
- Tourism generally: Goeldner (1994).

Literature reviews

- Exotic dance: Wahab et al. (2011).
- Lifestyle: Veal (1993).

- Museum visitor experiences: Kirchberg and Trondle (2012).

- Volunteer tourism: Wearing and McGehee (2013).

Systematic reviews

- Conduct: Boland et al. (2014).

- Examples:
  - alcohol: trading hour limitation impacts: Wilkinson et al. (2016);
  - arts participation: McCarthy et al. (2001);
  - events: research methods: Crowther et al. (2015); segmentation: Tkaczynski and Rundle-Thiele (2011);
  - gardening and older adults: Wang and MacMillan (2013); and
  - importance-performance analysis and tourism: Azzopardi and Nash (2013), Oh (2001).
  - park use – health-related: Evenson et al. (2016), Maller et al. (2002);
  - quality of life: Uysal et al. (2016).

- Sport/physical activity:
  - event legacy: Thompson et al. (2013);
  - Olympic Games impact on sport participation: Weed et al. (2009);
  - physical activity and the built environment: Zapata-Diomedi and Veerman (2016); and
  - race: Long et al. (2009), Long and Hylton (2014).
  - social media: Filo et al. (2015).

- Tourism:
  - host perceptions of tourism: Sharpley (2014).
  - technologies for tracking tourists: Shoval and Ahas (2016).

Journal content analysis

- Event tourism: Kim et al. (2013).

- Leisure journals: Henderson (2006: 5).

Meta-analysis

- Contingent valuation (willingness-to-pay) and the arts: Noonan (2003).

- General: Cooper et al. (2009), Mulrow (1994), Shelby and Vaske (2008).

- Leisure motivation scales: Manfredo et al. (1996).

- Outdoor recreation willingness-to-pay and economic values/benefit transfer: Shrestha and Loomis (2001).

- For qualitative research: Weed (2005).

- Response rates in web/internet surveys: Cook, Heath and Thompson (2000).

- Sport tourism research: Weed (2009).

- Youth sport programmes: Lindsey and Bacon (2015).

Style manuals

- American Psychological Association (APA) (2010) and www.apastyle.org; AGPS style manual: DCITA (2002).

- Electronic style manuals: APA guidelines at: www.apastyle.org/apa-style-help.aspx; Columbia guide: Walker and Taylor (2006).

Guide

- EndNote: Edhlund (2015)

References

American Psychological Association (APA) (2010). *Publication manual of the American Psychological Association,* 6th edn. Washington, DC: APA.

Azzopardi, E., and Nash, R. (2013). A critical evaluation of importance-performance analysis. *Tourism Management,* 35, 222–33.

Blackshaw, T. (Ed.) (2013). *Routledge handbook of leisure studies.* London: Routledge.

Bloyce, D., and Smith, A. (2010). *Sport policy and development.* London: Routledge.

Boland, A., Cherry, G.M., and Dickson, R. (Eds) (2014). *Doing a systematic review: a student's guide.* London: Sage.

Brukner, P., Khan, K., and Kron, J. (Eds) (2003). *Encyclopedia of exercise, sport and health.* Crows Nest, NSW: Allen & Unwin.

Cashman, R. (2006). *The bitter-sweet awakening: the legacy of the Sydney 2000 Olympic Games.* Sydney: Walla Walla Press.

Cook, C., Heath, F., and Thompson, T. L. (2000). Meta-analysis of response rates in web- or internet-based surveys. *Educational and Psychological Measurement,* 60, 821–36.

Cooper, H., Hedges, L. V., and Valentine, J. C. (Eds) (2009). *Handbook of research synthesis and meta-analysis,* 6th edn. New York: Russell Sage Foundation.

Critcher, C. (1989) A communication in response to: 'Leisure, lifestyle and status: a pluralist framework for analysis'. *Leisure Studies,* 8(2), 159–61.

Crowther, P., Bostock, J., and Perry, J. (2015). Review of established methods in event research. *Event Management,* 19(1), 93–107.

Darcy, S. (1998) *People with a disability and tourism: A bibliography*. Available at: www.researchgate.net/publication/228899578_People_with_a_Disability_and_Tourism_Bibliography.

DCITA (Department of Information Technology, Communications and the Arts) (2002). *Style manual for authors, editors and printers*, 6th edn. Milton, Qld: John Wiley & Sons.

Denzin, N., and Lincoln, Y. (Eds) (2005). *Sage handbook of qualitative research*. Thousand Oaks, CA: Sage.

Edhlund, B. M. (2015) *EndNote essentials*. Stallarholmen, Sweden: Form & Kunskab.

Elkington, S., and Stebbins, R. A. (2014). *The serious leisure perspective: an introduction*. London: Routledge.

Evenson, K. R., Jones, S. A., Holliday, K. M., Cohen, D. A., and McKenzie, T. L. (2016). Park characteristics, use, and physical activity: A review of studies using SOPARC (System for Observing Play and Recreation in Communities). *Preventive Medicine*, 86, 153–66.

Filo, K., Lock, D., and Karg, A. (2015). Sport and social media research: a review. *Sport Management Review*, 18(2), 166–81.

Goeldner, C. R. (1994). Travel and tourism information sources. In J. R. B. Ritchie and C. R. Goeldner (Eds), *Travel, tourism and hospitality research*, 2nd edn (pp. 81–90). New York: John Wiley.

Henderson, K. A. (2006). *Dimensions of choice: a qualitative approach to recreation, parks and leisure research, second edition*. State College, PA: Venture.

Jackson, E. L. (Ed.) (2006). *Leisure and the quality of life: impacts on social, economic and cultural development: Hangzhou consensus*. Hangzhou, China: Zhejiang University Press/World Leisure Organisation.

Jafari, J. (Ed.) (2000). *Encyclopedia of tourism*. London: Routledge.

Jameson, S. (2013). YouTube video on 'how to do a literature review': overview. *Journal of Hospitality, Leisure, Sport and Tourism Education*, 33, 137–40.

Jenkins, J., and Pigram, J. (Eds) (2003). *Encyclopedia of leisure and outdoor recreation*. London: Routledge.

Kim, J., Boo, S., and Kim, Y. (2013). Patterns and trends in event tourism study topics over 30 years. *International Journal of Event and Festival Management*, 4(1), 66–83.

Kirchberg, V., and Trondle, M. (2012). Experiencing exhibitions: a review of studies on visitor experiences in museums. *Curator*, 55(4), 435–52.

Levinson, D., and Christensen, K. (Eds) (1996). *Encyclopedia of world sport: from ancient times to the present*. Santa Barbara, CA: ABC-CLIO.

Lindsey, I., and Bacon, D. (2015). In pursuit of evidence-based policy and practice: a realist synthesis-inspired examination of youth sport and physical activity initiatives in England (2002–2010). *International Journal of Sport Policy and Politics*, doi: 10.1080/19406940.2015.1063528.

Long, J., and Hylton, K. (2014). Reviewing research evidence and the case of participation in sport and physical recreation by black and minority ethnic communities. *Leisure Studies*, 33(4), 379–99.

Long, J., Hylton, K., Spracklen, K., Ratna, A., and Bailey, S. (2009). *Systematic review of the literature on black and minority ethnic communities in sport and physical recreation*. London: Sport England.

Maller, C., Townsend, M., Brown, P., and St. Leger, L. (2002). *Healthy parks healthy people: the benefits of contact with nature in a park context: a review of current literature*. Report to Parks Victoria and International Park Strategic Partners Group, Melbourne: Faculty of Health and Behavioural Sciences, Deakin University. Available at: www.parkweb.vic.gov.au/resources/mhphp/pv1.pdf.

Manfredo, M. J., Driver, B. L., and Tarrant, A. (1996). Measuring leisure motivation: a meta-analysis of the recreation experience preference scales. *Journal of Leisure Research*, 28(3), 188–213.

McCarthy, K. F., Ondaatje, E. H., and Zakarus, L. (2001). *Guide to the literature on participation in the arts*. Santa Monica, CA: RAND.

Meyersohn, R. (1958). A comprehensive bibliography on leisure. In E. Larrabee and R. Meyersohn (Eds), *Mass leisure* (pp. 389–420). Glencoe, IL: Free Press.

Mountjoy, M., Anderson, L. B., Armstrong, N., and 21 others (2011). International Olympic Committee consensus statement on the health and fitness of young people through physical activity and sport. *British Journal of Sports Medicine*, 45, 839–48.

Mulrow, C. D. (1994). Rationale for systematic reviews. *British Medical Journal*, 309, 597–9.

Noonan, D. S. (2003). Contingent valuation and cultural resources: a meta-analytic review of the literature. *Journal of Cultural Economics*, 27(3/4), 159–70.

Oh, H. (2001). Revisiting importance–performance analysis. *Tourism Management*, 22(6), 617–27.

Page, S. J., and Connell, J. (Eds) (2012). *The Routledge handbook of events*. London: Routledge.

Pawson, R. (2006a). *Evidence-based policy: a realist perspective*. London: Sage.

Pawson, R. (2006b). Digging for nuggets: how 'bad' research can yield 'good' evidence. *International Journal of Social Research Methodology*, 9(2), 127–42.

Pendergast, T., and Pendergast, S. (Eds) (1999). *St. James encyclopedia of popular culture*. Detroit, MI: St. James Press.

Priest, N., Armstrong, R., Doyle, J., and Waters, E. (2008). Interventions implemented through sporting organisations for increasing participation in sport.

Cochrane Database of Systematic Reviews, 3, no pagination. Available at: www.cochrane.org.

Riley, R. W., and Love, L. L. (2000). The state of qualitative tourism research. *Annals of Tourism Research*, 27(1), 164–87.

Rojek, C., Shaw, S., and Veal, A. J. (Eds) (2006). *Handbook of leisure studies*. London: Palgrave.

Scraton, S., and Talbot, M. (1989). A response to 'Leisure, lifestyle and status: a pluralist framework for analysis'. *Leisure Studies*, 8(2), 155–8.

Sharpley, R. (2014). Host perceptions of tourism: a review of the research. *Tourism Management*, 42, 37–49.

Shelby, L. B., and Vaske, J. J. (2008). Understanding meta-analysis: a review of the methodological literature. *Leisure Sciences*, 30(2), 96–110.

Sherrow, V. (Ed.) (1996). *Encyclopedia of women and sports*. Santa Barbara, CA: ABC-CLIO.

Shoval, N., and Ahas, R. (2016). The use of tracking technologies in tourism research: the first decade. *Tourism Geographies*, doi: 10.1080/14616688.2016.1214977.

Shrestha, R. K., and Loomis, J. B. (2001). Testing a meta-analysis model for benefit transfer in international outdoor recreation. *Ecological Economics*, 39(1), 67–83.

Thompson, A., Schlenker, K., and Schulenkorf, N. (2013). Conceptualizing sport event legacy. *Event Management*, 17(2), 111–12.

Tkaczynski, A., and Rundle-Thiele, S. R. (2011). Event segmentation: a review and research agenda. *Tourism Management*, 32, 426–34.

United Nations Intergovernmental Panel on Climate Change (UNIPCC) (2014). *Climate change 2014: synthesis report*. Geneva: UNIPCC. Available at: www.ipcc.ch.

Uysal, M., Sirgy, M.J, Woo, E., and Kim, H. (2016). Quality of life (QOL) and well-being research in tourism. *Tourism Management*, 53, 244–61.

Veal, A. J. (1986). *Lifestyle: concept or buzzword?* Presentation to the International Sociological Association World Congress, Delhi, India, August.

Veal, A. J. (1989a). Leisure, status and lifestyle – a pluralist framework for analysis. *Leisure Studies*, 8(2), 141–53.

Veal, A. J. (1989b). Lifestyle, leisure and pluralism – a response. *Leisure Studies*, 8(3), 213–18.

Veal, A. J. (1993). The concept of lifestyle: a review. *Leisure Studies*, 12(4), 233–52.

Veal, A. J. (2000). *Lifestyle and leisure: a bibliography and review*. Available at: www.leisuresource.net.

Veal, A. J. (2009). *The Olympic Games: a bibliography.* School of Leisure and Tourism Studies, University of Technology, Sydney. Available at: www.uts.edu.au/sites/default/files/olympic_bib_.pdf.

Veal, A.J. (2012). *The Olympic Games: A bibliography.* Australian Centre for Olympic Studies, University of Technology Sydney. Available at: www.uts.edu.au/sites/default/files/olympic_bib_.pdf.

Veal, A. J. (2013). Lifestyle and leisure theory. In T. Blackshaw (Ed.), *Routledge handbook of leisure studies* (pp. 266–79). London: Routledge.

Wahab, S., Baker, L. M., Smith, J. M., Cooper, K., and Lerum, K. (2011). Exotic dance research: a review of the literature from 1970 to 2008. *Sexuality and Culture*, 15(1), 56–79.

Walker, J. R., and Taylor, T. (2006). *The Columbia guide to online style,* 2nd edn. New York: Columbia University Press.

Wang, D., and MacMillan, T. (2013). The benefits of gardening for older adults: a systematic review of the literature. *Activities, Adaptation and Aging,* 37(2), 153–81.

Wearing, S., and McGehee, N.G. (2013). Volunteer tourism: a review. *Tourism Management*, 38, 120–30.

Weaver, D. (Ed.) (2000). *Encyclopedia of ecotourism.* Wallingford, UK: CABI Publishing.

Weed, M. (2005). 'Meta interpretation': a method for the interpretive synthesis of qualitative research. *Forum: Qualitative Social Research*, 6(1), 1–21.

Weed, M. (2009). Progress in sports tourism research? A meta-review and exploration of futures. *Tourism Management*, 30(5), 615–28.

Weed, M., Coren, E., and Fiore, J. (2009). *A systematic review of the evidence base for developing a physical activity and health legacy from the London 2012 Olympic and Paralympic Games.* Canterbury, Kent: Centre for Sport, Physical Education and Activity Research, Canterbury Christ Church University. Available at: www.canterbury.ac.uk/social-applied-sciences/.

Wilkinson, C., Livingston, M., and Room, R. (2016). Impacts of changes to trading hours of liquor licences on alcohol-related harm: a systematic review 2005–2015. *Public Health Research and Practice*, 26(4), 1–7.

Zapata-Diomedi, B., and Veerman, J. L. (2016). The association between built environment features and physical activity in the Australian context: a synthesis of the literature. *BMC: Public Health*, 16, 484, doi: 10.1186/s12889-016-3154-2.

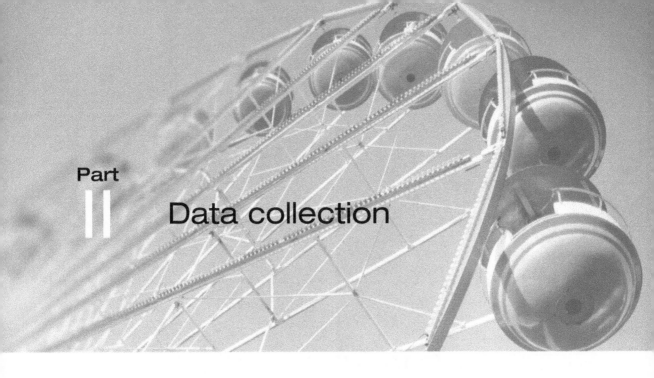

Part

II

Data collection

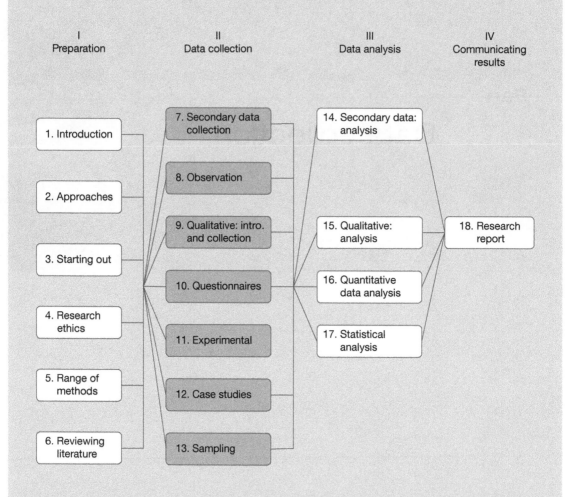

I
Preparation

II
Data collection

III
Data analysis

IV
Communicating results

1. Introduction

2. Approaches

3. Starting out

4. Research ethics

5. Range of methods

6. Reviewing literature

7. Secondary data collection

8. Observation

9. Qualitative: intro. and collection

10. Questionnaires

11. Experimental

12. Case studies

13. Sampling

14. Secondary data: analysis

15. Qualitative: analysis

16. Quantitative data analysis

17. Statistical analysis

18. Research report

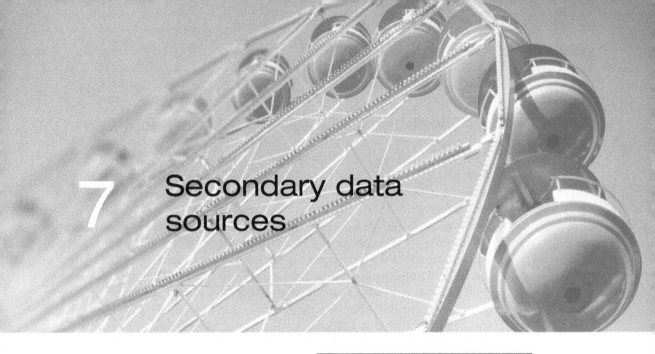

7 Secondary data sources

1. Introduction – measurement

1.1 Measuring leisure and tourism activity

Clear definition, and often measurement, is fundamental to research in any field of study. This is relevant to all forms of analysis, not just as it relates to secondary data, so this first part of the chapter is also relevant to the chapters which follow.

Since, in leisure and tourism, research invariably involves human beings, one dimension is the ways in which human beings relate to the field. A typology of individual engagement with leisure and tourism is presented in Table 7.1. It divides people into groups depending on whether they are involved with the field in a paid capacity, whether they are active/productive or engage in a consumption/receptive mode, the extent to which they are formally involved through things like volunteering or membership of organisations, and whether they are 'live' followers of the field or involved only via the media. Each of these categories gives rise to different sets of theoretical, and research issues and challenges.

Table 7.2 presents a five-fold typology of ways in which leisure and tourism activity can be measured.

Table 7.1 Typology of individual engagement with leisure and tourism

Action/ consumption	Type of engagement	Mode of engagement	Examples
Production/active	1. Professional	Full-time	Full-time professional athlete, official, manager, guide, musician
		Part-time	Part-time professional athlete, guide, musician
	2. Active leisure	Amateur Hobbyist	Amateur athlete, artist, musician, naturalist Casual participant
	3. Volunteer	Volunteer	Volunteer/unpaid coach, official, marshal, guide
Consumption/ receptive	1. Spectator/fan/ supporter	Committed live	Regular live audience member/ spectator/supporter/club member
		Occasional live	Occasional live audience member/ spectator, etc.
	2. Consumer/fan	Mediated	Watching on TV/DVD, listening on radio, online, reading sport/arts/ hobby print media

Table 7.2 Measuring leisure and tourism activity

Measure	Definition – relating to a defined community and a specified period of time (e.g. a week or year)	Leisure example for community X	Tourism example for community X
A Participation rate	The proportion of a defined population which engages in an activity.	6 per cent of the adult population go swimming at least once a week	5 per cent of the adult population make an overseas trip each year.
B Number of participants	Number of people who engage in an activity. (= A × pop'n. or C ÷ frequency of visit)	20,000 people swim at least once a week	700,000 residents visit country Y in a year.
C Volume of activity (visits)	Number of visits made or games played in an activity. (= B × visits/games per time-period*)	There are 1.2 million visits to swimming pools in a year.	Residents make 850,000 trips to country Y in a year.
D Time	a. Time spent on specific activity (= C × time per visit) b. The amount of leisure time available to the individual	a. Individuals play sport for 2 hours/week. b. Average individual has 5 hours leisure time/day.	a. The average tourist spends 5.5 nights in the area b. Average individual has 3.5 weeks holiday/year
E Time/space	a. Time/date when activity took place. b. Location of activity	a. Any of the above should refer to the year/season in which the activity took place. b. Any of the above should refer to the place in which the activity took place.	Any of the above should refer to the year/season in which the activity took place. Any of the above should refer to the place in which the activity took place.
F Expenditure	The amount of money spent per individual or community on leisure activities or goods or services. (= C × spend per visit or time-period)	Consumer expenditure on leisure is over £50 billion a year	Tourists visiting region Z spend £25 million in the region per annum
G Intensity	The energy and/or social commitment involved in an activity-experience.	See the serious leisure concept (Stebbins, 1982)	See Cohen's (1972) tourist typology.

* In tourism a further distinction is made between 'trips' (e.g. a complete holiday) and visits (i.e. places visited during the holiday)

** In tourism the measure 'bed-nights' is often used.

- *Percentage participation rate* is the most commonly used measure in leisure policy and planning research: it indicates the proportion of the population of a community participating or the proportions of particular social groups participating. This is particularly salient because of the public policy emphasis on boosting participation and equity and access for activities such as sport and the arts. By contrast, in tourism research the emphasis tends to be on the other four measures. In fact, the participation rate for tourism – the proportion of the population who go on holiday in the course of a year – is rarely compiled.

- *Number of participants* is equal to the participation rate multiplied by the population, so if the latter is rising, the number of participants can be rising even as the participation rate is falling.

- *Volume of activity* is equal to the numbers of participants multiplied by frequency of participation. It is one of the measures of greatest interest to facility managers because it indicates the number of tickets sold. In the case of tourism, this measure arises in three forms:
  – trips (the traveller's full, possibly multi-destination, itinerary);
  – visits (to a single destination or attraction); and
  – visitor-nights (overnight stay in a destination).

- *Time spent on an activity* is relevant in some sectors, such as electronic media, and is of key importance in a number of policy contexts. For example, the amount of time people spend taking exercise compared with the amount of time they spend in sedentary activities is vital in health-related policy.

- *Expenditure per visit and per trip* is, of course, the key measure for the private sector and increasingly in the public sector. It is the prime measure for tourism since, from the point of view of the host country or region, net economic benefits are its main justification.

- *Intensity* is most readily understood in relation to sport, where the amount of energy expended during exercise can be measured by such indicators as oxygen uptake (VO_2Max). In social terms it may be reflected in allocation of time (item E) and money (item F), but also in the type of involvement, such as membership of and leadership in organisations, the time-span of the individual's involvement and peer esteem. In leisure studies it is partly captured by the concept of 'serious' leisure (Elkington and Stebbins, 2014) as well as similar concepts such as involvement, commitment and specialisation (Veal, 2016).

1.2 Counting heads

As noted in Chapter 5, a key aspect of leisure/tourism policy-making, planning and facility management is the identification of levels of use – 'counting heads' or, in the case of audiences and spectators, counting 'bums on seats'. Table 7.3 shows a variety of sources of information on leisure participant/visitor numbers

Table 7.3 Counting heads: sources and methods – leisure*

Method	Data available	Additional data required to estimate numbers
Administrative – facility-based		
1. Individual ticket sales	Ticket sales per time-period	–
2. Bookings data	Facility bookings per time-period	Group size (by sample observation)
3. Season ticket/annual pass sales	Annual/season ticket sales	No. of trips per time-period per ticket (by survey)
4. Membership records/surveys	a. If member visits are automatically recorded: visits/time-period b. If not: visits/time-period from member survey	Number of members
5. Parking ticket sales data	Parking ticket sales per time-period	Vehicle occupancy (by observation)
Questionnaire-based surveys (see Chapter 10)		
6. Resident survey	% participating in activity and/or visiting particular facilities or facility types	Population (from census)
7. Tourist survey	Average frequency per time-period % visiting facility/facility type No. of visits during stay, length of stay	No. of tourists (from national/regional tourist body/local research)
8. On-site visitor interview surveys	% commuters, neighbours** (Tourists could be included here)	–
On-site visitor counts (see Chapter 8)		
Automatic counters		
9. Automatic vehicle counters	Number of vehicles per time-period	Vehicle occupancy (by observation)
10. Pedestrian counters	Number of persons per time-period	–
11. Video/time-lapse cameras/aerial photography	Number of persons/vehicles/craft present – sampled times, gives person/vehicle/craft-hours	Vehicle occupancy, average length of stay (by survey)
Visual/manual counts		
12. Entrance or exit flows	Number of visitors per time-period	–
13. Spot counts of numbers present	Number of persons present – sampled times, gives person-hours	Average length of stay (by survey)

* For more detailed discussion see Veal (2017, Chapter 12)

** Commuters and neighbours live in other council areas and use local facilities: commuters work in the study area and use facilities from workplace; neighbours use local facilities from home.

in three sections: administrative, or secondary, sources; questionnaire-based surveys; and direct counts. Because counting tourists involves people entering a country or region from elsewhere, typically for multiple trips and activities, it presents particular challenges and these are summarised in Table 7.4.

Table 7.4 Counting heads: sources and methods – tourism*

Method	Nature
Administrative	
1. Ports of entry short-term arrival/ departure data	All incoming passengers complete arrival cards, number of non-residents recorded
2. Public transport data	In situations where all visitors arrive by one or more public transport modes (e.g. island destinations by boat); visits = ticket sales (may need calibration for number of locals)
Questionnaire-based surveys (see Chapter 10)	
3. Road cordon survey: interview	• On major entry roads: total vehicle numbers noted by camera/traffic counter. • Sample of vehicles stopped: vehicle occupancy noted. • Driver interviewed re origin/destination, proportion tourists noted.
4. Road cordon survey: questionnaire	As above with additional self-completion mail-in questionnaire.
5. International visitors survey	Interviews with sample of departing tourists at airports: provides characteristics, itinerary, etc., but dependent on method 1 for actual numbers.
6. Domestic tourism survey	Survey of sample of residents on domestic tourism travel (e.g. > 1 overnight stay and > 40 km) over specified period: indicates proportion who have travelled in period.
7. On-site tourist survey	Interview a sample of tourists at known tourist gathering places. Filter tourists only. Dependent on other sources for actual numbers.
8. On-site facility visitor survey	Appropriate when one facility dominates the destination – e.g. a major national park. Interview a sample of all visitors to a leisure/tourist attraction: identify tourist proportion. Total visits to site available from other source.
9. Accommodation survey	Survey of accommodation operators to ascertain number of guests over a particular period (may need calibration for VFR (visiting friends and relatives)).
Direct counts/observation (see Chapter 8)	
10. Road cordon survey: automatic	Camera technology used to count all vehicles and record origin state/county/country of vehicle registration: proportion of non-local vehicles noted.

* For more detailed discussion see Veal (2017: Ch. 10).

Tables 7.3 and 7.4 clearly involve more than just secondary data but the full range of sources/methods is included here to make the point that none of these methods should be considered in isolation; indeed, for many estimation purposes, data from different sources must be combined. Observation and survey methods are discussed in Chapters 8 and 10 where further reference is made to Tables 7.3 and 7.4

Depending on how much information is gathered in the process, counting heads generally enables much more than presentation of numbers. It can facilitate examination of, explanation of and extrapolation of: trends in usage; performance levels (e.g. costs or income per visit); market reach; and social/economic impact. The process of analysing these various forms of data and using them to estimate visitor numbers is addressed in Chapter 14.

2. Introduction to secondary sources

In this chapter we consider the use of existing sources of data, as opposed to the collection of new data which is the subject of most of the rest of the text. The chapter examines mainly published statistical sources, such as the census and national leisure and tourism participation surveys, but other sources, such as archives and management data, are also included.

In undertaking research, it is clearly wise to use existing information where possible, rather than embarking on expensive and time-consuming new data-collection exercises. One aspect of this, systematic reviews/meta-analysis, has already been touched on in Chapter 6 in relation to the use of the literature. This can be seen as moving from literature review to secondary analysis and is discussed in Chapter 14. In searching the literature, the researcher may come across references to statistical or other data which are open to alternative analyses and interpretations or which may not have been fully analysed or exploited by the original collectors of the data. In other cases information may exist which was not originally collected for research purposes – for example, the administrative records of a leisure or tourism organisation – but which can provide the basis for research.

- *Primary* data are new data specifically collected in the current research project – the researcher is the *primary user* of such data.

- *Secondary data* already exist and were collected for some other (primary) purpose but can be used a second time in the current project – the researcher is the *secondary user*. Further analysis of such data is referred to as *secondary analysis*.

As with the literature, secondary data can play a variety of roles in a research project, from being the whole basis of the research to being a vital component or an incidental point of comparison. But to be seen as a research method in its own right in a project, the use of secondary data should contribute significantly to answering its research questions or testing hypotheses.

Some secondary data are available in a very 'raw' form – for example, organisational membership data – in which the dividing line between primary and secondary data becomes blurred. In other cases the data are highly processed: for example, the results of national leisure or tourism participation surveys. However, the data may still require considerable additional processing or formatting to be useful for the purpose in hand, and data from different sources may need to be combined in various ways. In still other cases, the data available in published form are not adequate for the purpose in hand and fresh analysis of the raw data is required – for example, involving accessing computer files of survey data for re-analysis. In this chapter we address just the sources of data. Analysis is addressed in Chapter 14.

2.1 Advantages and disadvantages of using secondary data

Some advantages and disadvantages of using secondary data are listed in Table 7.5.

A considerable amount of leisure and tourism data are collected on a regular basis at considerable cost, particularly by government agencies. Often the immediate policy requirements of the data are quite limited – for example, to announce a global figure on tourism numbers or numbers of participants in sport. In a sector where research funds are limited, it is unwise for the research community to waste such resources by failing to extract all possible research

Table 7.5 Advantages and disadvantages of using secondary data

Advantages
- Timing – data may be instantly available.
- Cost – cost of collecting new data avoided.
- Experience – the 'trial and error' experience of those who collected the original data can be exploited.
- Scale – secondary data may be based on larger samples than would otherwise be possible.
- Serendipity – inductive process of data analysis may yield serendipitous findings, which may not have arisen with primary, purpose-designed data collection.

Disadvantages
- Design – secondary data have been designed for another purpose, so may not be ideal for current project.
- Analysis limitations – if access to the raw data for re-analysis is not possible, potential for analysis/manipulation of the data for the current project may not be realised.

Table 7.6   Types of secondary data

Administrative/management data

National leisure participation surveys

Tourism surveys

Economic surveys

The census of population

Documentary sources

Opportunism

---

potential from them. This requires careful consideration of ways in which available data might be used, and it often calls for a quasi-inductive approach to research, posing the question: what can these data tell us?

2.2 Types of secondary data

Six main sources of secondary data are listed in Table 7.6. The inclusion of national leisure and tourism surveys might seem incongruous, since they are questionnaire-based surveys, and so it might be thought that they should be discussed in Chapter 10. But the class of surveys discussed here are large-scale and typically conducted on an annual basis so they take on the characteristics of 'official statistics'. The government agencies which commission them can be seen as the primary users, but they are also used by a variety of other organisations and individuals, including industry bodies and firms, other levels of government, consultants and academics. The categories listed in Table 7.5 are examined in turn in this chapter. Reference is made to examples in Britain and Australia. Similar data sets are available in most developed countries, and reference to international data collections is given in Table 7.8 and the Resources section.

3. Administrative/management data

3.1 Tourist arrivals and departures

At airports and international borders, governments collect data on individuals arriving and departing from the country via the familiar landing and departure cards. While the data are gathered for 'border protection' reasons, a by-product is information on tourist and resident arrivals and departures. For the most part, tourism agencies rely on their own surveys of international tourists because they provide more detailed information, as discussed in this chapter. However, the arrivals/departure data provide information which is internationally more complete and comparable, hence its use by organisations such as the World Tourism Organization (WTO) and the Organisation for Economic Cooperation and Development (OECD) (see the Resources section).

3.2 Licensing and taxing

Whenever governments impose heavy taxation and regulation, or even prohibition, on activities, it is usually because of a combination of moral or health fears about the activity, the potential for criminal involvement and an understanding of 'what the market will bear'. The by-product is that statistical data are collected on the activities, notably alcohol consumption, gambling and illicit drug use. While the type of data collected serves the needs of the taxation and regulatory authorities, rather than social researchers, it can still be of interest. For example, the growth in some categories of gambling, alcohol consumption, or illicit drug use and declines in others tells a social story.

3.3 Management data

Most leisure and tourism organisations generate routine data which can be of use for research purposes, and many have *management information systems* specifically designed to produce data upon which assessments of the performance of the organisation are based. Examples of such data, which may be available on an hourly, daily, weekly, monthly, seasonal or annual basis, are listed in Table 7.7. It is usually advisable to explore fully the nature, extent and availability of such data, and their potential utilisation, before embarking on fresh data collection. For example, if the manager of a facility is concerned about declining levels of visits, before initiating expensive procedures, such as surveys, to investigate the causes, it would be advisable to study the *available visitor data* to see whether the decline is across all services, and whether it is taking place at all times or only at certain times of the day, week, season or year.

Table 7.7   Management data

Visitor numbers (in various categories)

Visitor expenditure/income (in various categories)

Bookings and facility utilisation

Customer enquiries

Membership numbers and details

Customer complaints

Results of visitor/customer surveys

Expenditure of the organisation (under various headings)

Staff turnover/absenteeism, etc.

Numerous agencies are involved in collection of management data for their own administrative purposes, and in most cases the information is available in the annual reports of those organisations and sometimes on their websites. But generally, the data made public is presented only in summary form and the detail remains unpublished. Collation of such information, for example as input to a local plan, therefore becomes a research project in its own right. And if information is required at the national level, even in summary form, that also often requires considerable effort. There are some limited examples of such national collations – see the Resources section.

As noted in Chapter 5, the digitisation of financial transactions has placed in the hands of large retail companies and banks enormous quantities of information, referred to as Big Data. These are often linked with 'loyalty schemes', which involve customers providing additional data about themselves which can then be analysed alongside purchasing behaviour, providing companies with extensive data upon which to refine and focus marketing activities.

4. National leisure participation surveys

4.1 The national leisure survey phenomenon

In most developed countries surveys of leisure participation are conducted by government departments or agencies on a regular basis. These surveys, although they have limitations, are the main source of information, not only on overall levels of participation in leisure activities but also on differences in participation patterns between different groups in the community, such as the young and the old, men and women and occupational, income and ethnic groups. Any leisure researcher or professional should therefore be broadly familiar with these key data sources. In the United States such surveys have been conducted since the early 1960s, particularly on outdoor recreation (Cordell et al., 2005). Other countries began collecting data in the 1970s and 1980s.

International

Each country has tended to adopt different design principles, particularly in the way 'participation' is defined, as discussed later, so that the findings between different countries are generally not comparable. Table 7.8 refers to publications which summarise, for a number of countries, data on time-use (discussed later in this section), and leisure participation, including sport and cultural activity. The first four publications include single chapters devoted to individual countries. The two European Commission publications are, however, reports of surveys conducted across all 27 European Union member countries, while Schuster's (2007) compilation on cultural activities, includes the EU survey data and data from non-European countries in a large composite table.

Table 7.8 Publications summarising surveys of time-use, leisure and sport: countries included

Countries included	Fisher and Robinson (2010)	Cushman et al. (2005)	Nicholson et al. (2011)	Hallmann and Petry (2013)	European Commission	Schuster (2007)
	Time-use	Time-use, Leisure/ sport/arts, Tourism	Sport	Sport	Sport (2007), Cultural activities (2014)	Cultural activities
Australia	●	●	●	●		●
Austria					●	●
Belgium	●			●	●	●
Brazil	●			●		
Bulgaria	●		●		●	●
Canada		●	●	●		●
China			●	●		
Croatia					●	
Cyprus				●	●	●
Czech Republic					●	●
Denmark					●	●
Estonia	●			●	●	●
Finland	●		●	●	●	●
France	●	●		●	●	●
Germany	●	●	●	●	●	●
Greece					●	●
Hong Kong		●				
Hungary			●	●	●	●
India			●			
Ireland				●	●	●
Israel		●				
Italy	●				●	●
Japan	●	●	●	●		●
Korea	●					
Latvia					●	●
Lithuania	●				●	●
Luxembourg					●	●
Malta					●	●
Mexico				●		●
Netherlands	●	●	●	●	●	●

Table 7.8   *(continued)*

Countries included	Fisher and Robinson (2010)	Cushman et al. (2005)	Nicholson et al. (2011)	Hallmann and Petry (2013)	European Commission	Schuster (2007)
	Time-use	Time-use, Leisure/ sport/arts, Tourism	Sport	Sport	Sport (2007), Cultural activities (2014)	Cultural activities
New Zealand		●	●	●		●
Norway	●		●			●
Poland	●	●		●	●	●
Portugal					●	●
Romania					●	●
Russia		●				
Singapore			●			
Slovakia					●	●
Slovenia	●				●	●
South Africa			●	●		
Spain	●			●	●	●
Sweden	●				●	●
Turkey	●					●
Uganda				●		
UK/Britain/ England	●	●		●	●	●
USA	●	●	●	●		●

Sport and physical recreation

In both Britain and Australia, national surveys of sport and physical recreation participation have had a chequered history over the last 20 years, as shown in Table 7.9. It shows a pattern of spasmodic surveys during some periods, then a ten-year run of annual surveys in both countries, both of which have recently been replaced by new surveys. The British Taking Part Survey has been conducted for the longest period without alteration (12 years) and is continuing, but with some minor changes. Of particular note is the Active People Survey and its successor Active Lives Survey, which have an annual sample size of some 190,000. The large sample size provides a minimum sub-sample size of 500 for every local council, enabling analysis of local participation patterns. This demonstrates both the merits and drawbacks of secondary data. It is most unlikely that the £6 million a year which the APS/ALS costs to conduct would be available for purely research purposes: it is conducted to meet the policy requirements of Sport England (2016) and the UK Government (2015). This has implications for the design of the survey and the ways in which the data are analysed and published, and these features are discussed further in Chapter 14.

National leisure participation surveys are the main source of information available to researchers on overall participation levels in a range of leisure

Table 7.9 Sport participation surveys, Britain and Australia, 1996–2016

| Agency | England | | DCMS | Australia | |
	Sport England GHS			ASC etc.	ABS
1996	●				●
1997					●
1998					●
1999					●
2000				ERASS	●
2001	●			●	
2002				●	●■
2003				●	●
2004	APS		TPS	●	
2005	●		◆	●	
2006			◆	●	●■
2007	●		◆	●	
2008	●		◆	●	
2009	●		◆	●	●
2010	●		◆		●■
2011	●		◆		
2012	●		◆		●
2013	●		◆		
2014	●		◆		●
2015	●	ALS	◆	AusPlay	
2016	●	●	◆	●	
		↓	↓	↓	

GHS: General Household Survey
TPS: Taking Part Survey
ALS: Active Lives Survey
ERASS = Exercise, Recreation and Sport Survey
Shaded areas: last survey in the series

DCMS: Department for Culture, Media and Sport
APS: Active People Survey
ABS: Australian Bureau of Statistics
ASC, etc.= Australian Sport Commission + state governments

● sport and physical activity survey ◆ sport, culture and heritage survey ■ sport spectating survey ↓ continuing

activities. How they fit into the spectrum of methods for 'counting heads' is discussed at the end of the chapter. A number of issues arise in the use of these important databases, including questions of validity and reliability, sample size, the participation reference period used, the age range of the population covered, the range of activities included and availability of information on the social characteristics of respondents. These topics are discussed in turn here.

4.2 Validity and reliability

National leisure surveys suffer from the limitation of all interview surveys in that they are dependent on respondents' own reports of their patterns of leisure participation. How sure can we be, therefore, that the resultant data are accurate? We cannot be absolutely sure, as discussed in Chapter 10; however, a number of features of national surveys lend credence to their reliability and value as sources of data:

- national government statistical organisations have an enviable reputation for quality and professionalism in their work;
- the surveys are often based on large sample sizes; and
- the fact that there has been little dramatic variation in the findings of the various surveys over the years is reassuring (Gratton and Veal, 2005) – erratic and unexplainable fluctuations in reported levels of participation would have led to suspicions that the surveys were unreliable, but this has not happened.

Some commentators have questioned the validity of participation surveys, conducting experiments which show a tendency for respondents to exaggerate levels of participation substantially, at least in relation to some activities (Chase and Godbey, 1983; Chase and Harada, 1984). However, as Boothby (1987) suggests, for some groups, activities and surveys, there may also be under-reporting of levels of activity. While national survey data, especially when sponsored by governments, have the imprimatur of being 'official statistics', they are subject to all the limitations of questionnaire-based surveys as discussed in Chapter 10.

4.3 Sample size

Generally, the larger the sample size the more reliable and precise are the survey findings. The Australian survey discussed earlier is based on a sample of around 13,000 interviews and is therefore subject to only minimal 'statistical error' – a term explained in Chapter 13. The British survey, at 190,000, is much larger; in fact, it would be unnecessarily large if its only purpose was to provide national-level data, but it is designed to also provide data at the local council level, as noted earlier.

For many individual activities covered in the surveys, the proportion of the population participating is less than 1 per cent. However, even 1 per cent of the adult population of Britain is almost half a million people, so small percentages can represent large numbers of people. While this issue is discussed in more detail in Chapter 13, the constraints of a small sample size compared with a large sample size can be imagined from the following:

● Exercise, Recreation and Sport Survey (Australia): sample size 13,000: 1% of sample = 130;

● Active People Survey: national sample size 190,000: 1% of sample = 1900; and

● Active People Survey sub-sample for one council area: 500: 1% of sample = 5.

4.4 Key questions/specifications

Main question – participation reference period and duration

The level of participation depends substantially on the 'reference period' used; that is, the period of time to which the participation relates. Thus, for example, the proportion of the population who have been swimming in the 24 hours prior to being interviewed would be quite small, and the proportion who have done so in the last month or last year would be higher, while the proportion who have ever been swimming would be almost 100 per cent. Furthermore, in the case of physical activity, the *duration* of participation is important when considering the question of health benefits. Thus, for some activities, measuring only the proportion of participants who have participated for at least a minimum prescribed time, such as 30 minutes a week, would reduce the reported participation rate considerably. This is illustrated in Table 7.10 which shows, for a number of sports activities:

● the proportion of the population participating at least once in the last year compared with the proportion in the last four weeks (2002); and

● the proportion participating in the last month and, of those who have participated for at least 30 minutes in the last week (2008–9).

The second measure in each case reduces the participation rate by at least half, and in some cases by two thirds.

The published results from the Australian ERASS do not include the one-week measure for individual activities, but the proportion taking part in any form of exercise, recreation or sport activity in the year prior to interview in 2007–8 was 83.4 per cent, while the proportion who participated at least three times a week was just 49.3 per cent.

The one-year reference period is becoming the international norm (Cushman et al., 2005: 284). This practice has the advantage of covering participation in all seasons of the year in one survey and including most infrequent participants. It also enables comparison with other sectors, such as the arts, which use this

Table 7.10 Participation rates in sports, England, 2002, 2008–9

Sports*	2002, at least once in:		2008–9, at least once in:	
	Last year	**Last 4 weeks**	**Last month**	**Last week**
	% of persons aged 16 and over participating			
Walking	45.9	34.9	na	na
Swimming	34.8	13.8	13.2	7.6
Cycling	19.1	9.0	9.3	4.5
Football	9.1	4.9	7.4	5.1
Athletics**	1.0	0.3	6.4	4.2
Golf	12.1	4.8	3.5	2.1
Badminton	6.4	1.8	2.4	1.3
Tennis	7.0	1.9	2.4	1.3
Squash	3.8	1.3	1.2	0.7
Cricket	2.4	0.6	1.0	0.5
Equestrian	3.5	1.9	1.0	0.8
Bowls	3.8	1.3	1.0	0.6

Sources: 2002: Office for National Statistics General Household Survey: https://data.gov.uk/dataset/general_household_survey.
2008–9: Sport England: Active People Survey, www.sportengland.org/research/about-our-research/active-people-survey/

*Activities with at least 1% participation in last month in 2008–9 included.

**2002 definition is 'track and field' – 2008–9 includes all jogging, marathons, etc.

†National participation rates estimated from aggregated county figures.

measure. However, it has the disadvantage of introducing possible inaccuracies in respondents' recall of their activities over such a long time-period. Furthermore, for sport and physical exercise activity, policy-makers are interested in minimum frequency and duration which produce health benefits, so a one-week or two-week measure is becoming an additional norm for that sector. Use of the shorter reference period has the advantage of increased accuracy of recall but also the disadvantage that seasonal variation must be covered by interviewing at different times of the year and calculating an average.

Age-range

Participation surveys are restricted in terms of age-range covered. Some include respondents as young as 12 years old, while some cover only those aged 18 and over. Some also have upper age limits. The British and Australian surveys presented here cover people aged 16 and over. The reasons for not interviewing young children are threefold:

1. It may be difficult to obtain accurate information from very young children.

2. It may be considered ethically unacceptable to subject children to the sort of questioning which adults can freely choose to face or not (see Chapter 4).

3. There is a question as to when children are considered to engage in their own independent leisure activities as opposed to being under the control of parents.

Some surveys present data on children from 'proxy' interviews, in which questions about children's activities are answered by parents: an example is the Australian Bureau of Statistics (2009) survey of children's participation in culture and leisure activities. By contrast, the DCMS Taking Part Survey includes, for a sub-sample, direct interviews with children, but this is limited to children aged 11–15. Both of the new survey series plan to include data on children.

An age limit in the mid-teens has effects on the results, in that for some activities – for example, swimming or cycling – young teenagers may be a significant proportion of total participants. For other activities – for example, gardening or going to the opera – the age limit may be inconsequential because young people are not among the most frequent participants. When using data from leisure participation surveys, particularly when seeking to compare results from different surveys, it is therefore important to bear in mind the age-range covered.

Social/demographic characteristics

In addition to the basic information on participation, national leisure surveys generally include a wide range of background information on the people interviewed, including such variables as gender, occupation, age, education level reached, size of family or household unit and ethnicity or country of birth. This information can be used to examine levels of participation by different social groups from either an equity or a marketing point of view, and it can also be used to predict demand, as future changes in the underlying social structure of the community affect patterns of demand; this is explored in Chapter 14.

4.5 National time-use surveys

Time-use, or time-budget, research became a significant focus of international social research with the conduct of the UNESCO-funded *Multinational Comparative Time-Budget Research Project* in the 1960s (Szalai, 1972). In Britain, such surveys were conducted as long ago as the 1930s when the BBC used them to explore the public's patterns of use of broadcast media; while in Australia, they date back to the 1970s. In recent years, time-use surveys have been of particular interest because of the belief that people are becoming increasingly time-pressured. The most recent UK time-use surveys which permit analysis of trends in time-use were conducted in 2001 and 2005; a 2014–15 survey was conducted but results were not published at the time of writing (July 2017). UK time-use surveys are conducted in association with 14 other European countries under the auspices of the Harmonised European Time Use Survey which makes data available online (see the Resources section). The most recent in Australia were the 1997 and 2006 surveys conducted by the Australian Bureau of Statistics.

Time-use surveys ask respondents to keep a diary of their activities for one or two days, so they cover all aspects of time-use, including leisure, and are a

Table 7.11 Time use: Britain and Australia

	Britain, 2005	Australia, 2006
	Hours per week, persons aged 15+*	
Sleep	57.3	59.6
TV/video/radio/music	18.3	16.3
Other leisure	23.4	18.2
Paid work	19.8	24.1
Personal care	14.7	17.1
Domestic work/childcare	22.3	22.7
Travel and other	12.3	10.0
Total	168.0	168.0

Sources: Britain: data from Office for National Statistics: Time Use Survey, 2005, available at: www.ons.gov.uk. Australia: data from ABS (2006).

* Some differences between Britain and Australia may due to differences in definitions and some due to differing age structure.

key source of information for leisure studies. Compared with the participation surveys discussed earlier, the 'reference period' for a time-use survey is effectively one or two days. This overcomes the problem of recall accuracy involved in surveys which use longer recall periods, resulting in more reliable data, but drastically reduces the proportion of respondents engaging in any one activity. Apart from activities which large numbers of people engage in on most days, notably watching television and listening to the radio, time-use surveys are not ideal for studying individual leisure activities but are used to examine broad categories of time-use, as shown in Table 7.11.

While time-use surveys may give an adequate representation of day trips from home, they tend not to include holiday activity because of the obvious practical difficulties of sampling in the context of a domestic survey. There is, however, a parallel process of studying the time-budgets of holiday-makers at their destination. Douglas Pearce (1988) discussed the idea over two decades ago, drawing attention to a number of existing examples.

5. Tourism surveys

5.1 International and domestic tourism surveys

The information on each traveller gathered by the landing and departure cards discussed earlier in this chapter is typically limited to under 10 items, including country of origin, transport mode, length of stay, purpose of visit (holiday, business, visiting friends or relatives, etc.), gender, age and occupation and the area/destination where the traveller will be spending the most time. For data on such matters as tourist expenditure, destinations and satisfaction, questionnaire-based surveys are used. Typically, one survey is conducted of international visits to a country and another of domestic tourism trips within a country. The international survey tends to be conducted by face-to-face interviews of overseas visitors at ports of departure. For domestic tourism, the survey is conducted either as a face-to-face household survey or by telephone. Questions on overseas trips by residents are sometimes added to the domestic tourism survey and sometimes covered by including residents as a sub-sample of the international arrivals/departure survey.

Details of such surveys conducted in Britain and Australia are provided in Table 7.12. Quarterly or annual summaries of the results of the surveys are available online (see the Resources section).

5.2 Sample size

Samples sizes for national tourism surveys are large, typically in the tens of thousands. This is because information is required:

● on a quarterly as well as annual basis;

● for regional or country sub-samples (including breakdowns of demographics, expenditure, etc. for the sub-samples); and

● to provide a basis or grossing up to provide estimates of actual numbers of visits and visitor-nights (see Chapter 13, 'Confidence intervals applied to population estimates', for discussion of the sample-size implications of grossing up).

5.3 Definitions

As with leisure surveys, the data on tourist trips is influenced by the definition of 'tourist' and the reference time-periods used. Most definitions of tourism refer to a person staying away from their normal place of residence for at least one night and travelling a certain minimum distance to qualify as a tourist. This means that people who take a trip from London to Southend or Brighton, but do not stay overnight, are classified not as tourists but as day-trippers. However, many tourism surveys include day trips, usually defined by a minimum distance travelled (e.g. at least 40 km) and a minimum time away from home (e.g. 4 hours), because catering to day-trippers is a significant component of the tourism industry in many destinations.

Comprehensive data on border crossings are no longer collected in Europe because of the sheer volume of such crossings and the increasing liberalisation of travel regulations. Thus, while arrivals and departure data are collected by governments and their agencies for official purposes, the 'hard' data on tourism flows can, in reality, be every bit as 'soft' as the data on leisure participation (Edwards, 1991).

Table 7.12 National tourism survey details

UK: International Passenger Survey

Conducted by	Office for National Statistics
Frequency	Annual, continuous
Included	UK residents and international visitors to UK
Sample size	250,000
Method	Face-to-face interviews at major air/sea/Channel Tunnel port custom points

---

UK: UK Tourist Survey

Conducted by	Tourism commissions: Britain, England, Scotland, Wales
Frequency	Annual, continuous
Included	Residents aged 16+
Sample size	100,000
Trips included	Trips in last four weeks involving at least one night away from home.
Method	Face-to-face home-based interviews

Australia: International Visitor Survey

Conducted by	Tourism Research Australia
Frequency	Annual, continuous (quarterly and annual reports)
Included	Visitors to Australia
Sample size	40,000
Method	Face-to-face interviews in departure lounges of eight airports

---

Australia: National Visitor Survey

Conducted by	Tourism Research Australia
Frequency	Annual, continuous (quarterly and annual reports)
Included	Australian residents, 15+
Sample size	120,000
Trips included	Overnight stays >40km from home in last four weeks Daytrips >50km, >4 hours, in last week Overseas trips in last 3 months
Method	Telephone survey

Typical data collected	International destination: country Domestic destination: region Length of stay, nights; Purpose of trip (holiday, business, VFR, etc.); Expenditure; Transport mode used; Accommodation type used Information sources used; Leisure activities; Demographics (age, gender, etc.)

6. Economic/industry data

6.1 Household expenditure

In most developed countries, surveys of *household expenditure* are conducted on a regular basis. In Britain, the survey is an annual one and is called the *Expenditure and Food Survey*, while the Australian equivalent, the *Household Expenditure Survey*, is conducted every five years (see the Resources section). These surveys collect information from a cross-section of families throughout their respective countries on their weekly expenditure on scores of items, many of which relate to leisure and tourism. Table 7.13 indicates the range of leisure-related items included in such surveys. These economic data sources provide the basis for the regular leisure expenditure forecasting and market trend analysis reports produced by such organisations as the Sport Industries Research Centre at Sheffield Hallam University for the United Kingdom, and Richard K. Miller and Associates for the United States (details are in the Resources section).

6.2 Satellite accounts

Leisure and tourism industries – tourism, sport, gambling, etc. – are multi-sectoral, including direct service components, hospitality, transport, local government and so on. In national accounting systems which establish the economic scale and impact of industry sectors, leisure industries do not feature in their own right; their economic activity is spread across a range of the major industry sectors. Yet, were these components to be identified and information on them drawn together, they would be seen to be substantial industry sectors. Special projects have therefore been established in a number of countries, at the

Table 7.13   Household expenditure survey leisure items

Typical leisure expenditure items included in national household expenditure surveys

Alcoholic drink	Cinema, theatre, museums etc. admissions
Tobacco	Restaurant meals
Audio-visual, photographic, computer equipment	TV, video, internet costs
Games, toys, hobbies	Photographic
Computer software and games	Gambling (net losses)
Sporting, camping, outdoor recreation equipment	Newspapers, magazines, books, stationery
Gardening equipment, plants	Holidays – domestic and abroad
Pets, pet food	Transport (leisure about 30% of total)
Sports admissions, subscriptions, fees	

behest of interested government departments and agencies and industry groups, to establish satellite accounts to extract relevant data from across the national accounts and assemble it in an accessible form. The aim is to provide economic data on the leisure industries on an annual basis. It is not proposed to examine the results of these projects here, but sources are indicated in the Resources section.

7. The population census

Taking a census of the whole population, for taxation and other purposes, is a long-standing practice of governments, one of the most well-known historical example being the *Domesday Book*, compiled by William the Conqueror for the whole of England in the eleventh century.

7.1 The modern population census

The *population census* is an important source of information, and any aspiring leisure/tourism manager or researcher should be fully aware of its content and its potential. A complete census of the population is taken in Britain by the Office for National Statistics every 10 years; the latest was 2001, and before that, 1991, 1981 and so on. In Australia, because the population is growing relatively rapidly, the Australian Bureau of Statistics undertakes a census every five years. As in most countries, it is a statutory requirement for householders (and hoteliers, hospital managers, boarding school principals and prison governors) to fill out a census form on 'census night', indicating the number of people, including visitors, in the building, and their age, gender, occupation and so on. Some people escape the net, for instance some people sleeping rough or illegal immigrants, but generally the information is believed to be reliable and comprehensive.

Data from the census are available at a number of levels, from national down to the level of Enumeration Districts (EDs) (Collection Districts, CDs, in Australia), as indicated in Table 7.14. CDs are small areas, with populations of around 250 to 500, which a single census collection officer deals with on census night. By adding together data from a few CDs, a leisure facility manager can obtain data on the demographic characteristics of the population of the catchment area of the facility. An enormous amount of information is available on each of these areas, as listed in Table 7.15.

7.2 Uses of census data

It can be seen that none of the census information, with the possible exception of working hours, is concerned directly with leisure or tourism, so why should

Table 7.14   Census data: levels of availability

Britain	Australia
National	National
Regions	State
Counties	Postal codes
Local government areas	Local government areas
Parliamentary constituencies	State and federal Parliament electorates
Enumeration districts (EDs)	Collection districts (CDs)

Table 7.15   Census data available

Resident population

Number of males/females

Number/proportion in five-year age-groups (and single years for under-20s)

Numbers of people:
- with different religions
- by country of birth
- speaking different languages
- by country of birth of parents

Numbers of families/households:
- of different sizes
- with different numbers of dependent children
- which are single-parent families
- with various numbers of vehicles

Numbers of people:
- who left school at various ages
- with different educational/technical qualifications
- in different occupational groups
- by working hours
- unemployed
- living in different types of dwelling

the census be of interest to the leisure or tourism researcher? Among the uses, which are explored further in Chapter 14, are:

- planning facilities and conducting feasibility studies,

- area management/marketing,

- facility performance evaluation,

- market segmentation.

Table 7.16   Documentary sources

- Minutes of committee/council/board meetings/organisational archives
- Correspondence of an organisation or an individual
- Archives (may include both of the above and other papers)
- Popular literature, such as novels, magazines
- Newspapers, particularly coverage of specific topics and/or particular aspects, such as editorials, advertising or correspondence columns
- Brochures and advertising material
- Diaries
- Research literature (meta-analysis)

8. Documentary sources

Documentary sources lie somewhere between literature and management data as an information source for research. Typical examples are listed in Table 7.16. Many of such sources are important for historical research, either for a primarily historical research project, or as background for a project with a contemporary focus. In some cases the documents are a focus of research in their own right – for example, some research on women and sport has examined the coverage of women's sport in the media (e.g. Rowe and Brown, 1994). As the links between cultural and media studies and leisure and tourism studies increase, so analysis of media content, including television, is likely to increase (Critcher, 1992; Tomlinson, 1990).

9. Opportunism

Secondary data often give rise to what might be called opportunistic research, as discussed in Chapter 3. This applies to many of the government-sponsored surveys discussed above: data exist and have been used by the collecting agency only for limited purposes, or in internal policy-making processes which are not in the public domain. Examples include:

- the use of routinely collected playground accident data to study the effects of introducing new playground equipment (see Case study 11.6A); and

- the use of official data on sport participation to examine the validity of the claimed 'trickle-down' effect of hosting major sporting events (Veal et al., 2012).

Summary

This chapter is concerned with sources of secondary data; that is, data which have been collected by others for other purposes but might be utilised for current research purposes. There are potential cost and time-saving advantages to such a strategy and even an ethical dimension, which suggests that scarce resources should not be expended on new data collection if adequate data already exist. The chapter reviews a number of sources of secondary data commonly used in leisure and tourism research, namely: national leisure participation surveys; tourism surveys; economic data on consumer expenditure; the census of population; management data; and documentary sources. Analysis of such data is discussed in Chapter 14.

Test questions

1. What are the advantages and disadvantages of secondary data analysis?

2. What are some of the issues to be considered when making secondary use of data from major leisure or tourism participation surveys?

3. What are the names of the main surveys conducted in your country related to the following:
   a. leisure participation
   b. domestic tourism
   c. international tourism
   d. household expenditure?

4. The chapter lists nine sources of 'management data'. What are they?

5. The chapter lists seven types of 'documentary' source. What are they?

Exercises

No exercises are offered for this chapter, but exercises using secondary data are suggested in Chapter 14.

Resources

Websites

Systematic reviews

- Campbell Collaboration: systematic reviews in social policy area: www.campbellcollaboration.org.

- Cochrane Collaboration: systematic reviews in health/medical area: www.cochrane.org.

Tourist arrivals/departures

- Australia: www.abs.gov.au/ausstats/abs@.nsf/mf/3401.0

National collation of facility use data

- Museums and galleries, Australia: www.abs.gov.au, select Statistics > Culture and Recreation.

- Museums and galleries, UK: https://www.gov.uk/government/statistical-data-sets/museums-and-galleries-monthly-visits.

UK national leisure/tourism surveys

- Active People Survey: https://data.gov.uk/dataset/general_household_survey www.sportengland.org/research/about-our-research/active-people-survey/.

- International Passenger Survey: www.ons.gov.uk/surveys/informationfor households/householdandindividualsurveys/internationa lpassengersurveyips.

- Living Costs and Food Survey: www.ons.gov.uk, search on 'Living costs'.

- Population census: www.ons.gov.uk/census.

- Sport/culture participation: Department for Culture, Media and Sport (DCMS) Taking Part Survey: www.gov.uk/guidance/taking-part-survey.

- UK Time-use survey, 2014–15: www.timeuse.org/node/10831.

- UK Tourist Survey (domestic): www.visitbritain.org/insightsandstatistics/index.aspx.

Australia national surveys

- Arts participation: Australia Council for the Arts: www.australiacouncil.gov.au/research.

- Australian Bureau of Statistics data: www.abs.gov.au; select Statistics > Culture and Recreation.

- Exercise, Recreation and Sport Survey: www.ausport.gov.au/information/casro/ERASS.

- Household Expenditure Survey: www.abs.gov.au; search for '6530.0'.

- International Visitor Survey and National Visitor Survey: Tourism Research Australia: www.tra.gov.au/research.html.

- Population census: www.abs.gov.au; click on 'Census'.

International data

- Harmonised European Time Use Survey: https://www.h5.scb.se/tus/tus/Default.htm

- Organisation for Economic Cooperation and Development (OECD): www.oecd.org; search for 'Tourism' and 'Society at a glance', then locate Chapter 2 'Measuring Leisure in OECD Countries'

- World Tourism Organization: www.unwto.org.

Annual industry/consumer expenditure surveys

- UK annual leisure/sport industry reviews: Sport Industry Research Centre, Sheffield Hallam University: www.shu.ac.uk/research/specialisms/sport-industry-research-centre/what-we-do#this-section.

- USA annual leisure industry review: Richard K. Miller & Associates: www.rkma.com.

Sport, tourism satellite accounts

- Australia: www.abs.gov.au; search for 'Satellite accounts'.

- UK: for details of planning studies for sport and tourism accounts: www.ons.gov.uk/economy/nationalaccounts/satelliteaccounts/bulletins/uktourismsatelliteaccountuktsa/2015-06-26
  www.gov.uk/government/collections/sport-satellite-account-for-the-uk-statistics

Publications

- Arts/cultural surveys: Schuster (2007).

- Documentary sources: Kellehear (1993).

- Leisure surveys:
  - Australia: Veal (2003, 2005); and
  - international: Cushman et al. (2005).

- Measurement: Ekinci (2011).

- Outdoor recreation surveys, USA: Schuett et al. (2009).

- Sport and physical recreation surveys:
  - Australia: Eime et al. (2015), Veal (2003, 2005);
  - France: Aubel and Lefevre (2013);
  - international: Nicholson et al. (2011); and
  - UK: Fox and Rickards (2004), Gratton and Veal (2005), Rowe (2009).

- Time-use surveys: Fisher and Robinson (2010), Gershuny (2000), Pentland et al. (1999).

- Tourism data sources: Edwards (1991), UN World Tourism Organization (annual).

- Tourism satellite accounts: ABS (2016), Frechtling (2010).

References

ABS – see Australian Bureau of Statistics.

Aubel, O., and Lefevre, B. (2013). The comparability of quantitative surveys on sport participation in France (1967–2010). *International Review for the Sociology of Sport*, 50(6), 722–39.

Australian Bureau of Statistics (ABS) (2006). *How Australians use their time, 1997.* (Cat. No. 4153.0), Canberra: ABS.: Available at: www.abs.gov.au.

Australian Bureau of Statistics (ABS) (2009). *Children's participation in cultural and leisure activities.* (Cat. No. 4901.0), Canberra: ABS.

Australian Bureau of Statistics (ABS) (2016). *Australian national accounts: tourism satellite account, 2014–15* (Cat. No. 5249.0). Canberra; ABS

Boothby, J. (1987). Self-reported participation rates: further comment. *Leisure Studies*, 6(1), 99–104.

Chase, D., and Harada, M. (1984). Response error in self-reported recreation participation. *Journal of Leisure Research*, 16(4), 322–9.

Chase, D. R., and Godbey, G. C. (1983). The accuracy of self-reported participation rates. *Leisure Studies*, 2(2), 231–6.

Cohen, E. (1972). Towards a sociology of international tourism. *Social Research*, 39(1), 164–82.

Cordell, H. K., Green, G. T., Leeworthy, V. R., Stephens, R., Fly, M. J., and Betz, C. J. (2005). United States of America: outdoor recreation. In G. Cushman, A. J. Veal and J. Zuzanek (Eds), *Free Time and Leisure Participation: International Perspectives* (pp. 245–64). Wallingford, UK: CABI Publishing.

Critcher, C. (1992). Is there anything on the box? *Leisure studies and media studies*. *Leisure Studies*, 11(2), 97–122.

Cushman, G., Veal, A. J., and Zuzanek, J. (Eds) (2005). *Free time and leisure participation: international perspectives*. Wallingford, UK: CABI Publishing.

Edwards, A. (1991). The reliability of tourism statistics. *Economist Intelligence Unit: Travel and Tourism Analyst* (1), 62–75.

Eime, R. M., Sawyer, N., Harvey, J. T., Casey, M. M., Westerbeek, H., and Payne, W. R. (2015). Integrating public health and sport management: sport participation trends 2001– 2010. *Sport Management Review*, 18(2), 207–217.

Ekinci, Y. (2011). Measurement of variables. In E. Sirakaya-Turk, M. Uysal, W. E. Hammitt and J. J. Vaske (Eds.), *Research methods for leisure, recreation and tourism* (pp. 56–71). Wallingford, UK: CABI.

Elkington, S., and Stebbins, R.A. (2014). *The serious leisure perspective: an introduction*. London: Routledge.

European Commission (2007). *European cultural values: Special Eurobarometer 278/Wave 67*. Brussels: European Commission.

European Commission (2014). *Sport and physical activity: Special Eurobarometer 412*. Brussels: European Commission.

Fisher, K., and Robinson, J. (2010). *Daily routines in 22 countries: diary evidence of average daily time spent in thirty activities*. Technical Paper 2010-01, Oxford: Centre for Time Use Research, University of Oxford. Available at: www.timeuse.org.

Fox, K., and Rickards, L. (2004) *Sport and leisure: results from the sport and leisure module of the 2002 General Household Survey*. London: HMSO. Available at: www.statistics.gov.uk/downloads/theme_compendia/Sport&Leisure.pdf (accessed November 2010).

Frechtling, D. C. (2010). The tourism satellite account: a primer. *Annals of Tourism Research*, 37(1), 136–63.

Gershuny, J. (2000). *Changing times: work and leisure in postindustrial society*. Oxford: Oxford University Press.

Gratton, C., and Veal, A. J. (2005). Great Britain. In G. Cushman, A. J. Veal and J. Zuzanek (Eds), *Free time and leisure participation: international perspectives* (pp. 109–26). Wallingford, UK: CABI Publishing.

Hallmann, K., and Petry, K. (Eds) (2013). *Comparative sport development*. New York: Springer.

Kellehear, A. (1993). *The unobtrusive researcher: a guide to methods*. Sydney: Allen & Unwin.

Nicholson, M., Hoye, R., and Houlihan, B. (Eds) (2011). *Participation in sport: international policy perspectives*. London: Routledge.

Pearce, D. (1988). Tourist time budgets. *Annals of Tourism Research*, 15(1), 106–21.

Pentland, W. E., Harvey, A. S., Powell Lawton, M., and McColl, M. A. (Eds) (1999). *Time use research in the social sciences*. New York: Kluwer/Plenum.

Rowe, D., and Brown, P. (1994). Promoting women's sport: theory, policy and practice. *Leisure Studies*, 13(2), 97–110.

Rowe, N. (2009). The Active People Survey: a catalyst for transforming evidence-based sport policy in England. *International Journal of Sport Policy and Politics*, 1(1), 89–98.

Schuett, M. A., Warnick, R. B., and Lu, J. (2009). A qualitative analysis of national outdoor recreation surveys. *Journal of Park and Recreation Administration*, 27(2), 46–59.

Schuster, M. (2007). Participation studies and cross-national comparison: proliferation, prudence, and possibility. *Cultural Trends*, 16(2), 99–196.

Sport England (2016). *Toward a sporting nation: strategy, 2016–2021*. London: Sport England.

Stebbins, R. A. (1982). Serious leisure: a conceptual statement. *Pacific Sociological Review* (now *Sociological Perspectives*), 5, 251–72.

Szalai, A. (Ed.) (1972). *The use of time: daily activities of urban and suburban populations in twelve countries*. The Hague: Mouton.

Tomlinson, A. (Ed.) (1990). *Consumption, identity, and style: marketing, meanings, and the packaging of pleasure*. London: Comedia/Routledge.

UK Government (2015). *Sporting future: a new strategy for an active nation*. London: Cabinet Office.

Veal, A. J. (2003). Tracking change: leisure participation and policy in Australia, 1985–2002. *Annals of Leisure Research*, 6(3), 246–78.

Veal, A.J. (2005). Australia. In G. Cushman, A. J. Veal and J. Zuzanek (Eds), *Free time and leisure participation: international perspectives* (pp. 17–40). Wallingford, UK: CABI Publishing.

Veal, A. J. (2016). The serious leisure perspective and the experience of leisure. *Leisure Sciences*, 39(3), 205–223.

Veal, A. J. (2017). *Leisure, sport and tourism: politics, policy and planning*, 4th edn. Wallingford, UK: CABI Publishing.

Veal, A. J., Toohey, K., and Frawley, S. (2012). The sport participation legacy of the Sydney 2000 Olympic Games and other international sporting events hosted in Australia. *Journal of Policy Research in Tourism, Leisure and Events*, 4(2), 155–84.

World Tourism Organization (annual). *UNWTO: Tourism highlights*, 2016 edition. Madrid: UNWTO.

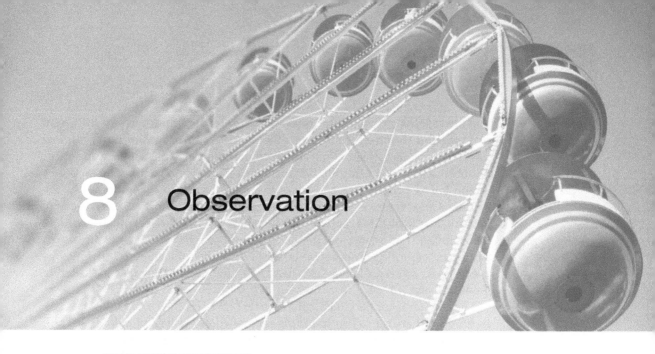

8 Observation

1. Introduction

The aim of this chapter is to draw attention to the importance of *looking* in research and to introduce some of the specific approaches of observational methods. It examines situations in which observation is particularly appropriate, outlines the main steps to be taken in designing and conducting an observation-based project and considers the role of various technologies in the process. Observation is a neglected technique in leisure and tourism research; nevertheless, while it is rarely possible to base a whole project on observation, the technique has a vital role to play, formally or informally, in most research strategies. Typically, observation is one of a number of techniques that may be used in a study, especially when 'head counting' is concerned, as indicated in Tables 7.3 and 7.4.

The chapter is located in Part II of the text which is concerned with data collection, but there is no corresponding separate data analysis chapter in Part III. This is because, in the case of quantitative observation, data can readily be analysed using simple spreadsheet collation, calculation and graphics. In the case of qualitative observation, the field notes to be analysed are similar to any other field-notes or interview transcripts and so are covered by the discussion of qualitative data analysis in Chapter 15. Some case studies are, however, included to demonstrate the outcomes of observational research.

Sometimes observational research is referred to as *unobtrusive methods*, since there is typically no involvement with the observed, who are generally not even aware that they are being observed. But the term unobtrusive methods is also used in relation to documentary sources, such as the media, organisational

Table 8.1 Types of observational research: quantitative and qualitative

Structured or systematic observation	Observation process subject to formal rules about what should be observed, how often, etc. – results typically recorded on a form and analysed quantitatively. Equivalent to the formal questionnaire-based approach in survey research.
Unstructured/ naturalistic/qualitative observation	No formal rules established; relatively informal recording or analysis procedures. Observer seeks to describe the phenomenon of interest and develop explanations and understandings in the process. Equivalent of the informal, in-depth interview.
Quasi-experimental observation	Researcher intervenes to change the environment and observes what happens – for example, changing the design of a children's playground. May be structured or unstructured.
Participant observation	The researcher is a participant in the milieu being studied – for example, the guided tour or the youth gang – rather than a separate, 'objective' researcher. May involve any of the above forms of observation. Discussed in Chapter 9.

records and diaries (see Kellehear, 1993); these sources are dealt with in the chapters on secondary data and qualitative methods. Here we concentrate on direct visual engagement with leisure or tourism sites.

A related idea is *visual research methods* (Annear et al., 2014), as mentioned in Chapter 5. This approach, however, is concerned not with observation on the part of the researcher but with engaging the research subjects in responding to visual cues, such as photographs, rather than the verbal cues of the question-naire/interview. Some visual approaches, such as Q methodology, can be seen as experimental and so are discussed in Chapter 11.

Observation involves *looking*. It can take a number of forms, as indicated in Table 8.1. Of importance here is that observational research can be quantitative, qualitative or a combination of both. There is also overlap with experimental methods and with participant observation, as discussed in Chapter 9.

2. Types and possibilities

2.1 Introduction

A number of types of situation where observation is appropriate or necessary can be identified, as listed in Table 8.2. These situations are discussed in turn here.

2.2 Children's play

Some research can be tackled only by means of observation. One example is children's play. Such research is concerned with such issues as:

- patterns of play in different environments;
- the types of playground equipment children of different ages prefer;

Table 8.2 Situations for observational research

1. Children's play
2. Level and type of use of informal leisure/tourism sites – counting heads
3. Spatial patterns of use of sites
4. Visitor profile
5. Deviant behaviour
6. Mystery shopping
7. Complementary research
8. Everyday life
9. Social behaviour

- whether boys' play patterns are different from those of girls; and

- whether there are differences in play patterns between children from different cultural backgrounds.

It is unlikely that such questions could be fully answered by interviewing children, particularly very young children. The obvious approach is to *observe* children at play and record their behaviour.

2.3 Informal spaces: counting heads

Structured observation methods can be used to estimate the level of use of informal recreation areas, such as beaches, urban parks or tourist sites, where there is no admission charge and therefore no ticket sales data to provide information on levels of use. Further, in such situations, there are often few formal constraints on capacity or spatial usage patterns, such as fixed seating.

Where the bulk of users arrive at a facility by private car and a charge is made for parking, indications of use levels may be provided by parking income. However, this does not account for non-vehicular use, and in some cases parking charges do not apply outside of certain hours, or there may be season permit holders who are not recorded every time they enter. To account for all vehicular use, it may be possible to install automatic vehicle counters to count the number of vehicles entering and leaving the site, as discussed later in the chapter. Vehicle counts, however, provide information on the number of *vehicles* using a site but not the number of *people*. To obtain estimates of the latter, it is necessary to supplement the vehicle counts by direct observation for a period of the time to ascertain the average number of persons in vehicles and, at some sites, to estimate the numbers arriving by foot or bicycle, who may not be recorded by the mechanical counting device.

Manual methods of counting usage levels are discussed in the next section on main elements of observational research.

2.4 Informal spaces: spatial/functional patterns of use

Observation is useful not only for gathering data on the number of users of a site but also for studying the way people make use of a site. This is particularly important in relation to the design and layout of leisure spaces, and their capacity. For example, if people tend to crowd close to entrances and parking areas (which they often do in outdoor sites), then where those entrances and parking areas are positioned will affect the pattern of use of the site. This can be used as a management/design tool to influence the pattern of use of a site.

Similarly, if, as has been found, people tend to locate themselves along *edges* – such as walls, fences, banks, areas of trees and shrubs – then this tendency can be used to influence the pattern of use of a site, by determining the nature and location of such edges (Ruddell and Hammitt, 1987). While this applies particularly to outdoor natural areas, it can also have some relevance in built-up areas, such as shopping malls, and in buildings, such as museums.

Buildings and open spaces for public use are often designed with little or no consideration as to how people will actually use them, or on the basis of untested assumptions about how they will be used. In reality it is often found that people do not actually behave as anticipated by the designers and some spaces are underused while others are overcrowded, or spaces are not actually used for the activities for which they were designed or equipped. The pattern of movement of people around exhibitions can affect the information absorbed, depending on the relative prominence and attraction of exhibits, as demonstrated in Case study 8.1. Observation is the means by which these aspects of space utilisation can be discovered.

2.5 Visitor profiles

Questionnaire-based site surveys are the typical means for researching demographic and group composition data which combine to provide a *visitor* or *user profile*. However, depending on the design of the questionnaire, and given that questionnaires in such situations are invariably quite brief, the information collected can miss vital features of the characteristics of the users of a site which can be identified by observation. For example, two music venues could have identical user age/gender/group size profiles but, because of the different types of music offered, could attract very different crowds, in terms of fashion, lifestyle and

---

Case study 8.1   Observation of museum visitor behaviour

In a book chapter reviewing a number of issues related to visitors to museums and visitor centres, Philip Pearce (1988: 90–113) at one point discusses the implications of visitors' decision to turn to the right on entering a museum and proceeding in an anti-clockwise direction, as opposed to turning left and proceeding in a clockwise direction. Research in the Telecom Museum in Victoria, Australia, as shown in Figure 8.1, shows that the two groups of visitors do indeed have different patterns of attention paid to the exhibits, as measured by the proportion of visitors who stop to view each exhibit. Further, those who turn right and proceed anti-clockwise have a higher level of attention throughout the exhibition – but this, it is argued, is likely to be due to the fact that they immediately encounter interactive exhibits, whereas those who turn to the left first encounter static, audio-visual exhibits. The methodology used is clearly simple but possibly time-consuming, depending on how long visitors stay and the extent to which more than one group can be studied at the same time. But it clearly produces data which are likely to be of interest to and readily understood and interpreted by managers.

▶

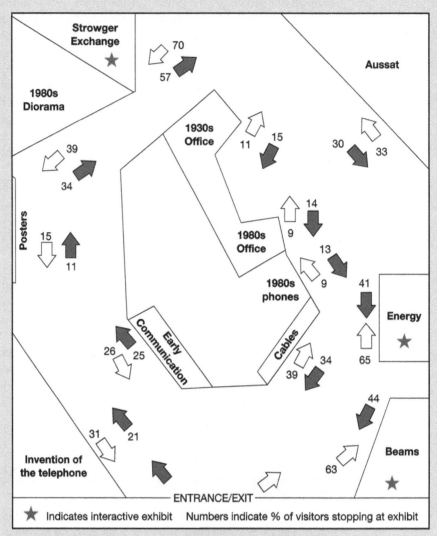

Figure 8.1 Visitor movement patterns in a museum

behaviour. Even at a single venue, an overall profile based on averages and percentages may hide the fact that it is used by a number of distinct user-groups. Questionnaire-based profiles may also miss distinctive usage patterns. For example, a park survey may indicate that there are x per cent mothers with young children, or single elderly users, but fail to pick up the fact that these groups attend at particular times and meet together and socialise. Of course, a questionnaire survey could pick up these features if it included appropriate questions, and if the sample was large enough and the analysis sophisticated enough, but this is not always the case. In addition to being a research approach in its own right, observational research can be used as a preliminary process to identify features of the user profile so that appropriate questions can be included in a questionnaire.

2.6 Deviant behaviour

The notion of *deviant* behaviour is a contested one, with one person's 'deviance' being another person's 'acceptable behaviour'. One term which has been used to cover this area is 'leisure on the margins of conventional morality' (Lynch and Veal, 2006: 317–338), covering such activities as the use of recreational drugs, graffiti and vandalism, various types of sexual activity, gambling and rowdy crowd behaviour or other forms of 'rule-breaking' in leisure settings. Deviant behaviour is a situation where observation is likely to be more fruitful than interviews. People are unlikely to tell an interviewer about their litter-dropping habits, their lack of adherence to the rules in a park, or their beer can-throwing habits at a football match. Finding out about such things requires observation – usually of a covert nature! This of course raises ethical issues, such as people's rights to privacy, as discussed in Chapter 4.

2.7 Mystery shopping

Mystery shopping is another potentially fruitful use of observation but one which is under-exploited in leisure and tourism. It involves a researcher playing the role of user/visitor/customer as a method of obtaining information on the quality of the experience enjoyed by users of a facility or product. The mystery shopper is required to make use of the facilities or services on offer on an *incognito basis*. The researcher has a checklist of features to observe – such as cleanliness, information availability and clarity, staff helpfulness – and makes a report after using the facilities or services. Such an approach draws on the expertise of the observer to assess quality of service and to record details, for example related to safety, which might not be noticed by routine users. Again, ethical and industrial relations issues may arise in such a study because of the element of deception involved in a researcher playing the part of a customer, typically on behalf of management.

2.8 Complementary research

Observation can provide essential quantitative or qualitative complements to other research methods.

Quantitative

Observation involving counts of users can be a necessary complement to inter-view surveys to correct for variation in sampling rates. For instance, in a typical tourist attraction, park or beach, two interviewers, working at a steady rate, may be able to interview virtually all (100 per cent) of users in the less busy periods in the early morning but manage to interview only a small proportion of the users (say 5 per cent) during the busy lunch hour and afternoon periods. In such a case, the final sample would over-represent early morning users and under-represent mid-day and afternoon users. If these two groups have different characteristics, the differential rate of sampling would likely have a biasing effect on, for example, the overall balance of views expressed by the users. Observational counts of the hourly levels of use can provide data to give an appropriate *weight* to the mid-day and afternoon users at the analysis stage. The process of *weighting* is described in more detail in Chapter 16.

Qualitative

Informal observation may provide complementary material for any study which is focused on a particular location or a type of location in order to set the research in context and provide some 'local colour'. More specifically, Seaton (1997) describes a project where interviewers involved in conducting interview surveys at various sites at an arts festival realised, from their own experience and observations, that the survey method had significant limitations. For example, obtaining an adequate sample of evaluative responses at the end of a performance was often impossible because audience members were in a hurry to depart from the venue; a short, standardised questionnaire designed in advance and used for a number of disparate performance-type events failed to capture the variety of experiences; and widespread resentment at the treatment of VIPs at the event was not captured by the questionnaire. An observational schedule was implemented which supplemented survey data by providing observers' own assessments of: audience profile based on type of cars in the car park; type of dress and age; satisfactions and resentments from audience responses; quality of catering by observation of refreshments and customer numbers; significance of friends and relatives of performers in the audience; and equipment and organisational issues. This had some of the features of the 'mystery shopping' technique discussed earlier.

2.9 Everyday life

The idea of simply observing *everyday life* as an approach to studying a society is associated with Britain's Mass Observation anthropological study of the British way of life in the 1930s and 1940s and with the work of Irving Goffman (1959). An anthology of mass observation sketches, published in 1984 (Calder and Sheridan, 1984) includes descriptions of everyday events in pubs, on the Blackpool seafront promenade and in the period of the wartime blitz in London. Goffman's work was more theoretical and concerned the ways individuals use space and interact in public and private places. An anthology of work in the Goffman style (Birenbaum and Sagarin, 1973) includes observational studies of such leisure activities as pinball, bars, card games and restaurants.

2.10 Social behaviour

Observation has been used in sociological research to develop ideas and theories about social behaviour in specific milieus and generally. The research of Fiske (1983) and Grant (1984) on the use of beaches and Marsh et al. (1978) on football fans are examples of this approach. These researchers use an interactive, inductive process to build explanations of social behaviour from what they observe. Very often a key feature of such studies is the way the researchers seek to contrast what they have observed with what has apparently been observed – or assumed to be taking place – by others, particularly those with influence or authority such as officials, police and the media. Observational research can challenge existing stereotypical interpretations of events and places.

3. Main elements of observational research

Observation seems to be essentially a simple research method with little 'technique' to consider. However, as with any research method, careful thought must go into the design, conduct and analysis stages of a project. In structured observation, what is mainly required from the researcher is precision, painstaking attention to detail, and patience. In unstructured observation, the same skills and attributes are required but, in addition, there is a need for a creative 'eye' which can perceive the significance and potential meanings of what is being observed and relate this to the research question. The main tasks in planning and conducting an observational project are as set out in Table 8.3.

As with the 'elements of the research process' outlined in Chapter 3, it is difficult to produce a list of steps which will cover all eventualities. In particular, if the approach is unstructured rather than structured, then a number of the steps discussed here, particularly those concerning counting, may be redundant.

3.1 Choice of site(s)

In the case of a provider-organisation's in-house or consultancy research, the sites to be studied may be fixed. But where there is an element of choice, some time should be devoted to inspecting and choosing sites which will not only

Table 8.3 Tasks/steps in an observation project

---

1. Choice of site(s)
2. Choice of observation point(s)
3. Choice of observation time-period(s)
4. Continuous observation or sampling?
5. Number and length of sampling periods
6. Deciding what to observe
7. Division of site into zones
8. Determination of information recording method
9. Conducting the observation
10. Analysing/interpreting data

---

offer the appropriate leisure/tourism behaviour but also provide suitable conditions for observation and/or will be representative of the range of types of site to be studied.

3.2 Choice of observation point(s)

Choice of observation points within a site is clearly important and needs to be done with care. Some sites can be observed in their entirety from one spot. In other cases, a circuit of viewing spots must be devised. For structured observation – for example, involving counting the number of people present or the flow of people passing a point over a period of time – it may be vital to conduct the observation from the same point(s) in various study periods, but for unstructured observation this may not be a consideration. Indeed, exploring and observing from different locations within a site may be desirable.

When unstructured but intensive observation of people's behaviour is involved, it may be necessary to choose observation points which are unobtrusive to avoid attracting attention, particularly in a confined space with relatively few people. This is related to the issue of the method of recording observations, as discussed in step 8 later in this chapter, since some forms of formal recording are more obvious than others.

3.3 Choice of observation time-period(s)

The choice of time-period is important because of variations in use of a site, by time of the year, day of the week, time of day or weather conditions, according to external social factors such as public holidays, or internal factors, such as the type of music – and hence of patron – offered on particular nights in a club. Observation to cover all time-periods may be very demanding in terms of resources, so some form of sampling of representative time-periods will usually be necessary.

3.4 Continuous observation or sampling?

The question of whether to undertake continuous observation or to sample different time-periods is related to the resources available and the nature of the site and the overall design of the project. The issue is particularly important if one of the aims of the research is to obtain an accurate estimate of the number of visitors to the site, when the terminology used to refer to the two approaches is *continuous counts* versus *spot counts*. It could, for example, be very expensive to place observers at the numerous gates of a large urban park for as much as 100 hours in a week to count the number of users during the entire time the park is open. Even if that were possible, it is unlikely that resources would be available to cover a whole year – except using automatic mechanical devices. A sampling approach must be adopted in most observation projects. Having decided to sample, it is of course necessary to decide how often to do this. This is discussed further under step 5.

If counting is being undertaken, there is also a decision to be made as to whether to count the number of people *entering* or *leaving* the site during specified time-periods or the number of people *present* at particular points in time. Counting the number of people present is referred to as a *spot count*. Counting the number of people entering or leaving over a period of time generally constitutes continuous counting, but if the time-periods are relatively short – for example, half an hour or an hour – then the results can be seen as a form of spot count. Counting the number of people present at particular points in time is generally less resource-intensive, since it can be done by one person regardless of the number of entrances to the site, and it can provide information on the spatial use of the site at the same time. Thus one person, at specified times, makes a circuit of the site and records the number of people present in designated zones (see step 7).

When unstructured observation is being undertaken, it is more likely that continuous observation will be adopted since the aim will generally be to observe the dynamics of events and behaviour at the site. However, the question of when to undertake such observation in order to cover all aspects of the use of the site still needs careful consideration.

3.5 Count frequency

When the study involves counts of users, how often should the counts be undertaken? This will depend to a large extent on the rate of change in the level of use of the site. For example, the six counts in Figure 8.2 are clearly insufficient since, if the broken line is the pattern of use observed in a research project

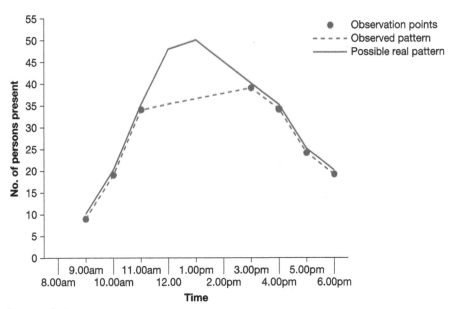

Figure 8.2 Counts of site use

but the unbroken line is the true pattern, the research would not have accurately represented the true situation. There is little advice that can be given to overcome this problem, except to sample frequently at the beginning of a project until the basic patterns of peaks and troughs in usage have been established; subsequently, it may be possible to sample less often.

3.6 What to observe

One approach to observing the spatial behaviour of visitors within a site is to record people's positions directly as indicated in Figure 8.3. In addition to observing numbers of people and their positions, it is possible to observe and record different types of activity. It is also possible, to a limited extent, to record visitor characteristics. For instance, men and women could be separately identified, and it is possible to distinguish between children and adults and to distinguish senior citizens; although, if a number of people are involved as counters, care will need to be taken over the dividing line between such categories as child, teenager, young adult, adult and senior person. It is also possible, again with care, to observe the size of groups using a site, especially if they are observed arriving or leaving at a car park.

These additional items of information would of course complicate the recording sheet, and symbols would be necessary to record the different types of person on a map. Care needs to be taken not to make the data collection so complicated that it becomes too difficult for the observers to observe and collect and leads to inaccuracies. This is one of those situations where it is necessary to consider carefully *why* the data are being collected and not to get carried away with data collection for its own sake.

In addition to observing people statically, or as they arrive at an entrance, it is also possible to observe visitors' movements through a site and illustrate the results graphically. A simple example is shown in Figure 8.4. Of course, care must be taken not to give offence by letting visitors become aware that they are

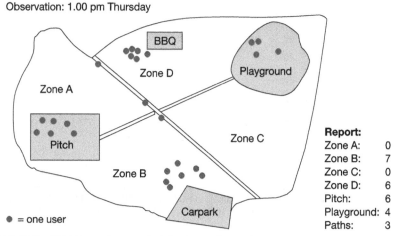

Figure 8.3 Mapping observed data: use of a park

Observation: 1.00–5.00 pm Thursday

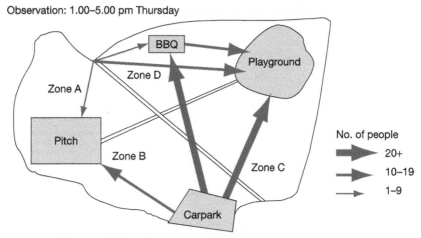

Figure 8.4 Flows within a site

being 'followed', but routes taken by visitors can be revealing for management. As discussed below, GPS methods can be used to perform this tracking, on a sampling basis.

Car registration numbers can be a useful source of information. First, they can provide information on where people have travelled from. Second, number plates can be used to trace the movement of vehicles within an area – for instance, within a national park with a number of stopping points.

3.7 Division of site into zones

In large sites, it is advisable to divide the site into areas or zones and record the number of people and their activities within those zones, as indicated in Figures 8.3 and 8.4. The zones should be determined primarily by management concerns – for example, in a park: the children's playground, the sports areas, the rose garden. But they should also be designed for ease of counting; ideally, zones should be such that they can be observed from one spot and should be clearly demarcated by natural or other features.

3.8 Recording information

Figure 8.5a provides an example of a counting sheet used in a structured observation project requiring counts of use in a study area with seven zones and the possibility of a variety of activities. The data collected using such a form are ideal for storage, manipulation and presentation in graphic form using a spreadsheet computer program as discussed in step 10 below. An alternative to this sort of form is to record data on copies of maps of the site, using numerals or dots, as in Figure 8.3 (with symbols for different types of activity).

Figure 8.5b is an example of a recording sheet for an unstructured observation exercise. There are fewer zones since the observation is likely to be more

a. Structured (recording numbers)

Site	Observer:	Date:	Start time:	Finish time:

Zone:							
Activity	A	B	C	D	E	F	G
Walking							
Sitting							
Playing sport							
Children playing							
Eating							
Total							

b. Unstructured (qualitative comments)

Site	Observer:	Date:	Start time:	Finish time:

	Comments:
Zone A	
Zone B	
Zone C	
Zone D	

Figure 8.5 Examples of observation recording sheets

intensive and time-consuming. In each zone, space is provided for free-form notes. The amount of space to reserve on the sheet depends on the length of time spent and the detail of the observation; it is possible that a whole page, or even more, may be required per zone per time-period, or that additional sheets could be used for different time-periods.

3.9 Conducting the observation

In the case of a structured observational project, if the project has been well planned, then the actual conduct should be straightforward. The main danger in a major project involving a lot of counting can be boredom, leading to inaccuracies in observing and recording data. It is therefore advisable to vary the work of those involved with, where appropriate, data collectors being involved in alternate spells of behavioural observation and counting and, where possible, being switched between sites. Counting can be done manually or using a hand-held mechanical counter.

In the case of unstructured observational projects, more demands are placed on the observer. Such a project is, in effect, a visual form of the qualitative type of research discussed in the next chapter. The observer is required to observe and describe what is going on at the site but must also engage directly with the research questions of the project in order to determine what to observe and what aspects of the observed scene should be described and recorded, and to at least begin the process of explanation.

3.10 Analysing data

In some cases of structured observation, the visual presentations of the sort presented in Figures 8.3 and 8.4 constitute the analysis. In other cases, data must be analysed and processed to present useable results. Four examples are presented here: presentation of usage patterns over the course of a day; estimating usage numbers from spot count data; weighting; and analysis of unstructured data.

Usage patterns

Consider the set of hourly counts shown in Table 8.4, which relate to the numbers of people present in a park, which opens at 8 a.m. and closes at 7 p.m. This pattern is illustrated graphically in Figure 8.6. This presentation may be sufficient for the project in hand, but it can be taken further, including converting the sample counts into an estimate of overall use numbers.

Estimating usage numbers

Table 8.5 sets out a process to estimate usage numbers from hourly spot count data. It is estimated in the example that there is an average of 95.1 people in the park over a 12-hour period, giving a total of 1141 *visitor-hours*. The number of visitor-hours is a valid measure of use in its own right and could be used to compare different sites or to compare the performance of the same site over time. But, for example, 12 visitor-hours could result from:

- one person visiting the park and staying all day;
- two people staying six hours each;
- 12 people staying one hour each; or
- 24 people staying half an hour each.

Table 8.4 Observed use of a park

Time	Walking	Sitting	Playing sport	Children playing	Total
	No. of people observed				
8 a.m.	5	1	0	2	8
9 a.m.	52	6	5	5	68
10 a.m.	44	19	10	7	80
11 a.m.	28	25	12	11	76
12 a.m.	31	40	25	13	109
1 p.m.	32	56	32	17	137
2 p.m.	37	46	23	22	128
3 p.m.	38	45	12	22	117
4 p.m.	39	40	33	32	144
5 p.m.	40	33	27	15	115
6 p.m.	42	20	12	12	86
7 p.m.	45	15	4	9	73
Total	433	346	195	167	1141
Average	36.1	28.8	16.3	13.9	95.1

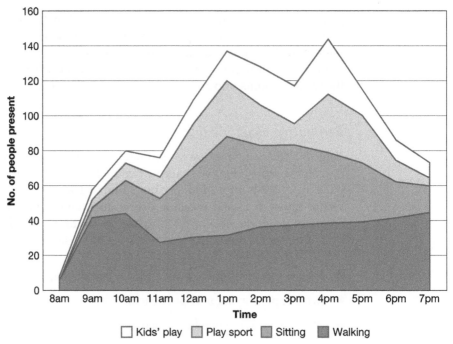

Figure 8.6 Park usage pattern

Table 8.5 Estimating visit numbers from count data

Data	Source	Result
A Average no. of users present	Counts (Table 8.4)	95.1
B No. of hours open	Table 8.4	12 hours
C No. of user-hours	A × B	1141*
D Average length of stay	User survey	0.5 hours
E No. of visits	C/D	2282

* Same as total number of people observed (Table 8.4), but would be different if counts were not made hourly.

So, if an estimate is required of the number of different *persons* visiting the park over the course of the day, additional information on the *length of stay* (item D) is necessary – this would usually be obtained from a questionnaire-based user survey, although it might possibly be obtained from detailed observation of a sample of groups. In the example in Table 8.5, the length of stay is 0.5 hour, so every user-hour represents two users, giving a total of 2282 visits for the day. Thus the number of visits is equal to the number of visitor-hours divided by the average length of stay.

Weighting

Details of user characteristics obtained from observation counts can be used as a check on the accuracy of sampling in interview surveys and may be used to *weight* the results of such surveys so that the final result is a better reflection of the characteristics of the users of the facility. This is similar to the time-of-day correction discussed earlier, but it relates to the personal characteristics of users rather than their time of use of the facility. For instance, if it was found by observation that half the users of a site were women, but in an interview survey only a third of those interviewed were women, the women in the sample could be given a greater weighting at the analysis stage so that their views and attitudes would receive due emphasis. The details of weighting are described more fully in Chapter 16.

Qualitative analysis

The raw form of the data from unstructured observation is likely to comprise a set of notes, possibly with some numbers, and probably with some diagrams. The immediate task for the researcher is therefore to ensure that these notes are in a readable form for future reference; this may involve writing or typing them out to provide a narrative. In the course of doing this, a start may be made on the analysis process. For example, the absence of a particular group of users on one occasion and their presence on another may be linked to the absence or presence of another group or some other change in the environment. The result is therefore likely to be an extended set of notes which can be seen as comparable with sets of notes or transcripts from other forms of qualitative research, as discussed in Chapter 9. Similar approaches to analysis are therefore appropriate, including identification of themes and patterns. The inductive interaction between data collection, data analysis and theory development which applies to qualitative research generally also applies to unstructured observational research. The computer software described in Chapter 15 for analysing informal interview transcripts might also be used to analyse notes from observational research.

4. Use of technology

In addition to the naked eye, a number of technological aids are available in observational research, as listed in Table 8.6. These are discussed in turn.

4.1 Automatic counters

Automatic counters are available for vehicles and pedestrians. Vehicle counters are based on one of four technologies:

- induction loop buried under the roadway: creates a magnetic field which detects vehicles passing through it – this option is relatively permanent, and expensive due to installation costs;

- pressure pad or tube: vehicles passing over the pad or tube complete an electrical circuit – this is cheaper than induction loop, but has limited life due to wear and tear;

- infra-red beam: vehicle is recorded when it breaks the beam – the cheapest option; and

- CCTV (closed circuit television): software can be used to analyse the images and count vehicles passing in view of the camera.

In each case, the device is attached to computerised equipment which can produce a variety of reports for users, for example, hourly, daily, weekly, monthly or annual counts and trend analysis. The technologies can generally detect vehicles of different types/sizes; for example, motorcycles, passenger vehicles and heavy vehicles.

Table 8.6 Type of technology

1. Automatic counters
2. GPS
3. Aerial photography
4. Still photography
5. Video
6. Time-lapse photography

Infra-red beams and CCTV can also be used to count pedestrian movements. But because pedestrians do not necessarily cross the beam one at a time, the counters may have to be *calibrated* using some direct observational data collected for a sample period. For example, direct visual counts may reveal that, in a certain location, a count of 100 on the automatic counter may represent, say, 120 individuals.

Cyclists sometimes use roadways, where they may be picked up by traffic counters, or they may use exclusive cycleways, where infra-red devices can be used. Where they share paths with pedestrians, the mix of pedestrians and cyclists would need to be determined by calibration based on direct observation as discussed earlier.

One of the disadvantages of these devices is their fixed nature; one device can monitor only one route or pathway. Locating a device at every point or entrance of interest may be expensive, and moving them around on a roster may be costly. Again, calibration using a period of direct visual counts may be the solution. For example, if direct counts revealed that the main entrance to a site typically accounted for half of all visits, the counts from an automatic counter located at that entrance would need to be doubled to provide an estimate of total visits.

4.2 GPS

Tracking visitors through a site or tourists around a destination is discussed earlier in this chapter. Various satellite and land-based radio and telephonic geographic positioning systems (GPS) devices may be used to assist in this task. Case study 8.2 provides a summary of a research project by Shoval and Isaacson (2007) which evaluated a number of such devices to track tourists' movements in urban areas.

Case study 8.2	Use of GPS: tourist tracking

Shoval and Isaacson (2007) examined the use of a number of devices to track tourist movements in a destination. Three experiments were conducted using combinations of three electronic technologies: satellite-based global positioning system (GPS), land-based time difference of arrival (TDOA) and cell sector identification (based on cell/mobile telephone systems). Single subjects, wearing one or more of these devices, conducted round trips in three different tourist destinations (Heidelberg, Germany, Jerusalem, Israel, and Nazareth/Akko, Israel). Graphical output of the subjects' routes is reproduced in the article and comments offered on the convenience of use by the subjects. While these procedures are described as experiments in the article, there is no comparison with traditional non-technological methods and the evaluation is minimal, so they should perhaps be more appropriately described as 'demonstrations'.

4.3 Aerial photography

The use of aerial photography is well developed in geography and geology, where a whole sub-discipline of *remote sensing* has developed using a variety of techniques. It can also be effective in leisure and tourism research. Where large areas are concerned, such as coastlines and estuaries, and where access is difficult and recreational use of the site is very scattered, aerial photography may be the only way to obtain estimates of levels and patterns of use. In harbours and estuaries, it is probably the best means of obtaining estimates of numbers of craft using the area since, as they are generally moving about in random patterns, it can be difficult to count manually on a crowded waterway. Needless to say, a good-quality camera is needed for such work.

This technique is currently becoming cheaper with the advent of inexpensive remote-controlled *drones*. At the time of writing, regulations for such devices, covering such issues of height limitations and privacy, are being developed in a number of jurisdictions.

4.4 Still photography

The value of ordinary, land-based photography as an adjunct to direct observation should not be overlooked. Digital photography and editing software have made the incorporation of photographs into research increasingly easy. The level of crowding of a site, its nature and atmosphere can be conveyed to the reader of a report with the aid of photographs. Particular problems – for instance, of erosion or of design faults – can be conveyed better visually than verbally – a picture speaks a thousand words. A 'photo-essay' can be composed around a number of themes or messages to convey simple research findings. The increased quality of cameras in mobile phones makes this a cheap and accessible option.

4.5 Video

Video can be used to record patterns of use of a site. As noted in relation to automatic counters and CCTV, software now exists to perform some types of analysis of digital images. The medium can provide a useful illustration of 'before' and 'after' situations, to illustrate the nature of problems on a site and the effect of measures to ameliorate the problems – for example, congestion, erosion or littering.

4.6 Time-lapse photography

Time-lapse photography lies somewhere between still photography and video. A time-lapse camera can be set up to take pictures of a scene automatically, say, every 10 seconds or every minute. The resultant sequence of pictures can then be projected as a film or video to show the speeded-up pattern of use of the area viewed. This is the technique used in wildlife documentaries which show a plant apparently growing before our eyes, but it can also be used to show the changing pattern of use of a leisure or tourism site.

5. Just looking

Finally, we should not forget just how important it is to use our eyes in research, even if the research project does not explicitly involve systematic observational data collection. Familiarity with a leisure activity or a leisure or tourism site helps in the design of a good research project and aids in interpreting data. Many studies have been based just on informal, but careful, observation. All useful information is not in the form of numbers. Careful observation of what is happening in a particular leisure or tourism situation, at a particular facility or type of facility or among a particular group of people, can be a more appropriate research approach in some circumstances than the use of questionnaires or even informal interviews. The good researcher is all eyes.

Summary

This chapter is concerned with the neglected technique of observation – *looking* – as a tool for research in leisure and tourism. It is noted that observation can be formalised or structured, involving counting of leisure and tourism site users and strict time- and space-sampling methods, or it can be informal or unstructured. In general, observation is non-intrusive in the study site, but 'contrived observation', as in the experimental method, is also possible. Participant observation is a further type of observational research but is dealt with in Chapter 9. Observational research spans the quantitative/qualitative methodological spectrum and can therefore involve both quantitative and qualitative analysis methods. A number of leisure and tourism situations is described in which observation methods might be used, including: children's play; the use patterns of informal leisure/tourism areas where no entrance fee is required and capacity and use patterns are not constrained by factors such as formal seating or booking systems; spatial and functional patterns of use of sites; user profiles; studying deviant behaviour; mystery shopping; research which is complementary to research conducted using other methods; everyday life; and social behaviour. The chapter outlines the observational research process in 10 steps: (1) choice of study site(s); (2) choice of observation point(s); (3) choice of observation time-period(s); (4) deciding on continuous observation or sampling; (5) deciding on the number and length of sampling periods; (6) deciding what to observe; (7) division of the study site(s) into zones; (8) recording observational information; (9) conducting the observation; and (10) analysing data. Finally brief consideration is given to various technological aids, including: automatic counters; GPS devices; and still, video and time-lapse cameras.

Test questions

1. Four types of observational research are identified at the beginning of the chapter. What are they?

2. A total of eight leisure or tourism situations is described where observation is a suitable, and sometimes the *most* suitable, form of research. Name three of these situations and explain in each case why observation is a particularly suitable research method.

3. What is the difference between spot counting and continuous counting?

4. In what forms can data from observational research be presented?

5. How can observational research findings assist in regard to weighting of survey data?

Exercises

1. Select an informal leisure or tourism site and position yourself in an unobtrusive location, but where you can see what is going on. Over a period of two hours, record what happens. Write a report on: how the site is used; who it is used by; how many people use it; what conflicts there are, if any, between different groups of users; and how the design of the space aids or hinders the activity which people engage in on the site.

2. Establish a counting system to record the number of people present in a selected leisure or tourism site at hourly intervals during the course of a day. Use the system to estimate the number of visitor-hours at the site for a two-hour period.

3. In relation to exercise 2: conduct interviews with three or four visitors each hour, and ask them how long they have stayed, or expect to stay, at the site. Establish the average length of stay and, using this information and the data from exercise 2, estimate the number of persons visiting the site in the course of the two-hour period.

4. Use photographs to record examples of neglect or damage to leisure or tourism sites known to you.

5. Examine recent volumes of a leisure or tourism journal and ascertain the proportion of articles using observational methods.

Resources

- General/methodological: Annear et al. (2014), Burch (1981), Kellehear (1993), Adler and Adler (1994); Structured and unstructured observation: Bryman and Bell (2015).

- Counting heads: Gartner and Hunt (1988), Tyre and Siderelis (1978).

- *En route* surveys: Gartner and Hunt (1988).

- Examples of leisure/tourism studies using observation:
  - Beach use: Bin et al. (2005), Fiske (1983), Grant (1984);
  - Children's play: Child (1983);
  - Countryside recreation: Glyptis (1981a, 1981b), Van der Zande (1985), Keirle and Walsh (1999);
  - Events: Seaton (1997);
  - Museums/zoos: Bitgood et al. (1988); Pearce (1988: see Case study 8.1); Ross et al. (2012).
  - Park use – health-related: Evenson et al. (2016);
  - Sporting crowds/riots: Cunneen et al. (1989); Football: Marsh et al. (1978); and
  - Urban parks: Floyd et al. (2008).

- GPS: Edwards et al. (2010), Shoval and Ahas (2016), Shoval and Isaacson (2007 – see Case study 8.2).

- Mystery shopping:
  - General: Dawson and Hillier (1995); and
  - Travel agents: Hudson et al. (2001).

- Photography: Annear et al. (2014), English (1988), Garrod (2008).

- Video: Arnberger and Eder (2008), Wuellner (1981).

- Visual methods: Annear et al. (2014); Johnson (2014).

References

Adler, P. A., and Adler, P. (1994). Observational techniques. In N. K. Denzin and Y. S. Lincoln (Eds), *Handbook of qualitative research* (pp. 377–92). Thousand Oaks, CA: Sage.

Annear, M. J., Cushman, G., Gidlow, B., and Keeling, S. (2014). A place for visual research methods in the field of leisure studies? Evidence from two studies of older adults' active leisure. *Leisure Studies*, 33(6), 618–43.

Arnberger, A., and Eder, R. (2008). Assessing user interactions on shared recreational trails by long-term video monitoring. *Managing Leisure*, 13(1), 36–51.

Birenbaum, A., and Sagarin, E. (Eds) (1973). People in places: the sociology of the familiar. London: Nelson.

Bin, O., Landry, C. E., Ellis, C.L., and Vogelsong, H. (2005). Some consumer surplus estimates for North Carolina beaches. *Marine Resource Economics*, 20, 145–61.

Bitgood, S., Patterson, D., and Benefield, A. (1988). Exhibit design and visitor behaviour. *Environment and Behaviour*, 20(4), 474–91.

Burch, W. R. (1981). The ecology of metaphor: spacing regularities for humans and other primates in urban and wild habitats. *Leisure Sciences*, 4(3), 213–30.

Bryman, A., and Bell, E. (2015). Breaking down the quantitative/qualitative divide, and Mixed methods research. Chapters 26–27 of *Business research methods*, 4th edn (pp. 625–60). Oxford: Oxford University Press.

Calder, A., and Sheridan, D. (1984). *Speak for yourself: a Mass Observation anthology, 1937–49*. London: Jonathan Cape.

Child, E. (1983). Play and culture: a study of English and Asian children. *Leisure Studies*, 2(2), 169–86.

Cunneen, C., Findlay, M., Lynch, R. and Tupper, V. (1989). *Dynamics of collective conflict: riots at the Bathurst Bike Races*. Sydney: Law Book Co.

Dawson, J., and Hillier, J. (1995). Competitor mystery shopping: methodological considerations and implications for the MRS Code of Conduct. *Journal of the Market Research Society*, 37(4), 417–43.

Edwards, D., Dickson, T., Griffin, T., and Hayllar, B. (2010). Tracking the urban visitor: methods for examining tourists' spatial behaviour and visual representations, in G. Richards and W. Munsters (Eds), *Cultural tourism research methods* (pp.104–14). Wallingford, UK: CABI.

English, F. W. (1988). The utility of the camera in qualitative inquiry. *Educational Researcher*, 17(5), 8–15.

Evenson, K. R., Jones, S. A., Holliday, K. M., Cohen, D. A., and McKenzie, T. L. (2016). Park characteristics, use, and physical activity: A review of studies using SOPARC (System for Observing Play and Recreation in Communities). *Preventive Medicine*, 86, 153–66.

Fiske, J. (1983). Surfalism and sandiotics: the beach in Oz popular culture. *Australian Journal of Cultural Studies*, 1(2), 120–49.

Floyd. M. F., Spengler, J. O., Maddock, J. E., Gobster, P. E., and Suau, L. (2008). Environmental and social correlates of physical activity in neighbourhood parks: an observational study in Tampa and Chicago. *Leisure Sciences*, 30(4), 360–75.

Garrod, B. (2008). Exploring place perception: a photo-based analysis. *Annals of Tourism Research*, 35(2), 381–401.

Gartner, W., and Hunt, J.D. (1988). A method to collect detailed tourist flow information. *Annals of Tourism Research*, 15(1), 159–72.

Glyptis, S.A. (1981a). People at play in the countryside. *Geography*, 66, 277–85.

Glyptis, S.A. (1981b). Room to relax in the countryside. *The Planner*, 67(5), 120–22.

Goffman, I. (1959). *The presentation of self in everyday life*. Garden City, NY: Doubleday/Anchor.

Grant, D. (1984). Another look at the beach. *Australian Journal of Cultural Studies*, 2(2), 131–38.

Hudson, S., Snaith, T., Miller, G., and Hudson, P. (2001). Distribution channels in the travel industry: using mystery shoppers to understand the influence of travel agency recommendations. *Journal of Travel Research*, 40(2), 148–54.

Johnson, A. (2014). Visual methods in leisure research. *World Leisure Journal*, 56(4), 317–23.

Keirle, I., and Walsh, S. (1999). Objective assessment of countryside recreation by observation. *Journal of Environmental Planning and Management*, 42(6), 875–87.

Kellehear, A. (1993). *The unobtrusive researcher: a guide to methods*. Sydney: Allen and Unwin.

Lynch, R., and Veal, A. J. (2006). *Australian leisure*, 3rd edn. Melbourne: Longman Australia.

Marsh, P., Rosser, E., and Harré, R. (1978). *The rules of disorder*. London: Routledge.

Pearce, P. L. (1988). *The Ulysses factor: evaluating visitors in tourist settings*. New York: Springer-Verlag.

Ross, S. R., Melbers, L. M., Gillespie, K. L., and Lukas, K. E. (2012). The impact of a modern, naturalistic exhibit design on visitor behavior: a cross-facility comparison. *Visitor Studies*, 15(1), 3–15.

Ruddell, E. J., and Hammit, W. E. (1987). Prospect refuge theory: a psychological orientation for edge effect in recreation environments. *Journal of Leisure Research*, 19(4), 249–60.

Seaton, A. V. (1997). Unobtrusive observational measures as a quality extension of visitor surveys at festivals and events: mass observation revisited. *Journal of Travel Research*, 35(4), 25–30.

Shoval, N., and Isaacson, M. (2007). Tracking tourists in the digital age. *Annals of Tourism Research*, 34(1), 141–59.

Shoval, N., and Ahas, R. (2016). The use of tracking technologies in tourism research: the first decade. *Tourism Geographies*, doi: 10.1080/14616688 .2016.1214977.

Tyre, G. L., and Siderelis, C. D. (1978). Instant-count sampling – a technique for estimating recreation use in municipal settings. *Journal of Leisure Research*, 10(2), 173–80.

Van der Zande, A. N. (1985). Distribution patterns of visitors in large areas: a problem of measurement and analysis. *Leisure Studies*, 4(1), 85–100.

Wuellner, L. H. (1981). The adult inhibition and peer disinhibition of preschool group play. *Journal of Leisure Research*, 13(2), 159–73.

9 Qualitative methods: introduction and data collection

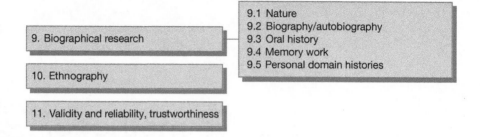

9. Biographical research

9.1 Nature
9.2 Biography/autobiography
9.3 Oral history
9.4 Memory work
9.5 Personal domain histories

10. Ethnography

11. Validity and reliability, trustworthiness

1. Introduction

This chapter addresses methods of research which involve the collection and analysis of *qualitative* information using the media of words, images or sounds, as distinct from numbers as used in quantitative methods. The chapter discusses the nature, history and advantages of qualitative methods, their role in research and the range of specific methods available, including in-depth interviews, group interviews/focus groups, participant observation, biographical methods, ethnographic approaches and the qualitative analysis of texts.

For most qualitative research methods, data collection, analysis and interpretation are intermingled rather than functionally and temporally separated as is generally the case in quantitative methods. Nevertheless, distinct data collection and analysis processes can be identified and analysis procedures tend to have common characteristics across the range of qualitative data-collection methods, so qualitative data *analysis* is discussed in Part III, Chapter 15.

1.1 The nature of qualitative methods

The term *qualitative* is used to describe research methods and techniques which use, and give rise to, qualitative rather than quantitative information; that is, information in the form of words, images and sounds. In general the qualitative approach tends to collect a great deal of detailed (sometimes referred to as 'rich' or 'thick') information about relatively few cases or subjects rather than the more limited information about a large number of cases or subjects which is typical of quantitative research. It is, however, possible to envisage qualitative research which actually deals with large numbers of cases. For example, a research project on sports spectators, involving observation and participation in spectator activity, could involve information relating, collectively, to tens of thousands of people.

Qualitative methods can be used for pragmatic reasons, in situations where formal, quantified research is not necessary or is not possible, but there can also be theoretical grounds for using such methods. Qualitative research is generally based on the belief that the people personally involved in a particular (leisure or tourism) situation are best placed to describe and explain their experiences, feelings and world view in their own words, and that they should be allowed to speak without the intermediary of the researcher and without being overly constrained by the framework imposed by the researcher.

One way in which qualitative research has been characterised is by referring to the *researcher* as 'research instrument', in contrast to, for example, the survey method where the research instrument is a questionnaire.

1.2 History and development

The history of the use of qualitative methods in leisure studies is different for North America, where the bulk of English-language leisure research activity has been conducted, and Britain and Australasia, which came later to the scene and have smaller research communities. The history in tourism studies, however, follows a similar trajectory worldwide.

The difference in regard to leisure is illustrated by the earliest large-scale empirical studies of leisure in the two countries. The American study *Leisure: a Suburban Study* by George Lundberg et al. (1934) was based primarily on time-budget diaries completed by almost 2500 respondents, and this was just one of 18 different survey formats used. The main results were presented in tables, although there are no statistical tests and the discussion is presented in a narrative style. By contrast, the earliest large-scale British study, Rowntree and Lavers's (1951) *English Life and Leisure*, while based on a substantial sample, used primarily qualitative methods, as indicated in Case study 9.1.

Case study 9.1	Early qualitative research: *English Life and Leisure*

In the earliest large-scale British study of leisure, *English Life and Leisure*, published in 1951, the authors describe their research method as follows:

> In making our study of contemporary life in England and Wales, we concluded that, besides the usual and methods of approaching the subject, we needed some means of letting a substantial number of men and women, of all ages and social classes, speak for themselves, in the hope that, as they told their individual stories, we should build up a living picture of English life and leisure. For such a purpose as we had in mind, formal interviewing, or the use of questionnaires, would have been useless, for many of the matters about which we desired information are intensely personal, and in any case we were interested more in behaviour than in such opinions as could be elicited by answers to short, set questions. We therefore decided to build up our picture of what people are like by a system of indirect interviewing. This method consists of making an acquaintance of an individual – the excuses for doing so are immaterial – and developing the acquaintance until his or her confidence is gained and information required can be obtained in ordinary conversation, without the person concerned ever knowing that there has been an interview or that any specific information was being sought. Such a method is laborious but effective. (Rowntree and Lavers, 1951: xii)

▶

Apart from likely ethics committee concerns about 'informed consent' on the part of interviewees, such an explanation would not look out of place in a twenty-first-century account of the rationale for use of qualitative methods. The first 121 pages of *English Life and Leisure* consist of individual 'case histories' of 220 (103 female, 117 male) of the almost 1000 people interviewed in 11 cities. These vary from just a few lines to almost a page in length and, although anonymous, are often remarkably candid. The scope of the interviews and case histories is indicated by the titles of the following 12 summary chapters which are:

- Commercialised Gambling
- How honest is Britain?
- Dancing
- Drink
- The cinema
- Reading habits
- Smoking
- The stage
- Adult education
- Sexual promiscuity
- Broadcasting [radio]
- Religion.

Half of the chapters include one or two small tables based on the survey respondents, but most of the discussion is qualitative in nature, including frequent short quotations from interviews.

Also of note is that the report includes perhaps the earliest example, in a leisure study, of the analysis of 'texts', in this case films. In a distinctive indicator of the times, the authors say:

When we started our investigations early in 1946 neither of us knew much about the cinema. We were not in any way hostile to it, but it so happened that preoccupation with other matters had prevented both of us from paying other than very infrequent visits to cinemas. We decided, however, that we must be in a position to write from first-hand knowledge, and one of us . . . has accordingly during the course of our investigations visited 125 cinemas of all types in London [and 10 other cities]. After every visit a careful analysis was made of the principal film shown, and our remarks in this section are based on these analyses. (Rowntree and Lavers, 1951: 232–3)

The section includes summary details of seven of the films, the researcher's own assessment of the 'desirability' of the 125 films viewed and a discussion of the censorship system. Desirability is assessed in a way which is unlikely to be seen in a contemporary study, using a five-category scale, as follows:

- broadly of cultural or educational value;
- reasonable entertainment but nothing more;
- harmless but inane;
- glorifying false values; and
- really objectionable.

The divide between qualitative and quantitative methods continued to be stronger in North America than in the United Kingdom; indeed, it has been argued that qualitative methods played a significant role in British leisure research as it entered its first major growth phase in the 1970s (Veal, 1994).

The difference in traditions is also reflected in research methods textbooks. For example, in the earliest English-language research methods textbook in the field, published in the United States in 1974, Richard Kraus and Lawrence Allen presented only the classical scientific model of research using quantitative methods. They recognised the existence of qualitative methods, but cautiously stated:

> Both forms of research represent important and valid approaches. However, there is a widely held view that the most significant kinds of research studies are those that are based on quantitative analysis, and that science must rely on actual measurement of scientific data. As a result, researchers tend to use quantitative measures wherever possible. . . . in such an individualistic and diversified field as recreation and leisure, there ought to be a place for research of a more intuitive or descriptive nature. (Kraus and Allen, 1974: 24–5)

They further stated that qualitative research methodology was 'less easily described', so there was no guidance on qualitative methods in their text. By contrast, the first British research methods textbook in the field, the first edition of this text, published in 1992, included a chapter on qualitative methods.

A shift in attitudes towards qualitative methods in leisure studies took place across the anglophone world during the 1980s, reflected in the publication of Karla Henderson's *Dimensions of Choice: A Qualitative Approach to Recreation, Parks and Leisure Research* (Henderson, 1991), later followed by a second edition (Henderson, 2006); and a similarly focused text for sport management appeared in 2009 (Edwards and Skinner, 2009). The shift was also reflected in the second edition of Kraus and Allen's textbook, published in 1998, in which they devoted a whole chapter to qualitative methods and one to documentary methods. The 'naturalistic perspective' was discussed alongside the scientific model and the first-edition observations noted earlier were cautiously modified. They stated that 'a strong case can be made that, in such an individualistic and diversified field as recreation and leisure, there ought to be a place for research of a more deeply probing, intuitive, or philosophical nature' (Kraus and Allen, 1998: 36).

The shift from an almost exclusively quantitative approach to a mix of quantitative and qualitative methods also took place in tourism studies. Ritchie and Goeldner's (1994) *Travel, Tourism and Hospitality Research* and Ryan's (1995) *Researching Tourist Satisfaction* both included chapters on qualitative methods, although the overall emphasis of the texts was quantitative. In 2004, a book of readings on *Qualitative Research in Tourism* (Phillimore and Goodson, 2004a) was published, with various contributions arguing strongly for the use of qualitative approaches, generally associating them with a critical/interpretive approach to tourism research. In that book, the editors provide a view of the evolutionary story (Phillimore and Goodson, 2004b), and Hollinshead (2004: 66) concludes that, in the early 2000s, tourism researchers were still not 'consummately skilful' in exploring ontology and selecting appropriate research methods.

Thus, in recent decades, qualitative methods have become widely accepted and are no longer seen as exceptional and in need of special justification. Arguably, in leisure studies qualitative studies are now dominant, while in tourism studies they are commonplace. Increasingly, in both areas, mixed methods are used. While, as discussed in Chapter 5, we should be cautious about invoking such terms as 'triangulation', it is often the case that research projects address more than one question and so multiple methods may be called for. This was illustrated in the historical example in Case study 9.1 and in a more contemporary example in Case study 9.2.

Case study 9.2   Mixed methods

Bennett et al. (2009) sought to replicate, in Britain in the 2000s, the influential research on class and culture conducted by Bourdieu (1984) in 1960s France. Their empirical work included four research vehicles, described in methodological appendices:

- 25 focus groups, to inform the researchers and provide input to the design of a questionnaire for a major sample survey;

- a questionnaire-based survey, with a sample of 1564 and a boost sample of 227 to ensure inclusion of various ethnic minorities;

- follow-up household semi-structured interviews with 30 individuals, selected from focus group and survey respondents together with their partners, to explore household dynamics, in contrast to individual behaviour etc. covered in the survey; and

- semi-structured interviews with 11 individuals occupying 'pinnacle positions in the corporate sector, political life or the civil service', who tend not to be picked up in the typical sample survey.

While the bulk of the book reports the results of the questionnaire-based survey, material from the other, qualitative, exercises is woven into the text.

---

2. Merits, functions, limitations

Kelly (1980), in making a plea for more qualitative leisure research over 30 years ago, suggested that qualitative research has the following advantages over quantitative research in the leisure context:

- The method corresponds with the nature of the phenomenon being studied – that is, leisure is a qualitative experience for the individual.

- The method 'brings people back in' to leisure research. By contrast, quantitative methods tend to be very impersonal – *real* people with names and unique personalities do not generally feature.

- The results of qualitative research are more understandable to people who are not statistically trained.

- The method is better able to encompass personal change over time. By contrast, much quantitative research tends to look only at current behaviour as related to current social, economic and environmental circumstances, ignoring the fact that most people's behaviour is heavily influenced by their life history and experience.

- Reflecting his first point, Kelly argued that leisure, including tourism, involves a great deal of face-to-face interaction between people – involving symbols, gestures, etc. – and qualitative research is well suited to investigating this.

- Kelly argues that qualitative techniques are better at providing an understanding of people's needs and aspirations, although some researchers in the psychological field in particular might disagree with him.

In this text, it has been argued that different methods are not inherently good or bad, but just more or less appropriate for the task in hand. Thus Kelly's comments relate to particular types of research with particular purposes. Qualitative methods would clearly be most appropriate if the focus of interest, following Kelly, is: the qualitative experience of leisure or tourism; personal leisure or tourism histories; the use of symbols, gestures, etc., in leisure/tourism contexts; people's leisure/tourism needs and aspirations; and/or communicating with an audience without statistical training.

Peterson (1994), speaking from a market researcher's perspective, lists the potential uses of qualitative research as:

- to develop hypotheses concerning relevant behaviour and attitudes;

- to identify the full range of issues, views and attitudes which should be pursued in larger-scale research;

- to suggest methods for quantitative enquiry – for example, in terms of deciding who should be included in interview surveys;

- to identify language used to address relevant issues (thus avoiding the use of jargon in questionnaires);

- to understand how a buying decision is made – questionnaire surveys are not very good at exploring *processes*;

- to develop new product, service or marketing strategy ideas – the free play of attitudes and opinions can be a rich source of ideas for the marketer;

- to provide an initial screening of new product, service or strategy ideas; and

- to learn how communications are received – what is understood and how – particularly related to advertising.

In the leisure and tourism research literature there is an apparent ongoing debate among proponents of quantitative and qualitative methods. This debate, however, has often been somewhat one-sided. Proponents of qualitative methods, in seeking to defend the approach in the face of assumed opposition, often ascribe views about the limitations of qualitative methods or the merits or quantitative methods to unnamed and unsourced proponents of the latter, sometimes bracketed with positivists. The quotation from Kraus and Allen noted earlier is a rare example of an explicit statement of the view that quantitative methods are innately superior to qualitative methods, but even here the authors distance themselves from the comment by referring to it as a 'widely held view', leaving open the possibility that they themselves might not subscribe to it. Phillimore and Goodson (2004b: 3–4) refer to qualitative research as being 'prone to criticisms that it is a 'soft', 'non-scientific' and inferior approach'. This is referenced to a paper by Guba and Lincoln (1998) which itself refers to just a single critical source, Sechrest (1992), who argues for the retention of quantitative methods in the particular context of public policy evaluation research.

While partisan proponents of qualitative methods are vigorous in promoting their virtues, like all methods, they also have their limitations. For example, Miles and Huberman, in their book *Qualitative Data Analysis* (1994), note the substantial increase in the prevalence of qualitative research in the social sciences but caution that:

> in the flurry of this activity, we should be mindful of some pervasive issues that have not gone away. These issues include the labour-intensiveness (and extensiveness over months or years) of [qualitative] data collection, frequent data overload, the distinct possibility of researcher bias, the time demands of processing and coding data, the adequacy of sampling when only a few cases can be managed, the generalizability of findings, the credibility and quality of conclusions, and their utility in the world of policy and action. (Miles and Huberman, 1994: 2)

In practice, Keith Hollinshead (2004: 67–8) observes in regard to tourism research: 'many qualitative approaches to research turn out to be poorly handled' and 'all too often qualitative researchers unquestioningly adopt a pre-formulated, generalised or etic orientation to their subject of study'. Similar comments are expressed by Dupuis (1999) in relation to qualitative leisure research.

3. The qualitative research process

3.1 Sequential vs recursive

Qualitative methods generally require, and enable, a more flexible, although no less rigorous, approach to overall research design and conduct than other approaches. Most quantitative research tends to be *sequential* in nature; the

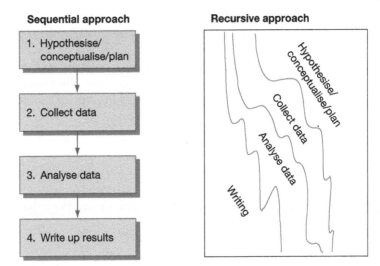

Figure 9.1 Sequential and recursive approaches to research

components of research as set out in Chapter 3 tend to be distinct and follow in a pre-planned sequence. This is inevitable because of the nature of the typical quantitative core data-collection task. Much qualitative research involves a more fluid relationship between the various elements of the research – an approach which might be called *recursive*. In this approach, hypothesis formation evolves as the research progresses, data analysis and collection take place concurrently and writing is also often evolutionary and ongoing rather than a separate process which takes place at the end of the project. The two approaches are represented diagrammatically in Figure 9.1.

Although the sequential and recursive models are presented here in the context of a contrast between quantitative and qualitative methods, in fact both quantitative and qualitative methods can involve sequential and recursive approaches. Thus it is possible for an essentially quantitative study to involve a variety of data sources and a number of small-scale studies, which build on one another in an iterative way. On the other hand, it is also possible for an essentially qualitative study to be conducted on a large scale, with a single data source – for example, a nationwide study of local council leaders, involving fairly standardised in-depth interviews.

3.2 Grounded theory

An important philosophical perspective in the analysis of qualitative data is the concept of *grounded theory* developed by two sociologists, Glaser and Strauss (1967). Grounded theory is concerned with the generation of theory from research, as opposed to research that tests *a priori* theory. It is therefore, in the terms discussed in Chapter 2, inductive rather than deductive. In this paradigm, theories and models should be *grounded* in real empirical observations rather than be governed by traditional methodologies and theories. In the generation of theory, the researcher approaches the data with no pre-formed notions in mind, instead seeking to uncover patterns and contradictions through close examination of the data. To achieve this, the researcher needs to be very familiar with the data, the subjects and the cultural context of the research. The process is a complex and personal one.

4. The range of qualitative methods – introduction

Qualitative techniques commonly used in leisure and tourism research and which are discussed in more detail in this chapter include: in-depth interviews; group interviews or focus groups; participant observation; textual analysis; biographical methods; and ethnography. The basic characteristics of these approaches are summarised in Table 9.1.

Table 9.1   Qualitative methods: summary

In-depth interviews	• Usually conducted with a relatively small number of subjects.
	• Interview guided by a checklist of topics rather than a formal questionnaire.
	• Interviews often digitally recorded and notes or verbatim transcript prepared.
	• Interviews typically take at least half an hour and may extend over several hours.
	• Repeat/follow-up interviews possible.
Group interviews/ focus groups	• Interviews/discussions conducted with a group, typically from 6 to 12.
	• Process is managed by a *facilitator* who guides the discussion.
	• Interaction between subjects takes place as well as between facilitator and subjects.
	• Proceedings generally digitally recorded and notes or verbatim transcript prepared.
Participant observation	• Researcher gathers information by being an actual participant with the subjects being studied.
	• Researcher may be known by the subjects as a researcher or may be *incognito*.
Biographical research	• Focuses on individual full or partial life histories.
	• May involve in-depth interviews but also documentary evidence and subjects' own written accounts.
Textual analysis	• Analysis of the content of 'texts', including print and audio-visual media.
Ethnography	• Utilises a number of the above techniques rather than being a single technique – borrowed from anthropology.

5. In-depth interviews

5.1 Nature

An in-depth interview, sometimes referred to as semi-structured, is character-ised by its length, depth and structure.

- *Length:* In-depth interviews tend to be much longer than questionnaire-based interviews, typically taking at least half an hour and sometimes several hours. The method may involve interviewing people more than once.

- *Depth:* As the name implies, the in-depth interview seeks to probe more deeply than is possible with a questionnaire-based interview. Rather than just asking a question, recording a simple answer, and moving on, the in-depth interviewer typically encourages respondents to talk, asks supplementary questions and asks respondents to explain their answers.

- *Structure:* The in-depth interview is therefore less structured than a questionnaire-based interview. While questionnaire-based interviews may be seen as *structured*, in-depth interviews are seen as *semi-structured* or *unstructured*, as discussed further later in this chapter. As a result, every interview in a qualitative study, although dealing with the same issues, will be different.

Arguably, interviews in general can be said to span part of a spectrum related to the extent to which the questions and their wording are fully pre-scribed in advance or not prescribed at all, and the extent to which responses are pre-coded or open-ended. This is shown in Table 9.2, which shows that questionnaire-based and in-depth interviews overlap in the middle of the spectrum.

Table 9.2 Questions, responses and interview types

Interview type	Question format	Responses	Interviewer/interviewee interaction
Structured A	Prescribed by questionnaire	Pre-coded	Formal, consistent
Structured B	Prescribed by questionnaire	Open-ended	Formal, consistent
Structured + semi-structured elements	Prescribed by questionnaire + supplementary	Open-ended	Mostly formal, consistent
Semi-structured	Checklist: question format not prescribed	Open-ended	Conversational, variable
Unstructured	Only the broad topic area is prescribed	Open-ended	Free-flowing conversational, variable

5.2 Purposes and situations

In-depth interviews tend to be used in three situations.

1. The subjects of the research may be relatively few in number, so a questionnaire-based, quantitative style of research would be inappropriate.

2. The information likely to be obtained from each subject is expected to vary considerably and in complex ways. An example would be interviews with the management staff of a leisure or tourism organisation, or interviews with the coaches of different sports teams. Each of these interviews would be different and would be a 'story' in its own right. In reporting the research, the unique nature and structure of each of these accounts would be of interest – data on 'what percentage of respondents said what' would not be relevant.

3. A topic may be explored as a preliminary stage in planning a larger study, possibly a quantitative study, such as a questionnaire-based survey.

5.3 Checklist

Rather than a formal questionnaire, the 'instrument' used for semi-structured in-depth interviews is often a *checklist* of topics to be raised, although a few key pre-determined, prescribed questions may be included. For example, a formal questionnaire might ask a question: 'Which of the following countries have you ever visited on holiday?' The informal interview checklist might simply include the words 'Countries visited'. The interviewer would shape the question according to the circumstances of a particular interview. If the interviewer is interested, for example, in the influence of childhood holiday experiences on adult visit patterns, in some interviews it may be necessary to ask a specific question such as: 'What overseas holiday trips did you take as a child?' In other interviews, in response to the interviewer's initial question, the interviewee might talk at length and volunteer detailed information on childhood trips unprompted. It is then not necessary to ask the separate question about childhood trips. Thus, in-depth interviews vary from interview to interview; they take on a life of their own.

The skill on the part of the interviewer is to ensure that all relevant topics are covered – even though they may be covered in different orders and in different ways in different interviews. This, however, assumes that the list of relevant topics is known from the beginning and is already covered by the checklist. In practice the qualitative research allows the range of topics – and hence the content of the checklist – to evolve during the research process. New topics may emerge from interviewees themselves.

The design of the checklist should nevertheless be as methodical as the design of a formal questionnaire – in particular, the items to be included on the checklist should be based on the conceptual framework for the study and the resultant list of data needs, whether this be detailed or general in nature, as discussed

This is part of a checklist devised in connection with a study of people's use of leisure time and attitudes towards leisure.

Current activities	How often?
	Why?
Explore each one – compare	Where? – home/away from home
	Who with?
	Meaning/importance
	Type of involvement
Activities would like to do	Why not?
Meaning of 'leisure' to you	
Constraints:	Home
	Work – time/energy/colleagues
	Family roles
	Being a woman/man
	Being a parent
	Money/costs
	Car/transport
Past activities	At school
	At college/university
	With family
Why changes?	
Facilities	Locally: favourite
	City: use/non-use – why?
Clubs/associations	
Personality	Skills
Dislikes	Aspirations

Figure 9.2   Example of a checklist for in-depth interviewing

in Chapter 3. An example of a checklist is included as Figure 9.2. The example given is in the form of a fairly terse list of topics. An alternative would be to include fully worded questions to initiate discussion of various topics, as would appear in a questionnaire; this may be advisable when a number of interviewers is involved. The problem with fully worded questions is that actually turning to the clipboard and reading out lengthy questions can interrupt the flow and informality of the interview. The more detailed the checklist, the more the interview would be described as *semi-structured*. If only a very brief checklist is used, or even none at all, the interview would be described as unstructured.

It should be noted that this typology and terminology would not be universally accepted among writers in the field: for example, Jennings (2005: 101) describes the questionnaire used in a structured interview as a 'checklist' and her corresponding entry for semi-structured and unstructured interviews is 'Field notes. Transcription and recording'. This terminology is not adopted here because it seems to confuse information elicitation with information recording.

5.4 The interviewing process

Conducting a good in-depth interview could be said to require the skills of a good investigative journalist. As Dean and his colleagues put it:

> Many people feel that a newspaper reporter is a far cry from a social scientist. Yet many of the data of social science today are gathered by interviewing and observation techniques that resemble those of a skilled newspaper [reporter] . . . at work on the study of, say, a union strike or a political convention. It makes little sense for us to belittle these less rigorous methods as 'unscientific'. We will do better to study them and the techniques they involve so that we can make better use of them in producing scientific information. (Dean et al., quoted in McCall and Simmons, 1969: 1)

There are two approaches to conducting an in-depth interview: standardised and informal or unstructured.

The standardised approach

A standardised approach is one in which the emphasis in a 'semi-structured' interview is on the 'structured' aspect and where some elements of the traditional scientific approach are replicated. The interaction between researcher and subject is, as far as possible, similar for all subjects. So prescribed questions are used, although the interviewer also improvises, depending on the flow of the interview. In this case, an important skill in interviewing is to avoid becoming so taken up in the conversational style of the interview that the interviewee is 'led' by the interviewer. The interviewer avoids agreeing – or disagreeing – with the interviewee or suggesting answers. This is more difficult than it sounds because in normal conversation, we tend to make friendly noises and contribute to the discussion. In this situation, the interviewer is torn between the need to maintain a friendly conversational atmosphere and the desire *not* to influence the interviewee's responses. Some of the carefully planned sequencing of questions which would be built into formal questionnaires must be achieved by the interviewer being very sensitive and quick thinking. For example, having discovered that the respondent does not go to the theatre, the interviewer should not lead the respondent by saying: 'Is this because of the cost?' Rather, the interviewee should be asked a more open question, such as: 'Why is that?' If the interviewee does not mention cost, but cost is of particular interest in the study, then the respondent might be asked a question such as: 'What about seat prices?' But this would be only *after* the interviewee has given his or her own unprompted reasons for not attending the theatre.

An important skill in interviewing of this sort is not to be afraid of silence. Some questions puzzle respondents, and they need time to think. The interviewer does not have to fill the space with noise under the guise of 'helping' the interviewee. The interviewee is allowed time to ponder. The initiative can be left with the respondent to ask for an explanation if a question is unclear. While it is pleasant to engender a conversational atmosphere in these situations, the semi-structured interview is in fact different from a conversation. The interviewer is meant to listen and encourage the respondent to talk – not to engage in debate.

The informal or unstructured approach

A more informal or unstructured approach is favoured by some researchers. Sherry Dupuis (1999), for example, sees the semi-structured approach as often inappropriately seeking to reflect the positivist paradigm in qualitative research. She argues that using qualitative methods involves full interaction with research informants, so interviewers should be free to engage in a relatively free-flowing two-way conversation with interviewees. But she also makes the further point that, if this is to happen, much more detail about this aspect of the research process should be reported in research accounts than is usually the case. Thus, for example, information gained by means of a full two-way conversation and exchange of views with an outgoing interviewee is arguably different in nature from information gained from interviews where the interviewee is more reserved.

The distinctions

Ryan (2000: 125) argues that the distinction between the standardised and non-standardised interview corresponds to the phenomenographic and phenomenological approach to research. In the first, researchers adopt a minimalist approach to intervention in the interview and subsequently analyse and interpret the transcript/output in the same way that any text would be analysed. In the second, researchers/interviewers are more active in eliciting responses to assist them to achieving an understanding of the interviewee's world-view during the course of the interview.

Whyte (1982) provides a sort of hierarchy in interviewer responses which vary in their degree of intervention in the interview. He also sees this as the interviewer exercising varying degrees of *control* over the interview. Beginning with the least intrusive style of intervention, Whyte's list is as shown in Table 9.3. It should be noted that, except for the sixth of these responses, introducing a new topic, the interviewer is essentially drawing on what subjects have already said and inviting them to expand on it. A simpler categorisation is Charmaz's (2006: 30–31) three-fold division into 'initial opening questions', 'intermediate questions' and 'ending questions'.

Table 9.3 Interviewing interventions – based on Whyte (1982)

1. 'Uh-huh'	A non-verbal response which merely indicates that the interviewer is still listening and interested.
2. 'That's interesting'	Encourages the subject to keep talking or expand on the current topic.
3. Reflection	Repeating the last statement as a question: e.g. 'So you don't like sport?'
4. Probe	Inviting explanations of statements: e.g. 'Why don't you like sport?'
5. Backtracking	Remembering something the subject said earlier and inviting further information: e.g. 'Let's go back to what you were saying about your school days'.
6. New topic	Initiating a new topic: e.g. 'Can we talk about other leisure activities – what about entertainment?'

5.5 Recording

Sound or video recording of in-depth interviews is common, although in some cases it might be felt that such a procedure could inhibit respondents. If recording is not possible, then notes must be taken during the interview or immediately afterwards. There can be great value in producing complete *verbatim* (word for word) transcripts of interviews from recordings. Manual transcription is a laborious process – one hour of interview taking as much as six hours to transcribe, although online services now exist which use voice-recognition technology to transcribe digitized recordings automatically. Transcripts are, however, necessary if the results of interviews are to be analysed in the most methodical and complete manner.

6. Focus groups

6.1 Nature

The idea of interviewing groups of people together rather than individually has become popular in market and community research. In this technique, the researcher plays the role of *facilitator, convenor* or *discussion leader* rather than interviewer. The aim of the process is much the same as in an in-depth interview, but in this case the participants interact with each other as well as with the researcher/facilitator.

6.2 Purposes

The technique can be used:

- when a particular group is important in a study but is so small in number that members of the group would not be adequately represented in a general community questionnaire-based survey – for example, members of minority ethnic groups or people with disabilities;

- when the interaction/discussion process itself is of interest – for example, in testing reactions to a proposed new product, or when investigating how people form political opinions; and

- as an alternative to the in-depth interview, when it may not be practical to arrange for individual in-depth interviews but people are willing to be interviewed as a group – for example, some youth groups or members of some ethnic communities.

6.3 Methods

A group will usually comprise between 6 and 12 participants. They may be chosen from a 'panel' of people who make themselves available to market researchers for this sort of exercise, or they may be chosen because they are members of a particular group of interest to the research – for instance, local residents in a particular area, members of a sports club, or a group of people on a holiday package. The members of the group may or may not be known to one another.

The usual procedure is to make a sound recording of the discussion and for the researcher to produce a written summary from the recording.

Many of the same considerations apply as in the in-depth interview situation: the process is informal but the facilitator still has a role in guiding the discussion and ensuring that all the aspects of the topic are covered – while also enabling unanticipated topics/views to emerge. In addition, in the group interview, the facilitator has the task of ensuring that everyone in the group has their say and that the discussion is not dominated by one or two vociferous members of the group.

7. Participant observation

7.1 Nature

In participant observation, the researcher becomes a participant in the social process being studied. The classic study of this type is Whyte's *Street Corner Society* (1955), in which the researcher spent several years living with an inner-city US Italian community. Direct leisure/tourism examples include Blackshaw's study of the leisure lives of working-class young males and Cole's (2005) study of tourism in an Indonesian village.

7.2 Purposes

In leisure and tourism, elements of participant observation are common in many types of research. For example, a researcher involved in studying the use of a park or resort can easily spend periods as a user of the facility. Many studies of individual sports and sports clubs are by participants in the sport and/or members of the club. Researchers of tourist destinations are invariably themselves visitors to those destinations. Traditionally, the process has involved considerable interaction of the researcher with the people being researched. In many cases some sort of participant observation is the only way of researching particular phenomena – for example, it would be difficult to study what really goes on in a drug sub-culture or in some youth sub-cultures using a questionnaire and clip-board. Becoming part of the group and immersed in its activities is the obvious way of studying the group.

7.3 Methods

Participant observation raises a number of practical/tactical, and sometimes ethical, challenges. For example, in some cases actually gaining admittance to the social setting of interest may be difficult, especially where close-knit groups are involved. Having gained admittance to the setting, the question arises as to whether to pose as a typical member of the group, whether to adopt a plausible disguise or persona (e.g. a 'journalist' or 'writer') or whether to admit to being a researcher.

Selection of informants within a group is an issue to be addressed by the participant observer in the same way that sampling must be considered by the survey researcher. The members of the study group who are most friendly and talkative may be the easiest to communicate with, but may not give a representative picture of the diversity of views and behaviour in the group.

In addition, there are practical problems to be faced over how to record information. When the researcher's identity as a researcher has not been revealed, the taking of notes in real time or the use of a recorder may be impossible. Even when researchers identify themselves as such, or assume a plausible identity, the use of such devices may interfere with the sort of natural relationship which researchers are trying to establish. The taking of regular and detailed notes is, however, the basic data recording method. This may be supplemented by photographs and even video and sound recordings in some instances. The ethical questions raised by researchers' relationship with informants are discussed in Chapter 4 (see Case study 4.1).

8. Analysing texts

8.1 Nature

The analysis of texts, such as plays and novels, is the very basis of some disciplines in the humanities, such as literature, media studies and cultural studies. As researchers from these disciplines have turned their attention to leisure and tourism issues, and as the relationships between leisure, tourism and *cultural products* have become recognised, the approach is playing an increasingly important role in leisure and tourism research. The term *text* is now used to embrace not just printed material but also pictures, posters, recorded music, film and television. Indeed, virtually any cultural product can, in the jargon, be *read* as *text*. The trend is reflected in the increasing use of the term *gaze* to describe the activity of both leisure and tourism researchers and the subjects of their research. The late John Urry stated the following:

> Tourism research should involve the examination of texts, not only written texts but also maps, landscapes, paintings, films, townscapes, TV programmes, brochures,

and so on . . . Thus, social research significantly consists of interpreting texts, through various mainly qualitative techniques, to identify the discursive structures which give rise to and sustain, albeit temporarily, a given tourist site. (Urry, 1994: 237–38)

It is not proposed to outline analysis techniques in detail in this text, since approaches vary considerably. These include the qualitative, literary 'reading' of texts, the *interpretation* of texts sometimes referred to as *hermeneutics* and the highly quantified form of analysis known as *content analysis*. The approach here is, rather, to introduce some examples of work in this area.

8.2 Novels and other literature

- Sönmez et al. (1993) examine the concept of leisure as portrayed in the novels of Kenyan author Ngugi wa Thiong'o. The analysis provides a perspective on a non-Western view of leisure and its place in a culture faced with the upheaval of the colonial and post-colonial experience.

- In two papers, Hultsman and Harper (1992, Harper and Hultsman, 1992) analyse a collection of 1930s essays on life in the 'Old South' of the USA to reveal new insights into leisure and class at that time.

- One chapter in Paul Barry's (2006: 414–44) biography of media businessman Kerry Packer, provides a fascinating insight into one, very rich, man's approach to 'serious leisure' (Stebbins, 1982) – in this case polo – illustrating the value of biographies as a source of material on leisure.

8.3 Mass media coverage

Media coverage of selected topics can be studied qualitatively and quantitatively by measuring the column centimetres devoted to the topic in newspapers or the time devoted to the topic on television. Examples include Godoy-Pressland's (2014) study of weekend newspaper sport coverage, Lenskyj's (2002) examination of press coverage of the Sydney 2000 Olympic Games and the analysis by Swart et al. (2013) of coverage of the 2010 South African FIFA World Cup.

8.4 Film

- MacCannell (1993) provides an extensive analysis of the tourist film *Cannibal Tours*, upon which he builds a detailed theoretical interpretation of the role of tourism in the modern world; Burns and Lester (2005) also examine this film.

- Rojek (1993) provides an analysis of Disney films and their role in contemporary culture, in his paper 'Disney culture'.

8.5 Material culture

- Hodder (1994), in his paper on 'The interpretation of documents and material culture', devotes relatively little space to documents, but concentrates on the idea of studying 'material culture' or artefacts. Among the latter he includes dress fashions, national flags and the archaeological study of garbage.

- Examples of the direct study of leisure and tourism-related cultural products in the research literature are studies of:

  - Music genres: Spracklen et al. (2014), Straw (1993).
  - Pornography: Paasonen et al. (2015).
  - Disney theme parks: Klugman et al. (1995), Rojek (1993).
  - Postcards: Cohen (1993).

8.6 Digital sources

The advent of the internet, mobile personal communication devices, social media and online commerce have led to the generation of enormous amounts of data on human behaviour, referred to in Chapter 5 as 'Big Data'. Corporate organisations which control these data banks can use them for their own purposes, but to the extent that many forms of such data are in the public domain, they also provide a source of quantitative and qualitative material for the social researcher (e.g. Christou and Sigal, 2016; Lupton, 2016).

9. Biographical research

9.1 Nature

Biographical research, or 'retrospective methods' (Snelgrove and Havitz, 2010), covers a range of techniques which involve researching all or a substantial part of the lives of individuals or groups of individuals. The most common example of such research is the conventional biography or autobiography, but the biographical approach includes a number of other research approaches and outputs, including oral history, memory work and personal domain histories. Detailed guidance on the conduct of biographical research is not given in this text, but a brief overview of the field is given here and sources of further information appear in the Resources section.

9.2 Biography/autobiography

Many published accounts of lives of business leaders, while often read for entertainment, also provide insight into how business and business leaders operate. There is, for example, an enormous literature on Walt Disney in which the biography of Disney himself and the story of the corporation are intertwined (e.g. Bryman, 1995; Foglesong, 2001; Project on Disney, 1995). In Australia, *The Rise and Fall of Alan Bond* (owner of breweries and television stations, among other things) and *The Rise and Rise of Kerry Packer* (owner of television stations, magazines and casinos), both by Paul Barry (1990, 2006), are notable examples of leisure business biographies.

9.3 Oral history

Oral history involves recording eyewitness accounts of events and typically storing the recordings and/or a transcription of them in an archive as a source for research. While such accounts range more widely than the interviewees' own lives, they are nevertheless personal accounts. An example is Parker's (1988) study of a British mining community during the miners' strikes of the 1980s – the book includes accounts by miners, Coal Board employees, police and community members.

9.4 Memory work

Memory work is a structured way of eliciting subjects' memories of events; it can be seen as a focus group aided by individual writing. Participants are asked to write a short account of an experience related to the research topic – for example, bullying at the workplace or successful selling. The written accounts are read aloud in focus group settings and discussed, and they may be followed up with further writing and/or interviewing (see Onyx and Small, 2001; Small, 2004).

9.5 Personal domain histories

In the 1980s, a technique termed 'personal leisure histories' was developed by Hedges (1986) to study the ways in which significant changes in life circumstances (marriage, birth of a child, change of job, health issues, etc.) impacted on patterns of leisure participation. While no known example exists, it seems clear that such a technique might be used to focus on other domains of life – hence the use of the term personal *domain* histories.

10. Ethnography

The ethnographic style of research is not one technique but an approach drawing on a variety of techniques. Generally, as applied to leisure and tourism research, it seeks to see the world through the eyes of those being researched, allowing them to speak for themselves, often revealed through extensive direct quotations in the research report. Often also, the aim is to debunk conventional, establishment, 'common sense' views of 'social problems', 'deviants', sexual and ethnic stereotypes and so on. In leisure studies, the approach has become particularly associated with 'cultural studies', for example, of youth sub-cultures and ethnic groups.

11. Validity and reliability, trustworthiness

The issues of validity – the extent to which research accurately represents what it is intended to represent – and reliability – the extent to which research is replicable – were discussed in Chapter 2, and it was noted there that some researchers prefer to use the term *trustworthiness* when discussing qualitative methods. Internal validity is concerned with the processes by which information is gathered from the subjects of the study. A case could be made that information collected by qualitative methods has a greater chance of being internally valid than information gathered by means of, for example, a short questionnaire, since in the qualitative data-collection situation more time and effort is generally taken to collect any one piece of information. Thus the exchange between interviewer and interviewee in an in-depth interview or the discussion in a focus group should increase the likelihood of interviewer/facilitator and interviewee/participants understanding one another.

External validity is concerned with the applicability of the findings beyond the subjects of the research. Typically, no formal claim of generalisability is made on the basis of qualitative study; but, as noted in Chapter 2, this strict rule is often implicitly ignored. It is noted in Chapter 13, that efforts are often made to select samples of subjects for qualitative research which have some semblance of representativeness, at least in terms of the qualitative diversity of the population being studied. It would be strange if researchers conducting qualitative research projects did not believe that there were *some* implications beyond the limited sample of subjects studied. Thus the belief is that what has been found is true of *some people* among the population from which the study subjects were drawn, but the extent cannot be quantified. In theoretical terms, if the findings of qualitative research are inconsistent with existing theory, it at least establishes that the theory is not *universally* valid. Furthermore, theoretical propositions arising from qualitative research *may* be more widely applicable.

Unlike the physical sciences, exact replicability of qualitative social research findings is clearly unlikely. However, accumulation of similar, or logically consistent, findings from a wide range of studies lends strength to the findings, not in a statistical sense but in terms of the robustness of the findings in different settings. There is a parallel in quantitative meta-analyses, where it can be argued that similar, but statistically insignificant, findings from a number of studies may be given some cumulative support if the level of significance of individual studies was affected by sample sizes.

Thus, while qualitative research cannot offer the rigorous tests of validity and reliability of quantitative research, the issues can be discussed, and some form of assessment of *trustworthiness* arrived at.

Summary

This chapter introduces the role of qualitative approaches in leisure and tourism research. One of the basic assumptions of qualitative research is that reality is socially and subjectively constructed rather than objectively determined. In this perspective, researchers are seen as part of the research process seeking to uncover meanings and understanding of the issues they are researching. In general, qualitative research involves the collection of a large amount of 'rich' information concerning relatively few people or organisations rather than more limited information from a large number of people or organisations.

Qualitative methods generally require a more flexible, recursive, approach to overall research design and conduct in contrast with the more linear, sequential approach used in most quantitative research. Hypothesis formation evolves as the research progresses; data collection and analysis take place concurrently and writing is also often an evolutionary process rather than a separate process which happens at the end of the project.

A range of qualitative methods is available to the researcher, including in-depth interviews, group interviews, focus groups, participant observation, textual analysis, biographical methods and ethnographic methods. The chapter outlines the nature and techniques involved in using each of these methods.

Validity and reliability of qualitative methods cannot be assessed using the rigorous, quantified tests of quantitative methods, but the issues can be addressed and assessed to give an assessment of what some have termed *trustworthiness*.

Test questions

1. Outline some of the merits of qualitative research.

2. Explain the difference between sequential and recursive approaches to research.

3. Outline Whyte's levels of interviewer intervention in an in-depth/informal interview.

4. In-depth interviews involve an interviewer: what is the equivalent in a focus group?

5. Name three types of biographical research.

6. How are the issues of validity and reliability approached in qualitative research?

Exercises

For exercises in qualitative methods, see Chapter 15.

Resources

- Auto-ethnography:
  - Leisure: Anderson and Austin (2011); and
  - Sport fandom: Knijnik (2015).

- Biographical methods:
  - Cultural biographies (teenagers and 'bedroom culture'): Lincoln (2005);
  - General: Atkinson (1998), Roberts (2002);
  - Leisure: Project on Disney (1995), Snelgrove and Havitz (2010);
  - Tourism: Ladkin (2004);
  - Personal domain histories: Hedges (1986); and
  - Memory work in tourism: Onyx and Small (2001), Paasonen et al. (2015), Small (2004).

- Digital leisure:
  - Leisure: Lupton (2016), Spracklen (2015); and
  - Tourism: Christou and Sigala (2016).

- Ethnography:
  - General: Davies (1997);
  - Leisure: Chick (1998), Lincoln (2005);
  - Sport: Spracklen et al. (2011); and
  - Tourism: Cole (2005), Pereiro (2010), Sandiford and Ap (1998).

- Focus groups: Greenbaum (2000), Krueger (2014), Morgan (1993), Stewart and Shamdasani (2014).

- Grounded theory:
  - General: Charmaz (2006), Glaser and Strauss (1967), Strauss (1987), Strauss and Corbin (1994);
  - Leisure: Dixon et al. (2013), Piggott (2010); and
  - Tourism: Connell and Lowe (1977).

- Informal/in-depth interviews:
  - General: Dunne (1995);
  - Musicians: Spracklen et al. (2014);
  - Outdoor recreationists: Moeller et al. (1980a, 1980b); and
  - Tourism: Jennings (2005); Jordan and Gibson (2004).

- Participant observation: Broughton et al. (2016); Leisure: Blackshaw (2003), Smith (1995), Wynne (1986); Outdoor recreation: Campbell (1970), Glancy (1986); Tourism: Cole (2005).

- Qualitative methods:
  - Leisure: Henderson (1991, 2006), Godbey and Scott (1990), Kelly (1980), Ruddell (2013);
  - Social science: Denzin and Lincoln (1994, 2006), Silverman (2015);
  - Sport studies/management: Andrews et al. (2005), Edwards and Skinner (2009); and
  - Tourism: Davies (2003), Jennings (2010), Peterson (1994), Phillimore and Goodson (2004b), Richards and Munsters (2010); Riley and Love (2000), Ruddell (2013), Walle (1997).

- Textual/visual:
  - General: Prior (2003);
  - Talk and text: Perakyla (2005);
  - Mass media: Billings and Tyler Eastman (2002), Jaimangal-Jones (2012), Lenskyj (2002), Swart et al. (2013); and
  - Tourism: Dinhopl and Gretzel (2016), Francesconi (2014), Albers and James (1988), Lester (2013), Litvin and Mouri (2009), Rakic and Chambers (2012).

- Trustworthiness: Guba and Lincoln (1998); Tourism: DeCrop (2004), Henderson (2006: 225–36).

References

Albers, P. C., and James, W. R. (1988). Travel photography: a methodological approach. *Annals of Tourism Research*, 15(1), 134–58.

Anderson, L., and Austin, M. (2011). Auto-ethnography in leisure studies. *Leisure Studies*, 31(2), 131–46.

Andrews, D. L., Mason, D. S., and Silk, M. L. (Eds) (2005). *Qualitative methods in sports studies*. Oxford: Berg.

Atkinson, R. (1998). *The life story interview*. London: Sage.

Barry, P. (1990). *The rise and fall of Alan Bond*. Sydney: Bantam/ABC.

Barry, P. (2006). *The rise and rise of Kerry Packer – Uncut*. Sydney: Bantam/ABC.

Bennett, T., Savage, M., Silva, E., Warde, A., Gayo-Cal, M., and Wright, D. (2009). *Culture, class, distinction*. London: Routledge.

Billings, A. C., and Tyler Eastman, S. (2002). Selective representation of gender, ethnicity and nationality in American television coverage of the 2000 Summer Olympics. *International Review for the Sociology of Sport*, 37(3/4), 351–70.

Blackshaw, T. (2003). *Leisure life: myth, masculinity and modernity*. London: Routledge.

Bourdieu, P. (1984). *Distinction: a social critique of the judgement of taste*. London: Routledge.

Broughton, K. A., Payne, L., and Liechty, T. (2016). An exploration of older men's social lives and well-being in the context of a coffee group. *Leisure Sciences*, doi: 10.1080/01490400.2016.1178200.

Bryman, A. (1995). *Disney and his worlds*. London: Routledge.

Campbell, F. L. (1970). Participant observation in outdoor recreation. *Journal of Leisure Research*, 2(4), 226–36.

Charmaz, K. (2006). *Constructing grounded theory*. London: Sage.

Chick, G. (1998). Leisure and culture: Issues for an anthropology of leisure. *Leisure Sciences*, 20(2), 111–33.

Christou, E., and Sigala, M. (2016). *Social media in travel, tourism and hospitality: theory, practice and cases*. London: Routledge.

Cohen, E. (1993). The study of touristic images of native people: mitigating the stereotype of a stereotype. In D. G. Pearce and R. W. Butler (Eds), *Tourism research: critiques and challenges* (pp. 36–69). London: Routledge.

Cole, S. (2005). Action ethnography: using participant observation. In B. W. Ritchie, P. Burns and C. Palmer (Eds), *Tourism Research methods: integrating theory with practice* (pp. 63–72). Wallingford, UK: CABI Publishing.

Connell, J., and Lowe, A. (1997). Generating grounded theory from qualitative data: the application of inductive methods in tourism and hospitality management research. *Progress in Tourism and Hospitality Research*, 3, 165–73.

Davies, B. (2003). The role of quantitative and qualitative research in industrial studies of tourism. *Journal of Travel Research*, 30(1), 59–63.

Davies, C. (1997). *Reflexive ethnography: a guide to researching selves and others*. London: Routledge.

DeCrop, A. (2004). Trustworthiness in qualitative tourism research. In J. Phillimore and L. Goodson (Eds), *Qualitative research in tourism: ontologies, epistemologies and methodologies*. London: Routledge, 156–69.

Denzin, N. K., and Lincoln, Y. S. (Eds) (1994). *Handbook of qualitative research*. Thousand Oaks, CA: Sage.

Denzin, N. K., and Lincoln, Y. S. (Eds) (2006). *Handbook of qualitative research*, 3rd edn. Thousand Oaks, CA: Sage.

Dinhopl, A., and Gretzel, U. (2016). Selfie-taking as touristic looking. *Annals of Tourism Research*, 57, 126–39.

Dixon, H. E. T., Igo, L. B., and Mcguire, F. A. (2013). Grounded theory methodology in research. In E. Sirakaya-Turk, M. Uysal, W. E. Hammitt and J. J. Vaske (Eds.), *Research methods for leisure, recreation and tourism* (pp. 127–39). Wallingford, UK: CABI.

Dunne, S. (1995). *Interviewing techniques for writers and researchers*. London: A. & C. Black.

Dupuis, S. (1999). Naked truths: towards a reflexive methodology in leisure research. *Leisure Sciences*, 21(1), 43–64.

Edwards, A., and Skinner, J. (2009). *Qualitative research in sport management*. Oxford, UK: Butterworth-Heinemann.

Foglesong, R.E. (2001). *Married to the mouse: Walt Disney World and Orlando*. New Haven, CT: Yale University Press.

Francesconi, S. (2014). *Reading tourism texts: A multimodal analysis*. Clevedon, UK: Channel View.

Glancy, M. (1986). Participant observation in the recreation setting. *Journal of Leisure Research*, 18(2), 59–80.

Glaser, B., and Strauss, A. L. (1967). *The discovery of grounded theory: strategies for qualitative research*. Chicago, IL: Aldine.

Godbey, G., and Scott, D. (1990). Reorienting leisure research – the case for qualitative methods. *Society and Leisure*, 13(1), 189–206.

Godoy-Pressland, A. (2014). The weekend as a male entity: how Sunday newspaper sports reporting centres around male activities, interest and language. *Leisure Studies*, 33(2), 148–63.

Greenbaum, T. L. (2000). *Moderating focus groups: a practical guide for group facilitation*. Thousand Oaks, CA: Sage.

Guba, E. G., and Lincoln, Y. S. (1998). Competing paradigms in qualitative research. In N. K. Denzin and Y. S. Lincoln (Eds), *The landscape of qualitative research: theories and issues* (pp. 195–220). Thousand Oaks, CA: Sage.

Harper, W., and Hultsman, J. (1992). Interpreting leisure as text: the whole. *Leisure Studies*, 11(3), 233–42.

Hedges, B. (1986). *Personal leisure histories*. London: Sports Council/Economic and Social Research Council.

Henderson, K. A. (1991). *Dimensions of choice: a qualitative approach to recreation, parks and leisure research*. State College, PA: Venture.

Henderson, K. A. (2006). *Dimensions of choice: a qualitative approach to recreation, park, recreation, tourism, sport, and leisure research*, 2nd edn. State College, PA: Venture.

Hodder, I. (1994). The interpretation of documents and material culture. In N. K. Denzin and Y. S. Lincoln (Eds), *Handbook of qualitative research* (pp. 393–402). Thousand Oaks, CA: Sage.

Hollinshead, K. (2004). A primer in ontological craft: the creative capture of people and places through qualitative research. In J. Phillimore and L. Goodson (Eds), *Qualitative research in tourism: ontologies, epistemologies and methodologies* (pp. 63–82). London: Routledge.

Hultsman, J., and Harper, W. (1992). Interpreting leisure as text: the part. *Leisure Studies*, 11(2), 135–46.

Jaimangal-Jones, D. (2012). More than worlds: analyzing the media discourses surrounding dance music events. *Event Management*, 16(3), 305–18.

Jennings, G. (2010). *Tourism research*, 2nd edn. Milton, Qld, Australia: John Wiley.

Jennings, G. R. (2005). Interviewing: a focus on qualitative techniques. In B. W. Ritchie, P. Burns and C. Palmer (Eds), *Tourism Research methods: integrating theory with practice* (pp. 99–117). Wallingford, UK: CABI Publishing.

Jordan, F., and Gibson, H. (2004). Let your data do the talking: researching the solo travel experiences of British and American women. In J. Phillimore and L. Godson (Eds), *Qualitative research in tourism: ontologies, epistemologies and methodologies* (pp. 215–35). London: Routledge.

Kelly, J. R. (1980). Leisure and quality: beyond the quantitative barrier in research. In T. L. Goodale and P. A. Witt (Eds), *Recreation and leisure: issues in an era of change* (pp. 300–14). State College, PA: Venture.

Klugman, K., Kuenz, J., Waldrop, S., and Willis, S. (1995). *Inside the mouse: the project on Disney*. Durham, NC: Duke University Press.

Knijnik, J. (2015). Feeling at home: an autoethnographic account of an immigrant football fan in Western Sydney. *Leisure Studies*, 34(1), 34–41.

Kraus, R., and Allen, L. (1974). *Research and evaluation in recreation, parks, and leisure studies*. Columbus, OH: Publishing Horizons.

Kraus, R., and Allen, L. (1998). *Research and evaluation in recreation, parks, and leisure studies*, 2nd edn. Needham Heights, MA: Allyn & Bacon.

Krueger, R.A. (2014). *Focus groups: a practical guide for applied research*. 5th edn. Newbury Park, CA: Sage.

Ladkin, A. (2004). The life and work history methodology: a discussion of its potential use for tourism and hospitality research. In J. Phillimore and L. Godson (Eds), *Qualitative research in tourism: ontologies, epistemologies and methodologies* (pp. 236–254). London: Routledge.

Lenskyj, H. J. (2002). *The Best Olympics Ever? Social Impacts of Sydney 2000*. Albany, NY: State University of New York Press.

Lester, J. (2013). *Mediating the tourist experience: from brochures to virtual encounters*. Farnham, UK: Ashgate

Lincoln, S. (2005). Feeling the noise: teenagers, bedrooms and music. *Leisure Studies*, 24(4), 399–414.

Litvin, S. W., and Mouri, N. (2009). A comparative study of the use of 'iconic' versus 'generic' advertising images for destination marketing. *Journal of Travel Research*, 48(2), 152–61.

Lofland, J., and Lofland, L. H. (1984). *Analyzing social settings: a guide to qualitative observation and analysis*, 2nd edn. Belmont, CA: Wadsworth.

Lundberg, G. A., Komarovsky, M., and McInerny, M. A. (1934). *Leisure: a suburban study*. New York: Columbia University Press.

Lupton, D. (2016). Foreword to special issue on digital leisure cultures: lively devices, lively data and lively leisure studies. *Leisure Studies*, 35(6), 709–11.

MacCannell, D. (1993). *The empty meeting grounds*. London: Routledge.

McCall, G. J., and Simmons, J. L. (Eds) (1969). *Issues in participant observation*. Reading, MA: Addison-Wesley.

Miles, M. B., and Huberman, A. M. (1994). *Qualitative data analysis*, 2nd edn. Thousand Oaks, CA: Sage.

Moeller, G. H., Mescher, M. A., et al. (1980a). The informal interview as a technique for recreation research. *Journal of Leisure Research*, 12(2), 174–82.

Moeller, G. H., Mescher, M. A., et al. (1980b). A response to 'A second look at the informal interview'. *Journal of Leisure Research*, 12(2), 187–88.

Morgan, D. L. (Ed.) (1993). *Successful focus groups: advancing the state of the art*. Newbury Park, CA: Sage.

Onyx, J., and Small, J. (2001). Memory-work: the method. *Qualitative Inquiry*, 7(6), 773–86.

Paasonen, S., Kyrola, K., Nikunen, K., and Saarenmaa, L. (2015). 'We hid porn magazines in the nearby woods': memory-work and pornography consumption in Finland. *Sexualities*, 18(4), 394–412.

Parker, T. (1988). *Red Hill: a mining community*. London: Coronet.

Perakyla, A. (2005). Analyzing talk and text. In K. Denzin and Y. S. Lincoln (Eds), *Handbook of qualitative research* (pp. 869–86). Thousand Oaks, CA: Sage.

Pereiro, X. (2010). Ethnographic research on cultural tourism: an anthropological view. In G. Richards and W. Munsters (Eds), *Cultural tourism research methods* (pp. 173–87). Wallingford, UK: CABI.

Peterson, K. I. (1994). Qualitative research methods for the travel and tourism industry. In J. R. B. Ritchie and C. R. Goeldner (Eds), *Travel, tourism and hospitality research*, 2nd edn (pp. 487–92). New York: John Wiley.

Phillimore, J., and Goodson, L. (2004a) Progress in qualitative research in tourism. In J. Phillimore and L. Goodson (Eds), *Qualitative research in tourism: ontologies, epistemologies and methodologies* (pp. 3–29). London: Routledge.

Phillimore, J., and Goodson, L. (Eds) (2004b). *Qualitative research in tourism: ontologies, epistemologies and methodologies*. London: Routledge.

Piggott, D. (2010). Listening to young people in leisure research: the critical application of grounded theory. *Leisure Studies*, 29(4), 415–33.

Prior, L. (2003). *Using documents in social research*. London: Sage.

Project on Disney (1995). *Inside the mouse: work and play at Disney World*. Durham, NC: Duke University Press.

Rakic, T., and Chambers, D. (Eds) (2012). *An introduction to visual research methods in tourism*. London: Routledge.

Richards, G., and Munsters, W. (Eds) (2010). *Cultural tourism research methods*. Wallingford, UK: CABI.

Riley, R. W., and Love, L. L. (2000). The state of qualitative tourism research. *Annals of Tourism Research*, 27(1), 164–87.

Ritchie, J. R. B., and Goeldner, C. R. (Eds) (1994). *Travel, tourism and hospitality research*, 2nd edn. New York: John Wiley.

Roberts, B. (2002). *Biographical research*. Buckingham, UK: Open University Press.

Rojek, C. (1993). Disney culture. *Leisure Studies*, 12(2), 121–36.

Rowntree, B. S., and Lavers, G. R. (1951). *English life and leisure: a social study*. London: Longmans, Green & Co.

Ruddell, E. (2013). Qualitative research in leisure, recreation and tourism. In E. Sirakaya-Turk, M. Uysal, W. E. Hammitt and J. J. Vaske (Eds), *Research methods for leisure, recreation and tourism* (pp. 114–26). Wallingford, UK: CABI.

Ryan, C. (1995). *Researching tourist satisfaction: issues, concepts, problems*. London: Routledge.

Ryan, C. (2000). Tourist experiences, phenomenographic analysis, post-positivism and neural network software. *International Journal of Tourism Research*, 2(1), 119–31.

Sandiford, P. J., and Ap, J. (1998). The role of ethnographic techniques in tourism planning. *Journal of Travel Research*, 37(1), 3–11.

Sechrest, L. (1992). Roots: back to our first generations. *Evaluation Practice*, 13(1), 1–7.

Silverman, D. (2015). *Interpreting qualitative data: methods for analysing talk, text and interaction*, 5th edn. London: Sage.

Small, J. (2004). Memory work. In J. Phillimore and L. Godson (Eds), *Qualitative research in tourism: ontologies, epistemologies and methodologies* (pp. 255–72). London: Routledge.

Smith, S. L. J. (1995). *Tourism analysis: a handbook, second edition*. Harlow, UK: Longman.

Snelgrove, R., and Havitz, M. E. (2010). Looking back in time: the pitfalls and potential of retrospective methods in leisure studies. *Leisure Sciences*, 32(3), 337–51.

Sönmez, S., Shinew, K., Marchese, L., Veldkamp, C., and Burnett, G. W. (1993). Leisure corrupted: an artist's portrait of leisure in a changing society. *Leisure Studies*, 12(4), 266–76.

Spracklen, K. (2015). *Digital leisure, the internet and popular culture*. Basingstoke, UK: Palgrave Macmillan.

Spracklen, K., Lucas, C., and Deeks, M. (2014). The construction of heavy metal identity through heritage narratives: a case study of extreme metal bands in the North of England, *Popular Music and Society*, 37(1), 48–64.

Spracklen, K., Timmins, S., and Long, J. (2011). Ethnographies of the imagined, the imaginary and the critically real: blackness, whiteness, the north of England and rugby league. *Leisure Studies*, 29(4), 397–414.

Stebbins, R.A. (1982). Serious leisure: a conceptual statement. *Pacific Sociological Review* (now *Sociological Perspectives*), 5(3), 251–72.

Stewart, D. W., and Shamdasani, P. N. (2014). *Focus groups: theory and practice*, 3rd edn. Newbury Park, CA: Sage.

Strauss, A., and Corbin, J. (1994). Grounded theory methodology. In N. K. Denzin and Y. S. Lincoln (Eds), *Handbook of qualitative research* (pp. 273–85). Thousand Oaks, CA: Sage.

Strauss, A. L. (1987). *Qualitative analysis for social scientists*. Cambridge: Cambridge University Press.

Straw, W. (1993). Characterising rock music culture: the case of heavy metal. In S. During (Ed.), *The cultural studies reader* (pp. 368–81). London: Routledge.

Swart, K., Linley, M., and Bob, U. (2013). The media impact of South Africa's historical hosting of Africa's first mega-event: sport and leisure consumption patterns. *International Journal of the History of Sport*, 30(16), 1976–93.

Urry, J. (1994). Cultural change and contemporary tourism. *Leisure Studies*, 13(4), 233–38.

Veal, A. J. (1994). Intersubjectivity and the transatlantic divide: a comment on Glancy (and Ragheb and Tate). *Leisure Studies*, 13(3), 211–16.

Walle, A. (1997). Quantitative versus qualitative tourism research. *Annals of Tourism Research*, 24(3), 524–36.

Whyte, W. F. (1955). *Street corner society*. Chicago: University of Chicago Press.

Whyte, W. F. (1982). Interviewing in field research. In R. G. Burgess (Ed.) *Field research: a sourcebook and field manual* (pp. 111–22). London: Allen & Unwin.

Wynne, D. (1986). Living on 'The Heath'. *Leisure Studies*, 5(1), 109–16.

10 Questionnaire surveys: typology, design and coding

1. Introduction	1.1 Definitions and terminology 1.5 Interviewer-completion or respondent-completion? 1.2 Roles 1.6 Types of questionnaire survey 1.3 Merits 1.4 Limitations
2. The household questionnaire survey	2.1 Nature 2.4 Time-use surveys 2.2 Conduct 2.5 National surveys 2.3 Omnibus surveys
3. The street survey	3.1 Nature 3.3 Quota sampling 3.2 Conduct
4. The telephone survey	4.1 Nature 4.4 National surveys 4.2 Conduct 4.3 Representativeness and response levels
5. The mail survey	5.1 Nature 5.3 Mail and user/site/visitor survey combos 5.2 The problem of low response rates
6. E-surveys	6.1 Nature and conduct 6.2 Advantages and disadvantages
7. User/on-site/visitor surveys	7.1 Nature 7.3 Uses of user surveys 7.2 Conduct 7.4 User/site/visitor and mail/ e-survey combo

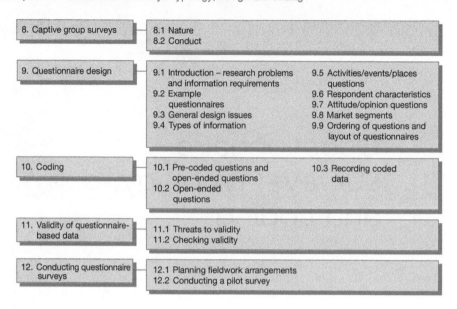

1. Introduction

This chapter presents an overview of the range of types of questionnaire survey and questionnaire design. Questionnaire surveys involve the gathering of information from individuals using a formally designed *questionnaire* or *interview schedule* and are arguably the most commonly used technique in leisure and tourism research.

The first part of the chapter discusses the merits of questionnaire methods and the distinction between interviewer-completion and respondent-completion questionnaire surveys, followed by an overview of the characteristics of: the household questionnaire survey; the street survey; the telephone survey; the postal or mail survey; on-site or user surveys; and captive group surveys.

The second half of the chapter considers the factors which must be taken into account in designing questionnaires for leisure and tourism studies. First, the relationships between research problems and information requirements are examined. This is followed by consideration of the types of information typically included in leisure and tourism questionnaires, the wording of questions, coding of questionnaires for computer analysis, the ordering and layout of questions and the problem of validity. Finally, some consideration is given to the special requirements of time-budget studies.

1.1 Definitions and terminology

A questionnaire can be defined as a 'a written/printed or computer-based schedule of questions and a *pro forma* for recording answers to the questions'. It is therefore both a means of eliciting information from respondents and a medium for recording answers.

The term *questionnaire survey* or *questionnaire-based survey* is used deliberately in this chapter to emphasise that the words *survey* and *questionnaire* mean two different things. There is a tendency in common parlance – and, unfortunately, in some research literature – to use the terms survey and questionnaire synonymously. For example, researchers have been known to make statements such as: '1000 surveys were distributed'. This is inappropriate; only *one* survey was involved – 1000 *questionnaires* were distributed. To distinguish the two terms:

- a questionnaire is a written/printed or computer-based schedule of questions; and

- a survey is the *process* of designing and conducting a study involving the gathering of information from a number of subjects.

A 'survey' does not always include a questionnaire; thus, for example, a study could involve a visual survey of beach crowding or a documentary survey of the contents of organisations' annual reports.

Alternative terms for the word questionnaire are 'research instrument' or 'survey instrument', which reference the science laboratory context. In addition, 'survey form' or 'question schedule' is sometimes used.

1.2 Roles

Questionnaire surveys are used when a specified range of information is required from individuals or organisations. The most common form of questionnaire-based survey is based on a representative sample of a defined population of individuals or organisations (as discussed in Chapter 13), although in some cases the whole population is included, as in a national census of the population (see Chapter 7). In both cases the aim is to make statements about the characteristics of the population, typically in the form of percentages, averages, relationships and trends.

Typically, questionnaire-based surveys are used to collect responses to questions which have a limited number of possible answers, for example, a person's gender or educational level. Some questions, however, can be open-ended, with an unspecified range of answers – for example, an open question on a visitor's complaints or suggestions regarding the management of a leisure or tourism facility.

Questionnaire-based surveys can play a role in the task of estimating the number of visits to leisure facilities and tourism destinations where visit numbers are not automatically gathered by administrative means, such as the sale of tickets. Examples include urban parks and tourism destinations that have car-borne access. This phenomenon is discussed in Chapter 7, where it is noted that information on visitor numbers may be gathered administratively (ticket sales, landing cards), by direct counts/observation or wholly or in part by questionnaire-based survey – see Tables 7.3 and 7.4.

1.3 Merits

Compared with the qualitative techniques discussed in Chapter 9, questionnaire surveys usually involve quantification – the presentation of results in numerical terms. This has implications for the way the data are collected, analysed and interpreted. In Chapter 9 a list of merits of qualitative methods, as put forward by Kelly, is presented. The merits of questionnaire surveys can be similarly examined. Some of the qualities of questionnaire surveys which make them useful in leisure and tourism research are set out below.

- Contemporary leisure and tourism are often mass phenomena, requiring major involvement from governmental, non-profit and/or commercial organisations, which rely on quantified information for significant aspects of their decision-making. Questionnaire surveys are an ideal means of providing some of this information.

- While absolute objectivity is impossible, questionnaire methods provide a transparent set of research procedures such that the way information was collected and how it was analysed or interpreted is clear for all to see, although, it must be said, journal articles vary in the amount of detail provided. Questionnaire survey data, which are invariably available in digital form, can often be re-analysed by others if they wish to extend the research or provide an alternative interpretation.

- Quantification can provide relatively complex information in a succinct, easily understandable, form, including graphics.

- Methods such as longitudinal surveys and annually repeated surveys provide the opportunity to study change over time, using comparable methodology.

- Leisure and tourism encompass a wide range of activities, with a range of characteristics such as frequency, duration and type of participation, expenditure, location, level of enjoyment and aspirations. Questionnaires are a good means of ensuring that a complete picture of a person's patterns of participation is obtained.

- While qualitative methods are ideal for exploring attitudes, meanings and perceptions on an individual basis, questionnaire methods provide the means to gather and record simple information on the incidence of attitudes, meanings and perceptions among the population as a whole, thus indicating not only that certain attitudes exist but also how widespread they are.

Comparison of this list and the one referring to qualitative methods at the beginning of Chapter 9 reinforces the view that each method has its merits and appropriate uses – the 'horses for courses' idea. Questionnaire surveys have a role to play when the research questions indicate the need for fairly structured data and generally when data are required from samples which are explicitly representative of a defined wider population. Examples of the role of questionnaire surveys versus other methods are shown in Table 10.1.

1.4 Limitations

Questionnaire-based surveys have a number of limitations, related to the fact that they are typically based on samples and rely on self-reported data.

Table 10.1 Use of questionnaire surveys compared with other methods – examples

Organisation/ Topic	Questionnaire survey	Qualitative methods	Other methods
Leisure facility/How to increase number of visitors	• User/visitor survey on what types of people use which services and when. • Community survey on socio-demographic characteristics of users vs non-users and perceptions of facility.	• Observation and/or focus groups on experience of visiting the facility – quality, atmosphere, service.	• Secondary analysis of ticket sales and utilisation data re. relative popularity of different activities/services.
Tourism Commission/Data for tourism strategic plan	• Intercept survey of visitors on accommodation used, sites visited, expenditure patterns and socio-demographic characteristics of visitors from different places.	• In-depth interviews or focus groups with visitors on quality of visitor experience • Focus groups with residents: attitudes towards tourists and tourist development.	• Arrival and departure data (if national study).
Individual researcher/The role of the holiday in leisure	• Household survey on socio-demographic characteristics and numbers of those who do and do not take holidays – measures of income, health and attitudes.	• In-depth interviews on meanings and importance of holidays and local leisure in individuals' lifestyles.	• Secondary analysis of official data on holiday entitlements and leave-taking.

Samples

Questionnaire surveys usually, but not always, involve only a proportion, or *sample*, of the population in which the researcher is interested. For example, the national surveys discussed in Chapter 7 are based on samples of only a few thousand to represent tens of millions of people. How such samples are chosen, how the size of the sample is decided and the implications of relying on a sample to represent a population are discussed in Chapter 13.

Self-reported data

As discussed in Chapter 2, questionnaire surveys rely on information from respondents. The accuracy of what respondents say depends on their own powers of recall, on their honesty and, fundamentally, on the format of the questions included in the questionnaire. There has been relatively little research on the validity or accuracy of questionnaire data in leisure and tourism studies, but some examples are indicated in the problems of validity and accuracy which arise from a number of sources, including exaggeration and under-reporting; accuracy of recall; and sensitivity:

- *Exaggeration/under-reporting:* Some research (see the Resources section) has suggested that respondents exaggerate levels of participation in some activities and under-report others. This may be conscious or unconscious and may be for reasons of prestige or lack of it – what Oppenheim (2000: 138) calls 'social desirability bias' – or a desire to be positive and friendly towards the interviewer, at least in a face-to-face situation. For example, if the interview is about sport or the arts, respondents may tend to exaggerate their interest in and involvement with sport or the arts, just to be helpful and positive.

- *Accuracy of recall:* Mistakes can be made in recalling events at all or in estimating frequency of involvement: for example, if someone claims to take part in an activity twice a week, is that equivalent to 104 times a year? Apart from seasonality, which could be addressed in the questionnaire, such factors as weather conditions, illness, public holidays and family and work emergencies may all reduce the actual level of participation. Even if the question attempts to avoid this problem by asking respondents about the actual number of occasions on which they have participated in a given time-period, respondents may be working from the 'once a week' notion and still over-estimate. Where alternative sources of information, such as club records, are available, it is possible to check the accuracy of questionnaire-based information. Studies of this phenomenon suggest substantial over-estimation in sporting/physical activity – examples are listed in the Resources section.

- *Sensitivity:* Sensitive topics can also give rise to under-estimation or over-estimation, and some leisure-related activities fall into this category: for example, Schaeffer (2000) provides information on responses regarding sexual activity and recreational drug use.

This suggests the need for careful questionnaire design and cross-checking/triangulation where possible, but also that the researcher and the user of research results should always bear in mind the nature and source of the data and not fall into the trap of believing that, because information is presented in numerical form and is based on large numbers, it represents immutable 'truth'.

1.5 Interviewer-completion or respondent-completion?

Questionnaire surveys can take one of two forms:

- *Interviewer-completed*: the questionnaire provides the *script* for an interview; an interviewer reads the questions out to the respondent and records the respondent's answers on the questionnaire – the classic 'clipboard' situation, where the method may also be referred to as *face-to-face* interviewing. When telephone surveys are involved, the interviewer may record answers on a computer.

- Respondent-completed, often referred to as *self-completion*: respondents read and fill out the questionnaire for themselves, on paper or online.

Each approach has its particular advantages and disadvantages, as summarised in Table 10.2. Interviewer-completion is more expensive in terms of interviewers' time (which usually has to be paid for), but the use of an interviewer usually ensures a more accurate and complete response. Respondent-completion can be cheaper and quicker but often results in low response rates, which can introduce bias into the results because those who choose not to respond or are unable to respond, perhaps because of language or literacy difficulties, may differ from those who do respond. When designing a questionnaire for respondent-completion, greater care must be taken with layout and presentation since it must be read and completed by 'untrained' people. In terms of design, respondent-completion questionnaires should ideally

Table 10.2 Interviewer-completion compared with respondent-completion

	Interviewer-completion	**Respondent-completion**
Advantages	More accuracy	Cheaper
	Higher response rates	Quicker
	Fuller and more complete answers	Relatively anonymous
	Design can be less 'user-friendly'	
Disadvantages	Higher cost	Patchy response
	Less anonymity	Incomplete response
		Risk of frivolous responses
		More care needed in design

consist primarily of *closed* questions – that is, questions which can be answered by ticking boxes. *Open-ended questions* – where respondents have to write out their answers – should generally be avoided in such a situation, since they invariably achieve only a low response. For example, in an interview, respondents will often give expansive answers to questions such as 'Do you have any comments to make on the overall management of this facility?' But they will not as readily write down such answers in a respondent-completion questionnaire.

There may, however, be cases when respondent-completion is to be preferred, or is the only practicable approach. For example, people to be surveyed may be widely scattered geographically, making face-to-face interviews impossibly expensive, so a mail or postal survey, which intrinsically involves respondent-completion, is an obvious choice. Furthermore, when a questionnaire deals with sensitive matters, respondents might prefer the anonymity of the respondent-completed questionnaire. Some of the issues connected with respondent-completion questionnaires are discussed more fully in the section on mail surveys.

It should be noted that some commentators, in discussions of research methods, draw a distinction between 'interview methods' and 'questionnaire methods'; this is clearly misleading because the interviewer-completed questionnaire-based survey clearly involves an interview, so the 'questionnaire method' may involve an interview, so is not distinct from the 'interview method'. Such comments invariably refer to a distinction between questionnaire-based methods and in-depth or semi-structured interviews, as discussed in Chapter 9.

1.6 Types of questionnaire survey

Questionnaire surveys in the leisure and tourism field can be divided into seven types: household surveys; street surveys; telephone surveys; mail surveys; e-surveys; user/on-site/visitor surveys; and captive group surveys. Each of these is discussed in more detail below, and some of their basic characteristics are summarised in Table 10.3.

2. The household questionnaire survey

2.1 Nature

Much of the quantified data in the field of leisure and tourism derive from household questionnaire surveys. While academics draw on the data extensively, the majority of such surveys are commissioned by government and

Table 10.3 Types of questionnaire survey – characteristics

Type	Completed by:	Cost	Sample	Possible length	Response rate
Household					
Standard	Either	Expensive	Whole population	Long	High
Time-use	Respondent	Expensive	Whole population	Long	High
Omnibus	Either	Medium per client	Whole population	Long	High
Street	Interviewer	Medium	Most of population	Short	Medium
Telephone	Interviewer	Medium	Land-line only	Short	High but falling
Mail	Respondent	Cheap	General or special	Varies	Low
E-survey	Respondent	Cheap	Email/internet only	Medium	Medium
On-site	Either	Medium	Site users only	Medium	High
Captive	Respondent	Cheap	Captive group only	Medium	High

commercial leisure and tourism organisations for policy or marketing purposes. The advantage of household surveys is that they are generally representative of the community – the samples drawn tend to include all age-groups, above a certain minimum, and all occupational groups. They also generally represent a complete geographical area – a whole country, a state or region, a local government area or a neighbourhood. Household surveys are therefore designed to provide information on the reported leisure or tourism behaviour of the community as a whole or a particular group drawn from the whole community – for example, the older population aged 65 and over, or young people aged 15–24.

While some household leisure/tourism surveys are specialised, many are broad-ranging in their coverage. That is, they tend to ask, among other things, about participation in a wide range of leisure activities, holiday-taking patterns or buying habits. This facilitates exploration of a wide range of issues which other types of survey cannot so readily tackle.

2.2 Conduct

Normally, household questionnaire surveys are interviewer-completed by face-to-face interview. However, it is possible for a questionnaire to be left at a respondent's home for respondent-completion and later collection, in which case the field-worker then has the responsibility of checking that questionnaires have been fully completed and perhaps conducting an interview in those situations where respondents have been unable to fill in the questionnaire, either because they have been too busy, have forgotten or have lost the questionnaire, or because of literacy or language problems or infirmity.

Being home-based, this sort of survey can involve quite lengthy questionnaires and interviews. By contrast, in the street, at a leisure or tourism facility, or over the telephone, it can be difficult to conduct a lengthy interview. General leisure participation surveys in particular, with their wide range of possible activities, often involve a very complex questionnaire which is difficult to administer 'on the run'. With the home-based interview, it is usually possible to pursue issues at greater length than is possible in other settings. An interview of three-quarters of an hour in duration is not out of the question, and 20–30 minutes is quite common.

A variation on the standard household questionnaire interview survey is to combine interviewer-completed and respondent-completed elements. This often happens with leisure surveys: the interviewer conducts an interview with one member of the household about the household – how many people live there, whether the dwelling is owned or rented, perhaps information on recreational equipment, or anything to do with the household as a whole. Then an individual questionnaire is left for each member of the household to complete, concerning their own leisure behaviour. The interviewer calls back later to collect these individual questionnaires.

The potential length of interviews, the problems of contacting representative samples and, on occasions, the wide geographical spread of the study area, mean that household surveys are usually the most expensive to conduct, per interview. Costs of the order of £30 or £35 per interview are typical, depending on the amount of analysis included in the price. When samples of several thousands are involved, the costs can therefore be substantial.

2.3 Omnibus surveys

While considering household surveys, mention should be made of the *omnibus* survey. These are surveys conducted by a market research or survey organisation with various questions included in the questionnaire on behalf of different clients. The main costs of conducting the survey, which lie in sampling and contacting respondents, are therefore shared by a number of clients. The cost of collecting fairly standard demographic and socio-economic information – such as age, gender, family structure, occupation and income – is also shared among the clients. With regular omnibus surveys many of the procedures, such as sampling and data processing, have become routinised, and interviewers are in place throughout the country already trained and familiar with the type of questionnaire and the requirements of the market research company – these factors can reduce costs significantly.

The British *General Lifestyle Survey* (GLS) (formerly *General Household Survey*) is an omnibus survey of 20,000 people run by the Office for National Statistics, the clients being government departments and agencies. In the years when leisure questions were included, the clients for those questions were the various national leisure/recreation agencies, such as the Sports Council and the Countryside Commission.

Although discussed here as a sub-category of household surveys, omnibus surveys may also be conducted using other formats, notably telephone and e-surveys.

2.4 Time-use surveys

Time-use, or time-budget, surveys are designed to collect information about people's use of time. Such information is generally collected as the main or subsidiary part of a household survey; in addition to answering a questionnaire, respondents are asked to complete a diary, typically covering a period of one or two days. Respondents are asked to record their waking-hours activities in a time-use diary, including starting and stopping times, together with information on where the activity was done, with whom, and possibly whether the respondent considered it to be paid work, domestic work or leisure. Secondary activities are also generally gathered, for example, listening to music while doing the housework. Radio and television-viewing audience data were traditionally collected using time-use diaries, but the practice for television is now to use people meters as discussed in Chapter 5. Home-based time-use surveys clearly cannot be used in relation to tourism activities, but the technique has been suggested for use with tourists to study their temporal and spatial behaviour at a destination (Pearce, 1988).

Coding and analysis of time-use data presents a considerable challenge, since hundreds of leisure and non-leisure activities must be given a code and the information must be processed for, say, 60 or 70 quarter-hour periods each day. Space does not permit a detailed treatment of this specialised topic here, but it can be followed up in the literature indicated in the Resources section.

2.5 National surveys

National leisure and tourism participation surveys, typically conducted by government statistical agencies, are discussed in Chapter 7 as a source of secondary data. These surveys are typically large-scale household or telephone surveys. Often their main secondary use is comparison with locally conducted surveys, the aim being to establish whether, on some participation measure, the local community is above or below the national average. If such comparisons are to be made, it follows that the local survey must be conducted in a similar way and the comparison questions in the questionnaire must be similarly worded. This clearly places a constraint on design, but, apart from the ability to make comparisons, it also has the advantage that the question format has been thoroughly tested.

3. The street survey

3.1 Nature

The street survey involves a relatively short questionnaire and is conducted, as the name implies, on the street – usually a shopping street or business area – or in squares or shopping malls, where a cross-section of the community might be expected to be found. The method can also be used to interview tourists to an area, in which case surveys are conducted at locations where tourists are known to congregate, such as the environs of major attractions, restaurant or tourist accommodation areas, or transport locations, such as airports or bus-stations. In the tourism case the survey could be seen as having some of the characteristics of the on-site, user or visitor survey, as discussed in section 7.

3.2 Conduct

Stopping people in the street or similar environments for an interview places certain limitations on the interview process. First, an interview conducted in the street cannot generally be as long as one conducted at someone's home – especially when the interviewee is in a hurry. Of course, some household interviews are very short because the interviewee is in a hurry or is a reluctant respondent, and some street interviews are lengthy because the respondent has plenty of time. As a general rule, however, the street interview must be shorter. Both in the home and street interview situation, before committing themselves to an interview, potential respondents often ask, 'How long will it take?' In the home-based situation, a reply of '15–20 minutes' is generally acceptable, but in the street situation, anything more than '5 minutes' would generally lead to a marked reduction in the proportion of people prepared to cooperate. The range of topics/issues/activities which can be covered in a street interview is therefore restricted, and this must be taken into account in designing the questionnaire.

The second limitation of the street survey is the problem of contacting a representative sample of the population. Certain types of people might not frequent shopping areas at all, or only infrequently – for example, people who are housebound for various reasons or those who have other people to do their shopping. Some types of tourist – for example, business tourists or those visiting friends or relatives – may not be found in the popular tourist areas. Such individuals might be of particular importance in some studies, so their omission can significantly compromise the results. Little can be done to overcome this problem; it has to be accepted as a limitation of the method. The other side of this coin is that certain groups will be over-represented in shopping streets – notably full-time home/child carers, the retired and the unemployed in suburban shopping areas, or office workers in business areas. It might also be the case that certain areas are frequented more by, for example, young people than old people or by men rather than women, so any sample would be representative of the users of the area, but not of the local population or visitor population as a whole.

3.3 Quota sampling

The means used to attempt to overcome the problem of unrepresentative samples is the technique of *quota sampling*, in which the interviewer is given a predetermined quota of different types of people – for example, by age, sex, occupation – to interview. The proportions in each category in the target population must be known in advance – for example, by reference to the Population Census or, in the case of international tourists, by reference to the official short-term arrivals and departure data (see Chapter 7). When the survey is complete, if the sample is still not representative with regard to the key characteristics, further adjustments can be achieved through the process of *weighting*, as discussed in Chapter 13.

4. The telephone survey

4.1 Nature

The telephone survey is particularly popular with political pollsters because of its speed and the ease with which a widespread sample of the community can be contacted. It is used extensively in market and academic research for these reasons.

An obvious limitation of the technique is that it excludes non-telephone subscribers – generally low-income groups and some mobile sections of the population. With telephones in virtually all homes in developed countries, this is not now as serious a problem as it was in the past. In the case of relatively simple surveys like political opinion polls, where the researcher has access to previous results from both telephone and face-to-face interviews, this problem may be overcome by the use of a correction factor – for instance, it might be known that inclusion of non-telephone subscribers always adds x per cent to the Labour vote. In certain kinds of market research the absence of the poorer parts of the community from the survey may be unimportant because they do not form a significant part of the market; but for much public policy and academic research, however, this can be a significant limitation.

An increasingly significant problem is the case of households which do not have a land-line telephone, relying only on mobile phones, which are not listed in directories. This is likely to involve mainly young people, who are an important target of much survey work. In some cases telephone companies can provide lists of non-business telephones to researchers, but typically without names or locations. Again, it may be possible to correct for this statistically if the characteristics of this group are known. One solution is the use of representative panels of respondents, as discussed in Chapter 5, or online or e-surveys, as discussed in section 6.

4.2 Conduct

Length of interview can be a limitation of telephone surveys, but not as serious as in the case of street interviews; telephone interviews of 10 or 15 minutes are acceptable.

The technique has its own unique set of problems in relation to sampling. Generally, the numbers to be called are selected at random from the telephone directory. Market research companies generally use Computer Assisted Telephone Interviewing (CATI), involving equipment and software which automatically dials random telephone numbers from a digital database. CATI systems also enable the interviewer to key answers directly into a computer, so dispensing with the printed questionnaire. This speeds up the analysis process considerably and cuts down the possibility of error in transcribing results from printed questionnaire to computer. It explains how the results of overnight political opinion polls can be published in the newspapers the next morning.

If a representative cross-section of the community is to be included, then it is necessary for telephone surveys to be conducted in the evenings and/or on weekends if those who have paid jobs or other day-time commitments are to be included.

A limitation of the telephone interview is that respondents cannot be shown such things as lists or images. This is particularly relevant to leisure and tourism surveys. In leisure participation surveys, respondents are frequently shown lists of activities and asked if they have participated in them. Such lists can include 20 or 30 items, which can be tedious to read out over the telephone. Similarly, in tourism studies respondents may be shown a list of places and asked which they have visited. Questionnaires which involve long checklists – for example, attitude dimensions – are also not easily administered by telephone.

It can be argued that telephones have an advantage over face-to-face interviews in that respondents may feel that they are more anonymous and may therefore be more forthcoming in their opinions. But it could also be argued that the face-to-face interview has other advantages in terms of eye contact and body language which enable the skilled interviewer to conduct a better interview than is possible over the telephone.

The main advantage of the telephone survey is that it is quick and relatively cheap to conduct. However, in some countries there is growing reluctance on the part of the public to cooperate with telephone surveys, resulting in the need to make a number of calls to contact cooperative respondents, thus increasing the costs and raising issues concerning representativeness.

4.3 Representativeness and response levels

An increasing number of problems arise in the conduct of telephone surveys, including consumer, technological, legal and social factors.

Reference has already been made to problems caused by the shift to mobile or cell phone technology: unlike land-line telephones, mobile phone numbers are not publicly listed and geographically identifiable, and people who rely entirely on mobile phones are not a cross-section of the whole community, so continued reliance on land-line telephones for surveys can result in biased samples. In developing countries, history is unfolding differently since the mobile phone has arrived in advance of universal access to land-line telephones.

Technological devices used to control and manage telephone access also present difficulties in contacting survey respondents, including user ID and answer machines/voice mail. Added to this, privacy legislation enables telephone subscribers to deny access for telemarketing, although bona-fide social research and government surveys are generally exempt.

In addition to consumer and technological change, surveyors note an increasing tendency for members of the public to refuse to cooperate with telephone surveys. Thus, one American organisation reports that, once contact is made, using standard survey techniques, while 58 per cent agreed to an interview in 1997, this had fallen to 38 per cent by 2003, although these figures increased to 74 per cent and 59 per cent when more rigorous techniques, including callbacks, were used (Pew Research Center, 2004).

The result of these changes is increased costs for telephone surveys as well as increased concerns about representativeness. The result is a trend towards online or e-surveys which, as discussed later in this chapter, face their own challenges.

4.4 National surveys

The comments about national surveys, made in relation to household surveys above, also apply to telephone surveys.

5. The mail survey

5.1 Nature

There are certain situations where the mail or postal method is the only practical survey technique to use. The most common example is where members
or customers of some national organisation are to be surveyed. The costs of
conducting face-to-face interviews with even a sample of the members or
customers throughout the country would be substantial – a mail survey is the
obvious answer. The mail survey has the advantage that a large sample can
be included. In the case of a membership organisation, there may be advantages in surveying the whole membership, even though this may not be necessary in statistical terms. It can, however, be very helpful in terms of the
internal politics of the organisation for all members to be given the opportunity to participate in the survey and to 'have their say'. While 'mail survey' is
the terminology used, this type of survey is increasingly being conducted via
email, with respondents being invited, by hard-copy mail or email, to log on
to a specified website to participate in an online survey, or e-survey, as discussed in section 6.

5.2 The problem of low response rates

The most notorious problem of postal surveys is low response rates. In
many cases as few as 25 or 30 per cent of those sent a questionnaire bother
to reply, and when surveys are poorly conceived and designed, the response
rate can fall to 3 or 4 per cent. Surveys with only 30 per cent response rates
are regularly reported in the research literature, but questions must
be raised as to their validity when 70 per cent of the target sample is not
represented.

What affects the response rate? Seven different factors can be identified, as
listed in Table 10.4 and discussed in turn below.

Table 10.4   Factors affecting mail survey response

---

a. The interest of the respondent in the survey topic
b. The length of the questionnaire
c. Questionnaire design/presentation/complexity
d. Style, content and authorship of the accompanying letter
e. Provision of a postage-paid reply envelope
f. Rewards for responding
g. Number and timing of reminders/follow-ups

---

a. Interest of the respondent in the survey topic

A survey of a local community about a proposal to route a six-lane highway through the neighbourhood would probably result in a high response rate, but a survey of the same community on general patterns of leisure behaviour would probably result in a low response rate. Variation among the population in the level of interest in the topic can result in a biased (that is, unrepresentative) response. For example, a survey on sports facility provision might evoke a high response rate among those interested in sport and a low response rate among those not interested – giving a false impression of overall community enthusiasm for sports facility provision. To some extent this can be corrected by weighting if the bias corresponds with certain known characteristics of the population (see Chapter 13). For example, if the membership records of the organisation being surveyed indicate a higher response rate from some geographical regions than from others, the membership record data could be used to weight the results to reflect the correct proportions.

b. Length of the questionnaire

It might be expected that a long questionnaire would discourage potential respondents. It can, however, be argued that other factors, such as the topic and the presentation of the questionnaire, are more important than the length of the questionnaire – that is, if the topic is interesting to the respondent and is well presented, then length of questionnaire and the time taken to complete it may be less of an issue. If the actual questionnaire is presented online, the potential respondent does not see the questionnaire but is typically advised about the time it will take to complete.

c. Questionnaire design/presentation/complexity

More care must be taken in design and physical presentation with any respondent-completed questionnaire. Typesetting, colour coding of pages, graphics and so on may be helpful. The online format typically makes this design process easier. Leisure and tourism surveys often present awesome lists of activities which can make a questionnaire look very complicated and demanding to complete.

d. The accompanying letter

The letter from the sponsor or researcher which accompanies the questionnaire may have an influence on people's willingness to respond. Does it give a good reason for the survey? Is it from someone or the type of organisation whom the potential respondent trusts or respects?

e. Postage-paid reply envelope

It is usual to include a postage-paid envelope for the return of a hard-copy questionnaire. Some believe that an envelope with a real stamp on it will produce a better response rate than a business-reply-paid envelope. Providing reply envelopes with real stamps is more expensive because, apart from the time spent in sticking stamps on envelopes, stamps are provided for both respondents and non-respondents.

f. Rewards

The question of rewards for taking part in a survey can arise in relation to any sort of survey but it is a device used most often in postal surveys. One approach is to send every respondent some small reward, such as a voucher for a firm's or agency's product or service, or even money. A more common approach is to enter all respondents in a draw for a prize. Even a fairly costly prize may be money well spent if it results in a substantial increase in the response rate, and when considered in relation to the cost of the alternative methods, such as a household survey involving face-to-face interviews. It could, however, be argued that the introduction of rewards causes certain people to respond for the wrong reasons and that it introduces a potential source of bias in responses. It might also be considered that the inclusion of a prize or reward 'lowers the tone' of the survey and places it in the same category as other, commercial, junk mail that comes through people's letter boxes every day.

g. Reminders/follow-ups

Sensible reminder and follow-up procedures are perhaps the most significant tool available to the researcher. They can include postcard/email/phone reminders, supplying a second copy of the questionnaire and offering a telephone interview, indicated in the sequence suggested in Table 10.5. Dillman et al. (2014) have conducted experiments with the offer of a telephone interview and note that this clearly increases the response rate but may provide different responses from the standard mail survey – this may be seen as a strength (a sort of triangulation) or a weakness.

Table 10.5 Mail survey follow-ups

Day	Reminders	Attachments	Comment
1	Initial mail-out	Questionnaire	–
8	Postcard reminder*	–	Email or telephone might be used if available and resources permit.
15	Letter reminder*	Copy of questionnaire	Copy of questionnaire is enclosed 'in case original has been mislaid'. Email might be used. Offer of telephone interview.
22	Final postcard reminder*	–	As above, email or phone might be used and offer of telephone interview.

(*if communication is via email, these will be email messages)

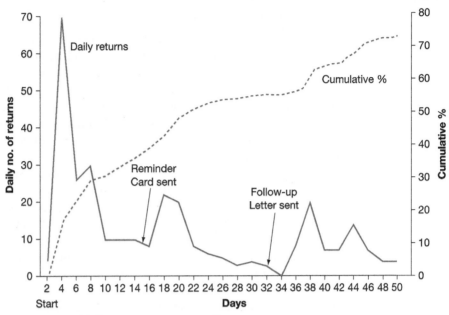

Figure 10.1 Mail survey response pattern

An example of the effects of follow-ups can be seen in Figure 10.1, which relates to a mail survey of residents' recreational use of a river estuary. It can be seen that the level of responses peaked after only 3 days and looked likely to cease after about 16 days, which would have given a potential response rate of just 40 per cent. The surges in responses following the sending of the later reminders can be seen, and the eventual result was a 75 per cent response rate, which is very good for this type of survey. The need for follow-ups must be considered when budgeting for a postal survey, since postage and printing costs are often the most significant item in such budgets.

The sending out of reminders means that it must be possible to identify returned questionnaires, so that reminders are not sent to those who have already replied. This means that questionnaires or envelopes must have an identifying number which can be matched with the mailing list. Some respondents resent this potential breach of confidentiality, but it cannot be avoided if only non-respondents are to be followed up. The confidentiality issue may be overcome if the identifier is placed on the reply envelope rather than the questionnaire. A further possibility is for the replies to be sent to a 'neutral' party, such as a solicitor or accountant. There is often a further advantage to being able to identify responses; they can be used to check the representativeness of the response. For instance, the questionnaire may not include respondents' addresses, but the geographical spread of the response can be examined if the identity of the responses is known, and any necessary weighting can then be carried out.

Gitelson and Drogin (1992) showed that sending final reminders with a personalised letter and sending it via certified/registered mail significantly increased the response rate compared with non-personalised letters and ordinary mail (see the summary in Case study 11.3).

How much is enough?

What level of response is acceptable? One answer would be to say that an adequate response has been achieved if the characteristics and responses of respondents are not significantly different from those of non-respondents. But how do you know the characteristics and responses of non-respondents? In some cases the researcher has access to some limited information on non-respondents – for example, their geographical location and other information which might be held on the database from which addresses were drawn. This can be used to make comparisons.

One approach which covers both characteristics and question responses is to compare early respondents with later respondents – if there is no difference, this may indicate that further pursuit of non-respondents is not necessary. It would of course be helpful to the research community if results of such examinations were publicly available so that conclusions could be drawn as to whether there is a general response rate at which further response patterns stabilise, whether there is no such rate or whether it is variable. Just a few researchers have conducted experiments on this question, and some examples are summarised in Chapter 11 in Case study 11.3. The Gitelson and Drogin (1992) study was a user/site/visitor and mail survey combo (described in the next subsection). Since the mail survey sample respondents and non-respondents had all been interviewed on-site, it was possible to compare the characteristics of the two groups in terms of the information from the on-site survey questionnaires.

5.3 Mail and user/site/visitor survey combos

A common practice is to conduct a brief face-to-face interview at a leisure or tourism site or event and ask respondents to complete a mail survey (or e-survey) questionnaire on their return home. This shortens the time taken to conduct the on-site interview but also means that respondents can give views about the facility or event when their visit has been completed in its entirety. In some cases the mail-back questionnaire may be provided after the on-site interview: in other cases addresses (or email addresses) may be obtained and the questionnaire sent to them.

6. E-surveys

6.1 Nature and conduct

E-surveys, or electronic or online surveys, are conducted via the internet. Standard 'hard-copy' mail has been the traditional medium for mail surveys and is still popular, but costs, speed and response rates, as discussed earlier, are increasingly seen as drawbacks of the method. Similarly, the growing problems

Table 10.6   Types of e-survey

Type	Request	Questionnaire	Completion	Return
1. Hybrid email/mail	Email	Attached text file	Manual or hard copy	Mail
2. Hybrid email	Email	Attached text file	Word-processor/ spreadsheet	Email + attached text file
3. Hybrid mail/inline	Mail	Online, interactive	Online	Online submission
4. Fully electronic – ad hoc	Email	Online, interactive	Online	Online submission
5. Fully electronic – panel	Email	Online, interactive	Online	Online submission

of traditional telephone surveys have been outlined earlier. The result has been increasing uses of the electronic or e-survey. A number of formats exist, ranging from simply using an email to transmit a traditional questionnaire, to a fully electronic, online format, as summarised in Table 10.6.

The first version simply uses email to replace the sending-out process. The second version uses email to send out and return, and uses a word-processor and/or spreadsheet rather than hard copy, but the questionnaire is still in traditional format. The final two versions involve an emailed request and online completion and return. Online questionnaires are interactive: the completion process is simplified for the respondent so that, when 'filter' questions are involved which require the respondent to skip certain questions and jump to a particular section of the questionnaire, this takes place automatically.

Commercial survey organisations, such as SurveyMonkey, offer e-survey services in which the customer/researcher specifies the questions to be included, then asks survey participants to access the survey organisation's website to take part in the survey. The customer/researcher can download the results on demand.

Many corporate organisations, such as banks, from time to time invite their online customers to complete online questionnaire surveys to obtain customer feedback on service quality. Similarly, while hotels still invite guests to complete a hard-copy feedback questionnaire on completion of their stay, it is now common for guests to receive an invitation to participate in an online survey via email some time after their return home.

An e-survey may be combined with a user/site/visitor in a similar way to the 'mail and user/site visitor survey combo' discussed above.

6.2 Advantages and disadvantages

The advantages of e-surveys to the researcher are the low cost and the speed with which they can be conducted. The fully electronic versions are designed to be very user-friendly, as noted earlier.

The disadvantage of the e-survey is that it is confined to those with access to the internet and, while the sending of reminders is cheap, the problem of low response may still be a problem for some surveys because they may be seen as part of the increasing volume of junk mail received via email.

7. User/on-site/visitor surveys

7.1 Nature

The terms *on-site*, *site*, *user* or *visitor* survey are used to refer to this type of survey. *On-site* and *site survey* tend to be used in the context of outdoor recreation studies, *user survey* in the context of indoor recreation facilities, and *visitor survey* when tourists or day-trippers are involved or for types of facility where visits are relatively infrequent, such as museums or zoos. A fourth term, *audience survey*, is used in the arts environment; for example, for surveys of theatre audiences. Researchers with a background in transport tend to use the term *intercept* survey, as discussed in Chapter 5. The term *user survey* is utilised in this section to cover all these situations.

The user survey is the most common type of survey utilised by managers in leisure and tourism. Surveys of local users and tourists are carried out at recreation or leisure facilities, and surveys of tourists are carried out at hotels and *en route* on various types of transport, particularly international air trips. As noted earlier in this chapter, general surveys of visitors to a tourist area often take the form of street surveys. Visitors are interviewed in the street, in squares/plazas or in seafront areas – anywhere where tourists are known to congregate. In this case the 'facility' is the tourist town or area, so the 'street survey' and the 'site survey' overlap, and consideration must be given to the features of both types of survey. In general, the site survey is more controlled than the street survey; interviewers are seen by respondents to be part of the management of the facility, and usually it is possible to interview users at a convenient time when they are not in a rush, as they may be in the street or shopping mall.

7.2 Conduct

User surveys can be conducted by interviewer- or respondent-completion. Unless carefully supervised, respondent-completion methods can lead to a poor standard in the completion of questionnaires and a low response level. As with all low response levels, this can be a source of serious bias in that those who reply may be unrepresentative of the users or visitors as a whole.

The usual respondent-completion survey involves handing users a questionnaire on their arrival at the site and collecting them on their departure, or conducting the whole procedure upon departure. Where respondent-completion is thought to be desirable or necessary, then sufficient staff should be employed to check all users leaving the site, to ask for the return of completed questionnaires, to provide replacements for questionnaires which have been mislaid and to assist in completing questionnaires, including completion by interview if necessary. Leaving a pile of questionnaires with a busy receptionist to hand out and collect rarely works well.

Conducting user surveys by interview is generally preferable to respondent-completion for the reasons discussed earlier in this chapter. The use of interviewers obviously has a cost disadvantage but, depending on the length of the interview, costs per interview are usually comparatively low. Typically, a user-survey interview will take about five minutes, but in some longer-stay facilities, such as a park or beach, significantly longer interviews are possible. Given the need to check through completed questionnaires, the gaps in user traffic and the need for interviewers to take breaks, it is reasonable to expect interviewers in such situations to complete about six interviews in an hour. Such estimates are, of course, necessary when planning project budgets and timetables.

The survey methods considered so far have been fairly multi-purpose: they could be used for market research for a range of products or services; by public agencies for a variety of policy-oriented purposes; or for academic research, which may or may not be policy- or management-oriented. User surveys are more specific. The most common use of such surveys is for policy, planning or management purposes. They are the type of survey which readers of this text are most likely to be involved with; they are the most convenient surveys for students to 'cut their teeth' on and the most common surveys for individual managers to become involved in. For these reasons, the roles of user surveys are considered in some detail.

7.3 Uses of user surveys

What can user surveys be used for? Four topics are discussed briefly in this sub-section: catchment area; user socio-demographic profile; user opinions and non-users.

Catchment area

What is the *catchment* or *market* area of the facility or service? It is the geographical area where most of the users come from. This can be important in terms of advertising policy. Management can concentrate advertising/marketing on its existing catchment area, or it can take conscious decisions to use marketing to attempt to extend its catchment area. But in order to adopt either of these approaches, it is first necessary to establish the current catchment area. Sometimes this information is already available from membership records; however, this does not always reflect the pattern of actual use. So in most cases it can be discovered only by means of a questionnaire-based survey in which home location is one of the questions.

User socio-demographic profile

What is the socio-economic/demographic profile of the facility users? It might be thought that a management capable of observation would be able to make this assessment without the need for a survey. This depends on the type of facility, the extent to which management is in continuous contact with users and the variability of the user profile. For example, a restaurant, hotel or resort manager might be very well informed on this because of the prices charged, but managers of beaches, urban parks, national/state parks or theatres might, for various reasons, be less well informed, or even misinformed.

Profile information can be used in a number of ways. As with data on catchment area, it can be used to consolidate or extend the market. Very often the commercial operator will opt to consolidate – to focus on a particular client group and maximise the market share of that group, by appropriate advertising, pricing and product development. On the other hand, in some situations decisions will be made to focus on a particular neglected 'demographic', especially if it comprises high-spenders. In the case of a public-sector facility the remit is usually to attract as wide a cross-section of the community as possible, so the data would be used to highlight those sections of the community not being catered for and therefore requiring marketing, pricing or product development attention. More broadly, a public agency responsible for a range of facilities could use the data to check whether the community is being appropriately provided for by all its facilities taken together.

User opinions

What are the opinions of users about the design, accessibility and service quality of the facility? Such opinion data are invariably collected in user surveys and are usually of great interest to managers, but the interpretation of the data it is not without its difficulties. If management is looking for pertinent criticisms, current users may be the wrong group to consult. Those who are most critical are no longer using the facility. Those using the facility may be reluctant to criticise because it undermines their own situation – if the place is so poor, why are they there? Those who are prepared to be critical may not be the sorts of clients for whom the facility is designed.

In some situations, people have little choice between facilities so criticisms are perhaps more easily interpreted. For example, parents' comments about the suitability of a neighbourhood park for children's play can be particularly pertinent when it is the only play area available in the neighbourhood.

When opinion data have been collected, it is often difficult to know precisely what to do with the results. Very often the largest group of users has no complaint or suggestion to make – either because they cannot be bothered to think of anything in the interview situation or because of the respondent selection process referred to earlier. Often the most common complaint is raised by as few as 10 per cent of users. If this is the most common complaint, then logically something ought to be done about it by the management – but it could also be said that 90 per cent of the users are not concerned about that issue, so perhaps there is no need to do anything about it! Very often, therefore, management can use survey results to suit their own preferences. If they want to do something about feature X, they can say that X was complained about by more users than anything else; if they do not want to do anything about X, they can say that 90 per cent of users are satisfied with X the way it is.

Managers mostly want to enhance and maximise the quality of the experience enjoyed by their visitors: it may not be criticism of specific features that is important but users' overall evaluation of the experience. Thus users can be asked to rate a facility or area using a scale such as very good/good/fair/ poor/very poor, or very satisfied/satisfied/dissatisfied/very dissatisfied. The results of such an evaluation can be used to compare users' evaluation of one facility with another – for example, in a system of parks. Or they could be used to examine the same facility at different times to see if satisfaction has increased or declined. This is of course related to evaluation/management-related research, as discussed in Chapters 1 and 2.

Non-users

User surveys by definition involve only current users of a facility or current visitors to an area. This is often cited as a limitation of such surveys, the implication being that non-users may be of more interest than users if the aim of management is to increase the number of users or visitors. Caution should, however, be exercised in moving to consider conducting research on non-users. For a start, the number of non-users is usually very large. For example, in a city of a million population, a facility which has 5000 users has 995,000 non-users! In a country with a population of 50 million, a tourist area which attracts a million visitors a year has 49 million non-visitors, and if management is interested in international visitors, they have around seven billion non-visitors! The idea that all non-users are potential users, and should therefore be researched, is therefore somewhat naive. Obviously, a more focused approach may be taken, but it may still be an expensive option.

At least, therefore, the user survey can help in focusing any research which is to be conducted on non-users. For example, in the case of a local leisure facility, the user survey defines the catchment area and, unless there is some reason for believing that the catchment area can or should be extended, the non-users to be studied are those who live within that area. Similarly, the user profile indicates the type of person currently using the facility and, again, unless there is a conscious decision to attempt to change that profile, the non-users to be studied are the ones with that profile living within the defined catchment area. Importantly, comparison between the user profile and the profile of the population of the catchment area, as revealed by population census data (see Chapter 7), can be used to estimate the numbers and characteristics of non-users in the area. Thus user surveys can reveal something about non-users.

7.4 User/site/visitor and mail/e-survey combo

In the earlier discussion of mail surveys in this chapter, the idea of a 'mail and user/site/visitor survey combo' is discussed, in which a short face-to-face on-site interview is followed by a request to the respondent to complete a mail survey or e-survey questionnaire on their return home.

8. Captive group surveys

8.1 Nature

The *captive group* survey is typically not referred to in other research methods texts. It refers to the situation where the people to be included in the survey comprise the membership of some group where access can be negotiated *en bloc*. Such groups include schoolchildren, adult education groups, clubs of various kinds and groups of employees – although all have their various unique characteristics. The ethical issues arising when such groups are 'volunteered' for research in this way are discussed in Chapter 4.

8.2 Conduct

A roomful of cooperative people can provide a number of respondent-completed questionnaires very quickly. Respondent-completion is less problematic in captive situations than in less controlled situations because it is possible to take the group through the questionnaire question by question and therefore ensure good standards of completion.

The most common example of a captive group is schoolchildren, since the easiest way to contact children under school-leaving age is via schools. The method may, however, appear simpler than it is in practice. Research on children for education purposes has become so common that education authorities are cautious about permitting access to children for surveys. Very often permission for any survey work must be obtained from the central education authority – the permission of the class teacher or head teacher is not sufficient.

While the most economical use of this technique involves using a respondent-completed questionnaire, interview methods can also be used. The essential feature is that access to members of the group is facilitated by their membership of that group and the fact that they are gathered together in one place at one time.

It is important to be aware of the criteria for membership of the group and to compare that with the needs of the research. In some cases an apparent match can be misleading. For example, attendees at a retired people's club meetings do not include all retired people – it excludes 'non-joiners' and the house-bound. While schools include all young people, care must be taken over their catchment areas, compared with the study area of the research, and with the mix of public-sector and private schools.

9. Questionnaire design

9.1 Introduction – research problems and information requirements

The important principle in designing questionnaires is to take it slowly and carefully and to remember why the research is being done. Very often research-ers move too quickly into 'questionnaire design mode' and begin listing all the things 'it would be interesting to ask'. In many organisations, a draft question-naire is circulated for comment and everyone in the organisation joins in. The process begins to resemble Christmas tree decorating – nobody must be left out, and everybody must be allowed to contribute their favourite bauble. This is not the best way to proceed!

The decision to conduct a questionnaire survey should itself be the culmina-tion of a careful process of thought and discussion, involving, as discussed in Chapter 3, consideration of all possible methods, not just surveys. The concepts and variables involved, and the relationships to be investigated, possibly in the form of hypotheses, theories, models or evaluative frameworks, should be clear and should guide the questionnaire design process, as illustrated in Figure 10.2. It is not advisable to *begin* with a list of questions to be included in the question-naire. The starting point should ideally be an examination of the management,

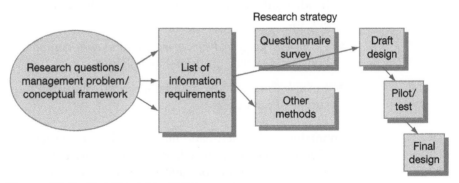

Figure 10.2 Questionnaire design process

planning, policy or theoretical questions to be addressed, followed by the drawing up of a list of information required to address the problems. This is outlined in Chapter 3 as elements 1–5 of the research process. Element 6, deciding the research strategy, involves determining which, if any, of the listed information requirements should be met by means of a questionnaire survey and which should be met by other methods. Questions should be included in the questionnaire only if they relate to requirements listed in element 5. This means that every question included must be linked back to the *research questions*.

In designing a questionnaire, the researcher should of course have sought out as much previous research on the topic or related topics as possible. This can affect the overall design of a project as discussed in Chapter 3. More specifically, if it is decided that the study in hand should have points of comparison with earlier studies, then those data items will need to be collected on a similar basis to that used in the earlier studies. Questionnaires from previous studies therefore become part of the input into the questionnaire design process.

9.2 Example questionnaires

Before considering questionnaire design in more detail, some examples of short questionnaires are presented in Case study 10.1, including typical questions used in household and site surveys, with interviewer-completed and respondent-completed examples:

● *Example A: site/street survey* is a questionnaire used to assess students' attitudes to campus social life. It is labelled as a site/street survey since, as it would be administered to students on-campus, it partly resembles a site or user survey; but since not all students may make use of the services being examined, it resembles a survey conducted in a street or shopping centre. It is presented as respondent-completed, but completion would probably best be conducted 'under supervision' – that is, completed and handed back to a survey worker at the time, rather than being handed out for later return, which would inevitably produce a low response rate. If the cooperation of the university authorities was obtained so that the questionnaire could be handed out and completed in class time, it would become a 'captive group' survey.

● *Example B: household survey* is an interviewer-completed questionnaire for a household survey on short-stay holidays.

● *Example C: site survey* is an interviewer-completed questionnaire for a site survey of park users.

Annotations in the left-hand margin of these example questionnaires indicate the type of question involved, as discussed later in the chapter. These example questionnaires cannot, of course, cover all situations, but they give a wide range of examples of questions and appropriate formats.

Case study 10.1   Example questionnaires

A: Site/street survey respondent-completed

	Campus Life Survey 2003		Office use
			#____
Standard pre-coded	1. Which of the following best describes your current situation?		qno
	Full-time student with no regular paid work	☐ 1	
	Full-time student with some regular paid work	☐ 2	__ status
	Part-time student with full-time job	☐ 3	
	Part-time student – other	☐ 4	

Standard pre-coded

1. Which of the following best describes your current situation?

Full-time student with no regular paid work	☐ 1
Full-time student with some regular paid work	☐ 2
Part-time student with full-time job	☐ 3
Part-time student – other	☐ 4

Office use: __ status

Pre-coded Multiple response – dichotomous

2. Which of the following university services have you used in the last 4 weeks?

Used campus cafe/bar	☐ 1	__ cafebar
Attended university club/association meeting	☐ 1	__ club
Attended a live music performance on campus	☐ 1	__ music
Watched a movie on campus	☐ 1	__ movie

Ranking

3. In thinking about the social and entertainment services provided on campus, what are the most important considerations for you? Please rank the items below in terms of their importance to you. Rank them from 1 for the most important to 5 for the least important.

	Rank	
Free or cheap access	___	__ cheap
Day time attractions	___	__ daytime
Acts, films, etc. not available elsewhere	___	__ unusual
Opportunities to socialise/meet people	___	__ meet
Cost	___	__ cost

Numerical – uncoded

4. Approximately how much do you spend in an average week on entertainment and social activities on and off campus?

£_____

____ spend

Likert scales

5. Please indicate the importance of the following to you in relation to campus life

	Very important	Important	Not at all important	
Relaxation	☐ 3	☐ 2	☐ 1	__ relax
Social interaction	☐ 3	☐ 2	☐ 1	__ social
Mental stimulation	☐ 3	☐ 2	☐ 1	__ mental

Open-ended Multiple response – categories

6. What suggestions would you make for improving campus social life?

_____

_____

__ sug1
__ sug2
__ sug3

Standard pre-coded

7. You are: Male ☐ 1   Female ☐ 2

__ gend

Numerical – uncoded

8. Your age last birthday was: ____ years

__ age

B: Household survey – interviewer-completed

Respondent No.	**Short Stay Holiday Survey** ____#
	Introductory remarks: Hallo. We are from St. Anthony's College and we are conducting a survey on people's short-stay holidays. Would you mind answering a few questions? It will take just a few minutes and the results will be kept confidential.
Pre-coded, factual	1. In the last six months, have you been on a short holiday trip of one, two or three nights away from home? Yes 1 – go to Q. 2 No 2 – go to Q.5 _____
Open-ended, factual, numerical	2. How many times did you go on such trips in the six months? Number of times: ___ go to q. 2 _____
Open-ended, factual	3. On your last trip, where did you go? _____ _____
	4. What were the main activities you engaged in on your visit?
Multiple response	a. Sightseeing 1 e. Arts activities/events 1 _____ b. Eating and drinking 1 f. Visit friends/relatives 1 _____ c. Sporting activities 1 g. Just doing nothing 1 _____ d. Walking 1 h. Other 1 _____
Simple pre-coded, factual	5. To what extent do you agree with the following statements?

5.

	Agree strongly	Agree	Neither	Disagree	Disagree strongly	
A short break is as valuable as long holiday	1	2	3	4	5	_____
Holidays make life worth living	1	2	3	4	5	_____

Pre-coded with showcard factual	6. Can you tell me which of the following age-groups you fall into?

Under 15	**A**
15–19	**B**
20–29	**C**
30–59	**D**
60+	**E**

         _____

Pre-coded with showcard factual	7. Which of the following best describes your current situation?

In full-time paid work	**A**
In part-time paid work	**B**
In full-time education	**C**
Full-time home/child care	**D**
Retired	**E**
Looking for work	**F**
Other	**G**

         _____

Pre-coded, factual, observed	THANK YOU FOR YOUR HELP
	Observe gender: Male 1 Female 2 _____

C: Site survey – interviewer-completed

The survey is being carried out for the local council to find out what users of the park think of the park, and what changes they would like to see. A total of 100 users of the park are interviewed at the only entrance, in batches of 10, on different days of the week, at different times of the day, and in different weather conditions.

Ramsey Street Park Survey ___
Excuse me: we are carrying out a survey for the council to find out what people think about the park. Could you spare a few minutes to answer a few questions?

Simple pre-coded

1. How often do you visit this park?

Every day	1
Several times a week	2
Once a week	3
Every 2 or 3 weeks	4
Once a month	5
Less often	6
First visit	7

Simple pre-coded, factual

2. Where have you travelled from today?

Home	1
Work	2
School/college/univ.	3
Other	4

Open-ended, factual

3. What suburb is that in?

_____

Simple pre-coded, factual

4. How long did it take you to get here?

5 minutes or less	1
6–15 minutes	2
16–30 minutes	3
31 minutes or more	4

Simple pre-coded, factual

5. How did you travel here?

Walk	1
Car	2
Motorbike	3
Bicycle	4
Bus/tram	5
Other	6

Open-ended, opinion

6. What do you like most about the park?

_____

Open-ended, opinion

7. What do you like least about the park?

_____

Attitude statement with show-card

8. Looking at the card, where would you place this park, in relation to others you know?

A. Way below average	**1**
B. Below average	**2**
C. Average	**3**
D. Above average	**4**
E. Well above average	**5**

Pre-coded, factual with showcard

9. Can you tell me which of these age-groups you fall into?

Under 15	**A**
15–19	**B**
20–29	**C**
30–59	**D**
60+	**E**

Pre-coded, factual

10. How many people are there in your group here today, including yourself?

Alone	1
Two	2
3–4	3
5 or more	4

Open-ended, factual, numerical

11. How many vehicles did your group arrive in?   ___

Observe, factual

THANK YOU FOR YOUR HELP

Observe:	Male	1
	Female	2

9.3 General design issues

Wording of questions

In wording the questions for a questionnaire, the researcher should:

- avoid jargon;
- simplify wherever possible;
- avoid ambiguity;
- avoid leading questions; and
- ask only one question at a time (i.e. avoid multi-purpose questions).

Examples of good and bad practice in question wording are given in Table 10.7.

Pre-coded vs open-ended questions

As illustrated in Figure 10.3, an *open-ended* question is one where the interviewer asks a question without any prompting of the range of answers to be expected, and writes down the respondent's reply verbatim. In a respondent-completed questionnaire, a line or space is left for respondents to write their answers. A closed or pre-coded question is one where the respondent is offered a range of answers to choose from, either verbally or from a show card or, in the case of a self-completed questionnaire, having the range of answers set out in the questionnaire and (usually) being asked to tick boxes.

In the open-ended case, there is no prior list. In the closed/pre-coded case, there is a list which is shown to the respondent. A third possibility, in an interviewer-administered survey, is a combination of the two, where the question is asked in an open-ended manner and no card is shown to the respondent, but

Table 10.7   Question-wording: examples of good and bad practice

Principle	Bad example	Improved version
Use simple language	What is your frequency of utilisation of retail travel outlets?	How often do you use travel agents?
Avoid ambiguity	Do you play sport very often?	Have you played any of the following sports within the last four weeks? (show list)
Avoid leading questions	Are you against the extension of the airport?	What is your opinion on the extension of the airport? Are you for it, against it or not concerned?
Ask just one question at a time	Do you use the local arts centre, and if so what do you think of its facilities?	Do you use the local arts centre? Yes/No What do you think of the facilities in the local arts centre?

Open-ended

What is the main constraint on your ability to study?

_____

Pre-coded/closed

Which of the following/items listed on the card is the main constraint on your ability to study? (show card – if interviewer-completed)

A. My job	☐$_1$
B. Timetabling	☐$_2$
C. Child care	☐$_3$
D. Spouse/partner	☐$_4$
E. Money	☐$_5$
F. Energy	☐$_6$
G. Other _____	☐$_7$

Card shown to respondent:

A. My job

B. Timetabling of the course

C. Child care

D. Spouse/partner

E. Money

F. Energy

G. Other _____

Figure 10.3 Open-ended vs pre-coded questions – example

the answer is recorded by the interviewer ticking the appropriate box on a pre-coded list on the questionnaire. If the answer does not fit any of the items on the list, it is written in an 'other' category and may be given a code at the analysis stage.

The advantage of the open-ended question is that the respondent's answer is not unduly influenced by the interviewer or by the questionnaire wording, and the verbatim replies from respondents can provide a rich source of varied material which might have been hidden by categories on a pre-coded list. Figure 10.4 gives an example of the range of responses which can result from a single open-ended question.

Because of convenience and saving any embarrassment respondents may have about divulging precise figures, pre-coded groups are often used when asking respondents about quantified information, such as age, income or expenditure. However, there is an advantage in using the open-ended approach for such data: that is in obtaining actual figures rather than group codes. This

Question: Do you have any complaints about this (beach/picnic) area?
(Site survey in a beachside national park with boating and camping. Number of responses in brackets)

Sand bars (22)

Parking (5)

Wild car driving (1)

Lack of beach area (1)

Too few shops (1)

Too few picnic tables (4)

No timber for barbecue (2)

Need more picnic space (3)

Need boat hire facilities (1)

Need active recn facilities (1)

Litter/pollution (74)

Urban sprawl (1)

Need wharf fishing access (1)

Lack of info. on walking trails (1)

Not enough facilities (3)

Slow barbecues (2)

Uncontrolled camping (1)

Lack/poor toilets (9)

Amenities too far from camp site (1)

Too much development (4)

(Speed) boats (44)

Need more trees for shade (1)

Yobbos drinking beer on beach (1)

Spear fishermen (1)

Water skiers (2)

Against nudism (3)

Loud music (1)

Dumped cars (1)

Traffic (1)

Poor roads (1)

Sand flies (1)

More barbecues (1)

Shells/oysters (1)

Need outdoor cafes (1)

Need more food places (1)

Water too shallow (1)

Uncontrolled boats (23)

Jet skis (39)

Surveys (1)

Should be kept for locals (1)

Seaweed (3)

Need showers (1)

Administration of National Park (1)

Maintenance & policing of Park (1)

Trucks on beach (2)

Anglers (1)

Crowds/tourists (26)

Having to pay entry fee (6)

Houses along waterfront (2)

Unpleasant smell (drain) (2)

Sales people (1)

Need electric barbecues (1)

Dogs (21)

No access to coast (1)

Park rangers not operating in interest of public (1)

Behaviour of others (20)

Access – long indirect road (1)

Need more shops (2)

Navigation marks unclear (1)

Need more taps (1)

Need more swings (1)

No first-aid facilities (1)

Need powered caravan sites (1)

Allow dogs (1)

Private beach areas (1)

Lack of restaurant (1)

Need rain shelters (1)

Can't spear fish (1)

No road shoulders for cyclists (1)

Remove rocks from swim areas (1)

Dangerous boat ramp pollutant activities (1)

Figure 10.4 Example of range of replies from an open-ended question

Source: Robertson and Veal (1987)

permits the flexible option of grouping categories in alternative ways when carrying out the analysis. It also enables *averages* and other measures to be calculated and facilitates a range of statistical analysis which is not possible with groups. The actual figure, rather than group code, is therefore often more useful for analysis purposes.

Open-ended questions have two major disadvantages. First, the analysis of verbatim answers to qualitative questions for computer analysis is laborious and may result in a final set of categories which are of no more value than a well-constructed pre-coded list. In the case of the answers in Figure 10.4, for example, for detailed analysis it may be necessary to group the answers into a manageable number of groups – this would be time-consuming and would involve a certain amount of judgement in grouping individual answers, which can be a source of errors. This process is discussed in more detail under *coding* later in this chapter. Often, therefore, an open-ended question is used in a pilot survey, the results from which are then used to devise a coded list of categories for the main survey.

The second disadvantage of the open-ended approach is that, in the case of respondent-completed questionnaires, response rates to such questions can be very low: people are often too busy or too lazy to write out free-form answers and may have literacy or language problems. When to use open-ended or closed questions is therefore a matter of judgement.

9.4 Types of information

Generally, the information to be gathered from questionnaire surveys can be divided into three groups:

1. Activities/events/places What?
2. Respondent characteristics Who?
3. Attitudes/motivations Why?

Table 10.8 lists some of the more common types of information collected under these three headings. The items covered are of course necessarily general in nature and do not cover all the specialised types of information which can be collected by questionnaire surveys. Some of these items of information require more intrusive questions than others – for example, income – and some can be difficult to ascertain accurately – for example, occupation or details of expenditure while on a tourist trip. They are not therefore all equally suitable for all survey situations.

9.5 Activities/events/places questions

Leisure and tourism activity is at the core of leisure and tourism research, and the procedure for measuring it is far from simple. A variety of possible measures of leisure and tourism activity was indicated earlier in Table 7.1, including the

Table 10.8   Range of information in leisure/tourism questionnaires

---

Activities and events/places

Site/visitor surveys
- Activities while on site or in the area
- Use of site attractions/facilities
- Frequency of visit
- Time spent on site
- Expenditure per head – amounts/purposes
- Travel-related information
- Trip origin (where travelled from)
  - Trip purpose
  - Home address
  - Travel mode
  - Travel time
- Accommodation type used

Household/telephone/postal surveys
- Leisure/travel aspirations/needs
- Evaluation of services/facilities available
- Psychological meaning of activities/satisfactions
- Reactions to development/provision proposals
- Values – re environment, etc.

Respondent characteristics – all survey types
- Gender
- Age
- Economic status (paid work, retired, etc.)
- Occupation/social class (own or 'head of household')
- Previous employment history
- Income (own or household)
- Education/qualifications

- Marital/family status
- Household type/family size
- Life-cycle
- Ethnic group/country of birth
- Residential location/trip origin
- Mobility – driving licence, access to private transport
- Party/group size/type (site/visitor surveys)

Attitude/motivation information – examples

Site/visitor surveys
- Reasons for choice of site/area
- Meaning/importance/values
- Satisfaction/evaluation of experience/services
- Comments on facility
- Future intentions/hopes

Household/telephone/postal surveys
- Leisure activities (including holidays) – what, where, how often, time spent, when, who with?
- Use of particular facilities/sites
- Travel mode to out-of-home leisure
- Expenditure patterns
- Past activities (personal leisure histories)
- Planned future activities

---

participation rate, the number of participants, the volume of activity or visits, the time spent, money spent, time/space measures and intensity. In any study consideration should be given as to which types of measure are necessary. The issues are discussed in turn here, in relation to leisure and tourism separately.

Leisure activities/events/places questions

In addition to *activity*, the terms *events* and *places* are used to reflect the scope of the phenomena being studied. For some research purposes, it is only necessary to know that a person has engaged in a generic activity – for example, 'visited a park'. In other cases it is necessary to know the geographical location, or 'place', of the activity – for example, 'visited a park within/outside the local government area'; or the precise facility – for example, 'visited X park'. Geographical location is obviously important for most tourism research. In other cases, it is not just the generic activity or the place that is of interest but also the specific organised event – for example, 'summer concert in the park'.

The problem of devising questions to gather information on leisure activities in leisure participation surveys is a difficult one. The difficulties centre on two main issues: whether to use an open-ended or pre-coded format; and the reference period for participation.

- An *open-ended format* question simply asks respondents to list the activities they have engaged in during their leisure time or free time over a specified period. Without any prompting, respondents may not understand the full scope of the word 'leisure' or 'free time' and might have difficulty in recalling all their activities. Using the term 'free time' might help a little, but it is still open to variation in interpretation. Providing people with a *coded* checklist of activities to choose from may be unwieldy, but it ensures that all respondents consider the same range of options. The disadvantage of the checklist is that its length may be daunting, particularly to the less literate, and activities later in the list may be under-represented. The time it takes to read the list may be a problem, testing respondents' patience. One compromise is to offer a checklist of 'types' of leisure activity, such as home-based activities, outdoor recreation, arts and entertainment, as an *aide-mémoire* for the respondent. The complexity is partly avoided by the tendency for separate surveys to be used for different categories of activity, such as sport and physical activity or arts and culture. However, this means that a person's leisure activity is not seen as a whole, and some activities, notably home-based activities and social activities, are omitted because they are not of interest to the policy agencies which fund most publicly available leisure participation surveys.

- The *reference period* for recalling activities is crucial to the nature of the findings. Table 10.9 shows the results from a 2001 survey in which respondents were asked about attendance at arts events in the previous four weeks, but if they had not participated in the previous four weeks, they were asked if they had participated in the last year. The results are plain to see. The time-period used to measure participation affects the absolute levels of participation recorded and also the apparent relative popularity of activities (see also Table 7.10). The shorter the time-period used, the more accurate the recall of respondents is likely to be, but shorter time-periods exclude large proportions of participants in those activities which are engaged in relatively infrequently. Furthermore, a time-period shorter than a year necessitates conducting the survey at a different time of the year in order to take account of seasonal variation in types and levels of participation.

Table 10.9   Attendance at arts events, England, 2003

	% of persons aged 16+ attending in the last:	
	12 months	**4 weeks**
Film at a cinema or other venue	59	22
Play or drama	25	4
Carnival, street arts or circus	26	4
Art, photography or sculpture exhibition	22	6
Craft exhibition	19	4
Pantomime	14	–
Cultural festival	8	2
Event connected with books or writing	8	2
Event including video or electronic art	7	2
A musical	26	4
Pop or rock concert	20	4
Classical music concert	10	2
Opera or operetta	6	1
Jazz concert	6	1
Folk or country and western concert	2	–
Other music	7	–
All types of live dance performance	12	–
Contemporary dance	4	–
Ballet	2	–
Other dance	7	–
Sample	6025	6025

Source: Fenn et al. (2004) – data not collected.

In addition to asking whether they have participated in an activity, respondents can also be asked *how often* they have participated and *how much time* was spent on the activity, as discussed in relation to measurement in Chapter 7. This can lead to very lengthy interviews for people who have engaged in a wide range of activities. To avoid this, in some surveys a particular leisure occasion, say, the last trip to the countryside, is explored in more detail – where the respondent went, who with, what day of the week and what time of day, what specific activities were engaged in and so on.

In local surveys or surveys focused on specific policy areas, it may be of interest to explore the use of specific, named, leisure facilities or tourist attractions – for example, visits to particular national parks or to sports centres – using a variety of approaches to measuring use.

In the case of site/user surveys, there is usually little problem in asking about activities, since the range of possible activities is limited. It is usual to ask people what activities they plan to engage in or have engaged in during their visit. Use of specific amenities at the site – such as refreshment facilities – are also generally explored.

Tourism activities/events/places

In the case of household questionnaire surveys concerned with tourism, the activity question concerns trips taken away from the home area over a specified time-period. As with local leisure activities, a major consideration is the recall time-period. For major holidays a one-year recall period is not out of the question; but for short breaks, asking about trips during that length of time may lead to inaccuracies in recall, so a shorter time-period of, say, three months is often adopted. This means that a survey must be conducted at different times of the year to capture seasonal variation.

A second time-period issue concerns the definition of tourist 'trip'. The definition used in a survey may follow an accepted definition of tourism: for example, a trip involving a stay away from home of one night or more. However, in some local tourism studies, *day trips* may also be of interest.

In addition to indicating trips taken, household tourism questionnaires also generally include questions on trip destination, length of stay, travel mode and type of accommodation used. Tourism surveys are usually much more concerned with economic matters than leisure surveys, so questions on the cost of the trip and of expenditure in various categories are often included.

For site surveys in a tourism context, including *en route* surveys, the activity questions asked of tourists may be similar to those asked of locals, but the reference period will of course be the period of their stay in the destination and again, there is often more interest in expenditure.

Media use

Questionnaires often include questions on media use, sometimes because it is considered a leisure activity, but also because such information can be useful when considering advertising policy. To obtain accurate information in this area would require a considerable number of questions on frequency of reading/viewing/listening and, in the case of electronic media, the type of programmes favoured. When the research is concerned with small-scale local facilities or services, television advertising is generally out of the question because of cost, so information on television watching need not be gathered. Similar considerations may apply to magazine and national newspaper reading. For many surveys, therefore, three questions are involved (show cards with lists of named media may be used):

● What (local) newspapers do you read regularly, that is, at least weekly?

● What (local) radio stations do you listen to regularly, that is, at least twice a week?

● What social media do you use?

9.6 Respondent characteristics

Characteristics of respondents are included in questionnaires because they are key variables in the study, as indicated in the research framework or the research questions, and/or because they are required to check the representativeness of the sample, for example in terms of age and gender. Table 10.10 lists typical characteristics/variables which arise. Each of these items can be discussed in terms of its technical features, but this discussion is provided on the text website.

9.7 Attitude/opinion questions

Attitudes and opinions are more complex aspects of questionnaire design. A range of techniques exists to explore people's opinions and attitudes, as listed in Figure 10.5. The first three formats, direct, open-ended questions, checklists and ranking, are straightforward, but the other formats presented merit some comment.

Likert scales

Scaling techniques are sometimes known as 'Likert scales' after the psychologist who developed their use and analysis. In this technique respondents are asked to indicate their agreement or disagreement with a proposition or the importance they attach to a factor, using a standard set of responses. One of the advantages of this approach is that the responses can be quantified, as discussed later under coding.

Ranking

Asking respondents to rank items in order of importance is a relatively straightforward process, provided the list is not too long: more than five or six items

Table 10.10   Respondent characteristics

Age

Economic status/occupation/socio-economic groups/class

Income

Marital, etc., status

Household type or group type (site survey)

Life-cycle stage

Ethnic group

Residential location, trip origin (site survey)

Housing information (type/tenure)

Transport (ownership/used)

a. Open-ended/direct

What attracted you to apply for this course?

_____

b. Checklist

Of the items on the card, which was the most important to you in applying for this course?

A. Good reputation
B. Easy access
C. Curriculum
D. Level of fees
E. Easy parking

c. Ranking

Please rank the items on the card in terms of their importance to you in choosing a course. Please rank them 1 for the most important to 5 for the least important.

	Rank
A. Good reputation	____
B. Easy access	____
C. Curriculum	____
D. Level of fees	____
E. Easy parking	____

d. Likert scales

Looking at the items on the card, please say how important each was to you in deciding to visit this area; was it: Very important, Quite important, Not very important or Not at all important?

	Very important	Quite important	Not very important	Not at all important
Good reputation	$\square_1$	$\square_2$	$\square_3$	$\square_4$
Easy access	$\square_1$	$\square_2$	$\square_3$	$\square_4$
Curriculum	$\square_1$	$\square_2$	$\square_3$	$\square_4$
Level of fees	$\square_1$	$\square_2$	$\square_3$	$\square_4$
Easy parking	$\square_1$	$\square_2$	$\square_3$	$\square_4$

e. Attitude statements

Please read the statements below and indicate your level of agreement or disagreement with them by ticking the appropriate box.

	Agree Strongly	Agree	No opinion	Disagree	Disagree strongly
In education, the learning experience is more important than the qualification	$\square_1$	$\square_2$	$\square_3$	$\square_4$	$\square_5$
Graduate course fees are too high	$\square_1$	$\square_2$	$\square_3$	$\square_4$	$\square_5$

f. Semantic differential

Please look at the list below and tick the line to indicate where you think this course falls in relation to each factor listed.

Difficult	|____|____|____|____|	Easy
Irrelevant	|____|____|____|____|	Relevant
Professional	|____|____|____|____|	Unprofessional
Dull	|____|____|____|____|	Interesting

Figure 10.5 Opinion or attitude question formats

could test respondents' patience. Again, quantitative analysis is possible – for example, in the form of average ranks.

Attitude statements

Attitude statements are a means of exploring respondents' attitudes towards a wide range of issues, including questions of a philosophical or political nature. Respondents are shown a series of statements and asked to indicate, using a scale, the extent to which they agree or disagree with them. Responses to both Likert scale questions and attitude statements can be scored, as indicated by the numerals beside the boxes in Figure 10.5. For example, 'agree strongly' could be given a score of 5, 'agree' a score of 4, and so on to 'disagree strongly' with a score of 1. In the analysis, scores can then be averaged across a number of respondents. So, for example, a group of people who mostly either 'agreed' or 'agreed strongly' with a statement would produce an average score between 4 and 5, whereas a group who 'disagreed' or 'disagreed strongly' would produce a low score, between 1 and 2.

Semantic differential

The semantic differential method involves offering respondents *pairs* of contrasting descriptors and asking them to indicate how the facility, place or service being studied relates to the descriptors. This technique is suitable for a respondent-completion questionnaire, since the respondent is required to place a tick on each line. It would be difficult to replicate this exactly in an interview situation with no visual prompts, such as in a telephone survey; the effect would be to reduce the possible answers to three: close to one end or the other and 'in the middle'. The choice of pairs of words used in a semantic differential list should arise from the research context and theory, and possibly pilot studies.

Repertory grid

A further development of this approach is the *repertory grid* technique, as discussed in Chapter 5. Here the pairs of words – called *personal constructs* – are elicited from the respondent. This technique is not explored further here, but references to examples of its use in leisure and tourism are given in the Resources section.

9.8 Market segments

The idea of market segmentation or lifestyle studies is introduced in Chapter 1. This involves classifying survey respondents according to a mix of activity, socio-demographic and attitude variables. All the necessary data items for this have therefore been discussed earlier. Actually determining market segments or lifestyle groupings is then an analytical task, and this is discussed in Part III of the text, notably in Chapter 17 under factor and cluster analysis.

9.9 Ordering of questions and layout of questionnaires

Survey introductory remarks

Should a questionnaire include introductory remarks – for example, explaining the purpose of the survey and asking for the respondent's assistance? In the case of a mail survey, such material is generally included in the covering letter. In other forms of respondent-completion questionnaire, a short note at the beginning of the questionnaire is advisable, although field-workers handing out questionnaires will usually provide the necessary introduction and explanation orally. In the case of interviewer-administered questionnaires, the remarks can be printed on the top of each questionnaire or can be included in interviewers' written instructions.

In practice, interviewers are unlikely to approach potential interviewees and actually read from a script: it is usually necessary to maintain eye contact. So interviewers must know in advance what they want to say. In the case of household surveys, potential interviewees may require a considerable amount of information and proof of identity from the interviewer before agreeing to be interviewed. But in the case of site interviews, respondents are generally more interested in knowing how long the interview will take and what sort of questions they will be asked – so only minimal opening remarks are necessary. For example, for a site survey, the introduction could be as brief as: 'Excuse me, we are conducting a survey of visitors to the area; would you mind answering a few questions?'

It is usually necessary for an interviewer to indicate what organisation they represent, and this can be reinforced by an identity badge. Market research or consultancy companies often instruct interviewers to indicate only that they represent the survey company and not the client. This can ensure that unbiased opinions are obtained, although in some cases it can raise ethical considerations if it is felt that respondents have a right to know what organisation will be using the information gathered.

One function of opening remarks can be to assure the respondent of confidentiality. In the case of site surveys, which are generally anonymous, confidentiality is easy to maintain. In the case of household surveys and some postal surveys, respondents can be identified, so assurances are generally necessary. The issue of confidentiality, including practical means of ensuring it, is an ethical issue and is discussed in Chapter 4.

Question order

It is important that an interview based on a questionnaire flow in a logical and comfortable manner. A number of principles should be borne in mind:

● Start with easy questions.

● Start with 'relevant' questions – for example, if the respondent has been told that the survey is about holidays, begin with some questions about holidays.

- Personal questions, dealing with such things as age or income, are generally best left to near the end. While they do not generally cause problems, and respondents need not answer those personal questions if they object, they are less likely to cause offence if asked later in the interview when a rapport has been established between interviewer and respondent. Similar principles apply in relation to respondent-completion questionnaires. It is sometimes suggested that this practice is unethical, in that people might not agree to cooperate if they knew in advance that personal questions would be asked. But since in leisure and tourism surveys the personal information is rarely deeply personal, and respondents can and do decline to answer such questions, the practice is widely seen as acceptable.

Layout

- *General:* A questionnaire should be laid out and printed in such a way that the person who must read it – whether interviewer or interviewee – can follow all the instructions easily and answer all the questions that they are meant to answer. In the case of respondent-completion questionnaires, extra care must be taken with layout because it can be very difficult to rectify faults once the survey process is underway. Clarity of layout, and the overall impression given by the questionnaire, can be all-important in obtaining a good response. Mail surveys and e-surveys, where the researcher does not have direct contact with the respondent, are the most demanding. A professionally laid-out questionnaire will pay dividends in terms of response rate and accuracy and completeness of responses.

- *Filtering:* Layout becomes particularly important when a questionnaire contains filters – that is, when answers to certain questions determine which subsequent questions must be answered. An example, with alternative ways of dealing with layout, is shown in Figure 10.6.

Layout 1

1. a. Have you studied at this university before?

    Yes $\Box_1$

    No $\Box_2$

  b. If YES: How long ago did you study here? ___ years

Layout 2

1. Have you studied at this university before?

    Yes $\Box_1$ Go to question 2

    No $\Box_2$ Go to question 3

2. How long ago did you study here? ___ years

Figure 10.6 Filtering: examples

- *Length:* A typeset format can reduce the number of pages considerably for a printed questionnaire, which may increase the response rate if the perceived length of the questionnaire is a factor. Even where interviewers are used, there are advantages in keeping the questionnaire as compact as possible for ease of handling. A two-column format, as used in Case study 10.1, example C, is worth exploring and can be easily achieved with word-processing packages.

- *Tick boxes and codes:* The questionnaire shown in Case study 10.1-A is designed for respondent-completion, and the layout therefore involves boxes for the respondent to tick. Boxes can, however, be laborious to type and lay out, so where an interviewer is being used, as in examples B and C, the interviewer can circle codes.

- *Office use column:* The 'office use' column, containing coding material, is not always necessary in interviewer-administered questionnaires but is included in examples A and B for exposition purposes. This type of layout can be used for respondent-completion in some situations – for example, in certain 'captive group' situations or where respondents are known to be highly literate and are unlikely to be deterred by the apparent technicalities of the layout.

10. Coding

Most questionnaire survey data are now analysed by computer. This means that the information in the questionnaire must be coded – that is, converted into generally numerical codes and organised in a systematic, 'machine-readable' manner.

10.1 Pre-coded questions and open-ended questions

Different procedures apply to pre-coded and open-ended questions and these are discussed in turn.

Pre-coded

The principle for coding of pre-coded questions is illustrated in many of the questions in the example questionnaires in Case study 10.1. For example, for question 1 in example A, the codes are as shown beside the boxes. Only one answer is possible, so only one *code* is recorded as the answer to this question.

Where the answer is already numerical, there is no need to code the answer because the numerical answer can be handled by the computer. For example, in question 4 of example A actual expenditure is asked for, which is a number and does not require coding.

Scaled answers, as in Likert scales and attitude statements, readily lend themselves to coding, as shown by the numerals in the examples given in Figure 10.5. In the case of the semantic differential, each of the sections of the response line can be numbered, say 1–4, so that answers can be given a numerical code, depending on where the respondent marks the line.

10.2 Open-ended questions

In the case of completely open-ended questions, quite an elaborate procedure must be followed to devise a coding system. As already suggested, the answers to open-ended questions can be copied from the questionnaires and presented in a report 'raw', as in Figure 10.4. If this is all that is required from the open-ended questions, then there is no point in spending the considerable labour necessary to code the information for computer analysis: the computer will merely reproduce what can be more easily achieved manually.

Computer analysis comes into its own if it is intended to analyse the results in more detail – for example, comparing the opinions of two or more groups. If such comparisons are to be made, it will usually be difficult to do so with, say,

---

Answers from 25 respondents to the question: 'What suggestions would you make for improving campus life?'

More live music ///	Better food ///
Upgrade facilities ///	Keep out non-students //
More weekday events //	Something with a theme, like a film festival //
More lunch-time events /	Better acoustics in main hall //
More evening events //	Events for socialising, e.g. barbecues //
Better PA system /	Events should start and finish on time ///
Cheaper drinks ///	More unusual acts, films, etc. . . . not just
Free transport from city /	what can be seen in town ///
More free events //	More participatory events – e.g. debates //
Less hard rock acts //	Free entry to all events //

Suggested coding system	
Comments on programme content	1
Comments on timing	2
Comments on facilities	3
Comments on costs	4
Comments on organisation	5
Other	6

Figure 10.7 Coding open-ended questions – example

50 or 60 different response groups to compare, especially if many of the responses are given by only one or two respondents. The aim then is to devise a coding system which groups the responses into a manageable number of categories. If a large sample is involved, it is advisable that the coding system be devised using a pilot survey, so that open-ended questions become pre-coded; but if this is not considered desirable, then a representative sub-sample of the main survey responses, say 50 or 100, might be used for the purpose. All responses are written down, noting the number of occurrences of each answer as in Figure 10.7. Then individual codes are given for the most frequent responses and the others are grouped into meaningful categories, as indicated. This is a matter of judgement. The aim is not to leave too many responses in the 'Other' category.

10.3 Recording coded data

Computer analysis is conducted using the coded information from a question-naire. This is best illustrated by an example – a completed questionnaire from Case study 10.1-A is set out in Figure 10.8.

In the 'office use' column, *spaces* are provided into which the codes from the answers can be written. The 'variable names' in the office column – qno, crse, lib, etc. – are explained in more detail in Chapter 16. Note the following:

- Questionnaire number, in the 'office use' column, is an identifier so that a link can be made between data in the computer and actual questionnaires – the example questionnaire is number 1.

- Question 1 – only one answer/code can be given.

- Question 2 – respondents can tick up to four boxes.

- Question 3 – five ranks must be recorded.

- Question 4 – asks for an actual number and this will be transferred into the computer without coding.

- Question 5 – consists of three Likert-scale items.

- Question 6 – an open-ended question. It is envisaged that some respondents might give more than one answer, so spaces have been reserved for three answers (although, in the example, only one has been given). The answers have a coding system (devised as discussed above) as follows:

Comments on programme content	1
Comments on timing	2
Comments on facilities	3
Comments on costs	4
Comments on organisation	5
Other	6

Campus Life Survey 2016

		Office use
		# _1_
		qno

1. Which of the following best describes your current situation?

Full-time student with no regular paid work ☐₁
Full-time student with some regular paid work ☑₂
Part-time student with full-time job ☐₃
Part-time student – other ☐₄

_2_ status

2. Which of the following university services have you used in the last 4 weeks?

Used campus cafe/bar ☑₁   _1_ cafebar
Attended a live music performance on campus ☑₁   _1_ music
Used campus sport facilities ☐₁   _0_ sport
Used campus travel service ☐₁   _0_ travel

3. In thinking about the social and entertainment services provided on campus, what are the most important considerations for you? Please rank the items below in terms of their importance to you. Rank them from 1 for the most important to 5 for the least important.

	Rank	
Free or cheap access	_1_	_1_ cheap
Daytime attractions	_4_	_4_ daytime
Acts, films, etc. not available elsewhere	_2_	_2_ unusual
Opportunities to socialise/meet people	_3_	_3_ meet
Quality of presentation	_5_	_5_ quality

4. Approximately how much do you spend in an average week on entertainment and social activities on and off campus?

£ _100_

_100_
spend

5. Please indicate the importance of the following to you in relation to campus life

	Very important	Important	Not at all important	
Relaxation opportunities	☑₃	☐₂	☐₁	_3_ relax
Social interaction	☑₃	☐₂	☐₁	_3_ social
Mental stimulation	☐₃	☐₂	☑₁	_1_ mental

6. What suggestions would you make for improving campus social life?

Provide more for minority tastes – less rock bands

_1_ sug1
_ _ sug2
_ _ sug3

7. You are: Male ☑₁   Female ☐₂   _1_ gend

8. Your age last birthday was: _18_ years   _18_ age

Figure 10.8 Completed questionnaire

The data from this particular completed questionnaire therefore become a single row of numbers, as shown in the first row of Figure 10.9, which shows how data from 15 completed questionnaires would look. How such a set of data may be analysed by computer is discussed in Chapter 16.

qno	status	cafebar	music	sport	travel	cheap	daytime	unusual	meet	quality	spend	relax	social	mental	sug1	sug2	sug3	gend	age
1	2	1	1	0	0	1	4	2	3	5	100	3	3	1	1			1	18
2	2	1	1	1	0	1	4	2	3	5	50	2	3	1	2	1		1	19
3	3	1	0	0	0	2	5	1	3	4	250	2	2	2	3	4		2	19
4	4	0	0	0	0	2	3	1	4	5	25	3	2	2	1	2	4	1	22
5	3	1	0	0	1	1	4	3	2	5	55	3	3	1				2	24
6	3	1	1	1	0	2	4	1	3	5	40	2	3	1	2			2	20
7	2	1	0	0	0	3	2	1	4	5	150	2	3	2	3			2	20
8	2	1	0	1	0	3	4	2	1	5	250	1	2	2	4	5		1	21
9	4	0	1	0	0	1	5	2	3	4	300	2	3	2				1	21
10	3	1	1	0	0	2	3	1	5	4	100	1	2	1	1	1		2	21
11	3	1	1	0	1	2	3	1	4	5	75	2	2	1	2	3		2	19
12	2	1	0	1	0	1	4	3	2	5	50	2	3	1				1	22
13	1	1	0	1	0	1	5	2	3	4	55	2	3	2	1	2		2	21
14	3	1	1	0	0	2	4	1	3	5	75	3	3	2	4			2	20
15	1	1	1	0	0	3	2	1	5	4	150	3	3	1	1	2	5	1	20

Figure 10.9   Data from 15 questionnaires

11. Validity of questionnaire-based data

11.1 Threats to validity

Questionnaire-based surveys are designed to gather information from individuals about their characteristics, behaviour and attitudes. Whether or not they actually achieve this depends on a number of possible threats to validity (as discussed in Chapter 2). Some of these are summarised in Table 10.11.

Table 10.11 Questionnaire surveys: threats to validity

Threat	Nature
General	
Non-response	Non-respondents may be significantly different from respondents, thus resulting in a biased sample.
Questionnaire design: lack of clarity	Leading questions, ambiguity, etc., results in inaccurate data.
Accuracy of recall	Respondents vary in their ability to recall activity or its timing/nature, especially over long time-periods.
Desire to impress	People have a natural desire to impress others, to give a good report of themselves, resulting in exaggeration of good points and down-playing of bad points.
Privacy concerns/ sensitivity	People may be reluctant to provide information at all on private/ sensitive matters, or may provide incomplete or inaccurate information.
Interviewee patience/ fatigue	Interviews perceived to be excessively long or uninteresting may lead to incomplete responses.
Physical context	If interview or questionnaire completion takes place in a distracting environment, inaccuracies or incompleteness may result.
Interviewer-administered	
Language/accent	Respondent may have difficulty with the language of the interview, and respondent or interviewer may have difficulty in understanding the other's accent.
Interviewer–respondent rapport	Particularly good or poor interviewer–respondent rapport may affect the accuracy and completeness of responses.
Interviewer consistency	If interviewer does not consistently follow instructions, or different interviewers interpret instructions differently, inaccuracies may result.
Respondent-completed	
Literacy	Respondents have difficulty in understanding questions or, in case of open-ended questions, in writing answers.
Non-completion	For a variety of reasons, some questions are not answered.

The principles of questionnaire design discussed earlier, and the principles of sampling outlined in Chapter 13, are designed to minimise threats to validity. To some extent the researcher must simply live with the limitations of the survey method and hope that inaccuracies are not significant and that some of them cancel each other out. There are, however, some measures which can be taken to check on the presence of this type of problem.

11.2 Checking validity

Some aspects of validity can be checked. The possibility of random or systematic error in responses may be checked by: the use of dummy questions or answer categories; semi-disguised duplication of questions; comparing time-periods; and referring to an alternative data source, where one exists. These possibilities are discussed in turn.

Dummy questions or answer categories

In a survey of recreation managers in Britain in the early 1980s, respondents were asked to indicate, from a list, what books and reports they had heard of and had read. Included in the list was one plausible-sounding, but non-existent title. A significant proportion of respondents indicated that they had heard of the report and a small proportion claimed to have read it! Such a response does not necessarily mean that respondents were lying – they may simply have been confused about the titles of particular publications. But it does provide cautionary information to the researcher on the degree of error in responses to questions, since it suggests that responses to the genuine titles may also include a certain amount of inaccuracy. For example, if 2 per cent of respondents claim to have read the non-existent report, this could suggest that all answers are subject to an error of plus or minus 2 per cent.

Semi-disguised duplication of questions

A similar approach is to include two or more questions in different parts of the questionnaire, which essentially ask the same thing. For example, an early question could ask respondents to rank a list of activities or holiday areas in order of preference. Later in the questionnaire, in the context of asking some detailed questions, respondents could be asked to indicate their favourite activity or holiday area. In the analysis, the responses could be tested for consistency.

Rather than detecting error, it is possible that this approach can discover that the interview or questionnaire completion experience itself has caused respondents to change their opinion, because it causes them to think through in detail something which they might previously have only considered superficially. In an Australian survey of gambling behaviour and attitudes towards a proposed casino development, Grichting and Caltabiano (1986) asked, at the beginning of the interview: 'What do you think about the casino coming to Townsville?

Are you for it or against it?' At the end of the interview they asked: 'Taking everything you have said into consideration, what do you think now about the casino coming to Townsville? Are you for it or against it?' It was found that about 'one in six respondents changed their attitude toward the casino during the course of the interview'.

Comparing time-periods

Bachman and O'Malley (1981) used data from a survey of marijuana and alcohol use among senior high school students to explore apparent inconsistencies in reported use levels in the last month and in the last year. Except for seasonal activities, it might be expected that use levels in the last month would be about one-twelfth of use levels for the whole year. It was found that use levels reported for the last month were very much higher than this, suggesting that either the one-month figures were exaggerated or the one-year figures were under-reported.

Ideally, such findings should be followed up with additional research to confirm the patterns in the case of alcohol and drug use, investigate its prevalence in relation to other types of leisure or tourism activity and suggest ways in which it might be taken into account in future survey work. There is little evidence of this being done. One study related to tourism has been conducted by Beaman et al. (2001), not only exploring the phenomenon of inaccurate recall but also suggesting how data might be corrected to take it into account. Two studies which investigate the problem using a different methodology are noted under 'Use of an alternative data source' next.

Use of an alternative data source

One area where alternatives to survey data are available is consumer expenditure on items subject to licensing and excise taxation, such as alcohol and tobacco consumption and gambling. No formal analysis of this type of data has been identified in the literature, but one source for Australia suggests that estimated expenditure on gambling (total net losses by gamblers) based on a household expenditure survey was A$2.1 billion in 2003–4, whereas the estimate based on gambling taxes collected by state governments was A$15.0 billion (Veal et al., 2013: 145, 157). While the latter figure includes expenditure by international tourists, this is partly offset by Australians' gambling expenditure overseas, and it is inconceivable that tourists accounted for more than a small proportion of the A$13 billion discrepancy. It is far more likely that when members of the household complete the Household Expenditure Survey questionnaire for the Australian Bureau of Statistics, gambling losses are grossly understated, both to the ABS and to fellow household members!

Two studies conducted at the University of Pennsylvania by David Chase and colleagues compared questionnaire survey results on estimated numbers of visits to swimming and tennis over two seasons with club sign-in records. In the first study (Chase and Godbey, 1983) it was found that over 75 per cent of respondents in both swimming and tennis clubs overestimated their visits, and in over 40 per cent of cases the error was greater than 100 per cent. The second, larger-scale study of a swimming club (Chase and Harada, 1984) confirmed the general picture, with survey respondents' estimate of previous season visits averaging 30, while the club records indicated that the actual frequency was 17.

Taking account of validity problems

There is no indication in the research and policy literature that those organisations and researchers conducting and using questionnaire survey results in the leisure and tourism area take the above findings on validity problems into account. The above discussions refer only to recall of factual information, but questions may also arise in regard to the validity of responses to questions on attitudes and aspirations. There does not seem to be much interest in exploring these problems among the leisure and tourism research community. Some of the issues have, however, been addressed by researchers in the medical sector, as the volume of papers edited by Stone et al. (2000) demonstrates.

12. Conducting questionnaire surveys

12.1 Planning fieldwork arrangements

The scale and complexity of the data collection, or fieldwork, process in survey research can vary enormously. At one extreme the process may be largely a matter of personal organisation on the part of the researcher; at the other extreme, a staff of hundreds may need to be recruited, trained and supervised. Fieldwork must be organised in any type of empirical study involving primary data collection, but because of the popularity of the survey method and the likelihood that it will involve organisation of individuals other than the single researcher, some attention is given to the task in this chapter.

Some of the items which need consideration are listed in Table 10.12. Brief notes on these tasks are presented here.

Table 10.12 Fieldwork planning tasks

a. Seek permissions – to visit sites, obtain records, etc.
b. Obtain lists for sampling – e.g. voters lists
c. Arrange printing – of questionnaires etc.
d. Check insurance issues
e. Prepare written instructions for interviewers
f. Prepare identity badges/letters for interviewers
g. Recruit interviewers and supervisors
h. Train interviewers and supervisors
i. Obtain quotations for any fieldwork to be conducted by other organisations
j. Appoint and train data coders/processors

a. Seek permissions

It is important to remember that permission is often needed to interview in public places, such as streets and beaches, because of local by-laws. Many areas which are thought of as 'public' are in fact the responsibility of some public or private organisation – for example, shopping centres and parks. Permission must be sought from these organisations to conduct fieldwork. It is also good practice to inform the local police if interviewing is being conducted in public places, in case of complaints or queries from the public.

b. Obtain lists

Obtaining lists, such as voters or membership lists, for sampling may seem routine, but often apparently straightforward tasks can involve delays, or the material may not be quite in the form anticipated and it takes time to process. Often research projects are conducted on very tight schedules, and delays of a few days can be crucial. Therefore, the earlier these routine tasks are tackled, the better.

c. Arrange printing

Printing (of questionnaires) sounds straightforward, but the in-house print shop has busy periods when it may not be possible to obtain a quick job turnround. Checking on printing procedures and turnround times at an early stage is therefore advisable.

d. Check insurance

When conducting fieldwork away from a normal place of work, insurance issues may arise, including public liability and workers' compensation for interviewers. In the case of educational institutions, staff and students are normally covered as long as they are engaged in legitimate university/college activities, but these matters should be checked with a competent legal authority in the organisation.

e. Prepare written instructions for interviewers

Provision of written instructions for interviewers is advisable and may cover:

- detailed comments on questionnaires and/or other instruments;
- instructions in relation to checking of completed questionnaires, etc., for legibility and completeness;
- instructions on returning questionnaires, etc.;
- dress and behaviour codes;
- roster details;
- 'wet weather' instructions, if relevant;

- instructions on what to do in the case of 'difficult' interviewees, etc.;

- details of time-sheets, payment, etc.; and

- contact telephone numbers.

A note on questionnaire-based interviewing is appropriate here. The general approach to interviewing when using a questionnaire is that the interviewer should be instructed to adhere precisely to the wording on the questionnaire. If the respondent does not understand the question, the question should simply be repeated exactly as before; if the respondent still does not understand, then the interviewer should move on to the next question. If this procedure is to be adhered to, then the importance of question wording and the testing of such wording in one or more pilot surveys is clear.

The above procedure is clearly important in relation to attitude questions. Any word of explanation or elaboration from the interviewer could influence, and therefore bias, the response. In relation to factual questions, however, it may be less important – a word of explanation from the interviewer may be acceptable if it results in obtaining accurate information.

f. Prepare identity badges/letters

If working in a public or semi-public place, fieldworkers should be clearly identified. A badge with the institutional logo and the fieldworker's given name is advisable. A letter from the research supervisor indicating that the fieldworker is engaged in legitimate research activity for the organisation may also be helpful.

g. Recruit interviewers and supervisors

Where paid interviewers, supervisors or other fieldworkers are to be used, it will be necessary to go through the normal procedures for employing part-time staff. Advice from the organisation's Human Resources Unit, or someone familiar with their procedures, will need to be sought.

h. Training

The length of training will vary with the complexity of the fieldwork and the experience of the fieldwork staff. Paid fieldworkers should be paid for the training session(s) (and this should be budgeted for). A two- or three-hour session is usually sufficient, but more may be necessary for a complex project. It is advisable for interviewers to practise interviews on each other, where possible, and report back on difficulties encountered.

i. Obtain quotations

In some cases certain aspects of the project are to be undertaken by other organisations – for example, data processing. Obtaining detailed quotations on price as early as possible is clearly advisable.

j. Appoint and train data processors

The coding, editing and processing of data for computer analysis is sometimes a significant task in its own right, requiring staff to be recruited. Recruitment and training procedures will need to be followed as for fieldworkers.

12.2 Conducting a pilot survey

Pilot surveys are small-scale 'trial runs' of a larger survey. Pilot surveys relate particularly to questionnaire surveys, but can in fact relate to trying out any type of research procedure. It is always advisable to carry out one or more pilot surveys before embarking on the main data-collection exercise. The purposes of pilot surveys are summarised in Table 10.13. The pilot can be used to test all aspects of the survey, not just question wording. Item e, 'Gain familiarity with respondents', refers to the role of the pilot in alerting the researcher to any characteristics, idiosyncrasies or sensitivities of the respondent group with which the researcher may not have been previously familiar. Such matters can affect the design and conduct of the main survey. Items h and i, concerned with the response rate and length of interview, can be most important in providing information to 'fine tune' the survey process. For example, it may be necessary to shorten the questionnaire and/or vary the number of field staff so that the project keeps on schedule and within budget.

In principle, at least some of the pilot interviews should be carried out by the researcher in charge, or at least by some experienced interviewers, since the interviewers will be required to report back on the pilot survey experience and contribute to discussions on any revisions to the questionnaire or fieldwork arrangements which might subsequently be made. The de-briefing session following the pilot survey is very important and should take place as soon as possible after the completion of the exercise, so that the details are fresh in the interviewers' minds.

Table 10.13 Pilot survey purposes

a. Test questionnaire wording
b. Test question sequencing
c. Test questionnaire layout
d. Code open-ended questions
e. Gain familiarity with respondents
f. Test fieldwork arrangements
g. Train and test fieldworkers
h. Estimate response rate
i. Estimate interview etc. time
j. Test analysis procedures

Summary

This chapter provides an introduction to questionnaire surveys, arguably the most commonly used data-collection vehicle in leisure and tourism research. The merits of questionnaire surveys are discussed, including the ability to quantify, transparency, succinctness in data presentation, the ability to study change over time, comprehensive coverage of complex phenomena and generalisability to the whole population. The second part of the chapter is devoted to discussing the features of seven different forms of the questionnaire survey: the household survey, the street survey, the telephone survey, the mail survey, the e-survey, the user/on-site/visitor survey and the captive group survey. The third part of the chapter considers questionnaire design and coding. Finally, the chapter considers fieldwork arrangements for questionnaire surveys, including the conduct of pilot surveys.

Test questions

1. What are the merits of questionnaire surveys?

2. Seven types of questionnaire survey are discussed in the chapter. What are they?

3. Outline the characteristics of three of these questionnaire survey types, in terms of: self- or interviewer-completion, cost, nature of the sample, possible length of questionnaire and likely response rate.

4. What type of survey would you conduct for a sample of 500 of the following:

   a. Tourists visiting a seaside resort
   b. Members of 'Greenpeace'
   c. The users of a theatre
   d. The users of a large urban park
   e. Overseas visitors to Great Britain
   f. People who do not play sport
   g. People who play sport
   h. People who stream commercial movies
   i. People aged 14 and over living in the local council area
   j. Young people aged 11–13 living in the local council area.

5. What is quota sampling?

6. What measures might be used to increase response rates in mail surveys?

7. What principles should be followed in wording questions in questionnaires?

8. What is the difference between pre-coded and open-ended questions, and what are the advantages and disadvantages of the two formats?

Exercises

1. Design a questionnaire in relation to one of the situations in Test Question 4 above. Assume the survey is being conducted on behalf of the site/facility management. Indicate hypothetical objectives of the study and compose the questionnaire, limiting it to 10 questions only.

2. Design a question on people's attitudes towards legalisation of drugs, using three alternative question formats.

3. If you are a member of a leisure/tourism class, invite members of the class to complete the questionnaire in Case study 10.1A and devise a coding system for the answers to open-ended questions based on the answers obtained.

4. Locate a published research report or thesis which includes a questionnaire survey and contains a copy of the questionnaire used (usually in an appendix) and provide a critique of the questionnaire design.

Resources

Websites

Time-budget diaries/time-use surveys by country: www.timeuse.org/information/access-data.

Publications

- Attitude measurement: McDougal and Munro (1994), Oppenheim (2000: ch. 11).

- E-surveys: Dillman et al. (2014).

- Intercept surveys: Denstadli (2000).

- Large-scale, national household surveys: see the Resources section in Chapter 7.

- Mail surveys: Dillman et al. (2014), Hammitt and McDonald (1982); Response rates: Frey (1991).

- Questionnaire design generally: Oppenheim (2000), Vaske (2008).

- Surveys in tourism: Denstadli (2000), Richards (2010); Feminist: Heimtun (2007).

- Repertory grid technique: Botterill (1989), Kelly (1955), Stockdale (1984).

- Surveys generally: Cushman and Veal (1993), Groves et al., (2009), Ryan (1995).

- Telephone surveys: Lavrakas (1993), Lepkowski et al. (2008).

- Time-budget diaries/time-use surveys: Burton (1971), Pentland et al. (1999), Szalai (1972); Tourists: Pearce (1988).

- Validity: exaggerated/unreliable, etc., responses to questionnaires: Bachman and O'Malley (1981), Beaman et al. (2001), Chase and Godbey (1983), Chase and Harada (1984), Oppenheim (2000: 138–9), Schaeffer (2000).

- Visitor (user) surveys vs conversion (coupon) surveys in tourism: Perdue and Botkin (1988).

References

Bachman, J. G., and O'Malley, P. M. (1981). When four months equal a year: inconsistencies in student reports of drug use. *Public Opinion Quarterly*, 45(4), 536–48.

Beaman, J., O'Leary, J. T., and Smith, S. (2001). The impact of seemingly minor methodological changes on estimates of travel and correcting bias. In A. G. Woodside, G. I. Crouch, J. A. Mazanec, M. Oppermann and M. Y. Sakai (Eds), *Consumer psychology of tourism, hospitality and leisure* (pp. 49–65). Wallingford, UK: CABI Publishing.

Botterill, T. D. (1989). Humanistic tourism? Personal constructs of a tourist: Sam visits Japan. *Leisure Studies*, 8(3), 281–94.

Burton, T. L. (1971). *Experiments in recreation research*. London: Allen & Unwin.

Chase, D., and Harada, M. (1984). Response error in self-reported recreation participation. *Journal of Leisure Research*, 16(4), 322–29.

Chase, D. R., and Godbey, G. C. (1983). The accuracy of self-reported participation rates. *Leisure Studies*, 2(2), 231–36.

Cushman, G., and Veal, A. J. (1993). The new generation of leisure surveys – implications for research on everyday life. *Leisure and Society*, 16(1), 211–20.

Denstadli, J. M. (2000). Analyzing air travel: a comparison of different survey methods and data collection procedures. *Journal of Travel Research*, 39(4), 4–10.

Dillman, D. A., Smyth, J. D., and Christian, L. M. (2014). *Internet, mail, and mixed-mode surveys: the tailored design method*, 4th edn. New York: Wiley.

Fenn, C., Bridgwood, A., Dust, K., Hutton, L., Jobson, M. and Skinner, M. (2004). *Arts in England 2003: attendance, participation and attitudes: findings of a study*

carried out by the Social Survey Division of the Office for National Statistics.
London: Arts Council England.

Frey, J. H. (1991). The impact of cover design and first questions on response
rates for a mail survey of skydivers. *Leisure Sciences*, 13(1), 67–76.

Gitelson, R. J., and Drogin, E. B. (1992). An experiment on the efficacy of a certified final mailing. *Journal of Leisure Research*, 24(1), 72–8.

Grichting, W. L., and Caltabiano, M. L. (1986). Amount and direction of bias in
survey interviewing. *Australian Psychologist*, 21(1), 69–78.

Groves, R. M., Fowler, F. J., and Couper, M. P. (2009) *Survey methodology*, 2nd
edn. Hoboken, NJ: Wiley.

Hammitt, W. E., and McDonald, C. D. (1982). Response bias and the need for
extensive mail questionnaire follow-ups among selected recreation samples.
Journal of Leisure Research, 14(3), 207–16.

Heimtun, B. (2007). From principles to practices in feminist tourism research: a
call for greater use if the survey method and the solicited diary. In I. Ateljevic,
A. Pritchard and N. Morgan (Eds), *The critical turn in tourism studies: innovative research methodologies* (pp. 245–59). Oxford: Elsevier.

Kelly, G. A. (1955). *The psychology of personal constructs*. New York: Norton.

Lavrakas, P. K. (1993). *Telephone survey methods: sampling, selection and supervision*, 2nd edn. Newbury Park, CA: Sage.

Lepkowski, J. M., Tucker, C., and Brick, J. M. (Eds) (2008). *Advances in telephone
survey methodology*. New York: John Wiley.

McDougall, G. H. G., and Munro, H. (1994). Scaling and attitude measurement
in travel and tourism research. In J. R. B. Ritchie and C. R. Goeldner (Eds),
Travel, tourism and hospitality research, 2nd edn (pp. 115–29). New York: John
Wiley.

Oppenheim, A. N. (2000). *Questionnaire design, interviewing and attitude measurement: new edition*. London: Pinter.

Pearce, P. L. (1988). *The Ulysses factor: evaluating visitors in tourist settings*. New
York: Springer-Verlag.

Pentland, W. E., Harvey, A. S., Powell Lawton, M., and McColl, M. A. (Eds)
(1999). *Time use research in the social sciences*. New York: Kluwer/Plenum.

Perdue, R. R., and Botkin, M. R. (1988). Visitor survey versus conversion study.
Annals of Tourism Research, 15(1), 76–87.

Pew Research Center for the People and the Press (2004). *Polls face growing resistance, but still representative, survey experiment shows*. Washington, DC: Pew
Research Center. Available at: http://people-press.org/report/211/.

Richards, G. (2010). The traditional quantitative approach. Surveying cultural
tourists: lessons from the ATLAS cultural tourism research project. In G.

Richards and W. Munsters (Eds), *Cultural tourism research methods* (pp. 13–32). Wallingford, UK: CABI.

Robertson, R. W., and Veal, A. J. (1987). *Port Hacking visitor use study*, Sydney: Centre for Leisure and Tourism Studies, University of Technology, Sydney.

Ryan, C. (1995). *Researching tourist satisfaction: issues, concepts, problems*. London: Routledge.

Schaeffer, N. C. (2000). Asking questions about threatening topics: a selective overview. In A. A. Stone et al. (Eds), *The science of self-report: implications for research and practice* (pp. 105–22). Mahwah, NJ: Lawrence Erlbaum.

Stockdale, J. (1984). People's conceptions of leisure. In A. Tomlinson (Ed.), *Leisure: politics, planning and people* (pp. 86–115). Eastbourne, UK: Leisure Studies Association.

Stone, A. A., Turkkan, J. S., et al. (2000). *The science of self-report: implications for research and practice*. Mahwah, NJ: Lawrence Erlbaum.

Szalai, A. (Ed.) (1972). *The use of time: daily activities of urban and suburban populations in twelve countries*. The Hague: Mouton.

Vaske, J. J. (2008). *Survey research and analysis: applications in parks, recreation and human dimensions*. State College, PA: Venture.

Veal, A. J., Darcy, S., and Lynch, R. (2013). *Australian leisure*, 4th edn. Melbourne: Longman Australia.

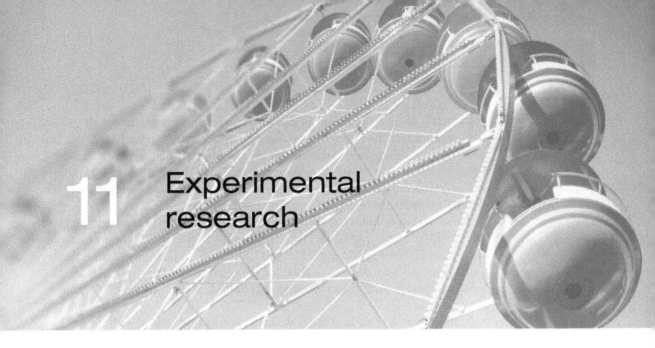

11 Experimental research

1. Introduction

The essence of the experiment is that the researcher aims to control all the relevant variables in the research environment and to vary selected variables and measure their effects on the subjects of the research. As discussed in Chapter 2, the experimental approach is closely associated with the positivist paradigm and is consistent with the classic scientific model of testing hypotheses and seeking to establish cause-and-effect relationships.

Use of the experimental method is generally believed to be rare in the leisure and tourism context, but when consideration is given to the full range of experimental and quasi-experimental methods used and the diversity of disciplinary contributions to the field, the body of experimental research in leisure and tourism research is found to be quite substantial, as demonstrated in section 5 of this chapter.

Being located in Part II of the text, this chapter is concerned with data collection, while data analysis is addressed in Part III. In the case of experimental methods, however, there is no corresponding separate analysis chapter in Part III because, in the leisure and tourism context, experimental data are invariably collected via questionnaire: thus the questionnaire survey method is embedded in the experimental method, or vice versa. Furthermore, as noted in Chapter 8, in cases where data are gathered by means of observation, the analysis of observations from subjects/cases is analogous to analysis of answers to questions, so the data file from an experimental study can be analysed in the same way as the data file from a questionnaire survey.

2. Principles of experimental research

2.1 Components

The essence of the experiment is that, ideally, the researcher controls all the relevant variables in the research environment. Selected variables are manipulated while others are held constant and the effects on subjects are measured. In the terminology of experimental study, the researcher is concerned with a *dependent variable*, an *independent* or *treatment variable*, a *treatment group* and a *control group*. There may be one or more of each of these variables in any one study:

- *Dependent variable:* The measurable outcome of the experiment, for example: participation in a leisure/tourism activity, level of satisfaction with a service; or level of fitness or health.

- *Independent or treatment variable:* A quality or characteristic of the subject or the environment that is varied or manipulated during the experiment, for example: provision of information/training; or the level and/or quality of service received.

- *Treatment or experimental group:* The group of participants or subjects receiving the treatment.

- *Control group:* A group of subjects not exposed to the treatment. The attributes of the control group may be matched with the attributes of the experimental or treatment group so that the two groups are as similar as possible or subjects may be randomly assigned to the two groups.

2.2 The classic experimental design

The classic or true design for experimental research, the pre-test–post-test control group design, is summarised in Figure 11.1 and involves five steps:

1. *Selection of a sample* of subjects (RS) from a population (sampling).

2. *Random allocation* of subjects two groups: R_t, the treatment group, and R_c, the control group.

3. In the pre-test observations (O_{t1}, O_{c1}), subjects in both groups are measured with respect to the dependent variable.

4. *Experimental treatment*, X, is applied to the treatment group.

5. *Post-test observations* (O_{t2}, O_{c2}): subjects in both groups are measured again with respect to the dependent variable.

6. *Examination of effects*: for the experimental treatment to be judged positive:

   - there should be no significant difference between O_{t1} and O_{c1}
   - there should be a significant difference between ($O_{t2} - O_{t1}$) and ($O_{c2} - O_{c1}$).

The concept of *significant* difference is discussed in Chapter 17.

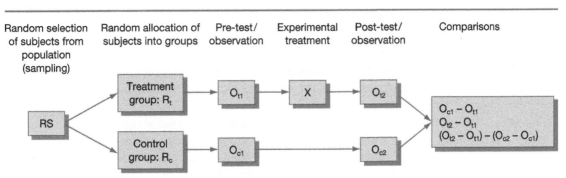

Figure 11.1 Classic experimental design

3. Validity

The aim of the classic design is to ensure, as far as possible, the *validity* of the research findings. As noted in Chapter 2, validity refers to the extent to which the information collected in a research study truly reflects the phenomenon being studied. There is generally a trade-off to be made between research validity and practicality and cost. While perfection is impossible, researchers should be aware of *threats to validity* and take these into account in the design of the experiment.

3.1 Threats to validity

Threats to the validity of experimental research fall into two main groups: *internal*, in which design components are compromised, and *external*, which relate to the application of the findings to the population to which the results are intended to apply. Some of these threats are summarised in Table 11.1.

Table 11.1   Threats to validity of experiments

Internal validity	Aspects of the experimental design which raise doubts as to whether change in dependent variable can be attributed entirely to the independent variable/treatment.
Maturation	Change occurs in study subject during the study period – e.g. fatigue.
History	Change in the external environment affects the study – e.g. weather conditions.
Testing	The test/observation process itself may affect subjects – e.g. asking questions raises awareness of, and therefore changes in, behaviour.
Instrumentation	Inconsistency or unreliability in the measuring instruments or observation procedures during a study – e.g. change in the way a questionnaire is designed.
Selection bias	Treatment group and control group have significantly different characteristics – e.g. one group markedly older than the other.
Mortality	Attrition of subjects from a study – likely to happen if treatment process is spread over a long period of time.
External validity	Extent to which results may be generalised beyond the study subjects and setting.
Reactive effects of testing	Tests/observation may sensitise subjects and affect behaviour responses, which would not happen in 'real life' – e.g. subjects wish to impress the researchers.
Effects of selection	Subjects may not be representative of wider population – e.g. when experiments conducted with tertiary students or city-centre dwellers. Also, the very fact of involvement with a study may cause subjects to behave differently from people generally – the 'Hawthorne effect'.

Reference is made to the 'Hawthorne effect', in which being part of a study affects people's behaviour. This was demonstrated many years ago in a study in the Hawthorne Plant of the Western Electric Company in the United States, which investigated the relationship between productivity and the brightness of lighting in the factory. As expected, productivity increased as illumination was increased. However, as brightness was decreased, productivity also rose. It was concluded that it was the attention the workers were receiving as a result of the study, rather than the lighting itself, that was affecting production.

3.2 Field experiments versus laboratory experiments

There is a trade-off between field experiments, or experiments in naturalistic settings, and laboratory experiments in relation to external and internal validity. 'Naturalistic' when applied to humans refers to everyday living settings, for example a person's home, workplace or leisure setting. In the case of leisure and tourism research, the equivalent of 'laboratory' is often an office, meeting room or classroom where data are elicited from subjects. In general, field experiments undertaken in natural leisure or tourism settings have greater external validity than laboratory-based experiments. On the other hand, laboratory-based experiments tend to have greater internal reliability than field experiments because of the greater control over extraneous variables. The decision on which type of experiment to conduct should be made only after careful consideration of the threats to internal and external validity described earlier, and consideration of the objectives of the research. The 'obvious' approach may not in fact be ideal. For example, it might appear obvious that gathering data from tourists at a holiday destination or from sports participants at a sports facility is appropriate; but if the interest is in general patterns of tourist or sporting behaviour, it might be best to avoid the possibility of subjects being over-influenced by any particular holiday/destination or sport/facility experience.

4. Quasi-experimental designs

4.1 Types of quasi-experimental design

In a natural science experiment, the subjects will be identical specimens or samples of organic or inorganic matter, or laboratory animals that are as near as possible identical, and are treated identically except for the experimental treatment. This is not possible in the sorts of social or organisational contexts with which leisure and tourism are involved. In such contexts, therefore, compromises must be made with the classic model and *quasi-experimental* designs must be devised.

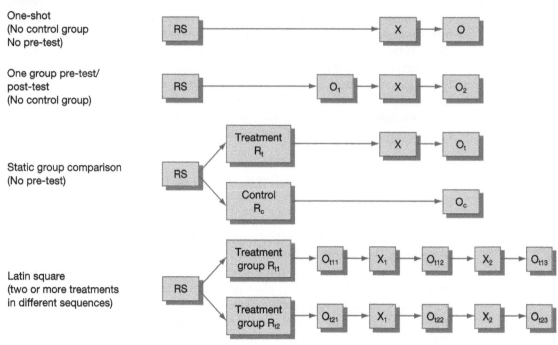

Figure 11.2   Quasi-experimental designs

Four common quasi-experimental designs are shown in Figure 11.2. They are: the one-shot design; the one group pre-test–post-test design, the static group design and the Latin square. Some designs simplify the classic model, for example by dispensing with a control group or the pre-test stage, while others complicate it, for example by adding additional treatments. They are often used where time, cost and practicality are important considerations, but there is typically a partial loss of validity associated with each design.

4.2 Experiments and projects

There is a tendency in some references to the experimental method to equate 'experiment' with 'research project'. But typically, a research project will comprise a series of experiments. In order to conduct an individual experiment, it is necessary to define the relevant dependent and independent/treatment variables. But a programme of experiments may evolve during the course of the project. Imagine a medical scientist searching for a drug to treat a virus: a number of possibilities may be explored before a successful treatment is discovered. This may take a number of experiments, even a number of projects. Thus an experimental project, or sequence of projects, may be much more exploratory, even inductive, than the formal hypothetical-deductive model of the single experiment.

5. Experimental methods in leisure and tourism research

Experiments involve research in a controlled environment in which the researcher is able to vary the conditions of the environment for research purposes. Opportunities to do this in leisure and tourism contexts, when people – customers, employees or the general public – are involved, are limited. This explains the preference for non-experimental methods, notably questionnaire-based surveys. Experimental or quasi-experimental methods are nevertheless used in a variety of leisure and tourism contexts, as indicated in Table 11.2, and these are discussed in turn in this section.

It is often assumed that the use of experimental methods is rare in leisure and tourism, but this is true only in relative terms. In an examination of six leisure studies journals over a six-year period, Havitz and Sell (1991) found that only 5 per cent used experimental methods, but this nevertheless amounted to 46 papers. However, in a 2001 review of the first category mentioned in Table 11.2, the consumer choice technique or discrete choice experiment, Crouch and Louviere (2001) identified over 40 published studies in the tourism, hospitality and leisure area, although less than half were in leisure/tourism journals. In the case of the second category, policy/management experimental projects, the number of studies would be much greater, although only a small proportion are reported in the peer-reviewed literature, and many tend to be

Table 11.2 Types and contexts of experiments in leisure and tourism research

1. Discrete choice experiments	Consumption or activity choice processes are studied by presenting subjects with hypothetical product descriptions with differing combinations of features and asking them to express their preferences.
2. Policy/management projects	Innovations in policy or management practice are tested out by experimental or pilot projects and evaluated using a variety of methods and with varying degrees of rigour.
3. Research methods experiments	Testing of innovative or alternative research methods or techniques, usually in the same setting, with the same subjects or split samples.
4. Psychological/ perceptual	Samples of subjects exposed to hypothetical situations/questions or images.
5. Sport-related	Studies of exercise effects, sport motivation, etc., using a variety of experimental methods.
6. Children's play	Observational studies of children with different play equipment/ environments.
7. Other examples	Action research; Q methodology; qualitative methods; training of tourism professionals; mental mapping; and physical models.

criticised for lack of methodological rigour. Then if we move into the areas of psychology and sport/exercise-related physiological research, which have considerable overlaps with leisure studies, the experimental method is dominant.

5.1 Discrete choice experiments (DCEs)

As noted in Chapter 5, discrete choice experiments (DCEs), based on the analytical technique of *conjoint analysis*, seek to explore people's decision-making processes in regard to choice of products or activities, including such phenomena as holiday types or destinations and leisure activities, services or facilities. The experimental feature of this approach is that, rather than researching people's actual decision-making, it involves asking subjects to make choices among hypothetical alternative products defined in terms of various combinations of features. In some cases the information is presented via a questionnaire on which subjects record their choices, so the approach could be seen as a particular form of questionnaire-based survey. In other cases subjects are presented with information on cards containing information on products with different combinations of features and are asked to sort them in order of preference. Two examples of DCEs in the leisure/tourism field are summarised in Case study 11.1. Conjoint analysis is discussed briefly in Chapter 18 as is multidimensional scaling, which is a similar process.

Case study 11.1 Discrete choice experiments: examples

In a review of the discrete choice experiment (DCE) literature, Crouch and Louviere (2001: 76) state that 'preference data elicitation procedures supported by careful experimental design and analysis can be used to tackle many of the questions facing managers and researchers who desire to understand tourism, hospitality and leisure choice processes with greater insight'. They identified over 40 discrete choice experiment studies using the approach. One is summarised as example A below. Other examples are listed in the Resources section of the chapter. In their paper Crouch and Louviere use the term 'choice modelling research' to describe the technique, while in other publications Louviere and collaborating authors have used the term 'simulated consumer choice or allocation experiments'

(Louviere and Woodworth, 1983) and 'stated choice methods' (Louviere *et al.* 2000). The term 'discrete choice experiment' has been adopted here from Kelly *et al.* (2007).

A. Eco-tourism

Kelly et al. (2007) conducted a DCE with visitors to the Whistler, British Columbia, ski resort to assess their preferences for 'eco-efficient' resorts. A sample of 1825 visitors were interviewed and asked for an email address to which an online questionnaire was sent for them to respond to after their visit. Of these, 876 submitted completed questionnaires. A list of 14 resort attributes was drawn up which would distinguish between an eco-efficient resort planning model, a 'business-as-usual' (i.e. current) model and a resource-intensive model. Thus, for example, looking at three attributes: 1. *form of development*: an eco-efficient resort would have a compact rather than a dispersed form; 2. *recreation activities*: an eco-efficient resort would exclude motorised sports; and 3. *energy needs*: in an eco-efficient resort a high proportion would be met from renewable resources. Respondents each received a questionnaire presenting one of 18 possible pairs of resorts, labelled A and B, with differing combinations of attributes and were asked to express their preference. A set of preference weights for each attribute/ value/category was produced, for day-visitors and overnight stayers. In general, it was found that a 'business-as-usual' model was the most pre-ferred, an eco-efficient model was second and a more resource-intensive model least popular. It should be noted that, having recruited respondents at a single site, the study of course had a built-in bias towards a resort of that type.

B. National Park site management

Bullock and Lawson (2008) conducted a DCE to explore visitors' preferred mix of management measures at a mountain trail, in Maine. As shown in Table 11.3, various types of resort were offered with different management, social and resource conditions. An on-site visitor survey was conducted with a sample of 450. Eighteen scenarios involving different combinations of the items/levels were devised and each respondent was asked to select between two. It was found that the most popular scenario, preferred by 45% of visitors, involved: no one turned away; visitors required to stay on-trail; use of fencing; many other visitors present; no visitors off-trail; and little visitor damage.

▶

Table 11.3   National park alternative management, examples

Items	Type 1	Type 2	Type 3
1. Visitors turned away?	None	Some, in busy times	Many in busy times
2. Visitors' freedom	Allowed off-trail	Asked to stay on trail	Must stay on trail
3. Access control	None	Signs	Rock borders
4. People on trail	Few others	Some others	Many others
5. People off trail	None	Some	Many
6. Visitor damage	Little	Some	Extensive

5.2 Policy/management experimental projects

Conducting experiments, often called *pilot projects*, *pilot programmes* or *trials*, is popular in the government sector, partly for the overt reason that it is wise to test effectiveness of policies on a small scale before implementing them more widely, but also because, to be somewhat cynical, they are much cheaper than a full-scale policy roll-out and can delay having to make a decision on such a roll-out. Invariably, such projects include an evaluation component, although this is not always adequately resourced or rigorously conducted. One of the earliest examples in the leisure sector in Britain took place in the late 1970s when a combination of government departments in Britain sponsored the 'Leisure and the Quality of Life' study which comprised 'four local experiments' designed to 'develop and increase a full range of leisure activities – cultural, recreational and sporting – and to record and learn as much as possible from the experience' (Department of the Environment, 1977: ix).

In some cases the declared policy-related experimentation is to increase levels of participation, often in sport and physical exercise but also in culture and leisure activities generally, as the Department of the Environment quotation exemplifies. However, invariably, the rationale behind the policy to boost participation is related to other policy areas, notably health and crime reduction in the case of sport and, more recently in Britain, 'social inclusion': the notion that all groups should enjoy the rights of citizenship, including engagement with social and cultural activity. In these cases, the criterion for the success of a project is not just participation itself, but also the resultant hoped-for improvements in health, crime reduction or social inclusion. The experimental model is therefore as shown in Figure 11.3. Two lots of measurements/observations are made, relating to participation and the social policy criterion, and the 'control' is often, in effect, the community at large: for example, the general level of sports participation or crime rates, related to the whole population or, in some cases, youth.

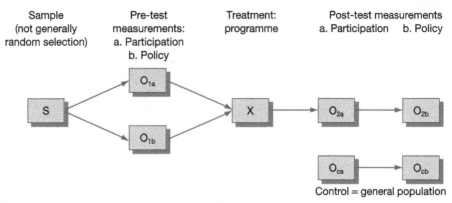

Figure 11.3 Experimental model of policy projects

Projects involving sport are particularly notable because, given its associa-tion with health, it involves not just social scientists but also medical, sport and human movement scientists. Thus both policy-makers and researchers involved are familiar with the experimental method, and it is often accepted in this envi-ronment that evidence-based policy should be based on rigorously conducted experiments. In order to provide such a basis for policy development, there-fore, a number of reviews of available research have been carried out to estab-lish what evidence exists on the effectiveness, or otherwise, of various types of experimental intervention. One of these is summarised in Case study 11.2, which also includes summaries of examples of individual studies.

Case study 11.2   Policy/management-related experimental studies

A. Sport participation: review

Priest et al. (2008) conducted a review of available literature on experiments/projects conducted by sporting organisations and designed to increase sport participation, involving the scanning of databases containing some 15,000 research publications. They note that interventions to boost sports participa-tion can take a variety of forms, including:

- mass media campaigns;
- information or education sessions;
- management or organisational change strategies;
- policy changes, for example to improve the socio-cultural environment to encourage people of specific age, gender or ethnicity to participate;
- changes to traditional or existing programmes, for example club- or associ-ation-initiated rule modification programmes; and
- provision of activities beyond traditional or existing programmes, for example 'Come and Try' initiatives (teaser or taster programmes), skill

▶

improvement programmes, and volunteer encouragement programmes (Priest et al., 2008: no pagination).

The aim of the review was to identify suitable studies, to evaluate them methodologically and to draw conclusions about the effectiveness of various forms of intervention in promoting sport participation. Their conclusions were:

> We found no controlled studies that met the inclusion criteria. We identified no uncontrolled studies, with pre- and post-test data, suitable to be included in . . . this review . . . and therefore assessed no studies for methodological quality. Despite using the most comprehensive search methods to date, no studies were identified that employed a controlled evaluation design. (Priest et al., 2008: no pagination)

This extraordinary finding indicates that, despite the involvement of health and sport scientists, along with social scientists, as discussed earlier, none of the studies identified conformed to the classic scientific model, with control groups and pre-intervention and post-intervention data. Even when relaxing the requirement for a control group (uncontrolled studies), no studies were found with pre-test and post-test data.

This is an extreme example of a problem recognised by others in attempting to review this field of study. Blamey and Mutrie (2004: 748) note one study which identified 253 publications for review but excluded 159 due to limitations in study design, and another where only 12 out of 254 papers satisfied the review criteria. Coalter (2007: 27–9) notes that this situation is not unique to sport and refers to discussion in the policy literature which suggests that the rigorous experimental criteria used in the natural sciences may not be appropriate in social policy areas and that, in any case, there is an absence of theoretical understanding of the causes of sport participation and non-participation to inform the design and evaluation or programmes/projects/experiments (Coalter, 2007: 171–4).

B. Sport and crime reduction

Nichols (2007), in his book *Sport and Crime Reduction*, presents eight case studies of projects designed to prevent young people from engaging in crime through participation in a sport-related programme. Just one project is described here. During a three-year period, 194 probationers volunteered to take part in a 12-week 'sports counselling' service which introduced them to a range of local council sporting facilities and courses such as lifesaving. No follow-up was undertaken in relation to sport participation, but the social outcome was measured by reconviction rates over the following two years. The reconviction rate for participants who completed the 12-week programme was significantly lower than for those who completed less than eight weeks and matched control groups who had not taken part in the programme at all.

Programme participants' self-esteem was also measured, at the beginning and end of the programme, and participation in the full course was found to make a significant positive difference.

C. Count me in: social inclusion through sport, culture

Count ME IN: the Dimensions of Social Inclusion through Culture and Sport is the title of a report prepared by the Centre for Leisure and Sport Research (2002) at Leeds Metropolitan University for the UK Department for Culture, Media and Sport. It presents the results of a study of 14 publicly funded short-term social projects which had the common aim of 'enhancing the quality of life in areas of disadvantage'. The 14 projects were made up of:

- *Sport:* three projects 'providing sporting opportunities as a constructive socially acceptable focus for the energies of young people'.
- *Arts and media:* six projects, two using the arts to 'stimulate public awareness of health issues', three 'directed to skills development among disaffected/vulnerable young people with a view to improving employment prospects' and one 'orientated to educational development'.
- *Heritage and libraries:* three projects, one 'designed to attract disadvantaged groups into the museum', one 'an arts in education project using heritage to stimulate imagination' and one 'a library service to develop communication in rural areas'.
- *Outdoor adventure:* two projects providing 'adventure education as a means of personal development and the fostering of self-confidence and self-esteem'.

The report notes that project managers generally report on progress to funding agencies using 'milestones' in the development of the project and 'outputs' in the form of such things as events staged and numbers of people attending. More challenging was assessing policy-related, social inclusion-related 'outcomes', such as improved health, access to employment, improved educational performance or crime reduction. Rather than project-by-project evaluations, chapters on a number of themes are presented, including education, employment, crime prevention, health, personal development and social cohesion. The report concludes by noting the practical and conceptual difficulties involved in evaluating outcomes of projects of this nature.

5.3 Experimenting with research methods

The practice of conducting experimental research to test the efficacy of different research methods has a long history in the leisure sector: for example, the report of one of the earliest research projects funded by the Sports Council in England, in the late 1960s, was entitled *Experiments in Recreation Research*

(Burton, 1971). While the basic methods being examined in this type of study are not themselves experimental methods, the experimental quality of the studies lies in using multiple methods or variations on methods in order to discover the effects of different research practices. Examples are presented in Case study 11.3. All examples are quasi-experimental although none conforms precisely to the designs indicated in Figure 11.2.

Case study 11.3   Experiments with research methods: examples

Experimental methods have been used in leisure and tourism contexts to compare the efficacy of different data-collection techniques. Some examples are presented here. A study on tourism tracking is summarised in Case study 8.2.

A. Attitude measurement techniques

Driscoll, Lawson and Niven (1994) conducted an experiment to collect the same data in two different ways. The data comprised respondents' assessment of 12 holiday destinations on the basis of 18 attributes. Using a postal survey method, one sample of 571 respondents was presented with 12 semantic differential (see Chapter 10) tables, one for each destination and each with 18 destination attributes. A second sample of 528 respondents was presented with a single grid, with destinations across the top and the 18 attributes down the side, and asked to score each country on each attribute. While in theory the two techniques were measuring the same thing, in practice it was found that the results obtained from the two methods differed significantly, even though the two samples were found to have similar socio-demographic profiles.

B. Mail survey follow-ups

Gitelson and Drogin (1992) conducted an experiment on the effectiveness of different forms of follow-up letter in a mail-back survey. Spectators at a Pennsylvania agricultural show were interviewed on-site to obtain basic socio-demographic information and addresses and were subsequently sent a questionnaire by mail. After sending a post-card reminder and a duplicate questionnaire, a response rate of 67 per cent had been achieved. The remaining 33 per cent were divided into three groups: all were sent a replacement questionnaire, but in addition, they received the following treatments with the following results:

- Group 1: non-personalised letter via ordinary mail: response rate 13 per cent.
- Group 2: personalised letter via ordinary mail: response rate 17 per cent.

- Group 3: personalised letter via certified/registered mail: response rate 43 per cent.

The use of certified/registered mail was clearly effective in increasing the response rate, although at additional cost. However, comparison of early and late respondents' survey results indicated that, in regard to the great majority of the data items in the questionnaire, the additional response had not made a significant difference.

C. Photographs vs written descriptions vs observation – ecological impacts

If managers/designers wish to gauge users' reactions to various levels and types of human impacts on ecological values at tourism/recreation sites, the use of written or photographic representation of the impacts would be a more convenient and cheaper method than gathering data on-site. But how accurately do they reflect on-site evaluations? This study, by Shelby and Harris (1985), used all three methods at 20 different campsites in five study areas. In each study area, for each of the methods, 30 visitors assessed the three or four sites within the area – so over 400 visitors were involved in the assessment. Participants assessed the acceptability of various types of impact and the overall desirability of the site on a five-point scale. In 90 per cent of cases, photograph-based assessments were not significantly different from on-site assessments, but written assessments differed more often.

5.4 Psychological/perceptual studies

The study of some psychological and perceptual aspects of leisure and tourism lends itself to experimental research, where subjects can be exposed to visual stimuli and their reactions or opinions recorded. Some examples are summarised in Case study 11.4.

| Case study 11.4 | Psychological/perceptual experiments |

A. Independence and psychological well-being

Most conceptualisations of leisure involve a personal sense of independence of action, of individuals feeling in control of that part of their lives. As a result of economic, social and physical factors, this sense of independence is often at risk among older people, resulting in reduced participation in leisure activity which in turn can have negative impacts on physical and psychological well-being. One way in which public agencies might intervene to counter this tendency is to provide courses which provide information about leisure opportunities and encourage and enable participation. Searle et al. (1995) report on an experiment designed to evaluate such an intervention. A treatment group and a control group, each of 15 persons aged 65 and over, were recruited and both groups completed pre-test and post-test questionnaires, 16 weeks apart, designed to assess general independence and psychological well-being. This was done using five scales: the Perceived Leisure Control Scale; Perceived Leisure Competence Scale; Life Satisfaction Index; Locus of Control Scale; and Leisure Boredom Scale (the use of scales in general is discussed in Chapter 5 and sources for these specific scales are given in the Resources section of that chapter). The treatment group attended a 16-week course and showed significant improvements in the post-test, compared with the control group, on four out of the five scales.

B. Landscape images

Landscape preservation and planning of scenic roads and trails within natural areas are guided in part by aesthetics. Planners and designers need to check their aesthetic judgements against those of the general public. Arranging for members of the public to provide assessments on-site is time-consuming and expensive, so photographs have been used. But just how this should be done, and how to interpret the results, has become a research area in its own right. In one such study by Wade (1982), 100 students and academic and support staff at two Virginia universities viewed a sequence of 10 scenic colour slides. Individuals viewed the slides alone and had control of the slide projector (today this would be done with computer images). At the end, they were asked to rank the views in order of preference. In another study using photography, Cherem and Driver (1983) used a different approach, this time involving on-site visits as well. A sample of users using a natural trail were presented with a relatively cheap camera and asked to take 10 photographs of views which they liked: the most popular views photographed were classified as 'consensus photographs'. In terms of quasi-experimental models depicted in Figure 11.2, these were 'one-shot' studies.

5.5 Sport-related experiments

Experiments are the main methodology used in the disciplines associated with sport and human movement, such as bio-mechanics and sport psychology. Two examples of such experiments are summarised in Case study 11.5.

Case study 11.5   Sport-related experiments

A. Mood and physical activity

One of the reasons why participation in sport and other forms of physical activity is encouraged is because of the health benefits it brings. This can be physical or mental. One aspect of poor mental health is depression. Kanning and Schlicht (2010) conducted a study to examine the effect of physical activity on mood. A sample of 13 subjects kept diaries over a 10-week period in which, on a daily basis, they recorded three randomly chosen distinct activities and how they felt before and after the activity. They found a positive relationship between physical activity and mood level, with the greatest effect being when people started the activity in a depressed mood. In this quasi-experimental method, the 'treatment' is selected, and the pre-test and post-test observations are under the control of the subjects. The method has some similarities with experience sampling method (ESM), as discussed in Chapter 5, but without the real-time prompts and recording.

B. Players and sporting equipment

Noting that elite tennis players are very particular about the tension at which their rackets are strung, Bower and Cross (2008) conducted experiments to examine the ability of elite players to detect differences in string tension and the efficiency of different string tensions in play. Participants in the study were 18 elite tennis players (i.e. nationally ranked or in the world top 1500, and aiming for a professional career) taking part in a tournament. Each participant compared two rackets with a string tension difference of 11 pounds, by using each racket to hit four balls projected by a machine. The test was conducted twice. If the player successfully detected a difference, the test was repeated with two rackets with a string tension difference of 6 pounds; if they were unsuccessful, the repeat involved rackets with a string tension difference of 17 pounds. Only 5 (28 per cent) players detected the 11-pound difference; but of these, only 2 could detect the 6-pound difference. Of the 13 (72 per cent) players who could not detect the 11-pound difference, 11 could not detect even the 17-pound difference. These findings were clearly at variance with the players' typical concern about string tension in their rackets. Other experiments, not summarised here, were conducted to test the rebound efficiency of rackets with different tensions.

5.6 Children's play

The study of children's play can be pursued by experimental methods because young children in particular spend much of their time in play environments controlled to a greater or lesser degree by adults. The play environment can be modified and changes in the children's behaviour observed without children being aware that a controlled experiment is being conducted. Some examples are presented in Case study 11.6.

Case study 11.6   Children's play experiments

A. Play equipment safety

Safety is of course a key consideration in children's play equipment design, and safety standards have developed over time. Howard et al. (2005) report on a project which assessed the effectiveness of the implementation of new standards promulgated in Canada in 1998. In Toronto, all school playgrounds were assessed against the new standards in 2000, and 136 were found to require replacement of dangerous equipment, while 225 were deemed satisfactory. By December 2001, the dangerous equipment had been removed from all 136 playgrounds, and 86 of these had received replacement equipment. This offered the opportunity to conduct a study with an experimental format – this might be termed an opportunistic experiment. The 86 playgrounds with replaced equipment were seen as the 'intervention' or treatment group, and 225 which required no replacement were the 'non-intervention' group. Data on injuries per 1000 students were collated for all playgrounds for the 10 months before and after the replacement of equipment. Injury rates declined between the two periods at the intervention schools while actually increasing at the non-intervention schools. This clearly supported the adoption of the new equipment safety standards.

B. Play equipment design

A study by Gramza et al. (1972) examined 4- to 5-year-old children's preferences for play equipment of differing complexity. Four groups of children were involved in the project, each experiencing two 12- to 15-minute sessions in a playroom. The project involved three A-frame climbing trestles: A, a plain trestle; B, a trestle modified by the addition of plain boards with a number of hand-foot holes; and C, a trestle with more additions, including irregular-shaped boards with hand–foot holes, a platform and a climbing rope. In Phase I the playroom contained trestles A and B and the number of children on each was recorded every five seconds for a 500-second period. This was repeated four weeks later. In Phase II the procedure was repeated with trestles A and C. It was found that the children were attracted to the more complex equipment and that their use of the equipment, in conjunction with other toys in the room, was creative and developed over time.

C. Adult inhibition and peer disinhibition

Children are socialised partly by adult guidance, rule-setting and enforcement (adult inhibition) and partly by peer influence, which may run counter to the adult rules (peer disinhibition). An experiment by Wuellner (1981) was designed to investigate the influence of these two factors. The experiment took place in a supervised playroom and involved a control group of pre-school children and two treatment groups playing for about 1.5 hours, with their behaviour video-recorded. One of the control groups was monitored for one day and the other for two days. The control group played without any intervention. For the treatment groups an area of the room, including some of the play equipment, was marked off by yellow tape on the floor and the experimenter, in the absence of the supervisor, indicated to the children that they should not play in that area because it was not fully set up (adult inhibition), and then departed and did not reappear. On the second day, a photograph of children playing in the 'no-go' area was displayed in the room (peer disinhibition). It was found that the adult inhibition effect was much more marked than the peer disinhibition, although the latter became more influential on the second day for the second treatment group.

5.7 Other examples

Action research

Action research is discussed in Chapter 5 and it is noted there that it has some features of an experimental design. The approach is depicted in Figure 5.1 as comprising four steps and it can be seen that:

- steps 1 and 2, which identify and assess a social problem, can be seen as the pre-test observation, with selection of a treatment group implied;
- step 3, the campaign for and achievement of action, is the treatment; and
- step 4, researching the results of the action, is the post-test observation.

One of the features of the experimental method is that the researcher controls the experimental process. In action research the researchers do not necessarily *control* the process, but the philosophy of action research is that they are involved with and therefore seek to have an *influence* on the process.

Q methodology

Q methodology, in which research participants arrange cards containing statements into a predetermined distribution, is also described in Chapter 5. While the approach can be seen as merely an elaboration of a questionnaire-based survey, the design and manipulation of the card-sorting process indicates a level of control which reflects features of the experimental approach.

Qualitative methods

Paradoxically, much qualitative research which is presented as distinct from the classic, positivist scientific experimental method, notably methodologies like participant observation and non-standardised interviewing, in which the researcher engages actively with the subjects, have features of the experimental method. The researcher's involvement with subjects can be seen as paralleling the 'treatment' in an experiment, although, of course, it is not in a controlled environment.

Training

Moscardo (1997) conducted experiments to assess the effectiveness of different exercises to train tourism professionals in *mindfulness*, defined as 'the active processing of information to create new categories, new definitions of situations, new routines for behaviour, and flexible and effective solutions to problems'. The study involved experimental and control groups. The experimental groups were exposed to a training exercise relating to the travel needs of seniors, followed by completion of a questionnaire on a possible holiday itinerary for seniors and people with disabilities. The control group completed the same questionnaire but without the training exercise. The experimental and control group questionnaire responses were then compared to determine the effects of the training.

Mental mapping

Walmsley and Jenkins (1991) used a mental mapping medium (discussed as 'perceptual mapping' in Chapter 5) to explore tourists' knowledge of a tourist destination. Two groups of visitors carried out the same exercise, to draw a map of a coastal resort, but subsequently completed different questionnaires related to 'locus of control' and active/inactive personality characteristics. The maps of the two groups were compared in terms of their identification of landmarks, districts and paths.

Physical models

In a study concerned with public reactions to reuse of heritage buildings, Black (1990) arranged for 1:25 models to be made of four heritage buildings and photographed them in three situations: 'as is now', with a 'small change' and 'large change', the changes indicating adaptation for commercial use as cafes/restaurants. A group of study participants were asked to scale the photographs on a range of features and the results were compared with a theoretical classification based on a limited number of physical characteristics. Arguably, this type of research might now be conducted using computer graphics.

Summary

Experimental methods are closely associated with the *positivist paradigm* and are consistent with the classic 'scientific' model of testing hypotheses and establishing cause-and-effect relationships. The essence of the experiment is that the researcher ideally controls all the relevant variables in the experiment. Selected variables are manipulated while others are held constant, and the effects on subjects are measured. Components of the experiment are: the treatment or experimental group; the control group; dependent variable; and the independent or treatment variable. The independent or treatment variable is manipulated during the experiment to examine its effect on the dependent variable. Typically, variables are measured before the treatment (pre-test) and after the treatment (post-test). Quasi-experimental designs vary this model by, for example, omitting a control group, omitting the pre-test or including more than one treatment group or treatment. Although *experimental methods* are usually associated with natural science and laboratories, it is possible to conduct some experiments in leisure and tourism contexts. Among these contexts are: discrete choice experiments (DCE); policy/management pilot or trial projects; experiments with research methods; psychological/perceptual studies; sport-related experiments and children's play.

Test questions

1. What are the defining characteristics of the experimental method?

2. Outline two examples of quasi-experimental models and indicate how they deviate from the classic experimental model.

3. Give three examples of contexts where experimental methods have been used in leisure or tourism research.

Exercises

1. Outline a true experimental research design to test the hypothesis that regular walking is a more effective way of achieving physical fitness than playing organised sport.

2. How could a leisure or tourism organisation set up an experiment to test the effectiveness of two forms of advertising? What elements of the 'classic' experimental design would need to be sacrificed? What type of quasi-experiment would this be?

Resources

- The classic work on experimental design for research: Campbell and Stanley (1972).

- Alternative research methods experiments: Burton (1971), Frey (1991), Gitelson and Drogin (1992), Perdue and Botkin (1988), Shoval and Isaacson (2007).

- Discrete choice experiments/stated choice method: Kelly et al. (2007), Crouch and Louviere (2001), Louviere and Woodworth (1983), Louviere et al. (2000). Examples:
  - Movie choice: Neelamegham and Jain (1999);
  - Park trail: Bullock and Lawson (2008);
  - Recreation specialisation: Oh and Ditton (2006);
  - Rock-climbing (and bibliography of environmental/recreation examples): Hanley et al. (2001);
  - Sport facility feature preferences: Bjørnskov Pedersen et al. (2011);
  - Sport tourism: Wiebke et al. (2008), Chalip and McGuirty (2004);
  - Theatre productions: Grisolia and Willis (2011), Willis and Snowball (2009);
  - Tourism and terrorism: Arana and Leon (2008); and
  - Tourists' art gallery choice: Caldwell and Coshall (2003).

- Experimenter effects in research: Rosenthal (1966).

- Leisure: Ellis et al. (2016), Havitz and Sell (1991), Oppewal (2011).

- Policy-related experiments: Batty (1977), Department of the Environment (1977), Long and Hylton (2014).

References

Arana, J. E., and Leon, C. J. (2008). The impact of terrorism on tourism demand. *Annals of Tourism Research*, 35(2), 299–315.

Batty, A. (1977). The action research background to the leisure experiments. In Department of the Environment (Ed.), *Leisure and the quality of life: a report on four local experiments* (pp. 3–16). London: HMSO.

Bjørnskov Pedersen, L., Kiil, A., and Kjær, T. (2011). Soccer attendees' preferences for facilities at the Fionia Park Stadium: an application of the discrete choice experiment. *Journal of Sports Economics*, 12(2), 179–99.

Black, N. (1990). A model and methodology to assess changes to heritage buildings. *Journal of Tourism Studies*, 1(1), 15–23.

Blamey, A., and Mutrie, N. (2004). Changing the individual to promote health-enhancing physical activity: the difficulties of producing evidence and translating it into practice. *Journal of Sports Sciences*, 22(8), 741–54.

Bower, R., and Cross, R. (2008). Elite tennis player sensitivity to changes in string tension and the effect on resulting ball dynamics. *Sports Engineering*, 11(1), 31–6.

Bullock, S. D., and Lawson, S. R. (2008). Managing the 'commons' on Cadillac Mountain: a stated choice analysis of Acadia National Park visitors' preferences. *Leisure Science*, 30, 71–86.

Burton, T. L. (1971). *Experiments in recreation research*. London: Allen & Unwin.

Caldwell, N., and Coshall, J. (2003). Tourists' preference structures for London's Tate Museum gallery: the implications for strategic marketing. *Journal of Travel and Tourism Marketing*, 14(2), 23–45.

Campbell, D. T., and Stanley, J. C. (1972). *Experimental and quasi-experimental designs for research*. Chicago: Rand McNally.

Centre for Leisure and Sports Research (2002). *Count me in: the dimensions of social inclusion through culture and sport, a report for the department for culture, media and sport*. Centre for Leisure and Sport Research, Leeds Metropolitan University.

Chalip, L., and McGuirty, J. (2004). Bundling sport events with the host destination. *Journal of Sport & Tourism*, 9(3), 267–82.

Cherem, G. J., and Driver, B. L. (1983). Visitor employed photography: a technique to measure common perceptions of natural environments. *Journal of Leisure Research*, 15(1), 65–83.

Christensen, J. E. (1982) On generalizing about the need for follow-up efforts in mail response surveys. *Journal of Leisure Research*. 14(3), 263–265.

Coalter, F. (2007). *A wider social role for sport*. London: Routledge.

Crouch, G. I., and Louviere, J. J. (2001). A review of choice modelling research in tourism, hospitality and leisure. In J. A. Mazanec, G. I. Crouch, J. R. B. Ritchie and A. G. Woodside (Eds), *Consumer psychology of tourism, hospitality and leisure*, Vol. 2 (pp. 67–86). Wallingford, UK: CABI Publishing.

Department of the Environment (1977). *Leisure and the quality of life: a report on four local experiments* (2 volumes). London: HMSO.

Driscoll, A., Lawson, R., and Niven, B. (1994). Measuring tourists' destination perceptions. *Annals of Tourism Research*, 21(3), 499–511.

Ellis, G., Lee, K. J., and Satchabut, T. (2016). Experimental designs in leisure studies. In G. J. Walker, D. Scott and M. Stodolska (Eds), *Leisure matters: the state and future of leisure studies* (pp. 333–44). State College, PA: Venture.

Frey, J. H. (1991). The impact of cover design and first questions on response rates for a mail survey of skydivers. *Leisure Sciences*, 13(1), 67–76.

Gitelson, R. J., and Drogin, E. B. (1992). An experiment on the efficacy of a certified final mailing. *Journal of Leisure Research*, 24(1), 72–8.

Gramza, A. F., Corush, J., and Ellis, M. J. (1972). Children's play on trestles differing in complexity: a study of play equipment design. *Journal of Leisure Research*, 4(3), 303–11.

Grisolia, J. M., and Willis, K. G. (2011) An evening at the theatre: using choice experiments to model preferences for theatres and theatrical productions. *Applied Economics*, 43(27), 3987–98.

Hanley, N., Mourato, S., and Wright, R. E. (2001). Choice modelling approaches: a superior alternative for environmental evaluation? *Journal of Economic Surveys*, 15(3), 435–62.

Havitz, M. E., and Sell, J. A. (1991). The experimental method and leisure/recreation research: promoting a more active role. *Society and Leisure*, 14(1), 47–68.

Howard, A. W., MacArthur, C., Willan, A., Rothman, L., Moses-McKeag, A., and MacPherson, A. K. (2005). The effect of safer play equipment on playground injury rates among school children. *Canadian Medical Association Journal*, 172(11), 1443–46.

Kanning, M., and Schlicht, W. (2010). Be active and become happy: an ecological momentary assessment of physical activity and mood. *Journal of Sport & Exercise Psychology*, 32(2), 253–61.

Kelly, J., Haider, W., Williams, P. W., and Englund, K. (2007). Stated preferences of tourists for eco-efficient destination planning options. *Tourism Management*, 28(3), 377–90.

Long, J., and Hylton, K. (2014). Reviewing research evidence and the case of participation in sport and physical recreation by black and minority ethnic communities. *Leisure Studies*, 33(4), 379–99.

Louviere, J. J., Hensher, D. A., and Swait, J. D. (2000). *Stated choice methods: analysis and applications*. Cambridge: Cambridge University Press

Louviere, J. J., and Woodworth, G. (1983). Design and analysis of simulated consumer choice or allocation experiments: an approach based on aggregate data. *Journal of Marketing Research*, 20(3), 350–67.

Moscardo, G. (1997). Making mindful managers: evaluating methods for teaching problem solving skills for tourism management. *Journal of Tourism Studies*, 8(1), 16–24.

Neelamegham, R., and Jain, D. (1999). Consumer choice process for experience goods: an econometric model and analysis. *Journal of Marketing Research*, 36(3), 373–86.

Nichols, G. (2007). *Sport and crime reduction: the role of sports in tackling youth crime*. London: Routledge.

Oh, C-O., and Ditton, R. B. (2006). Using recreation specialization to understand multi-attribute management preferences. *Leisure Sciences*, 28(4), 369–84.

Oppewal, H. (2011). Experimental research. In E. Sirakaya-Turk, M. Uysal, W. E. Hammitt and J. J. Vaske (Eds), *Research methods for leisure, recreation and tourism* (pp. 162–78). Wallingford, UK: CABI

Perdue, R. R., and Botkin, M. R. (1988). Visitor survey versus conversion study. *Annals of Tourism Research*, 15(1), 76–87.

Priest, N., Armstrong, R., Doyle, J., and Waters, E. (2008) Interventions implemented through sporting organisations for increasing participation in sport. *Cochrane Database of Systematic Reviews*, 3. Available at: http://onlinelibrary.wiley.com/doi/10.1002/14651858.CD004812.pub3/pdf/standard.

Rosenthal, R. (1966). *Experimenter effects in behavioral research*. New York: Appleton-Century-Crofts.

Searle, M. S., Mahon, M. J., Iso-Ahola, S., Sdrolias, H. A., and Van Dyck J. (1995). Enhancing a sense of independence and psychological well-being among the elderly: a field experiment. *Journal of Leisure Research*, 27(2), 107–24.

Shelby, B., and Harris, R. (1985). Comparing methods for determining visitor evaluations of ecological impacts: site visits, photographs and written descriptions. *Journal of Leisure Research*, 17(1), 56–67.

Shoval, N., and Isaacson, M. (2007) Tracking tourists in the digital age. *Annals of Tourism Research*, 34(1), 141–59.

Wade, G. (1982). The relationship between landscape preference and looking time: a methodological investigation. *Journal of Leisure Research*, 14(3), 217–22.

Walmsley, D. J., and Jenkins, J. M. (1991). Mental maps, locus of control, and activity: a study of business tourists in Coffs Harbour. *Journal of Tourism Studies*, 2(2), 36–42.

Wiebke, U., Ulrike, P., and Wolfgang, H. (2008) Trends in winter sport tourism: challenges for the future. *Tourism Review*, 63(1), 36–47.

Willis, K. G., and Snowball, J. D. (2009) Investigating how the attributes of live theatre productions influence consumption choices using conjoint analysis: the example of the National Arts Festival, South Africa. *Journal of Cultural Economics*, 33(2), 167–83.

Wuellner, L. H. (1981). The adult inhibition and peer disinhibition of preschool group play. *Journal of Leisure Research*, 13(2), 159–73.

12 Case study method

1. Introduction

A case study involves the study of an individual example – a case – of the phenomenon being researched. The aim is to seek to understand the phenomenon by studying one or more single examples. To some extent all social research is a case study at some level, since all research is geographically and temporally unique. Thus, for example, a survey of 500 visitors to a particular leisure or tourism site can be seen as a case study of the use of that site. Even a nationwide survey of the leisure or tourism activities of thousands of people in a Western country carried out in 2010, could be viewed, in one sense, as a case study of the activities of the population of one affluent country in the early twenty-first century.

The case study *research method* should be distinguished from other uses of the concept of cases, including in the law, where it refers to an individual crime, arrest and trial and may be important in setting precedents, and in medicine, where cases refer to individual patients. In both these examples, the case – either live or as a written record – becomes a vehicle for teaching, and in the business sector this is its exclusive use, the most well-known example being the Harvard Business School cases (Harvard Business School, nd).

2. Definitions

2.1 What is the case study method?

John Gerring (2016: 2.4) defines a *case* as 'a spatially and temporally delimited phenomenon of theoretical significance' and a *case study* as 'the intensive study of a single case or a small number of cases which also promises to shed light on a larger population of cases' (2.2). He argues that there is a continuum between the case study method and cross-case research: 'The fewer cases there are, and the more intensively they are studied, the more the work merits the appellation 'case study'' (2.2).

2.2 What the case study method is not

The fact that research projects using the case study method typically involve only one or a few cases suggests some similarity with qualitative research methods and in some texts the case study method is subsumed under 'qualitative methods' (e.g. Finn et al., 2000: 81). However, as leading authority Robert Yin states,

> the case study method is not just a form of 'qualitative research', even though it may be recognised among the array of qualitative research choices. . . . Some case study

research goes beyond being a type of qualitative research, by using a mix of quantitative and qualitative evidence. In addition, case studies need not always include the direct and detailed observational evidence marked by other forms of 'qualitative research'. (Yin, 2009: 19)

In fact, the use of a variety of types of data and types of analysis can be said to be a key feature of the case study method.

Some commentators (for example, Zikmund, 1997: 108) have implied that the case study method is used only for 'exploratory' purposes, but this is not the only possible purpose. As Yin (2009: 6) asserts, 'case studies are far from being only an exploratory strategy'. They can be the basis of substantive research projects in their own right, as the case studies summarised later in the chapter demonstrate.

2.3 Scale

Cases can consist of individuals, communities (villages, islands, cities), whole countries, organisations and companies, places and projects or events. These demographic and geographic dimensions are illustrated in Figure 12.1.

If a study involves just an individual or small group, such as a family, the methodological options are generally limited and are likely to be mostly qualitative (although studying an individual or small group over time could involve quantitative data). As we move up in scale the range of methods increases, both in terms of primary and secondary sources, including, for example, the use of information on a site and its environment and history and the social and demographic characteristics of the population of a community or country. Thus the sheer variety of types of data and types of data analysis would offer a 'rich' description of the case – the site or the country and its people. Furthermore, a

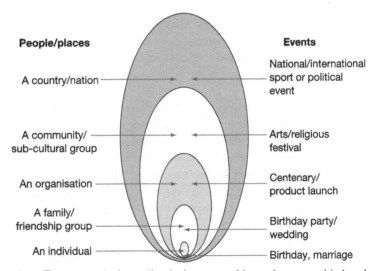

People/places

A country/nation

A community/
sub-cultural group

An organisation

A family/
friendship group

An individual

Events

National/international
sport or political
event

Arts/religious
festival

Centenary/
product launch

Birthday party/
wedding

Birthday, marriage

Figure 12.1 The case study method: demographic and geographic levels

case study at one level (for example, of a community or an organisation) could involve a variety of quantitative and qualitative methods and data sources involving components at lower levels (for example, questionnaire surveys of residents or employees, or financial and membership data).

3. Validity and reliability

Arguably, the multiple methodologies and data sources used by the typical case study method offer the possibility of achieving as high a level of internal validity as any single method discussed elsewhere in this text, since the limitations of one method or data source may be overcome by drawing on the qualities of another.

External validity – the extent to which findings apply beyond the specific case study – may also be aided by the use of multiple data sources, such as the use of secondary data from the wider population for comparative purposes and to establish the extent to which the case study is typical or unique – drawing on cross-case research as suggested by Gerring. Given that, in case study research, only one or a few cases are examined, the method does not seek to produce findings which are generally or universally representative. Thus a case study of an organisation does not include statements of the kind: 'this explains the behaviour of organisation X, therefore it will explain or predict the behaviour of the 50,000 similar organisations in similar situations or a significant proportion of them'. However, if research has *no* implications beyond the particular case at a particular time and place, there would be little point in conducting it. Referring again to Gerring:

> To conduct a case study implies that one has also conducted cross-case analysis, or at least thought about the broader set of cases. Otherwise, it is impossible for an author to answer the defining question of all case study research: what is this a case *of*? (Gerring, 2016: 13)

The relationship between case study research and the world beyond the case itself can be mediated by theory and policy issues, so conclusions might be in the form: 'this explains the behaviour of organisation X, which is inconsistent with theoretically based expectations, suggesting the possible need for some modification to the theory', or: 'this explains the behaviour of organisation X, suggesting that other types of organisation might be examined to see whether the explanation applies more widely'. Thus, while case study research may not result in generalisations about a population, it can have valid things to say in relation to theory in the case of explanatory research and in relation to policy in the case of evaluative research. Thus a number of scenarios can be envisaged in regard to theory and policy, as shown in Table 12.1.

Table 12.1 Case study research: theory and policy

Type of research	Research purpose	Case study outcomes
Explanatory research	Testing a single existing theory	Case study *confirms* applicability of theory in at least one setting or, alternatively, *raises doubts* as to applicability of theory and suggests modification or alternatives.
	Testing alternative/ competing theories	Case study demonstrates that one theory works better than the other in a particular situation, or that neither works universally.
	Developing theory where none exists	The task of the case study is to suggest *possible* theory.
Evaluative research	Testing effectiveness of a single policy	Case study *confirms* effectiveness of the policy in at least one setting or, alternatively, *raises doubts* as to effectiveness of the policy and possibly suggests modification or alternatives.
	Testing alternative/ competing policies	Case study demonstrates that one policy is more effective than the other in a particular situation, or that neither works universally.
	Establishing need for policy measures	The case study outlines the current problems and their likely causes and suggests the need for policy action.

Using the typology discussed in Chapter 1: in the case of *explanatory* research, a case study can be used to *test the applicability of an existing theory*. This might occur in situations where a theoretical proposition has never been tested empirically or where it has not been tested in a particular environment. Thus, in leisure studies, many propositions have in fact been developed using empirical evidence from sport, so a case study of non-sporting leisure activity could be used to test the universality of such propositions. Similarly, much tourism research is concerned with travel to varied places of interest in search of 'authenticity', so such ideas could be tested in the context of different types of holiday – for example, a case study of a caravan site visited by the same families at the same time every year. If the theory is found to be non-applicable in a case study situation, this does not necessarily 'disprove' it but can raise doubts as to its universal application.

In the case of policy-related *evaluative* research, the corresponding research task would be to test the effectiveness of a policy or type of management practice. For example, while the impact of promotional/advertising policy could be examined by use of aggregate national statistics on customer/participant numbers, it could also be examined by means of a case study of the experience in one or two communities or neighbourhoods, particularly if the results of the national statistical analysis were unclear or indicated an apparent lack of impact.

Reliability, in the sense of exact replication of research, is, of course, impossible in case study research, but the accumulation of evidence from a number of case studies may build a consensus around the findings of a programme of case study research and other evidence.

4. Merits of the case study approach

The particular merits of the case study method can be summarised as follows.

- the ability to place people, organisations, events and experiences in their social and historical context;
- the ability to treat the subject of study as a whole, rather than abstracting a limited set of pre-selected features;
- multiple methods – triangulation – are implicit and seen as a strength;
- the single, or limited number of, cases offers a manageable data-collection task when resources are limited;
- flexibility in data-collection strategy allows researchers to adapt their research strategy as the research proceeds; and
- there is no necessity to generalise to a defined wider population.

5. Design and conduct of case studies

While the case study method offers flexibility, it does not absolve the researcher from undertaking the usual initial preparatory steps – specifying research questions, reviewing the literature, establishing a theoretical framework and determining data needs and sources – as discussed in Chapter 3. As in any research, it is important to plan to avoid the problem of having collected a lot of data and not knowing what to do with it. The amount of flexibility offered is rarely unlimited – for example, in some circumstances it may be possible to interview people, or ask them for data, a number of times as new issues emerge in the course of the research, but in other circumstances this may not be possible.

In addition to the general guidance on the planning of research projects set out in Chapter 3, three specific issues are discussed here: defining the unit of analysis; selection of cases; and data gathering.

5.1 Defining the unit of analysis

While it might be a somewhat obvious point to make, it is necessary to be clear about the *unit of analysis* in case study research. For example, if the unit of analysis – the case – is a single leisure or tourism facility owned by a large organisation, it is important to keep the analysis at the facility level. For example, the policies and practices of the parent organisation are inevitably relevant, but they are 'given' influences on the facility management, so the research is not *about* the parent organisation. Conversely, data on the individual staff of the facility will form part of the research, but only insofar as they contribute to an understanding of the operation of the facility as a unit.

5.2 Selecting the case(s)

Of key importance in the case study method is the selection of the case or cases. This is, of course, comparable to sampling in a cross-case study. Four types of case selection can be considered.

- *Purposive:* Where more than one case is involved, the selection of cases is likely to be purposive – for example, in selecting a range of firms of similar or different sizes, in the same or different industries, in comparable or contrasting geographical locations or of similar or contrasting levels of profitability.

- *Illustrative:* Often the case(s) will be deliberately chosen to increase the likelihood of illustrating a particular proposition – for example, if the research is concerned with leadership success, then *successful* organisations with high-profile leaders may be deliberately chosen.

- *Typical/atypical:* The case may be chosen because it is believed to be typical of the phenomenon being studied, or it may be deliberately chosen as an extreme or atypical case. For example, a study examining the secrets of success in a particular industry might well select the *most* successful company for study.

- *Pragmatic/opportunistic:* In some cases the selection of cases may be pragmatic – for example, when the researcher has ready access to an organisation, possibly because he or she is an employee of it.

Whatever the rationale for the selection of a case or cases, it should be clearly articulated in the research report and the implications of the selection discussed.

5.3 Data gathering

A case study project generally uses a number of data sources and data-gathering techniques, including: the use of documentary evidence; secondary data analysis; in-depth interviews; questionnaire surveys; observation; and participant observation. The process of selecting data sources and collection techniques is the same as in any other research process, as discussed in Chapter 3. In that chapter, the idea that different data sources might be used in the same project to address different research questions or aspects of research questions is discussed. It is noted that all data collection should be linked to the research questions – even in cases where the research questions are being modified as the research progresses.

When a number of disparate data types and sources are involved, two other issues should be borne in mind:

- *consistency of the unit of analysis* – if, for example, participation data are involved, it is important that the data relate to the same geographical unit; and

- *temporal consistency* – ideally, all data should relate to the same time-period – this is related to the issue of the unit of analysis, since reorganisation – of, for example, a corporate body or administrative boundaries – can result in changes in the size, composition and functions of organisations over time.

6. Analysis

To the extent that the design of the case study, or parts of it, resembles that of more formalised research projects, with fixed research questions and corresponding data-collection and analysis procedures, the analysis process will tend to be deductive in nature; the data analysis will be designed to address the questions posed in advance. But a case study can involve qualitative methods with a recursive, more inductive format, as discussed in Chapters 9 and 15. Indeed, the flexibility of the whole case study approach suggests a more inductive approach. Thus the discovery, in the course of the research, of a previously unknown source of information might lead the researcher to ask the question: can this data add something to the research? While the new data source might help in addressing the existing research questions in unanticipated ways, it could also suggest whole new research questions.

Three main methods of analysis are outlined by both Burns (1994: 324–5) and Yin (2009: 106–18):

- *pattern matching* – relating the features of the case to what might be expected from some existing theory;

- *explanation building* – often an iterative process whereby a logical/causal explanation of what is discovered is developed by to-and-fro referencing between theory/explanation and data; and

- *time-series analysis* – explanations are developed on the basis of observing change over the time-period of the study.

In fact, all forms of analysis are possible within the context of a case study. It is the pulling together of the results of analyses of different sorts to form coherent conclusions which presents the challenge.

7. Case studies in practice

Four case studies of case studies conclude the chapter. The case studies provide brief details on each study, but further details can be followed up in the references provided.

7.1 Case study 12.1: *English Life and Leisure*

Case study 12.1 revisits the Rowntree and Lavers *English Life and Leisure* study previously examined for its qualitative content (Case study 9.1), but here noting the use of individual interview-based *case histories* of the leisure lives of individuals and a secondary/documentary source-based case study of a small town and its leisure infrastructure.

Case study 12.1	*English Life and Leisure*

Case study 9.1 refers to Rowntree and Lavers's (1951) study of *English Life and Leisure*, the earliest large-scale study of leisure in Britain, which began in 1947 during the post-World War II period of austerity. The study used a primarily qualitative approach which involved the case study method in two ways.

First, the bulk of the study involved interviews with almost 1000 individuals in 11 cities, and 220 of these are reported in a remarkable 121-page chapter of 'case histories', as described in Case study 9.1. Information from these and the rest of the interviews are then drawn on for the subsequent chapters on specific leisure activities.

Second, the report also includes a single chapter which is a case study of one small town, High Wycombe in Buckinghamshire, located between London and Oxford and with a population of 40,000. It is a purely descriptive account of the 30 or so social and special-interest clubs, cinema, library, dancing, music and drama facilities, outdoor recreation/sporting facilities and clubs, and a range of religious-based leisure facilities and organisations. Reports of the activities of the nine coach operators in the town offer an insight into day trips and holidays at this time, before the widespread ownership of cars:

> One of the largest companies sends on the average 20 coaches a week to London from October to the end of April. In 8 weeks they sent 100 coaches

to London filled with people going to see 'Skating Varieties'. They took 32 coach-loads of people to see a fight for the heavy-weight world championship. . . . During June 1949, one of the largest companies sent 367 coach-loads of people to the coast and to attractions in various towns. (Rowntree and Lavers, 1951: 403)

7.2 Case study 12.2: Euro Disneyland

Case study 12.2 presents a history of events over a 10-year period, in which the Euro Disney theme park and resort, north of Paris, was conceived, planned, developed and opened, up to its third year of operation, when it made its first profit following a series of losses. Based on participant observation, interviews and secondary sources, it covers a wide range of development, design, marketing and financial issues.

Case study 12.2   Euro Disneyland

Andrew Lainsbury's (2000) book, *Once Upon an American Dream*, is based on his experiences in a year spent working as a general hand (including a period playing Prince Charming) in the Euro Disneyland theme park and resort, north of Paris. Opened in 1992 amid much publicity and controversy over its appropriateness and viability in a European context, the development had a chequered history in its early years. The book has five main chapters, dealing with: (1) the development of the idea of a European Disneyland and the political activity of selecting and securing a site; (2) the design, or 'imagineering', of the project; (3) marketing of the project; (4) the financial struggles of the early years; and (5) the global Disney operation.

The book is written in a popular, narrative style but is underpinned by extensive endnotes and references. The historical accounts draw mostly on press coverage which, given the high profile of the Walt Disney Company, was extensive. Use is also made of the considerable body of literature on Disney, which comprises a mixture of popular and academic books, and papers in journals in such fields as cultural, media and American studies.

Numerous themes emerge in each of the chapters. Thus Chapter 1 provides an insight into the common phenomenon of countries and communities competing to attract industry and jobs, the financial and other 'deals' that are struck to attract enterprises, and the 'Not in My Back Yard' (NIMBY) politics of communities living in the immediate neighbourhood of proposed projects. The Disney project led to the establishment of the 'Association for the Protection of People Concerned by the Euro Disney Development'. Chapter 1 also discusses the clash of cultures between 'old Europe' and 'new America', an increasingly salient issue in an era of globalisation.

Much of Chapter 2 is design-oriented rather than business-oriented, but the 'vertical integration' practice of Walt Disney Company in developing not only the theme park but also the ancillary hotels and golf courses – which it failed to do in the original Disneyland in California – is outlined. Chapter 3 outlines the complex strategy for marketing the project, both before and after its opening.

The development made substantial losses in its early years, and Chapter 4 documents the various measures taken to 'rescue' the project by improving income and attendance, cutting costs and reorganising its finances. This resulted in the achievement of the first profits in 1995. The final chapter examines briefly the international development of Disney theme parks and the growth of competitors.

While the book does not present 'hard' research data, it uses a variety of perspectives, issues and data sources to explore the saga of Euro Disneyland and therefore presents a valid case study of a major transnational leisure/tourism investment project.

7.3 Case study 12.3: Nike, advertising and women

Case study 12.3 summarises research by Carty (1997) on a single aspect of the behaviour of a single organisation, the sports apparel multinational Nike. She uses a number of data sources but in particular illustrates the use of content analysis of print, poster and television advertising. The study focuses on the issue of whether Nike's rhetoric about treating women as respected customers is followed through in their advertising. We have discussed above, the proposition that, while conclusions from case studies can, strictly speaking, apply only to the case involved in the study, they would be of limited use if they did not at least raise the possibility of wider implications. Here the implication is that Nike may not be unique among multinational companies in its exploitative approach to women.

| Case study 12.3 | Nike, advertising and women |

Victoria Carty's (1997) study of the Nike sportswear company draws on a number of information sources and theoretical perspectives to explore and critique the *modus operandi* of the company, particularly in regard to its treatment of women. The main information sources are existing accounts of the development of Nike from the academic and popular literature and examples of Nike advertising on television and in print. Theoretical perspectives include theories of globalisation and postmodernism and the concept of 'global commodity chains', which geographically trace manufactured products from the point of consumption to the point of manufacture.

The thesis of the study is that Nike's advertising aimed at Western women consumers projects an image of the independent woman, while its manufacturing practices exploit Third World women who make up the majority of its manufacturing labour force employed at low wages and working in poor conditions in its own factories and those of its sub-contractors. The research seeks to demonstrate the validity of well-established theoretical frameworks which are critical of the role of multinational global corporations, particularly in the production of fashion products where the costs of manufacturing are heavily outweighed by the costs of marketing and the retail mark-up. Thus, using a case study of a single firm, the study seeks to 'illustrate the interdependencies between production and consumption, or economics and culture, as organized in the global economy'.

7.4 Case study 12.4: *Leisure, Lifestyle and the New Middle Class*

Wynne's (1998) *Leisure, Lifestyle and the New Middle Class* is a study of residents of a new middle-class housing estate using a questionnaire survey, in-depth interviews and ethnographic/participant observation methods, focusing on class situation and lifestyle groups and their distinctive pattern of use of the estate's leisure centre/club.

| Case study 12.4 | *Leisure, Lifestyle and the New Middle Class* |

Derek Wynne's (1998) *Leisure, Lifestyle and the New Middle Class: a Case Study* demonstrates clearly the use of multiple methods in a case study. It is a study of the residents of 'The Heath', a new middle-class southern England development of some 250 dwellings with its own leisure centre/club. The author lived in the development for three years and based his research on: a questionnaire survey of all residents; in-depth interviews with selected residents; and participant observation/ethnography. He uses the theoretical frameworks developed by Bourdieu, in his book *Distinction* (1984), to explore the social class situation and lifestyles of the 500 or so adult residents of The Heath. While the current occupational and educationally shaped social class positions of the residents were similar, their origins (working-class or middle-class parents) differed and were reflected in differing leisure patterns and cultural states. These differences were further reflected in the differences between two distinct user groups of the leisure centre/club: the 'drinkers' and the 'sporters'. Summaries of aspects of the case study can also be found in Wynne (1986).

Summary

This chapter considers the case study method which involves the study of a single case, or a small number of cases, of the phenomenon of interest, which contrasts with other methods discussed in the text which generally involve *cross-case* methods. But cross-case research may be embedded in a case study – for example, a study of a single community or tourist destination may involve a questionnaire-based survey of residents or visitors respectively. Thus case studies often use multiple methods, including any or all of the other methods discussed in the text. The chapter examines tasks in the design and conduct of case studies, including definition of the unit of analysis and selection of cases. Four case studies of contrasting leisure and tourism case studies complete the chapter.

Test questions

1. Define case study research and cross-case research.
2. Discuss the external validity challenges involved in case study research.
3. What are the four approaches to selecting cases discussed in the chapter?
4. Three approaches to case study analysis have been suggested in the literature. Name and describe these approaches.

Exercises

1. Consider a leisure or tourism facility/attraction known to you and outline the elements which might be involved in setting up a case study to explore the reasons for its success.
2. Read one of the example studies listed in the Resources section and identify the range of data sources used, methods of analysis and how the various types of information are drawn together to draw conclusions.

Resources

- General texts: Bromley (1986), Burns (1994: 312–31), Flyvbjerg (2006), Rose (2000), Stake (1995), Yin (2009).

- In leisure studies: Henderson (2006: 137–42).

- In tourism studies: Xiao and Smith (2005).

- Examples:
  - City governance and sport: Henry and Paramio Salcines (1998);
  - City governance and tourism: Long (2000);
  - Communities: Rowntree and Lavers (1951: ch. 14) – see also Case Studies 9.1, 12.1, 12.4;
  - Events: Harris (2014), Mules (2004);
  - Individuals: Saunders and Turner (1987);
  - Organisations and companies: Harris and Leiper (1995);
  - Places and projects: Hayllar et al. (2008), Murphy (1991);
  - Sport and social exclusion: four case studies: Collins (2014);
  - Sporting/social club in a residential community: Wynne (1986, 1998);
  - Tourism planning: Murphy (1991); and
  - Whole countries: Bramham et al. (1993), Williams and Shaw (1988).

References

Bourdieu, P. (1984). *Distinction: a social critique of the judgement of taste*. London: Routledge.

Bramham, R., Henry, I., Mommaas, H., and Van Der Poel, H. (Eds) (1993). *Leisure policies in Europe*. Wallingford, UK: CAB International.

Bromley, D. B. (1986). *The case-study method in psychology and related disciplines*. New York: John Wiley.

Burns, R. B. (1994). *Introduction to research methods*, 2nd edn. Melbourne: Longman Cheshire.

Carty, V. (1997). Ideologies and forms of domination in the organization of the global production and consumption of goods in the emerging postmodern era: a case study of Nike Corporation and the implications for gender. *Gender, Work and Organization*, 4(4), 189–201.

Collins, M. F. (2014). *Sport and social exclusion*, 2nd edn. London: Routledge.

Finn, M., Elliott-White, M. and Walton, M. (2000). *Tourism and leisure research methods*. Harlow, UK: Longman.

Flyvbjerg, B. (2006). Five misunderstandings about case-study research. *Qualitative Inquiry*, 12(2), 219–45.

Gerring, J. (2016). *Case study research: principles and practices*, 2nd edn. New York: Cambridge University Press (e-book version accessed).

Harris, R. (2014). The role of large-scale sporting events in host community education for sustainable development: an exploratory case study of the Sydney 2000 Olympic Games. *Event Management*, 18(2), 207–30.

Harris, R., and Leiper, N. (Eds) (1995). *Sustainable tourism: an Australian perspective*. Melbourne: Butterworth-Heinemann.

Harvard Business School (nd) *Harvard Business School Case Studies*. Cambridge, MA: Harvard University. Available at: www.hbsp.harvard.edu (accessed May 2017).

Hayllar, B., Griffin, T., and Edwards, D. (Eds) (2008). *City spaces, tourist places: urban tourism precincts*. Oxford: Butterworth-Heinemann.

Henderson, K. A. (2006). *Dimensions of choice: a qualitative approach to recreation, parks and leisure research*, 2nd edn. State College, PA: Venture.

Henry, I., and Paramio Salcines, J. L. (1998). Sport, culture and urban regimes: the case of Bilbao. In M. F. Collins and I. S. Cooper (Eds), *Leisure management: issues and applications* (pp. 97–112). Wallingford, UK: CAB International.

Lainsbury, A. (2000). *Once upon an American dream: the story of Euro Disneyland*. Lawrence, KS: University of Kansas Press.

Long, P. (2000). Tourism development regimes in the inner city fringe: the case of Discover Islington, London. In B. Bramwell and B. Lane (Eds), *Tourism collaboration and partnerships: politics, practice and sustainability* (pp. 183–99). Clevedon, UK: Channel View Publications.

Mules, T. (2004). Case study evolution in event management: the Gold Coast's Wintersun festival. *Event Management*, 9(1–2), 95–101.

Murphy, P. (1991). Data gathering for community-oriented tourism planning: a case study of Vancouver Island, British Columbia. *Leisure Studies*, 10(1), 65–80.

Rose, D. (Ed.) (2000). *Researching social and economic change: the uses of household panel studies*. London: Routledge.

Rowntree, B. S., and Lavers, G. R. (1951). *English life and leisure: a social study*. London: Longmans, Green & Co.

Saunders, D. M., and Turner, D. E. (1987). Gambling and leisure: the case of racing. *Leisure Studies*, 6(3), 281–300.

Stake, R. E. (1995). *The art of case study research*. Thousand Oaks, CA: Sage.

Williams, A. M., and Shaw, G. (1988). *Tourism and economic development: Western European Experience*. London: Belhaven.

Wynne, D. (1986). Living on 'The Heath'. *Leisure Studies*, 5(1), 109–16.

Wynne, D. (1998). *Leisure, lifestyle and the new middle class: a case study*. London: Routledge.

Xiao, H., and Smith, S. L. J. (2005). Case studies in tourism research: a state-of-the-art analysis. *Tourism Management*, 27(4), 738–49.

Yin, R. K. (2009). *Case study research: design and methods*, 4th edn. Thousand Oaks, CA: Sage.

Zikmund, W. G. (1997). *Business research methods*, 5th edn. Orlando, FL: Dryden Press.

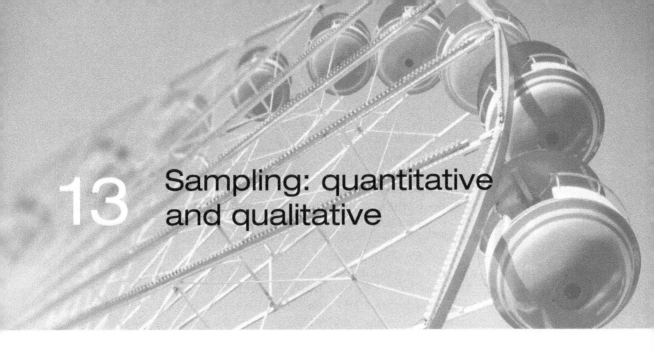

13 Sampling: quantitative and qualitative

1. Introduction: the idea of sampling

In most survey research and in some observational research, it is necessary to *sample*. Mainly because of costs, it is not usually possible to gather data from *all* the people, organisations or other entities which are the focus of the research. For example, if the aim of a research project is to study the leisure patterns or holiday-making behaviour of the adult population of a country, no one has the resources to conduct interviews with the millions of individuals who make up the adult population. The only time when the whole population is interviewed is every 5 or 10 years, when the government statistical agency conducts the official Census of Population – and the cost of collecting and analysing the data can be hundreds of millions of pounds or dollars.

At a more modest level, it would be virtually impossible to conduct face-to-face interviews with all the users of an urban park or a busy tourist area since, in busy periods, many hundreds might enter the site and leave in a short space of time. It might be possible to hand respondent-completion questionnaires to all users but, as discussed in Chapter 10, this approach has disadvantages in terms of quality and level of response. The usual procedure is to interview a sample – a proportion – of the users.

In Chapter 8, on observational methods, the problems of continuous counting of numbers of users of leisure and tourism sites were discussed, and it was noted that often available resources demand that sample counts be undertaken – that is, the numbers entering the site or present at the site are counted on a sample of occasions.

Sampling has implications not only for the way data are collected but also for the way they are analysed and interpreted.

2. Samples and populations

One item of terminology should be clarified initially. The total category of subjects which is the focus of attention in a particular research project is known as the *population*. A *sample* is selected from the population. The use of the term 'population' makes obvious sense when dealing with communities of people – for instance, when referring to the population of Britain or the population of London. But in social research, the term also applies in other instances; for example, the visitors to a resort over the course of a year constitute the *population of resort visitors*; and the users of a sports facility are the *population of users*.

The term 'population' can also be applied to non-human phenomena. For example, if a study of the physical characteristics of Australia's beaches found that there were 10,000 beaches in all, from which 100 were to be selected for study, then the 10,000 beaches can be referred to as the *population of beaches* and the 100 selected for study would be the sample. In some texts the word *universe* is used instead of population.

If a sample is to be selected for study, then two questions arise:

1. What procedures must be followed to ensure that the sample is representative of the population?

2. How large should the sample be?

These two questions are related since, other things being equal, the larger the sample, the more chance it has of being representative.

3. Representativeness

3.1 Random sampling

A sample which is not representative of the population is described as *biased*. The whole process of sample selection must be aimed at *minimising* bias in the sample. The researcher seeks to achieve representativeness and to minimise bias by adopting the principles of *random sampling*. This is not the most helpful term since it implies that the process is not methodical. This is far from the case – random does not mean haphazard! The meaning of random sampling is as follows:

> In random sampling all members of the population have an equal chance of inclusion in the sample.

For example, if a sample of 1000 people is to be selected from a population of 10,000, then every member of the population must have a 1 in 10 chance of being selected. In practice, most sampling methods involving human beings can only approximate this rule. The problems of achieving random sampling vary with the types of survey situation as discussed in Chapter 10.

3.2 Sampling for household surveys

The problem of achieving randomness can be examined in the case of a household survey of the adult residents of a country. If the adult population of the country is, say, 40 million and we wish to interview a sample of 1000, then every member of the adult population should have a 1 in 40,000 chance of being included in the sample. How would this be achieved? Ideally, there should be a complete list of all 40 million of the country's adults – their names should be written on slips of paper and placed in a revolving drum, physically or electronically, as in a lottery draw, and 1000 names should be drawn out. Each time a choice is made, everyone has a 1 in 40 million chance of selection – since this happens 1000 times, each person has a total of 1000 in 40 million or 1 in 40,000 chance of selection.

This would be a very laborious process. Surely, a close approximation would be to forget the slips of paper and the drum and choose every 40,000th name on the list. But where should the starting point be? It should be some random point between 1 and 40,000. There are published 'tables of random numbers', which can also be produced from computers, which can be used for this purpose. Strictly speaking, the whole sample should be chosen using random numbers, since this would approximate most closely to the 'names in a drum' procedure.

In practice, however, such a list of the population being studied rarely exists. The nearest thing to it would be the electoral registers of all the constituencies in the country. Electoral registers are fairly comprehensive because adults are required by law to register, but they are not perfect. Highly mobile/homeless people are often not included; many who live in multi-occupied premises are omitted. The physical task of selecting the names from such a list would be immense, but there is another disadvantage with this approach. If every 40,000th voter on the registers was selected, the sample would be scattered throughout the country. The cost of visiting every one of those selected, if the survey was for a face-to-face interview, would be very high.

In practice, therefore, organisations conducting national surveys compromise by employing 'multi-stage' sampling and 'clustered' sampling. Multi-stage means that sampling is not done directly but by stages. For example, if the country had, say, four states or regions, the proposed sample of 1000 would be sub-divided in the same proportions as the populations of the regions. Within each region, local government areas would then be divided into rural and urban and, say, four urban and two rural areas would be selected at random – with the intention of selecting appropriate sub-samples of perhaps 25, 40 or 50 from each area. These sub-samples could be selected from electoral registers, or streets could be selected and individuals contacted by calling on, say, every fifth house in the street. In any one street, interviewers may be instructed to interview, say, 10 or 15 people. By interviewing 'clusters' of people in this way, costs are minimised. But care must be taken not to reduce the number of clusters too much, since then the full range of population and area types would not be included.

Once a house has been selected for interview, a procedure must be devised for selecting a respondent from the household members; this is discussed in relation to telephone surveys next.

3.3 Sampling for telephone surveys

The traditional process for sampling for telephone surveys from the public residential telephone directories and the move to computer aided telephone interviewing (CATI) methods is described in Chapter 9. Some of the emerging difficulties with this method, given the rise of mobile telephones (also discussed in Chapter 9), threaten the representativeness of samples. Insofar as the resultant bias is age-related, this can be corrected by weighting; but if it reflects lifestyle differences, not much can be done about it. The printed or electronic directory is close to the list of people on the electoral register, as discussed earlier, except that, since there is typically only one land-line telephone per house, the list effectively refers to households rather than to individuals. As with household surveys, it is therefore necessary to use some procedure for selecting a respondent from among household members.

If, in face-to-face household surveys or telephone surveys, the interviewer was to interview the person who happened to answer the door or the telephone, this could result in bias, depending on local customs as to who in the household is more likely to answer the door or the phone. There is, of course, invariably a lower age limit for the survey, so persons under the prescribed age will not be selected. A typical procedure to 'randomise' the process of choosing among eligible household members is to ask to interview the person whose birthday is nearest to the interview date.

3.4 Sampling for site/user/visitor surveys

Conditions at leisure/tourism sites or facilities vary enormously, depending on the type and size of facility, the season, day of the week, time of day or the weather. This discussion can therefore be only in general terms. To ensure randomness, and therefore representativeness, it is necessary for interviewers to adhere to strict rules. Site interviewers operate in two ways:

1. ISUM: interviewer stationary, users mobile – for instance, when the interviewer is located near the entrance and visitors are interviewed as they enter or leave.

2. USIM: users stationary, interviewer mobile – for instance, when interviewing beach users or users of a picnic site.

In the ISUM case, the instructions interviewers should follow should be something like:

> When one interview is complete, check through the questionnaire for completeness and legibility. When you are ready with a new questionnaire, stop the next person to enter the gate. Stick strictly to this rule and do not select interviewees on any other basis.

The important thing is that interviewers should not avoid certain types of user by 'picking and choosing' whom to interview. Ideally, there should be some rule such as interviewing every fifth person to come through the door/gate; but, since users will enter at a varying rate and interviews vary in length, this is rarely possible, hence the 'next person to enter' method.

In the USIM case, the interviewer should be given a certain route to follow on the site and be instructed to interview, say, every fifth group they pass. Seated venues vary in design and formality. With theatres and concert halls, the interviewing will typically take place during intervals, in the circulation areas. The same may apply to sports venues, but for those sports with plenty of breaks in play, such as at cricket, it may also be possible to conduct interviewing in the seating areas.

Where interviewers are employed, the success of the process will depend on the training they are given, and this could involve observation of them at work to ensure that they are following the rules.

Sampling in site/visitor surveys leads inevitably to variation in the proportion of users interviewed at different times of the day (see Chapter 10). Where users tend to stay for long periods – as in the case of beaches – this may not matter; but where people stay for shorter periods and the type of user varies during the course of the day or week, the sample will probably be unrepresentative – that is, biased. This should be corrected by weighting as indicated at the end of the chapter.

When surveys involve the handing out of questionnaires for respondent-completion – as, for example, in a number of tourist *en route*/hotel surveys – unless field staff are available to encourage their completion and return, respondents will be self-selected. Busy hotel or leisure facility receptionists can rarely be relied upon to do a thorough job in handing out and collecting in questionnaires, unless the survey is a priority of the management and therefore closely supervised. Normally, a significant proportion of the population will fail to return the questionnaire – but it is unlikely that this self-selection process will be random. For example, people with difficulties in reading or writing, or people who are in a hurry, may fail to return their questionnaires. Those with 'something to say', whether positive or negative, are more likely to return their questionnaires than people who are apathetic or just content with the service, thus giving a misleading impression of the proportion of users who have strong opinions. Thus it can be seen that this type of 'uncontrolled' survey is at risk of introducing serious bias into the sample and should therefore be avoided if at all possible.

3.5 Sampling for street surveys and quota sampling

Although the technique of quota sampling can be used in other situations, it is most common in street surveys. The street survey is usually seen as a means of contacting a representative sample of the community, but in fact it can also be seen as a sort of site survey, the site being the shopping area. As such, a street survey which involved a random sample of the users of the street would be representative of the users of the shopping area rather than of the community as a whole – in a suburban shopping centre it could, for instance, have a high proportion of retired people or full-time home/child carers.

If the aim is in fact to obtain a representative sample of the whole community, then to achieve this, interviewers are given 'quotas' of people of different types to contact, the quotas being based on information about the community which is available from the census. For example, if the census indicates that 12 per cent of the population is retired, then interviewers would be required to include 12 retired people in every 100 interviewed. Once interviewers have filled their quota in certain age/gender groups, they are required to become more selective in whom they approach in order to fill the gaps in their quotas.

The quota method can be used only when background information on the target population is known – as with community surveys. In most user surveys this information is not known, so the strict following of random sampling procedures must be relied upon.

3.6 Sampling for mail surveys

The initial list of people to whom the questionnaire is sent in a mail survey may be the whole population (in the statistical sense) or a sample. If a sample is selected, it can usually be done completely randomly because the mailing list for the whole population is usually available.

The respondents to a mail survey form a sample; it is not randomly selected but self-selected. This introduces sources of bias similar to those in the uncontrolled self-completion site surveys discussed in section 3.4. There is little that can be done about this except to make every effort to achieve a high response rate, as discussed in Chapter 10. In some cases information may be available on the population which can be used to weight the sample to correct for certain sources of bias – for example, in the case of a national survey, the sample could be weighted to correct for any geographical bias in response because the geographical distribution of the population would be known. If, for example, the survey is of an occupational association and the proportion of members in various grades is known from records, then this can be used for weighting purposes. But ultimately, mail surveys suffer from an unknown and uncorrectable element of bias caused by non-response. All surveys experience non-response, of course, but the problem is greater with mail surveys because the level of non-response is usually greater.

3.7 Sampling for e-surveys

Often, when a population, such as the workforce or membership of an organisation, is to be studied by means of an e-survey, a complete listing of email addresses is available. The sampling process then resembles that of the mail survey: the entire population may be included or a specified proportion, for example, every fifth individual on the list. The challenges of non-response and representativeness are therefore the same as for mail surveys.

A common practice is for organisations, such as pressure-groups or local councils, to place an online questionnaire on their website and invite people to respond – that is, to self-sample. The resultant sample cannot therefore be said to be representative even of visitors to the website, since only those with sufficient interest and/or time will be motivated to take part in the survey. The sample is *certainly not*, as is sometimes implicitly claimed, representative of the general public.

3.8 Sampling for complex events and destination studies

As indicated in Chapter 5, events with a mix of multiple ticketed and non-ticketed venues and tourist destinations with multiple attractions present particular challenges for the researcher, not least in the task of sampling. Typically, research is required to provide information on a number of matters, including: the number of visitors to the destination/host community; number of visitors and locals attending individual sites and individual events; and socio-demographic profile, expenditure patterns and satisfactions/evaluation of visitors and local participants. This information will be gathered by one or more of the methods discussed in sub-sections 3.2–3.7. The sampling task, then, involves consideration of the protocols appropriate to the method. In addition, secondary data sources, such as ticket sales records, will be drawn upon. The unique challenge, therefore, is not the sampling and data collection *per se* but combining data from different sources to provide estimates for the whole event, particularly when an event involves large non-ticketed components and where a destination attracts significant numbers of day-trippers in addition to staying visitors.

3.9 Sampling/random assignment in experimental research

Experimental subjects are typically, in effect, a 'convenience' sample, as sometimes used in qualitative research, discussed at the end of the chapter. The group of students or members of an organisation are selected on the basis of convenient accessibility. In this case, the sample can at best be seen as likely to be representative of people in a similar situation – for example, 18- to 19-year-old leisure or tourism management students at a major urban university, mostly from middle-class backgrounds. But, of course, university environments vary, so the students may have different lifestyles from such students at other universities. The question of representativeness, or otherwise, is often established when experiments are replicated in other environments, and results are consolidated in systematic reviews of the research literature (see Chapter 6).

A sampling-related task in experimental research arises in relation to the random assignment of subjects to the experimental and control groups (see Chapter 11). Typically, the overall sample is of manageable size, so a list of names is available. The truly random way of proceeding is to use random numbers. For example, if there are 234 individuals in the overall sample, and the aim is to allocate half to the experimental group and half to the control group, the subjects should be numbered from 1 to 234, and 117 random numbers should be used to select the experimental group. In the past, tables of random numbers, often published as an appendix in statistics textbooks, were used to do this, but now 'random number generators' are available online (e.g. www. random.org). The online generator would be requested to produce 117 random numbers between 1 and 234.

4. Sample size

A popular misconception is that the size of a sample should be decided on the basis of its relationship to the size of the population – for example, that a sample should be, say, 5 per cent or 10 per cent of the population. *This is not so.* What is important is the absolute size of the sample, regardless of the size of the population. For example, a sample size of 1000 is equally valid, provided proper sampling procedures have been followed, whether it is a sample of the British adults (population 50 million), the residents of London (population 7 million), the residents of Brighton (population 100,000) or the students of a university (population, say, 15,000).

It is worth repeating that it is the *absolute size of the sample* which is important, not its size relative to the population. This rule applies in all cases, except when the population itself is small – this exception and its implications are discussed later in the chapter.

On the basis of what criteria, therefore, should a sample size be determined? The criteria are basically threefold:

1. the required level of precision in the results;

2. the level of detail in the proposed analysis; and

3. the available budget.

These issues are discussed in turn below. In addition, some comments are offered on:

4. reporting sample size issues;

5. application of confidence intervals to population estimates; and

6. sample size for small populations.

4.1 Level of precision – confidence intervals

The idea of the level of precision can be explained as follows. The question to be posed is: to what extent do the findings from a sample precisely reflect the population from which it is drawn? For example, if a survey was designed to investigate holiday-taking and it was found that 50 per cent of a sample of 500 people took a holiday in the previous year, how sure can we be that this finding – this *statistic* – is true of the population as a whole? How sure can we be, despite all efforts taken to choose a representative sample, that the sample is not in fact unrepresentative, and that the real percentage of holiday-taking in the population is in fact, say, 70 per cent or 30 per cent?

This question is answered in terms of *probabilities*. If the true population value is around 50 per cent, then, as long as random sampling procedures have been followed, the *probability* of drawing a sample which was so wrong that no one in the sample had been on holiday in the previous year would be very remote – almost impossible, one might say. On the other hand, the *probability* of coming up with, say, 48 or 49 per cent or 51 or 52 per cent would, one would think, be fairly high. The probability of coming up with 70 or 30 per cent would be somewhere in between.

Statisticians have examined the likely pattern of distribution of all possible samples of various sizes drawn from populations of various sizes and established that, when a sample is randomly drawn, the sample value of a statistic has a certain probability of being within a certain range either side of the real value of the statistic. That range is plus or minus twice the 'standard error' of the statistic. The size of the standard error depends on the size of the sample and is unrelated to the size of the population. A properly drawn sample has a 95 per cent chance of producing a statistic with a value which is within two standard errors of the true population value; so, conversely, there is a 95 per cent chance that the true population value lies within two standard errors of the sample statistic. This means that, if a hundred samples of the same size were drawn, in 95 cases we would expect the value of the statistic to be within two standard errors of the population value; in 5 cases, we would expect it to be outside the range. Since we do not generally actually know the population value, we have to rely on this theoretical statement of probability about the likely accuracy of our finding: we have a 95 per cent chance of being approximately right and a 5 per cent chance of being wrong.

This 'two standard errors' range is referred to as the '95 per cent confidence interval' of a statistic. The relationships between standard errors and level of probability is a property of the 'normal curve' – a bell-shaped curve with certain mathematical properties, which we are not able to pursue here. The idea of a normal curve and 95 per cent confidence intervals is illustrated in Figure 13.1. The general idea of probabilities related to the properties of certain types of 'distribution' is pursued in more detail in Chapter 17.

Tables have been drawn up by statisticians which give the confidence intervals for various statistics for various sample sizes, as shown in Table 13.1. Down the side of the table are various sample sizes, ranging from 50 to 10,000. Across the top of the table are statistics which one might find from a survey – for example, 20 per cent play tennis. The table shows 20 per cent together with 80 per cent because if it is found that 20 per cent of the sample play tennis, then clearly 80 per cent *do not* play tennis. Any conclusion about the accuracy of the statistic 20 per cent also applies to the corresponding statistic 80 per cent. In the body of the table are the *confidence intervals*.

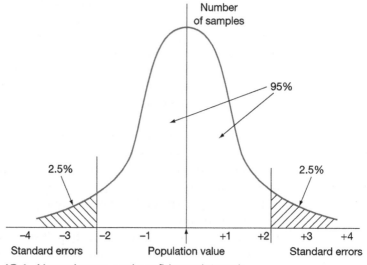

Figure 13.1 Normal curve and confidence intervals

Table 13.1 Confidence intervals related to sample size

Sample size	Percentages found from sample ('results')							
	50%	40 or 60%	30 or 70%	20 or 80%	10 or 90%	5 or 95%	2 or 98%	1 or 99%
	Confidence intervals (± %)							
50	±13.9	±13.6	±12.7	±11.1	±8.3	*	*	*
80	±11.0	±10.7	±10.0	±8.8	±6.6	*	*	*
100	±9.8	±9.6	±9.0	±7.8	±5.9	±4.3	*	*
150	±8.0	±7.8	±7.3	±6.4	±4.8	±3.5	*	*
200	±6.9	±6.8	±6.3	±5.5	±4.2	±3.0	±1.9	*
250	±6.2	±6.1	±5.7	±5.0	±3.7	±2.7	±1.7	*
300	±5.7	±5.5	±5.2	±4.5	±3.4	±2.5	±1.6	*
400	±4.9	±4.8	±4.5	±3.9	±2.9	±2.1	±1.4	±1.0
500	±4.4	±4.3	±4.0	±3.5	±2.6	±1.9	±1.2	±0.9
750	±3.6	±3.5	±3.3	±2.9	±2.1	±1.6	±1.0	±0.7
1000	±3.1	±3.0	±2.8	±2.5	±1.9	±1.3	±0.9	±0.6
2000	±2.2	±2.1	±2.0	±1.7	±1.3	±1.0	±0.6	±0.4
4000	±1.5	±1.5	±1.4	±1.2	±0.9	±0.7	±0.4	±0.3
10,000	±1.0	±1.0	±0.9	±0.8	±0.6	±0.4	±0.3	±0.2

* confidence interval greater than the percentage.

Interpretation of table: for example, for a sample size of 400, a finding of 30% is subject to a confidence interval of ±4.5 (that is to say, we can be 95% certain that the population value lies in the range 25.5% to 34.5%). For formula to calculate confidence intervals, see Appendix 17.1.

An example of how the table is interpreted is as follows: suppose we have a sample size of 500 and we have a finding that 30 per cent of the sample have a certain characteristic – say, have been away on holiday in the previous summer (so 70 per cent have *not* been away on holiday). Reading off the table, for a sample size of 500, we see that a finding of 30 per cent (and 70 per cent) is subject to a confidence interval of plus or minus 4.0. So we can be fairly certain that the population value lies in the range 26.0 per cent to 34.0 per cent.

An important point should be noted about these confidence intervals: to halve the confidence interval, it is necessary to quadruple the sample size. In the example above, a sample of 2000 people (four times the original sample) would give a confidence interval of plus or minus 2.0 per cent (half the original confidence interval). The cost of increasing the precision of surveys by increasing the sample is therefore very high.

Note that for smaller samples the confidence intervals become very large – for instance, for a sample of 50, the interval is plus or minus 13.9 per cent, meaning that a finding of 50 per cent can only be estimated to be within the range 36.1 to 63.9 per cent. For some statistics, for the smaller sample sizes, the confidence intervals are not calculable because the total margin of error is larger than the original statistic.

It should be noted that these confidence intervals apply only for samples which have been drawn using random sampling methods; other methods, such as multi-stage sampling, tend to produce larger confidence intervals, but the difference is often small, so the matter is not pursued here.

The implications of the precision criterion for deciding sample size now become clear. A sample size of, say, 1000 would give a confidence interval for a finding of 50 per cent of plus or minus 3.1 per cent. If that margin of error was not considered acceptable, then a larger sample size would be necessary. Whether or not it is considered acceptable depends on the uses to which the data will be put and is related to the type of analysis to be done, as discussed in section 4.2. An alternative way of considering these relationships between sample size and confidence interval is presented in Table 13.2. This presents, in the body of the table, the necessary sample size to achieve a given confidence interval.

4.2 Detail of proposed analysis

The confidence intervals in Table 13.1 illustrate further the second criterion concerning the choice of sample size: the type of analysis to be undertaken. If many detailed comparisons are to be made, especially concerning small proportions of the population, then too small a sample size may preclude very meaningful analysis. For instance, suppose a survey is conducted with a sample of 200 and it is found that 20 per cent of respondents went bowling and 30 per cent played tennis. The 20 per cent is subject to a margin of error of plus or minus 5.5 per cent and the 30 per cent is subject to a margin of plus or minus 6.3 per cent. Thus it is estimated that the proportions playing the two activities are as follows:

Bowling: between 14.5 and 25.5 per cent Tennis: between 23.7 and 36.3 per cent

Table 13.2 Necessary sample sizes to achieve given confidence intervals

Conf. interval	Percentages found from sample ('results')						
	50%	40 or 60%	30 or 70%	20 or 80%	10 or 90%	5 or 95%	1 or 99%
	Minimum necessary sample size						
±1%	9600	9216	8064	6144	3456	1824	380
±2%	2400	2304	2016	1536	864	456	*
±3%	1067	1024	896	683	384	203	*
±4%	600	576	504	384	216	114	*
±5%	384	369	323	246	138	73	*
±6%	267	256	224	171	96	*	*
±7%	196	188	165	125	71	*	*
±8%	150	144	126	96	54	*	*
±9%	119	114	100	76	43	*	*
±10%	96	92	81	61	35	*	*

The confidence intervals overlap, so we cannot conclude that there is any 'significant' difference in the popularity of the two activities, despite a 10 per cent difference given by the survey. This is likely to be very limiting in any analysis. If the sample were 500, the confidence intervals would be 3.5 per cent and 4.0 per cent respectively, giving estimates as follows:

Bowling: between 16.5 and 23.5 per cent Tennis: between 26.0 and 34.0 per cent

In this case the confidence intervals do *not* overlap, and we can be fairly certain that tennis *is* more popular than bowling.

The detail of the analysis, the extent of subdivision of the sample into sub-samples and the acceptable level of precision will therefore determine the necessary size of the sample. By and large this has nothing to do with the overall size of the original population, although there is a likelihood that the larger the population, the greater its diversity and therefore the greater the need for sub-division into sub-samples.

4.3 Budget

A further point is that it could be positively wasteful to expend resources on a large sample when it can be shown to be unnecessary. For example, a sample of 10,000 gives estimates of statistics with a maximum confidence interval of ±1 per cent. Such a survey could cost, say, £200,000 to conduct. To halve that confidence interval to ±0.5 per cent would mean quadrupling the sample size to 40,000 at an additional cost of £800,000. There can be very few situations where such expenditure would be justified for such a small return.

Ultimately, then, the limiting factor in determining sample size will be the third criterion, the resources available. Even if the budget available limits the sample size severely, it may be decided to go ahead and risk the possibility of an unrepresentative sample. If the sample is small, however, the detail of the analysis will need to be limited. If resources are so limited that the validity of quantitative research is questionable, it may be sensible to consider qualitative research which may be more feasible. Alternatively, the proposed research can be seen as a 'pilot' exercise, with the emphasis on methodology, preparatory to a more adequately resourced full-scale study in future.

4.4 Reporting sample size issues

How should the issue of sample size and confidence intervals be referred to in the report on the research? In some scientific research, complex statistical tests are considered necessary in reporting statistical results from surveys. In much social science research, and leisure and tourism research in particular, requirements are less rigorous. This is true to some extent in academic research but is markedly so in the reporting of policy/management research. While it is necessary to be aware of the limitations imposed by the sample size and to not make comparisons which the data cannot support, explicit reference to such matters in the text of a consultancy report is rare. A great deal of statistical jargon is not generally required: the lay reader expects the researcher to do a good job, and expert readers should be given enough information to check the analysis in the report for themselves. It is recommended that an appendix be included in reports indicating the size of the sampling errors. Appendix 13.1 gives a possible format.

In academic journals the rules are somewhat different, and there is an expectation that statistical tests (see Chapter 17) be 'up front'.

4.5 Confidence intervals applied to population estimates

The earlier comments are focused on confidence intervals applied to percentages of samples. Caution should be used when discussing *population estimates* based on sample surveys. In many cases the sample statistics are applied to the population as a whole to obtain estimates of, for example, total visits to a destination or type of facility, when even more care should be taken. A hypothetical worked example is outlined in Table 13.3. It might be thought that because the survey finding of the proportion of the population visiting a site (12 per cent) is subject to a confidence interval of ±2.0 per cent, this also applies to the estimated number of persons visiting and to the number of visits. But this is not so – both the number of persons and the number of visits are subject to a confidence interval of ±16.7 per cent. To obtain a confidence interval of ±2.0 per cent of the number of persons/visits – that is, to reduce it to an eighth of its current size – would require a sample size of at least 64,000.

4.6 Sample size and small populations

The earlier discussion of sample size assumes that the population is large – in fact, the statistical formulae used to calculate the confidence intervals are based on the assumption that the population is, in effect, infinite. The relationship between the size of confidence intervals and the size of the population becomes noticeable when the population size falls below about 50,000, as shown in Table 13.3. The table presents sample sizes necessary to produce 95 per cent confidence intervals of ±5 per cent and ±1 per cent for a sample finding of 50 per cent for different population sizes. Only the sample sizes for a 50 per cent finding are presented since, as shown in Table 13.1, the 50 per cent finding is the most demanding in terms of sample size: for a given sample size, the confidence intervals for other findings – for example, 30/70 per cent – is always smaller. The table first indicates the sample sizes for an infinite population, and these are the same as indicated for a ±5 per cent or ±1 per cent confidence interval in the first column of Table 13.4. The details of the formula relating confidence intervals to population size can be found in Krejcie and Morgan (1970).

Table 13.3 Confidence intervals applied to visit numbers

Item	Source	Number
Population	Census	500,000
Sample	Household survey	1000
% visiting a leisure/tourism site in a year	Household survey	12%
Percentage confidence interval	Table 13.1	±2.0%
Estimated number of persons	12% of 500,000	60,000
Conf. interval in terms of persons	±2% of 500,000	±10,000
Confidence interval as % of no. of persons	(10,000/60,000) × 100	±16.7%
Frequency of visit, times per year	Household survey	2.5
Estimated total visits	Calc.: 60,000 × 2.5	150,000
Confidence interval in terms of visits	Calc: 10,000 × 2.5	±25,000
Confidence interval as % of visits	Calc.: (25,000/150,000) × 100	16.7%

Table 13.4 Sample size and population size: small populations

Population size	Minimum sample sizes for confidence interval of ±5% and ±1% on a sample finding of 50%:	
	±5%	±1%
Infinite*	384	9602
10,000,000	384	9593
5,000,000	384	9584
1,000,000	384	9511
500,000	384	9422
100,000	383	8761
50,000	381	8056
25,000	378	6938
20,000	377	6488
10,000	370	4899
5000	357	3288
2000	322	1655
1000	278	906
500	217	475
200	132	196
100	80	99
50	44	50

* As in Tables 13.1 and 13.2.

5. Weighting

Situations where weighting of survey or count data may be required have been referred to at various points in this chapter. In Chapter 16 the procedures for implementing weighting using the SPSS computer package are outlined. Here we discuss the principles involved. Take the example of the data shown in Table 13.5. In the sample of 45 interviews, the number of interviews is spread fairly equally through the day, whereas more than half the actual users visit around the middle of the day (this information probably had been obtained by observation/counts). This can be a source of bias in the sample, since the mid-day users may differ from the others in their characteristics or opinions and they will be under-represented in the sample. The aim of weighting is to produce a weighted sample with a distribution similar to that of the actual users.

One approach is to 'gross up' the sample numbers to reflect the actual numbers: for example, the 9–11 am group is weighted by 25 ÷ 10 = 2.5, the 11–1 pm group is weighted by 240 ÷ 12 = 20, and so on, as shown in Table 13.6.

Table 13.5   Interview/usage data from a site/visitor survey

Time	# of interviews	%	Actual # of users (counts)	%
9–11 a.m.	10	22.2	25	5.7
11.01 a.m.–1 p.m.	12	26.7	240	55.2
1.01–3 p.m.	11	24.4	110	25.3
3.01–5 p.m.	12	26.7	60	2.7
Total	45	100.0	435	100.0

Table 13.6   Weighting

	A	B	C	D
Time	No. of interviews	No. of users	Weighting factors	Weighted sample no.
Source:	Survey	Counts	B/A	CxA
9–11 a.m.	10	25	2.5	25
11.01 a.m.–1 p.m.	12	240	20.0	240
1.01–3 p.m.	11	110	10.0	110
3.01–5 p.m.	12	60	5.0	60
Total	45	435		435

The weighting factors can be fed into the computer for the weighting to be done automatically, as discussed in Chapter 16. The initial weighting factors are equal to the user number divided by the sample number for that time-period. The weighted sample, therefore, is made to resemble the overall user numbers. It should be noted, however, that the sample size is still 45, not 435! If statistical tests are to be carried out, then it would be advisable to multiply the weighting factors by 0.103 (= 45/435) to bring the weighted sample total back to 45.

In this example, the basis of the weighting relates to the pattern of visits over the course of the day, which happened to be information which was available in relation to this particular type of survey. Any other data available on the population could be used – for example, if age structure is available from the census, then age-groups rather than time-periods might be used as the basis for weighting.

6. Sampling for qualitative research

As discussed in Chapter 9, qualitative research generally makes no claim to quantitative representativeness and, by definition, does not involve statistical calculation demanding prescribed levels of precision. Generally, therefore, the quantitative considerations outlined above are not relevant to qualitative research. This is not to say that representativeness is ignored entirely. As Karla Henderson (2006: 172) puts it: 'the researcher using a qualitative approach is not concerned about adequate numbers or random selection, but with trying to present a working picture of the broader social structure drawn from inter-views, observations, or text'. Thus if the population being studied includes young and old people, then both young and old people should ideally be included in the sample, unless an explicit decision has been made to concentrate on one age-group only. But the sample will not necessarily reflect the *proportions* of young and old in the study population. Miles and Huberman (1994: 28) list 16 'strategies' for qualitative sampling. Some of these are presented in Table 13.7.

In the research report, the qualitative sampling methods used should be ade-quately described. In all cases, just how individuals are selected and contacted should be indicated. For example, if the 'criterion' sampling method was used, what was the criterion used, and how were the people who met the criterion contacted? If a 'snowball' method was used, how was it started? If 'convenience' sampling was used, what was the convenience factor – friendship, family, col-leagues, students, neighbours? A table is often included, indicating key charac-teristics of sample members to give a broad indication of representativeness.

There are no generally hard and fast rules for determining the appropriate sample size in qualitative research. One criterion used in quantitative research also applies, namely the available budget and time. Some of the sampling meth-ods listed in Table 13.7 point towards a minimum sample size – for example,

Table 13.7   Selected qualitative sampling methods

Method	Characteristics
Convenience	Use of conveniently located persons or organisations – e.g. friends. colleagues, students, organisations in the neighbourhood, tourists visiting a local popular attraction.
Criterion	Individuals selected on the basis of a key criterion – e.g. age-group, membership of an organisation, purchasers of souvenirs.
Homogeneous	Deliberately selecting a relatively homogeneous sub-set of the population – e.g. university-educated male cyclists aged 20–30.
Opportunistic	Similar to 'convenience' but involves taking advantage of opportunities as they arise – e.g. studying major sporting event taking place locally, or a holiday resort where the researcher is holidaying.
Maximum variation	Deliberately studying contrasting cases. Opposite of 'homogeneous'.
Purposeful	Similar to 'criterion' but may involve other considerations, such as 'maximum variation', typicality.
Snowball	Interviewees used as source of suggestions for additional contacts.
Stratified purposeful	Selection of a range of cases based on set criteria, e.g. representatives of a range of age-groups or nationalities.

the range of groups to be covered in the 'criterion' and 'stratified-purposeful' methods. In grounded theory research, the sample size may be determined by the process of 'saturation', that is, the point at which further subjects stop producing new themes or theoretical categories (Charmaz, 2006: 113); in that case the sampling process is closely linked to the analysis process, as discussed in Chapter 15.

Summary

This chapter covers the topic of sampling, which is the process of selecting a proportion of the 'population' of subjects for study. It also examines the implications of sampling for data analysis. Two key issues are considered: *representativeness* of samples, and *sample size*. The researcher seeks representativeness by following the principles of *random sampling*, which means that, as near as possible, every member of the population has an equal chance of being selected. Different types of survey involve different practical procedures for achieving random sampling. If a sample has been randomly selected, the question still arises as to the extent to which the statistical findings from the sample truly reflect the population. Statistical procedures have been developed to assess the level of probability that a sample finding lies within a certain margin of the true population value. This margin is known as a *confidence interval*, and its size is related to the size of the sample, regardless of the size of the population – the larger the sample, the smaller the confidence interval or margin of statistical error. The necessary sample size for a study therefore depends on the precision required in the results, the detail of the analysis to be undertaken and the available budget. Finally, the chapter considers the practice of *weighting* to correct a sample for known bias and sampling for qualitative research.

Test questions

1. Define random sampling.

2. What is the opposite of a random/representative sample?

3. What is multi-stage sampling, and why is it used?

4. What is a confidence interval?

5. What determines the size of the sample to be used in a study?

6. What is weighting?

7. Name three methods which exist for sampling in qualitative research.

Exercises

1. Examine either a published research report or a journal article related to an empirical study and identify the procedures used to ensure a random sample. Is the information adequate?

2. Using the report in exercise 1, produce confidence intervals for a range of percentage statistics occurring in the report.

3. In the example comparing bowling and tennis in section 4.2, what would the confidence intervals be if the sample size was 4000?

4. Examine the results from a national recreation participation survey or a domestic or international tourism survey and produce confidence intervals for a number of the key findings.

5. Select two qualitative research reports/articles (see Resources, Chapter 9) and contrast the information provided on sampling methods used and assess their suitability.

Resources

- Sampling and the statistical implications of sampling are addressed in numerous statistics textbooks: Kidder (1981: ch. 4); Spatz and Johnston (1989: ch. 6).

- History of sampling: Brick (2011).

- Problem of mobile phones: AAPOR Cell Phone Task Force (2010), Link and Lai (2011).

- Sampling for qualitative methods: Miles and Huberman (1994).

- Sampling for telephone interviews: Lepkowski et al. (2008).

- Small populations: Krejcie and Morgan (1970).

References

AAPOR Cell Phone Task Force (2010). *New considerations for survey researchers when planning and conducting RDD telephone surveys in the U.S. with respondents reached via cell phone numbers*. Oakbrook Terrace, IL: American Association for Public Opinion Research. Available at: www.aapor.org.

Brick, J. M. (2011). The future of survey sampling. *Public Opinion Quarterly*, 74, 872–88.

Charmaz, K. (2006). *Constructing grounded theory*. London: Sage.

Henderson, K. A. (2006). *Dimensions of choice: a qualitative approach to recreation, parks and leisure research*, 2nd edn. State College, PA: Venture.

Kidder, L. (1981). *Selltiz, Wrightsman and Cook's research methods in social relations*. New York: Holt, Rinehart & Winston.

Krejcie, R. V., and Morgan, D. W. (1970). Determining sample size for research activities. *Educational and Psychological Measurement*, 30(4), 607–10.

Lepkowski, J. M., Tucker, C., and Brick, J. M. (Eds) (2008). *Advances in telephone survey methodology*. New York: John Wiley.

Link, M. W., and Lai, J. W. (2011). Cell-phone-only households and problems of differential nonresponse using address-based sampling design. *Public Opinion Quarterly*, 75(4), 613–35.

Miles, M. B., and Huberman, A. M. (1994). *Qualitative data analysis*, 2nd edn. Thousand Oaks, CA: Sage.

Spatz, C., and Johnston, J. O. (1989). *Basic statistics: tales of distribution*, 4th edn. Pacific Grove, CA: Brooks/Cole Publishing.

Appendix 13.1: Suggested appendix on sample size and confidence intervals

This is a suggested wording for an appendix or note to be included in research reports based on sample data. Suppose the survey has a sample size of 500.

Statistical note

All sample surveys are subject to a margin of statistical error. The margins of error, or 'confidence intervals' for this survey, with a sample of 500, are as follows:

Finding from the survey	95% confidence interval
50 per cent	± 4.4 per cent
40 per cent or 60 per cent	± 4.3 per cent
30 per cent or 70 per cent	± 4.0 per cent
20 per cent or 80 per cent	± 3.5 per cent
10 per cent or 90 per cent	± 2.6 per cent
5 per cent or 95 per cent	± 1.9 per cent
1 per cent or 99 per cent	± 0.9 per cent

This can be interpreted by example as follows: if 20 per cent of the sample are found to have a particular characteristic, there is an estimated 95 per cent chance that the true population percentage lies in the range 20 ± 3.5 per cent, i.e. between 16.5 per cent and 23.5 per cent. These margins of error have been taken into account in the analyses in this report.

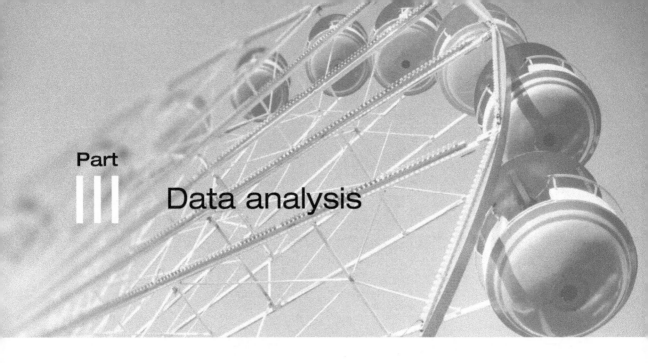

Part

III Data analysis

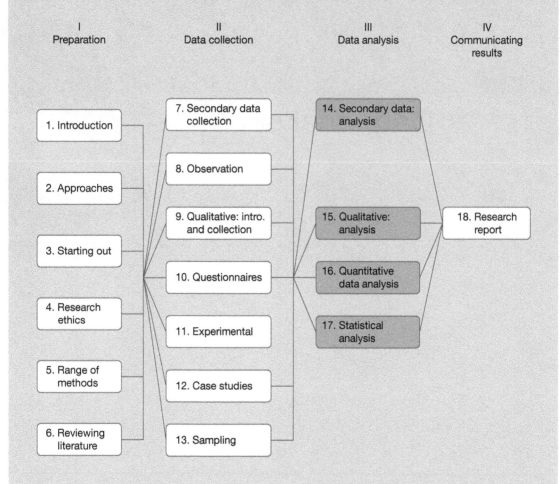

I Preparation	II Data collection	III Data analysis	IV Communicating results
1. Introduction	7. Secondary data collection	14. Secondary data: analysis	18. Research report
2. Approaches	8. Observation	15. Qualitative: analysis	
3. Starting out	9. Qualitative: intro. and collection	16. Quantitative data analysis	
4. Research ethics	10. Questionnaires	17. Statistical analysis	
5. Range of methods	11. Experimental		
6. Reviewing literature	12. Case studies		
	13. Sampling		

14 Analysing secondary data

1. Introduction

2. Case studies of secondary data analysis
   - 2.1 Income inequality and leisure participation
   - 2.2 Estimating demand for a leisure facility
   - 2.3 Tourism trend analysis
   - 2.4 Facility utilisation
   - 2.5 Facility catchment area
   - 2.6 Meta-analysis

1. Introduction

The secondary data phenomenon is described in Chapter 7, together with its various forms and sources. There are no specific analytical techniques or computer packages associated with such data, given its diversity. Most of the quantitative data is susceptible to relatively simple spreadsheet analysis. Where re-analysis of survey data is involved, the procedures outlined in Chapters 16 and 17 for the analysis stage of the primary project in which the data were gathered apply. Similarly, for qualitative data, the procedures in Chapter 15 apply. In this chapter, therefore, the aim is not to address the detail of analytical techniques but to provide summaries of examples of practical and imaginative uses of secondary data for leisure and tourism research purposes.

2. Case studies of secondary data analysis

Case study 11.6A, presented in Chapter 11, is an example of a quasi-experiment involving children's playground safety, but it can also be seen as an example of use of secondary data. The experiment involved before and after data on accident numbers in school playgrounds at the time of installation of new play equipment with higher safety standards. The accident statistics were collected routinely for legal, administrative and insurance purposes, but the researchers took the opportunity of using them for research purposes.

Six case studies of secondary data analysis are presented in this section.

2.1 Income inequality and leisure participation

Case study 14.1 relates to *The Spirit Level*, a book which is addressed to a popular/political audience and is based on analysis of secondary data from the United Nations and other sources. It makes the case that countries with a high degree of income equality perform better than countries with a low degree of income equality in relation to a range of quality of life measures. The book does not consider leisure, so this case study introduces some leisure-related data to the analysis.

Case study 14.1   *The Spirit Level* and sport

In *The Spirit Level: Why More Equal Societies Almost Always Do Better*, Richard Wilkinson and Kate Pickett (2009) use cross-national secondary data from the United Nations and other sources to make the case that the more equal the distribution of income in a country the more favourable are the outcomes on a range of indicators of human well-being, including life expectancy, infant mortality, physical and mental health, educational performance and the level of crime. The key point of the book is to demonstrate that, among wealthier countries, it is the *distribution* of income rather than its absolute level which determines the well-being of the society. The research has not been without its critics, but it raises interesting issues concerning public policy in the current era. The book does not, however, include leisure-related indicators, except for some data on working hours for a few of the countries. This has been remedied recently using data on time use and sporting and cultural participation (Veal, 2016) and volunteering (Veal and Nichols, 2017). With some qualifications, these studies find that leisure and volunteering conform to the *Spirit Level* thesis.

Here we further test the thesis in the leisure context with some more up-to-date data on sport participation in Europe. Data on sport participation are from *Eurobarometer 412*, a Europe-wide survey conducted by the European

Commission in 2013. This is related to a measure of income inequality, the Gini index, which is designed to take the value 0 where everyone in a country has the same income, and 100 in the theoretical situation where all income goes to one person. In Europe, the index ranges from 24.3 to 35.2. To test the *Spirit Level* initial proposition, that well-being is not related to absolute income, the relationship with Gross Domestic Product (GDP) per capita is also examined. The data are shown in Table 14.1 and the results plotted in Figures 14.1 and 14.2

Table 14.1 Sport participation, income inequality and GDP/head, European countries, 2013

Countries§	Participation in sport at least once a week (%)	Gini index of income inequality	GDP/head, $US
Portugal	28	34.2	21.8
Austria	45	27.0	45.9
Belgium	48	25.9	41.7
Cyprus	35	32.4	20.4
France	43	30.1	35.8
Germany	48	29.7	40.9
Greece	31	34.4	24.3
Ireland	52	30.0	38.9
Italy	30	32.8	31.4
Netherlands	58	25.1	43.0
Spain	46	33.7	30.1
UK	46	30.2	39.9
Denmark	68	26.8	39.6
Finland	66	25.4	38.7
Sweden	69	24.9	45.4
Czech Republic	36	24.6	27.5
Slovenia	51	24.4	28.2
Slovakia	33	24.2	23.8
Estonia	39	32.9	21.0
Hungary	39	28.3	19.2
Poland	27	30.7	21.2
Latvia	31	35.2	16.6
Lithuania	37	34.6	18.8

§ Excludes countries with population < 1million and/or GDP/head <$15k

Data sources: sport participation: Eurobarometer 412 (European Commission, 2013); income inequality: Eurostat; GDP/head: Groningen University Conference Board (Annual).

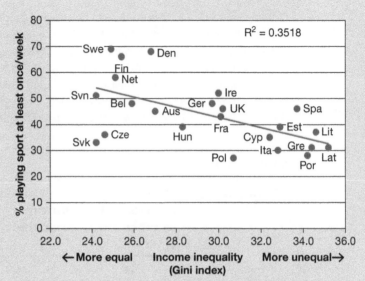

Figure 14.1   Sport participation and income inequality, European countries, 2013

Data source: see Table 1. R² is explained in Chapter 17

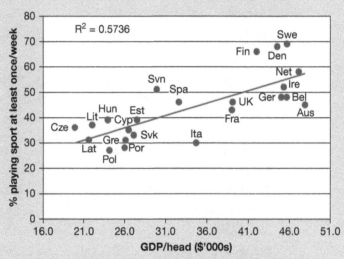

Figure 14.2   Sport participation and GDP/head, European countries, 2013

Data source: see Table 1. R² is explained in Chapter 17

Figure 14.1 shows clearly that, as income inequality increases, the level of sport participation declines, thus supporting the *Spirit Level* thesis. However, Figure 14.2 shows that an even stronger relationship is apparent, showing sport participation increasing with GDP per head. The *Spirit Level* thesis is therefore only partially supported, confirming the findings of the papers on leisure and volunteering (Veal, 2016; Veal and Nichols, 2017).

2.2 Estimating demand for a leisure facility

Case study 14.2 demonstrates an approach to estimating demand for a possible new facility based on national leisure participation data and the population census. This is the type of exercise which might be used in a feasibility study.

Case study 14.2   Estimating likely demand for a leisure facility

The problem

A developer or local council is considering whether to build a cinema on a particular site in a town centre, as part of a multi-purpose leisure complex. A cinema is used as an example, but the methodology could be applied equally to other types of facility. The town has a population of 100,000 and already has two 400-seat cinemas. The developer wants to know what demand exists in the area for such a facility. A range of approaches could be considered to investigate this question.

Possibilities

- *Existing facilities:* existing cinemas in the area could be examined to see whether they are overused or underused; that is, whether demand is already being adequately met by existing facilities. This, however, may not give the full answer, since it might be found that a well-managed, well-located cinema is well used while another, perhaps poorly managed and poorly located, is poorly used. It might also be difficult to obtain commercially sensitive data from potential competitors.

- *Resident survey:* an interview survey of local residents could be conducted to ask whether they would like to go to the cinema but do not do so at present because of lack of suitable facilities. Even if the time and money were available to conduct such a survey, the results could not be relied on as the main piece of information on which to base the decision because, while people's honesty and accuracy in recalling activities might be relied on in relation to activities which they have actually taken part in, asking them to predict their behaviour in hypothetical future situations is very risky.

- *Similar communities:* communities of similar population size and type could be examined to see what levels of cinema provision they have and how well they are used. Again, this may be a time-consuming process and somewhat 'hit-and-miss' because it is not easy to find comparable communities and because some of the data required, being commercially 'sensitive', may not be readily available.

- *Use of secondary data:* data from an appropriate national survey (NS) and the Population Census could be used to provide an approximate estimate of

▶

likely demand for cinema seats in the area. The aim is to provide an estimate of the level of demand which a community of the size of that in the study area is likely to generate and compare that with the level of demand already likely to be catered for by existing cinemas, to see whether or not there is a surplus of demand over supply.

The approach

The general approach is represented diagrammatically in Figure 14.3. The steps A to G shown in the diagram are discussed in turn below.

A. *Age-specific participation rates:* One of the features of cinema attendance is that it varies considerably by age. Cinema is attended more by young people than by older people. If, for example, the study town contains a higher-than-average proportion of young people, it would be expected that it would produce a higher than average demand for cinema, and vice versa. The hypothetical NS gives information on the percentage of people of different ages who go to the cinema, as shown in Table 14.2. It can be seen that teenagers are almost six times as likely to attend the cinema as the over-60s. The particular NS deals only with people aged 16 and over. Obviously, children under that age do go to the cinema; but there may be sufficient demand for an additional cinema even without taking account of the under-16s. So the under-16s can be ignored for the moment, only returning to them if necessary.

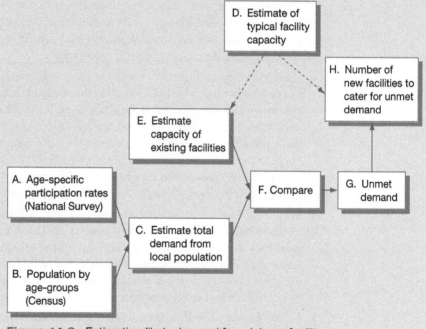

Figure 14.3 Estimating likely demand for a leisure facility

Table 14.2 Cinema attendance by age

Age group	%*
15–19 years	14.9
20–24	11.5
25–29	7.4
30–39	5.2
40–49	4.8
50–59	3.5
60+	2.5
Total/average	6.6

* % of age-group who go to the cinema in a week (from national survey).

B. *Population by age-groups:* Suppose the census gives the population of the town as 100,000, and the population aged 15 and over as 80,000. In Table 14.3, the age structure of the national population aged 15 and over is compared with that of the study town. Clearly, the town has a much younger age profile than the national average, with only just over half the proportion of over-55s and correspondingly larger proportions in the young age-groups. So it is clearly advisable to consider the question of age structure.

C. *Estimate total demand from local population:* Table 14.4 indicates how demand for cinema attendance would be estimated: attendances are estimated for each age-group and summed to give a total of 6543 attendances per week.

Table 14.3 Study town and national age structure compared

Age groups	National population* %	Study town population* %
15–19	12.5	19.5
20–24	11.9	19.0
25–29	10.6	14.2
30–39	20.1	21.1
40–49	14.2	9.0
50–59	11.8	7.7
60+	18.9	9.5
Total	100.0	100.0

* census data

▶

Table 14.4   Estimating demand for cinema attendance

	% of age-group participating per week (X)	Town population (Y)	Estimated demand*
Data source:	National survey	Census	XY/100
15–19 years	14.9	15,600	2324
20–24	11.5	15,200	1748
25–29	7.4	11,360	841
30–39	5.2	16,880	878
40–49	4.8	7,200	346
50–59	3.5	6,160	216
60+	2.5	7,600	190
Total/average	8.2	80,000	6543

* visits per week

D. *Estimate of typical facility capacity:* For this exercise, it is assumed that a typical 400-seat cinema auditorium requires 1500 ticket sales a week to be viable.

E. *Estimate capacity of existing facilities:* Two cinemas already exist in the town. If they have a seating capacity of 400 each, then they would accommodate some 3000 visits a week.

F. *Compare:* The total estimated demand is 6500 visits per week, and the existing cinemas have a capacity of 3000 per week.

G. *Unmet demand:* Unmet demand can therefore be estimated as about 3500 visits per week.

H. *Number of new facilities to cater for unmet demand:* It would take two typical 400-seat cinemas to cater for the unmet demand – that is, it is estimated that the town could support four cinemas.

Comment

The above approach does not predict demand precisely – it merely indicates a 'ball park' demand figure. A well-managed and programmed cinema might draw far more demand than is estimated. The national survey attendance rates relate to average attendances across the country, so clearly there are places where higher attendance rates occur as well as places where lower rates occur. What the exercise indicates is that, on the basis of data to hand, 6500 cinema attendances a week seems likely. This seems a very simple and crude calculation, but quite often investors – in the public and private sectors – fail to carry out even this sort of simple calculation to check on 'ball park' demand figures; investments are made on the basis of personal hunch, and then surprise is expressed when demand fails to materialise.

- *Forecasting note:* to provide a simple forecast of future demand, for, say, the year 2020, it would be necessary merely to insert population forecasts for the year 2020 into column B of Table 14.4 and rework the calculations.

- *Economic note:* while the exercise here has been outlined in terms of 'number of users or customers', use of household expenditure data, such as that discussed in Chapter 7, can convert the unit of analysis into expenditure.

2.3 Tourism trend analysis

Case study 14.3 is concerned with establishing trends from quarterly tourism arrivals data. Typically, such data have a seasonal pattern which must be 'smoothed out' to see the long-term trend, and one approach to this is to calculate a 'moving average'.

| Case study 14.3 | Tourism trend analysis |

Typically tourism statistics are produced on a monthly or quarterly basis, as in Table 14.5 (column A). Each quarterly figure of tourist arrivals reflects two factors: seasonal variation and longer-term trends. One way of examining the longer-term trend without the distraction of the seasonal variation is to produce a 'smoothed' series by calculating a 'moving average' (column B). The moving average consists of the average of the previous four quarters' figures. For example: the moving average figure for Oct–Dec, 2010, is the average of the four quarterly figures for 2010. The calculations can be done very easily with a spreadsheet program. The effect is to present a 'smoothed' trend series, as shown graphically in Figure 14.4.

In practice, the analysis of tourism trends, particularly as a basis for forecasting, is a much more complex process than indicated here. Some indication of this is given by Smith (1995: 125-130) and Frechtling (1996: 50:75). In particular, methods have been found to understand and modelling seasonal patterns, rather than just smoothing them out mathematically.

▶

Table 14.5   Tourist arrivals 2004–9

Year	Quarter		A. No. of arrivals, '000s	B. Moving average, '000s
2010	Jan–Mar	10-1	1511	
	Apr–Jun	10-2	1192	
	Jul–Sept	10-3	1420	
	Oct–Dec	10-4	1667	1448
2011	Jan–Mar	10-1	1505	1446
	Apr–Jun	10-2	1216	1452
	Jul–Sept	10-3	1381	1442
	Oct–Dec	10-4	1669	1443
2012	Jan–Mar	10-1	1567	1458
	Apr–Jun	10-2	1256	1468
	Jul–Sept	10-3	1444	1484
	Oct–Dec	10-4	1766	1508
2013	Jan–Mar	10-1	1651	1529
	Apr–Jun	10-2	1300	1540
	Jul–Sept	10-3	1535	1563
	Oct–Dec	10-4	1895	1596
2014	Jan–Mar	10-1	1779	1627
	Apr–Jun	10-2	1452	1665
	Jul–Sept	10-3	1643	1692
	Oct–Dec	10-4	2011	1721
2015	Jan–Mar	10-1	1950	1764
	Apr–Jun	10-2	1528	1783
	Jul–Sept	10-3	1774	1816
	Oct–Dec	10-4	2193	1861

Source: Australian Bureau of Statistics: 3401.0 – Short-term Visitor Arrival Estimates, Australia, at: www.abs.gov.au

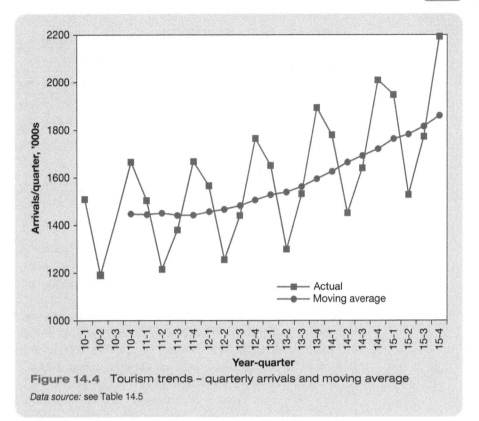

Figure 14.4 Tourism trends – quarterly arrivals and moving average

Data source: see Table 14.5

2.4 Facility utilisation

Facilities with a number of components, such as a leisure centre with different halls and specialist facilities or a convention centre with a variety of rooms and auditoria, usually routinely record booking data for each component, in terms of booking/no booking or an event in terms of numbers of users/ticket sales. Case study 14.4 demonstrates how such data might be used to assess utilisation as a basis for management action on programming, promotion or pricing.

Case study 14.4	Facility utilisation

Managers typically have information available on the use of facilities, but this is also often neglected as a source of data for research. As indicated in Case study 14.2, the level of utilisation of existing facilities is an important issue for managers and planners: this case study illustrates how existing data can be used to address this question.

Table 14.6 presents data which might be routinely collected on the level of use of particular areas of a leisure facility (e.g. various rooms or halls in an

▶

Table 14.6 Facility utilisation data

	Area A		Area B		Area C	
	Number	% utilisation	Number	% utilisation	Number	% utilisation
Capacity	300	100.0	120	100.0	500	100.0
Mon. usage	120	40.0	60	50.0	310	62.0
Tues. usage	150	50.0	40	33.3	210	42.0
Wed. usage	180	60.0	30	25.0	180	36.0
Thurs. usage	120	40.0	80	66.7	375	75.0
Fri. usage	100	33.3	95	79.2	430	86.0
Sat. usage	210	70.0	110	91.7	420	84.0
Sun. usage	250	83.3	40	33.3	310	62.0
Total for week	1130	53.8	455	54.2	2235	63.9

indoor leisure centre or various rides in a leisure park). The daily usage levels might be averaged over a number of weeks. For each of the areas it is necessary to estimate the daily capacity: this is a reasonable assessment of the number of users which would equate to the facility being deemed 'fully used' (see Veal, 2017: Ch. 12). The numbers of users are related to the capacity in the form of percentages, and these are graphed in Figure 14.5.

The graph shows a different pattern of use for Area A, compared with the other two areas. Area A is underused on Monday, Thursday and Friday, while areas B and C are underused between Sunday and Wednesday. This suggests the need for different programming and marketing policies for the various areas.

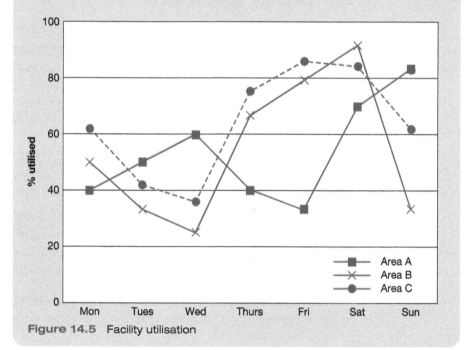

Figure 14.5 Facility utilisation

2.5 Facility catchment area

While information of visitors' residential location may be collected by means of on-site questionnaire-based surveys, in some cases that information is already available to management via membership or reservation data. Case study 14.5 shows an example of the use of such data to plot the catchment or market area of a facility. While the example assumes a leisure facility drawing visitors from an urban area, the method could be applied to a hotel or tourist attraction with a regional, national and even international catchment.

Case study 14.5   Facility catchment or market area

Leisure and tourism facilities often have available information on users' addresses which can be used to study the *catchment area* or *market area* – an important aspect of planning and management. Many leisure facilities, for example, have membership or subscriber lists. Hotels and resorts have details of home addresses of patrons.

Figure 14.6 shows how such data can be plotted on a map to produce a visual representation of the catchment or market area of the facility. Such information can be used either to concentrate marketing to increase sales in the existing area, or to focus marketing outside the identified area in order to extend the catchment or market area.

When very large numbers are involved, it may be necessary to sample membership or customer lists – for example, selecting every fifth or tenth member or patron on the list.

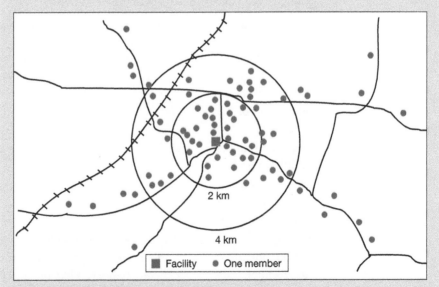

Figure 14.6   Catchment/market area
Source: Membership/patron address records

2.6 Meta-analysis

As discussed in Chapter 6, a meta-analysis of a number of existing studies on the same topic can be seen as a form of secondary data analysis. This applies particularly when the findings of the research are presented in the form of comparably quantitative indicators, as is the case with the study of interventions to promote sport participation as summarised in Case study 14.6.

Case study 14.6   Example of a meta-analysis

Study	Meta-analysis of the effectiveness of interventions (exercise programmes) to promote physical activity, related to context (i.e. alone/at home or group/organised environment).
Authors (Date)	Burke et al. (2006)
Data-bases searched	PsycINFO, PsycARTICLES, MEDLINE-OVID, SPORTDiscus
Keywords used in search	Physical activity interventions; exercise; aerobic; adherence; attendance; home-based exercise; exercise class; group exercise
Additional manual search	Following up references in existing review studies (five sources identified) and searching 13 identified journals
Initial number of studies identified	148
Criteria for inclusion	1. Study must compare two or more physical activity contexts. 2. Must include a statistical measure of the effectiveness of the context in promoting physical activity.
Net number of studies included	44
Combined number of study subjects	4578
Total population of effect sizes	1046
Effect sizes included	214
Outcomes of participation in a programme (= dependent variables)	102 variables identified in 5 categories: 1. adherence to programme; 2. social interaction; 3. quality of life; 4. physiological effectiveness; 5. functional effectiveness.

Type of programme (= independent variable)	1. true group (group with organised interaction) 2. collective (group, but no organised interaction) 3. home-based with contact 4. home-based without contact.
Descriptive statistics	Context; Age of participants; Gender; Clinical referral status; Activity level; Intervention level; Selection of participants.

Summary

The chapter presents six case studies demonstrating potential uses of secondary data, including: cross-national examination of inequality and sport participation, demand for new leisure facilities, analysis of trends in seasonal tourism data, assessment of levels of facility utilisation, analysis of a facility catchment area and meta-analysis.

Exercises

1. Take a leisure activity and a community of your own choice and, using data from a national leisure participation survey (see Chapter 7) and data from the population census, provide an estimate of the likely demand for the activity in the selected community, using the methodology outlined in Case study 14.2.

2. Conduct exercise 1 for tourism trips generated from a region of a country, using data from a domestic tourism survey.

3. In relation to exercise 1, what would be the implications of a predicted increase of 15 per cent in the number of people aged 60 and over and a 15 per cent decrease in the number of people aged 25 and under, over the next five years?

4. Undertake an exercise similar to Case study 14.4 for a leisure facility for which you can obtain usage data.

5. Undertake an exercise similar to Case study 14.5 for a leisure facility for which you can obtain user/member address data.

6. Select an activity from a national leisure participation survey and provide a *profile* of the activity, indicating the overall level of participation and how participation is related to age, gender, occupation and education.

7. Access quarterly tourist arrival data for a country of your choice over a 10-year period and calculate the trend as in Case study 14.3.

Resources

Secondary data sources

See the Resources section in Chapter 7.

Examples of studies

- Arts/culture:
  - arts audiences, secondary use of UK 'Taking Part' survey: Hand (2011); and
  - class/status, cross-national: Chan (2011).
- Free time: cross-national studies: Goodin et al. (2008).
- Leisure and gender: Veal (2011).
- Income inequality, cross-national studies:
  - leisure: Veal (2016); and
  - volunteering: Veal and Nichols (2017).
- Sport: national success: Shibli et al. (2010).
- Sport participation:
  - general, cross-national: Nicholson et al. (2011); and
  - and the Olympics: Sydney 2000: Veal et al. (2012); Vancouver 2010: Potwarka and Leatherdale (2016).
- Tourism trend analysis: Smith (1995: 125–130), Frechtling (1996: 50–75).

References

Burke, S. M., Carron, A. V., Eys, M. A., Ntoumas, N., and Estabrooks, P. A. (2006). Group versus individual approach? Meta-analysis of the effectiveness of interventions to promote physical activity. *Sport and Exercise Psychology Review*, 2(1), 13–29.

Chan, T. W. (Ed) (2011). *Social status and cultural consumption*. Cambridge: Cambridge University Press.

European Commission (2013). *Special Eurobarometer 412: sport and physical activity* Brussels: European Commission.

Frechtling, D. C. (1996). *Practical Tourism Forecasting*. Oxford: Butterworth-Heinemann.

Goodin, R. E., Rice, J. M., Parpo, A., and Eriksson, L. (2008). *Discretionary time: a new measure of freedom*. Cambridge: Cambridge University Press.

Groningen University Conference Board (Annual). *Total economy database*. Groningen, Sweden: GUCB. Available at: www.conference-board.org/data/economydatabase/.

Hand, C. (2011). Do arts audiences act like consumers? *Managing Leisure*, 16(2), 88–97.

Nicholson, M., Hoye, R., and Houlihan, B. (Eds) (2011). *Participation in sport: international policy perspectives*. London: Routledge.

Potwarka, L. R., and Leatherdale, S. T. (2016). The Vancouver 2020 Olympics and leisure-time physical activity rates among youth in Canada: any evidence of a trickle-down effect? *Leisure Studies*, 35(2), 241–57.

Shibli, S., Bigham, J., and Henry, I. (2010). Measuring the sporting success of nations. In I. Henry (Ed), *Transnational comparative research in sport* (pp. 61–81). London: Routledge.

Smith, S. L. J (1995). Tourism Analysis: A handbook. Harlow, UK: Longman.

Veal, A. J. (2011). Leisure participation patterns and gender: the survey evidence on Australian adults. *Annals of Leisure Research*, 14(2–3), 107–28.

Veal, A. J. (2016). Leisure, income inequality and the Veblen effect: cross-national analysis of leisure time and sport and cultural activity. *Leisure Studies*, 35(2), 215–40.

Veal, A. J. (2017). *Leisure, sport and tourism: politics policy and planning*, 4th edn. Wallingford, UK: CABI.

Veal, A. J., Frawley, S., and Toohey, K. (2012). The sport participation legacy of the Sydney 2000 Olympic Games and other international sporting events hosted in Australia. *Journal of Policy Research in Tourism, Leisure and Events*, 4(2), 155–84.

Veal, A. J., and Nichols, G. (2017). Volunteering and income inequality: cross-national relationships. *Voluntas*, 28(1), 379–99.

Wilkinson, R., and Pickett, K. (2009). *The spirit level: why more equal societies almost always do better*. London: Allen Lane.

15 Analysing qualitative data

1. Introduction

1.1 Data collection and analysis

This chapter addresses the task of analysing qualitative data. As indicated in Chapter 9, it is sometimes difficult to separate the collection and analysis processes for qualitative data, at least in a temporal sense; but there is nevertheless a clear difference between certain data-collection activities, such as interviewing someone with a sound recorder, and certain analysis activities, such as poring over interview transcripts. While, as discussed in Chapter 2, quantitative research can be inductive and qualitative research can be deductive, the qualitative approach lends itself to a more inductive process, especially when conducted on a small scale. This difference is illustrated in Figure 15.1, which presents a variation on the circular process of research depicted in Figure 2.1.

Traditionally, qualitative data were analysed by manual means, and this continues, but in recent years computer software has become available to aid the process. Computers replicate and speed up some of the more mechanical aspects of the manual processes but, of course, the task of organisation and interpretation remains with the researcher. The chapter

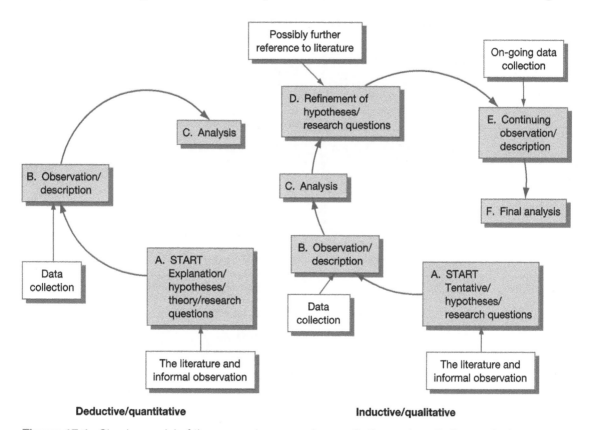

Figure 15.1 Circular model of the research process in quantitative and qualitative contexts

discusses both manual methods and computer-based methods. Since the most common form of qualitative data is interview or focus-group transcripts or notes, the following discussions are based on this form of data. Most of the procedures nevertheless apply, in adapted form, to other forms of data, such as mass or social media content or printed materials from organisational archives.

1.2 Data storage and confidentiality

Regardless of whether qualitative data are analysed manually or by computer, consideration should be given to the security and confidentiality of transcripts and digital files, particularly if sensitive material is involved. This raises ethical issues, as discussed in Chapter 4.

As a precaution, research material should ideally not be labelled with real names of organisations or people. Fictitious names or codes should be created. If it is felt that it will be necessary to relate recordings and transcripts back to original respondents at some later date, for example for second interviews, the list relating fictitious identities to real identities should be kept in a separate, secure place. Of course, actual names mentioned by respondents on recordings cannot easily be erased, and it is a matter of judgement as to whether it is necessary to disguise such names in transcripts, although in most cases they should be disguised in quotations in the research report. In some cases, however, it is necessary to create transcripts which are, in a way, less anonymous than the original. For example, an interviewee might say: 'I find it difficult to get on with John' – the transcript might change 'John' to 'David', but may need to identify John/David's position – for example, 'I find it difficult to get on with David [Supervisor]'.

Digitised research material stored on computer hard drives and other storage media is subject to the security risks of any digitised information. Some analysis software, including NVivo discussed in this chapter, offers password protection which may be a useful precaution.

1.3 Case study example

A case study of some in-depth interview data is used to illustrate qualitative data analysis – both manual and by computer, as shown in Case study 15.1.

Case study 15.1	Activity choice qualitative study

Figure 15.2 presents a very simple conceptual framework for studying leisure activity choice. Based on a model presented by Brandenburg et al. (1982) and further developed by Veal et al. (2013), it suggests that individuals' choice of leisure/tourism activity is influenced by background characteristics and experiences, present constraints and personal factors, but also by key events which trigger participation.

▶

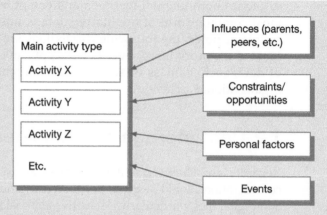

Figure 15.2 Outline conceptual framework for qualitative study of activity choice

While this example is expressed in terms of leisure as a whole, the framework would be suitable for analysis of a sector of leisure, such as sport, holiday-taking or the arts. Thus the activity choices, X, Y, Z, could relate to the whole range of leisure activities or a restricted sector. The model could be explored quantitatively, for example, by means of a questionnaire, but that would probably require prior definition of the three sets of influences and a set of key events. A qualitative approach enables the various factors and influences to be identified and analysed in a more exploratory manner. Interviews could be conducted using a checklist of the sort presented in Table 9.3.

Table 15.1 contains short extracts from three interviews with individuals about their leisure choices. The comments in the first column are explained later in the chapter. These transcripts are used to illustrate both manual and computer analysis of texts. The aim is to illustrate the mechanics of analysis in a way which could be readily replicated by the student. The length of the transcript extracts and their number has therefore been limited, so the substantive outcomes are incidental and not particularly meaningful taken in isolation. In a complete research exercise, full transcripts running to many pages would be involved and, although we are dealing with qualitative research, the number of interviews/transcripts in a study of this type would normally be more than three.

Table 15.1 Interview transcript extracts

Mark (Age 22, Male, Student, Income £8K)

	Q. What would you say is your most time-consuming leisure activity outside of the home at present?
Act.: Sport – football *Constraint: Commitments.* *Need to keep fit.* *Time, Money*	Well, I would say it's playing football, at least during the season. While the football's on, because of training twice a week and needing to be fairly serious about keeping fit I don't do much else: I probably only go to a pub once – or at most twice – a week. I don't have the time or the money to do much more.

Q. How were you introduced to football?

Influence: Parent+
Teacher ++
Event: Coaching clinic

Oh, I've always played . . . since I could run around I suppose. My dad says he spotted my talent – so-called – when I was a toddler, but it was one of the teachers at primary school that really encouraged me. He persuaded my mum to take me to a coaching clinic when I was about 8 or 9, then I got into the local under-11s.

Q. Why do you think you are attracted to football?

Personal: Competitive.
Team oriented. Active

Well, I'm pretty competitive – so I like sport generally. I like the team-spirit thing with football – I don't think I could do an individual sport where you didn't have a team around you. You make good friends. And it's fast and you're involved the whole time . . . I get bored playing cricket where you're standing around half the time.

Donna (Age 27, Female, FT Employed, Income £19K)

Q. What would you say is your most time-consuming leisure activity outside of the home at present?

Act.: Socialising

Just socialising I would say . . . you know, going out for a meal or a drink with friends . . . I go to the gym once or twice a week . . . and I like to swim a bit in the summer, but they don't take up much time overall.

Q. When did you first start going out socially on a regular basis?

Event: Earning money
Influence: Peers

I was about 16, I guess: the parents were a bit restrictive, but once I started earning a bit of money at weekends I managed to go out at least twice a week – to parties and to the cinema and stuff . . . my mum and dad didn't have any money to give me, so it wasn't until I started to work part-time that I could go out, sort of regularly. I've always had a fairly close-knit group of friends, girlfriends, about the same age as me, who've always gone out together . . . even with boyfriends – and one husband – arriving on the scene and disappearing from time to time!

▶

Q. What limits the number of times you go out socialising in a week?

Constraint:
Time, Money

Time and money! But mostly it's time these days – cos we don't always spend a lot.

Q. What are the essential ingredients for a good night out?

Personal:
Social – informal
Constraint: Time

It's all about people . . . people you know and people you might meet! Things like good food – and drink – or good music are important, but the enjoyment comes from doing it with your friends and knowing they have the same sorts of tastes and the same sense of fun. I am serious enough at work, I couldn't imagine myself spending a lot of time with some team sport with serious training and all that: I just don't have the time – or the inclination!

Lee (Age 23, Male, FT Employed, Income £22K)

Q. What would you say is your most time-consuming leisure activity outside of the home at present?

Event: Girlfriend
Personal: Anti-routine

it varies. I don't have any set pattern. Up until a couple of weeks ago I was going out with this girl and, apart from going round each other's house, we spent a lot of time going out, one way or another – to the pub, cinema, walking, shopping – it varied. Now that's stopped, it's still a bit of a mixture, but with various friends. I hate routine, so I don't get involved with anything regular.

Q. So what single thing – from among the mixture of things you do – would you say you spent most time doing in the last week?

Act.: Cinema

In the last week? Well, I haven't been out that much: it would have to be the movies: I went twice and one of them was one of those late-night double billers – about four hours.

Q. Are you a movie buff?

Event: Good review

I wouldn't go that far, but I like movies. I read reviews and that. The movie I saw on Tuesday had a lot of hype and I saw two or three good reviews. For once, the hype was justified: it was really good. Really good: better than the reviews – and that doesn't happen often.

2. Manual methods of analysis

2.1 Introduction

There are various ways of analysing interview transcripts or notes. The essence of any analysis procedure must be to return to the terms of reference, the conceptual framework and the research questions or hypotheses of the research, as discussed in Chapter 3. The information gathered should be sorted through and evaluated in relation to the concepts identified in the conceptual framework, the research questions posed or the hypotheses put forward. In qualitative research, those original ideas may be tentative and fluid. Questions and/or hypotheses and definitions and operationalisation of concepts may be detailed or general; the more detailed and specific they are, the more likely it is that they will influence the initial stages of the analysis. Conversely, the more general and tentative they are, the more likely it is that the data analysis process will influence their development and refinement. Data gathering, hypothesis formulation and the identification of concepts is a two-way, evolving process. Ideas are refined and revised in the light of the information gathered, as described in relation to the *grounded theory* approach and the *recursive* approach discussed in Chapter 9 and summarised in Figure 9.1. In Chapter 3 it is noted that the development of a conceptual framework and of research questions or hypotheses is the most difficult and challenging part of a research project.

In addition to the problem of ordering and summarising the data conceptually, the researcher is faced with the very practical problem of just how to approach the pile of interview notes or transcripts.

2.2 Reading

The basic activity in qualitative analysis is *reading* of notes, transcripts, documents or *listening* or *viewing* audio and video materials. In what follows, it is assumed that the material being analysed is text. While practical adaptations are necessary for audio and video material, the principles are the same. The reading is done initially in light of initial research questions and/or hypotheses and/or those which have evolved during the data-collection process.

2.3 Emergent themes

A typical approach to qualitative analysis is to search for *emergent themes* – the approximate equivalent of *variables* in quantitative research. Indeed, it has been argued that the practice mimics too closely the positivistic approach to research which many proponents of qualitative methods deprecate (Dupuis, 1999). There is certainly the temptation to begin adopting a quasi-quantitative approach to the process, identifying as themes only those which arise from the transcripts of a number of subjects. Clearly this would be inconsistent with the qualitative approach: a theme which emerges from just one subject is as valid as one which emerges from 10 subjects. The criterion for identification should be the extent to which the theme appears to be salient to the interviewee.

The themes may arise from the conceptual framework and research questions and therefore be consciously searched for in a deductive way, or they may emerge unprompted in a more inductive way. Typically, both processes will be at work.

Themes which emerge from the transcripts are 'flagged' in the left-hand margin of the transcripts in Table 15.1. The researcher's judgement of the strength with which the views are expressed is indicated here with one or more plus or minus signs. It is clear that other themes might be identified and alternative terms might be used for the items which are identified, illustrating the personal and subjective nature of qualitative analysis.

The 'developed' conceptual framework presented in Figure 15.3 shows how some of the themes/concepts/factors and relationships emerging from the interviews might begin to be incorporated into the conceptual framework. On the basis of information from short abstracts from three interviews, the conceptual framework is *developed* but not *fully* developed; it represents work in progress. The 'levels' referred to relate to discussion of computer-aided analysis discussed later in the chapter.

Emergent themes can play a role in the sampling process in the form of 'saturation'. This suggests that data gathering should stop when gathering fresh data 'no longer sparks new theoretical insights' (Charmaz, 2006:113).

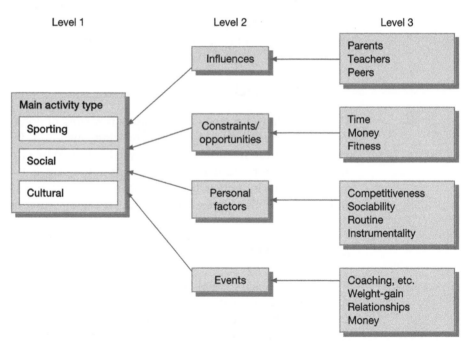

Figure 15.3   Developed conceptual framework for qualitative study of activity choice

2.4 Mechanics

The initial steps in qualitative analysis involve fairly methodical procedures to classify and organise the information collected.

Analysis can be done by hand on hard-copy transcripts, which should have a wide margin on one side to accommodate the 'flagging' of themes as discussed in section 2.3. Colour coding can be used in the flagging process and 'Post-it' notes may also be used to mark key sections.

Standard word-processor packages can be of considerable assistance in the analysis process. The space for flagging can then be secured using the 'columns' or tables facility in the word-processor. Word-processing packages also have facilities for:

- adding 'Comments' (e.g. in the Tracking facility in Word);

- blocking text with colour, underlining or bold;

- 'searching' to locate key words and phrases;

- paragraph and/or line numbering; and

- coding and cross-referencing using indexing or cross-referencing procedures.

A *cataloguing* approach can be used to group together interviewee comments associated with particular themes:

Constraint – time: Mark: p. 2, para. 3

Anna: p. 7, para. 4

Constraint – money: Mark: p. 2, para. 3

This is often necessary to keep track of topics across a number of interviews, but also because topics are typically covered several times in the same interview. A particular focus of the analysis may be related not only to particular substantive topics raised by the interviewer, and therefore related to particular questions, but also to, for example, underlying attitudes expressed by interviewees, which might arise at any time in an interview.

The catalogue becomes the basis for further analysis and writing up the results of the analysis. Being able to locate points in the transcripts where themes are expressed enables the researcher to check the wording used by respondents and explore context and related sentiments, and it facilitates the location of suitable quotations to illustrate the write-up of the results.

2.5 Analysis

In qualitative data analysis, it is possible to use techniques and presentation methods that are similar to those used in quantitative analysis. For example, in

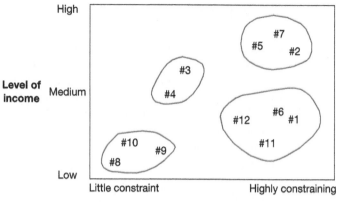

Figure 15.4 'Crosstabulation' of qualitative data

Figure 15.4 an analysis similar to a crosstabulation is shown, with 12 hypothetical interviewees 'plotted' on a two-dimensional space based on two variables derived from the interviews referred to above. The placing of the respondents depends on a qualitative assessment based on the interview transcripts. It can be seen that, in the example, the respondents fall into four groups. Given that this is a qualitative survey and the sample of interviewees is unlikely to be statistically representative, the *numbers* in each group are not important; it is the identification of the groups which is significant. Such a grouping would provide the basis for further analysis of the transcripts (see Huberman and Miles, 1994: 437).

Thus analysis of qualitative data has certain parallels with quantitative analysis, with themes corresponding to variables and relationships explored in ways which parallel crosstabulation and correlation. But they are parallels only, not equivalents. Whereas quantitative analysis generally seeks to establish whether certain observations and relationships are generally true in the wider population on the basis of statistical probability, qualitative analysis seeks to establish the existence of relationships on the basis of what individual people say and do. If only one person or organisation in the study is shown to behave in a certain way as a result of certain forces, this is a valid finding for qualitative research – the question of just how widespread such behaviour is in the wider society becomes a matter for other types of research.

Detailed analysis may be less important when the purpose of in-depth or informal interviews is to provide input into the design of a formal questionnaire. In that case the interviewer will generally make a series of notes arising from the interview which are likely to be of relevance to the questionnaire design process, and which can also provide input to the design process from memory of the interviewing experience, as long as the questionnaire design work is undertaken fairly soon after the interviews.

3. Qualitative analysis using computer software

3.1 Introduction

When the researcher is faced with a substantial number of lengthy documents to analyse, the decision may be made to ease the laborious process of coding and analysing by making use of one of the computer-aided qualitative data analysis software (CAQDAS) packages now available. As with statistical packages, it takes time to learn how to use qualitative analysis packages and to set up a system for an individual project, so a decision has to be made, on the basis of the size and complexity of the documentary material to be analysed, as to whether that investment of time will result in a net time saving, compared with manual analysis. Consideration should, however, be given to the fact that, once an analysis system has been set up, more analysis can be relatively quickly undertaken, possibly resulting in better quality of output than may have been possible using manual methods. Furthermore, looking to the future, a computerised analysis system can more easily be returned to at future dates for additional interrogation. Finally, even if the amount of data in a given project does not justify setting up a computerised analysis system, a smaller project may be an easier vehicle for learning to use and gain experience with a package. Familiarity and experience with a computer package merits an entry on a *curriculum vitae*.

It has been noted previously in this chapter that standard word-processing packages such as Microsoft Word offer facilities which can aid in sorting and locating material in transcripts. The standard word-processing package is, however, limited in its capabilities for this purpose. A number of purpose-designed CAQDAS packages are now on the market. One of the most commonly used, and which is demonstrated here, is NVivo, part of a stable of packages from QSR (Qualitative Solutions and Research Pty Ltd). This package requires considerable input from the researcher in, for example, identifying and coding themes and concepts in the texts being studied. Other packages, for example, Leximancer, deploy comparatively automatic coding and analysis procedures (see Sotiriadou et al. (2014) for a comparison between NVivo and Leximancer).

3.2 Interview transcripts

As with the manual analysis discussed earlier, the extracts of interview transcripts from the Activity Choice project as outlined in Case study 15.1 (Table 15.1) are used to demonstrate the operation of NVivo here. An ideal way for readers to engage with this section is to replicate the processes outlined on a computer. In what follows, it is assumed that the reader has access to a computer with NVivo installed.

Readers who wish to replicate the procedures should first either type the content of the transcripts into three files or download them from the text website. They should be in files named: Mark.doc; Donna.doc; and Lee.doc (a small font and wide margins are advised for ease of viewing on the NVivo screen). The suffix .doc (or .docx) indicates Word format, but NVivo will also accept text format (suffix .txt), rich text format (.rtf) or portable document format (.pdf). The files are introduced in the procedure 'Importing documents' (section 4.6).

4. NVivo

4.1 Introduction

NVivo is one of the most widely used CAQDAS packages. The software enables the researcher to index and coordinate the analysis of text stored as computer files. This includes primary material, such as interview transcripts and field notes, and other material such as newspaper clippings, reports and video clips. In addition, it assists in shaping and understanding data and in developing and testing theoretical assumptions about the data.

It is not possible in a short summary such as this to present all the features of the package – this is done in the online tutorials and 'Help' built into the package and in other specialist texts, such as that by Bazeley and Jackson (2013). Details of support materials are provided on the QSR website (see the Resources section). Just a few NVivo procedures, considered to be sufficient to get started with the package, are outlined here, as shown in Figure 15.5. Version 11 of the package was used in the preparation of these guidelines.

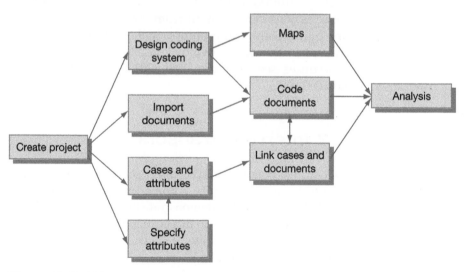

Figure 15.5   NVivo procedures covered

The NVivo opening *Welcome* screen, under *Get Started*, displays three icons: *New Project*, to create a new analysis projects, *Open Project*, to access an existing project, and *Help*. There is also a list of *Recent Projects*, including an already-loaded demonstration project. The right-hand part of the screen, under *Community*, contains messages from the QSR organisation.

4.2 Creating a project

To demonstrate the system, we start with *New Project*. This involves creating a named location for a research project, into which the documents to be analysed, such as interview transcripts, will be placed. The NVivo procedures to create a project for the Activity Choice project are shown in Figure 15.6.

1. Click on New *Project*
2. In the Title box enter: ActivityChoice
3. A file name (*ActivityChoice.nvp*) automatically appears in the *File Name* box – it will have a default location on your computer, but this can be altered by clicking on *Browse* and specifying a location of choice.
4. Click on *OK*.
5. The screen appears, as shown below.
6. At the top of the screen, a number of toolbar tabs appear: File, Home, External Data, etc.
7. The rest of the screen is divided into two main areas:
   - Left-hand side, the *Navigation View*: – clicking on one of the items at the bottom brings up a corresponding menu at the top.
   - Right-hand side, *List View* are – contents depends on *Navigation View* items, as discussed below.

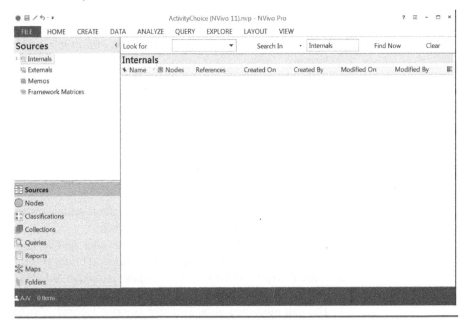

Figure 15.6   Create NVivo project – procedure

4.3 Saving

During an NVivo session, the program will periodically prompt the user to save the current version of the project. The user can save work done by using *File > Save*. Back-up copies of the project file should also be created at the end of a session.

4.4 Classifications, attributes and values

The NVivo package offers a hierarchical system for organising data, involving: *Classification*, *Attributes* and *Values*. *Classification* refers to types of data source: for example, individuals and organisations. In the example case study, we have only one data source, individuals; but in a real project, additional sources can be included as the project progresses. Attributes refer to the characteristics of the individual interviewees. At the top of the transcripts (Table 15.1) we have four attributes for each respondent: age; gender; employment status; and income. Each of these has a range of Values. Two of these, age and income, are numerical. The other two are categorical: for example, gender has the categories 'male' and 'female'. Before actual data can be uploaded, this list of attributes and values must be recorded in the NVivo system, as shown in Table 15.2.

Table 15.2   Attributes – procedure

---

1. Click on *Classifications* on the bottom left of the screen. Under the Classification heading, select *Node Classifications*.
2. Right-click in the right-hand blank area of the screen and select *New Classification*.
3. In the dialog box, 'Create a new classification' is already selected. In the Name box type *Individuals*. Click on *OK*. *Individuals* is now listed under *Name*.
4. Right-click on *Individuals* and select *New Attribute*.
5. In the dialog box, in the *Name* box type: *Age*. In the *Type* box select: *Integer*. Click on OK. The attribute *Age* should now be listed under *Name*.
6. Repeat steps 4 and 5 for the attribute *Income*.
7. Right-click on *Individuals* and select *New Attribute*.
8. In the dialog box, in the *Name* box type: *Gender*. In the *Type* box select: *Text*.
9. Click on the *Values* tab:
   - 'Unassigned' and 'Not applicable' default values are already in place;
   - click on *Add* and type in the value *Male*;
   - click on *Add* and type in *Female*, then click on *OK*; and
   - the attribute *Gender* should now be listed under *Attributes*.
10. Repeat steps 7–9 for attribute *Empstat* (employment status), with *Values FT Employed* and *Student*.
11. The four attributes, *Age, Empstat, Gender, Income*, should now be listed under Individual.

4.5 Cases and their attributes

We can now introduce our three interviewees as *cases* and record their individual socio-demographic attributes. Procedures are shown in Figure 15.7.

4.6 Importing documents

The interview transcript files from Case study 15.1 must now be imported into the ActivityChoice project file. It is assumed a text file exists for each interview, for example: Mark.docx; Donna.docx; and Lee.docx. These documents can be

---

1. Click on *Nodes* in the bottom left-hand corner of the screen, then under the *Nodes* menu click on Individuals.
2. Right-click in the blank Individuals area of the screen and select *New Node*.
3. In the New Node dialog box, type in the name *Mark*.
4. Still in the *New Node* dialog box, click on the *Attribute Values* tab, and in the *Classification* box drop-down list select *Individuals*.
5. In the *Attribute Values* dialog box, the four attributes are now listed:
   - for *Age* and *Income:* key in Mark's age in years (22) and income in £000s (8); and
   - from the drop-down values lists for *Gender* and *Empstat*, select *Male* then *Student*. Click on *OK*.
6. Repeat steps 2–5 for Donna (27, 19, Female, FT employed) and Lee (23, 22, Male, FT employed).
7. Save the project to disk using *File > Save*.

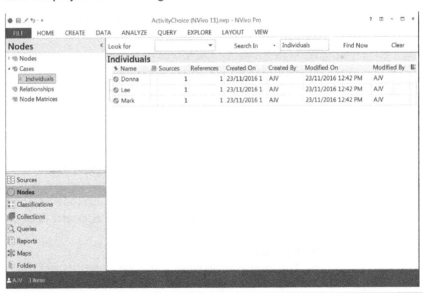

Figure 15.7 Cases and attributes – procedure

Table 15.3 Importing internal documents – procedure

1. In the lower left-hand menu, click on *Sources*.
2. In the menu which now appears above, click on *Internals*.
3. Click on *Internals* and select *New Folder*. Name the new folder *Interviews*.
4. Click on Interviews. The right-hand screen is now headed Interviews
5. Right-click in the *Interviews* blank space and select Import>Import Documents.
6. Use *Browse* to locate file Mark.docx and click on *OK*.
7. The *Document Properties* dialog box appears with Mark in the *Name* box: click on *OK*.
8. The file name Mark.docx should now be listed under *Interviews* with its date of creation.
9. Repeat steps 5–9 for Donna.docx and Lee.docx.
10. All three files will now be listed.
11. Save the modified project file, using *File>Save*

uploaded as shown in Table 15.3. It will be seen that other types of material can be incorporated, including sound and video material and external material such as links to websites. This demonstration is confined to dealing with text documents generated internally as part of the research project.

4.7 Linking individual interviewees/nodes and documents

The interview transcript files must now be linked with the three interviewees/ nodes, Mark, Donna and Lee. The procedure for this is shown in Table 15.4.

4.8 Setting up a coding system

As with questionnaires, documents such as interview transcripts must be *coded* in order to be analysed by computer. This involves setting up a *coding*

Table 15.4 Linking documents and cases – procedure

1. In the lower left-hand menu *Sources*, then *Internals* > *Interviews* on the menu, so that the three files appear listed in under the heading *Interviews*.
2. Click on the file icon on the left of the *Mark* file to highlight it.
3. Right click and select *Code Sources* > Code Sources at *Existing Nodes*.
4. The *Select Project Items* dialog box appears: Click on Nodes > Individuals and the list of three files will appear.
5. Click on *Select All*, then *OK*.
6. The three interviewees, with their attributes, are now linked with their respective interview transcripts – if you click on one of the names, the transcript for that respondent will appear in the space below.

system. A coding system can develop and evolve as the research progresses, but it has to start somewhere. In section 2.3 on manual coding above, the 'flagging' process is similar to the coding process involved here. On the basis of an initial conceptual framework (Figure 15.2) and reading short extracts from three interview transcripts, it was possible to develop a coding system which is displayed in the margin notes in Table 15.1 and reflected in the more developed conceptual framework in Figure 15.3. In a fully fledged project, the researcher would go on to read and code the full interview transcripts of the three example interviewees and other interviewees as well, and would apply the flagging/coding system to the other text read and would further develop the system in an inductive way. Coding systems using NVivo are developed in the same way. In the examples used in the rest of this chapter, the codes developed in the manual process are entered into the Activity Choice project to demonstrate the beginnings of a coding system.

The grouping of related concepts, as shown in Figure 15.3, are referred to in NVivo as *Tree Nodes.* Free-floating concepts, which have not been linked to any tree structure are referred to as *Free Nodes.* The procedures in Figure 15.8 describe the process for entering information presented in Figure 15.3 into the NVivo project file. The relevance of the three *levels* mentioned in Figure 15.3 should become apparent in this process.

1. In the lower left-hand menu, click on *Nodes*
2. Right click on *Nodes* and create a new folder called *Tree nodes.*
3. Click on *Tree nodes* so that the right-hand screen is labelled *Tree nodes.*
4. Right click in the right hand blank area and from the drop-down menu select *New Node,* type in the name *Main Activity* and click on *OK.* Main Activity is now listed under *Tree Nodes.*
5. Highlight *Main Activity* and right-click and in the drop-down menu select *New Node.* In the *New Node* dialog box, type in the name *Activity type* and click on *OK. Activity type* should now be listed, indented under *Main Activity.*
6. Repeat step 4 for: Influences, Constraints, Personal and Events.
7. Highlight *Activity type* and right-click. Select *New Node,* type in the name *Sporting* and click on *OK.*
8. Repeat step 6, adding *Social* and *Cultural. All three activity types are* now be listed under *Activity type.*
9. Repeat steps 6–7 for:
   - *Influences: Parents, Teachers, Peers*
   - *Constraints: Time, Money, Fitness*
   - *Personal: Competitive, Social-non-social, Anti-routine, Instrumental*
   - *Events:* Coaching etc., Weight-gain, Relationships, Money.

Figure 15.8 Setting up a coding system – procedure *(continued)*

The screen should then appear as follows.

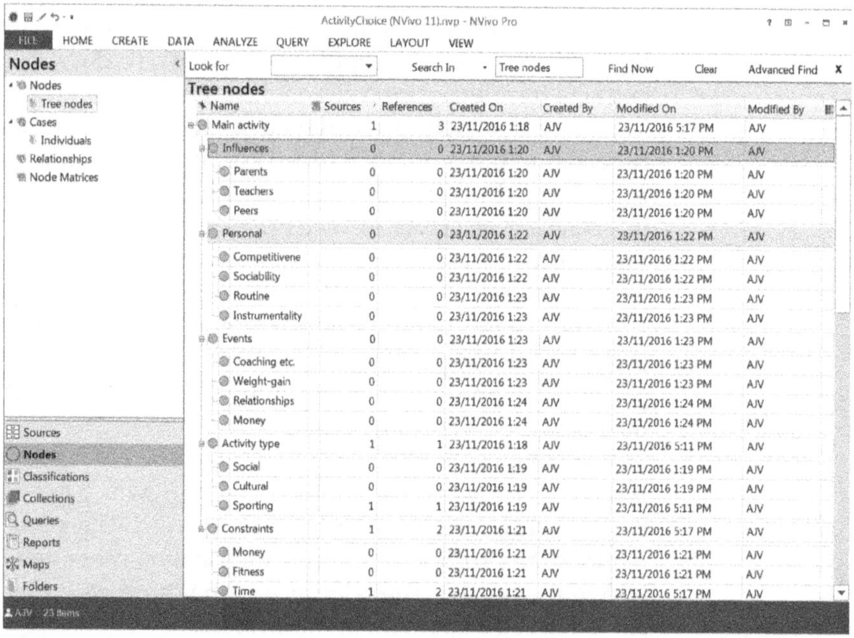

Figure 15.8 *(continued)*

4.9 Maps

The coding system can be depicted diagrammatically as a *map*. The procedures and output are shown in Figure 15.9. Note: this procedure was referred to as Maps in previous versions of the software.

NVivo's *project map* is equivalent to the idea of the *concept map*, as discussed in Chapter 3. The 'Mind map' and 'Concepts map' options can be used at the earliest stage in a project to develop concept maps.

4.10 Coding text

Once a coding system has been set up, documents, such as interview transcripts, can be coded. This process is outlined in Figure 15.10.

This illustration uses the coding system developed above, which arose from the manual analysis and theoretical framework outlined earlier in chapter, but the coder is not restricted to this framework: additional

1. In the Navigation area select *Nodes* and then *Tree Nodes* from the menu: the *Main Activity* node specified in Figure 15.8 will appear in the List View area.
2. In the Navigation View area, select *Maps*, which will now replace *Tree Nodes* in the List View area.
3. Right click in the List View area and from the menu, select *New Project Map*.
4. In the *New Model* dialog box enter a name for the model e.g. *Map1*, and click on *OK*.
5. A workspace for *Map1* appears at the top of the screen: click on the PROJECT MAP tab to bring up the Project Map Tools ribbon.
6. Click on Add Project Items.
7. In the *Add Project Items* dialog box, click on Nodes>*Tree Nodes*. *Main Activity* appears in the space to the right.
8. Click on the 'Main activity' plus sign, then on the plus signs for each characteristic. Then, to obtain the diagram below: tick the three items under 'Influences' and the four items under 'Events'. Then *OK*.
9. The diagram appears, with all the selected items in boxes stacked in the middle of the screen. Right click on the screen and the boxes will disappear and the items can then be moved around. To obtain the layout below, move 'Main activity' in place first, the 'Personal' then 'Influences' followed by its three items, then the other characteristics and items.

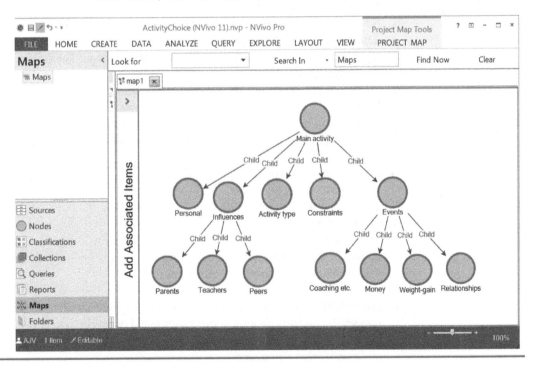

Figure 15.9 Maps – procedure

codes/nodes can be added as you go along. This reflects the qualitative methodology and is of course very likely to arise with longer interview transcripts. The procedure involves selecting 'At new node' at step 5b in Figure 15.10.

---

1. In the Navigation View area, select *Sources* then *Internals > Interviews*. The three interview transcript files appear in the right-hand screen.
2. Double-click on *Mark* and the transcript appears below.
3. A section of text is coded by highlighting: to have this highlighting indicated visually on the text after it has been coded: on the Windows menu, select *View > Highlight > Coding for Selected Items*.
4. A *Selected Project items* window will appear. Click on the + to the left of *Nodes*, click on *Tree nodes* and a *Main activity* box appears on the right-hand side: click on the + to the left of *Main activity*. *Activity type, constraints*, etc., will appear below. Click on the + to the left of *Activity type* and click on the box to the left of *Sporting*. Click OK.
5. To code the activity 'playing football' in Mark's transcript:
   a. Highlight *playing football*.
   b. Select *Analyze > Code*. The *Select Code Items* dialog box appears. (Option: as a shortcut, highlight *playing football* and right-click on the highlighted words. Click *Code* in the drop-down menu. The *Select Code Items* dialog box should appear. Continue to c.)
   c. In the *Select Code Items* dialog box, select *Tree nodes*. *Main Activity* appears.
   d. Click on the triangle on the left of the *Main Activity* listing and factors. *Personal, Influence, Activity type*, Events, etc., will be listed below.
   e. Click on the triangle on the left of *Activity type*, and *Sporting, Social, Cultural* will be listed below.
   f. Select *Sporting* and click *OK*.
   g. The text should appear highlighted.
   h. After the initial coding, additional references under the same node can be coded by clicking *Analyze*, then clicking the triangle under *Code*. Under *Recent Nodes*, click on the required code.
6. Repeat step 5 for:
   - text 'While the football's on, because of training twice a week and needing to be fairly serious about keeping fit I don't do much else: I probably only go to a pub once – or at most twice – a week', is coded as *Constraints > Time*; and
   - text: 'I'm pretty competitive – so I like sport generally' is coded as *Personal > Competitive*.
7. The result appears as below.
8. Repeat steps 2–7 for Donna and the statement 'I go to the gym once or twice a week' (result not shown below).

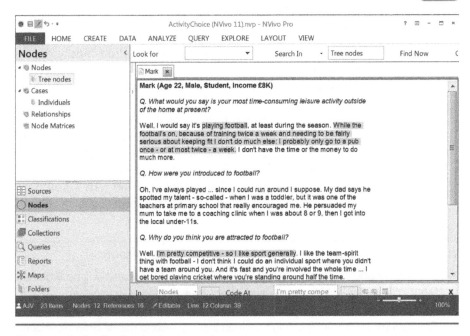

Figure 15.10 Coding text – procedure

4.11 Project summary

The Activity Choice project information is now assembled and coded, as summarised in Figure 15.11. Analysis involves exploring the content of the coded interview transcripts and the cases and their attributes.

4.12 Analysis: coding query

Software packages invariably include a wide range of procedures which is impossible to cover in a short summary such as this. Here we cover two very

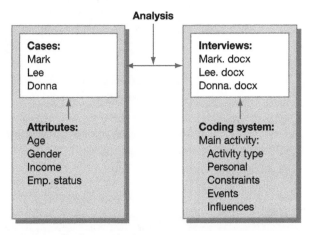

Figure 15.11 Activity Choice project summary

basic analysis procedures/issues which will be sufficient to get the researcher started. In reality, these procedures do not encompass data analysis as such, which is concerned with identifying relationships and meanings, discussed in a limited way in the manual analysis section of this chapter. The procedures covered here are related to data processing so that the analysis can begin. Two procedures are described below: *Coding Query* and *Matrix Coding Query*.

One of the simplest forms of analysis is simply to obtain a listing of all the sections of text coded in a certain way. Thus a listing of all passages in the transcripts coded with Sporting as the Main Activity is obtained as shown in Figure 15.12.

Rather than searching for text coded as a node in the coding system it is possible to search for any item of specified text. This would involve selecting *Text Search* instead of *Coding* at step 2 in Figure 15.12.

To select the text which has been coded *Sporting* as *Main Activity*:

1. In the Navigation View area, select *Queries*: the List View area will now be headed *Queries*.
2. Right click in the List View area and select *New Query > Coding*.
3. A *Coding Query* dialog box appears, including: Coded at *All Selected Nodes*.
4. To select by the *Node* 'Sporting': click on the '. . .' next to the *All Selected Nodes*. A *Select Project Items* window will appear. Click on the + to the left of *Nodes*. Then click on *Tree Nodes > Main Activity > Activity Type > Sporting > OK*. *Sporting* will appear next to the '. . .' button.
5. Click on *Run* query and a listing will appear in the Detail View area with the names of the cases, Mark and Donna, and a printout of the relevant text, as shown below.
6. The results of this query can be saved for future reference: right click in the result area and from the drop-down menu select *Story Query Results* and type in a name, e.g. Query_Sporting. This material can subsequently be accessed when required via the Navigation View area: *Queries > Results*.

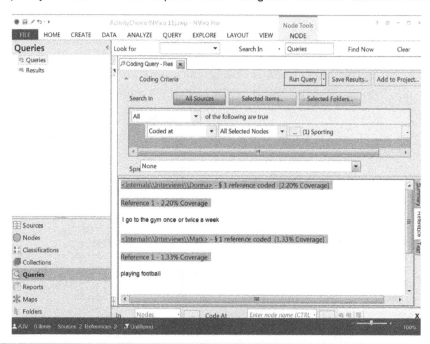

Figure 15.12   Queries – procedure

To divide interviewees engaging in sporting activities into males and females:

1. In the Navigation View area, select *Queries*: the List View area will now be headed *Queries*.
2. Right click in the List View area and select *New Query* > *Matrix Coding*.
3. In the *Matrix Coding Query* dialog box, under *Matrix Coding Criteria* and *Rows* and *Define More Rows*: *Selected Items* will be displayed.
4. Click on the *Select* button on the right. The *Select Project Items* dialog box will be displayed.
5. In the *Select Project Items* dialog box click on *Tree Nodes* to bring up *Main Activity*, then go down to *Sporting* (as in Figure 15.14 steps 5d–f) and click on *OK*.
6. On returning to the *Matrix Coding Query* dialog box, click on *Add to List* and *Tree Nodes/Main Activity/Activity Type/Sporting* will appear under *Name*.
7. Click the Columns tab and then Select.
8. In the *Select Project Items* dialog box select *Attributes* and then *Gender* then OK.
9. On returning to the *Matrix Coding Query* dialog box, click on *Add to List* and *Tree Nodes/Main Activity/Activity Type/Sporting* will appear under *Name*.
10. Click on *Run* and the results will be displayed in a table as follows:

	A: Case: Gender = Male	B: Case: Gender = Female
Sporting	1	1

11. This shows one male and one female coded as taking part in sport as their main activity: double clicking in the cells containing a number will bring up the relevant coded text.

Figure 15.13 Matrix coding query – procedure

4.13 Analysis: matrix coding query

The *Coding query* can be seen as the equivalent of a frequency count in questionnaire survey analysis; the equivalent of a crosstabulation is a *Matrix coding query*. Figure 15.13 shows the procedure for conducting such an analysis in the Activity Choice project to separate sports participants by gender.

Summary

The chapter is divided into two sections dealing respectively with manual and computer-aided qualitative data analysis methods.

Manual methods of data analysis involve 'flagging' issues or themes which emerge in texts such as interview transcripts. Such issues or themes may relate to an existing draft conceptual framework, to research questions and/or hypotheses; or, in a 'grounded theory', inductive approach, they may be used to build up a conceptual framework from the data. Since texts are invariably available as word-processed files, it is noted that certain features of word-processor packages, such as 'search' and 'list' or 'index', can be used to assist in the 'flagging' process. This provides a link to the custom-made Computer Aided Qualitative Data Analysis Software (CAQDAS) packages.

The second part of the chapter introduces the NVivo CAQDAS package, covering the setting up of a project file and a coding system, coding of data and some elementary analysis procedures. While the package has a large range of capabilities – including the handling of data other than interview transcripts – just a limited range of analysis procedures is presented in this short outline; but it is believed this is adequate for the qualitative researcher to make a start with computer-aided data analysis.

Test questions

1. What is an 'emergent theme'?

2. What are the two major activities involved in manual analysis of qualitative data?

3. What word-processor procedures might be used in 'manual' analysis of qualitative data?

4. What is the difference between a 'Node' and a 'Document' in NVivo?

Exercises

1. Download from the text website the three transcript files for the 'Activity choice' project used above – or type them out from Table 15.1 – and replicate the coding and analyses presented above. This can be done manually or by using NVivo.

2. Run the NVivo tutorials included with the package, particularly exploring features of NVivo not presented in this chapter.

3. Select an example of a quantitative and a qualitative research report from a recent edition of one of the leisure or tourism journals and consider whether the qualitative research project could have been approached using quantitative methods and whether the quantitative project could have been approached using qualitative methods.

4. Use the checklist in Table 9.3 to interview a willing friend or colleague. Assess your performance as an interviewer.

5. If you are studying with others, organise yourselves into groups of five or six and organise a focus-group interview, with one person as facilitator, choosing a topic of mutual interest, such as 'the role of education and qualifications in the leisure/tourism industries' or 'holiday choice processes', or 'fitness versus the enjoyment of sport'. Take turns in acting as convenor and assess each other's skills as convenor.

6. Using the issues of a newspaper for one week, provide a qualitative and quantitative analysis of the coverage of a topic of interest, such as: the environment, ethnic minorities, women and sport or overseas holiday locations.

7. Arrange to view a copy of *Cannibal Tours* and discuss the film in the light of MacCannell's (1993) essay on the film. Or view any Disney cartoon film and discuss it in relation to Rojek's (1993) paper.

Resources

Websites

- CATPAC – text analysis package – see Ryan (2000).

- Computer assisted qualitative data analysis network: www.surrey.ac.uk/sociology/research/researchcentres/caqdas/.

- Leximancer: http://info.leximancer.com/.

- NVivo: www.qsrinternational.com/ – includes a downloadable bibliography on qualitative data analysis sources.

- *Qualitative Research* journal: http://qrj.sagepub.com/.

- The Qualitative Report (portal): www.nova.edu/ssss/QR/.

Publications

- Analysis of qualitative data generally: Miles and Huberman (1994).

- Analysing talk and text: Perakyla (2005).

- Use of computer software packages in qualitative data analysis: Miles and Weitzman (1994), Richards and Richards (1994), Sotiriadou et al. (2014).

- Use of Leximancer software: Scott and Smith (2005), Sotiriadou et al. (2014).

- Use of NVivo software: Bazeley and Jackson (2013), Sotiriadou et al. (2014), Welsh (2002).

References

Bazeley, P., and Jackson, K. (2013). *Qualitative data analysis with NVivo*, 2nd edn. Thousand Oaks, CA: Sage.

Brandenburg, J., Greiner, W., Hamilton-Smith, E., Scholten, H., Senior, R., and Webb, J. (1982). A conceptual model of how people adopt recreation activities. *Leisure Studies*, 1(3), 263–76.

Charmaz, K. (2006). *Constructing grounded theory*. London: Sage.

Dupuis, S. (1999). Naked truths: towards a reflexive methodology in leisure research. *Leisure Sciences*, 21(1), 43–64.

Huberman, A. M., and Miles, M. B. (1994). Data management and analysis methods. In N. K. Denzin and Y. S. Lincoln (Eds), *Handbook of qualitative research* (pp. 428–44). Thousand Oaks, CA: Sage.

Miles, M. B., and Huberman, A. M. (1994). *Qualitative data analysis*, 2nd edn. Thousand Oaks, CA: Sage.

Miles, M., and Weitzman, E. (1994). *Computer programs for qualitative data analysis*. Thousand Oaks, CA: Sage.

MacCannell, D. (1993). *The empty meeting grounds*. London: Routledge.

Perakyla, A. (2005). Analyzing talk and text. In K. Denzin and Y. S. Lincoln (Eds), *Handbook of qualitative research* (pp. 869–86). Thousand Oaks, CA: Sage.

Richards, T. J., and Richards, L. (1994). Using computers in qualitative research. In N. K. Denzin and Y. S. Lincoln (Eds), *Handbook of qualitative research* (pp. 445–62). Thousand Oaks, CA: Sage.

Rojek, C. (1993). Disney culture. *Leisure Studies*, 12(2), 121–36.

Ryan, C. (2000). Tourist experiences, phenomenographic analysis, post-positivism and neural network software. *International Journal of Tourism Research*, 2(1), 119–31.

Scott, N., and Smith, A. E. (2005). Use of automated content analysis techniques for event image assessment. *Tourism Recreation Research*, 30(2), 87–91.

Sotiriadou, P., Brouwers, J., and Le, T-A. (2014). Choosing a qualitative data analysis tool: a comparison of NVivo and Leximancer. *Annals of Leisure Research*, doi:10.1080/11745398.2014.902292.

Veal, A. J., Darcy, S., and Lynch, R. (2013). *Australian leisure*, 4th edn. Sydney: Pearson Australia.

Welsh, E. (2002). Dealing with data: using NVivo in the qualitative data analysis process. *Forum: Qualitative Data Research*, 3(2), 1–9.

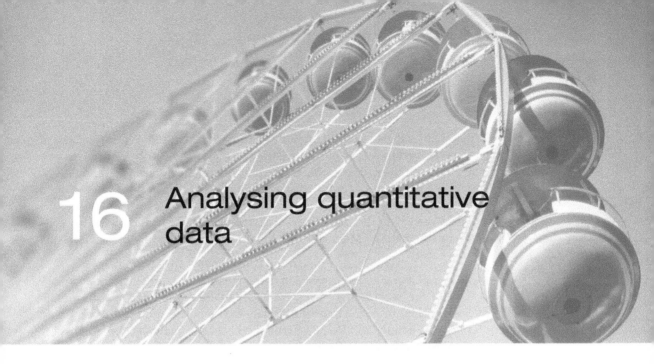

16 Analysing quantitative data

1. Introduction

2. Quantitative data analysis and types of research
- 2.1 Descriptive research
- 2.2 Explanatory research
- 2.3 Evaluative research
- 2.4 Overlaps
- 2.5 Reliability

3. Spreadsheet analysis

4. Statistical Package for the Social Sciences (SPSS)

5. Preparation
- 5.1 Cases and variables
- 5.2 Specifying variables
- 5.3 Starting up
- 5.4 Entering information about variables – Variable View window
- 5.5 Saving work
- 5.6 Entering data – Data View window

6. Analysis procedures
- 6.1 Starting an analysis session
- 6.2 Descriptives
- 6.3 Frequencies
- 6.4 Checking for errors
- 6.5 Multiple response
- 6.6 Recode
- 6.7 Mean, median and mode – measures of central tendency
- 6.8 Presenting the results – statistical summary
- 6.9 Crosstabulation
- 6.10 Weighting
- 6.11 Graphics

7. The analysis process

1. Introduction

In this chapter the analysis of quantitative data is addressed. While the focus is on data derived from questionnaire surveys, the processes can be used on any data with a number of cases for which data are available for a common set of variables. Two types of computer package are used:

● *Spreadsheets:* are the most widespread computer application used for general data analysis. Microsoft Excel is used to demonstrate certain analysis procedures.

● *Statistical packages:* are used to analyse statistical data in a research context. One of the most widely used packages is the Statistical Package for the Social Sciences (SPSS) and is used here for demonstration purposes. Other packages include *Minitab, BMD* (Biomedical Data analysis), *SAS* (Statistical Analysis System) and *Turbostats*.

Figure 10.8, in Chapter 10, contains a copy of a simple questionnaire which is used to demonstrate analysis processes in this chapter. Chapter 10 dealt with the procedure for coding the data from this questionnaire in a form suitable for computer analysis, as shown in Figure 10.9.

Before addressing the mechanics of data analysis, however, the typology of research discussed in Chapter 1 is discussed in relation to the analysis process.

2. Quantitative data analysis and types of research

In Chapter 1 it was noted that research might be of three kinds: descriptive, explanatory and evaluative. Before considering the process of analysing questionnaire survey data, these types of research and their relationship to analysis procedures to be covered in the chapter are discussed in turn below and summarised in Table 16.1.

Table 16.1 Research types and analytical procedures

Research type	Analytical procedures
Descriptive	Frequencies, Means
Explanatory	Crosstabulation, Comparison of means, regression
Evaluative	Frequencies – compared with targets or benchmarks
	Crosstabulations – comparing user/customer-groups
	Means – compared with some benchmark or target

2.1 Descriptive research

Descriptive research usually involves the presentation of information in a fairly simple form. Of the analytical procedures described in this chapter, the two most appropriate for descriptive research are:

- *frequencies*, which present counts and percentages of responses for single variables; and

- *means*, which present averages for numerical variables.

2.2 Explanatory research

Descriptive data do not, of themselves, *explain* anything. To explain the patterns in data or relationships between phenomena represented by the data, it is necessary to consider the question of *causality* – how to determine whether A is caused by B. In Chapter 2 it was noted that to establish causality, it is necessary to fulfil four criteria: association, time priority, non-spurious relation and rationale:

- *Associations* between variables can be explored using such procedures as *crosstabulations* (described in this chapter) and *regression* (described in Chapter 17).

- *Time priority* involves establishing that, for A to be the *cause* of B, then A must take place *before* B – this is sometimes testable in social science research and is sometimes obvious, but is generally more appropriate for the conditions of the natural science laboratory.

- *Non-spurious* relationships are those which 'make sense' theoretically (that is, for example, the relationship between A and B is not mediated by a third, extraneous variable C), and are not just a 'fluke' of the data. This can be approached using data analysis techniques. For example, suppose it is found that leisure and tourism expenditure is inversely related to age for the whole sample. If this relationship is also found for, say, men and women separately, and for other sub-groups – even random sub-samples – this suggests a non-spurious relationship.

- *Rationale*, or *theory*, is of course not produced by computer analysis but should be integral to the research design. As indicated in Chapter 2, the research may be *deductive* in nature, with pre-established hypotheses which are tested by the data analysis; or it may be *inductive*, in which development of theory and explanation building take place to a greater or lesser extent as part of the data analysis process. Either way, *explanation*, or the establishment of causality, is not complete without some sort of rational, conceptual explanation of the relationships found.

The example questionnaire from Chapter 10 offers only limited scope for *explanatory* research. For example, differences in attitudes between the various student groups – full-time and part-time or different age-groups, for example – may indicate that varying expectations from campus life may be a function of student group characteristics.

The particular procedures which are appropriate for explanatory analysis and which are covered in this chapter are the production of *crosstabulations*, which facilitate examination of the relationship between two or more variables based on frequencies, and the examination of the *means* of two or more variables. These procedures can establish whether or not statistical relationships exist between variables, but whether or not they are spurious and/or supported by theory involves reference to the theoretical or conceptual framework.

2.3 Evaluative research

Evaluative research basically involves comparisons between empirical findings and some benchmark derived from expectations, past figures, other similar facilities or programmes or target performance standards. The analysis called for, therefore, is relatively simple, generally involving comparisons between research findings and some benchmark value.

The example questionnaire developed in Chapter 10 could be used for evaluative purposes – for example, a low level of use of any of the services listed in question 2 could imply that the existing service is not performing well in meeting the demands of students, and low levels of use by particular groups could indicate a failure to meet the needs of all groups.

2.4 Overlaps

Analysis does not always fall exclusively into one of the three modes of research. For example, in presenting a descriptive account of the example Campus Life survey results, it would be natural to provide a breakdown of the participation patterns and preferences of the four student groups included. While this could be descriptive in form, it would begin at least to hint at explanation, in that any differences in the groups' patterns of behaviour or opinions would seem to call for explanation; the analysis would be saying 'these groups are different' and would be implicitly posing the question 'Why?' Insofar as the providers of campus services aimed to serve all sections of the student community, the data could be used in evaluating management practices and outcomes.

2.5 Reliability

In Chapter 2 reference was made to questions of *validity* and *reliability*. It has been noted that some attempt at testing validity – whether the data are measuring what they are intended to measure – can be achieved in the design of questionnaires. Reliability – whether similar results would be obtained if the research were replicated – is a difficult issue in the social sciences, but an approach can be made at the analysis stage. While statistical procedures are well suited to establishing the magnitude and strength of associations, the question of the reliability of such associations is more complex. Unlike the natural sciences, it is not always possible, for practical or resource reasons, to replicate research in the social sciences to establish reliability. While reference to previous research reported in the literature can be relevant and helpful in this respect, in fact, the changing essence of human nature over time and space means that consistency with previous research findings is by no means a guarantee of reliability. Indeed, the tracking of *change* is often the aim of social research.

If the sample is large enough, one approach to reliability is to split the sample into two or more sub-samples on a random basis, or on the basis of a selected variable, and see whether the results for the sub-samples are the same as for the sample as a whole. In the SPSS package this can be achieved using the procedure *split file*: the procedure is not covered here but is relatively straightforward to operate.

3. Spreadsheet analysis

Since most users of this text will be familiar with spreadsheet use, this section does not provide a guide to elementary spreadsheet procedures, but only to procedures specific to analysis of the type of data in a cases/variable form as, for example, arising from questionnaire surveys.

The shaded part of Figure 16.1 reproduces in spreadsheet format the data for 15 completed questionnaires from Figure 10.9. There is one change: the expenditure variable (*spend*) has been shifted to the end to sit alongside *age*, since both are uncoded numerical variables which are treated individually in the analysis. The unshaded part is produced by the FREQUENCY procedure provided in Excel. This procedure is described in Figure 16.2.

Spreadsheet analysis is suitable for a small data set when simple frequency tables are required. Certain statistical procedures, such as correlation and regression, can also be undertaken using a spreadsheet. But for larger data sets, particularly longer questionnaires, and more complex analyses, a statistical software package, as outlined next, is advisable.

4. Statistical Package for the Social Sciences (SPSS)

The main part of the chapter is organised as a step-by-step introductory manual for operating the Statistical Package for the Social Sciences (SPSS). It is envisaged that the reader will have access to a computer with SPSS available on it, so that the procedures described here can be tried out in practice.

The question arises as to the point at which it is worthwhile to invest time and energy in mastering a computer package for survey analysis rather than relying on a spreadsheet program, with which many people are already familiar. This of course depends on the scale and complexity of the task in hand and the likely future career path of the researcher. It is clear that a

Row	A	B	C	D	E	F	G	H	I	J	K	L	M	N	O	P	Q	R	S	T	U	V
1	qno	status	cafebar	music	sport	travel	cheap	daytime	unusual	meet	quality	relax	social	mental	sug1	sug2	sug3	gend		age		spend
2	1	2	1	1	0	0	1	4	2	3	5	3	3	1	1	1		1		18		100
3	2	2	1	1	1	0	1	4	2	3	5	2	3	1	2	1		1		19		50
4	3	3	1	0	0	0	2	5	1	3	4	2	2	2	3	4		2		19		250
5	4	4	0	0	0	0	2	3	1	4	5	3	2	2	1	2	4	1		22		25
6	5	3	1	0	0	1	1	4	3	2	5	3	3	1				2		24		55
7	6	3	1	1	1	0	2	4	1	3	5	2	3	1	2			2		20		40
8	7	2	1	0	0	0	3	2	1	4	5	2	3	2	3			2		20		150
9	8	2	1	1	1	0	3	4	2	1	5	1	2	2	4	5		1		21		250
10	9	4	0	1	0	0	1	5	2	3	4	2	3	2				1		21		300
11	10	3	1	1	0	0	1	3	1	5	4	1	2	1				2		21		100
12	11	3	1	1	0	1	2	3	1	4	5	2	2	1	1			2		21		75
13	12	2	1	0	1	0	2	4	3	2	5	2	3	1	2	3		1		19		50
14	13	1	1	0	1	0	1	5	2	3	4	2	3	2	1			2		22		55
15	14	3	1	1	0	0	2	4	1	3	5	3	3	2	4	2		2		21		75
16	15	1	1	1	0	0	3	2	1	5	4	3	3	1	1	2	5	1		20		150
17																						
18	Code	Freq	Freq	Freq	Freq	Freq	Freq	Freq	Freq	Freq	Freq	Freq	Freq	Freq	Freq	Freq	Freq	Freq	Cat.	Freq	Cat.	Freq
19	0	0	2	7	10	13	0	0	0	0	0	0	0	0	0	0	0	0	19	4	74	6
20	1	2	13	8	5	2	6	0	8	1	0	2	0	8	5	2	0	7	21	8	100	4
21	2	5	0	0	0	0	6	2	5	2	0	8	5	7	3	3	0	8	23	2	200	2
22	3	6	0	0	0	0	3	3	2	7	0	5	10	0	2	1	0	0	25	1		3
23	4	2	0	0	0	0	0	7	0	3	5	0	0	0	2	1	1	0				
24	5	0	0	0	0	0	0	3	0	2	10	0	0	0	0	1	1	0				
25	Total	15	15	15	15	15	15	15	15	15	15	15	15	15	12	8	2	15		15		15
26	Averages																			20.5		115

Figure 16.1   Survey data: spreadsheet analysis

1. Type: Code in cell A18.
2. Type: Freq in cell B18.
3. Type the codes 0, 1, 2, 3, 4, 5 in cells A19 to A24 respectively (0–5 covers all the codes used by variables *status* to *gend*.
4. Select cells B19 to B24 (the cells in which the results of the frequency counts will be placed, referred to in Excel as the 'bin array').
5. Type the following 'array formula' in the 'formula bar' (not shown in Figure 16.1):
   a. =FREQUENCY(B2:B16,$A19:$A24) and then press Ctrl + Shift + Enter together.
   b. The results will appear as shown in cells B19 to B24 in Figure 16.1.
   c. Note:
      ● When you have typed =FR Excel will offer you a pop-up FREQUENCY which you can select with a double click.
      ● You can select the cells B2:B16 rather than typing the cell references manually.
      ● The $A format is used in $A19:$A24 because the codes in cells A19:A24 will be utilised for all 17 coded variables, so in spreadsheet parlance, an absolute rather than a relative column location must be specified.
      ● General instructions on the use of the FREQUENCY formula are provide by the Excel Help facility.
6. The heading in cell B18 and the formulae in cells B19:B24 can now be copied to produce the frequencies for the other 16 variables: copy cells B18:B24 as one array and paste into cells C18:R24 in one 'copy and paste' operation.
7. Create totals in row 25 using normal spreadsheet procedures.
8. Example results, for *status*, are as follows:

Category	No.
Full-time student with no regular paid work	2
Full-time student with some regular paid work	5
Part-time student with full-time job	6
Part-time student – other	2
Total	15

9. For each variable, percentages can be created from the frequencies, and graphics can be created from the frequencies or the percentages using normal spreadsheet procedures.
10. Type category groupings for the non-coded variables, *age* and *spend*, in cells S18:S22 and U18:U20 respectively:
    ● cell S19: 19 indicates a group aged 19 and under
    ● cell S20: 21 indicates a group aged 20–21
    ● cell S21: 23 indicates a group aged 22–23
    ● cell S22: 25 indicates a group aged 24–25 (if blank, indicates '24 and over').
11. Select cells T19:T22, then type the following 'array formula' in the 'formula bar' (not shown in Figure 16.1):
    ● =FREQUENCY (T2:T16, S19:S22) (note: $S is not required, because the information is only being used for one variable) and then press Ctrl+Shift+Enter together.
    ● The results will appear as shown in cells T21 to T22 in Figure 16.1.
12. Results for *age* are therefore:

Age	No.
18–19	4
20–21	8
22–23	2
24–25	1

13. A similar process can be followed for the variable *spend*.
14. Totals, percentages and graphics can be produced as for the other variables. In addition, for the two non-coded variables, averages may be calculated.

Figure 16.2 Questionnaire survey data: steps in spreadsheet analysis

specialist survey package has far more capabilities than a spreadsheet, as this chapter and the next demonstrate. It should be noted that basic coding and data preparation is identical for both approaches and the basic data file is interchangeable between a spreadsheet and a survey analysis package such as SPSS. As noted in Chapter 15, it is also the case that familiarity and experience with a computer package merits an entry on a *curriculum vitae*.

SPSS for Windows is the version of the package which is available for IBM-compatible personal computers using the Microsoft *Windows* system. Version 23 of the package is referred to here. Most universities provide access to the software and further details and information on specialist guides can be found on the SPSS Inc. website (see the Resources section).

A full list of SPSS procedures can be found in the online SPSS manual which is included in the software package. In this chapter, five analysis procedures only are described:

- *descriptives* – key descriptive statistics for specified variables;
- *frequencies* – counts and percentages of individual variables;
- *crosstabs* – the crosstabulation of two or more variables;
- *means* – obtaining means/averages of appropriate variables; and
- *graphs* – the production of charts and graphs.

The areas covered in this chapter and the statistical procedures covered in Chapter 17 are summarised in Figure 16.3.

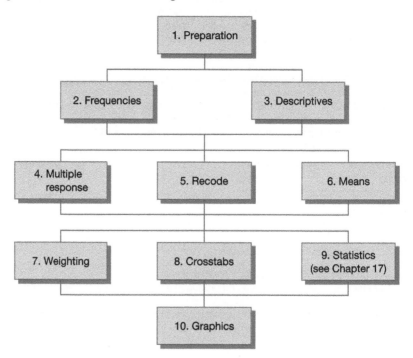

Figure 16.3 Survey analysis – overview

The chapter focuses on analysis of data from questionnaire surveys but, as noted above, SPSS can be used to analyse data from other sources also. Furthermore, although the package is ideally suited to dealing with numerical data, it can also handle non-numerical data. Any data organised on the basis of *cases* and a common range of *variables* for each case can be analysed using the package.

The chapter does not deal with procedures for logging into a computer, file handling or the installation of the SPSS software onto the computer; it is assumed that SPSS for Windows is already installed on a computer available to the reader. The information in the chapter provides an introduction to the basics only.

5. Preparation

5.1 Cases and variables

Statistical analysis packages deal with data which are organised in terms of *cases* and *variables*.

● A *case* is a single example of the phenomenon being studied and for which data have been collected – for example: an individual member of a community who has been interviewed; a participant in a leisure activity; an employee of a company; a visitor to a country; a leisure or tourism organisation; or a country for which data are available. So a *sample* is made up of a number of *cases*.

● A *variable* is an item of information which is available for all or some of the cases, which can take on different values or categories – for example, the *gender* of an individual, which can take on the category 'male' or 'female'; the *salary of an employee*, which can be any monetary value; the *number of employees* of a company; or the *population* of a country.

The use of *variables* is further discussed here, while *cases* arise when entering data, as discussed later in the chapter.

5.2 Specifying variables

In order to communicate with the package, it is necessary to identify each item of data in the questionnaire by a *variable name*. The questionnaire (Figure 10.8) is *annotated with variable names* in the 'Office Use' column. The question numbers and corresponding variable names are listed in Table 16.2, together with an additional nine items of information for each variable, which are required by the software. These items are discussed in turn.

Table 16.2 Variable names, labels and values

Question No.*	Name*	Type	Width**	Decimal places	Label	Values/Value labels	Missing values	Columns	Alignment	Measure/Data type
–	qno	Numeric	4	0	Questionnaire number	None	None	4	Right	Scale
1.	status	Numeric	1	0	Student status	1 F/T student – no work 2 F/T student – working 3 P/T student – F/T job 4 P/T student – other	None	4	Right	Nominal
2.	cafebar	Numeric	1	0	Campus cafe/bar in last 4 wks	1 Yes 0 No	None	4	Right	Nominal
	music	Numeric	1	0	Live campus music in last 4 wks	as for cafebar	None	4	Right	Nominal
	sport	Numeric	1	0	Sport facilities in last 4 wks	as for cafebar	None	4	Right	Nominal
	travel	Numeric	1	0	Travel service in last 4 wks	as for cafebar	None	4	Right	Nominal
3.	cheap	Numeric	1	0	Free/cheap (rank)	None	None	4	Right	Ordinal
	daytime	Numeric	1	0	Daytime events (rank)	None	None	4	Right	Ordinal
	unusual	Numeric	1	0	Not available elsewhere (rank)	None	None	4	Right	Ordinal
	meet	Numeric	1	0	Socialising (rank)	None	None	4	Right	Ordinal
	quality	Numeric	1	0	Quality of presentation (rank)	None	None	4	Right	Ordinal
4.	spend	Numeric	4	0	Expenditure on entertainment/month	None	None	4	Right	Scale
5.	relax	Numeric	1	0	Relaxation opportunities – importance	3 Very important 2 Important 1 Not at all important	None	4	Right	Scale
	social	Numeric	1	0	Social interaction – importance	as for relax	None	4	Right	Scale
	mental	Numeric	1	0	Mental stimulation – importance	as for relax	None	4	Right	Scale
6.	sug1	Numeric	2	0	Improvement suggestion – 1	1 Programme content§ 2 Timing 3 Facilities 4 Costs 5 Organisation	None	4	Right	Nominal
	sug2	Numeric	2	0	Improvement suggestion – 2	as for sug1	None	4	Right	Nominal
	sug3	Numeric	2	0	Improvement suggestion – 3	as for sug1	None	4	Right	Nominal
7.	gender	Numeric	1	0	Gender	1 Male 2 Female	None	4	Right	Nominal
8.	age	Numeric	2	0	Age	None	None	4	Right	Scale

* From Figure 10.8.
** max. no. of characters
§ See Figure 10.7 for derivation of coding system.

Name

- In addition to variables related to the eight questions in the questionnaire, there is a variable *qno* to record a reference number for each case or questionnaire.

- Every item of information on the questionnaire is given a *unique* name (no two variables with the same name).

- The length of variable names is limited to eight letters/numbers (no spaces), beginning with a letter. It is not permitted to use any of the following for variable names, because the SPSS program already uses these names for other purposes and would get confused!

ALL AND BY EQ GE GT LE LT NE NOT OR TO WITH

Three possible systems for naming variables are:

- practice adopted here, which is to use variables names which are full or shortened versions of how the item might be described – for example, *status* for student status, and *sug1* for improvement suggestion 1;

- use a generalised name such as *var* for variable; so a questionnaire with five variables would have variable names: *var1, var2, var3, var4, var5* – in fact SPSS has a system of 'default' variable names already set up in this form, which can be used instead of the customised names used here; and

- use of question numbers from the questionnaire – for example, *Q1, Q2a, Q2b* and so on.

Question 6 should be noted. It is an open-ended question, and respondents might wish to give any number of answers. In this case the designer of the questionnaire has assigned three variables to record up to three answers (*sug1*, *sug2* and *sug3*), on the assumption that a maximum of three answers would be given by any one respondent. Not all respondents will necessarily give three answers – this is no problem, because *sug2* and/or *sug3* can be left blank. Some may, however, give *more* than three answers, in which case it would not be possible to record the fourth and subsequent answers, and that information would be lost. If more than a handful of respondents give more than three answers, then a fourth variable (*sug4*) could be added. The decision on how many answers to allow for must depend on a pilot survey or preliminary scanning of the questionnaires. As an open-ended question, the coding system for question 6 applies to all three variables – *sug1, sug2, sug3* – and was devised from the range of free-form answers as discussed in Chapter 10.

Type

All the variables in the Campus Life survey questionnaire are *numeric* – that is, they can only be numbers. Other possibilities exist, including *date* and *string*, the latter meaning text comprising any combination of letters and numbers, but these options are not pursued here.

Width

Width specifies the maximum number of digits for the value of a variable. In the Campus Life survey questionnaire, all variables are single-digit except three:

- *qno:* width will depend on the size of the sample – here a width of four digits is indicated, indicating a maximum possible sample size of 9999;

- *cost:* width has been put at four, suggesting maximum possible individual weekly expenditure on entertainment of £9999 – which should accommodate all respondents!

- *sug1, sug2, sug3:* two digits allowing for 10 or more codes.

Decimal places

None of the variables in the Campus Life questionnaire includes *decimal places*, so the number of decimal places is set to zero for all of them. Many variables could, however, include decimals or dollars/cents, pounds/pence – for example, a person's height, or a tourist's expenditure per day.

Label

The variable *label* is fuller and more descriptive than the variable *name*, and there is no restriction on content or length. It can be included in output tables, making them more readily understandable by the reader. This is often necessary with long questionnaires with many variables, and particularly when the short variable *names* are not immediately recognisable.

Value labels

Value labels identify the codes used for each variable: e.g. for *gend*, 1 = male and 2 = female. In the case of the Campus Life questionnaire:

- The questionnaire number is just a reference number, so it has no value labels.

- Variables based on questions 1, 2 and 5 have specific codes or values (1, 2, 3, etc.) with value labels as specified in the questionnaire.

- Variables based on question 3 are ranks from 1 to 5 – they have therefore been specified in Table 16.2 as having no value labels. In fact, the values for these variables *could* be given value labels as follows: 1 = 'First', 2 = 'Second', 3 = 'Third', 4 = 'Fourth', 5 = 'Fifth'.

- The variable *cost* is an uncoded numerical sum of money and *age* is a number of years – they therefore have no value labels.

- The values/labels for the open-ended question, 6, were derived as shown in Figure 10.7.

Missing

If a respondent does not answer a question in a questionnaire, the data entry may be left blank, or a 'No answer' or 'Not applicable' code may be provided. The software will automatically treat a blank in the data as a 'missing value', but 'No answer' and 'Not applicable' codes can be provided and specified as *missing values*. The implications are that missing values are excluded when means and percentages are being calculated. In the Campus Life data set, the phenomenon of missing values becomes apparent in the case of variables *sug1*, *sug2* and *sug3*, since some respondents offer no suggestions at all, many offer only one and very few offer three – so there are usually numerous blanks in the data, particularly for *sug2* and *sug3*. In the case of the four variables associated with question 2, it would be possible for non-use of services to be left as a blank, giving rise to missing values, but in this case non-use has been coded as a zero. The *missing value* phenomenon is not pursued in detail in this chapter but is apparent in a number of the outputs from SPSS.

Columns

The number of columns or digits per variable is a presentational matter concerning the layout of the 'Data view' screen discussed in section 5.6. A variable can be *displayed* with any number of columns regardless of the specified *width* of the underlying variable. In the Campus Life example, the specification is four columns for all variables, enabling all the data to be seen on the 'Data view' screen at once without scrolling on most computer screens.

Alignment

Alignment is also presentational. As in a spreadsheet, or table, numerical data are easier to read if aligned to the right, while text is often more suitably aligned to the left.

Measure

Data can be divided into *nominal*, *ordinal* and *scale* types.

- *Nominal data* are made up of non-numerical *categories*, such as the status categories in question 1 and 'Yes/No' in question 2 of the example questionnaire. In this situation, while numerical codes are used in computer analysis, they have no numerical meaning – for example, code 2 is not 'half' of code 4 – the 1/0 codes could equally well be 6/7, A/B, or X/Y. It does not make sense, therefore, to calculate, for example, an average or mean of *nominal data* codes.

- *Ordinal data* reflect a *ranking*, as in question 3 of the example questionnaire; the 1, 2, 3 in this question represent the *order of importance*, but rank 3 cannot be interpreted as being '3 times as high as' rank 1. It is, however, possible to take an average or mean rank – for example, to speak of an 'average ranking'.

- *Scale data* are fully numerical – as in questions 4 (*spend*) and 8 (*age*) of the example questionnaire. Numerical information, such as a person's age, travel expenditure or frequency of participation in an activity, are scale data. In this case an answer of 4 *is* twice as high as an answer of 2, and averages or means are clearly appropriate.

The data type, or type of measure, of a variable affects the range of statistical analysis which can be performed and the appropriate formats for graphical presentation. These are discussed later, particularly in Chapter 17.

In Table 16.2 each variable is identified as nominal, ordinal or scale, as follows:

- *qno* is identified as a *scale* variable, although it will not be used in analysis;

- variables from questions 1, 2, 6 and 7 are *nominal*;

- variables from question 3 are *ordinal*;

- the question 4 variable, *spend*, and question 8 variable, *age*, are *scale* variables; and

- question 5 variables are 'Likert-style' variables, specified as *scale* variables for the reasons discussed next.

Attitude/Likert variables

Variables arising from *Attitude/Likert variables* (see Chapter 10) have been used extensively in psychological and market research and have come to be seen almost as *scale* variables when, in reality, they are just ordinal. Means are therefore accepted as an appropriate form of analysis when using such variables. The scores of 1 to 3 in question 5 in the Campus Life questionnaire can be treated as numerical indicators of the level of importance respondents attach to the items listed. The means can be interpreted as average 'scores' on importance. It is possible to sum scores in some circumstances.

Role

The default setting for all variables is *input*. This need not concern us here. The idea of an *output* variable will be apparent when the *Recode* procedure is discussed below.

5.3 Starting up

To start a SPSS Statistics session on a computer, activate the program as indicated in Table 16.3, then switch to the *Variable View* screen to start the process outlined in section 6.

Table 16.3   Starting a SPSS Statistics session

1. Start SPSS Statistics on your computer using the appropriate screen icon or *Start* and *All Programs*.
2. Two dialog boxes appear on the left of the screen, one labelled *New Files* and one *Recent Files*.
3. In *New Files*, double-click on *New Dataset*.
4. The *Data View* window, which will receive the data, appear, as in Figure 16.4. Clicking on the tab below brings up the *Variable View* window, which will receive information about the variables, as discussed above.

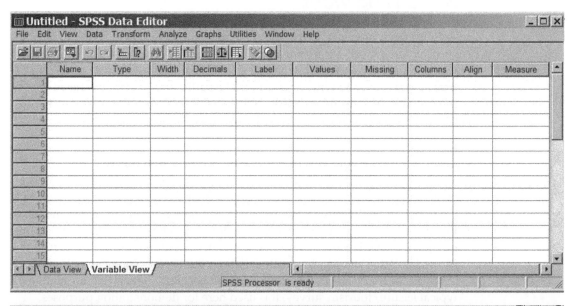

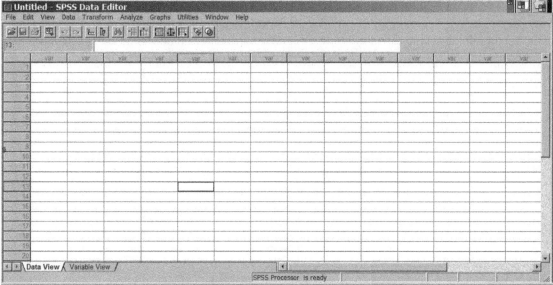

Figure 16.4   Blank Variable View and Data View windows

5.4 Entering information about variables – Variable View window

The information about the variables arising from a questionnaire, as shown in Table 16.3, must be typed into the *Variable View* window. The result of this exercise for the Campus Life questionnaire is as shown in Figure 16.5. It should be noted that for variables with identical value labels, the value labels can be copied and pasted.

5.5 Saving work

As with any computer work, the file should be saved to hard disk, memory stick or 'the cloud' from time to time during the course of preparation and when completed, and a backup copy should be made also. When saving for the first time, a file name will be required. The suffix for an SPSS datafile is .sav, so the example file could be called CampusLifeSurvey.sav. Once the file is *saved* the title 'CampusLifeSurvey' appears at the top of the screen.

5.6 Entering data – Data View window

Switching to the *Data View* window reveals that the variable names entered via the *Variable View* window have automatically been put in place across the top of the screen, and the system is ready to receive data. Data from the questionnaires can now be keyed in: one row on the screen per questionnaire, or *case*. Figure 16.6 shows the *Data View* window with data from the 15 cases/questionnaires shown in Figure 10.18. While a sample of 15 would generally be seen as too small for a typical leisure/tourism survey, it is used here for demonstration purposes.

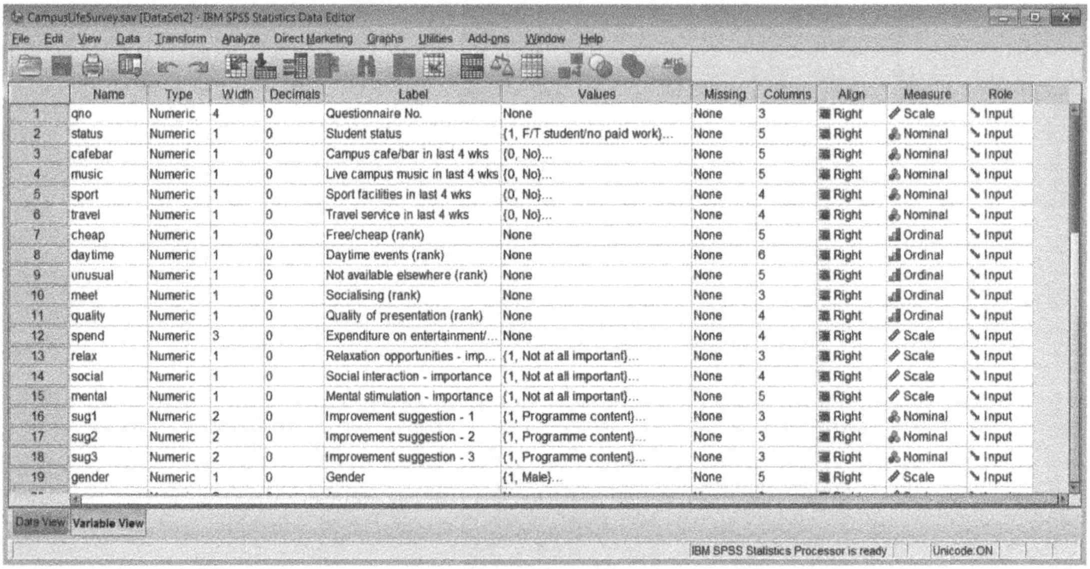

	Name	Type	Width	Decimals	Label	Values	Missing	Columns	Align	Measure	Role
1	qno	Numeric	4	0	Questionnaire No.	None	None	3	Right	Scale	Input
2	status	Numeric	1	0	Student status	{1, F/T student/no paid work}...	None	5	Right	Nominal	Input
3	cafebar	Numeric	1	0	Campus cafe/bar in last 4 wks	{0, No}...	None	5	Right	Nominal	Input
4	music	Numeric	1	0	Live campus music in last 4 wks	{0, No}...	None	5	Right	Nominal	Input
5	sport	Numeric	1	0	Sport facilities in last 4 wks	{0, No}...	None	4	Right	Nominal	Input
6	travel	Numeric	1	0	Travel service in last 4 wks	{0, No}...	None	4	Right	Nominal	Input
7	cheap	Numeric	1	0	Free/cheap (rank)	None	None	5	Right	Ordinal	Input
8	daytime	Numeric	1	0	Daytime events (rank)	None	None	6	Right	Ordinal	Input
9	unusual	Numeric	1	0	Not available elsewhere (rank)	None	None	5	Right	Ordinal	Input
10	meet	Numeric	1	0	Socialising (rank)	None	None	3	Right	Ordinal	Input
11	quality	Numeric	1	0	Quality of presentation (rank)	None	None	4	Right	Ordinal	Input
12	spend	Numeric	3	0	Expenditure on entertainment/...	None	None	4	Right	Scale	Input
13	relax	Numeric	1	0	Relaxation opportunities - imp...	{1, Not at all important}...	None	3	Right	Scale	Input
14	social	Numeric	1	0	Social interaction - importance	{1, Not at all important}...	None	4	Right	Scale	Input
15	mental	Numeric	1	0	Mental stimulation - importance	{1, Not at all important}...	None	5	Right	Scale	Input
16	sug1	Numeric	2	0	Improvement suggestion - 1	{1, Programme content}...	None	3	Right	Nominal	Input
17	sug2	Numeric	2	0	Improvement suggestion - 2	{1, Programme content}...	None	3	Right	Nominal	Input
18	sug3	Numeric	2	0	Improvement suggestion - 3	{1, Programme content}...	None	3	Right	Nominal	Input
19	gender	Numeric	1	0	Gender	{1, Male}...	None	5	Right	Scale	Input

Figure 16.5 Variable View window with variable names, labels, etc.

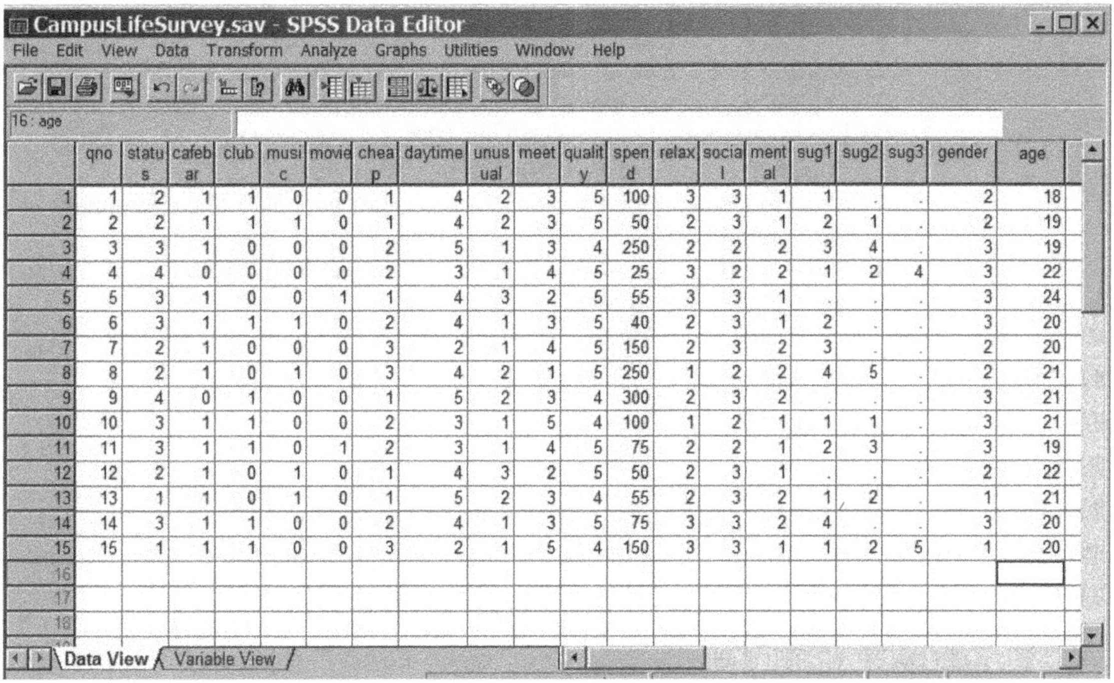

CampusLifeSurvey.sav - SPSS Data Editor

File   Edit   View   Data   Transform   Analyze   Graphs   Utilities   Window   Help

16 : age

	qno	status	cafebar	club	music	movie	cheap	daytime	unusual	meet	quality	spend	relax	social	mental	sug1	sug2	sug3	gender	age
1	1	2	1	1	0	0	1	4	2	3	5	100	3	3	1	1	.	.	2	18
2	2	2	1	1	1	0	1	4	2	3	5	50	2	3	1	2	1	.	2	19
3	3	3	1	0	0	0	2	5	1	3	4	250	2	2	2	3	4	.	3	19
4	4	4	0	0	0	0	2	3	1	4	5	25	3	2	2	1	2	4	3	22
5	5	3	1	0	0	1	1	4	3	2	5	55	3	3	1	.	.	.	3	24
6	6	3	1	1	1	0	2	4	1	3	5	40	2	3	1	2	.	.	3	20
7	7	2	1	0	0	0	3	2	1	4	5	150	2	3	2	3	.	.	2	20
8	8	2	1	0	1	0	3	4	2	1	5	250	1	2	2	4	5	.	2	21
9	9	4	0	1	0	0	1	5	2	3	4	300	2	3	2	.	.	.	3	21
10	10	3	1	1	0	0	2	3	1	5	4	100	1	2	1	1	1	.	3	21
11	11	3	1	1	0	1	2	3	1	4	5	75	2	2	1	2	3	.	3	19
12	12	2	1	0	1	0	1	4	3	2	5	50	2	3	1	.	.	.	2	22
13	13	1	1	0	1	0	1	5	2	3	4	55	2	3	2	1	2	.	1	21
14	14	3	1	1	0	0	2	4	1	3	5	75	3	3	2	4		.	3	20
15	15	1	1	1	0	0	3	2	1	5	4	150	3	3	1	1	2	5	1	20
16																				
17																				
18																				

Data View   Variable View

Figure 16.6   Data View window with data from 15 questionnaires

This is similar to the spreadsheet data file as shown in Figure 16.1. Indeed, if the data have already been typed into a spreadsheet and saved in a file, this file can be uploaded directly by SPSS. Go to File > Open > Data and, in the 'Open Data' dialog box, locate the file and change the 'Files of type' to the appropriate type – e.g. Excel.

Note: the device A > B > C, as used above and in subsequent presentations, indicates that, having selected A, this reveals a dialog box in which B should be selected, which in turn reveals another dialog box in which C should be selected.

Once the Data View and Variable View windows have been completed and the file saved, you are ready to begin analysis.

6. Analysis procedures

6.1 Starting an analysis session

The data file containing the data being used may already be on-screen (as in Table 16.2) since data entry has just been completed. If not, and in subsequent sessions, a file will need to be opened, as shown in Table 16.4.

Note that, in dialog boxes presented in analysis sessions, variables may be referred to either by their *name* or by their *labels*, according to the analyst's preference. You can switch between these two by clicking on Edit > Options > General. In the discussion that follows, variable *names* are used.

Table 16.4 Starting a SPSS analysis session

1. Start-up SPSS using the appropriate screen icon or *Start* and *All Programs*.
2. The dialog boxes as indicated in Table 16.3 appear.
3. If this is the computer on which your SPSS file was set up it will be listed in Recent Files and it can be selected by clicking on it. If your file is not displayed, select *Open another file* and locate your file in the appropriate location/medium.
4. The completed *Data View* and *Variable View* windows will now be displayed, ready for analysis to begin

6.2 Descriptives

The *Descriptives* procedure produces a range of statistics for specified variables. It is a useful initial procedure to run as a check on certain minimal information for all variables. The details for running the procedure and an example of the resultant output are shown in Figure 16.7. The *Output* is shown in a new window. Output files can be saved or selected output can be copied and pasted into a word-processing or PowerPoint-type document and edited as required.

Procedures

1. From the tabs at the top of the screen: select *Analyze > Descriptive Statistics > Descriptives*
2. Select all variables except *qno* and transfer them to the *Variable(s)* box, as in a 'cut and paste' operation.
3. Select Options and ensure that the following are ticked: *Mean, St. Deviation, Minimum, Maximum* then click on *Continue*.
4. Click on *OK* to produce the following output.

Output: Descriptive Statistics

	N	Minimum	Maximum	Mean	Std. Deviation
Student status	15	1	4	2.53	.915
Campus cafe/bar in last 4 wks	15	0	1	.87	.352
Live campus music in last 4 wks	15	0	1	.53	.516
Travel service in last 4 wks	15	0	1	.13	.352
Daytime events (rank)	15	2	5	3.73	.961
Not available elsewhere (rank)	15	1	3	1.60	.737
Socialising (rank)	15	1	5	3.20	1.082
Quality of presentation (rank)	15	4	5	4.67	.488
Expenditure on entertainment/month	15	25	300	115.00	87.076
Relaxation opportunities – importance	15	1	3	2.20	.676
Social interaction – importance	15	2	3	2.67	.488
Mental stimulation – importance	15	1	2	1.47	.516
First suggestion	12	1	4	2.08	1.165
Second suggestion	8	1	5	2.50	1.414
Third suggestion	2	4	5	4.50	.707
Gender	15	1	2	1.47	.516
Age	15	18	24	20.47	1.506

Figure 16.7 Descriptives procedure and output

In the example used, five statistics are produced for each variable (except *qno*).

N – total count

The total count is 15 for all variables – except the second and third suggestions (*sug2*, *sug3*) since only 12 respondents offered a second suggestion and only 8 offered a third; for the others, these variables were blank.

Minimum and Maximum

For coded variables, this is a check that nothing has been miscoded outside the coding range, e.g. 1–3. For the non-coded numerical variables, the maximum and minimum provided may be a useful finding.

Mean

The mean, or average, is the sum of all the values for that variable divided by the number of responses (N) for that variable. It is one measure of the idea of the 'middle' – or 'central tendency' of the values for a variable for this sample; other *measures of central tendency* are discussed under the *Frequencies* procedure below. The mean is generally a useful statistic for:

● numerical variables – in this case, mean Expenditure is £115 and the mean Age of the sample members is 20.47 years; and

● ordinal variables – for example, the average rank for the Free/cheap variable is 1.8.

In general, this is not a useful statistic for nominal/coded variables, but there are exceptions:

● Likert scales – Relaxation, Social interaction, Mental stimulation – as discussed in Chapter 10, the score can be seen as an index of importance, so the mean is an indicator of the average level of importance for the sample. In this example, Social interaction (mean 2.67) is the most important and mental stimulation (mean 1.47) is the least important.

● 1–0 variables (Campus cafe/bar to travel service): since non-users score zero, the mean effectively is the number of users divided by the total, which is the proportion of users: thus, for example, the proportion of users of the cafe/bar is 0.87 or 87 per cent.

Standard deviation

The standard deviation is a measure of the spread of values around the mean. In this example, among the variables which respondents were asked to rank, for the Quality of presentation, the standard deviation is 0.488, while that for Socialising is 1.082: this makes sense when we see from the maximum/minimum that for the former all responses were either 4 or 5, whereas for the latter they ranged from 1 to 5. The standard deviation is discussed further in Chapter 17.

6.3 Frequencies

The *Frequencies* procedure is the simplest form of descriptive analysis: it merely produces counts and percentages for individual variables – for example, the numbers and percentages of respondents registered in each student status group. The procedure can be run for one variable at a time or for a number of variables. It is advisable to begin the analysis of a data set by running *Frequencies* for one variable – so that the computer can read through the data and establish that the data file is in working order.

Frequencies for one variable

The steps to obtain a table for the variable *status* are set out in Figure 16.8, together with the resultant output. The *Output* window presents two tables. The first, *Statistics*, indicates the number of 'valid cases' on which the analysis is based – in this case 15. The second table, headed *Student status*, shows:

- *Frequency* – count of the numbers of students is each status group;
- *Percent* converts frequency numbers into percentages;
- *Valid Percent* is explained under 'missing values'; and
- *Cumulative Percent*, which adds percentages cumulatively: this may be useful for a variable like *spend* or *age*, but is not particularly useful for the variable *status*.

Procedures

1. Select *Analyze > Descriptive Statistics > Frequencies*. This opens the *Frequencies* dialog box.
2. In the *Frequencies* dialog box:
   a. select the variable *status* transfer it to the *Variable(s)* box for analysis (transfer back any other variables in the *Variables* box from previous analyses).
   b. make sure that *Display frequency tables* is ticked.
   c. select *OK* and the results will appear in a new *Output* window as shown below.

Output

Student status

N	Valid	15
	Missing	0

Student status

		Frequency	Percent	Valid Percent	Cumulative Percent
Valid	F/T student/no paid work	2	13.3	13.3	13.3
	F/T student/paid work	5	33.3	33.3	46.7
	P/T student – F/T job	6	40.0	40.0	86.7
	P/T student/Other	2	13.3	13.3	100.0
	Total	15	100.0	100.0	

Figure 16.8   Frequencies for one variable

Frequencies for a number of variables

If the single variable table has worked satisfactorily, frequency tables for all the variables can be obtained by transferring all the variables (except *qno*) into the *Variables* box in Step 2 in Figure 16.8. Running frequency tables for all variables is a common initial instruction in survey analysis: it is a good way of obtaining an overview of the results, and checking that all is well with the data. The results of this exercise for the example questionnaire are presented in the text website.

6.4 Checking for errors

After obtaining the *Frequencies* printout for all variables, check through the results to see if there are any errors. This could be, for example, in the form of an invalid code or an unexpected missing value. The error must be traced in the data file and corrected, perhaps by reference back to the original questionnaire. The data must then be corrected on the data window and the *Frequencies* table for that variable run again. *The corrected, 'clean' data file should then be saved.*

6.5 Multiple response

Questions 2 and 6 in the example questionnaire are *multiple response* questions. They are single questions with a number of possible responses and must be analysed using a number of variables. Particular multiple response analysis procedures are available to handle their particular characteristics. There are two types of multiple response question:

- *Multiple response – dichotomous*: question 2 on use of campus services is a dichotomous variable, because each answer category is essentially a yes/no (two values) variable; any one respondent could tick one, two, three or all four boxes, so each is a separate variable.

- *Multiple response – categories*: question 6, on suggestions for improvements, has three variables, *sug1, sug2, sug3*, each coded with the same five category values, as discussed earlier.

It can be seen from the text website that the normal *Frequencies* procedure produces output for these questions in a rather inconvenient format – four tables for question 2 and three tables for question 6. The *Multiple Response* procedure combines these multiple responses into a single table for each question. The procedure is operated as shown in Figure 16.9, together with the results for questions 2 and 6. It should be noted that percentages are given related to the number of respondents *and* to the total number of responses – which of these to use depends on the aims of the research.

Procedure

1. Select *Analyze > Multiple Response > Define Variable Sets*

Multiple response – dichotomous

2. Transfer *cafebar, music, sport* and *travel* into the *Variables in Set* box
3. Under *Variables Are Coded As*, select *Dichotomies*
4. In the *Counted value* box: type *1*
5. Give the 'set' a *Name* – e.g. *services*
6. Add a *Label* – e.g. *Services used*
7. Select *Add: $Services is listed in the Multiple Response Sets* box
8. A new variable, *$services*, is listed automatically
9. Select *Close*

Multiple response – categories

2. Transfer *sug1, sug2, sug3* into the *Variables in Set* box
3. Under *Variables Are Coded As,* select *Categories*
4. Enter *Range 1* through *5*
5. Add *Name*, e.g. *Sugs*
6. Add *Label*, e.g. *Suggestions for improvement*
7. Select *Add: $Sugs is listed in the Multiple Response set* box
8. A new variable *$sugs* is listed automatically
9. Select *Close*

To produce a table:

10. Select *Analyze > Multiple Response > Frequencies*
11. Transfer the new variable(s) into the *Table(s) for* box and click on OK.

Output

Group: $Service – Services used (Value tabulated = 1)

Dichotomy label	Name	Count	Pct of Responses	Pct of Cases
Campus cafe/bar in last 4 wks	cafebar	13	46.4	92.9
Live campus music in last 4 wks	music	8	28.6	57.1
Sport facilities in last 4 wks	sport	5	17.9	35.7
Travel service in last 4 wks	travel	2	7.1	14.3
Total responses		28	100.0	200.0

1 missing case; 14 valid cases

Group: $Sug – Suggestions for improvement

Category label	Code	Count	Pct of Responses	Pct of Cases
Programme content	1	7	31.8	58.3
Timing	2	6	27.3	50.0
Facilities	3	3	13.6	25.0
Costs	4	4	18.2	33.3
Organisation	5	2	9.1	16.7
Total responses	22	100.0	183.3	

3 missing cases; 12 valid cases

Figure 16.9   Multiple response – procedure and output

6.6 Recode

As the name implies, *Recode* is a procedure which can be used to change the codes of variable values. The procedure can be applied to scale, ordinal or nominal variables. This might be done for a number of reasons:

● presentational: when there is a large number of categories and several contain small numbers of responses especially with uncoded scale variables;

● theoretical: when different parts of the analysis call for different groupings of response categories;

● comparative: when comparisons with previous research require different groupings; and

● statistical: as discussed in Chapter 17.

Recode with scale and ordinal variables

Scale and ordinal variables are not pre-coded – the actual value given by respondents is recorded in the data file. In the case of scale variables in particular, this means that the *Frequencies* procedure outlined earlier produces a table with one line for every value in the data set – as can be seen in the text website for variables *spend* and *age*. With large samples this can produce impractically large tables with possibly hundreds of lines, which would be unreadable and unmanageable, particularly for crosstabulation (discussed in section 6.9). A *Recoded*, grouped, version of such variables can be produced using the method demonstrated in the first part of Figure 16.10.

Ordinal variables, such as those in question 3, can be recoded – for example, ranks first and second could be grouped together, and third and fourth, and so on. Similarly, Likert-type variables, as in question 5, can be recoded – for example, grouping 'very important' and 'important' together.

It might be asked: if the variable is to be grouped anyway, why not use groupings in the questionnaire, where respondents can tick a box? This is often done, but the advantage of not having the variable pre-coded is that it is possible to be flexible about what groupings are required and it is also possible to use such procedures as *Means* and *Regression*, which is not generally possible with pre-coded or nominal variables.

Recode with nominal/pre-coded variables

It is also possible to change the groupings of nominal or pre-coded variables using *Recode*. For example, analysis could be conducted comparing all full-time students and all part-time students – that is, two groups rather than four. This is illustrated in the second part of Figure 16.10.

Part 1 For a scale or ordinal variable

Example: recode the variable *spend* as follows:

Proposed groupings	New code	Value labels
0–50	1	£0–50
51–100	2	£51–100
101–200	3	£101–200
201+	4	£201 and over

Procedure

1. Selects the tab: *Transform > Recode into Different Variables*.
2. Transfer the variable to be recoded, *spend*, into the Input *variable -> Output variable* box.
3. In the *Output Variable* box, add a *Name* (e.g. *spendr*) and *Label* (e.g. *Spend on entertainment – recoded*).
4. Select *Old and New Values*.
5. In the *Old Value* box select *Range*. In the first box enter *1* and in the second box, enter *50*.
6. In the *New Value > Value* box, enter *1*, then click on *Add*. The *Old –> New* box should now contain '1 thru 50 --> 1'.
7. Repeat steps 5 and 6 for: *51* through *100 – Value 2*; and 101 through 200 – *Value 3*.
8. Select *Range through Highest*: enter *201*. In the *Value* box enter *4*, then click on *Add*.
9. The *Old–New* box now contains: 1 thru 50-->1; 51 thru 100 --> 2; 101 thru 200 --> 3; 201 thru Highest --> 4. Click on *Continue*.
10. Select *Change*, then *OK*. The new variable, *spendr*, now appears on the Data View and Variable View screens.
11. Add *Value Labels*, as above, via the *Variable View* window, as for any variable.
12. *Save* the data file with the new variable, if you will want to use it again.
13. Produce a *Frequencies* table for the recoded variable *spendr* in the usual way (Figure 16.8), to produce the output below.

Output

	Frequency	Percent	Valid Percent	Cumulative Percent
£ 0–50	4	26.7	26.7	26.7
£ 51–100	6	40.0	40.0	66.7
£ 101–200	2	13.3	13.3	80.0
£ 201+	3	20.0	20.0	100.0
Total	15	100.0	100.0	

Part 2. For a string (pre-coded) variable

Example: recode the variable *status* as follows:

Current coding	New code	Value labels
1. F/T student – no work	1	Full-time student
2. F/T student – working		
3. P/T student – F/T job	2	Part-time student
4. P/T student – other		

Procedure

1–4. Repeat steps 1–3 above, using variable *status*, recoded variable name *statusr* and label *Status – recoded*.
5. In the *Old Value* box select *Range*. In the first box enter *1* and in the second box, enter *2*.
6. In the *Value* box, enter *1*, then click on *Add*. The *Old –> New* box should now contain '1 thru 2 --> 1.
7. Repeat steps 5 and 6 for: *3* through *4 – Value 2*. The *Old –> New* box also now contains '3 thru 4 --> 2.
8. Select *Continue*
9. Select *Change*, then *OK*. The new variable, *statusr*, now appears on the *Data View* and *Variable View* screens.
10. Add *Value Labels*, as above, via the *Variable View* window, as for any variable.
11. *Save* the data file with the new variable, if you will want to use it again.
12. Produce a *Frequencies* table for the recoded variable *statusr* in the usual way, to produce the output below.

Figure 16.10 Recode procedures and output *(continued)*

Output

	Frequency	Percent	Valid Percent	Cumulative Percent
Full-time student	7	46.7	46.7	46.7
Part-time student	8	53.3	53.3	100.0
Total	15	100.0	100.0	

Figure 16.10 *(continued)*

6.7 Mean, median and mode – measures of central tendency

We have already considered the idea of measures of central tendency and the mean in the discussion of *Descriptives*. As noted there, a *mean* is the same as an *average* and is appropriate only for scale or ordinal data, not for nominal variables with codes which represent qualitative categories, except for the exceptions discussed earlier.

Here we also consider two other measures of central tendency:

- the *median*, which is the value for which there are as many members of the sample above as there are below; and

- the *mode*, which is the value which contains the largest number of sample members.

Two procedures are available in SPSS for producing means, as shown in Figure 16.11. Method 1 uses a feature of the *Frequencies* procedure:

- Example 1a shows that:
  - mean expenditure on entertainment among the sample is £115;
  - the median value is £75, which is lower than the mean because there are more people in the lower expenditure categories than in the higher categories; and
  - the mode is £50, £75, £100, £200 and £250, since all have two responses.
- Example 1b demonstrates the use of the procedure for producing mean scores for Likert-type scales – the median does not have a lot of meaning, but the mode, which is the most popular value for each variable, may be meaningful and useful in some situations.

Method 2 uses the *Means* procedure which produces means for sub-groups as well as for the whole sample. For example, mean expenditures on entertainment are shown for students of different statuses. Note that this moves beyond description into the area of possible *explanation*, since it reveals that a student's full-time/part-time and employment status may lead to different levels of expenditure.

Method 1. Using *Frequencies* procedure

a. Scale variable

1. Select *Analyze > Descriptive Statistics > Frequencies*.
2. Select *spend* and transfer to the *Variable(s)* box.
3. Select *Statistics* and click on *Mean*, *Median* and *Mode*.
4. Select *Continue*.
5. Select *OK* to run the *Frequencies* in the normal way.

Output (Frequency table not reproduced)

Statistics: Expenditure on entertainment/month

N Valid	15	Mean	115.00
Missing	0	Median	75.00
		Mode	50*

(*indicates multiple modes exist: the smallest value is shown).

b. Attitude statements/Likert scales

Use the procedure as in *a.*, above, to produce means for the three variables: *relax, social* and *mental*. Output as follows.

Output (Frequency table not reproduced)

	Relaxation opportunities – importance	Social interaction – importance	Mental stimulation – importance
N Valid	15	15	15
Missing	0	0	0
Mean	2.20	2.67	1.47
Median	2.0	3.0	1.0
Mode	2	3	1

Method 2. Using *Means* procedure

1. Select *Analyze > Compare Means > Means*.
2. Transfer *status* to the *Independent list* box.
3. Transfer *spend* to the *Dependent list* box.
4. Select *OK*. Means and standard deviations for each course group are produced, as below, showing different values for different groups.

(NB Dependent and independent variables are discussed in Ch. 17.)

Output

Expenditure on entertainment/week

Student status	Mean	N	Std. Deviation
F/T student/no paid work	102.50	2	67.175
F/T student/paid work	120.00	5	83.666
P/T student – F/T job	99.17	6	76.643
P/T student/Other	162.50	2	194.454
Total	115.00	15	87.076

Figure 16.11 Means procedures and output

6.8 Presenting the results – statistical summary

The layout of the frequency tables produced by the software contains more detail than is necessary for most reports. It is recommended that a *Statistical Summary* be prepared for inclusion in any report, rather than include a copy of the computer printout. The summary must be prepared with a word-processor, either typing it out afresh or editing the saved SPSS *Output* file. For example, the output from the *Frequencies, Recodes, Multiple response* and *Means* analysis covered so far, could be summarised as in Table 16.5.

Table 16.5   Campus Life Survey 2010: statistical summary

Sample size	15	*Expenditure on entertainment/month*	%
Student status	%	£0–50	26.7
F/T student/no paid work	13.3	£51–100	40.0
F/T student/paid work	33.3	£101–200	13.3
P/T student – F/T job	40.0	Over £200	20.0
P/T student/Other	13.3	Average	£115.00
Total	100.0		
		Suggestions for improvements	% of cases
Campus services used in the last 4 wks	%	Comments on programme content	58.3
Cafe/bar	86.7	Comments on timing	50.0
Live campus music	53.3	Comments on facilities	25.0
Sport facilities	33.3	Comments on costs	33.3
Travel service	13.3	Comments on organisation	16.7
Importance of factors in services	*avge rank.*	*Gender*	%
Free/cheap access	1.8	Male	53.3
Daytime events	3.7	Female	46.3
Not available elsewhere	1.6		%
Opportunities for socialising	3.2	*Age*	26.7
Quality of presentation	4.7	18–19	53.4
		20–21	20.0
		22 and over	

Importance of factors in campus services

	Very important	Important	Not Important	Mean score*
	%	%	%	
Relaxation opportunities	33.3	53.3	13.3	2.2
Social interaction	66.7	33.3	0.0	2.7
Mental stimulation	0.0	46.7	53.3	1.5

(* 3 = very important 2 = important 1 = not important.)

The following should be noted about the summary:

- The results from *Multiple Response* variables are presented in single tables.
- Recoded versions of *spend* and *age* are included.
- The mean *spend* and *age* and the mean scores for the attitude/Likert-type variables come from the *Means* procedure discussed earlier.
- It is generally not necessary to include raw frequency counts as well as percentages in reports, since the sample size is indicated: readers of the summary can work out the raw numbers for themselves if required.

6.9 Crosstabulation

Introduction

After calculation of frequencies and means, the most commonly used procedure used in survey analysis is probably crosstabulation. This relates two or more variables to produce tables of the sort commonly encountered in social research. In analysing the relationships between variables, crosstabulation marks the move from purely descriptive to explanatory analysis. The SPSS *Crosstabs* procedure and output are demonstrated in Part 1 of Figure 16.12.

Part 1 Crosstabs – Counts only

Procedure
1. Select *Analyze > Descriptive Statistics > Crosstabs*.
2. Transfer *music* to the *Columns* box.
3. Transfer *status* to the *Rows* box.
4. Select *OK*. Output is as below.

Output

Student status * Live campus music in last 4 wks Crosstabulation

		Live campus music in last 4 wks		Total
		No	Yes	
Student status	F/T student/no paid work	1	1	2
	F/T student/paid work	3	2	5
	P/T student – F/T job	2	4	6
	P/T student/Other	1	1	2
Total		7	8	15

Part 2 Crosstabs with row percentages

Procedure

1–3. Repeat steps 1–3 above.
4.   In the *Crosstabs* dialog box select *Cells*. The *Crosstabs: Cell Display* dialog box is presented.
5.   In the *Counts* box click on the tick in the Observed box to delete it.
6.   In the *Percentages* box, select *Row*.
7.   Select *Continue*, then *OK*. Output appears with percentages as follows.

Figure 16.12   Crosstabs – procedures and outputs *(continued)*

Output

Student status * Live campus music in last 4 wks Crosstabulation

		Live campus music in last 4 wks		
		No	Yes	Total
Student status	F/T student/no paid work	50.0%	50.0%	100.0%
	F/T student/paid work	60.0%	40.0%	100.0%
	P/T student – F/T job	33.3%	66.7%	100.0%
	P/T student/Other	50.0%	50.0%	100.0%
Total		46.7%	53.3%	100.0%

Part 3 Three-way crosstabulation

Procedure

1. Repeat steps 1–3 in Part 1 above.
4. In the *Crosstabs* dialog box: transfer *gender* into the *Layer* box.
5. Select *OK* to produce output as follows.

Output

Student status * Live campus music in last 4 wks *Gender Crosstabulation

Gender			Live campus music in last 4 wks		
			No	Yes	Total
Male	Student status	F/T student/no paid work	1	1	2
		P/T student – F/T job	2	3	5
		P/T student/Other	0	1	1
	Total		3	5	8
Female	Student status	F/T student/paid work	3	2	5
		P/T student – F/T job	0	1	1
		P/T student/Other	1	0	1
	Total		4	3	7

Figure 16.12   *(continued)*

Rows and columns

Having been specified as the *row* variable in Figure 16.17 Part 1, *status* appears down the side of the table, while the *column* variable, *music*, appears across the top. Specifying the two variables the other way around would produce a table with *status* across the top and *music* down the side.

Percentages

In most cases percentages are required in tables rather than just the raw figures. The Figure 16.12 Part 1 procedure includes percentages only for the row and column totals (which are the same as the percentages in the *Frequencies* tables for the individual variables). The cells in the body of the table contain only counts of the raw data, not percentages. To produce percentages in the body of the table, it is necessary to specify the 'cell contents'. There are four relevant options for individual cell contents:

● counts

● row percentages – where percentages add to 100 going across a row

- column percentages – where percentages add to 100 going down the column

- total percentages – where all cell percentages add to 100.

The choice of which percentages to use depends on the context and the purpose of the analysis – it generally becomes apparent in the course of discussing the contents of a table; often 'trial and error' is involved in testing out the use of particular percentages in particular situations. The procedures for producing row percentages in *Crosstabs* are shown in Part 2 of Figure 16.12.

Three-way crosstabulations

Often three-way crosstabulations are required. For example, the above table could be further subdivided by gender. This is demonstrated in Part 3 of Figure 16.12. Further subdivision is possible, although often sample size places limits on how far this can go.

6.10 Weighting

The weighting of data to correct for biased samples is discussed in Chapter 13, where the procedure for calculating a *weighting factor* is discussed. The simplest way of introducing a weighting factor to the SPSS process is to add the weights as an additional variable. For example, the 'weighting' variable might be called *wt* and the weight for each case typed into the data file like any other item of data.

To weight data, select *Data > Weight Cases*, specifying a weighting variable (e.g. *wt*). To save typing in the weights for every case, SPSS provides a logical procedure. For example, if all full-time students are to be given a weight of 1.3, it is possible to indicate this in the *Weight Cases* procedure. It is not intended to explain the detail of this procedure here – the reader is referred to the Help facility in the *Weight Cases* dialog box.

6.11 Graphics

Graphical presentation of data is an aid to communication in most situations. For example, most people can see trends and patterns in data more easily in graphic form. Computer packages generally offer the following graphic formats for data presentation:

- bar graph,
- stacked bar graph,

- pie chart,

- line graph,

- scatter plot.

Computers can produce all five formats from any one set of data. But all formats are not equally appropriate for all data types: the appropriate type of graphic depends on the type of data or level of measurement involved. The three data types therefore lend themselves to different graphical treatment. The relationships between these types of data and permitted graphical types are summarised in Table 16.6:

- The *bar graph* or *histogram* is perhaps the most commonly used graphic in leisure and tourism research. Because it deals with *categories* for each bar, any scale variable must first be divided into groups – using the *Recode* procedure. The 'stacked' bar graph includes information on two variables – the graphical equivalent of the crosstabulation.

- The *pie chart* is just that: it divides something into sections like a pie. The segments making up the pie chart must therefore add up to some sort of meaningful total – often the total sample or 100 per cent.

- The *line graph* is the most constrained and is used more generally in research in more quantified fields such as economics and the natural sciences. Strictly speaking, they should be used only with *scale* variables.

  - A line graph with a single *scale* variable indicates the distribution of a variable, although for the type of data in the example survey, this is probably best done by means of a bar chart.

Table 16.6 Data types and graphics (* Grouped)

	Data type		
	Nominal	**Ordinal**	**Scale**
Data characteristics	Qualitative categories	Ranks	Numerical
Example questions in Fig.10.20	1, 2, 6, 7	3, 5	4, 8
Mean/average possible	No	Yes	Yes
Types of graphic			
Bar graph	Yes	Yes	Yes*
Pie chart	Yes	Yes	Yes*
Line graph	No	No	Yes
Scatter plot	No	No	Yes

- A line graph can be used to show the relationship between two *scale* variables – with one variable on each axis. However, a fitted *regression* line, as discussed in Chapter 17, is generally more meaningful than a line traced through all observation points, as would happen with a line graph.
- A *scatter plot* is based on *two* scale variables but involves just plots of the observation points, rather than drawing a line through them. A 'best fit' line may however be produced based on *regression*, as discussed in Chapter 17.

Graphics are easily produced in SPSS using an optional feature of the *Frequencies* command, but this is not very flexible. A better option is the *Graphs* facility. Examples of graphics output from this facility are shown in Figure 16.13. Graphics can be copied and pasted into word-processing or PowerPoint-type documents. It is not proposed to consider graphics procedures in detail here; details can be found in the SPSS Graphs Help facility.

a. Bar chart
1. Select the tab Graphs > *Legacy Dialogs* > *Bar.*
2. In the *Bar Charts* dialog box select *Simple* and *Summaries for groups of cases,* then *Define.*
3. In the *Define Simple Bar* dialog box, transfer *status* to the *Category Axis* box.
4. In the *Bars Represent* box, select *N of cases* or *% of cases.* In example here, *% of cases* has been selected.
5. Select *OK* to produce the bar chart.

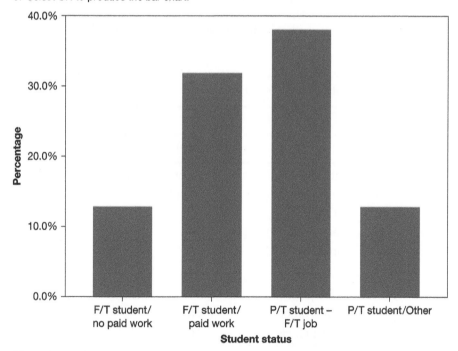

Figure 16.13   Graphics procedures and outputs *(continued)*

b. Stacked bar chart

1. Select *Graphs > Legacy Dialogs > Bar*.
2. In the *Bar Charts* dialog box, select Stacked and *Summaries for groups of cases*, then *Define*.
3. In the Define Stacked Bar dialog box, transfer *status* to the *Category axis* box and *gender* to the *Define Stacks by* box.
4. In the *Bars Represent* box, select *N of cases* or *% of cases*. In the example here, *N of cases* has been selected.
5. Select *OK* to produce the stacked bar chart.

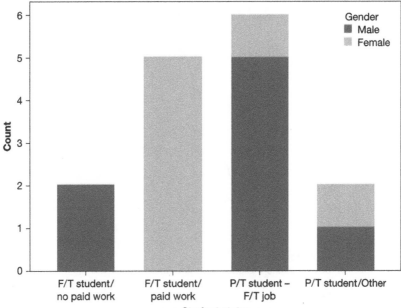

c. Pie chart

1. Select *Graphs > Legacy Dialogs > Pie*.
2. Select *Summary for Groups of Cases*, then *Define* to produce the dialog box: *Define Pie: Summaries for Groups of Cases*.
3. Transfer *status* to the *Define slices* box.
4. Select *N of cases* or *% of cases*. In the example here, *N of cases* has been selected.
5. Select *OK* to produce the pie chart.

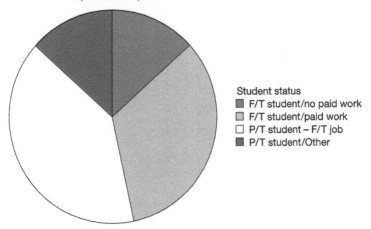

Figure 16.13   *(continued)*

d. Line graph

1. Select *Graphs > Legacy Dialogs > Line*.
2. Select *Line Simple,* then *Define* to produce the dialog box: *Define Simple Line: Summaries for Groups of Cases*.
3. Transfer *age* to the *Category axis* box.
4. Select *N of cases* or *% of cases*. In the example here, *N of cases* has been selected.
5. Select *OK* to produce the line graph.

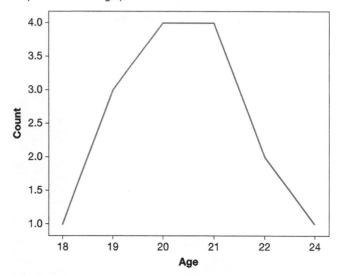

e. Scattergram

1. Select *Graphs > Legacy Dialogs > Scatter/Dot*.
2. Select *Simple Scatter,* then *Define* to produce the dialog box: *Simple Scatterplot*.
3. Transfer *spend* to the *Y-axis* box and *age* to the *X-axis* box.
4. Select *OK* to produce the scattergram (The default dots are hollow; solid black fill is obtained by right-clicking on the graphic and selecting: Edit content > In separate window).

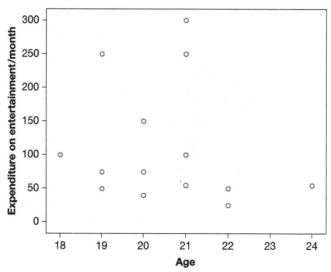

Figure 16.13 *(continued)*

7. The analysis process

The process described in this chapter is only a brief introduction to the mechanics of survey data analysis. While SPSS is capable of much more sophisticated analysis, mastery of the procedures presented here can provide a sound basis for a viable programme of investigation.

Summary

This chapter introduces the analysis of quantitative data, comprising a number of cases each with a common set of variables. The focus is on data from a questionnaire survey. The chapter opens with a discussion of the relationship between types of research (as presented in Chapter 1) and types of data analysis, including examination of levels of measurement and three corresponding variable types: nominal, ordinal and scale. Based on the introduction to coding in Chapter 10, a simple procedure for conducting some analysis using a spreadsheet is presented. The process of introducing survey data and information on variables into the SPSS computer package is then demonstrated. The chapter covers the following SPSS analysis procedures:

- *Frequencies* provides counts and percentages for individual and multiple variables.
- *Multiple response* creates single tables for the two or more variables arising from questions with multiple responses.
- *Recode* is used to create groups for scale variables and regroup pre-coded variables.
- *Means* calculates the means, or averages of variables and compares means medians and modal values for sub-samples.
- *Crosstabs* creates crosstabulations or frequency tables showing the relationships between two or more variables.
- *Weight* is used to weight data according to some criterion variable, as discussed in Chapter 13.
- *Graphs* produces graphical representations of data in various forms, including bar charts, pie charts, line graphs and scatter plots.

Test questions

1. Explain the difference between nominal, ordinal and scale variables and give examples.

2. What is the advantage of using an uncoded format for a scale variable in a questionnaire, rather than coding it into groups?

3. Outline the characteristics of the two types of multiple response question.

4. What are the two methods for obtaining means in SPSS?

Exercises

1. The major exercise for this chapter is to replicate the analyses presented in the chapter. This can be done by typing the data and variable definition data in Figures 16.5 and 16.6 or downloading them from the text website, and carrying out the instructions for the various procedures in the chapter.

2. Repeat each of the procedures in exercise 1 using at least one different variable in each procedure.

3. Conduct a survey of students using the questionnaire in Figure 10.8 and analyse the data using SPSS, following the analysis procedures outlined in this chapter.

Resources

SPSS

- Access and guidance: It is envisaged that most readers will have access to a teacher/tutor to assist as problems arise. The SPSS package itself includes a tutorial for beginners, and there are numerous books available on the use of SPSS. In higher education institutions, SPSS, as with other computer packages, is generally made available in computer laboratories on licence. Further training is available in SPSS, and other survey packages, through universities, commercial computer training organisations and the SPSS company itself in major centres around the world.

- The SPSS website is at: www.SPSS.com.

- A number of guides to the use of SPSS exist Carver and Nash (2005); Coakes (2012); George and Mallery (2005); Pallant (2016).

Text website

Full results from Frequencies procedure for all variables.

Questionnaire survey analysis generally

- It is difficult to locate published research reports which give full details of questionnaire surveys and their analysis. While many journal articles are based on survey research, they typically do not provide a copy of the questionnaire and provide only a brief summary of the analysis process – often only part of the analysis arising from the data.

- Few commercially published books are based primarily on questionnaire survey data, and, even when they are, full details are not always provided: one exception is Bennett et al. (1999), which provides not only a listing of the questions in the questionnaire but also a detailed discussion of the relationship between existing theory (by Bourdieu) and the empirical research described in the book.

- Government-sponsored survey reports, by the government statistical agency or other agencies, often contain these details – although inevitably they are generally either purely descriptive or related in a fairly straightforward manner to policy issues. Such reports are inconsistently available in libraries but are sometimes available on the internet, as indicated in the Resources section of Chapter 10.

- For an international review of survey evidence on leisure, time-use and tourism surveys in 17 countries, see Cushman et al. (2005).

References

Bennett, T., Emmison, M., and Frow, J. (1999). *Accounting for tastes: Australian everyday cultures*. Cambridge: Cambridge University Press.

Carver, R. H., and Nash, J. G. (2005). *Doing data analysis with SPSS version 12.0*. Belmont, CA: Thomson/Brooks/Cole.

Carver, R. H., Nash, J. G., and Gradwohl, J. (2011). *Doing data analysis with SPSS Version 18.0*, 5th edn. Belmont, CA: Thomson/Brooks/Cole.

Coakes, S. J. (2012). *SPSS analysis without anguish: (Version 20.0 for Windows)*. Brisbane: John Wiley & Sons.

Cushman, G., Veal, A. J., and Zuzanek, J. (Eds) (2005). *Free time and leisure participation: international perspectives*. Wallingford, UK: CABI Publishing.

George, D., and Mallery, P. (2005). *SPSS for Windows step by step: a simple guide and reference, 18.0 update*. Boston, MA: Pearson Education.

Pallant, J. F. (2016). *SPSS survival manual: a step by step guide to data analysis using SPSS*, 6th edn. Sydney: Allen & Unwin.

17 Statistical analysis

1. Introduction

2. The statistics approach

3. Data types and appropriate statistical tests

4. Chi-square

5. Comparing two means: the t-test

6. A number of means: one-way analysis of variance (ANOVA)

7. Factorial analysis of variance (ANOVA)

8. Correlation

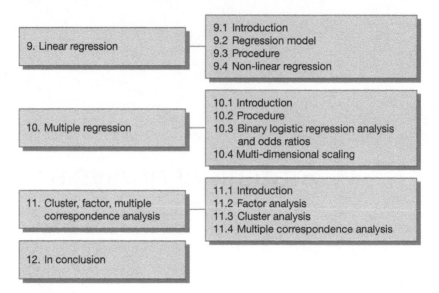

1. Introduction

This chapter provides an introduction to statistics, building on the outline of sampling theory presented in Chapter 13 and the introduction to the data analysis outlined in Chapter 16. It is *only* an introduction: it is not intended to be a complete course in statistics. Many textbooks cover approximately the same ground as covered in this chapter, but in more detail and greater depth, and reference to some of these texts is given in the Resources section. The outline of survey analysis in Chapter 16 deals with quantification and the generation and analysis of statistical information, but this chapter is concerned with more than just quantification. Given that, as discussed in Chapter 13, data based on samples are subject to a margin of error when generalising to the population from which they were drawn, this chapter examines how the accuracy of sample-based statistical data can be assessed and, in particular, how relationships between variables might be analysed and their statistical significance determined.

After discussing some general concepts related to the statistical method, the chapter covers a number of statistical tests which are appropriate for different types of data. In each case the SPSS procedures for carrying out the tests are described. At the end of the chapter some analysis procedures which are not covered by SPSS but are used in some leisure/tourism research are discussed in general terms.

2. The statistics approach

Some preliminary statistical concepts and ideas should be discussed, namely: the idea of probabilistic statements; the normal distribution; probabilistic statement formats; statistical significance; the null hypothesis; and dependent and independent variables.

2.1 Probabilistic statements

In general, the science of 'inferential statistics' seeks to make *probabilistic* statements about a *population* on the basis of information available from a *sample* drawn from that population. The statements are *probabilistic* because, as discussed in Chapter 13, it is not possible to be absolutely sure that any randomly drawn sample is truly representative of the population from which it has been drawn, so we can only estimate the *probability* that results obtained from a sample are true of the population. The statements which might be made on the basis of sample survey findings can be descriptive, comparative or relational:

- descriptive: for example, 10 per cent of adults play tennis;
- comparative: for example, 10 per cent of adults play tennis but 12 per cent play golf; and
- relational: for example, 15 per cent of people with high incomes play tennis but only 7 per cent of people with low incomes do so; there is a positive relationship between tennis-playing and income.

If they are based on data from samples, such statements cannot be made without qualification. The *sample* may indicate these findings, but it is not certain that they apply precisely to the population from which the sample is drawn, because there is always an element of doubt about any sample. Inferential statistics modifies the above example statements to be of the form:

- We can be 95 per cent confident that the proportion of adults that play tennis is between 9 per cent and 11 per cent.
- The proportion of golf players is *significantly* higher than the proportion of tennis players (at the 95 per cent level of probability).
- There is a positive relationship between level of income and level of tennis playing (at the 95 per cent level of probability).

2.2 The normal distribution

Descriptive statements and *confidence intervals* are discussed in general terms in Chapter 13 in relation to the issue of sample size. The probability or confidence interval statement is based on the *theoretical* idea of drawing repeated samples of the same size from the same population. The sample drawn in any one piece of research is only one of a large number of *possible* samples which *might* have been drawn. If a large number of samples *could* be drawn, such an exercise would produce a variety of results, some very unrepresentative of the population but most, assuming random sampling procedures are used, tending to produce results close to the true population values. Statistical theory – which we are unable to explore in detail here – is able to quantify this tendency, so that we can say that, in 95 or 99 out of 100 such samples, the values found from the sample will fall within a certain range on either side of the true population value – hence the idea of confidence intervals as discussed in Chapter 13.

The theory relates to the bell-shaped *normal distribution* which would result if repeated samples were drawn and the values of a statistic (for example, the proportion who play tennis) plotted, as shown in Figure 17.1. The *normal curve* which would result if a very large number of samples was drawn is shown in Figure 13.1. The population value of a statistic (such as a percentage or the average of a variable) lies at the centre of the distribution, and the value of the statistic found from a sample in a particular research project is just one among

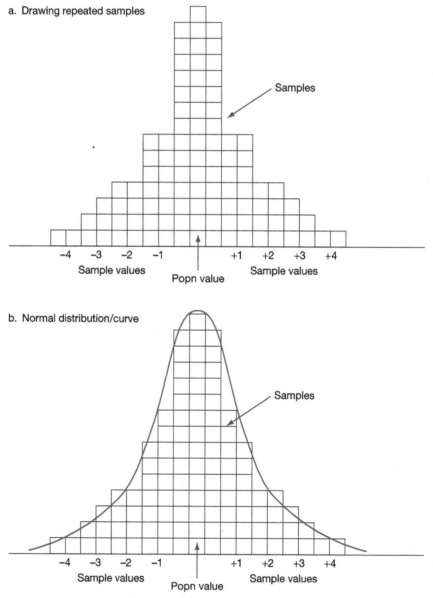

Figure 17.1 Drawing repeated samples and the normal distribution

the many sample possibilities. The probabilistic statement is made on the basis of this distribution, which has theoretically known properties for different samples and measures, such as percentages and means.

This idea of levels of probability concerning the accuracy of sample findings, based on the theoretical possibility of drawing many samples, is common to most of the statistical procedures examined in this chapter.

2.3 Probabilistic statement formats

It is customary in social research to use probability levels of 95 per cent or 99 per cent – and occasionally 90 per cent or 99.9 per cent. As probability estimates these can be interpreted exactly as in everyday language – for example, when we say '90 per cent certain', '50:50' or '9 times out of 10', we are making probabilistic statements. So, if a survey finding is *significant* (a concept discussed further in section 2.4) at the '99 per cent level', we are saying that we believe that there is a 99 per cent chance that what we have found is true of the population. There is therefore, conversely, a 1 per cent chance that what we have found is *not* true. If we can only say that something is significant at the lower 95 per cent level, we are less confident – there is a 5 per cent chance that what we have found is not significant. Thus the terminology *highly significant* is sometimes used in relation to findings at the 99 per cent level and *significant* for the 95 per cent level.

In some cases, instead of the computer-generated results of statistical tests using these conventional cut-off points, they present the exact probability – for example, it might be found that a result is significant at the 96.5 per cent level or the 82.5 per cent level. It is then left up to the researcher to judge whether such levels are acceptable.

Note also, that sometimes the result is expressed as 1 per cent rather than 99 per cent, or as 5 per cent rather than 95 per cent. A further variation is to express the probability as a proportion rather than a percentage – for example, 0.05 rather than 5 per cent, or 0.01 rather than 1 per cent. Similarly, the exact calculations may be expressed as proportions – for example, 0.035 rather than 3.5 per cent or 96.5 per cent.

In the following, therefore, in each row the three forms are equivalent.

5%	95%	0.05
1%	99%	0.01
0.1%	99.9%	0.001
3.5%	96.5%	0.035
7.5%	92.5%	0.075

In computer printouts from SPSS, if the probability is below .0005, it sometimes comes out as .000 because it is printed only to three decimal places. In some research reports and computer printouts, results which are significant at the 5 per cent level are indicated by * and those significant at the 1 per cent level are indicated by **.

In the examples and discussions in this chapter, the 5 per cent/95 per cent value is used as the criterion level of tests of significance.

2.4 Significance

The second common feature of statistical tests and procedures is that they deal with the idea of *significance*. A *significant* difference or relationship is one which is *unlikely to have happened by chance*. So, for example, the bigger the difference between two sample percentages, the more likely it is that the difference is *real* and not just a statistical chance happening.

For example, if it was found from a sample that 10 per cent of women played tennis and 11 per cent of men played tennis, we would be inclined, even from a common-sense point of view, to say that the difference is not significant. If another sample were selected, we would not be surprised to find a larger difference between the two figures, for them to be exactly the same or even the opposite way around: it is 'too close to call'. However, whether or not such a small difference is *statistically* significant depends on the sample size. If the findings were based on a small sample, say around 100 people, 50 men and 50 women, the difference would not be significant – the chances of getting a different result from a different sample of 100 people from the same population would be high – one person more or less in each group would change the proportion by 2 per cent. But if the sample were large – say 1000 men and 1000 women – then a small difference of even one percentage point might be found to be statistically significant, since in this case the difference would represent not just one or two persons, but 10 persons. So if the result is based on such a large sample, we can be much more confident that it is 'real' and would be reproduced if another sample of similar size were drawn.

Statistical theory enables us to quantify and assess significance – that is, to say what sizes of differences are significant for what sizes of sample.

Statistical significance should not, however, be confused with *social, theoretical* or *managerial* significance. For example, if the finding that 10 per cent of women and 11 per cent of men played tennis was based on a sample of, say, 10,000 people, it would be *statistically* significant, but this does not make the difference significant in any social sense. For all practical purposes, on the basis of such findings, we would say that men's and women's tennis playing rates are the same or very similar. This is a very important point to bear in mind when reading research results based on statistics; large samples can produce many 'statistically significant' findings; but that does not necessarily make them 'significant' in any other way.

2.5 The null hypothesis

A common feature of the statistical method is the concept of the *null hypothesis*, referred to by the symbol H_0. It is based on the idea of setting up two mutually incompatible hypotheses, so that only one can be true. If one proposition is true then the other is untrue. The null hypothesis usually proposes that there is *no difference* between two observed values or that there is *no relationship* between variables. There are therefore two possibilities:

H_0 – Null hypothesis: there is *no* significant difference or relationship.
H_1 – Alternative hypothesis: there *is* a significant difference or relationship.

Usually it is the *alternative* hypothesis, H_1, that the researcher is interested in, but statistical theory explores the implications of the *null* hypothesis.

In terms of the types of research approach discussed in Chapter 2, this is very much a *deductive* approach: the hypothesis is set up in advance of the analysis. However, as noted in Chapter 2, this may be set in the context of an exploratory or even inductive project in which a number of relationships is explored, but the testing of each relationship is set up as a deductive process.

The use of the null hypothesis idea can be illustrated by example. Suppose, in a study of leisure participation patterns using a sample of 1000 adults, part of the study focuses on the relative popularity of golf and tennis. The null hypothesis would be that the participation levels are the same.

H_0 – tennis and golf participation levels are the same; and
H_1 – tennis and golf participation levels are significantly different.

Suppose it is found that 120 people (12%) play tennis and 120 (12%) play golf. Clearly, there is no difference between the two figures; they are consistent with the null hypothesis. The null hypothesis is accepted and the alternative hypothesis is rejected.

But suppose the numbers playing tennis were found to be 121 (12.1%) and the number playing golf was 120 (12.0%). Would we reject the null hypothesis and accept the alternative, that tennis and golf participation levels are different? From what we know of samples, clearly not: this would be too close to call. Such a small difference between the two figures would still be consistent with the null hypothesis. So how big would the difference have to be before we reject the null hypothesis and accept that there is significant difference? A difference of 5, 10, 15? This is where statistical theory comes in: to provide a test of what is and is not a *significant difference*. This is basically what the rest of this chapter is all about: providing tests of the relationship between sample findings and the null hypothesis for different situations. The null hypothesis is used in each of the tests examined.

2.6 Dependent and independent variables

The terminology *dependent variable* and *independent variable* is discussed in Chapter 1 and is frequently used in statistical analysis. If there is a significant relationship between a dependent and an independent variable, the *implication* is that changes in the former are caused by changes in the latter: the independent variable *influences* the dependent variable.

For example, if it is suggested that the level of holiday-taking is influenced by a person's income level, then the level of holiday-taking is the *dependent* variable and income is the *independent* variable. Even though a certain level of income does not *cause* people to go on holiday, it makes more sense to suggest that level of income facilitates or constrains the level of holiday-taking, than to suggest the opposite. So it makes some sense to talk of holiday-taking being *dependent* on income. One variable can be dependent

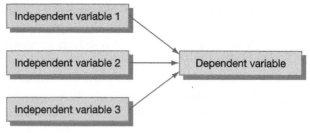

Figure 17.2   Dependent and independent variables

on a number of independent variables, as illustrated in Figure 17.2 – for example, it may be hypothesised that holiday-taking is dependent on income *and* occupation *and* age.

3. Data types and appropriate statistical tests

The idea of levels of measurement, or types of data, was introduced at the beginning of Chapter 16, when nominal, ordinal and scale data types were discussed. The higher the level of measurement, the greater the range of analysis that can be carried out on the data. For example, it is possible to calculate means/averages of ordinal and scale data but not of nominal data. Consequently, different statistical tests are associated with different levels of measurement. The rest of the chapter sets out different statistical tests to be used in different situations, as summarised in Table 17.1. The tests all relate to comparisons between variables and relationships between variables. The appropriate type of test to be used depends on the format of the data, the level of measurement and the number of variables involved.

In what follows:

- Data from a questionnaire survey similar to that used in Chapter 16 are used to illustrate the various tests, but with a larger sample and additional leisure and tourism participation variables added.

- Listings of the additional questions and variables used are included as Appendix 17.1 and the expanded data file can be found on the website for this text.

- The variable *statusr* (student status recoded) in the data set is produced as shown in Figure 16.10.

- As in Chapter 16, the examples have been created using SPSS for Windows, Version 23.

- For readers who are mathematically inclined, formulae for various of the test statistics are shown in Appendix 17.2.

Table 17.1 Types of data and statistical test

Task	Format of data	No. of variables	Types of variable	Test
Relationship: 2 variables	Crosstabulation of frequencies	2	Nominal	Chi-square
Difference: 2 paired means	Means: whole sample	2	Two scale/ordinal	t-test – paired
Difference: 2 means – independent samples	Means: 2 sub-groups	2	a. Scale/ordinal (means) b. Nominal (2 groups only)	t-test – independent samples
Relationship: 2 variables	Means: 3+ sub-groups	2	a. Scale/ordinal (means) b. Nominal (3+ groups)	One-way analysis of variance
Relationship: 3+ variables	Means: crosstabulated	3+	a. Scale/ordinal (means) b. 2+ nominal	Factorial analysis of variance
Relationship: 2 variables	Individual measures	2	Two scale/ordinal	Correlation
Linear relationship: 2 variables	Individual measures	2	Two scale/ordinal	Linear regression
Linear relationship: 3+ variables	Individual measures	3+	Three or more scale/ordinal	Multiple regression
Relationships: large numbers of variables	Individual measures	Many	Large numbers of scale/ordinal	Factor analysis Cluster analysis

4. Chi-square

4.1 Introduction

The Chi-square test (symbol: χ^2, pronounced 'ky', to rhyme with sky) can be used in a number of situations, but its use is demonstrated here in relation to crosstabulations of two *nominal* variables – the familiar tables produced from such packages as SPSS. When examining crosstabulations, it is possible to use 'common sense' and an underlying knowledge of the size of confidence intervals, as discussed in Chapter 13, to make an approximate judgement as to whether there is any sort of relationship between the two variables involved in the table. However, unless the pattern is very clear, it can be difficult to judge whether the overall differences are *significant*. The chi-square test is designed to achieve this.

Table 17.2 Alternative expressions of hypotheses

	Option 1	Option 2	Option 3
Null hypothesis (H₀):	There is *no* relationship between full time/part-time status and gender.	Male and female full-time/part-time status is the same.	Observed and expected values are not significantly different.
Alternative hypothesis (H₁)	There *is* a relationship between full time/part-time status and gender.	Male and female full-time/part-time status is different.	Observed and expected values are significantly different.

4.2 Null hypothesis

The null hypothesis is that *there is no difference in full-time/part-time status between male and female students:* that is:

H_0 – there is *no* relationship between student status and gender in the population of students.
H_1 – there *is* a relationship between status and gender in the population of students.

Note that the proposition being tested can therefore be expressed in three ways, as shown in Table 17.2. The terms 'observed' and 'expected' in Option 3 are explained in section 4.4.

4.3 Procedure

Figure 17.3 shows the SPSS procedures to obtain a crosstabulation with a chi-square test, and the resultant output. The example chosen relates student full-time/part-time status (*statusr*) to gender (*gender*). The interpretation of this output is discussed below.

4.4 The value of Chi-square

The cells of the table include counts and column percentages, as discussed in relation to crosstabulations in Chapter 16. But they also include *expected counts.* These are the counts which *would be expected if the null hypothesis were true* – that is, if there was no difference between males and females in their full-time/part-time status. In this case we have an equal number of men and women in the sample, so the expected values show a 50:50 split for each status.

Procedure

1. Select *Analyze > Descriptive Statistics > Crosstabs.*
2. Transfer the variable *statusr* to the *Row(s)* box and *gender* to the *Column(s)* box.
3. Select *Statistics*. In the *Crosstabs: Statistics* dialog box, select *Chi-square*, then *Continue.*
4. Select *Cells*, then, in the *Crosstabs: Cells Display* dialog box:
   - in *Counts*: select *Observed* and *Expected*
   - in *Percentages*: select *Column*, then *Continue.*
5. Select *OK* to produce the output below (*Case Processing Summary* table omitted).

Output

Student status recoded * Gender Crosstabulation

			Gender		Total
			Male	Female	
Student status recoded	Full-time	Count	18	9	27
		Expected Count	13.5	13.5	27.0
		% within Gender	66.7%	33.3%	54.0%
	Part-time	Count	7	16	23
		Expected Count	11.5	11.5	23.0
		% within Gender	30.4%	69.6%	46.0%
Total		Count	25	25	50
		Expected Count	25.0	25.0	50.0
		% within Student status recoded	50.0%	50.0%	100.0%

Chi-Square Tests **(key items highlighted)**

	Value	df	Asymp. Sig. (2-sided)	Exact Sig. (2-sided)	Exact Sig. (1-sided)
Pearson Chi-Square	**6.522**[a]	**1**	**.011**		
Continuity Correction[b]	5.153	1	.023		
Likelihood Ratio	6.676	1	.010		
Fisher's Exact Test				.022	.011
Linear-by-Linear Association	6.391	1	.011		
N of Valid Cases	50				

a. 0 cells (.0%) have expected count less than 5. The minimum expected count is 11.50.
b. Computed only for a 2 × 2 table.

Figure 17.3 Chi-square test: procedure and output

Chi-square is a statistic based on the sum of the differences between the counts and the expected counts: the greater this sum, the greater the value of Chi-square. However, if the differences between the observed and expected counts in the table are simply added, it will be found that the positives cancel out the negatives, giving zero. Chi-square is therefore based on the sum of the *squared values of the differences*. The SPSS package calculates the value of Chi-square, so it is not necessary to know the details of the formula (shown in Appendix 17.2). It is sufficient to understand that Chi-square is a statistical measure of the difference between the observed and expected counts in the table.

In the example in Figure 17.3, the value of Chi-square is 6.522. We are using the 'Pearson' value, devised by the statistician Karl Pearson – the other values given do not concern us here.

How should this value of Chi-square be interpreted? We have noted that the greater the difference between the observed and expected values, the greater the value of Chi-square. Our null hypothesis is that there is *no* difference between the two sets of values. But clearly, we would accept some *minor* differences between two sets of values and still accept the null hypothesis. But just how big would the differences have to be before we would reject the null hypothesis and conclude that there *is* a difference between male and female full-time/part-time status?

For a given size of table (in this case, two cells by two), statisticians have been able to calculate the likelihood of obtaining various values of Chi-square when the null hypothesis is true. As with the normal distribution discussed in Chapter 16, this is based on the theoretical possibility of drawing lots of samples of the same size. This is shown in Figure 17.4. It shows that, for a particular table size, if the null hypothesis is true, some differences in observed and expected counts can be expected from most samples drawn from a given population, so a *range of values* of Chi-square can be expected. Most values of Chi-square would be expected to be fairly small; some larger values would occur, but only rarely – they are unlikely.

Therefore, any value of Chi-square in the range to the right of the 5 per cent point in the diagram is considered unlikely and *inconsistent with the null hypothesis*: we *reject* the null hypothesis. If it is in the range to the left of the 5 per cent point, we *accept* the null hypothesis.

In Figure 17.3, the output tells us the value of Chi-square for the table, 6.522, and the likelihood, or probability, of this value: 0.011, or 1.1 per cent. Our value of Chi-square is therefore an unlikely one (it has a likelihood/probability of less than 5 per cent), so we reject the null hypothesis and conclude that there *is* a significant difference between the proportions of male and female students with full-time and part-time status.

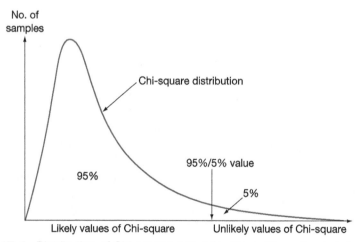

Figure 17.4 Distribution of Chi-square assuming the null hypothesis is true

4.5 Degrees of freedom

The values of Chi-square depend on the table size. This is measured by the *degrees of freedom*, calculated by: *the number of rows minus one* multiplied by *the number of columns minus one*. So, for the table in Figure 17.3, the degrees of freedom are: $(2 - 1) \times (2 - 1) = 1 \times 1 = 1$. This is shown in the output table under *df*.

One rule for the application of Chi-square is that there should not be more than one-fifth of the cells of the table with *expected counts* of less than five, and none with an *expected count* of less than one. The output indicates whether such cells exist. Note (a) at the bottom of the table indicates that no cells have an expected count of less than 5, and the minimum expected count is 11.5, so there is no problem. Grouping of some of the values by recoding can be used to reduce the number of cells and thus increase the expected frequencies. In fact, this was done in the example with the recoded variable – if the analysis is run with the original *status* variable, the test infringes the expected counts rule and is invalid.

4.6 Reporting

How should the results of statistical tests such as Chi-square be reported? Four solutions can be considered, as follows.

1. Include the results of the test in the table in the research report, as in Table 17.3. The commentary might then merely say: 'The relationship between full-time/part-time status and gender was significant at the 5 per cent level.'

2. Include the test results in the text. For example: 'The relationship between full-time/part-time status and gender was significant at the 5 per cent level ($\chi^2 = 6.5$, 1 DF).'

Table 17.3 Presentation of Chi-square test results

Status	Male	Female	Total
	%	%	%
Full-time student	66.7	33.3	54.0
Part-time student	30.4	69.6	46.0
Total	100.0	100.0	100.0
Sample size:	25	25	50

$x^2 = 6.52$, DF 1, significant at the 5% level

3. Make the statistics less intrusive by including a note in the report or paper indicating that all tests were conducted at the 5 per cent level and that test values are included in the tables, or are listed in an appendix, or even excluded altogether for non-technical audiences.

4. Use the * and ** approach to indicate significant and highly significant results in tables, as discussed in section 2.3.

5. Comparing two means: the t-test

5.1 Introduction

So far we have dealt only with proportions or percentages, either singly or in crosstabulations; but many research results are in the form of averages – for example, the average age of a group of participants in an activity, the average holiday expenditure of visitors from different countries, or the average score of a group on a Likert scale. In statistical parlance, an average is referred to as a *mean*. Means can be calculated only for *ordinal* and *scale* variables, not nominal variables.

The simplest form of analysis is to compare two means to see whether they are significantly different. For example, we might want to test whether the average age of golf players in a sample is significantly different from that of the tennis players, or whether the average amount spent on holidays by a group of people is greater or less than the amount spent on the arts and entertainment. In this situation, the null hypothesis is expressed as follows:

H_0 – Null hypothesis: there is *no* difference between the means.
H_1 – Alternative hypothesis: there *is* a difference between the means.

For this situation, rather than Chi-square, a statistic referred to as 't' is calculated – but the interpretation is similar. This is based on a formula involving the sample size and the two means to be compared. If there is *no difference* between two means in the population (H_0) then, for a given sample size, t has a known 'distribution' of likely values, as illustrated in Figure 17.5 in comparison with the Chi-square distribution. High values are rare, so if the value from a sample is high – in the top 5 per cent of values for that sample size – then we reject H_0 and accept H_1; that is, we conclude that there *is* a significant difference at the 5 per cent level of probability respectively. Note that, because 't' can take on negative or positive values there are two 'tails' to its distribution – hence the reference to 'two-tailed test' in some of the output discussed below.

There are two situations where we might want to compare means:

● To compare the means of two variables which apply to the whole sample – for example, comparing the average amount spent on holidays with the

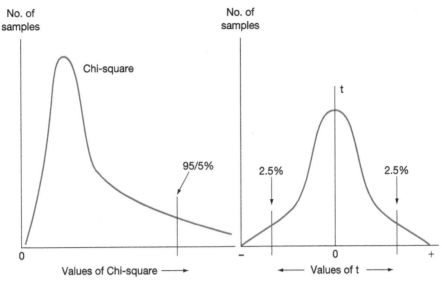

Figure 17.5 Chi-square and t distributions

average amount spent on the arts and entertainment (for everybody in the sample). This is known as a *paired samples test*.

- To compare the means of one variable for two sub-groups – for example, comparing the average age of men in the sample with that of women. The sample is divided into two sub-groups, men and women; this is known as a *group* or *independent samples* test.

5.2 Paired samples test

Figure 17.6 presents two examples of the paired samples test. The output provides a range of statistics with which we are not concerned here – including a correlation, which is discussed later in the chapter. The items of interest are depicted in bold in Figure 17.6.

Example 1 compares the frequency of playing sport/fitness with the frequency of visiting national parks.

- The people in the sample play sport/fitness on average 12.2 times in three months and visit national parks on average 9.8 times, a difference of 2.4. The question is whether this difference is significant.

- The value of t is 1.245 and its (2-tail) significance is 0.219 or 21.9 per cent.

- The result is consistent with the null hypothesis (0.219 is much higher than 0.05).

- We therefore accept the null hypothesis, that the difference between the level of sport playing and the level of visits to national parks is *not significant*.

Procedure

1. Select *Analyze > Compare Means > Paired Samples T-Test*.
2. Transfer the first variable to the *Paired variables* box, then transfer the second variable.
3. Select *OK* to obtain t-test output.

Output

Example 1: First variable: Playing Sport, second variable: Visiting National Parks

Paired Samples Statistics

		Mean	N	Std. Deviation	Std. Error Mean
Pair 1	**Play sport/fitness**	**12.20**	50	13.095	1.852
	Visit national park	**9.80**	50	8.804	1.245

Paired Samples Correlations (IGNORE)

		N	Correlation	Sig.
Pair 1	Play sport/fitness & Visit national park	50	.274	.054

Paired Samples Test

		Paired Differences					t	df	Sig. (2-tailed)
		Mean	Std. Deviation	Std. Error Mean	95% Confidence Interval of the Difference				
					Lower	Upper			
Pair 1	**Play sport/fitness – Visit national park**	**2.400**	13.631	1.928	−1.474	6.274	**1.245**	49	**.219**

Example 2: Visit national parks vs Going out for a meal

Paired Samples Statistics

		Mean	N	Std. Deviation	Std. Error Mean
Pair 1	**Visit national park**	**9.80**	50	8.804	1.245
	Go out for meal	**6.54**	50	3.157	0.446

Paired Samples Correlations – IGNORE

		N	Correlation	Sig.
Pair 1	Visit national park & Go out for meal	50	−.044	.759

Paired Samples Test

		Paired Differences					t	df	Sig. (2-tailed)
		Mean	Std. Deviation	Std. Error Mean	95% Confidence Interval of the Difference				
					Lower	Upper			
Pair 1	**Visit national park – Go out for meal**	**3.26**	9.484	1.341	0.565	5.955	**2.431**	49	**.019**

Figure 17.6 Comparing means: t-test: paired samples – procedure and output

Example 2 compares the frequency of visiting national parks and going out for a meal. In this case:

- the difference in the mean frequencies is 3.26;
- the value of t is 2.431;
- its significance level is 0.019, which is below 0.05; and
- so we reject the null hypothesis and conclude that there *is a significant difference* between the frequency of visiting national parks and going out for meals.

5.3 Independent samples test

Figure 17.7 compares male and female entertainment expenditure.

- Male expenditure is £110, female is £138.60, a difference of £28.60;
- t has a value of –1.25 and a significance level of 0.219; and
- 0.219 is above 0.05, consistent with the null hypothesis, so we accept that there is no significant difference between the two expenditure figures.

Procedure
1. Select *Analyze > Compare Means > Independent Samples T-Test*.
2. Transfer the variable for which the mean is required (spend) to the *Test variables box*.
3. Transfer the variable to be used to divide the sample into two groups (*gender*) to the *Grouping variable* box.
4. Select *Define groups* and enter the values used to divide the sample into two groups (in the example: 1 for Male and 2 for Female). Select *Continue* and the two values appear in brackets following the name of the grouping variable: *gender*(1, 2).
5. Select *OK* to obtain t-test.

Output

Group Statistics

	Gender	N	Mean	Std. Deviation	Std. Error Mean
Entertainment, £ p.m.	**Male**	25	**110.00**	77.607	15.521
	Female	25	**138.60**	84.613	16.923

Independent Samples Test

	Levene's Test for Equality of Variances		t-test for Equality of Means						
	F	Sig.	t	df	Sig. (2-tailed)	Mean Difference	Std. Error Difference	95% Confidence Interval of the Difference	
								Lower	Upper
Equal variances assumed	.431	.514	**–1.245**	48	**.219**	–28.600	22.963	–74.770	17.570
Equal variances not assumed			–1.245	47.646	.219	–28.600	22.963	–74.779	17.579

Figure 17.7 Comparing means: t-test: independent samples – procedure and output

Procedure

To obtain a table comparing means:

1. *Select Analyze > Compare Means > Means.*
2. Transfer the variables for which means are required (*sportfit, theatre, npark, meal, hols*) to the *Dependent list* box.
3· Transfer the grouping variable (*status*) to the *Independent list* box
4. In *Options,* ensure that *Mean* and *Number of cases* are in the *Cell statistics* box.
5. Select *OK* to produce the output.

Output

Student status		Play sport/fitness	Visit theatre	Visit national park	Go out for meal	Holiday expenditure
F/T student/no paid work	Mean	9.69	2.62	9.77	6.46	328.46
	N	13	13	13	13	13
F/T student/paid work	Mean	9.64	2.93	8.64	4.00	342.50
	N	14	14	14	14	14
P/T student – F/T job	Mean	19.06	2.25	8.63	8.19	425.63
	N	16	16	16	16	16
P/T student/Other	Mean	6.29	3.29	14.86	8.00	752.86
	N	7	7	7	7	7
Total	Mean	12.20	2.68	9.80	6.54	422.90
	N	50	50	50	50	50

Figure 17.8   Comparing ranges of means: procedure and output

6. A number of means: one-way analysis of variance (ANOVA)

6.1 Introduction

The t-test was used to examine differences between means two at a time. *Analysis of variance* (ANOVA) is used to examine *more than two* means at a time. This begins to resemble the crosstabulation process, but with *means* appearing in the cells of the table instead of counts. An example is shown in Figure 17.8, which compares mean leisure participation levels and holiday expenditure for the various student status groups. Here the question which we seek to answer with ANOVA is whether, for each activity/expenditure item, the mean for the different groups of students are different from the overall mean – that is, whether participation/expenditure is related to student status.

The null hypothesis is that all the means are equal to the overall mean. How different must the group means be from the overall mean before we reject this hypothesis? Before conducting the ANOVA test, we consider the concept of *variance*.

6.2 Variance

Whether or not the means are in effect from *one* population (with *one* mean) or from *different* sub-populations (with *different* means) depends not only on the differences between the means but also on the 'spread', or *variance*, of the cases upon which they are based. Figure 17.9 shows four examples of three means, with the associated spread of cases around them. The 'spread' of sample values is referred to as the *variance* and can be measured by adding up the differences between the scores of individual cases and the mean score.

A. The means are well spaced and there is very little overlap in the cases – there *is* a significant difference between the means.

B. The means are closer together and there is considerable overlap, suggesting that they may be from the same population.

C. The means are spaced as in A, but the spread around the means is greater and so overlap is considerable, suggesting uncertainty as to whether or not the means are significantly different.

D. The clearest case of overlap – so we can be fairly certain that the three sets of data are from the same population.

A visual presentation of this type of information, although in a different format, can be obtained using the *Boxplot* feature within the *Graphics* procedure of SPSS.

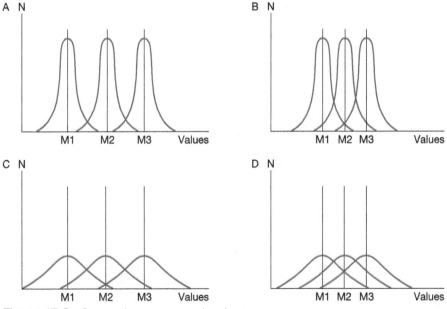

Figure 17.9   Comparing means and variances

6.3 ANOVA: analysis of variance

Whether or not the means are significantly different from the overall mean depends on:

- the spread of the separate sub-group means around the overall mean – the *between-groups* variance – the greater the between-groups variance, the *greater* the likelihood of significant difference; and

- the spread of each of sub-group cases around the sub-group mean – the *within-groups* variance – the greater the within-groups variance, the *less* the likelihood of significant difference.

Analysis of variance is based on the ratio of these two measures, which produces a statistic referred to as F. As with the other statistics examined, values of F for a given number of degrees of freedom (based on sample sizes and number of groups) have a known probability distribution in the null hypothesis situation. High values are unlikely and result in the rejection of the null hypothesis.

The SPSS procedures for analysis of variance and examples of output are shown in Figure 17.10.

Procedure
1. Select *Analyze > Compare Means > One-way ANOVA*.
2. Transfer variables for which means are required (*sportfit, theatre, npark, meal, hols*) to *Dependent list box*.
3. Transfer grouping variable (*status*) to the *Independent list box*.
4. Select *OK* to produce the output.

Output

ANOVA

		Sum of Squares	df	Mean Square	F	Sig.
Play sport/fitness	Between Groups	1171.650	3	390.550	2.485	.072
	Within Groups	7230.350	46	157.182		
	Total	8402.000	49			
Visit theatre	Between Groups	6.446	3	2.149	.411	.746
	Within Groups	240.434	46	5.227		
	Total	246.880	49			
Visit national park	Between Groups	219.871	3	73.290	.942	.428
	Within Groups	3578.129	46	77.785		
	Total	3798.000	49			
Go out for meal	Between Groups	148.752	3	49.584	6.715	.001
	Within Groups	339.668	46	7.384		
	Total	488.420	49			
Holiday expenditure	Between Groups	968661.162	3	322887.054	6.644	.001
	Within Groups	2235593.338	46	48599.855		
	Total	3204254.500	49			

Figure 17.10   One-way analysis of variance – procedure and output

In Figure 17.10, it can be seen from the figures in bold that:

- For the first three activities, significance is above 0.05, so the null hypothesis is accepted and it is concluded that participation in these activities is not related to student status.
- For the last two activities, going out for a meal and holiday expenditure, significance is below 0.05, so the null hypothesis is rejected and we conclude that there is a relationship between these activities and student status.

7. Factorial analysis of variance (ANOVA)

7.1 Introduction

As with one-way analysis of variance, factorial analysis of variance deals with *means*. But while the former deals with means of groups determined on the basis of *one* variable, the latter is designed for sets of means grouped by more than one classifying variable, or *factor*. An example is shown in Figure 17.11, which presents a table of mean frequency of theatre-going by the two factors *status* and *gender*, with no statistical test at this stage.

Procedure
1. Select *Analyze > Compare Means > Means*.
2. Transfer *theatre* to the *Dependent list* box.
3. Transfer *status* to the *Independent list* box.
4. Click on *Next* to get *Layer 2 of 2*, then *gender* to the *Independent list* box.
5. Select *OK* to obtain the output.

Output Visit theatre

Student status	Gender	Mean	N	Std. Deviation
F/T student/no paid work	Male	3.11	9	1.833
	Female	1.50	4	2.380
	Total	2.62	13	2.063
F/T student/paid work	Male	1.56	9	1.130
	Female	5.40	5	2.191
	Total	2.93	14	2.433
F/T student – F/T job	Male	1.40	5	2.074
	Female	2.64	11	2.730
	Total	2.25	16	2.543
P/T student/Other	Male	3.50	2	2.121
	Female	3.20	5	1.643
	Total	3.29	7	1.604
Total	Male	2.24	25	1.786
	Female	3.12	25	2.587
	Total	2.68	50	2.245

The above might be presented in a report as follows:

Figure 17.11 A table of means – procedure and output (*continued*)

Table X.   Frequency of visiting theatre, by status and gender

Course	Mean no. of visits in three months		
	Male	Female	Total
F/T student/no paid work	3.1	1.5	2.6
F/T student/paid work	1.6	5.4	2.9
P/T student – F/T job	1.4	2.6	2.3
P/T student/Other	3.5	3.2	3.3
Total	2.2	3.1	2.7

Figure 17.11 *(continued)*

It can be seen that:

- from the Total column, there is little difference in frequency of attendance by status, with the lowest mean frequency 2.3 and the highest 3.3;

- from the Total row, there is little difference in frequency of attendance by gender (male 2.2, female 3.1); and

- but when the two variables are put together, considerable differences emerge, with the lowest mean frequency at 1.4 and the highest at 5.4.

Analysis of variance examines this 'crosstabulation of means' and determines whether the differences revealed are significant. As with the one-way analysis of variance, the procedure examines the differences *between* group means and the spread of values *within* groups.

The null hypothesis is that there is no interaction between the variables – that the level of theatre-going of the students in the various categories is not affected by gender. A table of 'expected counts' consistent with the null hypothesis could be produced as for the Chi-square example, but the values would be means rather than numbers of cases.

7.2 Procedure

Figure 17.12 shows the results of a factorial analysis of variance on the above data. It can be seen from the F probabilities in bold, that the relationship between:

- theatre-going and status alone is not significant (Sig. = 0.250);

- theatre-going and gender is not significant (Sig. = 0.242); and

- theatre-going and course and gender together is significant at the 5 per cent level (Sig. = 0.019) – so the null hypothesis is rejected: the interaction between gender and status with regard to theatre-going is significant.

Procedure

1. Select *Analyze > General Linear Model > Univariate*.
2. Select the *Dependent* variable – the one for which the means are to be calculated (*theatre*).
3. Select the *Fixed Factors* – the two variables affecting the dependent variable (*status* and *gender*).
4. In the *Post Hoc* box dialog box, transfer *status* and *gender* to the *Post Hoc tests for* box, then select *LSD*, then click *Continue*.
5. Select *OK* to obtain the output.

Output

Dependent Variable: Visit theatre (**key items in bold**)

Source	Type III Sum of Squares	df	Mean Square	F	Sig.
Corrected Model	66.523(a)	7	9.503	2.213	.052
Intercept	299.090	1	299.090	69.650	.000
status	18.308	3	6.103	1.421	**.250**
gender	6.041	1	6.041	1.407	**.242**
status * gender	47.424	3	15.808	3.681	**.019**
Error	180.357	42	4.294		
Total	606.000	50			
Corrected Total	246.880	49			

a R Squared = .269 (Adjusted R Squared = .148)

Figure 17.12   Factorial analysis of variance – procedure and output

8. Correlation

8.1 Introduction

Correlation can be used to examine the relationships between two or more *ordinal or scale* variables. If two variables are related in a systematic way, they are said to be *correlated*. They can be:

- *positively* correlated (as one variable increases, so does the other);
- *negatively* correlated (as one variable increases, the other decreases); or
- *un-correlated* (there is no relationship between the variables).

It is often helpful to think of correlation in visual terms. Relationships between income and the four variables are shown in Figure 17.13, illustrating two types of correlation. The graphics were produced using the graphics *Scatterplot* procedure discussed in Chapter 16. Each dot represents one person (or case or observation). The correlation coefficients, r, are explained below.

a. **No apparent relationship between national park visiting and income – almost zero correlation (r = 0.024)**

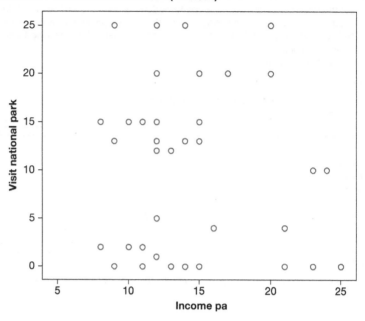

b. **Holiday expenditure clearly increases with income – high correlation (r = 0.91)**

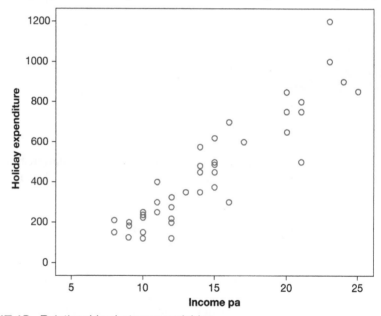

Figure 17.13 Relationships between variables

Correlation can be measured by means of the *correlation coefficient,* usually represented by the letter *r.* The coefficient has the following characteristics:

● zero if there is no relationship between two variables;

● +1.0 if there is perfect positive correlation between two variables;

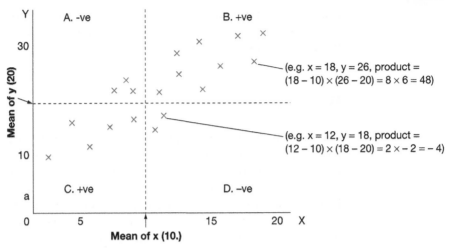

Figure 17.14 Correlation

- −1.0 if there is perfect negative correlation between two variables;
- between 0 and +1.0 if there is *some* positive correlation;
- between 0 and −1.0 if there is *some* negative correlation; and
- the closer the coefficient is to 1.0, the higher the correlation, for example:
  - 0.9 is a *high positive* correlation;
  - 0.2 is a *low positive* correlation; and
  - −0.8 is a *high negative* correlation.

The correlation coefficient is calculated by measuring how far each data point is from the mean of each of the two variables and multiplying the two differences. In Figure 17.14 it can be seen that the result will be a positive number for data points in the top right-hand and bottom left-hand quadrants (B and C) and negative for data points in the other two quadrants (A and D). The calculations are shown for two of the data points by way of illustration. If most of the data points are in quadrants B and C, a positive correlation will result, while if most of the data points are in A and D, a negative correlation will result. If the data points are widely scattered in all four quadrants, then the negatives cancel out the positives, resulting in a low value for the correlation. This explains in very broad terms the basis of the positive and negative correlations, and high and low correlations. It is beyond the scope of this text to explain how the 'perfect' correlation is made to equal one, but, for those with the requisite mathematics, this can be deduced from the formula for r, which is given in Appendix 17.2.

8.2 Significance of *r*: null hypothesis

The *significance* of a correlation coefficient depends on its size and also the sample size, and it is assessed by a t-test. The null hypothesis is that the correlation is zero. The t-test therefore indicates only whether the correlation coefficient is *significantly different from zero*. Quite low coefficients can therefore emerge as 'significant' if the sample is large enough.

8.3 Procedure

The procedures for producing correlation coefficients between pairs of variables are shown in Figure 17.15. The output is in the form of a symmetrical matrix, so that, for example, the correlation between sport and income is the same as between income and sport. For each pair of variables, the output includes the correlation coefficient, the sample size and Sig., the probability/significance related to the t-test. The starring system discussed above is used to indicate significance at the 5 per cent (*) and 1 per cent (**) levels. As with other tests, if the probability is below the 0.05 or 0.01 levels, we reject the null hypothesis and conclude that the correlation is significantly different from zero.

Procedure

1. Select *Analyze > Correlate > Bivariate*.
2. Transfer variables to be included (*inc, sportfit, theatre, npark, meal, hols*) to the *Variables* box.
3. Select *OK* to produce output.

Output

Correlations matrix

		Income pa	Play sport	Visit theatre	Visit national park	Go out for meal	Holiday expenditure
Income pa	Pearson Correlation	1.000	-.439**	.460**	.024	.076	.915**
	Sig. (2-tailed)	.	.001	.001	.866	.598	.000
	N	50	50	50	50	50	50
Play sport	Pearson Correlation	-.439**	1.000	-.679**	.274	.454**	-.368**
	Sig. (2-tailed)	.001	.	.000	.054	.001	.008
	N	50	50	50	50	50	50
Visit theatre	Pearson Correlation	.460**	-.679**	1.000	-.292*	-.286*	.379**
	Sig. (2-tailed)	.001	.000	.	.039	.044	.007
	N	50	50	50	50	50	50
Visit national park	Pearson Correlation	.024	.274	-.292*	1.000	-.044	.058
	Sig. (2-tailed)	.866	.054	.039	.	.759	.688
	N	50	50	50	50	50	50
Go out for meal	Pearson Correlation	.076	.454**	-.286*	-.044	1.000	.119
	Sig. (2-tailed)	.598	.001	.044	.759	.	.410
	N	50	50	50	50	50	50
Holiday expenditure	Pearson Correlation	.915**	-.368**	.379	.058	.119	1.000
	Sig. (2-tailed)	.000	.008	.007	.688	.410	.
	N	50	50	50	50	50	50

Figure 17.15 Correlation matrix – procedure and output

** Correlation is significant at the 0.01 level (2-tailed). * Correlation is significant at the 0.05 level (2-tailed).

9. Linear regression

9.1 Introduction

Linear regression takes us one step further in this type of quantitative analysis – in the direction of 'prediction'. If the correlation between two variables is consistent enough, then one variable can be used to predict or estimate the other. In particular, easily measured and predicted variables (such as age or income) can be used to predict variables which are more difficult or costly to measure (such as participation in leisure or tourism activity). For example:

- Knowledge of the relationship between age and leisure participation can be used in planning leisure facilities for a community: the future age structure of the community can be relatively easily estimated and, with this information, future demand for leisure activities can be estimated.

- Relationships between income per head and amount of overseas air travel per head in different countries or over various time-periods can be used to predict growth of air travel as incomes rise or fall.

The procedures described here are just one format in which the relationships between variables of interest can be examined. If the variables can be quantified, then the techniques enable the strength and nature of the relationship to be quantified also.

9.2 Regression model

To predict one variable on the basis of another, a *model* or equation is needed of the type:

Example 1: Leisure participation = *some number* multiplied by AGE
Example 2: Demand for overseas travel = *some number* multiplied by INCOME.

Suppose leisure participation is measured in terms of the number of visits or days participation for some activity over the course of a year, and demand for overseas travel is measured by the number of overseas trips in a year. Regression analysis produces an equation of the form:

Example 1: Days participation = a + bAGE
Example 2: Trips = a + bINCOME.

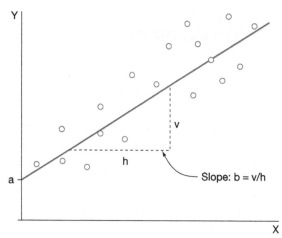

Figure 17.16   Regression line

The *coefficients* or *parameters*, a and b, are determined from examination of existing data, using *regression analysis*. The process of finding out the values of the parameters is referred to as *calibration* of the model.

In general terms this is represented by the equation y = a + bx, where y stands for participation or travel demand and x stands for age or income. Note that here *participation* and *travel demand* are the *dependent variables* and AGE and INCOME are the *independent variables*.

In visual terms this describes a 'regression line' fitted through the data, with 'intercept' or 'constant' of *a* and 'slope' of *b*, as shown in Figure 17.16. The regression procedure finds the 'line of best fit' by finding the line which minimises the sum of the (squared) differences between it and the data points, and specifies this line by giving values for a and b.

9.3 Procedure

Examples of regression output are shown in Figure 17.17. The program produces a large amount of output with which we are not concerned here – only the items in bold are discussed. However, the output illustrates the point that regression is an involved process and only the broad outlines are dealt with in this text. The output relates to *multiple* regression, which involves more than one independent variable, as discussed in the next section – but here we have only one independent variable, income.

The items we are interested in are the value of the regression coefficient, R (similar to the correlation coefficient, *r*), the value of R^2, which is an indicator of how well the data fit the regression line, its test of significance, and the coefficients listed under B. For Example 1 in Figure 17.17, the relationship between income and holiday expenditure:

● the value of R is 0.915;

● R^2 is 0.836;

Procedure

1. Select *Analyze > Regression > Linear*.
2. Select *dependent* and *independent* variables.
3. Select *OK* to produce the output.

Output (key items in bold)

Example 1: Income (independent) by holiday expenditure (dependent)

Model Summary

Model	R	R Square	Adjusted R Square	Std. Error of the Estimate
1	**.915**	**.836**	.833	104.51

a   Predictors: (Constant), Income pa

ANOVA

Model		Sum of Squares	df	Mean Square	F	Sig.
1	Regression	2679971.336	1	2679971.336	**245.361**	**.000**
	Residual	524283.164	48	10922.566		
	Total	3204254.500	49			

a   Predictors: (Constant), Income pa   b   Dependent Variable: Holiday expenditure

Coefficients

		Unstandardized Coefficients		Standardized Coeffs	t	Sig.
Model		B	Std. Error	Beta		
1	**(Constant)**	**−323.493**	49.890		−6.484	.000
	Income pa	**52.563**	3.356	.915	15.664	.000

a   Dependent Variable: Holiday expenditure

Example 2: Income (independent) by theatre-going (dependent)

Model Summary

Model	R	R Square	Adjusted R Square	Std. Error of the Estimate
1	**.460**	**.212**	.195	2.01

a   Predictors: (Constant), Income pa

ANOVA

Model		Sum of Squares	df	Mean Square	F	Sig.
1	Regression	52.284	1	52.284	**12.896**	**.001**
	Residual	194.596	48	4.054		
	Total	246.880	49			

a   Predictors: (Constant), Income pa   b Dependent Variable: Visit theatre

Coefficients

		Unstandardized Coefficients		Standardized Coeffs	t	Sig.
Model		B	Std. Error	Beta		
1	**(Constant)**	**−.617**	.961		−.642	.524
	Income pa	**.232**	.065	.460	3.591	.001

a   Dependent Variable: Visit theatre

Figure 17.17   Regression analysis – procedure and output

- probability (as measured by an F test) is 0.000 which makes it highly significant; and
- the *constant* (a) is −323.493 and the *coefficient* or *slope* (b) for income is 52.563.

The regression equation is therefore:

Holiday expenditure ($ pa) = −323.493 + 52.563 * income (in £000s pa)

This regression line can be plotted onto a graph, as shown in Figure 17.18, using the SPSS *Curve estimation* procedure.

With this equation, if we knew a student's income we could estimate their level of holiday expenditure, either by reading it off the graph or by calculating it. For example, for a student with an income of £10,000 a year:

Holiday expenditure = −323.49 + 52.56 * 10 = −323.49 + 525.60 = £202.11

So we would estimate that such a student would spend £202 on holidays in a year. Of course, we are not saying that *every* student with that income will spend this sum: the regression line/equation is a sort of average; it is not precise.

Procedure
1. Select *Analyze > Regression > Curve Estimation*.
2. Transfer *hols* to *Dependents* box and *inc* to *Independent* box
3. Select *OK* to produce output.

Output

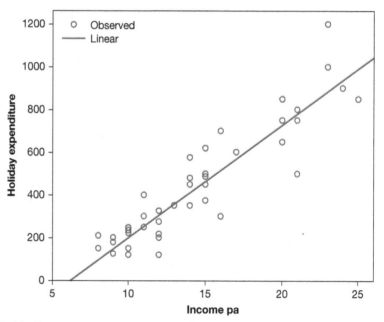

Figure 17.18 Regression line: curve estimation – procedure and output

Example 2 in Figure 17.17 produces similar output for the relationship between theatre-going and income. In this case the resultant regression equation would be:

Theatre-going (frequency in 3 months) = −0.62 + 0.23 * income

9.4 Non-linear regression

In Figure 17.19 the relationship between the two variables is *non-linear* – that is, the relationship indicated is curved, rather than being a straight line. The *Curve fit* procedure offers a number of models which may produce lines/curves which fit the data better than a simple straight line. Theory or trial and error may lead to a suitable model. In Figure 17.19 a 'cubic' model is presented, in which the independent variable is raised to the power of three – this results in the curved line indicated and a small increase in the value of R^2 to 0.843. This emphasises the importance of examining the data *visually*, as done here, and not relying just on correlation coefficients.

Procedure
1. Select *Analyze > Regression > Curve Estimation*.
2. Select *dependent* and *independent* variables (*hols* and *inc*).
3. Under *Models* select *Cubic*.
4. Select *OK* to produce output.

Output

Independent: inc

Dependent	Mth	Rsq	d.f.	F	Sigf	b0	b1	b2	b3
hols	CUB	.843	46	82.43	.000	494.351	−113.10	10.5471	−.2118

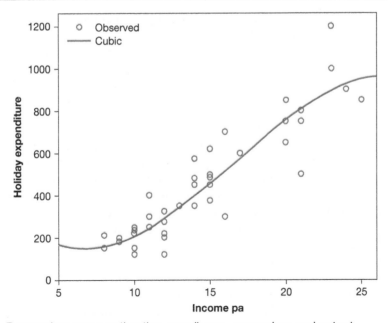

Figure 17.19 Regression: curve estimation, non-linear – procedure and output

10. Multiple regression

10.1 Introduction

Multiple regression is linear regression involving more than one independent variable. For example, we might hypothesise that sports participation is dependent not just on income but also on age, or that overseas travel is dependent not just on income but also on the price of airfares. Thus our models, or regression equations, would be:

Example 1: Sports participation = a + b * income + c * age
Example 2: Travel = a + b * income + c * fares

In *linear* regression, as discussed in the previous section, the procedure fits a straight line to the data – the line of *best fit*. In *multiple* regression, the procedure fits a *surface* to the data – the surface of best fit. It is possible to visualise this in three dimensions (one dependent and two independent variables), with the axes forming a three-dimensional box, the observations suspended in space and the regression surface being a flat plane somewhere within the box. SPSS offers a 3-D graphical option to represent this in the *Scattergram* procedure. When additional variables are included, then four, five or 'n' dimensions are involved; and it is not possible to visualise the process, but the mathematical principles used to establish the regression equation are the same.

10.2 Procedure

An example, in which theatre-going is related to income and age, is shown in Figure 17.20. It will be noticed that the value of R has risen from 0.46 in the single variable case (Figure 17.17, Example 2) to 0.58, indicating an improvement in the 'fit' of the data to the model. The model equation is now:

Theatre-going (per 3 months) = −0.349 + 0.056 * income + 0.0227 * age

It is possible, in theory, to continue to add variables to the equation. This should, however, be done with caution, since it frequently involves *multicollinearity*, where the independent variables are themselves inter-correlated. The 'independent' variables should be, as far as possible, just that: independent. Various tests exist to check for this phenomenon. Often, in leisure and tourism, a large number of variables is involved, many inter-correlated but each contributing something to the leisure or tourist phenomenon under investigation. Multivariate analysis procedures, such as cluster and factor analysis, discussed in section 11, are designed partly to overcome these problems.

A technique often used in leisure research is *structural equation modelling (SEM)*, or *path analysis* in which a network of equations is established to model a particular social process. An example is shown in Figure 17.21, relating to

Procedure

1. Select *Analyze* > *Regression* > *Linear*.
2. Transfer theatre to dependent box and age, income to independents box.
3. At *Method*, select *Enter* for all the selected variables to be included immediately, or *Stepwise* for the program to select and include variables in order of influence.
4. Select OK to produce the output.

Output (key items in bold)

Variables Entered/Removed[b]

Model	Variables Entered	Variables Removed	Method
1	**Age, Income pa**[a]	.	Enter

a   All requested variables entered.   b   Dependent Variable: Visit theatre

Model Summary

Model	R	R Square	Adjusted R Square	Std. Error of the Estimate
1	**.580**[a]	**.336**	.308	1.87

a   Predictors: (Constant), Age, Income pa

ANOVA[b]

Model		Sum of Squares	df	Mean Square	F	Sig.
1	Regression	83.023	2	41.512	**11.907**	**.000**[a]
	Residual	163.857	47	3.486		
	Total	246.880	49			

a   Predictors: (Constant), Age, Income pa   b   Dependent Variable: Visit theatre

Coefficients[a]

		Unstandardized Coefficients		Standardized coefficients	t	Sig.
Model		B	Std. Error	Beta		
1	(Constant)	**-3.493**	1.316		-2.654	.011
	Income pa	**.056**	.084	.111	.662	.511
	Age	**.227**	.076	.497	2.969	.005

a   Dependent Variable: Visit theatre

Figure 17.20   Multiple regression – procedure and output

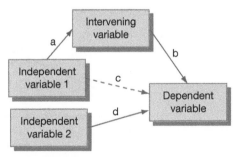

Figure 17.21   Structural equation modelling

health and fitness. This suggests that exercise regime affects a person's fitness which in turn affects health. But engaging in exercise might also affect health directly because it produces a sense of well-being. There are direct and indirect influences among the variables and SEM seeks to identify and quantify them using regression equations. Special computer packages are available to do this, as indicated in the Resources section.

10.3 Binary logistic regression analysis and odds ratios

Data in binary form – for example, male/female or participant/non-participant – can be quantified by use of one and zero. Mathematically, statistics such as means and correlation coefficients can be calculated with such data, but they violate some of the principles behind statistical tests, such as the assumption that data are normally distributed. The oddity of the data can be seen in Figure 17.22, which portrays one scale variable and one binary variable, with a regression line and correlation coefficient indicated. If the scale variable, were to be replaced by a second binary variable, all the cases would be located at four points only: 0,0; 0,1; 1,1; and 1,0. *Binary logistic regression* is designed to cope with these situations. The relationship is described by *odds ratios*. An odds ratio describes the relative strength of the association between an independent variable and categories of the dependent variables. For example, in examining the relationship between cultural participation (yes/no) and gender (male/female), odds ratio of 1.4 for females and 0.6 for males would indicate that females are 1.4 times more likely to participate in sport than males and males are 0.6 times as likely to participate as females. The advantage of binary logistic regression over, for example, a series of Chi-square tests, is that all independent variables can be modelled in a single procedure with the odds ratios for each being considered against each other. Sources and examples are provided in the Resources section.

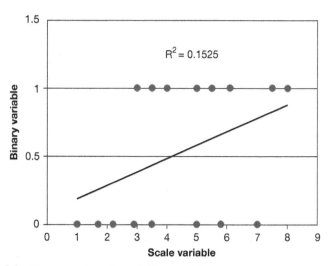

Figure 17.22 Binary and scale variable graphic

10.4 Multi-dimensional scaling

Nominal data can be handled in combination with scale/ordinal data, as indicated in Table 17.1, but when relationships between a number of nominal variables are involved, *multi-dimensional scaling* is one solution. It typically creates a visual representation of the pattern of proximities (i.e. similarities or distances) amongst variables. Sources and examples are indicated in the Resources section.

11. Cluster, factor, multiple correspondence analysis

11.1 Introduction

Cluster, factor and multiple correspondence analysis techniques are used when the number of independent variables is large and there is a desire to group them in some way. The theoretical counterpart to this is that there are some complex phenomena which cannot be measured by just one or two variables but require a 'battery' of variables, each contributing some aspect to the make-up of the phenomenon. Examples are:

- a person's 'lifestyle' or 'psychographic' group (made up of variables such as leisure and work patterns, income and expenditure patterns, values, age, and family/household situation); and

- a person's characteristics as a tourist – a 'tourist type' (made up of variables such as travel experience, expenditure patterns, products desired and satisfactions sought).

Each of these is often researched using a large number of data items – for example, lifestyles/psychographics have been measured by asking people as many as 300 questions about their attitudes to work, politics, morals, leisure, religion and so on. The techniques may be:

- *exploratory* – the analytical process is used to discover any factors/clusters which may exist in the data; or

- *confirmatory* – the analytical process is used to test the existence of one or more hypothesised clusters or factors.

11.2 Factor analysis

Factor analysis is based on the idea that certain variables 'go together', in that people with a high score on one variable also tend to have a high score on

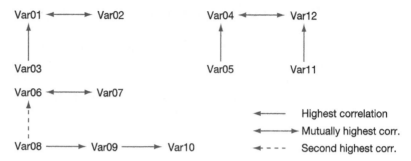

Figure 17.23   Simple manual factor analysis

certain others, which might then form a group. For example, people who go to the theatre might also visit galleries; people with strong pro-environment views might be found to favour certain types of holiday. Analysis of this type of phenomenon can be approached using a simple, manual technique based on a correlation matrix of the variables (as discussed in section 8.3). This is illustrated in Figure 17.23, where groupings of variables are produced by indicating which variables have their highest and second highest correlations with each other. In this case the process results in three groupings of variables.

This manual procedure takes account of only the highest and second-highest correlations, but variables will have a range of lower-order relationships with each other which are difficult to take account of using this manual method. A number of lower-order correlations may, cumulatively, be more significant than a single highest correlation. Factor analysis is a mathematical procedure which groups the variables taking account of *all* the correlations. The details of the method are, however, beyond the scope of this text.

11.3 Cluster analysis

Cluster analysis is another 'grouping' procedure, but it focuses on the individuals directly rather than the variables. Imagine a situation with two variables, age and some behavioural variable, and data points plotted in the usual way, as shown in Figure 17.24. It can be seen that there are three broad 'clusters' of respondents – two young clusters and one older cluster. Each of these clusters might form, for example, particular market segments.

With just two variables and a few observations, it is relatively simple to identify clusters visually. But with more variables and hundreds of cases, this would be more difficult. Cluster analysis involves giving the computer a set of rules for building clusters. It first calculates the 'distances' between data points, in terms of a range of specified variables. Those points which are closest together are put into a first-round 'cluster', and a new 'point' halfway between the two is put in their place. The process is repeated to form a second round of clustering, and a third and fourth and so on, until there are only two 'points' left. The result is usually illustrated by a 'dendrogram', of the sort shown in Figure 17.25.

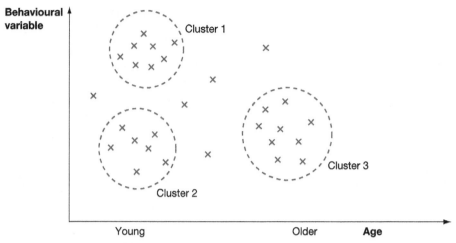

Figure 17.24 Plots of 'clusters'

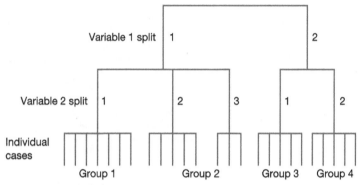

Figure 17.25 Dendrogram

11.4 Multiple correspondence analysis

Factor and cluster analysis can be applied only to scale/numerical data – for example, frequency of participation. While some mathematical operations can be undertaken with binary variables (participant/non-participant = 1/0) and Likert-type variables, when more complex nominal variables are involved, for example social class or ethnicity, this is not possible. Multiple Correspondence Analysis (MCA) is a procedure which overcomes this difficulty: it is a form of cluster analysis for nominal data. Again, the detail is beyond the scope of this text, but sources and examples are given in the Resources section.

MCA has been used particularly in research on cultural participation patterns in recent years. This is partly as a result of the significance of the work of French sociologist Pierre Bourdieu, who used the technique in his seminal work *Distinction* (Bourdieu, 1984). MCA was used to plot various occupational/social classes in French society along with their typical patterns of leisure participation and cultural tastes and consumption in a space defined by cultural and economic capital. An extract from a much larger diagram is shown in Figure 17.26. Bennett et al. (2009) have recently replicated Bourdieu's study using British data.

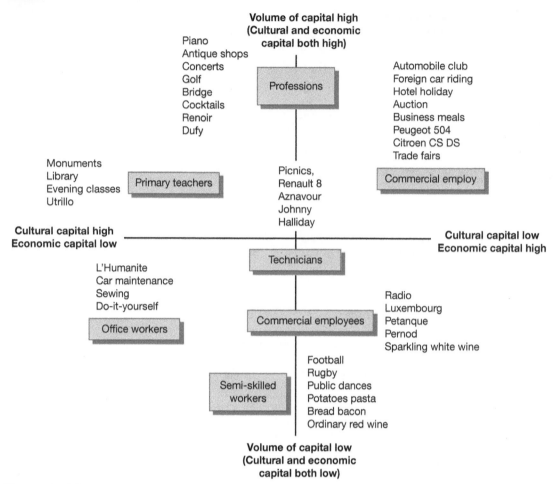

Figure 17.26 Multiple Classification Analysis: from Bourdieu's diagram of the spaces of social position and lifestyle

Source: Redrawn excerpt from Bourdieu (1984: 128).

12. In conclusion

Much leisure and tourism research, even of a quantitative nature, is conducted without the use of the techniques covered in this chapter. This is a reflection of the descriptive nature of much of the research in the field, as discussed in Chapter 1, the nature of the data involved and the needs of the audience or client for the research. Often in leisure and tourism the need is for 'broad brush' research findings: accuracy is required, but a high level of precision is not. Contrast this with medical research, where precision can be literally a matter of life or death. To some extent the level of use of statistical techniques is related to disciplinary traditions. Thus, for example, the use of statistical techniques in the American *Journal of Leisure Research* is quite common as a result of the heavy involvement of psychologists in American leisure research; whereas in the British journal *Leisure Studies* statistical techniques are less often deployed, reflecting the British tradition of qualitative sociology. In the case of tourism journals, statistical techniques such as regression and correlation tend to arise quite often because of the strong economic dimension of some tourism research.

Many leisure or tourism researchers could therefore find that they rarely make use of the techniques presented in this chapter, but they should be able to interpret research reports which do make use of them, and it may be valuable to be able to utilise them if called upon.

As has been stressed throughout this text, data collection and analysis should be determined by a theoretical, conceptual or evaluative framework. At the analysis stage the researcher should, ideally, not be wondering what to relate to what and choosing variables and analyses in an *ad hoc* manner. While a certain amount of inductive exploration and even serendipity is inevitable, ideally there should be a basic analysis plan from the beginning. Key variables and the question of relationships between them should have been thought about in advance, for example as a result of an early 'concept mapping' exercise, as discussed in Chapter 3. Thus, while the examples given in this chapter may appear *ad hoc* and 'data driven', in a real research project the procedures used should be theory driven or problem or hypothesis driven.

Summary

This chapter builds on Chapter 13, which introduces the idea of sampling and its effects, and on Chapter 16, which deals with the analysis of questionnaire survey data using the package SPSS. Here, the principles and processes involved in statistical analysis are introduced. The phenomenon of statistics, in this context, refers not just to quantification but to the processes required to generalise findings from samples to the wider population. Statistical concepts are initially introduced, including: the idea of probabilistic statements; the normal distribution; significance; the null hypothesis; and dependent and independent variables. The chapter then outlines SPSS procedures and presents outputs for a number of statistical tests, as follows.

- Chi-square – for examining the relationship between two variables in a frequency table;
- the t test – for comparing the significance of the difference between two means;
- one-way analysis of variance (ANOVA) – for examining the relationship between two variables as expressed by a set of means;
- factorial analysis of variance (ANOVA) – for examining the relationship between one dependent variable and two independent variables based on means;

- correlation – the relationship between two scale variables;

- linear regression – which establishes the 'line of best fit' between two variables;

- multiple regression – which examines the relationship between one dependent variable and two or more independent variables; and

- cluster, factor and multiple correspondence analysis – which deal with summarising the relationships among large numbers of variables.

Test questions and exercises

It is suggested that the reader replicate the various analyses set out in this chapter, first using the data in text website and then using their own data set. This can be based on data which may have been collected for Chapter 16 but will involve adding a range of scale variables to the questionnaire, similar to those listed in Appendix 17.1.

Resources

Websites

- SPSS software: www.spss.com

- Structural equation modelling (SEM):
  - Amos software: www.spss.com/amos/
  - Lisrel software: www.ssicentral.com/lisrel/index.html
  - Semnet discussion group: www2.gsu.edu/~mkteer/semnet.html

Publications

- Many excellent statistics textbooks are available which cover the range of techniques included in this chapter and, of course, much more. Texts vary in terms of the degree of familiarity with algebra that they assume on the part of the reader, so readers with limited mathematical knowledge should 'shop around' to find a text which deals with the topic in conceptual terms rather than in detailed mathematical terms. However, a certain amount of mathematical aptitude is, of course, essential. Examples of general research methods texts which include statistics are Ryan (1995) and Burns (1994); and a specialist text, Spatz (2010).

- Cluster analysis: Downward and Riordan (2009).

- Multidimensional scaling: Borg and Groenen (2005).

- Multiple correspondence analysis: Le Roux and Rouanet (2010); examples: Bourdieu (1984), Bennett et al. (2009).

- Odds ratios, example: Hand (2009).

- Structural equation modelling (SEM): Kline (2015); student motivation: Han and Yeon (2015).

- For text on SPSS, see Chapter 16.

References

Bennett, T., Savage, M., Silva, E., Warde, A., Gayo-Cal, M., and Wright, D. (2009). *Culture, class, distinction*. London: Routledge.

Bourdieu, P. (1984). *Distinction: a social critique of the judgment of taste*. London: Routledge and Kegan Paul.

Borg, I., and Groenen, P. J. F. (2005). *Modern multidimensional scaling*. New York: Springer.

Burns, R. B. (1994). *Introduction to research methods*, 2nd edn. Melbourne: Longman Cheshire.

Downward, P., and Riordan, J. (2009). Social interactions and the demand for sport: cluster demand in economics. In D. Byrne and C. C. Ragin (Eds), *Sage handbook of case-based methods* (pp. 392–409). London: Sage.

Han, H., and Yeon, H. (2015). Driving forces in the decision to enrol in a hospitality and tourism graduate program. *Journal of Hospitality, Leisure, Sport and Tourism Education*, 17(1), 14–27.

Hand, C. (2009). Modelling patterns of attendance at performing arts events: the case of music in the United Kingdom. *Creative Industries Journal*, 2(3), 259–71.

Kline, R. B. (2015). *Principles and practice of structural equation modelling*, 4th edn. New York: Guilford Press.

Le Roux, B., and Rouanet, H. (2010). *Multiple correspondence analysis*. Thousand Oaks, CA: Sage.

Ryan, C. (1995). *Researching tourist satisfaction: issues, concepts, problems*. London: Routledge.

Spatz, C. (2010). *Basic statistics: tales of distribution*, 10th edn. Boston MA: Cengage Learning.

Appendix 17.1: Details of example data used – variable details and data

Additional questions (added to the questionnaire in Figure 10.8)

What is your approximate gross income in £ per year: £_____ | _____ inc

Approximately how many times have you engaged in the following activities |
  in the last 3 months: |
                                                                                |
    a. Sporting/fitness activity   ____ times | _____ sport

    b. Been to live theatre   ____ times | _____ spectate

    c. Visited a national park   ____ times | _____ npark

    d. Been out for a meal   ____ times | _____ meal
                                                                                |
Approximately how much did you spend on holidays |
    in the last year?   £____ | _____ hols

Additional variables added to SPSS data file

inc	Numeric	5	0	Income pa, $'000s	None	None	8	Right	Scale
sport	Numeric	5	0	Played sport - times in last 3 months	None	None	8	Right	Scale
theatre	Numeric	5	0	Visit theatre - times in last 3 months	None	None	8	Right	Scale
npark	Numeric	5	0	Visit national park - times in last 3 months	None	None	8	Right	Scale
hols	Numeric	5	0	Holiday expenditure	None	None	8	Right	Scale
statusr	Numeric	5	0	Student status - recoded	1 Full-time 2 Part-time	None	7	Right	Nominal

Statusr is a recoded variable, as discussed in Chapter 16

A copy of the data file can be found on the text website.

Appendix 17.2: Statistical formulae

- **95 per cent Confidence interval for normal distribution for percentage p**

$$C.I. = 1.96 \sqrt{\frac{p\,(100 - p)}{n - 1}}$$

Where n = sample size

- Chi-square

$$\chi^2 = \sqrt{\Sigma((O - E)/E)^2}$$

- **t for difference between means**

$$t = \sqrt{\frac{(\bar{x}_1 - \bar{x}_2)}{(s_1^2/n_1 + s_2^2/n_1)}}$$

- **Standard Deviation**

$$SD = \sqrt{\frac{\Sigma(x - \bar{x})^2}{n}}$$

- **Correlation Coefficient**

$$r = \sqrt{\frac{\Sigma((x - \bar{x})(y - \hat{y}))^2}{(s_1^2/n_1 + s_2^2/n_2)}}$$

- **Value of t for Correlation Coefficient**

$$t = r\sqrt{(N - 2)/(1 - r)^2}$$

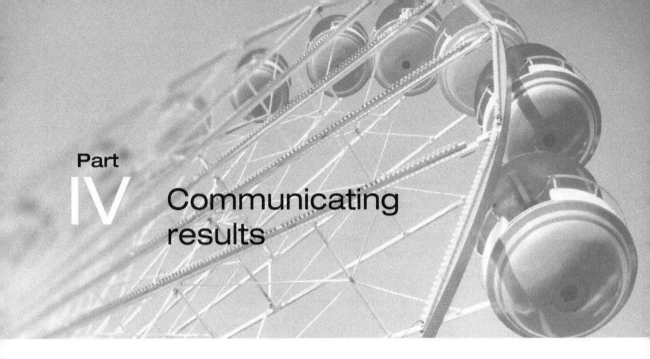

Part

IV

Communicating results

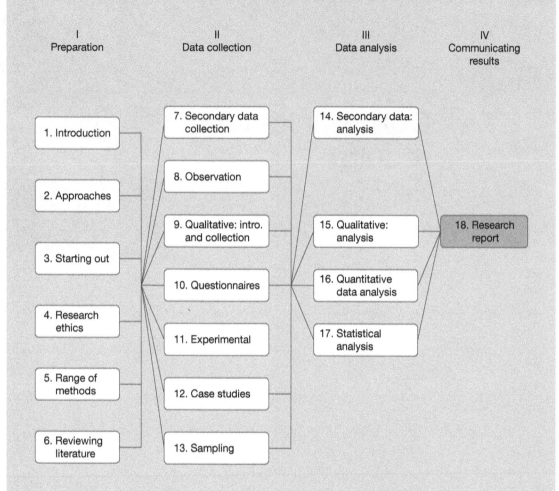

I	II	III	IV
Preparation	Data collection	Data analysis	Communicating results

1. Introduction

2. Approaches

3. Starting out

4. Research ethics

5. Range of methods

6. Reviewing literature

7. Secondary data collection

8. Observation

9. Qualitative: intro. and collection

10. Questionnaires

11. Experimental

12. Case studies

13. Sampling

14. Secondary data: analysis

15. Qualitative: analysis

16. Quantitative data analysis

17. Statistical analysis

18. Research report

18 Preparing a research report

1. Introduction

This chapter outlines key aspects of the reporting of research results. It concentrates primarily on the preparation and presentation of written research reports, including content, structure and layout, and considers the varying requirements and conventions of different reporting formats. The chapter concludes with a consideration of non-written formats, particularly the oral presentation.

2. Written research reports

2.1 Types/styles

Written reports of research are a key element of the world of management and planning and of academe. In management/planning, reports come in a variety of forms, as discussed in Chapter 1, including position statements, market profiles, market research, market segmentation/lifestyle/psychographic studies, feasibility studies, leisure/recreation needs studies, tourism strategies/marketing plans, forecasting studies, impact studies, performance appraisals and industry/sector studies. The results of academic studies are produced in article, report, book, or thesis format.

In this chapter we deal with three report formats: (1) management/planning/project reports in general, (2) academic articles and (3) theses. The first of these may arise in a management/planning context or may arise from a funded academic project when the researcher reports to the funding body; this style of report is referred to as a *project report* in the discussion that follows. Project reports prepared for a policy or practitioner readership are referred to as *management reports*. In North America, the word 'dissertation' is generally used rather than 'thesis'. The main distinguishing characteristics of the three styles of report are summarised in Table 18.1.

The medium is the message, and in this case the medium is the written report. The ability to prepare a report and to recognise good-quality and poor-quality reports should be seen as a key element in the skills of the aspiring manager or researcher. While form is no substitute for good content, a report which is poorly presented can undermine or even negate good content. While the researcher should of course focus primarily on achieving high-quality substantive content, the presentational aspects raised in this chapter also merit serious attention.

2.2 Getting started

In discussing research proposals in Chapter 3, it was noted that researchers invariably leave too little time for report writing. Even when adequate time has been allocated in the timetable, this is often whittled away and the writing of the report is delayed, leaving too little time. There is a tendency to put off report writing because it is difficult and it is often felt that, with just a little more data analysis or a little more reading of the literature, the process of writing the report will become easier. This is rarely the case – it is invariably difficult!

A regrettably common practice is for writers of research reports to spend a great deal of their depleted time, with the deadline looming, writing and preparing material which could have been attended to much earlier in the process. There are often large parts of any report which can be written before

Table 18.1   Types of research report

Feature	Management/ planning/project report	Academic article	Thesis
Authors	In-house staff, external consultants or funded academics	Academics	Honours, masters or doctoral students
Content	Report of commissioned or grant-funded project	Report of academic research	Report of academic research
Brief	Provided by commissioning organisation or outlined in grant application	Generally self-generated (although may arise from commissioned work)	Generally self-generated (although may arise in part from grant-funded project)
Quality assurance	In-house: internal; consultants/academics: reputation of consultants/ researchers	Anonymous refereeing process (see Chapter 1)	Supervision + examination by external examiners
Readership	Professional managers/ planners, possibly elected or appointed board/council/ committee members	Primarily academic	Primarily academic
Published status	May or may not be publicly available	Publicly available (often online) in published academic journals	Publicly available in libraries and online; findings often published in summary form in one or more academic articles
Length	Varies	In the social/ management sciences, including leisure/ tourism: generally 5000–7000 words	In the social/management sciences, including leisure/tourism: Honours: c. 20,000 words Masters: c. 40,000 words PhD: c. 70,000 words +
Emphasis	Emphasis on findings rather than links with the literature/theory and methodology (but the latter must be described)	Methodology, theory, literature as important as the findings	Methodology, theory, literature as important as the findings

data analysis is complete, or even started. Such parts include the introduction, statement of objectives, outline of theoretical or evaluative framework, literature review and description of the methodology. In addition, time-consuming activities such as arranging for maps, illustrations and cover designs to be produced need not be left until the last minute!

Furthermore, as St Pierre (2005) has argued, writing involves *thinking* and can be seen as part of the research process rather than something which follows the completion of the research process.

2.3 Report components

Reports generally include certain standard components, although some are unique to certain report styles, as shown in Table 18.2. The components listed are discussed in turn.

Cover

For a project report the cover should include minimal information, such as title, author(s) and publisher or sponsor. The lavishness and design content will vary with the context and the resources available.

If the report is available for sale, it should include an International Standard Book Number (ISBN) on the back cover. The ISBN is a 13-digit product identifier for books and other published materials used by publishers, booksellers and libraries. The ISBN system is overseen by the London-based International ISBN Agency and registered with the International Organization for Standardization (ISO) in Geneva. ISBNs are allocated by National ISBN Agencies, which are often national libraries which, under national legislation, generally receive free deposit copies of all publications produced in their country. The ISBN makes it easy to order publications through book retailers and ensures that the publication is catalogued in library systems around the world.

Title page

The title page is the first page inside the cover of a project report. It may include much the same information as the cover or considerably more detail, as indicated in Table 18.2. In some cases, as in commercially published books, some of the detail is provided on the reverse of the title page.

List of contents

Lists of contents are required in project reports, and theses and may include just chapter titles but usually also include details of sub-sections. An example of a contents list is shown in Figure 18.1. Word-processor packages include procedures for compiling tables of contents and lists, such as tables and diagrams.

Summary – executive summary/abstract/synopsis

A summary is required for all three styles of report except for very short project reports. The summary is called *executive summary* in a report, *abstract* in an

Table 18.2 Report style and components

	Content	Management/Planning/ Research report	Academic article	Thesis
Cover	• Title of report • Author(s) • Institution/publisher • ISBN (if published) back cover	All items listed left	Not applicable	Prescribed by university regulations
Title page	• Title of report • Author(s) • Institution/publisher • Address, phone, website*, etc.* • Sponsoring body • Date of publication* • If the report is for sale: ISBN*. (* sometimes on reverse of title page)	All items listed left	Cover page containing: • Title of article • Author(s) • Institutional affiliation • Contact details (omitted by editors for anonymous refereeing)	Prescribed by university regulations
Contents page(s)	See Figure 18.1 for example	As in Figure 18.1	Not applicable	As in Figure 18.1 but less detailed section numbering
Summary	Summary of *whole* report, including background, aims, methods, main findings, conclusions and (where applicable) recommendations.	Executive Summary: Length of report: 20 pp: ½–1 page 21–50 pp: 3–4 pp 50–100 pp: 5–6 pp	Abstract: Length: typically about 300 words	Synopsis: Length: typically 3–5 pages

Preface/Foreword

Optional. Contains background information, sometimes an explanation of authors' involvement with the project. Foreword may be a commentary written by a significant individual not directly involved in the project. Not applicable in academic article, where such information may be included in an endnote.

Acknowledgements

- Funding organisations
- Liaison officers of funding organisations
- Members of steering committees
- Organisations/individuals providing access to information, etc.
- Staff employed (e.g. including interviewers, coders, computer programmers, secretaries, word-processors)
- Individuals (including academic supervisors) who have given advice, commented on report drafts, etc.
- (Collectively) Individuals who responded to questionnaires, etc.

Main body of report

Discussed separately.

Appendices

Text/statistical material included for the record but which, because of its size, would interrupt the flow if included in the main body of the report.

CONTENTS

Figure 18.1 Example report contents page

article or *synopsis* in a thesis. The typical length also varies, depending on the context.

An executive summary is sometimes thought of as the summary for the 'busy executive' who does not have time to read the whole report, but it really refers to the idea that it should contain information necessary to take *executive action* on the basis of the report.

A summary should cover the *whole* of the report, article or thesis, as indicated in Table 18.2; it is *not* the introduction. The summary should, of course, be written *last*.

Preface/foreword

A preface or foreword (not 'forward'!) is used for a variety of purposes. Usually it explains the origins of the study and outlines any qualifications or limitations. Acknowledgements of assistance may be included if there is no separate 'acknowledgements' section. Sometimes a significant individual is asked to write a foreword, such as the director of an institution, a government minister or an eminent academic.

Acknowledgements

Copyright matters may also be included. It is clearly a matter of courtesy to acknowledge any assistance received during the course of a research project. People and institutions who might be acknowledged are listed in Table 18.2.

2.4 Main body of the report – technical aspects

Clearly, the main body of the report is its most important component. The substantive content is discussed in the next section; here we consider a number of technical aspects of organisation and presentation, as listed in Table 18.3.

Table 18.3 Main body of report: technical aspects

Section numbering
Paragraph numbering
'Dot point' lists
Page numbering
Headers/footers
Heading hierarchy
Typing layout/spacing
Tables and graphics
Referencing
Which person?

Section numbering

In project reports it is usual to number not only the major sections/chapters, but also sub-sections within chapters, as shown in the example in Figure 18.1. Once a numbering system is established, it should be carried through consistently throughout the report. Word-processor packages provide style *templates* to facilitate this process.

In project reports, section numbers may extend to several levels. For example, within section 4.2, there could be sub-sections: 4.2.1, 4.2.2, etc. Further levels can become cumbersome and are generally not required throughout the report, so if there is an occasional need for further sub-sub-sections, it is often advisable to use a simple a., b., c. or (i), (ii), (iii), etc.

Journal articles rarely include section numbering; when it is included, it is typically one level only.

In theses, chapters are numbered, and possibly one level of sections within chapters, but sub-section numbering is not generally used.

Paragraph numbering

In some reports, notably government reports, paragraphs are individually numbered, although this is rare. This can be useful for reference purposes when a report is being discussed in committees, etc. Paragraphs can be numbered in a single series for the whole report or chapter by chapter: in Chapter 1: paragraphs 1.1, 1.2, 1.3, etc.; in Chapter 2: paragraphs 2.1, 2.2, 2.3, etc., and so on.

'Dot point' lists

'Dot point' lists are very common in project reports and quite common in the other reporting formats. This device assists the reader to understand the structure of the material and to visually scan a document. Project reports are often discussed in committee or written comments are offered in various consultation exercises, and this process is eased by dot-point lists, although numbered lists may be even more helpful: it is easier to refer to and to locate 'item 5' than 'the fifth dot point'.

Where possible, grammatical rules should be followed in dot-point lists. For example, in Table 18.4, the list is, in effect, all one sentence. There are therefore, semicolons at the end of each list item, a full stop at the end and no capital letters at the beginning of each item. Some publishers, however, have 'house

Table 18.4 Dot-point list example

In preparing a research report, the author should take account of:

- the likely readership;
- the requirements of the funding agency, as indicated in the study brief;
- printing or other distribution format;
- likely costs; and
- delivery of a clear message.

---

styles' which omit this punctuation. The principle is difficult to follow when the individual dot points are lengthy, perhaps themselves involving more than one sentence: in this case each dot point in a sequence should be treated as one or more complete sentences with capital letters and full stops.

Page numbering

One problem in putting together long reports, especially when different authors are responsible for different sections, is to organise page numbering so that it follows on from chapter to chapter. This can be eased by numbering each chapter separately, for example: Chapter 1: pages 1.1, 1.2, 1.3, etc.; Chapter 2: pages 2.1, 2.2, 2.3, etc. and so on. Such a numbering system can also aid readers in finding their way around a report. Word-processors can be made to produce page numbers in this form by using the header and/or page-numbering facilities.

It is general practice for the title page, contents page(s), acknowledgements, and the executive summary pages to be numbered as a group using roman numerals (as in this text) and for the main body of the report to start at page 1 with normal numbers. Word-processors will facilitate this.

Headers/footers

Word-processing packages provide the facility to include a running header or footer across the top or bottom of each page. This can be used to indicate sections or chapters, as in this text, or, in the case of a consultancy report, can be used to indicate title and authorship of the report, perhaps even displaying the consultancy logo on each page.

Heading hierarchy

In the main body of the report, a hierarchy of heading styles should be used, with the major chapter/section headings being in the most prominent style and with decreasing emphasis for sub-section headings. For example:

1. Chapter Titles
1.1 Section Headings
1.1.1 Sub-section Headings

Such a convention helps readers to know where they are in a document. When a team is involved in writing a report, it is clearly sensible to agree to these heading styles in advance. Word-processor systems provide a report with 'styles' which standardise heading formats and section-numbering systems, linked to assembly of tables of contents.

Typing layout/spacing

Essays and books tend to use the convention of starting new paragraphs by indenting the first line. Report style is to separate paragraphs by a blank line and not to indent the first line. Report style also tends to have more headings. For a document in report style, it is usual to leave wide margins, which raises the question as to whether it is necessary to print documents in 1.5 or double space format or whether single spacing is adequate (and more friendly to the environment!). Different journals have different format specifications for submission of articles, typically on the journal website. Universities provide their own guidelines for the layout of theses.

Tables and graphics

Balance: When presenting the results of quantitative research, an appropriate balance must be struck between the use of tables, graphics and text. In most cases, very large or complex tables are consigned to appendices and simplified and/or graphical versions included in the body of the report. It may be appropriate to place *all* tables in appendices and provide only 'reader-friendly' graphics in the body of the report. The decision on which approach to use depends partly on the complexity of the data to be presented, but mainly on the type of audience.

Tables/graphics vs text: Tables, graphics and text each have a distinctive role to play in the presentation of the study findings:

- tables provide information;

- graphics illustrate that information so that patterns can be seen in a visual way; while

- the text should be telling a story or developing an argument and 'orchestrating' tables and graphics to support that task.

There seems to be little point in the text of a report simply repeating what is in a table or graphics. The text should at least highlight the main features of the data; ideally it should develop an argument or draw conclusions based on the data. In the example in Figure 18.2, Commentary A merely repeats what is in the table: it says nothing to the reader about the difference between men's and women's participation patterns, which is presumably the purpose of the exercise. Commentary B, on the other hand, is more informative, pointing out particular features of the data in the table.

Statistical tests: In the more quantitative disciplines there is a convention that, in academic reports such as journal articles and theses, the results of statistical tests (see Chapter 17) should be mentioned in the text, even if the information is also available in a table. Thus, for example, a sentence in the text might read: 'Mean weekly frequency of participation by men (2.1) is significantly higher than for women (1.7, $t = 5.6$, $p < 0.001$, see Table 2)'. Clearly the information in brackets 'clutters' the text and makes it less reader-friendly if a number of such insertions is involved. It seems unnecessary to include this information in the text if it can be seen in the table; and the information on the t-test may be meaningless to readers without statistical knowledge. In less quantitative fields of study, it is not necessary to include the information in brackets, particularly the

Table X. Participation in top 5 sports/physical activities, persons aged 16+, Great Britain, 1986

Activity	% Participating in four weeks prior to interview (most popular quarter)	
	Males	Females
Walking	21	18
Football	6	*
Snooker/billiards	17	3
Swimming – indoor	9	10
Darts	9	3
Keep-fit/yoga	1	5

Source: General Household Survey, OPCS

* less than 0.05%.

Commentary A

The table indicates that the top five sports and physical recreation activities for men are walking, with 21% participation, snooker/billiards (17%), indoor swimming (9%), darts (9%) and football (6%), whereas for women the five most popular activities are walking (18%), indoor swimming (10%), keep-fit/yoga (5%), snooker/billiards (3%) and darts (3%).

Commentary B

Men and women may have more in common in their patterns of leisure activity than is popularly imagined. The table indicates that four activities – walking, swimming, snooker/billiards and darts – are included in the top five most popular sport and physical recreation activities for both men and women. While in general men's participation levels are higher than those of women, the table shows that women's participation rate exceeds that of men for two of the activities, namely keep-fit/yoga and swimming.

Figure 18.2 Table and commentaries

t-test result, in the text if it is available in a table. In management reports, results of statistical tests are often not included at all, although they may have been carried out, and such terms as 'significantly different' or 'not significantly different' may be used.

Presentation: Diagrams and tables should, as far as possible, be complete in themselves. That is, the title should be informative and the columns, rows or axes should be fully labelled so that the reader can understand them without necessarily referring to the text. The table in Figure 18.2 follows these principles. Thus tables or graphics presenting data from leisure and tourism surveys or other data sources should include information on:

- the geographical area to which the data refer;
- the year(s) to which the data refer or the year collected;

- gender and age-range of the sample or population to which the data relate;

- sample size, where relevant; and

- units of measurement.

Reproductions of secondary data should indicate the source of data, but tables or graphics presenting results from the primary data collection of the study, such as a survey, do not need to indicate this on every table and diagram. However, some consultants tend to do this for intellectual property reasons, so that if a user copies just one table or diagram, then its source is still indicated.

Referencing

References to the literature and other sources in academic reports should follow appropriate referencing conventions, as discussed in Chapter 6. This may, however, be inappropriate for the non-academic readerships of management reports. While sources should be acknowledged in such reports, it is generally appropriate to do so in an unobtrusive manner – for example, by use of the endnote rather than author/date reference style. In some management reports the 'review of the literature' is relegated to an appendix, with just the conclusions being presented in the body of the report.

Which person?

In academic reports, it is conventional to report the conduct and findings of research in an *impersonal* style – for example, to say: 'A survey was conducted' rather than 'I/we conducted a survey'; and 'It was found that . . .' rather than 'I/we found that . . .'. Some believe that this attempt to appear 'scientific' is inappropriate in the social sciences, particularly in qualitative research where the researcher personally engages with the research subjects (see Dupuis, 1999). First-person (I, we) accounts are therefore sometimes, but not commonly, used in some leisure and tourism reports. The first-person plural is also quite commonly used by consultants in management reports, especially when the consultants wish to convey the impression that they are bringing particular team skills and experience to bear on a project.

The impersonal style can appear odd or pretentious when authors refer to their own work. Thus, for me to say: 'Veal (2002) has argued that leisure is pluralistic' seems odd, and for me to say: 'The author has argued that leisure is pluralistic (Veal, 2002)' seems pretentious. The solution in such a situation is either to use the first person – 'I have argued that leisure is pluralistic (Veal, 2002)' – or to 'de-centre' the author – 'It has been argued that leisure is pluralistic (Veal, 2002)'.

2.5 Main body of the report – structure

It could be said that the three most important aspects of a research report are: (1) structure, (2) structure and (3) structure! The *structure* of a report is of fundamental importance and needs to be thoroughly considered and discussed, particularly when a team is involved. While all reports have certain structural features in common, the important aspects of any one report concern the underlying argument and how that relates to the objectives of the study and any data collection and analysis involved. This is linked fundamentally to the *research objectives*, the *theoretical or evaluative framework* and the *overall research strategy*, as discussed in Chapter 3.

Before writing starts, it can be useful to decide not only on the report structure and format but also target word lengths for each chapter or section. While an agreed structure is a necessary starting point, it is also necessary to be flexible. As drafting gets going, it may be found that what was originally conceived as one chapter needs to be divided into two or three chapters, or what was thought of as a separate chapter can be incorporated into another chapter or into an appendix. Throughout, consideration needs to be given to the overall length of the report, in terms of words or pages.

When a questionnaire survey is involved, there is a tendency for some to structure the presentation according to the sequence of questions in the questionnaire and, correspondingly, the sequence of tables as they are produced by the computer analysis. This is not an appropriate way to proceed! Questionnaires are structured for ease of interview, for the convenience of interviewer and/or respondent: they do *not* provide a suitable sequence and structure for a report. The report should be structured around the substance of the research problem or 'narrative', as discussed in section 2.8.

The table of contents, as shown in Figure 18.1, indicates the formal broad structure of the report to the reader. The example relates to project reports and theses, which tend to be lengthy, to be divided into chapters and to have tables of contents. Journal articles are shorter and do not have tables of contents, but structure is, of course, still important. There is a conventional overall structure for journal articles involving about seven sections, as shown in Table 18.5. This structure is not hard and fast: in particular, not all articles are empirical, so 'methods' and 'results' sections are not universal.

In the case of a project report, the contents page indicates the general organisation of the report and should make the reader aware of the structure, but it is only a broad indication. It is rarely enough on its own: the structure must be *explained* to the reader – often more than once. Being clear in your own mind

Table 18.5 Conventional academic article structure

- Background/introduction/justification for the research/nature of the problem/issue
- Review of the literature
- Specific outline of problem/issue/hypotheses
- Methods
- Results
- Conclusions
- References

about structure is one thing; conveying it to the reader can be quite another. Thus it is good practice, particularly in the case of a lengthy report/thesis, to provide an outline of the structure of the whole report in the introductory chapter, and outlines of each chapter in the introduction to the chapter. Summaries are useful at the end of each chapter, and these can be revisited and summarised at the end of the report when drawing conclusions together. It is advisable to provide numerous references backwards and forwards, as reminders to the reader as to where you are in the overall narrative of the report. When a list of 'factors', 'issues' or 'topics' is about to be discussed in turn, it is useful to list the factors or issues to be discussed, and then summarise at the end of the section to indicate what the review of factors or issues has achieved.

Articles are, of course, shorter, so organising the structure is less of a challenge. There is no table of contents as such, although the abstract – typically just a paragraph – is usually printed at the beginning of an article and can give some impression. But the logic and structure should also be fully explained within the body of the article.

2.6 Between methods and results

All empirical research reports, regardless of format, should include a clear summary of the methods used to gather data. In journal articles, the description is often quite short, because of the limitation of word length. In management reports, the description may be short in the body of the report because of the type of readership, but there is scope to provide more detail in appendices. In a thesis, an extensive and explicit description of methods used is essential.

In all formats, but particularly in a thesis, the *choice* of methods should also be discussed. Why was a particular method selected? What alternatives were considered, and why were they rejected? Such a discussion should be related to the nature of the research questions/hypotheses. It is not sufficient merely to list the characteristics and merits of the methods chosen, but to indicate why those *particular* characteristics were appropriate in *this particular project*. Factors to consider in selecting a research method are discussed at the end of Chapter 5, and these should be referred to in justifying the choice of method.

Part of the reporting of results of empirical research involves provision of some very basic information on the success of the chosen method in achieving a suitable sample of subjects for study. Since this is technical in nature and not concerned directly with the substantive findings, it can be reported in the 'methods' section, although it is often reported as the first part of the 'results' sections. This component of the report should provide information on:

- the size of the sample achieved;
- response rates and an indication as to whether they are deemed to be acceptable or likely to have caused bias;

- characteristics of the sample, particularly if they can indicate the *representativeness* of the sample (see Chapter 13) – thus a sample from a household or community survey might be compared with the known age/gender structure of the local population from the population census data for the area, while the age structure of a site-survey sample might be compared with junior/adult ticket sales ratios or information from other similar surveys; and

- any measures taken to correct sample bias by means of weighting, and a description of that process.

2.7 Audiences and style

The style, format and length of a report is largely influenced by the type of audience at which it is aimed. The amount of technical jargon used and the detail with which data are presented will be affected by this question of audience. Audiences may be of three kinds:

- *Popular audience:* consisting of members of the general public who might read a report of research in a newspaper or magazine – full research reports are therefore not generally written for a popular readership.

- *Decision-makers:* groups, such as elected members of councils, government ministers, members of boards of companies, or senior executives, who may not have a detailed knowledge of a particular field, or may have a particular knowledge, which might be technical, managerial or political.

- *Experts:* professionals or academics who are familiar with the broad subject matter of the research.

2.8 Report functions: record and narrative

A research report can be thought of in two ways: first, the report as *narrative*, and second, the report as *record*. Balancing these demands as the report is being put together can be a major challenge.

Report as narrative

Narrative means that a report has to tell a *story* to the reader. The writer of the report therefore needs to think of the flow of the argument – the 'story' – in the same way that the writer of a novel has to consider the plot. The report as narrative may call for presentation of only simplified factual information or key features of the data, possibly in graphical form, to demonstrate and illustrate the argument. The narrative of a research report usually develops as indicated in Figure 18.3. The items listed may emerge in a variety of chapter-section configurations. For example, sections A and B could be one chapter/section or three or four, depending on the complexity of the project.

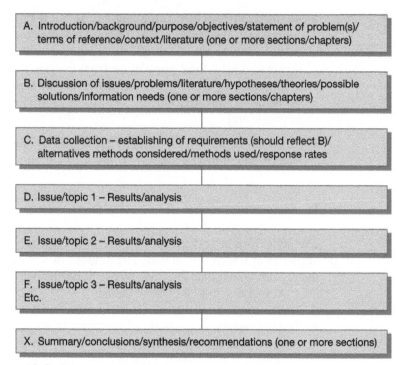

Figure 18.3   Report as narrative – structure

The introductory section(s), A, should reflect the considerations which emerged in the initial steps in the planning stages of a project (components 1, 2 and 6 in Figure 3.1). The term 'context' is used to include the environment in which the research is situated, including any initial literature review which may be involved. Section(s) B should reflect components 3–5 and 7–8 in the research planning process and may include further reference to the literature.

In sections B and C, it is important that the relationships between data requirements and the research questions and theoretical or evaluative framework be explained, as discussed in Chapter 3. It should be clear from the discussion why the data are being collected – and how this relates to the planning/ management/theoretical issues raised; how it was anticipated that the information collected would solve or shed light on the problems/issues raised, or aid decision-making.

In section C, methodology should be described in detail; it should be clear why particular techniques were chosen, how samples or subjects were selected and what data-collection instruments were used. Where sample surveys are involved, full information should be given on response rates and sample sizes obtained and some indication given of the consequences in terms of confidence intervals, as discussed in Chapter 13. These technical aspects of the results of any survey work can be included in the methodology section of the report or in the first of the results sections.

The results/analysis sections (D, E, F, etc.) should ideally be structured by the earlier conceptual or theoretical discussion (B) around issues and elements of the research problem.

Sometimes conclusions are fully set out in the results/analysis section(s), and all that is required in the final conclusions section is to reiterate and draw them together. In other cases, the final section includes the final stage of analysis and the drawing of conclusions from that analysis.

In writing the final section, it is vital to refer back to the terms of reference/objectives of the study to ensure that all objectives have been met.

Not all research reports include 'recommendations'. Recommendations are most likely to arise from evaluative research and in policy/management contexts where the brief has explicitly asked for them. It should, of course, be clear *to whom* any recommendations are addressed.

The report as 'record'

The report as *record* means that a report is often also a reference source where future readers may wish to look for information. Being a good record may involve including extensive detailed information which would interfere with the sequence of the narrative. The report as record is likely to call for the presentation of detailed information – even data which were collected but did not prove particularly relevant for the overall study conclusions.

It is wise to think beyond the immediate readership and use of a research report, and think of it also as the definitive record of the research conducted. It should therefore contain a summary of all the relevant data collected in a form which would be useful for any future user of the report. This means that, while data may be presented in the main body of the report in a highly condensed and summarised form in order to produce a readable narrative, it should *also* be presented in as much detail as possible 'for the record'. To avoid interfering with the narrative, data included for record purposes can be placed in appendices or, when large amounts of data are involved, in a separate statistical volume.

In the case of questionnaire survey data, it can be a good idea to provide a statistical appendix which includes tables from all the questions in the order they appear in the questionnaire, as discussed in Chapter 16. Any reader interested in a specific aspect of the data is then able to locate and use it. The main body of the report can then be structured around issues and need not be constrained by the structure of the questionnaire.

2.9 Research reports: conclusions

Ultimately, the writing of a good research report is an art and a skill which develops with practice. Reports can be improved enormously as a result of comments from others – often because the writer has been 'too close' to the report for too long to be able to see glaring faults or omissions. The researcher/writer can also usually spot opportunities for improvement if he or she takes a short break and returns to the draft report with 'fresh eyes'.

Finally, *checking and double-checking the report for typing, spelling and typographical errors is well worth the laborious effort!*

3. Other media

While the written report is still the most common medium for the communication of research results, this is likely to change in future. In particular, the researcher is often required to present final or interim results of research in person, and some sort of audio-visual aids are usually advisable, including hand-outs, posters, computers and video devices.

3.1 Oral presentations

The oral presentation, typically aided by computer-based visuals using such packages as Microsoft PowerPoint, is typically used by consultants presenting results of a project to clients, by academics and others presenting to academic or professional conferences, and by students as part of a coursework or thesis process.

An important point to bear in mind in regard to the audio-visual presentation is the obvious fact that it is *not* the same as a written report. The presentation must be designed as a medium/message in its own right. The information to be presented must fit into the time allotted and must be suitable for the medium. Therefore, a conscious selection of material must typically be made. This will normally be explained at the beginning of the presentation, but constant references to what is *not* being covered in the presentation because of lack of time are an indication of an unprofessional approach. For example, if there are six 'key findings' from a study, rather than rushing to cover all six, it is in most cases better to say to an audience: 'There are six findings from the study, and in this presentation I am going to concentrate on the three most important.'

It goes without saying that the presenter should *practise* presenting the material to ensure that it fits into the time allotted. Such practice sessions can be seen as the equivalent of various drafts of the written report. Typically, it is necessary to be selective in making such a presentation. Judgement must be used in deciding what to include and what to leave out. As with the writing of abstracts and synopses, this can be a considerable challenge. Practice runs help in this process since programs such as PowerPoint include a 'rehearse timings' procedure which helps in deciding how long to spend on particular parts of the presentation and what to leave out on grounds of time.

Reading from a prepared script is rarely as successful as talking directly to an audience. However, if a prepared script *is* being used, then practising the presentation so that the presenter is very familiar with the script is even more advisable; then frequent eye contact can be made with the audience.

Arranging and reviewing video-recordings of practice runs of a presentation can pay dividends.

3.2 Use of PowerPoint-type software

Most of the readers of this text are students, who sit through hundreds of PowerPoint-type presentations during the course of their studies. Students are therefore experienced judges of what is and is not a good presentation. These notes distil just a few of the 'dos and don'ts'.

- Don't stand in front of the screen!

- Don't overcrowd slides. The standard slide templates available in programs such as PowerPoint provide a default font size and a default number of 'dot points' on a slide. This is for a good reason. Viewing an image when preparing it on a personal computer screen from less than a metre is different from viewing the same image projected on a screen in a lecture hall or meeting room. Thus, a table or graphic with 30 lines of data may be readable in a printed report and when viewed half a metre from a personal computer screen, but it may not be readable to someone 20 metres from a projection screen. This means that tables or diagrams appearing in reports must often be simplified or subdivided. For example, the most important, say, 10 lines of a table or items in a graphic must be selected, or the table or graphic must be divided into two or more sequential slides. As an example, the PowerPoint slides available for this text include eight slides for Figure 18.1: one containing the main chapter/section headings only (the headings in capital letters) and one each for the detail of each chapter/section and the references, appendices, etc. One of the worst things to hear from a presenter is: 'You probably won't be able to read this from the back of the room but . . .' A practice run-through with a full-size screen viewed from the back of a room is advisable.

- Note that simple typefaces, notably the 'sans serif' varieties such as Calibri or Arial, are easier to read in screen-based presentations than serif typefaces, such as Times New Roman.

- Use graphics. The PowerPoint-type presentation is a *visual* medium. Ideally, therefore, graphical images should be mixed with verbal material. Photographs, and even video material, from the research process and/or relating to the research subject can make a presentation 'come alive'. On the other hand, excessive use of such material can be a distraction and may limit time available for presentation of key material. A balance must be struck.

- Be careful about colour. Maximum contrast aids viewing. Yellow lettering on an orange background may look effective in close-up on a computer screen but could be unreadable when projected. Lighting conditions in rooms vary, and projector colour definition can also vary: it is better to play it safe. Similarly, photographs which look good on a small screen may not impress when projected on a large screen in room without dimmed lighting.

- Use the *dynamic* features of the program. PowerPoint-type programs include 'animation'. While items flying into view from all directions may be a distraction, the sequential appearance of, for example, items in a dot-point list at least concentrates the viewer/listener on the item which the presenter is currently talking about. This works even more effectively with graphics.

Again, using an example from the PowerPoint slides made available with this book: in the case of Figure 3.1, which summarises the 10 components of the research process, the 10 boxes appear sequentially, so that the presenter can talk about each component in turn as it appears on screen.

3.3 Poster presentations

- Poster presentations are offered at some conferences and are a particularly useful entrée for research students new to the conference circuit. A poster presentation involves summarising research on a card, typically about 420 x 600mm (A2), which is pinned up in a room or lobby area with others, rather like pictures in a gallery. Conference delegates may examine the posters at will, often with the author on hand at specified times to answer questions and engage in discussion. Typically, the content will comprise a copy of the Abstract, summaries of key methods and findings and copies of diagrams/ tables. Clearly, such a presentation format must be highly selective and must be readable to someone standing in front of the poster.

4. A final comment

Research is a creative process which, in the words of Norbert Elias with which we began this text, aims to 'make known something previously unknown to human beings . . . to advance human knowledge, to make it more certain or better fitting . . . the aim is . . . discovery'. It is hoped that this text will provide some assistance in that process of discovery and that the reader will enjoy some of the satisfactions and rewards which can come from worthwhile research.

Summary

This chapter considers the preparation of what is generally the final outcome of a research project, namely a written report. It considers the varying demands of three types of report: the management/planning/research project report, the academic journal article and the thesis, each with different audiences, different constraints and different conventions. The chapter reviews the various ancillary components of a report, including the cover, cover page, title page, list of contents, synopsis/abstract/executive summary, preface/foreword and acknowledgements. It then considers the main body of the report in terms of technical aspects, largely to do with format, and structure and content. Structure is emphasised as the key feature of a research report, particularly in their longer formats. The roles of the report and narrative and as record are discussed. Finally, some guidance is offered on oral presentations with use of PowerPoint-type aids, and poster presentations.

Test questions/exercises

No specific exercises are offered here. By now the reader should be capable of venturing into the world of research by carrying out a research project from beginning to end.

Resources

The best reading relevant to this chapter is the critical reading of research reports. As regards non-print media, most readers of this text have ample opportunity in the course of their academic and/or professional lives to see numerous examples of good and bad audio-visual presentations from which they can discern good and bad practice!

- Writing as method: St Pierre (2005).

- Writing research reports: Tierney (2013).

- Writing about leisure: Roberts (2016).

- Use of PowerPoint: Horvath and Lodge (2015).

References

Dupuis, S. (1999). Naked truths: towards a reflexive methodology in leisure research. *Leisure Sciences*, 21(1), 43–64.

Horvath, J. C., and Lodge, J. M. (2015). It's not PowerPoint's fault, you're just using it wrong. *The Conversation*, 26 June. Available at: http://theconversation.com/its-not-powerpoints-fault-youre-just-using-it-wrong-43783.

Roberts, K. (2016): Writing about leisure. *World Leisure Journal*, doi: 10.1080/16078055. 2016.1261645

St Pierre, E. A. (2005). Writing: a method of inquiry Part II: Writing as a method of nomadic inquiry. In N. K. Denzin and Y. S. Lincoln (Eds), *Handbook of qualitative research*, 2nd edn, (pp. 967–73). Thousand Oaks, CA: Sage.

Tierney, P. (2013). Communicating research results. In E. Sirakaya-Turk, M. Uysal, W. E. Hammitt, and J. J. Vaske (Eds), *Research methods for leisure, recreation and tourism* (pp. 249–63). Wallingford, UK: CABI.

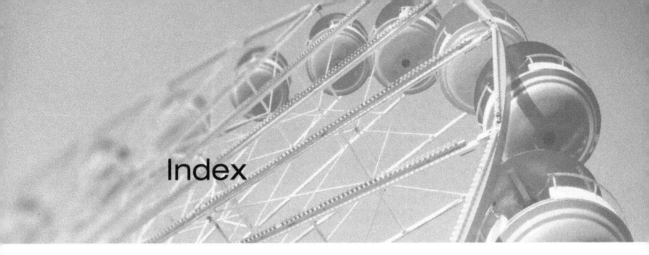

Index